MARKET
SHARE
REPORTER

ISSN 1052-9578

MARKET SHARE REPORTER

AN ANNUAL COMPILATION

OF REPORTED MARKET SHARE

DATA ON COMPANIES,

PRODUCTS, AND SERVICES

2 0 0 1

ROBERT S. LAZICH, Editor

Detroit
New York
San Francisco
London
Boston
Woodbridge, CT

Robert S. Lazich, *Editor*

Editorial Code & Data Inc. Staff

Susan Turner, *Contributing Editor*
Joyce Piwowarski, *Programmer/Analyst*

Gale Group Staff

Brian Rabold, *Coordinating Editor*

Mary Beth Trimper, *Composition Manager*
Wendy Blurton, *Senior Buyer*
Nekita McKee, *Buyer*

Gary Leach, *Graphics Artist*
Cindy Baldwin, *Production Design Manager*

TABLE OF CONTENTS

TABLE OF TOPICS

The *Table of Topics* lists all topics used in *Market Share Reporter* in alphabetical order. One or more page references follow each topic; the page references identify the starting point where the topic is shown. The same topic name may be used under different SICs; therefore, in some cases, more than one page reference is provided.

INTRODUCTION

Market Share Reporter (MSR) is a compilation of market share reports from periodical literature. The eleventh edition covers the period 1997 through 2000; while dates overlap slightly with the tenth edition, the eleventh edition of *MSR* has completely new and updated entries. As shown by reviews of previous editions plus correspondence and telephone contact with many users, this is a unique resource for competitive analysis, diversification planning, marketing research, and other forms of economic and policy analysis. Features of the 2001 edition include—

- More than 2,000 entries, all new or updated.
- SIC classification, with entries arranged under 511 SIC codes.
- Corporate, brand, product, service and commodity market shares.
- Coverage of private and public sector activities.
- North American coverage.
- Comprehensive indexes, including products, companies, brands, places, sources, and SICs.
- Table of Topics showing topical subdivisions of chapters with page references.
- Graphics.
- Annotated source listing—provides publishers' information for journals cited in this edition of *MSR*.

MSR is a one-of-a-kind resource for ready reference, marketing research, economic analysis, planning, and a host of other disciplines.

Categories of Market Shares

Entries in *Market Share Reporter* fall into four broad categories. Items were included if they showed the relative strengths of participants in a market or provided subdivisions of economic activity in some manner that could assist the analyst.

- *Corporate market shares* show the names of companies that participate in an industry, produce a product, or provide a service. Each company's market share is shown as a percent of total industry or product sales for a defined period, usually a year. In some cases, the company's share represents the share of the sales of the companies shown (group total)—because shares of the total market were not cited in the source or were not relevant. In some corporate share tables, brand information appears behind company names in parentheses. In these cases, the tables can be located using either the company or the brand index.

- *Institutional shares* are like corporate shares but show the shares of other kinds of organizations. The most common institutional entries in *MSR* display the shares of states, provinces, or regions in an activity. The shares of not-for-profit organizations in some economic or service functions fall under this heading.

- *Brand market shares* are similar to corporate shares with the difference that brand names are shown. Brand names include equivalent categories such as the names of television programs, magazines, publishers' imprints, etc. In some cases, the names of corporations appear in parentheses behind the brand name; in these cases, tables can be located using either the brand or the company index.

- *Product, commodity, service, and facility* shares feature a broad category (e.g. household appliances) and show how the category is subdivided into components (e.g. refrigerators, ranges, washing machines, dryers, and dishwashers). Entries under this category cover products (autos, lawnmowers, polyethylene, etc.), commodities (cattle, grains, crops), services (telephone, child care), and facilities (port berths, hotel suites, etc.). Subdivisions may be products, categories of services (long-distance telephone, residential phone service, 800-service), types of commodities (varieties of grain), size categories (e.g., horsepower ranges), modes (rail, air, barge), types of facilities (categories of hospitals, ports, and the like), or other subdivisions.

- *Other shares.* MSR includes a number of entries that show subdivisions, breakdowns, and shares that do not fit neatly into the above categorizations but properly belong in such a book because they shed light on public policy, foreign trade, and other subjects of general interest. These items include, for instance, subdivisions of governmental expenditures, environmental issues, and the like.

Coverage

The eleventh edition of *Market Share Reporter* covers essentially the same range of industries as previous editions. However, all tables are *new* or represent *updated* information (more recent or revised data). Also, coverage in detail is different in certain industries, meaning that more or fewer SICs are covered or product details *within* SICs may be different. For these reasons, it is recommended that previous editions of *MSR* be retained rather than replaced.

Changes in Coverage. Beginning with the fifth edition, *MSR's geographic area of coverage became North America—Canada, the United States, and Mexico. As in all past editions, the vast majority of entries are for the United States. In the first four editions of MSR,* international data were included at greater or lesser intensity depending on availability of space. This necessitated, among other things, frequent exclusion of data organized by states or regions of the United States—which are popular with users.

In order to provide better service to users, a companion publication, called *World Market Share Reporter (WMSR),* is available. *WMSR* features global market share information as well as country-specific market share and/or market size information outside North America. At the same time, *MSR* features more geographical market shares in the North American area.

MSR reports on *published* market shares rather than attempting exhaustive coverage of the market shares, say, of all major corporations and of all products and services. Despite this limitation, *MSR* holds share information on nearly 3,300 companies, more than 1,600 brands, and more than 1,800 product, commodity, service, and facility categories. Several entries are usually available for each industry group in the SIC classification; omitted groups are those that do not play a conventional role in the market, e.g., Private Households (SIC 88).

Variation in coverage from previous editions is due in part to publication cycles of sources and a different mix of brokerage house reports for the period covered (due to shifting interests within the investment community).

As pointed out in previous editions, *MSR* tends to reflect the current concerns of the business press. In addition to being a source of market share data, it mirrors journalistic preoccupations, issues in the business community, and events abroad. Important and controversial industries and activities get most of the ink. Heavy coverage is provided in those areas that are—

- large, important, basic (autos, chemicals)
- on the leading edge of technological change (computers, electronics, software)
- very competitive (toiletries, beer, soft drinks)
- in the news because of product recalls, new product introductions, mergers and acquisitions, lawsuits, and for other reasons
- relate to popular issues (environment, crime), or have excellent coverage in their respective trade press.

In many cases, several entries are provided on a subject each citing the same companies. No attempt was made to eliminate such seeming duplication if the publishing and/or original sources were different and the market shares were not identical. Those who work with such data know that market share reports are often little more than the "best guesses" of knowledgeable observers rather than precise measurements. To the planner or analyst, variant reports about an industry's market shares are useful for interpreting the data.

Publications appearing in the March 1999 to June 200 period were used in preparing *MSR*. As a rule, material on market share data for 2000 were used by preference; in response to reader requests, we have included historical data when available. In some instances, information for earlier years was included if the category was unique or if the earlier year was necessary for context. In a few other cases, projections for 2001 and later years were also included.

"Unusual" Market Shares

Some reviewers of the first edition questioned—sometimes tongue-in-cheek, sometimes seriously—the inclusion of tables on such topics as computer crime, endangered species of fish, children's allowances, governmental budgets, and weapons system stockpiles. Indeed, some of these categories do not fit the sober meaning of "market share." A few tables on such subjects are present every edition—because they provide market information, albeit indirectly, or because they are the "market share equivalents" in an industrial classification which is in the public sector or dominated by the public sector's purchasing power.

Organization of Chapters

Market Share Reporter is organized into chapters by 2-digit SIC categories (industry groups). The exception is the first chapter, entitled *General Interest and Broad Topics*; this chapter holds all entries that bridge two or more 2-digit SIC industry codes (e.g. retailing in general, beverage containers, advanced materials, etc.) and cannot, therefore, be classified using the SIC system without distortion. Please note, however, that a topic in this chapter will often have one or more additional entries later—where the table could be assigned to a detailed industry. Thus, in addition to tables on packaging in the first chapter, numerous tables appear later on glass containers, metal cans, etc.

Within each chapter, entries are shown by 4-digit SIC (industry level). Within blocks of 4-digit SIC entries, entries are sorted alphabetically by topic, then alphabetically by title.

SIC and Topic Assignments

MSR's SIC classifications are based on the coding as defined in the *Standard Industrial Classification Manual* for 1987, issued by the Bureau of the Census, Department of Commerce. This 1987 classification system introduced significant revisions to the 1972 classification (as slightly modified in 1977); the 1972 system is still in widespread use (even by the Federal government); care should be used in comparing data classified in the new and in the old way.

The closest appropriate 4-digit SIC was assigned to each table. In many cases, a 3-digit SIC had to be used because the substance of the table was broader than the nearest 4-digit SIC category. Such SICs always end with a zero. In yet other cases, the closest classification possible was at the 2-digit level; these SICs terminate with double-zero. If the content of the table did not fit the 2-digit level, it was assigned to the first chapter of *MSR* and classified by topic only.

Topic assignments are based on terminology for commodities, products, industries, and services in the SIC Manual; however, in many cases phrasing has been simplified, shortened, or updated; in general, journalistically succinct rather than bureaucratically exhaustive phraseology was used throughout.

Organization of Entries

Entries are organized in a uniform manner. A sample entry is provided below. Explanations for each part of an entry, shown in boxes, are provided on the facing page.

☆ 961 ☆ [1]

Personal Care Appliances (SIC 3634) [2] [3]

Electric Toothbrush Market [4]

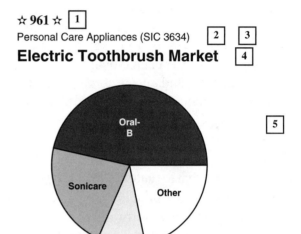

[5]

The $229 million market is shown in percent. Braun makes Oral-B; Optiva Corp. makes Sonicare; Teledyne makes Water Pik. [6]

	($ mil.)	Share [7]
Oral-B	$ 107.5	46.94%
Sonicare	49.6	21.66
Water Pik	22.2	9.69 [8]
Other	49.7	21.70

Source: *Advertising Age*, April 3, 2000, p. 10, from Information Resources Inc. [9]

[1] *Entry Number.* A numeral between star symbols. Used for locating an entry from the index.

[2] *Topic.* Second line, small type. Gives the broad or general product or service category of the entry. The topic for Electric Toothbrush Market is Personal Care Appliances.

[3] *SIC Code.* Second line, small type, follows the topic. General entries in the first chapter do not have an SIC code.

4 *Title.* Third line, large type. Describes the entry with a headline.

5 *Graphic.* When a graphic is present, it follows the title. Some entries will be illustrated with a pie or bar chart. The information used to create the graphic is always shown below the pie or bar chart.

6 *Note Block.* When present, follows the title and is in italic type. The note provides contextual information about the entry to make the data more understandable. Special notes about the data, information about time periods covered, market totals, and other comments are provided. Self-explanatory entries do not have a note block.

7 *Column headers.* Follow the note block. Some entries have more than one column or the single column requires a header. In these cases, column headers are used to describe information covered in the column. In most cases, column headers are years (2000) or indicators of type and magnitude ($ mil.). Column headers are shown only when necessary for clarity of presentation.

8 *Body.* Follows the note block or the column header and shows the actual data in two or more columns. In most cases, individual rows of data in the body are arranged in descending order, with the largest market share holder heading the list. Collective shares, usually labelled "Others" are placed last.

9 *Source.* Follows the body. All entries cite the source of the table, the date of publication, and the page number (if given). In many cases, the publisher obtained the information from another source (original source);

in all such cases, the original source is also shown.

Continued entries. Entries that extend over two adjacent columns on the same page are not marked to indicate continuation but continue in the second column. Entries that extend over two pages are marked *Continued on the next page.* Entries carried over from the previous page repeat the entry number, topic (followed by the word *continued*), title, and column header (if any).

Use of Names

Company Names. The editors reproduced company names as they appeared in the source unless it was clearly evident from the name and the context that a name had been misspelled in the original. Large companies, of course, tend to appear in a large number of entries and in variant renditions. General Electric Corporation may appear as GE, General Electric, General Electric Corp., GE Corp., and other variants. No attempt was made to enforce a uniform rendition of names in the entries. In the Company Index, variant renditions were reduced to a single version or cross-referenced.

Use of Numbers

Throughout *MSR*, tables showing percentage breakdowns may add to less than 100 or fractionally more than 100 due to rounding. In those cases where only a few leading participants in a market are shown, the total of the shares may be substantially less than 100.

Numbers in the note block showing the total size of the market are provided with as many significant digits as possible in order to permit the user to calculate the sales of a particular company by multiplying the market total by the market share.

In a relatively small number of entries, actual unit or dollar information is provided rather than share information in percent. In such cases, the denomination of the unit (tons, gallons, $) and its magnitude (000 indicates multiply by 1,000; mil., multiply by 1,000,000) are mentioned in the note block or shown in the column header.

Data in some entries are based on different kinds of currencies and different weight and liquid measures. Where necessary, the unit is identified in the note block or in the column header. Examples are long tons, short tons, metric tons or Canadian dollars, etc.

Graphics

Pie and bar charts are used to illustrate some of the entries. The graphics show the names of companies, products, and services when they fit on the charts. When room is insufficient to accommodate the label, the first word of a full name is used followed by three periods (...) to indicate omission of the rest of the label.

In the case of bar charts, the largest share is always the width of the column, and smaller shares are drawn in proportion. Two bar charts, consequently, should not be compared to one another.

Sources

The majority of entries were extracted from newspapers and from general purpose, trade, and technical periodicals normally available in larger public, special, or university libraries. All told, 1,025 sources were used; of these, 520 were primary print sources, Many more sources were reviewed but lacked coverage of the subject. These primary sources, in turn, used 505 original sources.

In many cases, the primary source in which the entry was published cites another source for the data, the original source. Original sources include other publications, brokerage houses, consultancies and research organizations, associations, government agencies, special surveys, and the like.

Many sources have also been used from the World Wide Web. The citation includes the Web address, the date the article was retrieved, and, if possible, the title of the article or report. In many cases Web pages have no title or author name. As well, it is not uncommon for Web pages to be moved or temporarity out of operation.

Since many primary sources appear as original sources elsewhere, and vice-versa, primary and original sources are shown in a single Source Index under two headings. Primary sources included in *MSR* almost always used the market share data as illustrative material for narratives covering many aspects of the subject. We hope that this book will also serve as a guide to those articles.

Indexes

Market Share Reporter features five indexes and three appendices.

- Source Index. This index holds 1,025 references in two groupings. *Primary sources* (520) are publications where the data were found. *Original sources* (505) are sources cited in the primary sources. Each item in the index is followed by one or more entry numbers arranged sequentially, beginning with the first mention of the source.

- Place Names Index. This index provides references to cities, states, parks and regions in North America and elsewhere. References are to entry numbers.

- Products, Services, Names and Issues Index. This index holds more than 1,800 references to products, personal names and services in alphabetical order. The index also lists subject categories that do not fit the definition of a product or service but properly belong in the index. Examples include *budgets, conglomerates, crime, defense spending, economies, lotteries*, and the like. Some listings are abbreviations for chemical substances, computer software, etc. which may not be meaningful to those unfamiliar with the industries. Wherever possible, the full name is also provided for abbreviations commonly in use. Each listing is followed by one or more references to entry numbers.

- Company Index. This index shows references to nearly 3,300 company names by entry number. Companies are arranged in alphabetical order. In some cases, the market share table from which the company name was derived showed the share for a combination of two or more companies; these combinations are reproduced in the index.

- Brand Index. The Brand Index shows references to more than 1,500 brands by entry number. The arrangement is alphabetical. Brands include names of publications, computer software, operating systems, etc., as well as the more conventional brand names (Coca Cola, Maxwell House, Budweiser, etc.)

- Appendix I - SIC Coverage. The first appendix shows SICs covered by *Market Share Reporter*. The listing shows major SIC groupings at the 2-digit level as bold-face headings followed by 4-digit SIC numbers, the names of the SIC, and a *page* reference (rather than a reference to an entry number, as in the indexes). The page shows the first occurrence of the SIC in the book. *MSR*'s SIC coverage is quite comprehensive, as shown in the appendix. However, many 4-digit SIC categories are further divided into major product groupings. Not all of these have corresponding entries in the book.

- Appendix II - NAICS/SIC Conversion Guide. The SIC system is presently being revised, with SIC codes being replaced with North American Industry Classification System (NAICS) codes. NAICS is a six digit classification system that covers 20 sectors and 1,170 industries. The first two digits indicate the sector, the third indicates the subsector, the fourth indicates the industry group, the fifth indicates the NAICS industry, and the sixth indicates the national industry. This book is organized around the "old" SIC system because so many still use it. The appendix has both a SIC to NAICS and a NAICS to SIC look-up facility. More information on NAICS can be obtained form the Census Bureau Web site at: http://www.census.gov/naics.

- Appendix III - Annotated Source List. The third appendix provides publisher names, addresses, telephone and fax numbers, and publication frequency of primary sources cited in *Market Share Reporter*, 11th Edition.

What's New

Several recent changes have been made to *Market Share Reporter*. Beginning with the ninth edition, titles of periodicals, movies and software are rendered in italics. Personal names have been moved to the *Products, Services, Names and Issues Index*. Amusement parks and state parks will now be found in the *Places Index*. With the increasing use of the North American Industrial Classification System (NAICS), we have included SIC/NAICS and NAICS/SIC conversion tables. We hope the readers find these additions of use.

Available in Electronic Formats

Diskette/Magnetic Tape. *Market Share Reporter* is available for licensing on magnetic tape or diskette in a fielded format. The complete database may be ordered. The database is available for internal data processing and nonpublishing purposes only.

Online. *Market Share Reporter* is accessible online as File MKTSHR through LEXIS-NEXIS and as part of the MarkIntel service offered by Thomson Financial Services' I/PLUS Direct. For more information, contact LEXIS-NEXIS, P.O. Box 933, Dayton, OH 45401-0933, phone (937)865-6800, toll-free (800)227-4908, Website: http://www.lexis-nexis.com; or Thomson Financial Services, 22 Pittsburgh St., Boston, MA 02210, phone: (617)345-2701, toll-free: (800)662-7878.

CD-ROM. *Market Share Reporter* is available on CD-ROM as part of *Market Share Reporter and Business Ranking Worldwide*. For more information call 1-800-877-GALE.

Acknowledgements

Market Share Reporter is something of a collective enterprise which involves not only the editorial team but also many users who share comments, criticisms, and suggestions over the telephone. Their help and encouragement is very much appreciated. *MSR* could not have been produced without the help of many people in and outside of The Gale Group. The editors would like to express their special appreciation to Mr. Brian Rabold (Coordinating Editor, Gale Group) and to the staff of Editorial Code and Data, Inc.

Comments and Suggestions

Comments on *MSR* or suggestions for improvement of its usefulness, format, and coverage are always welcome. Although every effort is made to maintain accuracy, errors may occasionally occur; the editors will be grateful if these are called to their attention. Please contact:

Editors
Market Share Reporter
The Gale Group
27500 Drake Road
Farmington Hills, Michigan 48331-3535
Phone:(248)699-GALE
or (800)347-GALE
Fax: (248) 699-8069

General Interest and Broad Topics

★ 1 ★

Animal Health

Animal Health Products - 1998

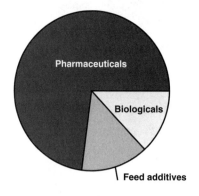

Pharmaceuticals includes insecticides and dosage-form medications used in disease prevention and treatment programs.

	($ mil.)	Share
Pharmaceuticals	$ 3,100	73.03%
Feed additives	595	14.02
Biologicals	550	12.96

Source: *Broiler Industry*, September 1999, p. 12, from Animal Health Institute.

★ 2 ★

Assets

U.S. Financial Assets

Data show share of assets. Banks once had over 50% of the market.

Banks	25.4%
Pensions	24.4
Insurers	17.4
Investment cos.	14.9
Savings & loans	9.4
Other	8.4

Source: *Investor's Business Daily*, November 22, 1999, p. 1, from Cato Institute.

★ 3 ★

Building Materials

Largest Building Material Firms - 1999

Firms are ranked by revenues in billions of dollars.

Owens-Illinois	$ 5.7
Owens-Corning	5.0
Corning	4.8
USG	3.6
Armstrong World Inds.	3.4
Vulcan Materials	2.3
Johns Manville	2.1

Source: *Fortune*, April 17, 2000, pp. I-63.

★ 4 ★

Cheerleading

Cheerleading Market by Region

There are an estimated 3.3 million cheerleaders in the United States. The market includes pompons, uniforms and cheerleading camps.

South	36%
North Central	30
West	17
Northeast	17

Source: *New York Times*, July 17, 1999, p. B1, from American Sports Data.

★5★

Connectivity

Home-Networked Households

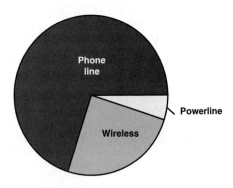

An estimated 6 million homes are expected to be wired for communications and entertainment by 2003.

	2001	2003
Phone line	81%	70%
Wireless	15	25
Powerline	4	5

Source: *IEEE Spectrum*, December 1999, p. 31, from Yankee Group.

★6★

Consumer Spending

Popular Brands for Teenagers

Data show the three ''coolest'' brands, based on a survey of 2,000 consumers ages 12 to 19. Figures are for Spring 1999.

Nike	29%
Tommy Hilfiger	16
Old Navy	8
Gap	8
Abercrombie & Fitch	8
Levi Strauss	7
FUBU	7

Source: *New York Times*, August 28, 1999, p. B1, from Teenage Research Unlimited and U.S. Census Bureau.

★7★

Consumer Spending

Teen Spending - 1999

Teenagers spent $141 billion during the year, an increase from $122 billion in 1997.

Clothing	34%
Entertainment	22
Food	15
Cosmetics/personal care products	8
Sporting goods and clothing	6
Reading materials	3
Other	11

Source: *Inc.*, December 1999, p. 33, from Teenage Research Unlimited and *React*.

★8★

Finance

Financial Institutions - 1999

Data show the breakdown of assets.

Pension funds	29.6%
Commercial banks	22.1
Investment companies	21.7
Insurance companies	14.8
Other	11.4

Source: *New York Times*, October 23, 1999, p. B4, from Federal Reserve Board of Governors.

★9★

Flooring

Floor Covering Sales - 1998

Total sales reached $16.9 billion.

Carpet & area rugs	63.1%
Resilient	16.1
Ceramic	10.9
Hardwood	7.2
Laminate	2.7

Source: *Floor Covering Weekly*, July 1999, p. 1.

★ 10 ★

Gifts and Parties

Social Expressions Industry - 1999

Chain drug stores generated $2.6 billion in products for social occasions. The market is shown by segment.

Greeting cards 78.5%
Gift wrap, ribbons, bows 12.0
Party supplies 9.5

Source: *Chain Drug Review*, March 13, 2000, p. 63, from Racher Press.

★ 11 ★

Homefurnishings

Housewares Industry Sales

Sales are shown in millions of dollars.

	($ mil.)	Share
Electrics	$ 10,428	18.06%
Tabletop	7,853	13.60
Cookware/bakeware	7,619	13.20
Decorative accessories	6,555	11.35
Space organizers	4,328	7.50
Cleaning products	3,762	6.52
Furniture	3,640	6.31
Kitchen tools/accessories	3,256	5.64
Other	10,290	17.82

Source: ''An Inside Look at Housewares.'' Retrieved January 26, 2000 from the World Wide Web: http://www. exposemagazine.com.

★ 12 ★

Media

Largest Entertainment Firms - 1999

Firms are ranked by revenues in billions of dollars.

Time Warner . . . . $ 27.3
Walt Disney 23.4
Viacom 12.8
CBS 7.5
USA Networks 3.2

Source: *Fortune*, April 17, 2000, pp. I-63.

★ 13 ★

Media

Largest Media Companies - 1998

Companies are ranked by revenues in billions of dollars.

GE . . . . $ 100.5
Sony 56.6
Time Warner 26.8
Walt Disney 22.9
Viacom/CBS 18.9
News Corp. 13.6
Seagram 12.3

Source: *Time*, September 20, 1999, p. 52.

★ 14 ★

Media

Where People Get Their News

Television 49.5%
Newspaper 25.5
Radio 11.0
News magazine 5.0
Internet 4.9
Other 4.1

Source: *Brill's Content*, March 2000, p. 76.

★ 15 ★

Nutrition

U.S. Nutrition Industry

The $25.8 billion industry is shown in percent. Natural product retailers are still the largest channel, followed by mass market retailers.

Natural food 34%
Vitamins 21
Herbs/botanicals 15
Personal care 13
Sports nutrition 6
Other 11

Source: Retrieved February 17, 2000 from the World Wide Web: http://www.store.yahoo.com/nbj/aninov99.html, from *Nutrition Business Journal*.

★ 16 ★

Packaged Goods

Best-Selling New Products - 1998

Sales are shown in millions of dollars.

Frito-Lay Wow chips . . . . $ 347
Downy Care fabric softener 176
Colgate Total 152
Polaroid Platinum 149
Gillette Mach 3 razor and blades 147
Thermasilk hair-care products 120
Febreze (Procter & Gamble) 107

Source: *USA TODAY*, July 6, 1999, p. B1, from Information Resources Inc.

★ 17 ★

Packaging

Beverage Container Demand - 2003

Metal 48.7%
Plastic 25.2
Glass 14.9
Paper 11.2

Source: *Plastics News*, August 23, 1999, p. 3, from Freedonia Group Inc.

★ 18 ★

Packaging

Cosmetic and Toiletry Packaging

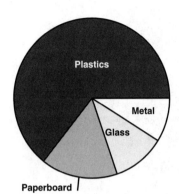

Demand is shown in millions of units.

	1998	2003	Share
Plastics	8,286	10,455	64.84%
Paperboard	2,323	2,538	15.74
Glass	1,612	1,740	10.79
Metal	1,322	1,392	8.63

Source: *Modern Plastics*, December 1999, p. 16, from Freedonia Group Inc.

★ 19 ★

Packaging

Cosmetic/Toiletry Container Demand - 2003

Plastics 65%
Paperboard 16
Glass 11
Metal 8

Source: *Plastics News*, July 26, 1999, p. 3, from Freedonia Group Inc.

★ 20 ★

Pets

Top Pets in North America

Population is shown in millions.

Cats 66.1
Dogs 58.2
Small animals (ferrets, rabbits, etc.) 12.7
Parakeets 11.0
Freshwater fish 10.8
Reptiles 7.5

Continued on next page.

★ 20 ★ *Continued*
Pets

Top Pets in North America

Population is shown in millions.

Finches	7.3
Cockatiels	6.3
Canaries	2.5

Source: *USA TODAY*, May 11, 2000, p. D1, from *The Top 10 of Everything 2000*.

★ 21 ★
Pipes

Pipe Demand - 2003

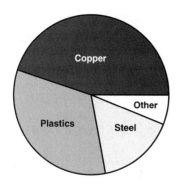

Total demand is expected to reach 14.7 billion feet.

Copper	45%
Plastics	33
Steel	16
Other	6

Source: *Plastics News*, June 7, 1999, p. 3, from Freedonia Group.

★ 22 ★
Promotional Products

Largest Promotion Product Groups - 1998

Companies are ranked by net revenues in millions of dollars.

DraftWorldwide	$ 176.9
Wunderman Cato Johnson	140.1
Cyrk-Simon Worldwide	137.8
Alcone Marketing	123.5
Gage Marketing Group	99.4

Source: "PROMO 100." Retrieved November 11, 1999 from the World Wide Web: http://www.promomagazine/ Magazines/Promo.

★ 23 ★
Recycling

How Old Newspapers Are Used

Newsprint	33.4%
Net exports	23.6
Recycled paperboard	16.5
Tissue	6.7
Printing/writing	2.0
Containerboard	0.1
Other	17.7

Source: *Waste Age*, October 1999, p. 28, from American Forest & Paper Association.

★ 24 ★
Research

Top R&D Spenders

Spending is shown in billions of dollars.

General Motors Corp.	$ 7.90
Ford Motor Co.	6.30
Lucent Technologies	5.09
IBM	4.47
Hewlett-Packard Co.	3.35
Motorola Inc.	2.89
Merck & Co.	2.86
DuPont	2.75

Source: *Assembly*, December 1999, p. 12, from Technical Insights.

★ 25 ★

Research

Who Funds Research Funds

Funding is shown in billions of dollars.

	($ bil.)	Share
Federal	$ 22.3	65.20%
University	5.8	16.96
Industry	2.1	6.14
State/local	2.0	5.85
Nonprofit	2.0	5.85

Source: *Wired*, April 2000, p. 89, from Arbitron.

★ 26 ★

Research

Who Spends Research Funds

Spending is shown in billions of dollars.

	($ bil.)	Share
Industry	$ 169.3	68.35%
Federal	65.8	26.56
University	5.8	2.34
Nonprofit	3.9	1.57
State/local	2.9	1.17

Source: *Wired*, April 2000, p. 89, from Arbitron.

★ 27 ★

Storage

Garage Storage Unit Sales

Sales are for the year ended June 1999. Data are for the hardware/home improvement channel.

Shelving	34%
Wire	30
Totes	12
Clear	9
Cabinets	2
Drawers	2
Workbeches	1
Other	10

Source: *Do-It-Yourself Retailing*, January 2000, p. 81, from Vista Sales and Marketing.

★ 28 ★

Surfacing

Surfacing Dollar Shares

Sales are for the year ended September 1999.

Concrete	55%
Concrete repair	26
Cement	13
Asphalt	3
Stucco	3

Source: *Do-It-Yourself Retailing*, January 2000, p. 81, from Vista Sales and Marketing.

★ 29 ★

Windows and Doors

Nonresidential Entry Doors

	1998	2002
Steel	53%	53%
Aluminum	36	37
Wood	6	7
Other	5	3

Source: *Wood Digest*, April 2000, p. 62, from Ducker Research Company.

★ 30 ★

Windows and Doors

Residential Entry Doors

	1998	2002
Steel	74%	74%
Wood	24	24
Fiberglass	2	2

Source: *Wood Digest*, April 2000, p. 62, from Ducker Research Company.

★ 31 ★
Windows and Doors

Window and Door Sales in Canada - 1997

Total sales reached $3.9 billion in 1997.

	($ mil.)	Share
Wood and metal	$ 3,320	84.95%
PVC windows and doors	588	15.05

Source: Retrieved January 5, 2000 from the World Wide Web: http://www.trade.port.org/ts/countries/canada/mrr/mark0196.html, from Industry Canada.

SIC 01 - Agricultural Production - Crops

★ 32 ★

Produce (SIC 0100)

Produce Sales by Segment

Vegetables, misc.	36.2%
Fruit, misc.	12.5
Apples	10.5
Potatoes	6.9
Tomatoes	6.5
Citrus fruit	6.0
Lettuce	5.3
Other	6.1

Source: *Supermarket Business*, October 15, 1999, p. 99.

★ 33 ★

Rice (SIC 0112)

Rice Acreage by State - 1998

Area planted in thousands of acres.

	Acres	Share
Arkansas	1,540	46.04%
Louisiana	625	18.68
California	480	14.35
Texas	285	8.52
Mississippi	270	8.07
Missouri	145	4.33

Source: *Rice Journal*, May 15, 1999, p. 18, from U.S. Department of Agriculture.

★ 34 ★

Corn (SIC 0115)

Seed Corn Market

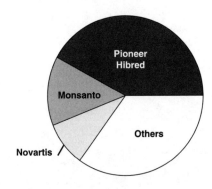

Market shares are shown in percent.

Pioneer Hibred	42%
Monsanto	14
Novartis	9
Others	35

Source: *Financial Times*, September 13, 1999, p. 4, from AgrBioForum V1N2.

★ 35 ★

Corn (SIC 0115)

U.S. Corn Market - 1998

Feed	58%
Export	17
Food	8
Sweetener	6
Ethanol	6
Change in stocks	5
Seed	1

Source: *Doane's Agricultural Report*, December 10, 1999, p. 49.

★ 36 ★
Soybeans (SIC 0116)

U.S. Soybean Market - 1998

Domestic meal	37%
Bean exports	27
Exported as meal	10
Domestic oil	10
Change in stocks	8
Seed	6
Exported as oil	2

Source: *Doane's Agricultural Report*, December 10, 1999, p. 49.

★ 37 ★
Cotton (SIC 0131)

Cotton Seed Market

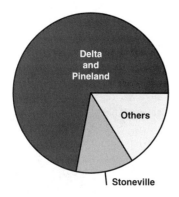

Market shares are shown in percent.

Delta and Pineland	72%
Stoneville	12
Others	16

Source: *Financial Times*, September 13, 1999, p. 4, from AgBioForum V1N2.

★ 38 ★
Potatoes (SIC 0134)

Alberta's Potato Market

The farm gate cash receipts reach approximately $60 million annually. Data show acreage by variety.

	Acres	Share
Russet burbank	3,280	31.99%
Ranger russet	1,692	16.50
Russet norkotah	1,268	12.37
Shepody	927	9.04
Atlantic	516	5.03
Other	2,571	25.07

Source: "Alberta Potato Industry." Retrieved July 21, 1999 from the World Wide Web: http://www.cadvision.com/Home_Pages.

★ 39 ★
Vegetables (SIC 0161)

Largest Growers in the North

Companies are ranked by vegetable acreage.

R.D. Offutt Co.	65
Hartung Brothers Inc.	17
Heartland Farms Inc.	11
Tri-Campbell Farms	10
Wysocki Produce Farm Inc.	8
Paramount Farms Inc.	8
Walther Farms	7
Black Gold Farms	7
Okray Family farms Inc.	6
Charles H. West Farms Inc.	6

Source: *AVG*, October 1999, p. 17.

★ 40 ★
Vegetables (SIC 0161)

Largest Growers in the South

Companies are ranked by vegetable acreage.

Navajo Agricultural Products Industry	27
Martori Farms	10
Rousseau Farming Co.	7
Pasquinelli Produce Co.	5
Wyatt Hidalgo Farms	5
Greer Farms	5

Continued on next page.

★ 40 ★ *Continued*

Vegetables (SIC 0161)

Largest Growers in the South

Companies are ranked by vegetable acreage.

Sakata Farms Inc.	3
Waymon Farms	3
Starr Produce Co.	3
Griffin Ranches Inc.	2

Source: *AVG*, October 1999, p. 24.

★ 41 ★

Vegetables (SIC 0161)

Largest Growers in the Southeast

Companies are ranked by vegetable acreage.

A. Duda & Sons Inc.	24
Pacific Tomato Growers Ltd./Triple E Produce Group	16
Thomas Produce Co.	12
Hundley Farms Inc.	12
Six L's Packing Co. Inc.	12
Zellwin Farms Co.	8
Gargiulo Inc.	8
Suwannee Farms/Eagle Island Farms	6

Source: *AVG*, October 1999, p. 40.

★ 42 ★

Vegetables (SIC 0161)

Largest Growers in the West

Companies are ranked by vegetable acreage.

Grimmway Farms	42
Tanimura & Antie	39
Larsen Farms	28
D'Arrigo Bros. Co. of California Inc.	24
Bruce Church LLC	24
Boskovich Farms Inc.	17
Ocean Mist Farms/Boutonnet Farms	15
P.J. Taggares Co.	15
Nunes Vegetables Inc.	14
Dresick Farms Inc.	13

Source: *AVG*, October 1999, p. 32.

★ 43 ★

Vegetables (SIC 0161)

Pumpkin Acres Harvested - 1997

Illinois	7,631
New York	5,388
Ohio	4,758
Michigan	4,603
Pennsylvania	4,265

Source: *New York Times*, October 30, 1999, p. A12, from United States Department of Agriculture.

★ 44 ★

Vegetables (SIC 0161)

U.S. Avacado Market

Calavo	55%
Other	45

Source: *Latin Trade*, January 2000, p. 22.

★ 45 ★

Fruit (SIC 0170)

Non-Citrus Fruit Production

Data show the value of crop production, in millons of dollars.

Grapes, all	$ 2,447.3
Strawberries	686.4
Avocados	251.6
Prunes, dried basis	210.3
Apples	176.2
Peaches	165.1
Nectarines	98.8
Plums	75.8
Olives	68.5
Cherries, sweet	63.3

Source: ''Crop Information.'' Retrieved January 5, 2000 from the World Wide Web: http://fruits and nuts.ucdavis. edu/acreage.html.

3 1833 03718 9674

★ 46 ★
Fruit (SIC 0171)
Largest Berry Growers

Companies are ranked by berry acreage.

Cherryfield Foods	9,250
Jasper Wyman & Son	7,016
Northland Cranberries	2,548
Merrill Blueberry Farms	2,300
A.D. Makepeace Co.	1,742
Atlantic Blueberry Co.	1,320
Haines & Haines	1,187
Coastal Berry Co.	1,180
Guptill Farms	1,038
Kirk Produce Sunrise Growers	1,030

Source: *Fruit Grower*, September 1999, p. 7.

★ 47 ★
Fruit (SIC 0172)
Largest Grape Growers

Companies are ranked by grape acreage.

E&J Gallo Winery	16,310
Giumarra Vineyards Corp.	10,000
Golden State Vintners	9,500
Delicato Vineyards/San Bernabe Vineyard	9,020
The McCarty Co.	7,500
Sun World International	7,407
Vino Farms	7,353
Dole Food Co.	7,000
Sunmet	6,375
Scheid Vineyards	5,600

Source: *Fruit Grower*, September 1999, p. 7.

★ 48 ★
Fruit (SIC 0172)
Largest Grape Producers

Data are in thousands of tons.

	(000)	Share
California	5,900	90.02%
Washington	275	4.20
New York	189	2.88
Other	190	2.90

Source: *Wines & Vines*, November 1999, p. 16.

★ 49 ★
Nuts (SIC 0173)
California's Almond Market

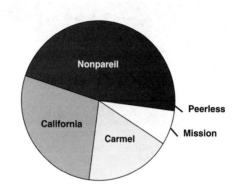

Nonpareil	45%
California	28
Carmel	18
Mission	7
Peerless	2

Source: *The Manufacturing Confectioner*, August 1999, p. 67.

★ 50 ★
Nuts (SIC 0173)
Largest Nut Growers

Firms are ranked by nut acreage.

Paramount Farming Co./Paramount Citrus	48,077
Farmland Management Services	15,264
Premiere Partners	8,949
Diamond Agraindustries	8,619
Dole Food Company	8,300
Lassen Land Co.	7,317
Farmers Investment Co.	7,181
Braden Farms	6,629
Ka'U Agribusiness Co.	6,474
Capital Agricultural Property Services . . .	6,366

Source: *Fruit Grower*, September 1999, p. 8.

★ 51 ★

Nuts (SIC 0173)

Popular Types of Nuts

Data show the preferred types of nuts grown and consumed in the United States. The average American eats 2.25 pounds a year.

Almonds	25%
Pecans	22
Walnuts	17
Pistachios	8
Hazelnuts	3
Others	25

Source: *USA TODAY*, February 16, 1999, p. A1, from USDA Economic Research Service.

★ 52 ★

Fruit (SIC 0175)

Largest Apple/Pear Growers

Companies are ranked by apple/pear acreage. Stemilt Management is the leader although figures were unavailable.

Naumes	5,946
Brewster Heights Packing	5,650
Evans Fruit Farm	5,044
Broetje Orchards	4,200
Borton & Sons	3,167
Capital Agricultural Property Services . . .	2,797
Northwestern Fruit and Produce Co.	2,761
Bowman Agricultural Enterprises	2,746
Fruit Hill Orchard	2,657
Kropf Orchards & Storage	2,500

Source: *Fruit Grower*, September 1999, p. 7.

★ 53 ★

Fruit (SIC 0175)

Largest Apple Producers

Production in millions of 42-pound boxes.

Washington	123.7
New York	28.8
Michigan	25.0
California	19.6
Pennsylvania	11.9

Source: *New York Times*, October 26, 1999, p. A14, from U.S. Department of Agriculture and U.S. Apple Association.

★ 54 ★

Fruit (SIC 0175)

Largest Stone Fruit Growers

Firms are ranked by stone fruit acreage.

Gerawan Farming	4,650
Fowler Packing Co.	3,455
Southern Orchard Lane Packing	3,400
Taylor Orchards	3,312
Sun World International	3,190
California Prune Packing	3,162
ITO Packing Co.	2,906
Thiara Brothers Orchards	2,700
R.W. DuBose & Son	2,300
Evans Farms	2,250

Source: *Fruit Grower*, September 1999, p. 8.

★ 55 ★

Fruit (SIC 0175)

Top Apple Producers - 1999

Data show estimated millions of bushels. The USDA estimates the crop at 251.5 million bushels.

	(mil.)	Share
Washington	123.7	51.74%
New York	26.5	11.08
Michigan	25.5	10.66
California	15.0	6.27
Pennsylvania	11.0	4.60
Other	37.4	15.64

Source: *Fruit Grower*, October 1999, p. 5, from USApple.

★ 56 ★
Flowers (SIC 0181)

Largest Carnation Producers

California

Colorado

Pennsylvania

Other

Data are in thousands of stems. Consumption of standard carnations reached 1.2 billion stems, or an average 4.3 stems per person.

	(000)	Share
California	56,360	89.32%
Colorado	5,872	9.31
Pennsylvania	398	0.63
Other	471	0.75

Source: *Florist's Review*, December 1999, p. 51, from United States Department of Agriculture.

★ 57 ★
Flowers (SIC 0181)

Largest Cut Flower Producers

The United States exported $284 million in greenhouse and nursey products in 1998. Data are in thousands of wholesale dollars. Figures refer to operations with sales in excess of $100,000.

California	$ 266,683
Florida	27,398
Washington	16,434
Hawaii	14,531
Colorado	11,330
Oregon	10,364
Michigan	10,022
New Jersey	8,959

Source: *Florist's Review*, December 1999, p. 51, from United States Department of Agriculture.

★ 58 ★
Flowers (SIC 0181)

Largest Flowering Potted Plant Growers

Companies are ranked by square footage, in millions.

Hines Horticulture	6.0
Kurt Weiss Greenhouses	5.2
Color Spot Nurseries	3.6
Nurserymen's Exchange	2.8
Woodburn Nursery & Azaleas	2.3

Source: *Greenhouse Grower*, May 2000, p. 34.

★ 59 ★
Flowers (SIC 0181)

Largest Fresh-Cut Flower Growers

Companies are ranked by square footage, in millions.

Kitayama Brothers	2.1
Sun Valley Floral Farms	2.0
Johannes Flowers Inc.	1.6
Burgett Floral	1.4
Pajaro Valley Greenhouses	1.3

Source: *Greenhouse Grower*, May 2000, p. 34.

★ 60 ★
Flowers (SIC 0181)

Largest Rose Producers

Data are in thousands of stems. Data include hydrid tea or sweetheart.

	(000)	Share
California	226,025	69.48%
Colorado	17,912	5.51
Pennsylvania	5,090	1.56
New York	4,547	1.40
Wisconsin	3,828	1.18
Michigan	3,316	1.02
Other	64,590	19.86

Source: *Florist's Review*, December 1999, p. 51, from United States Department of Agriculture.

★ 61 ★

Flowers (SIC 0181)

Largest Sources of Chrysanthemums

Data are in thousands of stems.

	(000)	Share
Colombia	41,126	76.60%
Netherlands	5,845	10.89
Ecuador	4,207	7.84
Costa Rica	1,583	2.95
Mexico	227	0.42
Dominican Republic	118	0.22
Others	585	1.09

Source: *Florist's Review*, December 1999, p. 51, from United States Department of Agriculture.

★ 62 ★

Flowers (SIC 0181)

Largest Sources of Lillies

Data are in thousands of stems.

	(000)	Share
Netherlands	28,461	64.79%
Costa Rica	4,960	11.29
Chile	3,340	7.60
Mexico	2,234	5.09
Colombia	2,198	5.00
Dominican Republic	1,242	2.83
Ecuador	747	1.70
Others	744	1.69

Source: *Florist's Review*, December 1999, p. 51, from United States Department of Agriculture.

★ 63 ★

Green Goods (SIC 0181)

Green Goods Sales - 1999

Total sales reached $21 billion.

	($ bil.)	Share
Evergreens	$ 8.08	37.24%
Bedding/ground plants	4.07	18.76
Shrubs/flowering trees	3.71	17.10
Flowering plants	2.63	12.12
Fruit/nut plants	1.56	7.19
Foliage plants	1.06	4.88
Bulbs	0.59	2.72

Source: *Nursery Retailer*, February/March 2000, p. 74.

SIC 02 - Agricultural Production - Livestock

★ 64 ★

Hogs (SIC 0213)

Largest Hog Producers

Annual production is shown in millions.

Smithfield Foods	11.6
ContiGroup	2.9
Seaboard Corporation	2.6
Prestage Farms	2.2

Source: *New York Times*, April 7, 2000, p. C1, from Smithfield Foods, National Pork Producers Council, and *Successful Farming*.

★ 65 ★

Hogs (SIC 0213)

Largest Pork Packers - 1998

Data show number of hogs killed, in millions.

Smithfield Foods	77
IBP	65
Swift	39
Excel	38
Farmland	33

Source: *Pork*, September 1999, p. 14, from National Pork Producers Council.

★ 66 ★

Hogs (SIC 0213)

Largest Pork Processors

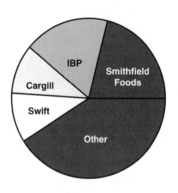

Data show share of pork processing.

Smithfield Foods	21%
IBP	18
Cargill	10
Swift	10
Other	41

Source: *New York Times*, April 7, 2000, p. C1, from Smithfield Foods, National Pork Producers Council, and *Successful Farming*.

★ 67 ★

Hogs (SIC 0213)

Largest Pork Producers - 1999

Data show thousands of sows. Shares of the group are shown based on 2.59 million sows produced by the top 50 firms.

	(000)	% of Group
Smithfield Foods/Murphy	675	26.06%
ContiGroup Companies	162	6.25
Seaboard Corporation	145	5.60
Prestage Farms	121	4.67
Cargill	110	4.25

Continued on next page.

★ 67 ★ *Continued*
Hogs (SIC 0213)

Largest Pork Producers - 1999

Data show thousands of sows. Shares of the group are shown based on 2.59 million sows produced by the top 50 firms.

	(000)	% of Group
Tyson Foods	110	4.25%
Iowa Select Farms	90	3.47
Purina Farms (Koch)	80	3.09
Farmland Industries/Alliance	67	2.59
Goldsboro Hog Farm	66	2.55
Other	964	37.22

Source: *Successful Farming*, October 1999, p. 15.

★ 68 ★
Sheep and Lamb (SIC 0214)

Sheep/Lamb Inventory by State - 1999

Data show breeding sheep, one year old or older. As of January 1, 1999 there were 5.31 million breeding sheep.

	(000)	Share
Texas	1,050.0	19.76%
Wyoming	500.0	9.41
California	390.0	7.34
Utah	360.0	6.77
Montana	345.0	6.49
Other	2,669.1	50.23

Source: *The Shepard*, March 1999, p. 9.

★ 69 ★
Cows (SIC 0215)

Dairy Cows by State

Data are in thousands for April 1999.

California	1,456
Wisconsin	1,395
New York	700
Pennsylvania	615
Minnesota	545
Texas	342
Idaho	310

Source: *Dairy Herd Management*, June 1999, p. 70, from United States Department of Agriculture.

★ 70 ★
Poultry (SIC 0250)

Leading Broiler Firms - 1999

Firms are ranked by average weekly ready-to-cook production in millions of pounds.

Tyson Foods Inc.	154.30
Gold Kist Inc.	58.83
Perdue Farms Inc.	47.78
Pilgrim's Pride Corporation	38.22
ConAgra Poultry Cos.	34.90
Wayne Farms, ContiGroup	25.34
Sanderson Farms Inc.	20.58
Cagle's Inc.	19.74
Foster Farms	15.43

Source: *WATT PoultryUSA*, January 2000, p. 18C.

★ 71 ★
Poultry (SIC 0251)

Largest Poultry Firms - 1999

Data show millions of hens. The top 62 firms own 209.8 million birds.

Cal-Maine Foods Inc.	19.9
Rose Acre Farms	16.2
Michaels Foods	15.0
DeCoster Egg Farms	12.6
Buckeye Egg Farm	10.5
Fort Recovery Equity	8.0
Moark Productions Inc.	6.5
Midwest Poultry Services	5.7

Source: *Egg Industry*, January 2000, p. 10.

★ 72 ★
Eggs (SIC 0252)

Egg Sales by Packaging

Shares are for the second quarter of the year. Data refer to supermarket sales.

12CT	77.5%
18CT	15.1
6CT	3.5
Bulk	3.0

Source: *Egg Industry*, August 1999, p. 20, from A.C. Nielsen.

★ 73 ★

Eggs (SIC 0252)

Egg Production by State

Data show billions of eggs.

Ohio	8.1
Iowa	6.7
California	6.6
Pennsylvania	6.1
Indiana	5.8
Georgia	5.1
Texas	4.4
Arkansas	3.4

Source: *Egg Industry*, February 2000, p. 10, from U.S. Department of Agriculture.

★ 74 ★

Eggs (SIC 0252)

Leading Fresh Egg Markets - 1999

Los Angeles	
New York City	
Philadelphia	
Boston	
Chicago	

Sales are shown in millions of dollars in selected markets. Figures are for the year ended September 4, 1999.

Los Angeles	$ 148.0
New York City	125.8
Philadelphia	60.7
Boston	60.3
Chicago	58.9

Source: *Grocery Headquarters*, January 2000, p. 45, from A.C. Nielsen.

★ 75 ★

Turkeys (SIC 0253)

Largest Turkey Processors - 1997

Sales are shown in millions of pounds.

Butterball Turkey Co.	900
Jennie-O Foods	766
Wampler	685
Cargill	514
Shady Brook Farms	498
Carolina Turkeys	450

Sara Lee Foods	415
Lewis Rich Turkey Co.	360

Source: "Turkey Statistics." Retrieved December 14, 1999 from the World Wide Web: http://www.turkeyfed.org/press/stats/stats.html, from *Turkey World*.

★ 76 ★

Turkeys (SIC 0253)

Largest Turkey Producers

Data are in millions of pounds.

	(mil.)	Share
North Carolina	1,300	18.57%
Minnesota	1,000	14.29
Missouri	598	8.54
Virginia	533	7.61
Arkansas	496	7.09
California	443	6.33
South Carolina	356	5.09
Indiana	352	5.03
Pennsylvania	233	3.33
Other	1,689	24.13

Source: *Christian Science Monitor*, November 23, 1999, p. 24, from U.S. Bureau of the Census.

★ 77 ★

Dogs (SIC 0271)

Top Dog Breeds - 1999

Data show the number of registered breeds.

Labrador retrievers	154,897
Golden retrievers	62,652
German shepard	57,256
Dachshund	50,772
Beagles	49,080
Poodles	45,852
Chihuahuas	42,013
Rottweilers	41,776
Yorkshire terriers	40,684

Source: Retrieved February 1, 2000 from the World Wide Web: http://www.akc.org/breeds/top50.cfm, from American Kennel.

★ 78 ★

Equines (SIC 0272)

Horse Registrations - 1999

Data are estimated, in thousands.

	No.	Share
Quarter Horse	130,000	64.15%
Thoroughbred	36,500	18.01
Tennessee Walking Horse	14,000	6.91
Arabian	11,500	5.68
Anglo & Half-Arabian	4,041	1.99
Morgan horse	3,500	1.73
Saddlebred	3,100	1.53

Source: *Equus*, November 1999, p. 265.

★ 79 ★

Equines (SIC 0272)

Top Equine Owning States

Texas
California
Tennessee
Florida
Pennyslvania
Oklahoma
Ohio

Population is shown as of January 1, 1999, in thousands. Equines include horses, ponies, mules, burros and donkeys.

Texas	600
California	240
Tennessee	190
Florida	170
Pennyslvania	170
Oklahoma	170
Ohio	160

Source: *DVM News Magazine*, May 1999, p. 6E, from United States Department of Agriculture.

★ 80 ★

Aquaculture (SIC 0273)

Aquaculture Sales in Florida

Data show value of sales in thousands of dollars.

	($ 000)	Share
Clams	$ 12,712	41.39%
Other aquatics	12,063	39.28
Alligator hide/meat	3,189	10.38
Tilapia	1,067	3.47
Sport/game fish	1,044	3.40
Catfish	637	2.07

Source: Retrieved January 18, 2000 from the World Wide Web: http://www.nass.usda.gov/fl/misc/98aqua14.htm.

★ 81 ★

Farming (SIC 0291)

Organic Cropland by State

Data are in acres.

Idaho	107,955
California	96,851
North Dakota	88,581
Montana	59,362
Minnesota	56,275
Wisconsin	41,245
Colorado	35,127
Iowa	34,276

Source: *USA TODAY*, April 26, 2000, p. A1, from Agriculture Department Agricultural Outlook.

★ 82 ★

Farming (SIC 0291)

Organic Farmers by State

California	633
Washington	299
Wisconsin	279
Ohio	226
Oregon	216

Source: *Wall Street Journal*, September 10, 1999, p. W10, from OrgancicFarming Research Foundation.

SIC 07 - Agricultural Services

★ 83 ★

Vet Services (SIC 0740)

Largest Vet Practices

Veterinary Center of America	
	National PetCare Centers
Your Pet's Choice	
	National Veterinary Associates

Data show number of practices.

Veterinary Center of America 192
National PetCare Centers 72
Your Pet's Choice 60
National Veterinary Associates 30

Source: *TRENDS Magazine*, August/September 1999, p. 14.

★ 84 ★

Farm Loans (SIC 0761)

Top Agricultural Banks

Banks are ranked by total agricultural loans. Data are in millions of dollars.

Wells Fargo BL NA . . . . $ 2,078.0
US Bank NA 1,336.0
NationsBank 1,295.0
Sanwa Bank California 838.1
NatiosnBank NA 838.1
Keybank NA 827.9
Regions Bank 582.3
Union Planters NB 541.2

Source: *Ag Lender*, July 1999, p. 4.

★ 85 ★

Lawn Care (SIC 0780)

Lawn & Garden Care - 1998

Retail sales reached $30.2 billion. Lawn & garden sales generated roughly 8.4% of the $89.2 billion in sales generated by the top 500 home improvement centers. The category came in second to lumber.

	($ bil.)	Share
Lawn care	$ 8.5	28.52%
Landscaping	6.4	21.48
Flower gardening	3.9	13.09
Vegetable gardening	2.0	6.71
Tree care	1.7	5.70
Shrub care	1.6	5.37
Insect control	1.6	5.37
Indoor plants	1.1	3.69
Other	3.0	10.07

Source: *National Home Center News*, July 19, 2000, p. 55, from National Gardening Association.

★ 86 ★

Lawn Care (SIC 0782)

Leading Lawn Maintenance Firms

Data are in millions of dollars.

TruGreen-Chemlawn . . . . $ 820.0
TruGreen LandCare 450.0
Environmental Industries Inc.. . . . . . . 436.0
The Davey Tree Expert Co. 314.0
The Brickman Group 150.0
Bartlett Tree Experts 104.0
Randall & Blake 56.4
The Weed Man 50.0
The Lawn Doctor Inc. 50.0
Gothic Landscape 39.0

Source: "State of the Industry Report." Retrieved December 3, 1999 from the World Wide Web: http://www. lawnandlandscape.com.

SIC 10 - Metal Mining

★ 87 ★

Gold (SIC 1041)

Top Gold Producers

Production is shown in thousands of ounces.

	(000)	Share
Newmont Gold Company	3,004.0	26.32%
Barrick Gold Corporation	2,386.7	20.91
Rio Tinto	1,134.8	9.94
Homestake Mining Company	702.5	6.15
Echo Bay Mines	555.7	4.87
Placer Dome Inc.	518.0	4.54
Amax Gold Inc.	432.7	3.79
Pegasus Gold Inc.	369.6	3.24
Other	2,310.1	20.24

Source: "Stats." Retrieved April 10, 2000 from the World Wide Web: http://www.nma.org/Gold%20Producers.htm, from The Gold Institute.

★ 88 ★

Silver (SIC 1044)

Silver Production in North America - 1998

Data are in millions of ounces.

Mexico	92.5
United States	62.8
Canada	36.2

Source: "Gold." Retrieved April 10, 2000 from the World Wide Web: http://www.silverinstitute.org/producti.htm.

★ 89 ★

Silver (SIC 1044)

Top Silver Producers in North America - 1998

Data are in millions of ounces.

Industrias Penoles (Mexico)	36.4
Grupo Mexico (Mexico)	16.1
Cominco Ltd. (Canada)	13.3
Homestake Mining (U.S.)	11.7
Noranda Inc. (Canada)	11.2

Source: "Gold." Retrieved April 10, 2000 from the World Wide Web: http://www.silverinstitute.org/producti.htm.

★ 90 ★

Silver (SIC 1044)

Top U.S. Silver Producers

Production is shown in millions of ounces.

	(mil.)	Share
Rio Tinto	12.5	19.84%
Echo Bay	11.0	17.47
Coeur d'Alene	8.4	13.33
Asarco	5.4	8.60
Hecla	4.9	7.83

Continued on next page.

★ **90** ★ *Continued*

Silver (SIC 1044)

Top U.S. Silver Producers

Production is shown in millions of ounces.

	(mil.)	Share
Kinross Gold	4.7	7.50%
Cominco	4.3	6.82
Sunshine	4.2	6.74

Source: "Stats." Retrieved April 10, 2000 from the World Wide Web: http://www.nma.org/Silver%20Producers.htm.

SIC 12 - Coal Mining

★ 91 ★

Coal (SIC 1220)

Top Mines in West Virginia

Data are in millions of short tons. Top companies include Mingo Logan Coal, McElroy Coal, Performance Coal, Consolidated Coal, Catenary Coal and U.S. Steel Mining.

Mountaineer	7.4
McElroy	6.6
UBBMC Montcoal Eagle	5.7
Robinson Run No. 95	5.6
Loveridge	5.4
Samples	4.9
No. 50	4.8
Shoemaker	4.8
Federal No. 2	4.8

Source: *Mining Engineering*, May 1999, p. 105.

SIC 13 - Oil and Gas Extraction

★ 92 ★

Natural Gas (SIC 1311)

Natural Gas Reserves - 1999

The leading firms in North America are ranked by reserves in trillons of cubic feet.

ExxonMobil	16.3
BP Amoco	12.0
Burlington Resources	7.4
Shell Oil	7.0
Anardarko/Union Pacific	5.8
Arco	5.2
Texaco	4.2

Source: *Wall Street Journal*, April 4, 2000, p. A10, from NPD Group.

★ 93 ★

Oil (SIC 1311)

Crude Oil Leaders - 1999

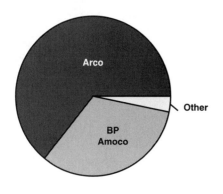

Production is shown as of November 1999.

Arco	61%
BP Amoco	31
Other	3

Source: *New York Times*, January 4, 2000, p. C1, from Alaska Oil and Gas Conservation Commission and Energy Information Administration.

★ 94 ★

Oil (SIC 1311)

Oil Production by State - 1999

Data show thousands of barrels annually produced. Total production reached 2.13 billion barrels.

	(000)	Share
Louisiana	531,245	24.88%
Texas	514,649	24.11
Alaska	382,761	17.93
California	311,667	14.60
Oklahoma	67,450	3.16
New Mexico	63,741	2.99
Wyoming	60,433	2.83
Other	203,021	9.51

Source: *World Oil*, February 2000, p. 60.

★ 95 ★

Oil Rigs (SIC 1381)

Oil Rig Ownership - 1999

Rig ownership is shown by fleet size.

More than 20 rigs	54.4%
2-5 rigs	17.4
11-20 rigs	13.8
6-10 rigs	10.2
1 rig	4.2

Source: *World Oil*, October 1999, p. 56.

★ 96 ★

Oil Wells (SIC 1381)

Oil Well Drilling - 1999

Data show the number of wells drilled by region.

Alberta	3,463
Saskatchewan	927
British Columbia, onshore	126
Manitoba	12
Newfoundland, offshore	3
Nova Scotia, offshore	2
Northwest Territories, onshore	1

Source: *World Oil*, February 2000, p. 85.

SIC 14 - Nonmetallic Minerals, Except Fuels

★ 97 ★
Crushed Stone (SIC 1420)

Crushed Stone Production in the Eastern U.S. - 1999

Pennsylvania	
New York	
Virginia	
New Jersey	
Maryland	

Data are in millions of metric tons for the third quarter 1999.

Pennsylvania	30.4
New York	18.1
Virginia	17.5
New Jersey	7.0
Maryland	6.8

Source: *Pit & Quarry*, January 2000, p. 20.

★ 98 ★
Sand and Gravel (SIC 1440)

Leading Aggregate Firms in North America - 1999

Selected companies are ranked by sales in millions of dollars.

Vulcan Materials	$ 1,810
Hanson Building Materials America	1,740
Lafarge Corp.	1,419
Martin Marietta Materials	1,126
U.S. Aggregates	298
Southdown	164

Source: *Rock Products*, March 2000, p. 16.

★ 99 ★
Sand and Gravel (SIC 1440)

Sand and Gravel Production in the Eastern U.S. - 1999

Data are estimated in millions of metric tons for the third quarter 1999.

Pennsylvania	6.5
New Jersey	4.9
Massachusetts	3.8
Maine	3.4
New Hampshire	3.0

Source: *Pit & Quarry*, January 2000, p. 20.

★ 100 ★
Phosphate Rock (SIC 1475)

Phosphate Market by Finished Product

Data are in thousands of short tons. Florida provides rougly 75% of the nation's phosphate supply.

	(000)	Share
Diammonium phosphate	10,727.0	69.87%
Monoammonium phosphate	1,781.0	11.60
Triple super phosphate	1,589.0	10.35
Phosphoric acid	690.0	4.49
Superphosphoric acid	566.4	3.69

Source: ''Phosphate Rock.'' Retrieved April 10, 2000 from the World Wide Web: http://www.flaphos.org/Facts97.html.

SIC 15 - General Building Contractors

★ 101 ★

Construction (SIC 1500)

Construction Industry in Canada - 1998

Ontario	30.6%
Alberta	18.9
Quebec	18.7
British Columbia	16.9
Atlantic Canada	5.6

Source: *Globe and Mail*, July 7, 1999, p. B8, from Canadian Construction Association.

★ 102 ★

Residential Construction (SIC 1521)

Housing Starts by Region

	1999	2000
South	45.8%	46.2%
West	24.2	25.1
Midwest	20.7	20.5
Northeast	9.3	9.6

Source: *Builder*, January 2000, p. I30.

★ 103 ★

Residential Construction (SIC 1521)

Real Estate Leaders in Atlanta, GA - 1998

Firms are ranked by transaction sides closed.

Coldwell Banker Buckhead Brokers	17,588
RE/MAX Greater Atlanta	15,459
Northside Realty	10,665
Harry Norman Realtors	7,801
Prudential Atlanta/Georgia Realty	7,786

Source: *Realtor Magazine*, July 1999, p. 42.

★ 104 ★

Residential Construction (SIC 1521)

Real Estate Leaders in Boston, MA - 1998

Firms are ranked by transaction sides closed.

Hunneman/Coldwell Banker	16,303
The DeWolfe Co. Inc.	12,000
Jack Conway & Co. Realtors	3,846
RE/MAX First Choice Real Estate	3,389
Hammond Residential Real Estate	1,879

Source: *Realtor Magazine*, July 1999, p. 42.

★ 105 ★

Residential Construction (SIC 1521)

Real Estate Leaders in Chicago, IL - 1998

Firms are ranked by transaction sides closed.

Colwell Banker Residential Brokerage . . . 27,400
Baird & Warner Inc. 14,000
Koenig & Strey Inc. 6,914
RE/MAX Naperville/RE/MAX Enterprises . 4,254
Century 21 Dabbs group 3,997

Source: *Realtor Magazine*, July 1999, p. 42.

★ 106 ★

Residential Construction (SIC 1521)

Real Estate Leaders in Cleveland, OH

Data show number of permits. Pulte has a 3% share.

Pulte 283
Ryan Homes 188
Gross Builders 184
Whitlach & Co. 170
Wagler Homes 166

Source: *Crain's Cleveland Business*, March 1, 1999, p. 12.

★ 107 ★

Residential Construction (SIC 1521)

Real Estate Leaders in Detroit, MI - 1998

| Real Estate One Inc. |
| Century 21 Town & Country |
| Coldwell Banker Schweitzer Real Estate |
| Century 21 Associates |
| Prudential Chamberlain |

Firms are ranked by transaction sides closed.

Real Estate One Inc. 10,532
Century 21 Town & Country 8,096
Coldwell Banker Schweitzer Real Estate . . 6,863
Century 21 Associates 5,100
Prudential Chamberlain 3,967

Source: *Realtor Magazine*, July 1999, p. 42.

★ 108 ★

Residential Construction (SIC 1521)

Real Estate Leaders in Los Angeles, CA - 1998

Firms are ranked by transaction sides closed.

Coldwell Banker Residential Brokerage . . 39,427
Fred Sands Realtors 17,717
Prudential California Realty 9,492
First Team Real Estate - Orange County . . 8,575
RE/MAX/Beach Cities/Westside Properties . 5,432

Source: *Realtor Magazine*, July 1999, p. 42.

★ 109 ★

Residential Construction (SIC 1521)

Real Estate Leaders in New York City, NY - 1998

Firms are ranked by transaction sides closed.

Coldwell Banker New York Metro 33,440
William Ravels Real Estate & Home
    Service 8,100
Prudential Long Island Realty 6,500
Burgdorff Realtors 6,200
Douglas Ellimann 4,177

Source: *Realtor Magazine*, July 1999, p. 42.

★ 110 ★

Residential Construction (SIC 1521)

Real Estate Leaders in Philadelphia, PA - 1998

Firms are ranked by transaction sides closed.

Fox & Roach Realtors 21,006
Century 21 Alliance 2,395
RE/MAX Eastern Inc. 2,047
RE/MAX 2000 1,587
RE/MAX Services Inc. 1,564

Source: *Realtor Magazine*, July 1999, p. 42.

★ 111 ★
Residential Construction (SIC 1521)

Real Estate Leaders in San Francisco, CA - 1998

Firms are ranked by transaction sides closed.

Coldwell Banker Northern California	24,053
Prudential California Realty	7,561
Alain Pinel, Realtors	5,920
Pacific Union Real Estate Group	5,000
Dutra Realty Enterprises Inc.	3,300

Source: *Realtor Magazine*, July 1999, p. 42.

★ 112 ★
Residential Construction (SIC 1521)

Top Builders - 1999

Companies are ranked by number of closings.

Pulte Corp.	26,622
Kaufman and Broad Home Corp.	22,460
D.R. Horton	19,041
Centex Corp.	18,832
Lennar Corp.	12,589
The Ryland Group	10,193
NVR	9,316
U.S. Home Corp.	9,246
Beazer Homes USA	7,804
Del Webb Corp.	7,737

Source: *Builder*, May 2000, p. 138.

★ 113 ★
Residential Construction (SIC 1521)

Top Builders in Detroit, MI - 1999

Firms are ranked by total revenues in millions of dollars.

Barton Malow Co.	$ 969.5
Walbridge Aldinger Co.	775.0
Etkin Skanska Construction Co.	262.5
Turner Construction Co.	210.0
JM Olson Corp.	167.5

Source: *Crain's Detroit Business*, March 13, 2000, p. 14.

★ 114 ★
Residential Construction (SIC 1521)

Top Public Home Builders - 1999

Companies are ranked by gross revenues in billions of dollars.

Centex Corp.	$ 5.7
Pulte Home Corp.	3.8
Kaufman and Broad Home Corp.	3.8
D.R. Horton	3.3
Lennar Corp.	3.1
NVR	2.0
The Ryland Group	2.0
U.S. Home Corp.	1.8
Del Webb Corp.	1.7

Source: *Builder*, March 2000, p. 75.

★ 115 ★
Residential Construction (SIC 1522)

Top Multifamily Markets - 1999

Spending on multifamily properties (apartments or condominums) reached $8.4 billion for the first four months of the year.

Orlando, FL	5,946
Dallas, TX	5,310
Houston	4,311
Phoenix, AZ	3,515
Washington D.C.	3,184

Source: *Building Design & Construction*, August 1999, p. 23, from U.S. Department of Commerce.

★ 116 ★
Nonresidential Construction (SIC 1542)

Top Hotel Design Firms - 1998

Companies are ranked by lodging fees in millions of dollars.

Wimberly Allison Tong & Goo	$ 37.3
Carl Ross Design	25.2
Hirsch Bedner Associates	24.7
Wilson & Associates	23.0
Arthur Shuster	15.0
RTKL Associates	14.9
DiLeonardo International	13.0
Concepts 4	10.1

Source: *Hotel & Motel Management*, November 15, 1999, p. 1.

SIC 16 - Heavy Construction, Except Building

★ 117 ★

Contracting (SIC 1600)

Leading Owners of Construction - 1998

The companies are ranked by amount of construction in progress, in billions of dollars.

General Motors Corp.	$ 4.3
Ford Motor Co.	2.7
E.I. Du Pont de Nemours	2.0
Merck & Co.	1.7
Southern Co.	1.7
Intel Corp.	1.6
Sprint PCS Group	1.6
Philip Morris Cos. Inc.	1.4

Source: *ENR*, November 22, 1999, p. 36.

★ 118 ★

Contracting (SIC 1600)

Top Contractors - 1998

Firms are ranked by revenues in billions of dollars.

Bechtel Group Inc.	$ 9.7
Fluor Daniel Inc.	9.6
Kellogg Brown & Root	6.8
CENTEX Construction Group	3.7
Foster Wheeler Corp.	3.6
The Turner Corp.	3.6
Skanska (USA) Inc.	3.0
Peter Kiewit Sons Inc.	2.9
Bovis Construction Corp.	2.2
Gilbane Building Co.	2.2

Source: *ENR*, May 31, 1999, p. 79.

★ 119 ★

Contracting (SIC 1600)

Top Contractors in Canada - 1998

Sales are shown in millions of dollars.

PCL Construction Group Inc.	$ 2,219.4
Ledcor Industries Ltd.	750.0
BFC Construction Corporation	644.5
Ellis-Don Construction Ltd.	617.7
Axor Group Inc.	380.0
Canron Construction	335.0
Flint Energy Services Ltd.	292.0
Dominion Construction Company Inc.	271.1

Source: *Heavy Construction News*, June 1999, p. 20.

★ 120 ★

Bridge Construction (SIC 1611)

Top Bridge Designers - 1998

Firms are ranked by design revenues in millions of dollars.

URS Grenier Woodward-Clyde	$ 88.5
Parsons Brinckerhoff Inc.	70.5
HNTB Corp.	49.6
Parsons Corp.	35.5
Greenman-Pedersen Inc.	30.0
The Louis Berger Group	29.8
T.Y. Lin International	29.3

Source: *ENR*, July 1999, p. 46.

★ 121 ★

Highway Construction (SIC 1611)

Top Highway Designers - 1998

Firms are ranked by design revenues in millions of dollars.

Parsons Brinckerhoff Inc.	$ 200.1
The Louis Berger Group	127.9
HNTB Corp.	108.9
Parsons Corp.	106.6
URS Grenier Woodward-Clyde	96.3
Jacobs Sverdrup	84.0
PBS&J	80.0

Source: *ENR*, July 1999, p. 46.

SIC 17 - Special Trade Contractors

★ 122 ★
Remodeling (SIC 1700)

Top Remodeling Categories

Spending is shown in millions of dollars.

Painting & paper hangers	$ 12.6
Roofing	11.7
Kitchen & bath	10.0
HVAC	9.7
Windows & doors	8.1
Plumbing	7.3
Flooring	7.2
Room additions	6.2
Siding	3.2

Source: *Wood Digest - Industry Trends Report*, April 2000, p. 32.

★ 123 ★
Contracting - Painting (SIC 1721)

Top Painting Contractors - 1998

Cannon Sline Inc.
J.L. Manta Inc.
Protherm Services Group LLC
Bryant-Durham Elec. Co. Inc.
Swanson & Youngdale Inc.
Techno Coatings Inc.
Avalotis Corp.
Ascher Brothers Co. Inc.

Firms are ranked by revenues in millions of dollars.

Cannon Sline Inc.	$ 45.2
J.L. Manta Inc.	37.6
Protherm Services Group LLC	31.2
Bryant-Durham Elec. Co. Inc.	30.3
Swanson & Youngdale Inc.	$ 29.3
Techno Coatings Inc.	28.7
Avalotis Corp.	20.4
Ascher Brothers Co. Inc.	19.6

Source: *ENR*, October 11, 1999, p. 74.

★ 124 ★
Contracting - Electrical (SIC 1731)

Top Electrical Contractors -1998

Firms are ranked by revenues in millions of dollars.

EMCOR Group Inc.	$ 1,237.8
Integrated Electrical Services Inc.	1,100.0
Building One Services Corp.	916.1
Quanta Services Inc.	449.9
MYR Group Inc.	436.6
SASCO Group	401.0
Mass. Electric Construction Co.	375.9
Cupertino Electric Inc.	249.6
Rosendin Electrical Inc.	208.0

Source: *ENR*, October 11, 1999, p. 62.

★ 125 ★
Contracting - Wall/Ceiling (SIC 1741)

Top Wall/Ceiling Contractors - 1998

Firms are ranked by revenues in millions of dollars.

Performance Contracting Group Inc.	$ 194.6
KHS&S Contractors	112.3
National Construction Enterprises Inc.	110.3
Midwest Drywall Co. Inc.	98.2
Nastasi & Associates Inc.	94.2
Anson Industries Inc.	77.1
Eliason & Knuth Cos. Inc.	70.3
Acousti Engineering Co. of Florida	63.0
Nastasi White Inc.	59.0

Source: *ENR*, October 11, 1999, p. 74.

★ 126 ★
Contracting - Asbestos (SIC 1742)

Leading Asbestos Contractors - 1998

Firms are ranked by revenues in millions of dollars.

LVI Services Inc.	$ 102.6
NSC Corp.	86.7
PDG Environmental Inc.	36.8
MARCOR Remediation Inc.	34.5
IREX Contracting Group	30.3
Specialty Systems Inc.	20.7
Philip Services Corp.	19.8
Precision Environmental Co. Inc.	17.3

Source: *ENR*, October 11, 1999, p. 76.

★ 127 ★
Contracting - Sheet Metal (SIC 1761)

Top Sheet Metal Contractors - 1998

Firms are ranked by revenues in millions of dollars.

Kirk & Blum	$ 69.6
Scott Co. of California	49.0
Hill Mechanical Group	46.5
EMCOR Group Inc.	44.2
Holaday-Parks Inc.	40.0
Cal-Air Inc.	37.9
Crown Corr Inc.	36.0
Anson Industries Inc.	33.7

Source: *ENR*, October 11, 1999, p. &1.

★ 128 ★
Roofing (SIC 1761)

Residential Roofing Market - 2003

The market is expected top reach 170 million squares.

	(mil.)	Share
Asphalt shingles	131.5	77.35%
Roll roofing	17.0	10.00
Roof tile	7.8	4.59
Wood shingles and shakes	3.6	2.12
Built-up roofing	3.4	2.00
Modified bitumen roofing	1.7	1.00
Metal roofing	1.6	0.94
Elastometric roofing	1.4	0.82
Other	2.0	1.18

Source: *Building Material Dealer*, April 2000, p. 31, from Freedonia Group.

★ 129 ★
Siding (SIC 1761)

Residential Siding Market - 2003

The market is expected top reach 81 million squares.

	(mil.)	Share
Vinyl	42.9	52.96%
Wood	12.7	15.68
Stucco, stone, concrete & related	8.2	10.12
Fiber cement	8.1	10.00
Brick	7.9	9.75
Metal and other	1.2	1.48

Source: *Building Material Dealer*, April 2000, p. 31, from Freedonia Group.

★ 130 ★
Contracting - Steel Erection (SIC 1791)

Top Steel Erection Contractors - 1998

Firms are ranked by revenues in millions of dollars.

Schuff Steel Inc.	$ 189.9
Midwest Steel Inc.	130.7
The Broad Group	84.0
The Williams Group	76.0
Sowles Co.	46.6
Derr Construction Co.	38.3
Interstate Iron Works Copr.	36.8
Area Erectors	31.0
Allstate Steel Co.	29.0

Source: *ENR*, October 11, 1999, p. 68.

★ 131 ★
Contracting - Excavation/Foundation (SIC 1794)

Top Excavation/Foundation Contractors - 1998

Firms are ranked by revenues in millions of dollars.

Hayward Baker Inc.	$ 103.3
Ryan Incorporated Central	90.0
Manafort Brothers Inc.	88.7
Malcolm Drilling Co. Inc.	84.1
AGRA Foundations Inc.	70.0
Philip Services Corp.	69.2
McKinney Drilling Co.	67.5
Independence Excavating Inc.	59.4
Case Foundation Co.	57.8

Source: *ENR*, October 11, 1999, p. 68.

★ 132 ★

Contracting - Demolition and Wrecking (SIC 1795)

Top Demolition/Wrecking Contractors - 1998

Firms are ranked by revenues in millions of dollars.

Penhall Co.	$ 95.0
Philip Services Corp.	59.3
North American Site Developers Inc.	39.8
Cleveland Wrecking Co.	35.1
Bierlein Cos. Inc.	32.1
ICONCO Inc.	27.2
P&P Contractors Inc.	26.3
The Millgard Corp.	26.3

Source: *ENR*, October 11, 1999, p. 76.

SIC 20 - Food and Kindred Products

Food (SIC 2000)

Largest Food and Drink Companies - 1998

Firms are ranked by sales in bilions of dollars. Data are for the U.S. and Canada.

Philip Morris Companies Inc.	$ 31.4
PepsiCo. Inc.	22.3
Coca-Cola Co.	18.8
ConAgra Inc.	17.9
IBP Inc.	12.8
Sara Lee Corp.	10.8
Anheuser-Busch Companies Inc.	9.2
H.J. Heinz Co.	9.2
Nabisco Inc.	8.4
Bestfoods	8.3

Source: *Prepared Foods*, July 1999, p. 16.

Food (SIC 2000)

Largest Food and Drink Firms in Canada - 1998

Sales are shown in billions of dollars.

McCain Foods Ltd.	$ 5.1
The Seagram Company Ltd.	4.6
Maple Leaf Foods Inc.	3.2
George Weston Ltd.	2.6
Kraft Canada Inc.	2.2
Molson Breweries	1.9
Groupe Saputo Inc.	1.9
Nestle Canada Inc.	1.6
Cott Corp.	1.4

Source: *Food in Canada*, September 1999, p. 1, from Ernst & Young.

Food (SIC 2000)

Largest Food Firms - 1999

Firms are ranked by revenues in billions of dollars.

Conagra	$ 24.5
Sara Lee	20.0
Archer Daniels Midland	14.2
IBP	14.0
Farmland Industries	10.7
H.J. Heinz	9.3
Bestfoods	8.6
Nabisco Group Holdings	8.2
Tyson Foods	7.3

Source: *Fortune*, April 17, 2000, pp. I-63.

Food (SIC 2000)

Largest Meat/Poultry/Food Processors

Firms are ranked by sales in billions of dollars.

ConAgra	$ 24.0
IBP	13.3
Cargill	9.0
Tyson	6.4
Sara Lee	4.5
Smithfield	3.8
Hormel	3.2
Oscar Mayer	2.5
Gold Kist	2.3

Source: Retrieved January 1, 2000 from the World Wide Web: http://www.stagnito.com/np/index.html.

★ 137 ★

Food (SIC 2000)

Largest Packaged Food Companies - 1998

Companies are ranked by sales in millions of dollars.

Philip Morris	$ 27.3
PepsiCo.	11.6
Heinz	9.2
Nabisco Holdings	8.4
Bestfoods	8.3
Sara Lee	8.2
Kellogg	6.7

Source: *Chemical Market Reporter*, July 19, 1999, p. 6, from Schroder & Co. Inc.

★ 138 ★

Food (SIC 2000)

Largest Snack/Baked Goods Makers

Firms are ranked by snack and baked good sales in billions of dollars.

Frito-Lay Inc.	$ 7.4
Nabisco Inc.	6.9
Flowers Industries Inc.	4.0
Interstate Bakeries Corp.	3.4
Keebler Corp.	2.7
Campbell Soup Co.	2.3
Kraft Foods Inc.	2.3
The Pillsbury Co.	1.9
The Earthgrains Co.	1.9

Source: *Snack Food & Wholesale Bakery*, December 1999, p. 30.

★ 139 ★

Food (SIC 2000)

Leading Health Food Categories - 1999

The market is shown in billions of dollars.

Natural	$ 25.4
Functional foods	14.2
Vitamins/minerals	13.2
Organic	4.2
Herbs	3.6

Source: *Cereal Foods World*, November-December 1999, p. 747.

★ 140 ★

Food (SIC 2000)

Medical/Specialty Food Market - 1998

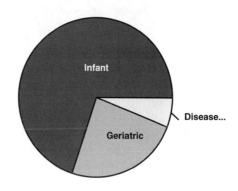

The market was valued at $5.41 billion.

	($ bil.)	Share
Infant	$ 3.78	69.87%
Geriatric	1.30	24.03
Disease specific	0.32	6.10

Source: "Introduction to U.S. Markets for Medical Specialty Foods." Retrieved February 1, 2000 from the World Wide Web: http://www.just-food.com, from Frost & Sullivan.

★ 141 ★

Food (SIC 2000)

Natural Food Store Sales - 1999

Sales are shown in millions of dollars for the year ended October 1999.

Beverages, non-dairy	$ 169.2
Cereal, cold	119.7
Tea	118.9
Beverages, carbonated	91.4
Milk, organic	65.8
Juices, refrigerated	60.7
Potato chips, regular	30.0

Source: *Supermarket Business*, March 15, 2000, p. 44, from A.C. Nielsen and SPINS.

★ 142 ★
Food (SIC 2000)

Shelf-Stable Food Sales - 1998

Sales are shown in millions of dollars.

Salad dressings	$ 1,300
Salad, fresh-cut	1,200
Sauces	1,100
Mayonnaise	1,000
Gravy and sauce mixes	860
Mexican sauces	827
Mustard and ketchup	743

Source: "Salad Dessing and Sauce Trends." Retrieved January 11, 2000 from the World Wide Web: http://www.dressings-sauces.org/trends.html, from Association for Dressings and Sauces.

★ 143 ★
Meat Processing (SIC 2011)

Commercial Cattle Slaughter Market - 1998

Market shares are shown in percent.

IBP	28.8%
Excel	18.0
ConAgra	16.8
Farmland	6.8
Other	29.6

Source: "Market Share of Top Packers." Retrieved May 16, 2000 from the World Wide Web: http://www.ag.ndsu.nodak.edu.

★ 144 ★
Meat Processing (SIC 2011)

Steer/Heifer Slaughter Market - 1998

Market shares are shown in percent.

IBP	32.7%
Excel	22.2
ConAgra	18.8
Farmland	8.3
Other	18.0

Source: "Market Share of Top Packers." Retrieved May 16, 2000 from the World Wide Web: http://www.ag.ndsu.nodak.edu.

★ 145 ★
Meat Snacks (SIC 2011)

Top Meat Snacks - 1999

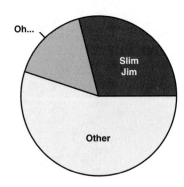

Supermarket sales reached $117 million for the year ended July 18, 1999.

	($ mil.)	Share
Slim Jim	$ 34.0	29.06%
Oh Boy! Oberto	18.4	15.73
Other	64.6	55.21

Source: *Supermarket News*, September 27, 1999, p. 59, from Information Resources Inc.

★ 146 ★
Lunch Meat (SIC 2013)

Top Lunch Meat Brands - 1999

The $2.7 billion market is shown in percent for the year ended March 28, 1999.

	($ mil.)	Share
Oscar Mayer	$ 591	21.89%
Louis Rich	129	4.78
Butterball	105	3.89
Other	1,875	69.44

Source: *Brandweek*, July 5, 1999, p. 8, from Information Resources Inc.

★ 147 ★
Meat (SIC 2013)

Top Packaged Meats

Sales are in millions of dollars for the year ended September 4, 1999.

Lunchmeat, sliced, refrigerated	$ 2,394.5
Frankfurters, refrigerated	1,576.2
Bacon, refrigerated	1,576.0

Continued on next page.

★ 147 ★ *Continued*
Meat (SIC 2013)

Top Packaged Meats

Sales are in millions of dollars for the year ended September 4, 1999.

Sausage, dinner	$ 1,016.6
Sausage, breakfast	798.0
Lunchmeat, deli pouches, refrigerated	613.8
Lunchmeat, nonsliced, refrigerated	251.3
Bratwurst & knockwurst	155.3
Franks, cocktail, refrigerated	104.6

Source: *Grocery Headquarters*, December 1999, p. 37, from A.C. Nielsen.

★ 148 ★
Meat (SIC 2013)

U.S. Meat Sales -1999

Beef sales have increased with the growth of high protein, low carbohydrate diets. Consumer sales reached $36.7 billion for the first nine months of the year.

Beef	40.0%
Pork	28.4
Chicken	27.4
Turkey	4.2

Source: *Los Angeles Times*, November 3, 1999, p. 1.

★ 149 ★
Poultry (SIC 2015)

Best-Selling Frozen Poultry Brands - 1999

Sales are shown in millions of dollars for the 12 weeks ended June 12, 1999.

Tyson	$ 53.6
Banquet	42.3
Cagles	10.6
Barber	8.4
Private label	84.2

Source: *Frozen Food Age*, September 1999, p. 1, from Information Resources Inc.

★ 150 ★
Poultry (SIC 2015)

Largest Poultry Firms

Tyson Foods	25.0%
Gold Kist	8.6
Perdue Farms	7.9
ConAgra Poultry	5.5
Pilgrim's Pride	4.1
Wayne Poultry	4.1
Sanderson Farms	2.7
Cagle's	2.5
Foster Farms	2.5
Other	37.1

Source: *Poultry & Egg Marketing*, November/December 1999, p. 14, from National Chicken Council.

★ 151 ★
Dairy Products (SIC 2020)

Dairy Product Sales - 1998

Sales are shown in millions of dollars.

Juice, refrigerated	$ 3,620.0
Eggs	2,140.0
Yogurt	1,770.0
Dough, refrigerated	1,340.0
Cottage cheese	841.5

Source: *Supermarket News*, March 20, 2000, p. 42, from International Deli-Bakery Association.

★ 152 ★
Dairy Products (SIC 2020)

Largest Dairy Firms - 1998

The top firms in the U.S. and Canada are ranked by sales in millions of dollars.

Kraft Foods	$ 4.3
Suiza Foods	2.8
Land O'Lakes Inc.	2.7
Dean Foods Co.	2.5
Dairy Farmers of America	2.3
Schreiber Foods Inc.	1.3
Leprino Foods Co.	1.3
Kroger Foods	1.3
Saputo Group	1.1
Parmalat Canada	1.1

Source: *Dairy Foods*, July 1999, p. 13.

★ 153 ★

Dairy Products (SIC 2020)

Largest Dairy Product Producers - 1998

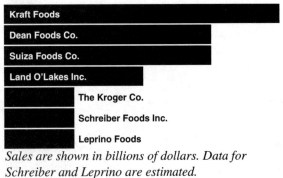

Kraft Foods

Dean Foods Co.

Suiza Foods Co.

Land O'Lakes Inc.

The Kroger Co.

Schreiber Foods Inc.

Leprino Foods

Sales are shown in billions of dollars. Data for Schreiber and Leprino are estimated.

Kraft Foods	$ 4.2
Dean Foods Co.	2.8
Suiza Foods Co.	2.6
Land O'Lakes Inc.	2.2
The Kroger Co.	1.4
Schreiber Foods Inc.	1.4
Leprino Foods	1.2

Source: *Refrigerated & Frozen Foods*, June 1999, p. 47, from Information Resources Inc. InfoScan.

★ 154 ★

Butter (SIC 2021)

Leading Butter/Margarine Markets - 1999

Sales are shown in millions of dollars in selected markets. Figures are for the year ended September 4, 1999.

New York City	$ 187.4
Philadelphia	105.7
Los Angeles	101.1
Boston	88.3
Chicago	82.4

Source: *Grocery Headquarters*, January 2000, p. 45, from A.C. Nielsen.

★ 155 ★

Margarine (SIC 2021)

Top Margarine Brands in Canada - 1999

Shares are shown based on estimated sales of $293.9 million for the year ended December 31, 1999.

Lipton	57.9%
Parmalat	11.4
Canbra	3.1
Innovative Foods	2.8
Thibault	1.3
Baxter	0.2
Private label	21.2
Other	2.1

Source: ''Report on Market Share.'' Retrieved June 8, 2000 from the World Wide Web: http://www. marketingmag.ca, from A.C. Nielsen MarketTrack.

★ 156 ★

Cheese (SIC 2022)

Cheese Product Sales - 1998

Shares are shown based on supermarket sales for the year ended January 3, 1999.

	($ mil.)	Share
Natural cheese, not shredded . .	$ 1,989.9	29.71%
Yogurt, refrigerated	1,753.7	26.18
Natural cheese, shredded	1,387.6	20.72
Cottage cheese	761.3	11.37
Sour cream	512.5	7.65
Dips, refrigerated	293.3	4.38

Source: *Refrigerated and Frozen Foods*, June 1999, p. 36, from Information Resources Inc. Infoscan.

★ 157 ★

Cheese (SIC 2022)

Cheese Sales Volumes - 1999

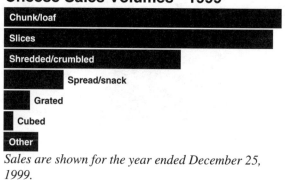

Sales are shown for the year ended December 25, 1999.

Chunk/loaf	32.8%
Slices	32.2
Shredded/crumbled	20.6
Spread/snack	7.0
Grated	2.7
Cubed	0.5
Other	4.2

Source: *Dairy Foods*, April 2000, p. F, from A.C. Nielsen and IDFA Cheese Market Research Project.

★ 158 ★

Cheese (SIC 2022)

Leading Cheese Markets - 1999

Sales are shown in millions of dollars in selected markets. Figures are for the year ended September 4, 1999.

Los Angeles	$ 389.3
New York City	389.3
Chicago	206.9
Philadelphia	197.5
Boston	190.9

Source: *Grocery Headquarters*, January 2000, p. 45, from A.C. Nielsen.

★ 159 ★

Cheese (SIC 2022)

Top Cheese Snack Makers - 1998

Shares are shown for the year ended January 3, 1999.

Frito-Lay Inc.	56.9%
Planters	9.2
Wise Foods	6.9
Bachman	2.3
Golden Flake	2.1
Private label	10.7
Other	11.9

Source: *Snack Food & Wholesale Bakery*, June 1999, p. SI38, from Information Resources Inc.

★ 160 ★

Cheese (SIC 2022)

Top Cheese Snacks - 1998

Shares are shown for the year ended January 3, 1999.

Cheetos	51.4%
Planters	9.2
Cheez Doodles	5.7
Chee-tos Cheesy Checkers	5.5
Bachman Jax	2.3
Golden Flake	2.1
Snyders of Berlin	1.0
Private label	10.2
Other	12.6

Source: *Snack Food & Wholesale Bakery*, June 1999, p. SI38, from Information Resources Inc.

★ 161 ★

Cheese (SIC 2022)

Top Natural Cheese Brands - 1998

Shares are shown based on supermarket sales of $1.3 billion for the year ended January 3, 1999.

Kraft	28.9%
Sargento	12.9
Healthy Choice	3.1
Crystal Farms	2.8
Sorrento	1.4
Kraft Free	1.2
Churry Provincia	1.2

Continued on next page.

★ 161 ★ *Continued*

Cheese (SIC 2022)

Top Natural Cheese Brands - 1998

Shares are shown based on supermarket sales of $1.3 billion for the year ended January 3, 1999.

Sargento Double Cheese	0.9%
Sargento Preferred Light	0.9
Private label	40.5
Other	6.2

Source: *Refrigerated and Frozen Foods*, June 1999, p. 36, from Information Resources Inc. Infoscan.

★ 162 ★

Cheese Spreads (SIC 2022)

Top Aerosol Cheese Spreads - 1998

Total supermarket sales reached $71.9 million for the year ended January 3, 1999.

Nabisco Easy Cheese	98.4%
Crystal Farms Cheezoid	0.7
Private label	0.4

Source: *Snack Food and Wholesale Bakery*, June 1999, p. 75, from Information Resources Inc.

★ 163 ★

Cheese Spreads (SIC 2022)

Top Cheese Spread/Ball Brands - 1998

Total sales reached $261.8 million for the year ended January 3, 1999.

	($ mil.)	Share
Kaukana	$ 19.9	7.6%
Alouette	18.2	6.9
Price	16.0	6.1
Precious	14.9	5.7
Private label	39.5	15.1

Source: *Snack Food and Wholesale Bakery*, June 1999, p. 75, from Information Resources Inc.

★ 164 ★

Cheese Spreads (SIC 2022)

Top Refrigerated Cheese Spreads - 1998

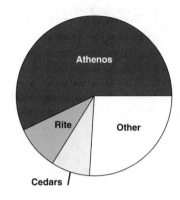

Total supermarket sales reached $33.8 million for the year ended January 3, 1999.

	($ mil.)	Share
Athenos	$ 19.2	56.6%
Rite	3.0	9.0
Cedars	2.8	8.1
Other	8.8	26.3

Source: *Snack Food and Wholesale Bakery*, June 1999, p. 75, from Information Resources Inc.

★ 165 ★

Dairy Creamer (SIC 2023)

Top Dairy Creamer Brands - 1998

Shares are shown based on total sales of $293.9 million for the year ended September 13, 1998.

	($ mil.)	Share
Carnation Coffee Mate	$ 153.2	79.01%
Borden Cremora	26.1	13.46
Community	1.9	0.98
Cain's	0.5	0.26
International Delight	0.2	0.10
N Rich	0.1	0.05
Preamer	0.1	0.05
Other	11.8	6.09

Source: *MMR*, November 16, 1998, p. 22, from Information Resources Inc.

★ **166** ★

Frozen Desserts (SIC 2024)

Best-Selling Frozen Food Novelties

Sales are shown in millions of dollars for the 12 weeks ended June 12, 1999. Data are for the single serving market.

Klondike	$ 30.2
Popsicle	29.0
Drumstick	24.4
Dole Fruit & Juice	13.3
Private label	78.1

Source: *Frozen Food Age*, September 1999, p. 1, from Information Resources Inc.

★ **167** ★

Frozen Desserts (SIC 2024)

Frozen Novelty Sales - 1999

Sales are shown in millions of dollars for the year ended December 28, 1999.

	($ mil.)	Share
Klondike	$ 116.6	6.70%
Popsicle	104.7	6.01
Drumstick	96.2	5.53
Dole Fruit & Juice	49.6	2.85
Haagen-Dazs	47.8	2.75
Eskimo Pie	41.6	2.39
Dove Bar	40.8	2.34
Wells' Blue Bunny	39.7	2.28
Private label	287.8	16.53
Other	916.2	52.62

Source: *Dairy Foods*, March 2000, p. 57, from Information Resources Inc.

★ **168** ★

Frozen Desserts (SIC 2024)

Leading Pudding/Dessert Markets - 1999

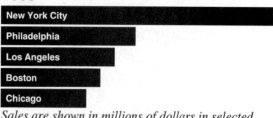

Sales are shown in millions of dollars in selected markets. Figures are for the year ended September 4, 1999.

New York City	$ 38.7
Philadelphia	18.8
Los Angeles	16.0
Boston	14.0
Chicago	11.6

Source: *Grocery Headquarters*, January 2000, p. 45, from A.C. Nielsen.

★ **169** ★

Frozen Desserts (SIC 2024)

Top Frozen Yogurt/Tofu Brands - 1999

Sales are shown in millions of dollars for the year ended December 28, 1999.

	($ mil.)	Share
Dreyer's/Edy's	$ 46.4	17.85%
Ben & Jerry's	34.9	13.42
Turkey Hill	20.6	7.92
Haagen-Dazs	17.5	6.73
Breyer's	12.5	4.81
Kemps	12.0	4.62
Blue Bell	6.4	2.46
Mayfield	5.7	2.19
Private label	49.1	18.88
Other	54.9	21.12

Source: *Dairy Foods*, March 2000, p. 57, from Information Resources Inc.

★ 170 ★

Frozen Desserts (SIC 2024)

Top Refrigerated Pudding/Mousse/ Gelatin Parfaits

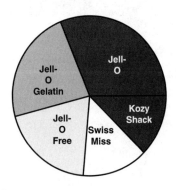

Total supermarket sales reached $476.9 million for the year ended January 3, 1999.

	($ mil.)	Share
Jell-O	$ 126.3	26.5%
Jell-O Gelatin Snacks	95.4	20.0
Jell-O Free	79.0	16.6
Swiss Miss	58.4	12.2
Kozy Shack	53.2	11.2

Source: *Snack Food and Wholesale Bakery*, June 1999, p. 75, from Information Resources Inc.

★ 171 ★

Frozen Desserts (SIC 2024)

Top Sherbert/Sorbet/Ice Brands - 1999

Sales are shown in millions of dollars for the year ended December 28, 1999.

	($ mil.)	Share
Haagen-Dazs	$ 24.0	12.37%
Dreyer's/Edy's	19.8	10.21
Blue Bell	9.5	4.90
Ben & Jerry's	7.2	3.71
Kemps	6.0	3.09
Wells' Blue Bunny	4.0	2.06
Prairie Farms	3.2	1.65
Perry's	2.6	1.34
Private label	57.4	29.59
Other	60.3	31.08

Source: *Dairy Foods*, March 2000, p. 57, from Information Resources Inc.

★ 172 ★

Ice Cream (SIC 2024)

Best-Selling Ice Cream Brands - 1999

Sales are shown in millions of units for the 12 weeks ended June 12, 1999.

Breyer's	79.4
Dreyer's Edy's Grand	23.2
Blue Bell	15.0
Haagen-Dazs	12.4
Private label	79.4

Source: *Frozen Food Age*, September 1999, p. 1, from Information Resources Inc.

★ 173 ★

Ice Cream (SIC 2024)

Ice Cream Product Sales - 1999

Data show sales in millions of units for the year ended October 10, 1999. Data are for food stores only.

Ice cream	1,124.0
Frozen yogurt/tofu	79.6
Sherbert/sorbets	78.6

Source: *Supermarket Business*, January 15, 2000, p. 51, from Information Resources Inc.

★ 174 ★

Ice Cream (SIC 2024)

Popular Ice Cream Flavors - 1999

Sales are shown in millions of dollars for the year ended December 28, 1999.

Vanilla	$ 161.8
Chocolate	54.1
Neopolitan	45.0
Cookies & cream	19.8
Chocolate chip	17.0
Mint chocolate chip	15.8
Vanilla/chocolate	13.5
Cookie flavor	12.5

Source: *Dairy Foods*, March 2000, p. 57, from Information Resources Inc.

★ 175 ★
Ice Cream (SIC 2024)

Premium Ice Cream Market

Haagen Daz	47.5%
Ben & Jerry's	40.7
Starbuck's	9.2
Other	1.8

Source: Retrieved January 20, 2000 from the World Wide Web: http://www.activemedia-guide.com/prem_icecream.htm, from U.S. Business Reporter.

★ 176 ★
Milk (SIC 2026)

How Milk Is Used - 2000

A total of 165 billion pounds (milk equivalent) are expected to be produced in 2000.

	(bil.)	Share
Cheese	61.9	38.30%
Fluid use	57.0	35.27
Butter, creamery	26.6	16.46
Frozen desserts	14.4	8.91
Evaporated & condensed	1.7	1.05

Source: *Dairy Foods*, January 2000, p. 49, from Food and Agricultural Policy Research Institute.

★ 177 ★
Milk (SIC 2026)

Largest Milk Producers

Suiza
Dean Foods
Other

Market shares are shown in percent.

Suiza	20%
Dean Foods	13
Other	67

Source: *Advertising Age*, January 10, 2000, p. 4.

★ 178 ★
Milk (SIC 2026)

Leading Milk Processors - 1999

Suiza Foods
Dean Foods
Kroger
Dairy Farmers of America
Prairie Farms Cooperative
Southern Foods Group
Safeway Stores - Dairy Div.
Others

Data show estimated wholesale sales in millions of dollars.

	($ mil.)	Share
Suiza Foods	$ 2,600	10.99%
Dean Foods	2,300	9.73
Kroger	1,400	5.92
Dairy Farmers of America	1,000	4.23
Prairie Farms Cooperative	850	3.59
Southern Foods Group	800	3.38
Safeway Stores - Dairy Div.	700	2.96
Others	14,000	59.20

Source: *Dairy Foods*, January 2000, p. 13.

★ 179 ★
Milk (SIC 2026)

Milk Consumption by Type - 1998

Milk, lowfat	43.0%
Milk, plain whole	33.4
Milk, skim fat free	16.9
Milk, flavored	5.5
Buttermilk	1.2

Source: "Steady, Slow Decline in U.S. Milk Drinking." Retrieved April 26, 2000 from the World Wide Web: http://www.beveragemarketing.com, from Beverage Marketing Corp.

★ 180 ★
Milk (SIC 2026)

Refrigerated Soy Milk Market

The market is valued at $300 million.

White Wave 78%
Other 22

Source: *Forbes*, May 15, 2000, p. 324.

★ 181 ★
Milk (SIC 2026)

Top Soy Milk Brands in Canada

So Good 25.3%
Sunrise 23.2
Sensational Soy 9.5
Other 41.0

Source: *Marketing Magazine*, December 13, 1999, p. 3.

★ 182 ★
Yogurt (SIC 2026)

Top Yogurt Brands - 1998

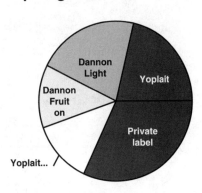

Total supermarket sales reached $1.75 billion for the year ended January 3, 1999.

	($ mil.)	Share
Yoplait	$ 177.3	10.1%
Dannon Light	176.5	10.1
Dannon Fruit on the Bottom . . .	110.4	6.3
Yoplait Light	96.6	5.5
Private label	257.4	14.7

Source: *Snack Food and Wholesale Bakery*, June 1999, p. 75, from Information Resources Inc.

★ 183 ★
Yogurt (SIC 2026)

Top Yogurt Vendors - 1999

Total sales reached $1.78 billion for the year ended March 28, 1999.

	($ mil.)	Share
Dannon	$ 552.2	31.02%
General Mills	533.0	29.94
Kraft Foods	177.8	9.99
Stonyfield Farm	43.6	2.45
Borden	25.4	1.43
Johanna Farms	23.7	1.33
Private label	260.1	14.61
Other	164.2	9.22

Source: *Advertising Age*, July 5, 1999, p. 26, from Information Resources Inc.

★ 184 ★
Baby Food (SIC 2032)

Baby Food Market

Gerber 73%
Beech-Nut 13
Heinz 11
Other 3

Source: *Wall Street Journal*, February 29, 2000, p. B16.

★ 185 ★
Baby Food (SIC 2032)

Baby Food Sales - 1998

Data show share of supermarket sales.

Formula 72.2%
Strained 12.4
Junior 6.9
Juices 3.8
Other 4.7

Source: *Progressive Grocer*, July 1999, p. 55.

★ 186 ★

Baby Food (SIC 2032)

Leading Baby Food Markets

Sales are shown in millions of dollars in selected markets.

Los Angeles	$ 240.3
New York City	188.5
Philadelphia	107.0
Chicago	84.6
Boston	72.3

Source: *Grocery Headquarters*, January 2000, p. 45, from A.C. Nielsen.

★ 187 ★

Infant Formula (SIC 2032)

Baby Formula Market - 1999

Shares are shown for the four weeks ended July 3, 1999.

Ross Laboratories	54.6%
Similac	31.8
Gerber	11.9
Generics	1.7

Source: *New York Times*, September 6, 1999, p. 13, from A.C. Nielsen.

★ 188 ★

Infant Formula (SIC 2032)

Baby Formula Sales by Type - 1999

Sales of baby formula in supermarkets reached $3 billion for the year ended January 2, 2000.

	($ mil.)	Share
Formula, powdered	$ 1,500.0	50.35%
Formula, liquid concentrate	939.5	31.53
Formula, ready to drink	539.9	18.12

Source: *Supermarket News*, February 21, 2000, p. 69, from Information Resources Inc.

★ 189 ★

Infant Formula (SIC 2032)

Infant Formula Market

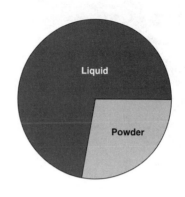

	(bil.)	Share
Liquid	2.9	72.5%
Powder	1.1	27.5

Source: *Washington Post*, September 11, 1999, p. E1, from PBM Products.

★ 190 ★

Infant Formula (SIC 2032)

Top Baby Formula Brands - 1998

Shares are shown based on total sales of $1.01 billion for the year ended September 13, 1998.

	($ mil.)	Share
Enfamil	$ 395.9	39.16%
Similac	233.8	23.13
Prosobee	126.8	12.54
Isomil	114.1	11.29
Lactofree	46.5	4.60
Nutramigen	35.5	3.51
Carnation Good Start	29.2	2.89
Carnation Alsoy	13.0	1.29
Other	16.2	1.60

Source: *MMR*, November 16, 1998, p. 22, from Information Resources Inc.

★ 191 ★
Soup (SIC 2032)

Soup Market Shares

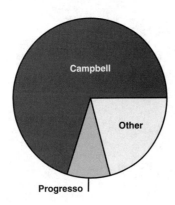

The $3.2 billion market is shown in percent.

Campbell 70%
Progresso 9
Other 21

Source: "Campbell Soup Reports Disappointing Earnings."
Retrieved May 30, 2000 from the World Wide Web: http://
www.library.northernlight.com.

★ 192 ★
Canned Food (SIC 2033)

Canned Fruit Sales - 1998

Supermarket sales reached $1.4 billion. Share of category sales are shown in percent.

Peaches 19.5%
Applesauce 16.4
Pineapple 16.1
Berries 9.4
Fruit, mixed 9.1
Pears 8.8
Other 20.7

Source: *Progressive Grocer*, July 1999, p. 56.

★ 193 ★
Canned Food (SIC 2033)

Canned Pasta Market

Market shares are shown in percent.

Franco American 58%
Other 42

Source: *Forbes*, April 3, 2000, p. 106.

★ 194 ★
Canned Food (SIC 2033)

Canned Vegetable Sales - 1998

Supermarket sales reached $3.4 billion. Category sales are shown in percent.

Beans 22.2%
Tomatoes 13.4
Corn 11.7
Beans, baked 11.2
Carrots and peas 7.2
Other 34.3

Source: *Progressive Grocer*, July 1999, p. 56.

★ 195 ★
Canned Food (SIC 2033)

U.S. Applesauce Market - 1998

The market was valued at $112 million.

Mott's 54.6%
Other 45.4

Source: Retrieved February 11, 2000 from the World Wide
Web: http://www.library.northernlight.com.

★ 196 ★
Jellies and Jams (SIC 2033)

Leading Jam/Spread Markets - 1999

Sales are shown in millions of dollars in selected markets. Figures are for the year ended September 4, 1999.

New York City . . . . $ 95.9
Los Angeles 79.4
Philadelphia 51.5
Boston 51.3
Chicago 47.0

Source: *Grocery Headquarters*, January 2000, p. 45, from
A.C. Nielsen.

★ 197 ★
Jellies and Jams (SIC 2033)
U.S. Jelly/Jam Market - 1999

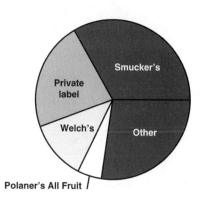

Shares are shown based on total sales of $671.9 million for the year ended March 28, 1999.

	($ mil.)	Share
Smucker's	$ 224.0	33.34%
Private label	150.5	22.40
Welch's	79.0	11.76
Polaner's All Fruit	36.0	5.36
Other	182.4	27.15

Source: *Supermarket News*, August 30, 1999, p. 51, from Information Resources Inc.

★ 198 ★
Juices (SIC 2033)
Best-Selling Frozen Juices - 1999

Total sales reached $1.08 billion for the year ended March 28, 1999.

	($ mil.)	Share
Orange juice concentrate	$ 515.1	47.51%
Drink/cocktail drink concentrate	207.9	19.18
Lemonade/limeade concentrate	90.2	8.32
Blended fruit juice concentrate	84.5	7.79
Apple juice concentrate	72.3	6.67
Grape juice concentrate	48.3	4.46
Other	65.8	6.07

Source: *Beverage Industry*, July 1999, p. 34, from Information Resources Inc.

★ 199 ★
Juices (SIC 2033)
Cranberry Beverage Market

The market was valued at $750 million for the year ended July 1999.

Ocean Spray	53%
Other	47

Source: *Supermarket News*, November 15, 1999, p. 54, from Information Resources Inc.

★ 200 ★
Juices (SIC 2033)
Largest Refrigerated/Frozen Juice Producers - 1998

Sales are shown in millions of dollars.

Tropicana Beverage Group	$ 1,600
The Minute Maid Co.	495
Citrus World Inc.	468
McCain Citrus Inc.	350
Welch's	120

Source: *Refrigerated & Frozen Foods*, June 1999, p. 47, from Information Resources Inc. InfoScan.

★ 201 ★
Juices (SIC 2033)
Ready-to-Drink Chilled Juice Market in Canada - 2000

Shares are shown based on sales of $380.7 million for the year ended February 26, 2000.

Tropicana	57.8%
Minute Maid	7.0
Oasis	6.3
Beatrice	5.6
Private label	16.4
Other	6.9

Source: "Report on Market Share." Retrieved June 8, 2000 from the World Wide Web: http://www.marketingmag.ca, from industry sources.

★ 202 ★

Juices (SIC 2033)

Refrigerated Orange Juice Market

Tropicana 41%
Minute Maid 20
Florida's Natural 9
Private label 20

Source: *Chicago Tribune*, November 15, 1999, p. 3, from Information Resources Inc.

★ 203 ★

Juices (SIC 2033)

Shelf-Stable Juices/Nectars Market in Canada - 1999

Shares are shown based on sales of $698.6 million for the year ended February 26, 2000.

Sun-Rype 22.6%
Del Monte 20.8
McCain 15.0
Lassonde 7.6
Minute Maid 5.5
Private label 20.0

Source: ''Report on Market Share.'' Retrieved June 8, 2000 from the World Wide Web: http://www.marketingmag.ca, from *Beverage Digest*.

★ 204 ★

Juices (SIC 2033)

Super Premium Juice Market

Odwalla Inc. 60%
Other 40

Source: *Supermarket News*, February 28, 2000, p. 31.

★ 205 ★

Dried Fruit (SIC 2034)

Fruit Snack Market - 1998

Shares are shown based on sales for the year ended January 3, 1999.

	($ mil.)	Share
General Mills	$ 224.6	28.75%
Sun-Maid Growers of California . .	150.6	19.28
Favorite Brands International . . .	82.0	10.50

	($ mil.)	Share
Brach & Brock Confections . . .	$ 32.7	4.19%
Dole	25.6	3.28
Paramount Farms (Sunkist)	21.0	2.69
Mariani Packing Co.	18.3	2.34
Private label	84.4	10.80
Other	142.0	18.18

Source: *Snack Food & Wholesale Bakery*, June 1999, pp. SI-69, from Information Resources Inc.

★ 206 ★

Dried Fruit (SIC 2034)

Leading Dried Fruit Brands - 1998

Shares are shown based on sales of $124.1 million for the year ended January 3, 1999. Market does not include fruit roll-ups or raisins.

Sun-Maid 16.5%
Ocean Spray Craisins 15.0
Mariani 13.2
Seneca 7.5
Home 5.5
Other 42.3

Source: *Snack Food & Wholesale Bakery*, June 1999, pp. SI-69, from Information Resources Inc.

★ 207 ★

Raisins (SIC 2034)

Top Raisin Brands - 1998

Shares are shown based on sales of $216.9 million for the year ended January 3, 1999.

Sun-Maid 55.8%
Dole 11.4
Del Monte 2.4
Champion 1.7
Private label 25.3
Other 3.4

Source: *Snack Food & Wholesale Bakery*, June 1999, pp. SI-69, from Information Resources Inc.

★ 208 ★
Guacamole (SIC 2035)

Guacamole Market Leaders

Shares are shown based on supermarket sales.

Calavo	27.7%
AvoMex	18.4
IMO	15.9
Other	38.0

Source: "Marketing Promotion News." Retrieved November 19, 1999 from the World Wide Web: http://www.calavo.com.

★ 209 ★
Ketchup (SIC 2035)

Ketchup Market in Canada

Heinz	65%
Other	35

Source: Retrieved May 2, 2000 from the World Wide Web: http://www.husa.com/annualreport/home.html.

★ 210 ★
Mustard (SIC 2035)

Best-Selling Mustards

French's	
Grey Poupon	
Gulden's	
Dijonnaise	

Sales are shown in millions of dollars.

French's	$ 48.0
Grey Poupon	44.3
Gulden's	19.4
Dijonnaise	12.0

Source: *Brandweek*, January 24, 1999, p. 14, from Information Resources Inc.

★ 211 ★
Peanut Butter (SIC 2035)

Peanut Butter Market

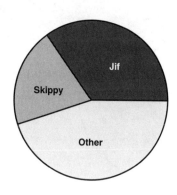

The $829 million market is shown in percent.

	($ mil.)	Share
Jif	$ 290	34.98%
Skippy	162	19.54
Other	377	45.48

Source: *Advertising Age*, January 31, 2000, p. 22, from Information Resources Inc.

★ 212 ★
Pickles and Olives (SIC 2035)

Leading Pickles/Olives/Relish Markets - 1999

Sales are shown in millions of dollars in selected markets. Figures are for the year ended September 4, 1999.

New York City	$ 77.9
Los Angeles	70.8
Philadelphia	44.0
Boston	43.7
Chicago	41.8

Source: *Grocery Headquarters*, January 2000, p. 45, from A.C. Nielsen.

★ 213 ★
Salad Dressings (SIC 2035)

Salad Dressing Market - 1998

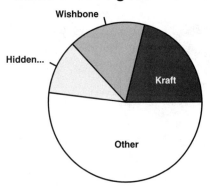

The $1.8 billion market is shown in percent for the year ended January 1999.

	($ mil.)	Share
Kraft	$ 268	20.62%
Wishbone	210	16.15
Hidden Valley Ranch	144	11.08
Other	678	52.15

Source: *Supermarket News*, May 10, 1999, p. 37, from Information Resources Inc.

★ 214 ★
Sauces (SIC 2035)

Asian Sauce Market

Sales are in the club store segment.

Yoshida	75%
Other	25

Source: "Heinz Expands its U.S. Condiments Business." Retrieved May 2, 2000 from the World Wide Web: http:// www.prnewswire.com.

★ 215 ★
Spreads (SIC 2035)

Spread and Syrup Sales - 1998

Supermarket sales are shown in millions of dollars.

	($ mil.)	Share
Peanut butter mixes	$ 752.12	31.62%
Maple syrup	525.78	22.10
Jams and jells	419.70	17.64
Marmalades	234.39	9.85
Honey	159.82	6.72
Chocolate syrup	145.42	6.11
All other breakfast syrup/spreads	141.49	5.95

Source: *Progressive Grocer*, July 1999, p. 58, from Information Resources Inc.

★ 216 ★
Frozen Vegetables (SIC 2037)

Best-Selling Mixed Vegetable Brands

Sales are shown in millions of dollars for the year ended June 12, 1999.

Green Giant Create A Meal!	$ 27.1
Bird's Eye	14.1
Birds Eye Farm Fresh	10.5
Pictsweet	6.0
Private label	38.8

Source: *Frozen Food Age*, September 1999, p. 1, from Information Resources Inc.

★ 217 ★
Frozen Vegetables (SIC 2037)

Frozen Sidedish Market - 1999

Shares are shown based on supermarket sales of $235.8 million for the year ended January 3, 1999.

	($ mil.)	Share
Green Giant Pasta Accents	$ 38.2	16.20%
Ore-Ida	29.7	12.60
Larry's	28.1	11.92
Green Giant Rice Originals	16.1	6.83
Pagoda Café	15.7	6.66
Stouffer's	12.4	5.26
Stouffer's Lean Cuisine	10.5	4.45
Other	85.1	36.09

Source: *Refrigerated & Frozen Foods*, June 1999, p. 84, from Information Resources Inc. InfoScan.

★ 218 ★

Frozen Vegetables (SIC 2037)

Frozen Vegetable Market - 1998

Shares are shown based on supermarket sales of $1.6 billion for the year ended January 3, 1999.

Pillsbury Co. (Green Giant) 13.5%
Agilink Foods (Birds Eye, Freshlike) 13.0
United Foods (Pictsweet) 6.1
Private label 40.7
Other 26.7

Source: *Refrigerated & Frozen Foods*, June 1999, p. 47, from Information Resources Inc. InfoScan.

★ 219 ★

Frozen Vegetables (SIC 2037)

Largest Frozen Vegetable/Fruit Producers - 1998

Sales are shown in millions of dollars.

Simplot Food Group . . . . $ 1,400
Lamb-Weston Inc. 1,300
Agrilink Foods 719
Pillsbury Co. 650
McCain Foods USA 612
Heinz Frozen Food Co. 602
NORPAC Foods 259
Nestle USA 250
Agripac Inc. 185

Source: *Refrigerated & Frozen Foods*, June 1999, p. 47, from Information Resources Inc. InfoScan.

★ 220 ★

Frozen Vegetables (SIC 2037)

Leading Frozen Vegetables Markets - 1999

Sales are shown in millions of dollars in selected markets. Figures are for the year ended September 4, 1999.

New York City . . . . $ 216.9
Philadelphia 122.1
Los Angeles 106.0
Chicago 90.3
Boston 82.7

Source: *Grocery Headquarters*, January 2000, p. 45, from A.C. Nielsen.

★ 221 ★

Frozen Foods (SIC 2038)

Best-Selling Frozen Dinners/Entrees - 1999

Sales are shown in millions of dollars for the year ended June 20, 1999.

Stouffer's . . . . $ 128.9
Healthy Choice 78.9
Marie Callender's 62.3
Weight Watcher's Smart Ones 52.7
Stouffer's Lean Cuisine 44.0

Source: *Frozen Food Age*, September 1999, p. 1, from Information Resources Inc.

★ 222 ★

Frozen Foods (SIC 2038)

Best-Selling Hand-Held Entrée Brands - 1999

Sales are shown in millions of dollars for the 12 weeks ended June 12, 1999.

Hot Pockets	$ 43.9
Lean Pockets	18.2
Croissant Pockets	13.2
Red Baron Pouches	9.8

Source: *Frozen Food Age*, September 1999, p. 1, from Information Resources Inc.

★ 223 ★

Frozen Foods (SIC 2038)

Best-Selling Hand-Held Entrees - 1999

Shares are shown based on total supermarket sales of $815.1 million for the year ended January 3, 1999.

	($ mil.)	Share
Hot Pockets	$ 195.1	23.94%
Lean Pockets	81.9	10.05
Croissant Pockets	61.6	7.56
Red Baron Pouches	44.3	5.43
Delimex	33.7	4.13
White Castle	33.0	4.05
Tina	33.0	4.05
Healthy Choice	28.7	3.52
State Fair	25.1	3.08
Other	278.7	34.19

Source: *Refrigerated & Frozen Foods*, June 1999, p. 57, from Information Resources Inc.

★ 224 ★

Frozen Foods (SIC 2038)

Best-Selling Meat Substitutes

Sales are shown in millions of units for the year ended June 12, 1999.

Morningstar Farms	$ 3.5
Gardenburger	3.3
Moran	1.5
Steak-Umm	1.5
Private label	2.9

Source: *Frozen Food Age*, September 1999, p. 1, from Information Resources Inc.

★ 225 ★

Frozen Foods (SIC 2038)

Best-Selling Potatoes/Fries/ Hashbrowns - 1999

Sales are shown in millions of dollars for the 12 weeks ended June 12, 1999.

Ore-Ida	$ 36.1
Ore-Ida Golden Crinkles	18.5
Ore-Ida Tater Tots	14.0
Ore-Ida Golden Fries	7.1
Private label	49.7

Source: *Frozen Food Age*, September 1999, p. 1, from Information Resources Inc.

★ 226 ★

Frozen Foods (SIC 2038)

Frozen Food Sales - 1998

Sales are shown in millions of dollars.

Dinners/entrees	$ 4,800
Ice cream/sherbert	4,100
Pizza	2,100
Vegetables, plain	1,700

Continued on next page.

★ 226 ★ *Continued*
Frozen Foods (SIC 2038)

Frozen Food Sales - 1998

Sales are shown in millions of dollars.

Poultry	$ 1,400
Breakfast food	886
Seafood	877
Potatoes/onions	842

Source: ''Industry at a Glance.'' Retrieved January 26, 2000 from the World Wide Web: http://www.affi.com, from Information Resources Inc.

★ 227 ★
Frozen Foods (SIC 2038)

Frozen Waffle Market in Fort Worth, TX

Dallas/Fort Worth residents consume $10.1 million in frozen waffles annually.

Eggo	60.2%
Other	39.8

Source: ''Frozen Waffles in Fort Worth.'' Retrieved February 11, 2000 from the World Wide Web: http://www.library.northernlight.com.

★ 228 ★
Frozen Foods (SIC 2038)

Hand-Held Food Market - 1999

Chef America
Camino Real
Schwan's Sales Enterprises
ConAgra Frozen Foods
Delimex
White Castle
Other

Shares are shown based on total supermarket sales of $815.1 million for the year ended January 3, 1999.

Chef America	44%
Camino Real	7
Schwan's Sales Enterprises	5
ConAgra Frozen Foods	4
Delimex	4
White Castle	4
Other	32

Source: *Refrigerated & Frozen Foods*, June 1999, p. 57, from Information Resources Inc. InfoScan.

★ 229 ★
Frozen Foods (SIC 2038)

Largest Snack/Appetizer/Sidedish Producers - 1998

Sales are shown in millions of dollars.

Kraft Foods Inc.	$ 1,200
Schwan's Sales Enterprises	764
House of Raeford Farms Inc.	500
The Pillsbury Co.	487
Anchor Food Products Inc.	400
Sargento Foods Inc.	346
Chef America Inc.	330

Source: *Refrigerated & Frozen Foods*, June 1999, p. 47, from Information Resources Inc. InfoScan.

★ 230 ★

Frozen Foods (SIC 2038)

Natural Frozen Foods Market

Data show estimated share of sales of frozen entrees, pizzas and convenience foods.

Amy's Kitchen	70%
Other	30

Source: *Grocery Headquarters*, September 1999, p. 46, from A.C. Nielsen.

★ 231 ★

Frozen Foods (SIC 2038)

Top Frozen Appetizer Brands - 1998

Shares are shown based on supermarket sales of $413.3 million for the year ended January 3, 1999.

Totino's	23.5%
Bagel Bites	18.5
Totino's Pizza Rolls	7.2
Poppers	6.6
Hot Pockets	5.3
Farm Rich	3.8
Cheese Bites	2.8
La Choy	2.2
Other	30.1

Source: *Snack Food & Wholesale Bakery*, June 1999, pp. SI-79, from Information Resources Inc.

★ 232 ★

Frozen Foods (SIC 2038)

Top Frozen Dips Brands - 1998

Shares are shown based on supermarket sales of $3.2 million for the year ended January 3, 1999.

Calavo	85.2%
T.G.I. Friday's	3.2
Private label	5.0
Other	6.6

Source: *Snack Food & Wholesale Bakery*, June 1999, pp. SI-79, from Information Resources Inc.

★ 233 ★

Frozen Foods (SIC 2038)

Top Pot Pie Brands

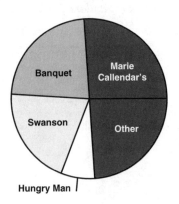

The $295 million market is shown in percent.

	($ mil.)	Share
Marie Callendar's	$ 76	25.76%
Banquet	69	23.39
Swanson	60	20.34
Hungry Man	20	6.78
Other	70	23.73

Source: *Advertising Age*, November 1, 1999, p. 65.

★ 234 ★

Frozen Foods (SIC 2038)

Top Refrigerated Appetizer Brands - 1998

Shares are shown based on supermarket sales of $3.2 million for the year ended January 3, 1999.

AFC	22.3%
Holly Farms	18.7
Kikka	15.2
Other	43.8

Source: *Snack Food & Wholesale Bakery*, June 1999, pp. SI-79, from Information Resources Inc.

★ 235 ★
Frozen Foods (SIC 2038)

Veggie Burger Market - 2000

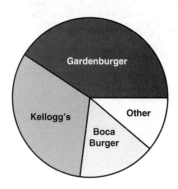

Shares are for the week ended April 8, 2000.

Gardenburger 41%
Kellogg's 32
Boca Burger 16
Other 11

Source: "Gardenburger Announces Fiscal 2Q 2000 Results." Retrieved May 1, 2000 from the World Wide Web: http://www.prnewswire.com.

★ 236 ★
Frozen Pizza (SIC 2038)

Best-Selling Frozen Pizza Brands

Sales are shown in millions of units for the year ended June 20, 1999.

Tombstone 17.1
DiGiorno 13.5
Tony's 12.4
Red Baron 8.9
Freschetta 7.4

Source: *Frozen Food Age*, September 1999, p. 1, from Information Resources Inc.

★ 237 ★
Frozen Pizza (SIC 2038)

Best-Selling Pizza Kits - 1998

Shares are shown based on supermarket sales of $143.8 million for the year ended January 3, 1999.

	($ mil.)	Share
Mama Rosa	$ 84.3	58.62%
Pizzeria Uno	3.6	2.50
Our Old Italian	3.5	2.43
Reno's	3.4	2.36
Private label	25.6	17.80
Other	23.4	16.27

Source: *Refrigerated & Frozen Foods*, June 1999, p. 47, from Information Resources Inc. InfoScan.

★ 238 ★
Frozen Pizza (SIC 2038)

Leading Frozen Pizza Snack Markets - 1999

Sales are shown in millions of dollars in selected markets. Figures are for the year ended September 4, 1999.

Chicago . . . . $ 134.7
New York City 93.9
Los Angeles 76.7
Philadelphia 68.9
Boston 53.3

Source: *Grocery Headquarters*, January 2000, p. 45, from A.C. Nielsen.

★ 239 ★
Frozen Pizza (SIC 2038)

Top Frozen Pizza Brands - 1998

Shares are shown based on supermarket sales of $2. 105 billion for the year ended January 3, 1999.

	($ mil.)	Share
DiGiorno	$ 293.0	13.92%
Tombstone	275.7	13.10
Tony's	174.7	8.30
Red Baron	169.5	8.05
Totino's	160.4	7.62
Freschetta	109.2	5.19
Stouffer's	74.8	3.55
Jack's	71.6	3.40
Celeste	66.2	3.14

Continued on next page.

★ 239 ★ *Continued*

Frozen Pizza (SIC 2038)

Top Frozen Pizza Brands - 1998

Shares are shown based on supermarket sales of $2. 105 billion for the year ended January 3, 1999.

	($ mil.)	Share
Private label	$ 103.0	4.89%
Other	607.0	28.83

Source: *Refrigerated & Frozen Foods*, June 1999, p. 80, from Information Resources Inc. InfoScan.

★ 240 ★

Frozen Pizza (SIC 2038)

Top Frozen Pizza Brands - 1999

Shares are shown based on supermarket sales for the year ended March 26, 2000.

DiGiorno	14.0%
Tombstone	13.8
Red Baron	8.0
Tony's	7.6
Totino's	7.1
Stouffer's	3.9
Jack's Original	3.4
Celeste Pizza for One	3.0
Other	39.2

Source: *Milling & Baking News*, May 23, 2000, p. 1, from Information Resources Inc.

★ 241 ★

Frozen Pizza (SIC 2038)

Top Frozen Pizza Makers - 1999

Shares are shown based on supermarket sales of $2. 105 billion for the year ended January 3, 1999.

Private label	4.9%
Other	17.6
Kraft Foods Pizza Div.	34.9
Schwan's Sales Enterprise	26.2
Pillsbury Co.	9.7
Nestle USA	3.6
VDK Frozen Foods	3.1

Source: *Refrigerated & Frozen Foods*, June 1999, p. 37, from Information Resources Inc. InfoScan.

★ 242 ★

Flour (SIC 2041)

Leading Flour Markets - 1999

Sales are shown in millions of dollars in selected markets. Figures are for the year ended September 4, 1999.

New York City	$ 18.1
Los Angeles	15.1
Chicago	10.7
Philadelphia	9.3
Boston	8.6

Source: *Grocery Headquarters*, January 2000, p. 45, from A.C. Nielsen.

★ 243 ★

Cereal (SIC 2043)

Leading Cereal Markets - 1999

Sales are shown in millions of dollars in selected markets. Figures are for the year ended September 4, 1999.

New York City	$ 482.4
Los Angeles	419.9
Philadelphia	294.7
Chicago	249.3
Boston	246.8

Source: *Grocery Headquarters*, January 2000, p. 45, from A.C. Nielsen.

★ **244** ★
Cereal (SIC 2043)

Top Cereal Makers - 1998

Shares are shown based on supermarket sales.

Kellogg	32.1%
General Mills	32.0
Post General Foods	16.5
Quaker Oats	9.1
Store brands	7.8
Malt-O-Meal	2.5

Source: *Detroit Free Press*, June 18, 1999, p. A1, from Bloomberg News and Information Resources Inc.

★ **245** ★
Rice (SIC 2044)

Rice Mix Market

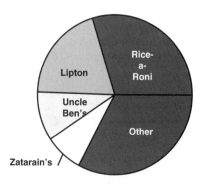

Rice-a-Roni	30.0%
Lipton	20.0
Uncle Ben's	10.0
Zatarain's	7.5
Other	32.5

Source: *Times-Picauyne*, November 28, 1999, p. F1, from Roper Starch Worldwide Inc and Zatarain's.

★ **246** ★
Baking Needs (SIC 2045)

Baking Mix Market in Canada

Sales are shown in millions of dollars for the year ended October 9, 1999.

	($ mil.)	Share
Cake mixes	$ 32.0	72.23%
Cookie mixes, dry	6.2	14.00
Brownie mixes	6.1	13.77

Source: *Marketing Magazine*, December 6, 1999, p. 2.

★ **247** ★
Baking Needs (SIC 2045)

Baking Product Sales - 1998

Supermarket sales are shown in millions of dollars.

	($ mil.)	Share
Cooking and salad oils	$ 1,538.20	24.13%
Mixes, baking	1,292.20	20.27
Sugar	1,214.40	19.05
Flour, stuffing, breading and other	1,147.00	17.99
Chips and other	390.10	6.12
Canned and dry millk	377.96	5.93
Cake frosting, RTS	236.44	3.71
Cake and cookie decoration . . .	105.33	1.65
Yeast, dry	72.93	1.14

Source: *Progressive Grocer*, July 1999, p. 55.

★ **248** ★
Baking Needs (SIC 2045)

Leading Baking Mix Markets

Sales are shown in millions of dollars in selected markets. Figures are for the year ended September 4, 1999.

Boston	$ 72.3
New York City	57.3
Los Angeles	54.4
Philadelphia	35.4
Chicago	33.0

Source: *Grocery Headquarters*, January 2000, p. 45, from A.C. Nielsen.

★ 249 ★

Dough (SIC 2045)

Refrigerated Dough Market - 1999

Shares are shown for the year ended July 18, 1999.

Pillsbury	77.4%
Merico	0.8
Private label	21.6

Source: Retrieved January 1, 2000 from the World Wide Web: http://jasper.sosland.com/cgi-bin/.c// pageitems_body?, from Information Resources Inc.

★ 250 ★

Dry Dishes (SIC 2045)

Dry Side Dish Market

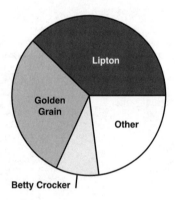

Betty Crocker

The category had sales of $428 million for the year ended October 10, 1999. Golden Grain makes Rice-A-Roni and Noodle-Roni.

	($ mil.)	Share
Lipton	$ 164	38.32%
Golden Grain	128	29.91
Betty Crocker	38	8.88
Other	98	22.90

Source: *Advertising Age*, December 6, 1999, p. 74, from Information Resources Inc.

★ 251 ★

Pet Food (SIC 2047)

Pet Food Market in Mexico

Ralston-Purina	30%
Mars Mexico	15
Quaker Pet Foods	10
Other	45

Source: "Pet Food Market." Retrieved September 21, 1999 from the World Wide Web: http://atn-riae.agr.ca/public/htmldocs/e2124.htm.

★ 252 ★

Pet Food (SIC 2047)

Pet Food Market Leaders - 1998

Data are estimated.

Ralston Purina	15.4%
Friskies PetCare	12.4
Heinz	11.9
Hill's	7.6
Doane/Windy Hill	7.4
Iams	5.0
Kal Kan	4.9
Nutro	2.7
Other	32.7

Source: *Veterinary Product News*, April 1999, p. 26, from *Pet Food Industry*, John Maxwell Jr., and Davenport & Co.

★ 253 ★

Pet Food (SIC 2047)

Pet Food Sales - 1998

Sales are shown in millions of dollars.

Ralston Purina	$ 1,622.0
Friskies	1,309.5
Heinz	1,256.9
Hill's	804.4
Doane/Windy Hill	785.9
Iams	524.5
Kal Kan	514.0

Source: *Feedstuffs*, August 16, 1999, p. 4, from Brakke Consulting Inc., John Maxwell Jr., and *Pet Food Industry*.

★ 254 ★
Pet Food (SIC 2047)

Pet Food Sales in Canada - 1998

Sales are shown in millions of dollars for the year ended October 10, 1998. Data show sales at supermarkets, which account for 54.2% of pet category sales.

Meal & kibbled dog food . . . . $ 90.7
Luxury canned cat food 73.0
Dry cat food 63.8
Specialty canned dog food 33.7
Dog biscuits 20.6
Dog treats 12.8
Maintenance canned dog food 7.3
Cat treats 5.4
Soft moist dog food 4.3
Semi-moist cat food 3.5
Maintenance canned cat food 3.2

Source: *Canadian Grocer*, March 1999, p. 1, from A.C. Nielsen MarketTrack.

★ 255 ★
Pet Food (SIC 2047)

Pet Food Vendors - 1998

Ralston Purina 17%
Nestle 16
Heinz 15
Hill's 8
Mars/Kal Kan 7
Doane 6
Iams 5
Other 26

Source: *Pet Product News*, October 1999, p. 34, from Salomon Smith Barney.

★ 256 ★
Pet Food (SIC 2047)

Premium Pet Food Market

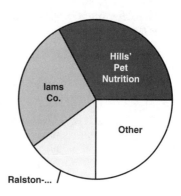

Shares are shown of the $2.5 billion market.

Hills' Pet Nutrition Inc. 33%
Iams Co. 27
Ralston-Purina Co. 15
Other 25

Source: *Los Angeles Times*, August 12, 1999, p. C1, from Procter & Gamble Co.

★ 257 ★
Pet Food (SIC 2047)

Top Cat Food Brands - 1998

Brands are ranked by sales of $1.21 billion for the year ended January 21, 1999.

	($ mil.)	Share
Friskies	$ 195.3	16.14%
Fancy Feast	163.5	13.51
9 Lives Plus	150.8	12.46
Friskies Fancy Feast	111.5	9.21
9 Lives	82.4	6.81
Whiskas	63.1	5.21
Friskies Alpo	54.2	4.48
Friskies Special Diet	36.0	2.98
Other	353.2	29.19

Source: *MMR*, May 17, 1999, p. 36, from Information Resources Inc.

★ 258 ★

Pet Food (SIC 2047)

Top Dry Dog Food Brands - 1998

Shares are shown based on total sales of $2.43 billion for the year ended January 1, 1999.

	($ mil.)	Share
Kal Kan Pedigree Mealtime . . .	$ 343.2	23.98%
Purina Dog Chow	264.0	18.45
Purina ONE	218.1	15.24
Purina Puppy Chow	142.5	9.96
Purina Kibbles 'n Chunks	98.3	6.87
Ken-L Ration Kibbles 'n Bits 3x . .	90.3	6.31
Ken-L Ration Gravy Train	56.7	3.96
Purina Fit & Trim	55.5	3.88
Other	162.4	11.35

Source: *MMR*, May 17, 1999, p. 61, from Information Resources Inc.

★ 259 ★

Bakery Products (SIC 2050)

Largest Bakery Product Producers - 1998

Sales are shown in millions of dollars.

Pillsbury Co.	$ 2,200
Sara Lee US Foods	830
Mrs. Smith's Bakeries Inc.	650
Kellogg Co.	580
Earthgrains Co.	480
Rich Products Corp.	445
Otis Spunkmeyer	200
Edwards Baking Co.	175

Source: *Refrigerated & Frozen Foods*, June 1999, p. 47, from Information Resources Inc. InfoScan.

★ 260 ★

Bakery Products (SIC 2050)

Leading Bread/Baked Goods Markets

Sales are shown in millions of dollars in selected markets. Figures are for the year ended September 4, 1999.

New York City	$ 723.9
Los Angeles	559.2
Chicago	424.3
Boston	420.9
Philadelphia	361.0

Source: *Grocery Headquarters*, January 2000, p. 45, from A.C. Nielsen.

★ 261 ★

Bakery Products (SIC 2050)

Private Label Bakery Products

Data show the category leaders in the private label industry. Dollar shares are shown in percent.

Pies & cakes	50.4%
Fresh bread & rolls	28.9
Pastry/doughnuts	20.9
English muffins	15.7
Bakery snacks	6.1

Source: *Supermarket News*, April 17, 2000, p. 42, from Information Resources Inc.

★ 262 ★

Bakery Products (SIC 2050)

Supermarket Bakery Sales

White bread and rolls	19.3%
Cakes, decorated	17.2
Bread and rolls, variety	11.3
Cakes, custom decorated	10.0
Doughnuts, yeast-raised	7.9
Bagels, croissants, muffins	7.8
Pies	7.1

Continued on next page.

★ 262 ★ *Continued*
Bakery Products (SIC 2050)
Supermarket Bakery Sales

Cakes, layer 6.1%
Other 13.3

Source: *Supermarket Business*, March 15, 2000, p. 96.

★ 263 ★
Bagels (SIC 2051)
Bagel Sales by Type

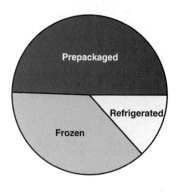

Data show unit sales in supermarkets for the year ended July 18, 1999.

	(mil.)	Share
Prepackaged	174.8	49.48%
Frozen	131.5	37.22
Refrigerated	47.0	13.30

Source: *Wall Street Journal*, September 28, 1999, p. B6, from Information Resources Inc.

★ 264 ★
Bagels (SIC 2051)
Refrigerated Bagel Market

Lender's 69%
Other 31

Source: "Aurora Foods Completes Lender's Bagles." Retrieved May 2, 2000 from the World Wide Web: http://www.aurorafoods.com.

★ 265 ★
Bagels (SIC 2051)
Top Bagel Brands - 1999

Shares are shown based on supermarket sales for the year ended July 18, 1999.

Thomas' 26.3%
Sara Lee 15.0
Lender's Bagle Shop 12.4
Earth Grains 7.3
Oroweat 3.8
Brownberry 1.4
Lender's Bake Shop 1.3
New York Bagel Boys 1.2
Western Bagel 1.0
Private label 18.0
Other 12.3

Source: *Snack Food & Wholesale Bakery*, September 1999, p. 22, from Information Resources Inc.

★ 266 ★
Bakery Products (SIC 2051)
Donut Sales by Type - 1999

Sales are shown for the four weeks ended April 25, 1999.

	($ 000)
Donuts, fresh	$ 38,294.0
Snack cake/donuts, refrigerated	230.8

Source: Retrieved January 1, 2000 from the World Wide Web: http://www.aibonline.org/SERICES/.e/ StatisticsAndTrends, from *Modern Baking*.

★ 267 ★
Bakery Products (SIC 2051)
Muffin Sales by Type

Sales are shown for the four weeks ended April 25, 1999.

	($ 000)	Share
English muffins, fresh	$ 29,584.2	64.40%
Muffins, fresh	13,687.1	29.80
English muffins, refrigerated . . .	2,072.4	4.51
Muffins, frozen	576.1	1.25
Muffins, refrigerated	16.7	0.04

Source: Retrieved January 1, 2000 from the World Wide Web: http://www.aibonline.org/SERVICES/.e/ StatisticsAndTrends, from *Modern Baking*.

★ 268 ★
Bakery Products (SIC 2051)

Top Packaged Sweet Pastries - 2000

Sales are shown in millions of units for the first three months of the year. McKee Foods had 45% of the market for this period.

Little Debbie Nutty Bar	16.8
Little Debbie Swiss Rolls	15.8
Little Debbie Oatmeal Crème Pie	15.0
Little Debbie Fudge Brownie	7.7
Little Debbie Fudge Round	6.8
Hostess Twinkie	5.3
Little Debbie Devil Squares	4.9
Little Debbie Zebra Cakes	4.8
Hostess Chocolate Cupcakes	4.3

Source: *USA TODAY*, May 15, 2000, p. 2B, from Information Resources Inc. Infoscan.

★ 269 ★

Bakery Products (SIC 2051)

Top Snack Cake Brands - 1999

Brand shares are shown based on sales of $972.2 million for the year ended October 10, 1999.

Little Debbie	25.0%
Hostess	10.2
Tastykake	5.7
Hostess Twinkies	5.7
Hostess Ding Dong's	2.8
Nabisco SnackWell's	2.2
Little Debbie Zebra Cakes	2.2
Hostess Ho Hos	2.2
Drake's	2.1
Private label	6.6
Other	35.3

Source: *Snack Food & Wholesale Bakery*, December 1999, p. 18, from Information Resources Inc.

★ 270 ★

Bakery Products (SIC 2051)

Unit Cake Sales

Sales are shown in billions of dollars. In 1998, wedding cakes sales reached $141 million; custom cakes sales reached $1.6 billion; all occasion cake sales reached $1.8 billion.

	(000)	Share
Cupcakes/brownies, fresh	50,173.1	80.88%
Cakes, fresh	9,835.4	15.86
Cheesecakes, frozen	1,718.2	2.77
Cakes, refrigerated	233.5	0.38
Snack cakes/donuts, refrigerated	71.6	0.12

Source: Retrieved January 1, 2000 from the World Wide Web: http://www.aibonline.org/SERVICES/.e/ StatisticsAndTrends, from *Modern Baking*.

★ 271 ★

Bread (SIC 2051)

Commercial Bread Market in Mexico

Shares are shown for the year ended July 18, 1999.

Bimbo	90%
Other	10

Source: Retrieved January 1, 2000 from the World Wide Web: http://jasper.sosland.com/cgi-bin/.c// pageitems_body?, from Information Resources Inc.

★ 272 ★

Bread (SIC 2051)

Top Frozen Bread Brands - 1998

Shares are shown based on supermarket sales of $188.9 million for the year ended January 3, 1999.

	($ mil.)	Share
Pepperidge Farm	$ 57.2	30.28%
New York	35.4	18.74
Cole's	33.2	17.58
Mamma Bella	14.4	7.62
Private label	12.2	6.46
Other	36.5	19.32

Source: *Refrigerated & Frozen Foods*, June 1999, p. 37, from Information Resources Inc. InfoScan.

★ 273 ★
Toaster Pastries (SIC 2051)

Top Toaster Pastry Brands - 1998

Shares are shown based on supermarket sales for the year ended January 3, 1999.

Kellogg's Pop Tarts	70.2%
Nabisco Toastettes	4.8
Kellogg's Pop-Tarts Pastry Swirls	2.6
Flavorkist Toastem	2.2
Private label	15.7
Other	4.5

Source: *Snack Food & Wholesale Bakery*, June 1999, pp. SI-28, from Information Resources Inc.

★ 274 ★
Cookies (SIC 2052)

Cookie Unit Sales - 1999

Unit sales are shown in millions of dollars for the year ended January 30, 2000. Total sales reached 2. 358 billion.

	(mil.)	Share
Nabisco Oreo	204.9	8.69%
Nabisco Chips Ahoy!	166.5	7.06
Nabisco Snackwells	74.9	3.18
Keebler Chips Deluxe	74.1	3.14
Little Debbie Nutty Bar	73.7	3.13
Nabisco Newtons	71.2	3.02
Keebler Fudge Shoppe	61.2	2.60
Other	1,631.5	69.19

Source: *Baking Business*, April 2000, p. 1, from Information Resources Inc.

★ 275 ★
Cookies (SIC 2052)

Top Cookie Makers

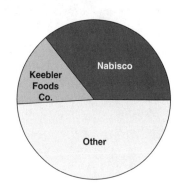

Keebler's share is estimated.

Nabisco	36%
Keebler Foods Co.	15
Other	49

Source: *Wall Street Journal*, April 7, 2000, p. 3B, from Information Resources Inc.

★ 276 ★
Cookies (SIC 2052)

Top Cookie Markets - 1998

Data show food store sales in millions of dollars.

New York City	$ 289.3
Los Angeles	176.7
Chicago	128.7
Baltimore/Washington	93.6
Philadelphia	93.5
Boston	92.5

Source: *Supermarket Business*, July 1999, p. 39, from Information Resources Inc.

★ 277 ★
Crackers (SIC 2052)

Graham Cracker Market

Honey Maid	49%
Keebler	18
Private label	33

Source: *Advertising Age*, February 28, 2000, p. 101, from Information Resources Inc.

★ 278 ★
Crackers (SIC 2052)

Top Cracker Brands - 1999

Shares are shown based on sales for the year ended November 7, 1999.

Nabisco Ritz	13.2%
Sunshine Cheez-It	7.8
Pepperidge Farm Goldfish	6.7
Nabisco Premium	6.4
Nabisco Triscuit	5.4
Nabisco Wheat Thins	5.3
Nabisco Grahams	4.6
Other	50.6

Source: *Snack Food & Wholesale Bakery*, January 2000, p. 16, from Information Resources Inc.

★ 279 ★
Crackers (SIC 2052)

Top Cracker Makers

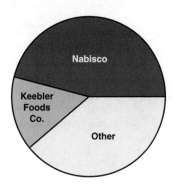

Keebler's share is estimated.

Nabisco	46%
Keebler Foods Co.	15
Other	39

Source: *Chicago Tribune*, April 5, 2000, p. 3B.

★ 280 ★
Crackers (SIC 2052)

Top Cracker Markets - 1998

Data show food store sales in millions of dollars.

New York City	$ 181.8
Los Angeles	136.6
Chicago	85.3
Boston	81.1
Baltimore/Washington	79.2
Philadelphia	77.4

Source: *Supermarket Business*, July 1999, p. 39, from Information Resources Inc.

★ 281 ★
Frozen Bakery Products (SIC 2053)

Frozen Sweet Goods Market - 1998

Shares are shown based on supermarket sales of $375.8 million for the year ended January 3, 1999.

	($ mil.)	Share
Pillsbury Toaster Strudel	$ 142.7	38.03%
Sara Lee	67.7	18.04
Pepperidge Farm Three Layer Cake	40.6	10.82
Pepperidge Farm	23.5	6.26
Mrs. Smith's	22.3	5.94
Marie Callender's	14.2	3.78
Pepperidge Farm Dessert Classics	9.2	2.45
Other	55.0	14.66

Source: *Refrigerated and Frozen Foods*, June 1999, p. 36, from Information Resources Inc.

★ 282 ★
Frozen Bakery Products (SIC 2053)

Top Frozen Bagel Brands - 1998

Shares are shown based on supermarket sales of $175.9 million for the year ended January 3, 1999.

	($ mil.)	Share
Lender's	$ 86.1	48.95%
Lender's Big & Crusty	46.3	26.32
Private label	23.4	13.30
Other	20.1	11.43

Source: *Refrigerated & Frozen Foods*, June 1999, p. 37, from Information Resources Inc. InfoScan.

★ 283 ★
Frozen Bakery Products (SIC 2053)

Top Frozen Bagel Brands - 1999

Shares are shown based on supermarket sales for the year ended July 18, 1999.

Lender's	49.1%
Lender's Big N Crusty	26.7
Sara Lee	5.0
Sara Lee Flavor	1.4
Bagels Forever	1.2
Private label	13.3
Other	3.3

Source: *Snack Food & Wholesale Bakery*, September 1999, p. 22, from Information Resources Inc.

★ 284 ★
Frozen Bakery Products (SIC 2053)

Top Frozen Pie Brands - 1999

Sales are shown for the year ended July 18, 1999.

	($mil.)	Share
Mrs. Smith's	$ 104.30	38.88%
Sara Lee	50.90	18.97
Edwards	23.90	8.91
Mrs. Smith's Special Recipe	18.60	6.93
Mountain Top	13.90	5.18
Mrs. Smith's Restaurant Classics	13.20	4.92
Other	43.48	16.21

Source: Retrieved January 1, 2000 from the World Wide Web: http://jasper.sosland.com/cgi-bin/.c// pageitems_body?, from Information Resources Inc.

★ 285 ★
Sugar (SIC 2061)

Leading Sugar/Sugar Substitute Markets - 1999

Sales are shown in millions of dollars in selected markets. Figures are for the year ended September 4, 1999.

New York City	$ 66.4
Los Angeles	57.6
Philadelphia	41.8
Chicago	34.2
Boston	30.4

Source: *Grocery Headquarters*, January 2000, p. 45, from A.C. Nielsen.

★ 286 ★
Breath Fresheners (SIC 2064)

Best-Selling Breath Fresheners - 1999

Shares are shown based on sales of $51.3 million for the year ended October 10, 1999.

Sweet Breath	31.9%
BreathAsure	23.9
Binaca	20.5
Orablast	4.4
BreathAsure D	3.6
Binaca Blasters	2.7
Crystal	2.6
Other	11.4

Source: *Chain Drug Review*, January 3, 2000, p. 38, from Information Resources Inc.

★ 287 ★
Breath Fresheners (SIC 2064)

Top Breath Freshener/Mint Brands - 1999

Shares are shown for the third quarter of the year.

Tic Tac	26.2%
Altoids	24.8
BreathSavers	20.1
Certs Cool Mint Drops	9.0

Continued on next page.

★ 287 ★ *Continued*
Breath Fresheners (SIC 2064)

Top Breath Freshener/Mint Brands - 1999

Shares are shown for the third quarter of the year.

Certs Powerful Mints	6.7%
Certs	6.0
Smint	2.4
Other	4.8

Source: *The Manufacturing Confectioner*, January 2000, p. 42, from Information Resources Inc.

★ 288 ★
Breath Fresheners (SIC 2064)

Top Breath Freshener/Mint Makers - 1999

Shares are shown for the third quarter of the year.

Ferrero USA Inc.	26.3%
Callard & Bowser-Suchard	24.8
Warner Lambert	23.0
Nabisco Foods Group	20.1
Chupa Chups USA	2.4
Other	3.4

Source: *The Manufacturing Confectioner*, January 2000, p. 42, from Information Resources Inc.

★ 289 ★
Breath Fresheners (SIC 2064)

Top Plain Mint Brands - 1999

Shares are shown for the third quarter of the year.

LifeSavers	36.5%
Van Melles Mentos	13.8
LifeSavers Wint-O-Green	7.9
Brock	7.9
Brach's	6.2
Farley's	5.3
Richardson After Dinner	3.1
Other	19.3

Source: *The Manufacturing Confectioner*, January 2000, p. 42, from Information Resources Inc.

★ 290 ★
Breath Fresheners (SIC 2064)

Top Plain Mint Makers - 1999

Shares are shown for the third quarter of the year.

Nabisco Foods Group	44.4%
Brach's Confections	16.5
Van Melle USA Inc.	14.2
Farley Candy Co.	5.3
Richardson Brands Inc.	3.1
Bobs Candies Inc.	2.1
Other	14.4

Source: *The Manufacturing Confectioner*, January 2000, p. 42, from Information Resources Inc.

★ 291 ★
Confectionery Products (SIC 2064)

Confectionery Sales in Canada

Sales are shown in millions of Canadian dollars for the year ended March 27, 1999.

Chocolate bars	$ 142.4
Gum	57.4
Nonchocolate confections	41.7
Boxed chocolates	34.5
Licorice	12.4
Hard roll candy	6.3
Mini mints	3.5

Source: *The Manufacturing Confectioner*, January 2000, p. 8, from A.C. Nielsen MarketTrack.

★ 292 ★

Confectionery Products (SIC 2064)

Leading Candy Markets

Sales are shown in millions of dollars in selected markets. Figures are for the year ended September 4, 1999.

New York City . . . . $ 200.8
Los Angeles 157.4
Chicago 114.8
Philadelphia 112.1
Boston 100.5

Source: *Grocery Headquarters*, January 2000, p. 45, from A.C. Nielsen.

★ 293 ★

Confectionery Products (SIC 2064)

Lollipop Sales Leaders - 1999

Shares are shown based on convenience store sales for the year ended August 8, 1999.

Tootie Roll Industries 45.98%
Topps 20.02
Uniconfis 5.20
Spangler 3.84
Favorite Brands International 3.48
Other 21.48

Source: *The Manufacturing Confectioner*, November 1999, p. 21, from MSA Watch.

★ 294 ★

Confectionery Products (SIC 2064)

Nonchocolate Chewy Candy Market - 1999

Shares are shown for the third quarter of the year. Data refer to candy larger than 3.5 oz.

Starburst 10.8%
Farley's 8.6
Skittles 5.1
Hershey's Classic Caramels 4.9
Tootsie Roll 4.9

Brach's 3.5%
LifeSavers GummiSavers 3.1
Other 59.1

Source: *The Manufacturing Confectioner*, January 2000, p. 41, from Information Resources Inc.

★ 295 ★

Confectionery Products (SIC 2064)

Nonchocolate Chewy Candy Market Leaders - 1999

Shares are shown for the third quarter of the year. Data refer to candy smaller than 3.5 oz.

Skittles 12.5%
Starburst 12.2
Van Melles Mentos 11.5
Van Melles Air Heads 9.1
LifeSavers GummiSavers 8.9
LifeSavers 3.3
Y&S Twizzler 3.0
Starburst Fruit Twists 3.0
Other 36.5

Source: *The Manufacturing Confectioner*, January 2000, p. 41, from Information Resources Inc.

★ 296 ★

Confectionery Products (SIC 2064)

Top Bagged/Boxed Licorice Brands - 1999

Shares are shown for the second quarter of the year. Data are larger than 3.5 oz.

Y&S Twizzler 66.2%
American Licorice 15.4
Good & Plenty Licorice 4.9
Starburst Fruit Twists 4.2
Kenny's 2.9
Bassetts 1.7
Other 4.7

Source: *The Manufacturing Confectioner*, September 1999, p. 63, from Information Resources Inc.

★ 297 ★
Confectionery Products (SIC 2064)

Top Bagged/Boxed Licorice Makers - 1999

Shares are shown for the second quarter of the year.

Hershey Chocolate USA 66.6%
American Licorice Co. 15.7
Leaf North America 4.9
Mars Inc. 4.2
Kenny's Candy Co. 2.9
Other 5.7

Source: *The Manufacturing Confectioner*, September 1999, p. 63, from Information Resources Inc.

★ 298 ★
Confectionery Products (SIC 2064)

Top Diet Candy Brands - 1999

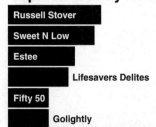

Shares are shown based on sales for the year ended February 27, 2000.

Russell Stover 13.8%
Sweet N Low 13.3
Estee 9.6
Lifesavers Delites 9.3
Fifty 50 . . . . 6.2
Golightly 6.1
Other 41.7

Source: *Professional Candy Buyer*, May/June 2000, p. 1, from Information Resources Inc.

★ 299 ★
Confectionery Products (SIC 2064)

Top Gummi Brands - 1999

Sales are shown in millions of dollars for the year ended June 5, 1999. The category reached $159.8 million.

	($ mil.)	Share
Gummisavers	$ 37.2	23.28%
Trolli	27.2	17.02
Brach's	12.9	8.07
Farley's	9.8	6.13
Black Forest	6.2	3.88
Private label	11.5	7.20
Other	55.0	34.42

Source: *Professional Candy Buyer*, July/August 1999, p. 1, from A.C. Nielsen and Favorite Brands.

★ 300 ★
Confectionery Products (SIC 2064)

Top Hard Sugar Candies - 1998

Shares are shown based on sales of $382.5 million for the year ended January 3, 1999.

	($ mil.)	Share
Lifesavers	$ 49.9	13.0%
Jolly Rancher	49.4	12.9
Werther's	42.0	11.0
Tootsie Roll Pops	29.3	7.7
Hershey's TasteTations	25.2	6.6

Source: *Snack Food & Wholesale Bakery*, June 1999, pp. SI-79, from Information Resources Inc.

★ 301 ★
Confectionery Products (SIC 2064)

Top Hard Sugar/Rolled Candy Brands - 1999

Shares are shown for the third quarter of the year.

LifeSavers 13.1%
Jolly Rancher 12.8
LifeSaver Crème Savers 10.3
Werthers 8.5
Starburst 6.6

Continued on next page.

★ 301 ★ *Continued*
Confectionery Products (SIC 2064)

Top Hard Sugar/Rolled Candy Brands - 1999

Shares are shown for the third quarter of the year.

Hershey's Tastetations	5.3%
Tootie Roll Pops	5.3
Pearson Nips	4.7
Other	33.4

Source: *The Manufacturing Confectioner*, January 2000, p. 41, from Information Resources Inc.

★ 302 ★
Confectionery Products (SIC 2064)

Top Marshmallow Brands - 1998

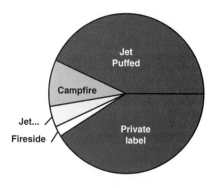

Shares are shown based on sales of $123 million for the year ended January 3, 1999.

	($ mil.)	Share
Jet Puffed	$50.7	41.2%
Campfire	11.1	9.0
Jet Puffed Funmallows	4.4	3.6
Fireside	2.7	2.2
Private label	47.9	39.0

Source: *Snack Food & Wholesale Bakery*, June 1999, pp. SI-79, from Information Resources Inc.

★ 303 ★
Confectionery Products (SIC 2064)

Top Non-Chocolate Candy Brands - 1998

Shares are shown based on sales of $1.04 billion for the year ended January 3, 1999.

Y&S Twizzler	10.2%
Starburst	6.8
Farley's	4.6
Hershey's Classic Caramel	3.0
Private label	3.4
Other	72.0

Source: *Snack Food & Wholesale Bakery*, June 1999, pp. SI-79, from Information Resources Inc.

★ 304 ★
Confectionery Products (SIC 2064)

Top Novelty Candy Brands - 1999

Shares are shown for the third quarter of the year.

Pez	8.2%
Sweet Tarts	5.9
Topps Push Pop	4.7
Hot Tamales	4.5
Topps Ring Pop	4.5
Mega Warheads	4.4
Sunmark Shock Tarts	3.6
Other	64.2

Source: *The Manufacturing Confectioner*, January 2000, p. 42, from Information Resources Inc.

★ 305 ★
Confectionery Products (SIC 2064)

Top Novelty Candy Makers - 1999

Shares are shown for the third quarter of the year.

Sunmark Inc.	25.1%
The Topps Company Inc.	11.7
Pez Candy	8.2
Cap Toys Inc.	5.5
Foreign Candy Co. Inc.	5.1
Just Born Inc.	4.6
Other	39.8

Source: *The Manufacturing Confectioner*, January 2000, p. 42, from Information Resources Inc.

★ 306 ★

Confectionery Products (SIC 2064)

Top Seasonal Candy Markets - 1999

| New York City |
| Los Angeles |
| Baltimore/Washington |
| Chicago |
| San Antonio/Corpus Christi |

Sales at food stores are shown in millions of dollars for the year ended March 28, 1999.

New York City	$ 42.0
Los Angeles	38.8
Baltimore/Washington	27.8
Chicago	25.9
San Antonio/Corpus Christi	21.9

Source: *Supermarket Business*, June 1999, p. 28, from Information Resources Inc.

★ 307 ★

Confectionery Products (SIC 2064)

Top Seasonal Candy Sales

Seasonal unit sales are shown.

Hershey's Kiss Holiday	112,123
M&M/Mars M&M's Plain Holiday	94,936
Bob's 12ct Candy Canes Peppermint	90,820
M&M/Mars M&M's Peanut Holiday	63,642
Hershey Reese's Mini Holiday	49,119
Palmer Gold Coins	45,360
Pez Favorite Assorted Shipper	33,358
Bob's Red & Green Candy Cane	30,900
Fannie May Christmas Pop	26,043
Bob's 12ct Candy Canes Cherry	25,277

Source: *Candy Business*, March/April 2000, p. 1, from Efficiency Market Services.

★ 308 ★

Confectionery Products (SIC 2064)

Top Specialty Candy Makers - 1998

Sales are for the year ended December 27, 1998.

	($ mil.)	Share
Bobs Candies	$ 22.2	20.48%
R.M. Palmer	19.3	17.80
Russell Stover Candies	17.6	16.24
Spangler Candy	11.4	10.52
Frankford Candy	8.1	7.47
Allen Candy	7.5	6.92
Other	22.3	20.57

Source: *Wall Street Journal*, December 14, 1999, p. 4A, from Information Resources Inc.

★ 309 ★

Confectionery Products (SIC 2064)

Top Specialty Nut/Coconut Candy Brands - 1999

Shares are shown for the third quarter of the year.

Leaf Pay Day	34.2%
Brach's	17.2
Brach's Maple Nut Goodies	4.6
Pearson's	4.3
Planters	3.2
Lance	3.0
Russell Stover	2.9
Other	30.6

Source: *The Manufacturing Confectioner*, January 2000, p. 40, from Information Resources Inc.

★ 310 ★

Confectionery Products (SIC 2064)

Top Specialty Nut/Coconut Candy Makers - 1999

Shares are shown for the third quarter of the year.

Leaf North America	34.6%
Brach's Confections	21.8
Pearson Candy Co.	4.3
Standard Candy Co. Inc.	4.1

Continued on next page.

★ 310 ★ *Continued*
Confectionery Products (SIC 2064)

Top Specialty Nut/Coconut Candy Makers - 1999

Shares are shown for the third quarter of the year.

Nabisco Foods Group	3.2%
Ferrara Pan Candy Co. Inc.	3.0
Lance Inc.	3.0
Other	26.0

Source: *The Manufacturing Confectioner*, January 2000, p. 40, from Information Resources Inc.

★ 311 ★
Cough Drops (SIC 2064)

Top Cough Drop Brands - 1999

Shares are shown for the third quarter of the year.

Halls	29.5%
Ricola	10.3
Cold Eeze	7.5
Ludens	7.4
Robitussin	4.8
Sucrets	3.6
Halls Plus	3.3
Private label	12.8
Other	20.8

Source: *The Manufacturing Confectioner*, January 2000, p. 42, from Information Resources Inc.

★ 312 ★
Cough Drops (SIC 2064)

Top Cough Drop Makers - 1999

Shares are shown for the third quarter of the year.

Warner Lambert	34.7%
Ricola Inc.	10.3
Whitehall Robins	8.0
Quigley Corporation	7.5
Ludens Inc.	7.4
Private label	12.8
Other	19.3

Source: *The Manufacturing Confectioner*, January 2000, p. 42, from Information Resources Inc.

★ 313 ★
Snack Bars (SIC 2064)

Nutrition Bar Leaders - 1999

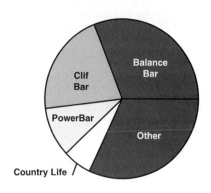

Shares are shown based on sales at natural-food retailers. Figures are as of October 24, 1999.

Balance Bar	31%
Clif Bar	21
PowerBar	10
Country Life	6
Other	32

Source: *Investor's Business Daily*, January 12, 2000, p. A10, from Information Resources Inc. and SPINS Scan.

★ 314 ★
Snack Bars (SIC 2064)

Top Snack Bar Brands - 1999

Shares are shown for the third quarter of the year.

Kelloggs Rice Krispie Treats	11.6%
Kelloggs Nutri Grain	10.8
Quaker Chewy	10.1
Quaker Fruit & Oatmeal	5.0
Sunbelt	5.0
Slim Fast	4.9
Other	52.6

Source: *The Manufacturing Confectioner*, January 2000, p. 42, from Information Resources Inc.

★ 315 ★
Snack Bars (SIC 2064)

Top Snack Bar Makers - 1999

Shares are shown for the third quarter of the year.

Kellogg Co.	28.1%
Quaker Oats Company	16.6

Continued on next page.

★ 315 ★ *Continued*

Snack Bars (SIC 2064)

Top Snack Bar Makers - 1999

Shares are shown for the third quarter of the year.

McKee Baking Co.	8.6%
Slim Fast Foods Co.	6.9
Nabisco Foods Group	5.7
General Mills	5.5
Private label	5.6
Other	2.3

Source: *The Manufacturing Confectioner*, January 2000, p. 42, from Information Resources Inc.

★ 316 ★

Chocolate (SIC 2066)

Chocolate Candy Boxed/Bagged Makers - 1999

Shares are shown for the third quarter of the year.

Hershey Foods	46.1%
Mars Inc.	31.3
Nestle USA Inc.	6.4
Brachs Confections	3.2
Leaf North America	2.4
Storck USA LP	1.4
Farley Candy Co.	1.4
Ferrero USA Inc.	0.8
Other	7.0

Source: *The Manufacturing Confectioner*, January 2000, p. 40, from Information Resources Inc.

★ 317 ★

Chocolate (SIC 2066)

Chocolate Candy Sales - 1999

Chocolate candy (non-seasonal) sales are shown in millions of dollars.

	($ mil.)	Share
Chocolate candy box/bag > 3.5 oz.	$ 484.4	53.78%
Chocolate candy snack size	244.6	27.16
Chocolate candy bar < 3.5 oz.	128.0	14.21
Chocolate covered cookie/wafer	43.7	4.85

Source: *Discount Merchandiser*, February 2000, p. 3, from Information Resources Inc.

★ 318 ★

Chocolate (SIC 2066)

Chocolate Candy Sales Leaders - 1999

Shares are shown based on convenience store sales for the year ended August 8, 1999.

Hershey	51.25%
M&M/Mars	33.25
Nestle	11.32
Tootsie Roll Industries	1.81
Other	2.37

Source: *The Manufacturing Confectioner*, November 1999, p. 21, from MSA Watch.

★ 319 ★

Chocolate (SIC 2066)

Chocolate Candy Snack/Fun Size Brands - 1999

Shares are shown for the third quarter of the year. Data refers to boxes and bags larger than 3.5 oz.

Snickers	17.1%
Reese's	15.5
Kit Kat	12.1
Milky Way	7.0
Butterfinger	5.7
Three Musketeers	5.5
Nestle Crunch	5.3
Peter Paul Almond Joy	4.7
Twix	4.1
Other	23.0

Source: *The Manufacturing Confectioner*, January 2000, p. 40, from Information Resources Inc.

★ 320 ★
Chocolate (SIC 2066)

Chocolate Candy Snack/Fun Size Makers - 1999

Shares are shown for the third quarter of the year.

Hershey Foods	40.3%
Mars Inc.	38.5
Nestle USA Inc.	17.7
Leaf North America	1.8
Other	1.7

Source: *The Manufacturing Confectioner*, January 2000, p. 40, from Information Resources Inc.

★ 321 ★
Chocolate (SIC 2066)

Top Boxed/Bagged Chocolate Candies - 1999

Shares are shown for the third quarter of the year. Data refers to boxes and bags larger than 3.5 oz.

M&Ms	20.0%
Hershey's	11.5
Hersey's Kisses	6.4
Hershey's Nuggets	6.0
Snickers	5.9
Reese's	5.1
York Peppermint Patty	3.5
Nestle Treasures	2.4
Other	39.2

Source: *The Manufacturing Confectioner*, January 2000, p. 40, from Information Resources Inc.

★ 322 ★
Chocolate (SIC 2066)

Top Chocolate Candy Brands - 1998

Shares are shown based on sales of $3.2 billion for the year ended January 3, 1999. Data are for non-seasonal candy.

M&Ms	6.6%
Russell Stover	5.4
Hershey's	4.6
M&Ms (less than 3.5 oz)	3.7
Snickers Snack Size	3.3
Hershey's Kisses	3.0
Reese's Snack Size	3.0
Hershey's	2.5
Snickers	2.4%
Kit Kat Snack Size	2.3
Other	63.2

Source: *Snack Food & Wholesale Bakery*, June 1999, pp. SI-79, from Information Resources Inc.

★ 323 ★
Chocolate (SIC 2066)

Top Chocolate Candy Markets - 1999

New York City
Los Angeles
Chicago
Baltimore/Washington
Philadelphia

Sales at food stores are shown in millions of dollars for the year ended March 28, 1999.

New York City	$ 88.2
Los Angeles	73.3
Chicago	53.0
Baltimore/Washington	44.6
Philadelphia	32.6

Source: *Supermarket Business*, June 1999, p. 28, from Information Resources Inc.

★ 324 ★
Chocolate (SIC 2066)

Top Chocolate Snack Candy Makers - 1999

Shares are for the second quarter of the year.

Hershey Chocolate USA	42.1%
Mars Inc.	38.1
Nestle	17.5
Russell Stover	1.1
Leaf North America	0.7
Other	0.5

Source: *The Manufacturing Confectioner*, September 1999, p. 62, from Information Resources Inc. InfoScan.

★ 325 ★
Gum (SIC 2067)

Bubble Gum Market Shares - 1998

The market is shown by flavor. The market is valued at nearly $500 million.

Original	58.8%
Mixed fruit	12.7
Grape	9.5
Strawberry	7.9
Watermelon	6.3
Others	4.8

Source: Retrieved March 13, 2000 from the World Wide Web: http://www.retailmerchandising.net.

★ 326 ★
Gum (SIC 2067)

Gum Sales Leaders - 1999

Shares are shown based on convenience store sales for the year ended August 8, 1999.

William Wrigley Jr.	49.45%
Adams	28.54
Nabisco	13.56
Amurol	3.53
Hershey	2.45
Other	2.47

Source: *The Manufacturing Confectioner*, November 1999, p. 21, from MSA Watch.

★ 327 ★
Gum (SIC 2067)

Top Gum Makers - 1999

Sales are for the year ended July 18, 1999.

Wrigley's	$ 286
Warner-Lambert Co.	96
Nabisco Foods Group	34
Leaf	26

Source: *Advertising Age*, September 1999, p. 4, from Information Resources Inc.

★ 328 ★
Nuts (SIC 2068)

Leading Nuts Markets - 1999

Sales are shown in millions of dollars in selected markets. Figures are for the year ended September 4, 1999.

New York City	$ 68.0
Los Angeles	51.6
Boston	36.1
Chicago	29.9
Philadelphia	28.9

Source: *Grocery Headquarters*, January 2000, p. 45, from A.C. Nielsen.

★ 329 ★
Nuts (SIC 2068)

Top Nut Makers - 1998

Market shares are shown for the year ended January 3, 1999.

Planters Co.	46.8%
Nutcracker	3.1
John B. Sanfilippo & Sons Co.	3.0
Mauna Loa	2.1
Blue Diamond	2.0
Sunkist	1.8
Private label	22.8
Other	18.4

Source: *Snack Food & Wholesale Bakery*, June 1999, p. SI47, from Information Resources Inc.

★ 330 ★
Nuts (SIC 2068)

Top Snack Nut Brands - 1998

Shares are shown based on total sales of $1.01 billion for the year ended January 1, 1999.

	($ mil.)	Share
Planters	$ 452.5	44.76%
Nutcracker	31.1	3.08
Mauna Loa	20.9	2.07

Continued on next page.

★ 330 ★ *Continued*

Nuts (SIC 2068)

Top Snack Nut Brands - 1998

Shares are shown based on total sales of $1.01 billion for the year ended January 1, 1999.

	($ mil.)	Share
Fisher	$ 17.1	1.69%
Sunkist	16.6	1.64
Hoody	13.0	1.29
Blue Diamond	10.3	1.02
Diamond	10.1	1.00
Other	439.4	43.46

Source: *MMR*, November 6, 1999, p. 20, from Information Resources Inc.

★ 331 ★

Fats and Oils (SIC 2070)

Leading Shortening/Oil Markets - 1999

Sales are shown in millions of dollars in selected markets. Figures are for the year ended September 4, 1999.

New York City	$ 127.6
Los Angeles	94.2
Philadelphia	50.0
Boston	42.4
Chicago	37.7

Source: *Grocery Headquarters*, January 2000, p. 45, from A.C. Nielsen.

★ 332 ★

Olive Oil (SIC 2079)

Top Olive Oil Brands - 1999

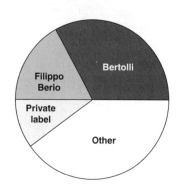

The category reached sales of $343 million for the year ended February 27, 2000.

	($ mil.)	Share
Bertolli	$ 112	32.65%
Filippo Berio	60	17.49
Private label	35	10.20
Other	136	39.65

Source: *Advertising Age*, April 3, 2000, p. 12, from Information Resources Inc.

★ 333 ★

Beverages (SIC 2080)

Largest Beverage Companies - 1998

Sales are shown in billions of dollars.

Coca-Cola Co.	$ 18.8
Diageo	18.1
Nestle SA	13.0
PepsiCo. Inc.	11.0
Anheuser-Busch	8.5
The Seagram Co.	4.6
Miller Brewing Co.	4.1
Cadbury Schweppes	3.2
Danone Group	3.1

Source: *Beverage Industry*, June 1999, p. 22.

★ 334 ★

Beverages (SIC 2080)

Largest Beverage Marketers - 1998

Sales are shown in billions of dollars for North America.

Coca-Cola Company	$ 18.8
Coca-Cola Enterprises	13.4
PepsiCo.	11.3
Anheuser-Busch	9.2
The Seagram Company Ltd.	4.6
Philip Morris	4.1
FEMSA	2.8
Panamerican Beverages	2.7
Southern Wine & Spirits	2.6
Cadbury Schweppes	1.9

Source: *Beverage World*, July 1999, p. 55.

★ 335 ★

Beverages (SIC 2080)

Largest Bottlers - 1998

Sales are shown in millions of dollars.

Coca-Cola Enterprises	$ 13,414
Pepsi Bottling Group	7,041
Whitman Corp.	1,635
The American Bottling Co.	1,000
Honickman Affiliates	1,000

Source: *Beverage Industry*, June 1999, p. 34.

★ 336 ★

Beverages (SIC 2080)

U.S. Beverage Market - 1998

Shares are shown based on total gallons consumed of 49.3 billion.

Soft drinks	30.7%
Milk	12.9
Beer	12.1
Coffee	11.9
Fruit beverages	8.2
Bottled water	7.6
Tea	5.2
Wine	1.1
Other	10.1

Source: "New Beverage Marketing Report Surveys Beverage Market." Retrieved April 26, 2000 from the World Wide Web: http://ww.just-drinks.com, from Beverage Marketing Corporation.

★ 337 ★

Beer (SIC 2082)

Beer Market by Segment

Packaged	89.7%
Draught	10.3

Source: *Discount Merchandiser*, December 1999, p. 55, from *Beverage World*.

★ 338 ★

Beer (SIC 2082)

Beer Market in San Antonio, TX

BudCo.	50%
Halo	29
Coors Distributing	8
Other	3

Source: Retrieved January 13, 2000 from the World Wide Web: http://www.amcity.com/sanantonio/stories/1999/12/20/story2.html, from *Wholesale Beer Distributors Report*.

★ 339 ★

Beer (SIC 2082)

Beer Sales by Segment - 1999

Sales are shown in millions of dollars for the year ended January 22, 2000.

	($ mil.)	Share
Regular beer	$ 8,206.4	50.03%
Light beer	7,280.8	44.39
Ale	344.1	2.10
Malt liquor	314.6	1.92
Malt beverages	166.0	1.01
Stout/porter	90.6	0.55

Source: *Supermarket Business*, April 15, 2000, p. 112, from A.C. Nielsen.

★ 340 ★

Beer (SIC 2082)

Largest Beer Wholesalers - 1998

Data are in millions of cases.

The Reyes Family	27.0
Ben E. Keith Beers	27.0
Manhattan Beer Distributors Inc.	21.1
JJ Taylor Companies Inc.	20.3
Hensley & Company	18.8

Continued on next page.

★ 340 ★ *Continued*
Beer (SIC 2082)

Largest Beer Wholesalers - 1998

Data are in millions of cases.

Silver Eagle Distributors	18.4
The Sheehan Family	18.4
Topa Equities Ltd. Inc.	17.6
C. Mark Pirrung and John A. Economos	17.4
The Banko Family	15.4

Source: *Beverage World*, September 1999, p. 48.

★ 341 ★
Beer (SIC 2082)

Mexico's Beer Market - 1998

Bottles	82.3%
Cans	17.0
Kegs	0.7

Source: *MB*, October 1999, p. 46, from Mexico's National Beermakers Association.

★ 342 ★
Beer (SIC 2082)

Top Beer Brands - 1999

Budweiser	19.3%
Bud Light	14.4
Miller Franchise	8.3
Coors Light	8.1
Busch	4.8
Milwaukee's Best	3.3

Miller Genuine Draft	2.8%
Miller High Life	2.8
A-B Natural Light	2.3
Other	33.8

Source: *Beverage Industry*, February 2000, p. 8, from Maxwell Consumer Report.

★ 343 ★
Beer (SIC 2082)

Top Beer Makers - 1998

Anheuser-Busch	47%
Miller	19
Coors	9
Pabst	3
Other	22

Source: *Financial Times*, April 8, 2000, p. 9, from Impact Databank.

★ 344 ★
Beer (SIC 2082)

Top Beer Makers - 1999

Anheuser Busch	49.0%
Miller	20.9
Coors	10.8
Stroh	6.8
S&P Industries	2.3
Genessee	0.8
Boston Beer	0.7
Others	8.7

Source: *Beverage World 2000 Databank*, Annual, p. 26, from Beverage Marketing Corp.

★ 345 ★
Beer (SIC 2082)

Top Imported Beer Brands - 1999

Corona Extra	25.3%
Heineken	18.0
Labatt's Blue	5.5
Becks	4.3
Guinness	3.7
Foster	3.5
Molson Ice	3.2
Bass Ale	2.6

Continued on next page.

★ 345 ★ *Continued*

Beer (SIC 2082)

Top Imported Beer Brands - 1999

Tecate	2.6%
Other	22.6

Source: *Beverage Industry*, February 2000, p. 8, from Maxwell Consumer Report.

★ 346 ★

Wine (SIC 2084)

Top Cooler Brands in Canada - 2000

Shares are shown based on sales of 3.95 million of liter cases for the year ended February 28, 2000.

Mike's Hard Lemonade	29.6%
Mike's Hard Cranberry Lemonade	17.6
Seagram's Wildberry Vodka	5.6
Mike's Hard Lemon Ice Tea	4.8
Vex Hard Lemonade	3.5
Bacardi Breezer Caribbean Key	2.5
Wildberry Xtra	2.4
Vex Hard Cranberry Lemonade	2.4
Captain Morgan Spiked Cherry	2.0
Original Stuff Vodka Grape	1.9
Other	27.7

Source: "Report on Market Share." Retrieved June 8, 2000 from the World Wide Web: http://www. marketingmag.ca, from industry sources.

★ 347 ★

Wine (SIC 2084)

Top Wine Producers

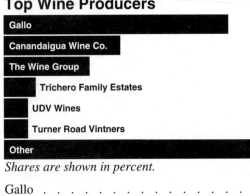

Shares are shown in percent.

Gallo	28.5%
Canandaigua Wine Co.	14.6
The Wine Group	11.3
Trichero Family Estates	3.8
UDV Wines	3.1
Turner Road Vintners	3.1
Other	35.6

Source: *Forbes*, December 13, 1999, p. I70, from Adams Business Media.

★ 348 ★

Wine (SIC 2084)

Wine Shipments by Class

Data are estimated in millions of gallons.

	(mil.)	Share
Not over 14% alcohol	479	87.41%
Sparkling	37	6.75
Over 14% alcohol	32	5.84

Source: *Wines & Vines*, March 2000, p. 16, from Gomberg, Fredrikson & Associates and U.S. govt. sources.

★ 349 ★
Liquor (SIC 2085)

Alcoholic Cider Market

Sales are shown in thousands of cases. The market was valued at $111 million.

Hornsby's	1,025
Cider Jack	835
Woodchuck	725
Hard Core	375
Woodpecker	345

Source: ''Cider.'' Retrieved January 25, 2000 from the World Wide Web: http://www.beveragebusiness.com/art%2Darch/99estes10.html, from *Impact's Annual Beer Study*.

★ 350 ★
Liquor (SIC 2085)

Bourbon Consumption by Age

60 and over	50.0%
40-49	21.7
50-59	16.1
30-39	7.5
20-29	4.6

Source: *USA TODAY*, June 22, 1999, p. 3B, from Impact Databank.

★ 351 ★
Liquor (SIC 2085)

Gin Consumption by Age

60 and over	35.8%
50-59	29.2
30-39	26.5
40-49	4.2
20-29	4.0
Under 20	0.2

Source: *USA TODAY*, June 22, 1999, p. 3B, from Impact Databank.

★ 352 ★
Liquor (SIC 2085)

Spirits Consumption in Canada

Sales are shown by type.

Vodka	18.0%
Liquor	18.0
Rum	14.8
Dry gin	12.0
Brandy	9.6
Scotch	7.3
Whisky	6.1

Source: Retrieved January 1, 2000 from the World Wide Web: http://www.tradeport.org/ts/countries/canada/mrr/mark0025.html.

★ 353 ★
Liquor (SIC 2085)

Tequila Consumption by Age

20-29	52.4%
30-39	15.1
40-49	12.8
60 and over	10.6
50-59	9.1

Source: *USA TODAY*, June 22, 1999, p. 3B, from Impact Databank.

★ 354 ★
Liquor (SIC 2085)

Top Blended American Whiskies - 1998

Seagram's 7 Crown	44.4%
Kessler	15.2
Calvert Extra	3.7
Fleischmann's Preferred	3.6
Beamis & Star	3.2

Source: Retrieved January 1, 2000 from the World Wide Web: http://www.beveragenet.net/cheers/1998/0998/998burbn.asp, from *Adams Liquor Handbook, 1998*.

★ 355 ★

Liquor (SIC 2085)

Top Bourbon and Straight American Whiskies - 1998

Jim Beam	25.8%
Jack Daniels Black	24.1
Early Times	7.4
Evan Williams	7.0
Ancient Age	4.6
Other	31.1

Source: Retrieved January 1, 2000 from the World Wide Web: http://www.beveragenet.net/cheers/1998/0998/998burbn.asp, from *Adams Liquor Handbook*.

★ 356 ★

Liquor (SIC 2085)

Top Domestic Vodka Brands - 1998

Sales are shown in thousands of 9-liter cases.

	(000)	Share
Smirnoff	5,970	21.02%
Popov Vodka	2,330	8.20
Gordon's Vodka	2,040	7.18
McCormick Vodka	1,418	4.99
Barton Vodka	1,290	4.54
Total Kamchatka	1,047	3.69
Wolfschmidt	1,000	3.52
Skol Vodka	960	3.38
Gilbey's Vodka	960	3.38
Other	11,390	40.10

Source: Retrieved January 1, 2000 from the World Wide Web: http://www.beveragenet.net/cheers/1998/0998/998burbn.asp, from *Adams Handbook Advance, 1999*.

★ 357 ★

Liquor (SIC 2085)

Top Imported Vodka Brands

Sales are shown in thousands of cases.

	(000)	Share
Absolut	3,650	58.80%
Stolichnaya	1,230	19.81
Ketel One Vodka	450	7.25
Finlandia	220	3.54
Tanqueray Sterling	180	2.90
Others	478	7.70

Source: Retrieved January 1, 2000 from the World Wide Web: http://www.beveragenet.net/cheers/1998/0998/998burbn.asp, from *Adams Handbook Advance, 1999*.

★ 358 ★

Liquor (SIC 2085)

Top Premium Spirits Brands - 1998

Market shares are shown in percent. The premium sector is composed of brands selling at retail for at least $10 per 750 ml bottle.

Bacardi	4.9%
Absolut	2.6
Jack Daniel's	2.4
Jim Beam	2.2
Jose Cuervo	2.1
Other	85.8

Source: *Research Alert*, March 19, 1999, p. 8, from Impact Databank.

★ 359 ★

Liquor (SIC 2085)

Top Tequila Brands - 1998

Data are in thousands of 9 liter cases.

	(000)	Share
Jose Cuervo/1800	2,926	44.53%
Montezuma	660	10.04
Sauza	515	7.84
Giro	425	6.47
Juarez	330	5.02
Other	1,715	26.10

Source: Retrieved January 1, 2000 from the World Wide Web: http://www.beveragenet.net/cheers/1998/0998/998burbn.asp, from *Adams Handbook Advance, 1999*.

★ 360 ★
Liquor (SIC 2085)

Vodka Consumption by Age

30-39	44.1%
60 and over	27.0
40-49	10.3
50-59	10.2
20-29	8.4

Source: *USA TODAY*, June 22, 1999, p. 3B, from Impact Databank.

★ 361 ★
Bottled Water (SIC 2086)

Non-Carbonated Bottled Water Market in Canada - 2000

Shares are shown based on sales of $77.2 million for the year ended March 25, 2000.

Evian	20.0%
Montclair	11.5
Aquafina	10.3
Danone	9.2
Naya	5.9
Aberfoyle	3.9
Dasani	3.0
Volvic	2.7
Cristalline	0.4
Private label	26.9
Other	6.2

Source: "Report on Market Share." Retrieved June 8, 2000 from the World Wide Web: http://www. marketingmag.ca, from industry sources.

★ 362 ★
Bottled Water (SIC 2086)

Top Bottled Water Makers

Perrier Group	29.4%
Suntory Water Group	9.0
McKesson Corporation	7.4
Danone International	6.6
Pepsi-Cola	3.8
Crystal Geyser	2.6
Other	41.2

Source: *Beverage World 2000 Databank*, Annual, p. 26, from Beverage Marketing Corp.

★ 363 ★
Bottled Water (SIC 2086)

Top Carbonated Water Brands - 1999

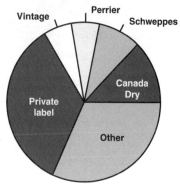

Total sales reached $524.1 million for the year ended July 28, 1999.

	($ mil.)	Share
Canada Dry	$ 67.0	12.78%
Schweppes	45.0	8.59
Perrier	30.0	5.72
Vintage	29.0	5.53
Private label	184.0	35.11
Other	169.1	32.26

Source: *Beverage Industry*, September 1999, p. 13, from Information Resources Inc.

★ 364 ★
Bottled Water (SIC 2086)

Top Noncarbonated Bottled Water Brands - 1999

Shares are shown based on sales for the year ended March 28, 1999.

Evian	7.1%
Poland Spring	6.9
Arrowhead	5.1
Aquafina	4.3
Dannon	4.1
Zephyrhills	3.8
Deer Park	3.6
Private label	22.8
Other	65.1

Source: *Beverage Industry*, July 1999, p. 40, from Information Resources Inc.

★ 365 ★
Soft Drinks (SIC 2086)

Best-Selling Drinks at Convenience Stores in Southern Texas - 1999

Data show 20-ounce beverage share for the 12 weeks ended September 4, 1999.

Coca-Cola	18.5%
Dr. Pepper	15.1
Big Red	9.2
Sprite	8.4
Diet Coke	5.8
Pepsi	5.4
Mountain Dew	4.3
Other	33.3

Source: *Beverage Industry*, February 2000, p. 34, from A. C. Nielsen.

★ 366 ★
Soft Drinks (SIC 2086)

Fountain Drink Market in Canada - 1998

Coca-Cola Co.	62.8%
Pepsi/7Up	29.7
Other	7.5

Source: *Beverage Digest*, May 28, 1999, p. 1.

★ 367 ★
Soft Drinks (SIC 2086)

New Age Beverage Market

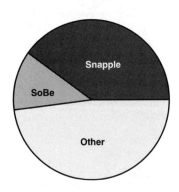

Sales of this broad, ill-defined category reached $438 million for the year ended December 5, 1999.

Snapple	$ 174.8	39.91%
SoBe	53.0	12.10
Other	210.2	47.99

Source: *Supermarket News*, February 21, 2000, p. 68, from Information Resources Inc.

★ 368 ★
Soft Drinks (SIC 2086)

New Age Beverage Sales - 1999

Data are in millions of cases.

	(mil.)	Share
Retail PET water	474.1	40.6%
Sports beverages	212.0	18.1
Single-serve fruit beverages	189.2	16.2
RTD tea	171.7	14.7
Sparkling water	62.7	5.4
Premium soda	24.1	2.1
Vegetable/fruit juice blends	16.9	1.4

Source: *Beverage World*, March 15, 2000, p. 19, from Beverage Marketing Corp.

★ 369 ★
Soft Drinks (SIC 2086)

Popular Soft Drinks for Asians

Data show the most purchased drinks, based on a survey. There are 10.8 million Asian Americans.

Coca-Cola 53%
7Up 12
Pepsi 9
Sprite 6
Dr. Pepper 1

Source: *Brandweek*, November 8, 1999, p. 18.

★ 370 ★
Soft Drinks (SIC 2086)

Soft Drink Market - 1998

Coca-Cola Co.. . . . . 44.5%
Pepsi-Cola Co. 31.4
Dr. Pepper/Seven-Up 14.4
Cott Corp. 2.7
National Beverage 2.0
Royal Crown 1.3
Monarch Co. 0.5
Seagram's 0.3
Big Red 0.3
Other 2.6

Source: *Atlanta Journal-Constitution*, June 1, 1999, p. E1, from *Beverage Digest*.

★ 371 ★
Soft Drinks (SIC 2086)

Soft Drink Market by Packaging in Canada

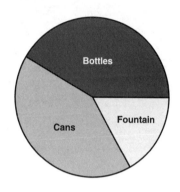

Bottles 41.5%
Cans 41.5
Fountain 16.9

Source: Retrieved January 18, 2000 from the World Wide Web: http://www.bizlink.com, from Canadian Soft Drink Association.

★ 372 ★
Soft Drinks (SIC 2086)

Soft Drink Market by Segment

Regular 74.2%
Diet 25.8

Source: *Discount Merchandiser*, December 1999, p. 55, from *Beverage World*.

★ 373 ★
Soft Drinks (SIC 2086)

Soft Drink Sales Leaders at Mass Merchandisers - 1999

Market shares are shown in percent.

Coca-Cola Co.. . . . . 33.8%
PepsiCo.. . . . . 33.1
Dr. Pepper/Seven Up 14.6
Triarc Cos. 0.6

Source: *Beverage Industry*, March 2000, p. 24, from Information Resources Inc.

★ 374 ★

Soft Drinks (SIC 2086)

Soft Drink Sales Leaders in Drug Stores - 1999

Market shares are shown in percent.

Coca-Cola Co. 43.2%
PepsiCo. 37.6
Dr. Pepper/Seven Up 14.8
Triarc Cos. 0.6

Source: *Beverage Industry*, March 2000, p. 24, from Information Resources Inc.

★ 375 ★

Soft Drinks (SIC 2086)

Sports Drink Market - 1998

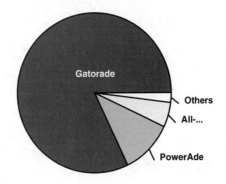

Gatorade 82.0%
PowerAde 11.4
All-Sport 4.9
Others 1.7

Source: *Wall Street Journal*, December 10, 1999, p. B4, from *Beverage Digest*.

★ 376 ★

Soft Drinks (SIC 2086)

Sports Drink Market by Segment

Liquid 94.2%
Powder 5.8

Source: *Discount Merchandiser*, December 1999, p. 55, from *Beverage World*.

★ 377 ★

Soft Drinks (SIC 2086)

Top Diet Drinks - 1999

Shares are shown of the diet market.

Diet Coke 32.7%
Diet Pepsi 18.3
Caffeine Free Diet Coke 6.7
Caffeine Free Diet Pepsi 3.7
Diet Dr. Pepper 3.7
Pepsi One 3.3
Diet Mountain Dew 3.2
Diet 7 Up 2.2
Other 26.3

Source: *Beverage World*, March 15, 2000, p. 19, from Beverage Marketing Corp.

★ 378 ★

Soft Drinks (SIC 2086)

Top Noncarbonated Soft Drink Brands - 1999

Shares are shown for the year ended June 12, 1999.

Snapple (Triarc) 40.5%
Ocean Spray 14.7
Arizona 13.7
Lipton/Pepsi 10.8
SoBe 9.3
Mistic (Triarc) 5.0
Nestea/Coke 4.7
Other 6.3

Source: *USA TODAY*, August 3, 1999, p. 2B, from *Beverage Digest*.

★ 379 ★

Soft Drinks (SIC 2086)

Top Soda Makers in Canada - 1998

Coca-Cola Co. 39.4%
Pepsi/7Up 34.3
Cadbury Schweppes 9.7
A&W 0.3
Others 16.3

Source: *Beverage Digest*, May 28, 1999, p. 1.

★ 380 ★
Soft Drinks (SIC 2086)

Top Soft Drink Brands - 1998

Shares are for the year ended March 21, 1999. Market includes take-home outlets only, including supermarkets, mass merchandisers, convenience outlets, drug chains and mini-marts.

Coke Classic	16.4%
Pepsi-Cola	15.0
Diet Coke	7.1
Mountain Dew	6.9
Other	54.6

Source: *Advertising Age*, August 23, 1999, p. 3, from Beverage Digest's Green Sheet.

★ 381 ★
Soft Drinks (SIC 2086)

Top Soft Drink Brands - 1999

Data show millions of cases.

	(mil.)	Share
Coca-Cola Classic	2,060.6	20.3%
Pepsi-Cola	1,436.8	14.1
Diet Coke	860.3	8.5
Mountain Dew	719.1	7.1
Sprite	681.7	6.7

Source: *Financial Times*, April 4, 2000, p. 22, from Beverage Marketing.

★ 382 ★
Soft Drinks (SIC 2086)

Top Soft Drink Markets - 1999

Sales are shown in millions of dollars of February 28, 1999.

Los Angeles	$ 623.9
New York City	543.1
Chicago	428.1
Baltimore/Washington D.C.	261.3
Dallas/Ft. Worth	231.9

Source: *Supermarket Business*, May 1999, p. 74, from Information Resources Inc.

★ 383 ★
Soft Drinks (SIC 2086)

Top Soft Drink Producers - 1999

Market shares are shown in percent.

Coca-Cola Co.	44.1%
Pepsi-Cola	31.0
Dr. Pepper/Seven Up	14.5
Cott Corporation	2.8
National Beverage	2.0
Triarc/Royal Crown	1.1
Seagram Mixers	0.3
Monarch	0.3
Big Red	0.3
Other	3.6

Source: "Soft Drink Sales Increased 0.6% in 1999." Retrieved April 13, 2000 from the World Wide Web: http://www.just-drinks.com, from Beverage Marketing Corp.

★ 384 ★
Soft Drinks (SIC 2086)

Top Soft Drinks in Canada - 1999

Shares are shown based on sales of 632 million 192-oz cases for the year ended December 31, 1999.

Coca-Cola	38.6%
Pepsi-7 Up	35.4

Continued on next page.

★ 384 ★ *Continued*

Soft Drinks (SIC 2086)

Top Soft Drinks in Canada - 1999

Shares are shown based on sales of 632 million 192-oz cases for the year ended December 31, 1999.

Canada Dry	5.1%
Crush	2.7
Schweppes	1.1
Dr. Pepper	0.5
A&W	0.4
Other	16.2

Source: "Report on Market Share." Retrieved June 8, 2000 from the World Wide Web: http://www.marketingmag.ca, from *Beverage Digest*.

★ 385 ★

Seafood (SIC 2091)

Canned Fish Sales - 1998

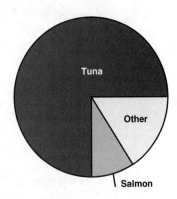

Share of supermarket category sales are shown in percent.

Tuna	74.7%
Salmon	9.0
Other	16.3

Source: *Progressive Grocer*, July 1999, p. 56.

★ 386 ★

Seafood (SIC 2091)

Leading Canned Seafood Markets - 1999

Sales are shown in millions of dollars in selected markets. Figures are for the year ended September 4, 1999.

New York City	$ 155.8
Los Angeles	84.0
Philadelphia	66.5
Boston	65.8
Chicago	43.4

Source: *Grocery Headquarters*, January 2000, p. 45, from A.C. Nielsen.

★ 387 ★

Seafood (SIC 2092)

Best-Selling Frozen Fish Brands - 1999

Sales are shown in millions of dollars for the 12 weeks ended June 20, 1999.

Gorton's	$ 30.3
Van de Kamp's	23.3
Mrs. Paul's	18.1
SeaPak	8.8
Private label	35.2

Source: *Frozen Food Age*, September 1999, p. 1, from Information Resources Inc.

★ 388 ★

Seafood (SIC 2092)

Best-Selling Frozen Seafood Brands - 1998

Shares are shown based on supermarket sales of $896.1 million for the year ended January 3, 1999.

	($ mil.)	Share
Gorton's	$ 147.3	14.12%
Van de Kamp's	131.7	12.62
Mrs. Paul's	96.3	9.23
SeaPak	40.7	3.90
Singleton	27.4	2.63

Continued on next page.

★ 388 ★ *Continued*
Seafood (SIC 2092)

Best-Selling Frozen Seafood Brands - 1998

Shares are shown based on supermarket sales of $896.1 million for the year ended January 3, 1999.

	($ mil.)	Share
Contessa	$ 21.7	2.08%
Sealord	20.0	1.92
Private label	117.1	11.22
Other	441.2	42.28

Source: *Refrigerated & Frozen Foods*, June 1999, p. 74, from Information Resources Inc. InfoScan.

★ 389 ★
Seafood (SIC 2092)

Frozen Seafood Market - 1998

Shares are shown based on supermarket sales of $896.1 million for the year ended January 3, 1999.

VDK Frozen Foods	27.3%
Gorton's	18.9
Rich-SeaPak	4.6
Singleton	3.1
Contessa	2.5
Private label	25.7
Other	17.9

Source: *Refrigerated & Frozen Foods*, June 1999, p. 47, from Information Resources Inc. InfoScan.

★ 390 ★
Seafood (SIC 2092)

Seafood Supermarket Sales

Fish	39%
Shrimp	31
Prepared entrees, uncooked	13
Prepared entrees, cooked	12
Other	5

Source: *Supermarket Business*, November 15, 1999, p. 96.

★ 391 ★
Coffee (SIC 2095)

Coffee Sales by Segment - 1999

Sales are shown in millions of dollars for the year ended July 18, 1999.

	($ mil.)	Share
Coffee, ground	$ 2,109.4	60.81%
Coffee, instant	602.0	17.35
Coffee, ground decaffinated	339.6	9.79
Coffee, whole bean	238.2	6.87
Coffee, instant decaffinated	179.9	5.19

Source: *Supermarket Business*, November 15, 1999, p. 49, from Information Resources Inc.

★ 392 ★
Coffee (SIC 2095)

Leading Coffee Markets - 1999

Sales are shown in millions of dollars in selected markets. Figures are for the year ended September 4, 1999.

New York City	$ 212.5
Los Angeles	143.3
Chicago	103.9
Boston	101.3
Philadelphia	100.1

Source: *Grocery Headquarters*, January 2000, p. 45, from A.C. Nielsen.

★ 393 ★
Coffee (SIC 2095)

Top Decaffinated Coffee Brands - 1998

The $196.9 billion market is shown for the year ended September 13, 1998.

	($ mil.)	Share
Folgers	$ 54.6	27.73%
Taster's Choice Original	38.9	19.76
Maxwell House Sanka	34.9	17.72
General Foods International	28.9	14.68

Continued on next page.

★ 393 ★ *Continued*

Coffee (SIC 2095)

Top Decaffinated Coffee Brands - 1998

The $196.9 billion market is shown for the year ended September 13, 1998.

	($ mil.)	Share
Maxwell House	$ 16.2	8.23%
Caffee D Vita	3.7	1.88
Maxwell House Café Cappuccino	2.9	1.47
Other	16.8	8.53

Source: *MMR*, November 16, 1998, p. 18, from Information Resources Inc.

★ 394 ★

Coffee (SIC 2095)

Top Ground Coffee Brands - 1998

The $2.43 billion market is shown for the year ended September 13, 1998.

	($ mil.)	Share
Folgers	$ 667.3	27.46%
Maxwell House	457.6	18.83
Maxwell House Master Blend	200.0	8.23
Folgers Coffee House	170.0	7.00
Hills Brothers	81.5	3.35
Chock Full O'Nuts	65.8	2.71
Maxwell House Lite	65.8	2.71
Yuban	63.1	2.60
Other	658.9	27.12

Source: *MMR*, November 16, 1998, p. 18, from Information Resources Inc.

★ 395 ★

Snacks (SIC 2096)

Best-Selling Corn Chips - 1999

Shares are shown based on sales of $520.2 million for the year ended January 30, 2000.

Frito-Lay Fritos	43.3%
Fritos Scoops	22.7
Doritos 3Ds	12.5
Bugles	7.9
Frito Lay Fritos Racerz	2.2
Sabrositas	2.2

Fritos Chili and Scoops	1.7%
Other	7.5

Source: *Snack Food & Wholesale Bakery*, March 2000, p. 20, from Information Resources Inc.

★ 396 ★

Snacks (SIC 2096)

Best-Selling Potato Chip Brands - 1999

Sales are shown in millions of dollars for the year ended March 28, 1999.

Lay's	$ 783
Ruffles	392
Lay's Wow	142
Ruffles Wow	118
Wavy Lay's	114
UTZ	55
Wise	52
Herr's	43
Private label	161

Source: *New York Times*, July 21, 1999, p. C1, from NPD Group Inc. and Information Resources Inc.

★ 397 ★

Snacks (SIC 2096)

Best-Selling Potato Chips

Shares are shown based on sales for the year ended March 28, 1999.

Lay's	33.5%
Ruffles	16.8
Lay's WoW!	6.1
Ruffles WoW!	5.0
Wavy Lay's	4.9
Utz	2.3
Wise	2.2
Herr's	1.8
Ruffles The Works	1.6
Private label	6.9
Other	23.9

Source: *Snack Food & Wholesale Bakery*, August 1999, p. 8, from Information Resources Inc.

★ 398 ★

Snacks (SIC 2096)

Best-Selling Potato Chips - 1999

Shares are shown based on unit sales of 1.5 billion for the year ended December 5, 1999.

	(mil.)	Share
Lay's	612.6	40.84%
Ruffles	185.7	12.38
Wavy Lay's	106.1	7.07
Wise	51.0	3.40
Utz	40.1	2.67
Lay's WoW!	38.1	2.54
Ruffles WoW!	34.0	2.27
Private label	122.2	8.15
Other	310.2	20.68

Source: *Discount Merchandiser*, March 2000, p. 3, from Euromonitor.

★ 399 ★

Snacks (SIC 2096)

Best-Selling Tortilla/Tostada Chip Brands - 1999

Shares are shown based on sales of $1.8 billion for the year ended July 18, 1999.

Doritos	38.5%
Tostitos	29.8
Baked Tostitos	5.2
Santitas	3.1
Doritos WoW	2.6
Tostitos	2.3
Mission	2.1
Padrinos	1.3
Private label	4.3
Other	10.8

Source: *Snack Food & Wholesale Bakery*, November 1999, p. 13, from Information Resources Inc.

★ 400 ★

Snacks (SIC 2096)

Chicago's Potato Chip Market - 1999

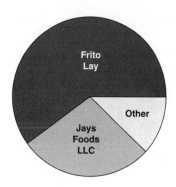

Frito Lay's share is estimated.

Frito Lay	60%
Jays Foods LLC	28
Other	12

Source: *Crain's Chicago Business*, September 27, 1999, p. 3, from Information Resources Inc.

★ 401 ★

Snacks (SIC 2096)

Fruit Roll Up Market - 1998

Shares are shown for the year ended January 3, 1999.

Betty Crocker Fruit Roll Up	18.2%
Betty Crocker Fruit by the Foot	13.9
Betty Crocker Gushers	11.2
Farley's Rugrats	7.1
Sunkist	4.9
Betty Crocker String	4.5
Private label	5.9
Other	34.3

Source: *Snack Food & Wholesale Bakery*, June 1999, p. SI38, from Information Resources Inc.

★ 402 ★

Snacks (SIC 2096)

Rice/Corn Cake Market Shares - 1998

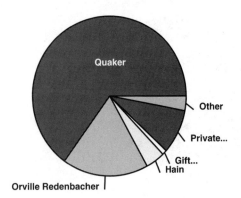

Shares are shown for the year ended January 3, 1999.

Quaker	65.1%
Orville Redenbacher	18.3
Hain	3.9
Gift of Nature	1.0
Private label	8.6
Other	3.1

Source: *Snack Food & Wholesale Bakery*, June 1999, p. SI38, from Information Resources Inc.

★ 403 ★

Snacks (SIC 2096)

Snack Food Sales - 1999

Sales are shown in millions of dollars for food/drug/ mass stores.

Potato chips	$ 2,840.9
Tortilla chips	1,833.4
Crackers, flavored snack	915.0
Pretzels	641.8
Crackers, cheese	629.6
Cheese snacks, puffed	489.5
Corn chips	378.8
Popcorn, popped	148.4
Caramel corn	142.3

Source: *Supermarket Business*, March 15, 2000, p. 58, from A.C. Nielsen.

★ 404 ★

Snacks (SIC 2096)

Top Chocolate-Covered Salted Snacks - 1998

Shares are shown based on sales for the year ended January 3, 1999.

Nestle Flipz	84.2%
Choczels	3.8
Snyder's of Hanover	2.4
Toadally Snax	1.8
Palmer	1.5
Other	6.3

Source: *Snack Food & Wholesale Bakery*, June 1999, pp. SI-40, from Information Resources Inc.

★ 405 ★

Snacks (SIC 2096)

Top Microwavable Popcorn Brands - 1998

Shares are shown based on sales of $667.4 million for the year ended January 3, 1999.

Orville Redenbacher	14.8%
Pop Secret	14.4
Orville	12.0
Orville Redenbacher Budders	12.0
Private label	10.6
Other	36.2

Source: *Snack Food & Wholesale Bakery*, June 1999, pp. SI-40, from Information Resources Inc.

★ 406 ★

Snacks (SIC 2096)

Top Popcorn Brands - 1998

Shares are shown based on sales of $62.5 million for the year ended January 3, 1999.

Orville Redenbacher	29.2%
Jolly Time	16.2
Jiffy Pop	11.7
Cousin Willies	1.6
Private label	32.5
Other	8.8

Source: *Snack Food & Wholesale Bakery*, June 1999, pp. SI-40, from Information Resources Inc.

★ 407 ★
Snacks (SIC 2096)

Top Popcorn/Caramel Corn Brands - 1998

Shares are shown based on sales of $254.8 million for the year ended January 3, 1999.

Crunch & Munch	15.8%
Houston Harvest	15.3
Cracker Jack	9.3
Smart Food	8.8
Chester's	5.0
ACT II	3.2
Jays O-ke-Doke	2.7
Wise	2.7
Private label	7.5
Other	29.7

Source: *Snack Food & Wholesale Bakery*, June 1999, pp. SI-40, from Information Resources Inc.

★ 408 ★
Snacks (SIC 2096)

Top Pretzel Brands - 1999

Shares are shown based on sales of $573.2 million for the year ended December 5, 1999.

	($ mil.)	Share
Rold Gold Pretzels	$ 161.8	28.23%
Snyders of Hanover Pretzels	108.8	18.98
Snyder's of Hanover Old Thyme Pretzels	19.4	3.38
Combo Pretzels	16.9	2.95
Bachman Pretzels	16.4	2.86
Herr's Pretzels	12.6	2.20
Utz Pretzels	11.5	2.01
Private label	70.2	12.25
Other	155.6	27.15

Source: *Discount Merchandiser*, March 2000, p. 3, from Euromonitor.

★ 409 ★
Snacks (SIC 2096)

Top Pretzel Makers - 1998

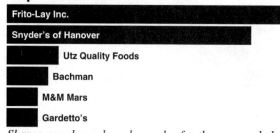

Shares are shown based on sales for the year ended January 3, 1999.

	($ mil.)	Share
Frito-Lay Inc.	$ 156.0	26.6%
Snyder's of Hanover	138.7	23.6
Utz Quality Foods	26.6	4.5
Bachman	21.6	3.7
M&M Mars	17.4	3.0
Gardetto's	17.0	2.9

Source: *Snack Food & Wholesale Bakery*, June 1999, pp. SI-40, from Information Resources Inc.

★ 410 ★
Snacks (SIC 2096)

Top Snack Mix Brands - 1999

The market is valued at $239.4 million for the year ended December 5, 1999.

General Mills Chex Mix	46.1%
Gardetto's Snack Ens	16.1
Sunshine Cheez It Party Mixes	11.1
Sunshine Cheez It Snack Mixes	10.6
Pepperidge Farm Goldfish Party Mix	4.3
Nabisco Ritz Party Mix	3.1
Other	8.7

Source: *Snack Food & Wholesale Bakery*, February 2000, p. 18, from Information Resources Inc.

★ 411 ★

Ice (SIC 2097)

Leading Ice Markets - 1999

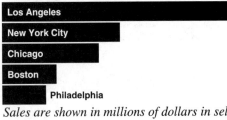

Los Angeles	
New York City	
Chicago	
Boston	
Philadelphia	

Sales are shown in millions of dollars in selected markets. Figures are for the year ended September 4, 1999.

Los Angeles	$ 26.0
New York City	10.5
Chicago	8.5
Boston	5.4
Philadelphia	3.9

Source: *Grocery Headquarters*, January 2000, p. 45, from A.C. Nielsen.

★ 412 ★

Pasta (SIC 2098)

Frozen Pasta Market - 1998

Shares are shown based on supermarket sales of $252.3 million for the year ended January 3, 1999.

	($ mil.)	Share
Rosetto	$ 64.7	25.73%
Mrs. T's	36.4	14.47
Italian Village	26.3	10.46
Celentano	18.6	7.40
Private label	14.5	5.77
Other	91.0	36.18

Source: *Refrigerated & Frozen Foods*, June 1999, p. 47, from Information Resources Inc. InfoScan.

★ 413 ★

Pasta (SIC 2098)

Leading Pasta Markets - 1999

Sales are shown in millions of dollars in selected markets. Figures are for the year ended September 4, 1999.

New York City	$ 128.9
Los Angeles	58.9
Philadelphia	54.4
Boston	52.3
Chicago	38.9

Source: *Grocery Headquarters*, January 2000, p. 45, from A.C. Nielsen.

★ 414 ★

Pasta (SIC 2098)

Pasta Sales - 1998

Data show estimated sales in millions of pounds.

Spaghetti	308
Elbows	121
Noodles	70
Twirls	52
Penne/mostaccoli	51
Capellini	49
Ziti	42
Shells	39
Vermicelli	36
Linguine	36

Source: "I Love Pasta." Retrieved January 21, 2000 from the World Wide Web: http://ilovepasta.org/ industrystatistics.html, from National Pasta Association.

★ 415 ★

Pasta (SIC 2098)

Refrigerated Pasta Market - 1998

Shares are shown based on supermarket sales of $148.8 million for the year ended January 3, 1999.

	($ mil.)	Share
Contadina Dalla Casa Buitoni	$ 74.3	49.93%
Di Giorno	40.2	27.02
Monterey Pasta Co.	5.0	3.36
Mallard's	2.7	1.81
Private label	14.5	9.74
Other	12.1	8.13

Source: *Refrigerated & Frozen Foods*, June 1999, p. 47, from Information Resources Inc. InfoScan.

★ 416 ★

Pasta (SIC 2098)

Top Pasta Brands - 1999

Sales are shown for the year ended July 18, 1999.

	($ mil.)	Share
Barilla	$ 100.2	9.03%
Ronzoni	93.1	8.39
Mueller's	91.8	8.27
Creamette	82.5	7.43
San Giorgio	73.3	6.60
American Beauty	65.7	5.92
Other	603.4	54.36

Source: Retrieved January 1, 2000 from the World Wide Web: http://jasper.sosland.com/cgi-bin/.c// pageitems_body?, from Information Resources Inc.

★ 417 ★

Food Preparations (SIC 2099)

Dessert Topping Market - 1999

Catogory sales reached $1.0 billion in supermarkets.

RTS desserts	40.5%
Pudding and pie filling mixes	21.1
Gelatin	20.6
Prepared toppings (not frostings)	14.0
Maraschino cherries	3.8

Source: *Progressive Grocer*, July 1999, p. 56.

★ 418 ★

Lunch Kits (SIC 2099)

Lunch Kit Market

Lunch kit sales have reached $688 million. Market shares are shown in percent.

Oscar Mayer's Lunchables	78%
Other	22

Source: *Food & Beverage Marketing*, March 1999, p. 26.

★ 419 ★

Marinades (SIC 2099)

Marinade Market Shares

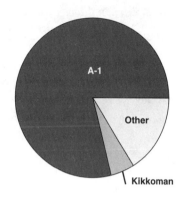

The marinade category has grown from $43 million in 1996 to $163 million as of November 7, 1999. According to the source 52% of consumers marinate steak vs. 25% for chicken and fish.

	($ mil.)	Share
A-1	$ 128.4	78.77%
Kikkoman	7.8	4.79
Other	26.8	16.44

Source: *Advertising Age*, December 20, 1999, p. 3, from Information Resources Inc.

★ 420 ★

Spices (SIC 2099)

Spice/Seasoning Market Leaders

Shares are shown as of December 27, 1998 and November 7, 1999.

	1998	1999
McCormick	37.2%	38.5%
Specialty Brands	6.0	5.3
Tone Brothers	3.3	2.7
Albeto Culver	3.3	3.0
Goya Foods	2.8	2.7
A&A Spice & Food	2.4	2.5
Mojave Foods	1.9	1.8
Private label	11.3	11.2

Source: *Supermarket Business*, January 15, 2000, p. 17, from Information Resources Inc.

★ 421 ★

Spices (SIC 2099)

Spices and Extract Sales - 1998

Supermarket sales are shown in millions of dollars.

	($ mil.)	Share
Spices, herbs, seasonings . . .	$ 853.21	58.86%
Salt	253.07	17.46
Pepper	210.27	14.50
Extracts and food coloring . . .	133.13	9.18

Source: *Progressive Grocer*, July 1999, p. 58, from Information Resources Inc.

★ 422 ★

Syrup (SIC 2099)

Maple Syrup Production - 1999

Total production reached 1.2 million gallons.

	(000)	Share
Vermont	370,000	30.83%
New York	195,000	16.25
Maine	187,000	15.58
Ohio	95,000	7.92
Wisconsin	75,000	6.25
Michigan	73,000	6.08
Pennsylvania	67,000	5.58
Other	138,000	11.50

Source: *USA TODAY*, March 8, 2000, p. A1, from National Agricultural Statistics Service.

★ 423 ★

Syrup (SIC 2099)

Top Syrup Brands - 1999

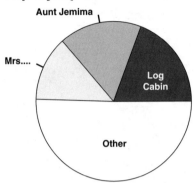

Shares are shown based on sales of $471.5 million for the year ended November 7, 1999.

	($ mil.)	Share
Log Cabin	$ 89.0	18.88%
Aunt Jemima	82.0	17.39
Mrs. Butterworth's	63.0	13.36
Other	237.5	50.37

Source: *Advertising Age*, December 20, 1999, p. 44, from Information Resources Inc.

★ 424 ★

Taco and Tortilla Kits (SIC 2099)

Top Tortilla/Taco Kit Brands - 1999

Sales are shown for the year ended July 18, 1999.

	($ mil.)	Share
Mission	$ 198.6	26.29%
Old El Paso	107.5	14.23
Guerrero	95.8	12.68
Taco Bell	55.8	7.39
Ortega	25.8	3.41
Dianes	17.0	2.25
Tia Rosa	16.2	2.14
Other	238.8	31.61

Source: Retrieved January 1, 2000 from the World Wide Web: http://jasper.sosland.com/cgi-bin/.c// pageitems_body?, from Information Resources Inc.

SIC 21 - Tobacco Products

★ 425 ★
Tobacco (SIC 2100)

Largest Tobacco Firms - 1999

The largest tobacco firms are ranked by revenues in billions of dollars.

Philip Morris	$ 61.7
R.J. Reynolds Tobacco	11.3
Universal	4.0
Dimon	1.9
UST	1.4

Source: *Fortune*, April 17, 2000, pp. I-74.

★ 426 ★
Tobacco (SIC 2100)

Tobacco Product Sales - 1999

Total sales at chain drug stores reached $3.9 billion.

Cigarettes	69.8%
Cigars	12.5
Lighters, accessories	11.2
Smokeless tobacco	5.4
Pipes, pipe tobacco	1.1

Source: *Chain Drug Review*, March 13, 2000, p. 55, from Racher Press.

★ 427 ★
Cigarettes (SIC 2111)

Tobacco Market in Canada

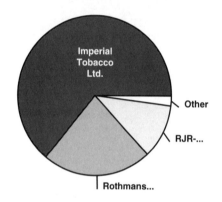

Market shares are shown in percent.

Imperial Tobacco Ltd.	64%
Rothmans Benson & Hedges Inc.	23
RJR-Macdonald Inc.	11
Other	2

Source: *Globe and Mail*, June 8, 1999, p. B7, from company reports.

★ 428 ★
Cigarettes (SIC 2111)

Top Cigarette Brands - 1999

Shares are shown for the second quarter of the year.

Marlboro	35.2%
Newport	7.7
Doral	6.6
Winston	5.2
GPC	5.0
Other	40.3

Source: *Advertising Age*, August 30, 1999, p. 4, from Maxwell Report.

★ 429 ★

Cigarettes (SIC 2111)

U.S. Cigarette Market

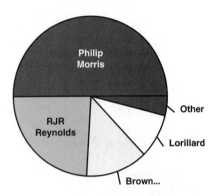

Philip Morris	.50%
RJR Reynolds	24
Brown & Williamson	13
Lorillard	9
Other	4

Source: *Washington Post*, September 15, 1999, p. E1, from Salomon Smith Barney and Goldman Sachs.

★ 430 ★

Cigars (SIC 2121)

Boxed Cigar Sales - 1998

$75 - $100	26%
$40 - $74.99	23
$20 - $39.99	12
Under $20	6
Over $100	6

Source: Retrieved February 11, 2000 from the World Wide Web: http://www.gosmokeshop.com.

★ 431 ★

Smokeless Tobacco (SIC 2131)

Smokeless Tobacco Market

The market is valued at $2 billion.

Skoal	39.5%
Copenhagen	33.7
Other	26.8

Source: *Brandweek*, February 7, 2000, p. 6, from A.C. Nielsen.

★ 432 ★

Snuff (SIC 2131)

Moist Snuff Market

The $1.8 billion market is shown in percent.

UST	.76%
Conwood	13
Other	11

Source: *Forbes*, May 29, 2000, p. 72.

★ 433 ★

Chewing Tobacco (SIC 2141)

Chewing Tobacco Market

Shares are for December 1999.

UST	.75.9%
Conwood	.13.4
Swedish Match	6.3
Swisher Intl	0.3
Other	1.1

Source: *Wall Street Journal*, March 30, 2000, p. A3, from Credit Suisse First Boston and Baseline.

SIC 22 - Textile Mill Products

★ 434 ★

Textiles (SIC 2200)

Largest Textile Product Firms - 1999

The largest textile firms are ranked by revenues in billions of dollars.

Shaw Industries	$ 4.1
Mohawk Industries	3.0
Springs Industries	2.2
Westpoint Stevens	1.8
Burlington Industries	1.6
Pillowtex	1.5
Interface	1.2
Unifi	1.2

Source: *Fortune*, April 17, 2000, pp. I-74.

★ 435 ★

Textiles (SIC 2200)

U.S. Textile Market

Distribution is shown by pounds.

Apparel	36%
Floorcoverings	25
Industrial	23
Homefurnishings	16

Source: *Textile World*, January 2000, p. 26, from Fiber Organon.

★ 436 ★

Apparel (SIC 2250)

Woven Apparel Imports - 1998

Market shares are shown based on imports of $28.1 billion.

Women's & girl's suits & ensembles	30.4%
Men's & boy's suits & ensembles	22.8
Men's and boy's shirts	10.8
Women's & girl's shirts & blouses	7.9
Men's and boy's overcoats	6.5

Women's & girls' overcoats	4.2%
Bras, girdles & garters	4.0
Track suits, ski suits & swimwear	3.7
Other	9.7

Source: *Textile Asia*, April 1999, p. 117.

★ 437 ★

Hosiery (SIC 2251)

Sheer Hosiery Market

The market reached an estimated $300 million in department stores.

Hanes Hosiery	30%
No Nonsense	20
Other	50

Source: *WWD Fairchild 100 Supplement*, November 1999, p. 98.

★ 438 ★

Hosiery (SIC 2251)

Top Pantyhose Brands - 1999

Shares are shown based on sales of $899.5 million for the year ended February 27, 2000.

Leggs Sheer Energy	13.7%
No Nonsense	11.7

Continued on next page.

★ 438 ★ *Continued*

Hosiery (SIC 2251)

Top Pantyhose Brands - 1999

Shares are shown based on sales of $899.5 million for the year ended February 27, 2000.

Leggs Silken Mist	7.2%
Just My Size	5.6
Leggs Everyday	5.4
Leggs	4.1
No Nonsense Sheer Endurance	3.8
Private label	19.7
Other	28.8

Source: *Supermarket Business*, May 15, 2000, p. 76, from Information Resources Inc.

★ 439 ★

Hosiery (SIC 2252)

Largest Sock Knitters

Data show annual sales in millions of dollars.

Renfro	$ 286
Sara Lee Sock Co.	265
Great American Knitting	164
V.I. Prewett Mills	150
Kentucky Derby Hosiery	105

Source: *Textile World*, October 1999, p. 30, from industry reports.

★ 440 ★

Carpets (SIC 2273)

Carpet & Rug Shipments - 1999

Data are forecasted.

	(mil.)
Needlepunch & other	145%
Rugs & misc.	125
Automotive & industrial	80
Woven	30
Artificial grass	30
Tufted broadloom	1

Source: *Textile World*, June 1999, p. 62, from U.S. Dept. of Commercer and Carpet & Rug Institute.

★ 441 ★

Carpets (SIC 2273)

Carpet Market Leaders

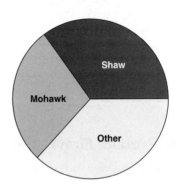

Shaw	35%
Mohawk	28
Other	37

Source: *Forbes*, November 15, 1999, p. I74.

★ 442 ★

Carpets (SIC 2273)

Top Carpet Makers - 1998

Sales are shown in millions of dollars.

Shaw/Queen	$ 930
Mohawk/World/Durkan	560
Interface	365
Beaulieu/Lotus	310
Lees	280
Collins & Aikman	170
Mannington Carpet	150
Milliken	125
J&J Industries	120
US Axminster	65

Source: "Total Sales for Commercial Carpets." Retrieved December 2, 1999 from the World Wide Web: http://www.floorfocus.com/FeatAllComm.html, from *Floor Focus*.

SIC 23 - Apparel and Other Textile Products

★ 443 ★

Apparel (SIC 2300)

Apparel Sales by Segment - 1999

Total sales reached $183.8 billion.

	($ mil.)	Share
Women's	$ 96,006	52.22%
Men's	56,514	30.74
Boy's	13,515	7.35
Girl's	9,932	5.40
Other	7,892	4.29

Source: "NPD Reports U.S. Apparel Sales." Retrieved February 29, 2000 from the World Wide Web: http://library.northernlight.com, from NPD Group.

★ 444 ★

Apparel (SIC 2300)

Canada's Sports Clothing Sales - 1998

Data show estimated retail sales in thousands of dollars. Total sales reached $1.372 billion.

Warmup/track suits	$ 315,000
Sweat shirts	227,000
Bathing suits	138,000
Sweat pants	136,000
Ski jackets	79,000
Golf shirts	71,000
Snow/ski suits	56,000
Ski pants	41,000

Source: Retrieved January 21, 2000 from the World Wide Web: http://strategis.ic.gc.ca/SSG, from Industry Canada.

★ 445 ★

Apparel (SIC 2300)

Fleecewear Market Leaders - 1999

Selected market shares are shown in percent.

Russell	29.1%
Adidas	14.5
Champion	13.0
Other	43.4

Source: "Athletic Apparel Market Share Report." Retrieved May 1, 2000 from the World Wide Web: http://www.businesswire.com, from SportsTrend.Info.

★ 446 ★

Apparel (SIC 2300)

Infant and Toddler Apparel Sales - 1998

Total infant and toddler apparel sales reached $7.12 billion.

	($ mil.)	Share
Bottoms	$ 1,874	26.32%
Tops	1,428	20.06
Underwear and sleepwear	1,274	17.89
Tailored clothing	766	10.76
Nightwear/robes	733	10.29
Sweats and warmups	611	8.58
Other	434	6.10

Source: *Discount Merchandiser*, October 1999, p. 3, from NPD Group Inc.

★ 447 ★

Apparel (SIC 2300)

Largest Sports Licensee Sales - 1999

Companies are ranked by estimated sales in millions of dollars.

Logo Athletic	$ 200
VF Knitwear	190
Champion	188
Pro Player	175
Nike	162
New Era	123
Starter	120
Haddad	110

Source: *Sports Business Journal*, February 7, 2000, p. 25, from *Sporting Goods Business*.

★ 448 ★

Apparel (SIC 2300)

Men's Apparel Sales by Fiber

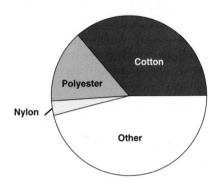

Cotton had nearly 60% of the entire apparel market.

Cotton	36.8%
Polyester	14.6
Nylon	3.1
Other	46.5

Source: *DNR*, April 10, 2000, p. 21, from NPD Group.

★ 449 ★

Apparel (SIC 2300)

Outerwear Apparel Market - 1999

Market shares are shown in percent.

Columbia	27.8%
Adidas	17.7
Other	54.5

Source: "Athletic Apparel Market Share Report." Retrieved May 1, 2000 from the World Wide Web: http://www.businesswire.com, from SportsTrend.Info.

★ 450 ★

Apparel (SIC 2300)

Protective Apparel Market

Baxter Healthcare and Kimberly-Clark control about 56% of the market.

Surgical packs, components, drapes	37%
Medical gloves	32
Protective wearing clothing	20
Other	11

Source: *Medical & Healthcare Marketplace Guide*, 1999, pp. I-693.

★ 451 ★

Apparel (SIC 2300)

Sports Apparel Market - 2000

Shares are shown for the first quarter of the year.

Nike	21.1%
Adidas	13.1
Columbia Sportswear	10.2
Champion Products	4.8
Russell Athletic	4.4
Reebok	3.1
Bike Athletic	2.3
Ridgeview	1.6
Other	39.4

Source: ''Athletic Apparel Market Share Report.''
Retrieved May 1, 2000 from the World Wide Web: http://
www.businesswire.com, from SportsTrend.Info.

★ 452 ★

Apparel (SIC 2300)

Sports Licensed Apparel Sales - 1998

Sales are shown in millions of dollars.

	($ mil.)	Share
T-shirts	$ 1,080	41.22%
Fleece tops	441	16.83
Jackets	393	15.00
Knit shirts	333	12.71
Caps/hats	202	7.71
Shorts	62	2.37
Fleece pants	55	2.10
Warm-ups	54	2.06

Source: *Discount Merchandiser*, November 1999, p. 143,
from National Sporting Goods Association.

★ 453 ★

Apparel (SIC 2300)

Top Jeans Producers - 1998

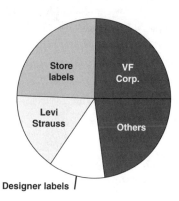

The $12 billion market is shown by company.

VF Corp.	25.1%
Store labels	24.5
Levi Strauss	16.3
Designer labels	11.6
Others	22.5

Source: *Los Angeles Times*, November 6, 1999, p. C1, from
Tactical Retail Solutions and *Bridge News*.

★ 454 ★

Apparel (SIC 2300)

U.S. Apparel Imports

*Shares are shown based on imports for the year
ended July 31, 1999.*

Mexico	14.36%
Canada	9.90
China	7.03
Pakistan	5.18
China (Taiwan)	4.73
South Korea	4.31
Other	54.49

Source: *Bobbin*, November 1999, p. 67, from U.S. Department of Commerce and major shippers reports.

★ 455 ★
Apparel (SIC 2300)

Women's Plus-Sized Apparel Market

Studies show the typical American woman is size 12, stands 5'4'' and weighs 144 pounds. 23% of the plus-size market is devoted to size 23 and over.

Sportswear	49%
Tailored/dress	22
Intimate	18
Outerwear	5
Swim/activewear	4
Other	2

Source: *WWD*, April 3, 2000, p. 2, from NPD American Shoppers Panel and Strategic Information Services.

★ 456 ★
Apparel (SIC 2325)

Men's Khaki Sales

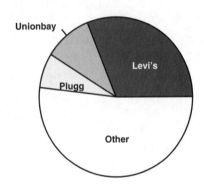

Levi's	31.3%
Unionbay	9.5
Plugg	7.3
Other	51.9

Source: *DNR*, May 22, 2000, p. 16.

★ 457 ★
Apparel (SIC 2325)

Young Men's Jeans Market - 1998

Market shares are shown in percent.

Levi's	51.7%
FUBU	7.4
Plugg	3.9
Other	37.0

Source: *DNR*, March 19, 1999, p. 27.

★ 458 ★
Apparel (SIC 2325)

Young Men's Slacks Market - 1998

Market shares are shown in percent.

Levi's	25.2%
Union Bay	10.5
Bugle Boy	8.5
Plugg	6.8

Source: *DNR*, March 19, 1999, p. 27.

★ 459 ★
Apparel (SIC 2330)

Women's Apparel Sales by Fiber

Cotton	37.4%
Polyester	24.3
Nylon	10.3
Rayon	8.4
Wool	4.9
Silk	3.4
Other	11.3

Source: *WWD*, October 26, 1999, p. 9, from NPD Group.

★ 460 ★
Apparel (SIC 2330)

Women's Apparel Sales by Size - 1998

Misses	51%
Large sizes	20
Juniors	12
Petite	4
Other	13

Source: *WWD*, August 24, 1999, p. 5.

★ 461 ★
Apparel Accessories (SIC 2380)

Women's Apparel Accessory Sales - 1999

Sales are from October 1998 - September 1999. The female accessories market reached $3.2 billion.

Wallets	16%
Gloves/mittens	15
Handbags	13
Belts	11
Caps/hats	10
Scarfs/shawls	8
Other	5

Source: *Footwear News*, November 29, 1999, p. 13, from NPD American Shoppers Panel.

★ 462 ★
Homefurnishings (SIC 2392)

Bath Product Sales - 1998

Bath towels

Bath/accent rugs

    Shower curtains

    Bath accessories

Sales are shown in millions of dollars.

	($ mil.)	Share
Bath towels	$ 2,376	54%
Bath/accent rugs	924	21
Shower curtains	572	13
Bath accessories	528	12

Source: *Home Textiles Today 2000 Business Annual Supplement*, 2000, p. 54.

★ 463 ★
Homefurnishings (SIC 2392)

Leading Home Textile Firms - 1999

Companies are ranked by estimated sales in millions of dollars.

Westpoint Stevens	$ 1,868
Springs	1,740
Pillowtex	1,538
Mohawk Industries Inc.	470
Dan River	441
Crown Crafts	357
Burlington	300

Croscill Home Fashions	$ 283
Pacific Coast	230
Glenoit Corporation	225

Source: *Home Textiles Today*, January 3, 2000, p. 12.

★ 464 ★
Homefurnishings (SIC 2392)

Retail Bedding Sales - 1998

The $2.3 billion market is shown in percent.

Sheets/pillowcases	29%
Comforters	20
Bed pillows	13
Blankets	8
Bed-in-the-bag	6
Decorative pillows	6
Mattress pads	4
Throws	4

Source: *Home Textiles Today 2000 Business Annual Supplement*, 2000, p. 50.

★ 465 ★
Homefurnishings (SIC 2392)

Table Linen Sales - 1999

The kitchen textiles and table linen market is shown by segment.

	($ mil.)	Share
Tablecloths	$ 253	23%
Kitchen towels	231	21
Place mats	198	18
Napkins	110	10
Dishcloths	99	9
Potholders and mitts	88	8

Source: *Home Textiles Today*, February 14, 2000, p. 10.

★ 466 ★
Slipcovers (SIC 2392)

Manufactured Slipcover Market

Sure Fit	85%
Other	15

Source: *High Points*, November 1999, p. 24.

SIC 24 - Lumber and Wood Products

Wood (SIC 2400)

Wood Used by Furniture Makers - 1996

HW dimension	25%
Particleboard	24
HW lumber	22
MDF	17
HW plywood	6
Other	6

Source: *Forest Products Journal*, November/December 1999, p. 53.

Paneling (SIC 2421)

Canadian Paneling Production

Data are in cubic meters.

	(meters)	Share
Oriented strand board	6,304,538	56.11%
Particleboard	2,347,003	20.89
Construction plywood	1,760,364	15.67
Fiberboard	823,556	7.33

Source: *Wood Technology*, October 1999, p. 35, from Statistics Canada.

Paneling (SIC 2421)

Structural Paneling Sales

Data are in billions of cubic feet.

	1997	1998
U.S.	28.4	29.0
Canada	8.4	9.7

Source: *Wood Technology*, October 1999, p. 36, from American Paneling Association and Statistics Canada.

Paneling (SIC 2421)

U.S. Paneling Production

Data are in millions of square feet. Structural panels are in a 3/8 inch basis; particleboard is in a 3/4 inch basis; medium denity fiberboard is a 3/4 inch basis; hardboard is a 1/8 inch basis.

	(mil.)	Share
Structural panel	29,003	73.79%
Particleboard	4,592	11.68
Hardboard	4,300	10.94
MDF	1,410	3.59

Source: *Wood Technology*, October 1999, p. 35, from American Particleboard Association, Composite Panel Association, and American Hardboard Association.

Cabinets (SIC 2434)

Largest Cabinet Makers - 1999

Firms are ranked by sales in millions of dollars.

Masco Corp.	$ 2,000
MasterBrand Cabinets Inc.	600
American Woodmark Corp.	327
Omega Cabinets Ltd.	278
Elkay Mfg. Co., Cabinet Group	200
Triangle Pacific Corp.	177
RSI Home Products	174
Cardell Kitchen & Bath Cabinetry	143
Republic Industries Inc.	125

Source: *Wood & Wood Products*, March 2000, p. 60.

★ 472 ★
Veneer (SIC 2435)

Popular Veneer Woods - 1998

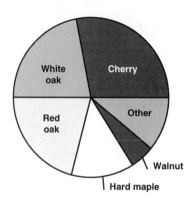

Total production reached 7.23 billion square feet.

Cherry	28%
White oak	22
Red oak	21
Hard maple	13
Walnut	5
Other	11

Source: *Wood & Wood Products*, September 1999, p. 15, from *Hardwood Plywood and Veneer News*.

★ 473 ★
Pallets (SIC 2448)

Popular Types of Pallets

Data show the most frequently purchased types of pallets, based on a survey. Pallets are shipped for warehousing and shipping.

Wood	91%
Wood composites	4
Plastic	4
Other	1

Source: *Modern Materials Handling*, May 2000, p. 67, from National Wood Pallet and Container Association.

★ 474 ★
Manufactured Homes (SIC 2451)

Manufactured Home Industry - 1998

A total of 372,843 homes were shipped during the year.

	Units	Share
Champion Enterprises	68,264	18.31%
Fleetwood Enterprises	66,222	17.76
Oakwood Homes	38,237	10.26
Clayton Homes	28,429	7.62
Cavalier Homes	24,387	6.54
Skyline Corp.	17,286	4.64
Palm Harbor Homes	15,352	4.12
American Homestar	12,373	3.32
Other	102,293	27.44

Source: Retrieved January 1, 2000 from the World Wide Web: http://www.mfghome.org/statistics/98top25.html, from *Manufactured Home Merchandiser*.

★ 475 ★
Manufactured Homes (SIC 2451)

Top Manufactured Home Builders - 1999

Companies are ranked by shipments.

Champion Enterprises	71,761
Fleetwood Enterprises	62,506
Oakwood Homes Copr.	37,496
Clayton Homes	28,344
Cavalier Homes	22,377
Skyline Corp.	15,300
Palm Harbor Homes	15,000
American Homestar Corp.	12,311
Horton Homes	9,142

Source: *Builder*, May 2000, p. 178.

★ 476 ★
Decking (SIC 2490)

Wood-Substitute Decking Market

The wood substitute market accounts for only 3% of the entire $2.5 decking market.

Trex	85%
Other	15

Source: *Investor's Business Daily*, April 27, 2000, p. A12.

★ 477 ★

Fire Logs and Starters (SIC 2499)

Top Fire Log/Firestarter Brands - 1999

Shares are shown based on sales of $145.4 million for the year ended February 27, 2000.

Duraflame 17.2%
Duraflame Xtratime 13.6
Pine Mountain 10.2
Starter Logg 7.5
Northland 5.0
Duraflame Anytime 3.6
Duraflame Crackleflame 2.6
Hearthlogg 2.6
Private label 22.9
Other 14.8

Source: *Supermarket Business*, May 15, 2000, p. 70, from Information Resources Inc.

SIC 25 - Furniture and Fixtures

★ 478 ★
Furniture (SIC 2500)

Furniture Market Leaders - 1998

Companies are ranked by shipments shown in millions of dollars.

Furniture Brands International . . . . . $ 1,960.3
LifeStyle Furnishings 1,744.7
La-Z-Boy 1,244.0
Klaussner 725.0
Ashley 651.0
Ethan Allen 610.8
Ladd 571.1
Sauder 530.0
Bassett 397.6
Bush Furniture 384.3

Source: *Furniture Today*, May 10, 1999, p. 9.

★ 479 ★
Furniture (SIC 2500)

Largest Upholstered Seating Manufacturers

Sales are shown in millions of dollars. The top 50 firms in North America reported sales of $8.22 billion. Figures for Furniture Brands and LifeStyle are for 1997.

La-Z-Boy Inc. . . . . $ 1,000
Furnituer Brands Intl. 935
Klaussner Furniture Brands 720
Gobal 580
LifeStyle Furnishings Intl. Ltd. 450
Herman Miller Inc. 410
Flexsteel Industries Inc. 236
Futorian Furnishings Inc. 200
Ethan Allen Inc. 190
Ashley Furniture Industries Inc. 172

Source: "1999 UDM Top 50." Retrieved January 21, 2000 from the World Wide Web: http://www.fdmmag.com/top50.htm.

★ 480 ★
Furniture (SIC 2500)

Ready-to-Assemble Furniture Market

Office furniture

Entertainment furniture

Bedroom furniture

Homefurnishings

The industry had sales of $1.9 billion.

Office furniture 53%
Entertainment furniture 23
Bedroom furniture 17
Homefurnishings 9

Source: "NPD HomeTrak Reports Almost $2B in RTA Sales." Retrieved April 24, 2000 from the World Wide Web: http://www.businesswire.com, from NPD HomeTrak.

★ 481 ★
Furniture (SIC 2500)

Ready-to-Assemble Furniture Sales

Unit sales are shown in percent.

Home entertainment 29.0%
Office 23.5
Bedroom 12.3
Kitchen 6.7
Storage 5.1
Other 23.4

Source: *Furniture Today*, August 9, 1999, p. 8, from NPD Group.

★ 482 ★

Furniture (SIC 2500)

Top Furniture Markets

Chicago, IL	
New York City, NY	
Los Angeles, CA	
Detroit, MI	
Washington D.C.	
Atlanta, GA	
Philadelphia, PA	

Sales are shown in millions of dollars.

Chicago, IL . . . . $ 940.1
New York City, NY 510.5
Los Angeles, CA 503.5
Detroit, MI 496.9
Washington D.C. 494.2
Atlanta, GA 454.6
Philadelphia, PA 362.7

Source: *Wall Street Journal*, January 28, 2000, p. W10, from American Furniture Manufacturers Association.

★ 483 ★

Mattresses (SIC 2515)

Mattress Market by Size - 1998

Mattress and foundation shipments reached 36.32 million units shipped.

Queen-size 31.6%
Twin-size 29.8
Other 38.6

Source: "About the Industry." Retrieved February 29, 2000 from the World Wide Web: http://www.sleepproducts.org, from International Sleep Products Association.

★ 484 ★

Fixtures (SIC 2541)

Top Fixture Makers - 1998

Companies are ranked by sales in millions of dollars.

Lozier Corp. . . . . $ 300.0
Madix Store Fixtures 170.0
Oklahoma Fixture Co. 75.0
MII Inc. 60.0
Met Merchandising Concepts 60.0

Ready Fixtures . . . . $ 55.0
J.D. Store Equipment 46.0
Dann Dee Display Fixtures 45.2
Sifa Sinthesi Inc. 42.0

Source: *VM + SD*, October 1999, p. 39.

★ 485 ★

Fixtures (SIC 2541)

Top Woodworking/Store Fixture Makers - 1998

Companies are ranked by sales in millions of dollars.

LA Darling Co. . . . . $ 200.0
Madix Store Fixtures 182.0
Ontario Store Fixtures 176.0
Oklahoma Fixture Co. 72.0
Alexandria Moulding 70.0
Hamilton Fixture 65.1
Mll Inc. 62.0
Goer Mfg. Co. 52.5
Vira Manufacturing Inc. 42.5

Source: *Wood & Wood Products*, April 2000, p. 60.

SIC 26 - Paper and Allied Products

★ 486 ★

Paper (SIC 2600)

Largest Paper/Forest Product Firms - 1999

Firms are ranked by revenues in billions of dollars.

International Paper	$ 24.5
Georgia-Pacific	17.7
Kimberly-Clark	13.0
Weyerhaeuser	12.2
Smurfit-Stone Container	7.3
Fort James	7.1
Boise Cascade	6.9
Champion International	5.2
Temple-Inland	4.0
Willamette Industries	4.0

Source: *Fortune*, April 17, 2000, pp. I-63.

★ 487 ★

Paper (SIC 2611)

Top Kraft Paper Makers - 1999

Total capacity reached 3.3 milliion tons in North America.

Longview Fibre	15.2%
Smurfit-Stone Container	13.6
International Paper	12.1
Gaylord Container	8.3
Georgia-Pacific	7.7
Other	43.1

Source: *Pulp & Paper*, December 1999, p. 6.

★ 488 ★

Pulp (SIC 2611)

Top Pulp Makers in North America - 1999

Market shares are shown in percent.

Weyerhaeuser Co.	12.7%
Georgia-Pacific Corp.	8.5
International Paper Corp.	7.1
Parsons & Whittemore Inc.	6.2
Bowater Inc.	5.3
Champion Corp.	4.9
Other	55.3

Source: *Pulp & Paper*, August 1999, p. 11.

★ 489 ★

Paper (SIC 2621)

Top Newsprint Makers - 1999

Market shares are shown in percent. Data are for North America.

Abitibi	22.0%
Bowater	17.1
Donohue	12.8
Kruger	6.2
Fletcher Challenge Canada	4.5
Other	37.4

Source: *Wall Street Journal*, December 22, 1999, p. B4, from Deutsche Banc Alex. Brown and *Pulp & Paper Week*.

★ 490 ★
Paper (SIC 2621)

Top Uncoated Groundwood Makers

Shares are shown for North America.

Abitibi-Consolidated	29.5%
Pacifica Papers	8.6
Bowater	7.5
Alliance	6.7
Stora Port Hawkesbury	5.2
Kruger	5.0
Other	37.5

Source: *Pulp & Paper*, September 1999, p. 11.

★ 491 ★
Paper (SIC 2671)

Coated Free-Sheet Market - 1999

Shares are shown based on capacity. Data are for North America.

Sappi Fine Paper	18.0%
Consolidated Papers	13.8
Westvaco	12.0
Mead	11.8
Champion International	8.3
Potlatch	6.3
International Paper	4.9
Other	24.9

Source: *Pulp & Paper*, March 2000, p. 9.

★ 492 ★
Tape (SIC 2672)

Top Household Tape Brands - 1998

Brands are ranked by sales of $329.1 million for the year ended January 31, 1999.

	($ mil.)	Share
Scotch	$ 142.9	43.42%
Manco	54.4	16.53
Scotch Magic	46.8	14.22
Manco Duck	13.0	3.95
Tartan	11.0	3.34
Quick Stik	4.9	1.49

	($ mil.)	Share
3M	$ 3.8	1.15%
Manco EZ Start	2.7	0.82
Action	2.1	0.64
Other	47.5	14.43

Source: *MMR*, May 17, 1999, p. 61, from Information Resources Inc.

★ 493 ★
Feminine Hygiene Products (SIC 2676)

External Protection Market

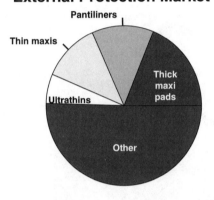

Private label led the way over retail brand tampons for sales growth with 6.5% rise in unit volume and 9.8% gain in dollar volume. Retail unit shares are shown in percent. Tampax is the top brand.

Thick maxi pads	18.6%
Pantiliners	12.9
Thin maxis	11.7
Ultrathins	5.7
Other	51.1

Source: *Nonwovens Industry*, January 2000, p. 36.

★ 494 ★
Feminine Hygiene Products (SIC 2676)

Feminine Protection Market - 1999

Shares are shown based on sales of $1.91 billion for the year ended October 10, 1999. Top producers include Procter & Gamble, Playtex, Personal Products and Kimberly-Clark.

Tampax	14.4%
Always	13.6
Always Ultra	8.6
Playtex Gentle Glide	8.3
Kotex	8.1

Continued on next page.

★ **494** ★ *Continued*

Feminine Hygiene Products (SIC 2676)

Feminine Protection Market - 1999

Shares are shown based on sales of $1.91 billion for the year ended October 10, 1999. Top producers include Procter & Gamble, Playtex, Personal Products and Kimberly-Clark.

Stayfree	7.3%
Kotex Security	4.2
O.B.	3.8
Private label	6.6
Other	25.1

Source: *Chain Drug Review*, January 3, 2000, p. 48, from Information Resources Inc.

★ **495** ★

Feminine Hygiene Products (SIC 2676)

Leading Feminine Hygiene Markets - 1999

Sales are shown in millions of dollars in selected markets. Figures are for the year ended September 4, 1999.

Los Angeles	$ 7.1
New York City	6.3
Chicago	4.9
Philadelphia	3.6
Boston	2.2

Source: *Grocery Headquarters*, January 2000, p. 45, from A.C. Nielsen.

★ **496** ★

Feminine Hygiene Products (SIC 2676)

Top Tampon Brands - 1998

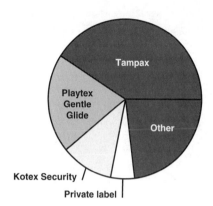

Tampax	40.5%
Playtex Gentle Glide	20.3
Kotex Security	11.3
Private label	5.3
Other	22.6

Source: *Chain Drug Review*, February 1, 1999, p. 53.

★ **497** ★

Sanitary Paper Products (SIC 2676)

Adult Incontinence Market - 1999

Shares are shown based on sales of $581.1 million for the year ended October 10, 1999.

Depend (Kimberly-Clark)	31.6%
Depend Poise (Kimberly-Clark)	18.7
Serenity (Personal Products)	9.9
Depend Overnight (Kimberly-Clark)	2.7
Attends (Procter & Gamble)	1.9
Compose (Intellitecs)	1.4
Other	33.8

Source: *Chain Drug Review*, January 3, 2000, p. 35, from Information Resources Inc.

★ 498 ★

Sanitary Paper Products (SIC 2676)

Disposable Paper Products Market in Canada

The market is shown in percent.

Personal 47.2%
Tissue 40.2
Household 12.6

Source: "Disposable Paper Products Market." Retrieved April 20, 2000 from the World Wide Web: http://library. northernlight.com, from Euromonitor.

★ 499 ★

Sanitary Paper Products (SIC 2676)

Disposable Paper Products Market in United States

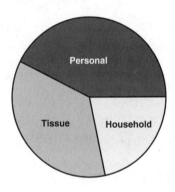

The market is shown in percent.

Personal 42.5%
Tissue 35.8
Household 21.7

Source: "Disposable Paper Products Market." Retrieved April 20, 2000 from the World Wide Web: http://library. northernlight.com, from Euromonitor.

★ 500 ★

Sanitary Paper Products (SIC 2676)

Incontinence Product Leaders - 1999

Shares are shown based on sales for the year ended January 2, 2000. Other is nearly all private label.

Kimberly Clark 54.1%
Johnson & Johnson 9.6
Procter & Gamble 1.7
Medco 1.5
Intellitecs 1.1
Sun Mark 0.4
Other 31.6

Source: *Supermarket Business*, March 15, 2000, p. 63, from Information Resources Inc.

★ 501 ★

Sanitary Paper Products (SIC 2676)

Incontinence Product Market Shares - 1999

Shares are shown based on sales for the year ended January 2, 2000.

	Units (mil.)	Share
Depend	14.4	23.68%
Depend Poise	13.9	22.86
Serenity	7.4	12.17
Depend Overnight	1.1	1.81
Compose	0.8	1.32
Attends	0.6	0.99
Other	22.6	37.17

Source: *Supermarket Business*, March 15, 2000, p. 63, from Information Resources Inc.

★ 502 ★

Sanitary Paper Products (SIC 2676)

Leading Diaper Markets - 1999

Sales are shown in millions of dollars in selected markets. Figures are for the year ended September 4, 1999.

Los Angeles	$185.5
New York City	137.0
Philadelphia	68.7
Boston	59.6
Chicago	52.1

Source: *Grocery Headquarters*, January 2000, p. 45, from A.C. Nielsen.

★ 503 ★

Sanitary Paper Products (SIC 2676)

Mexico's Diaper Market

Mexico consumes roughly 250 million diapers a month.

Kleen Bebe	50%
Other	50

Source: *Mexico Business Monthly*, July 1999, p. 7.

★ 504 ★

Sanitary Paper Products (SIC 2676)

Top Diaper Brands - 1999

The $4.05 billion market is shown in percent for the year ended July 18, 1999.

	($ mil.)	Share
Huggies Ultratrim	$873.6	21.57%
Luvs Ultra Leakguards	484.5	11.96
Pampers Baby Dry	426.5	10.53
Huggies Pull Ups	318.4	7.86

	($ mil.)	Share
Pampers Baby Dry Stretch	$316.0	7.80%
Pampers Premium	237.7	5.87
Huggies Supreme	175.5	4.33
Dryers	133.3	3.29
Huggies Pull Ups Goodnites	107.8	2.66
Other	977.7	24.13

Source: *MMR*, November 1, 1999, p. 29, from Information Resources Inc.

★ 505 ★

Sanitary Paper Products (SIC 2676)

Top Diaper Makers - 1998

Kimberly-Clark	40.7%
Procter & Gamble	37.9
Drypers	3.4
Private label	16.4
Other	1.6

Source: *Investor's Business Daily*, September 22, 1999, p. A10, from Salomon Smith Barney.

★ 506 ★

Sanitary Paper Products (SIC 2676)

Top Diaper Vendors - 1999

Kimberly Clark Corp.	42.7%
Procter & Gamble	37.0
Drypers Corp.	3.5
Hygienic Prods.	0.6
Private label	15.6
Other	0.6

Source: *Discount Merchandiser*, March 2000, p. 62, from Information Resources Inc.

★ 507 ★

Sanitary Paper Products (SIC 2676)

Top Disposable Cup Brands

Brands are ranked by sales of $424 million for the year ended January 21, 1999.

	($ mil.)	Share
Solo	$96.5	22.87%
Dixie	49.5	11.73
Dixie Coordinates	33.2	7.87
Dart	28.1	6.66
Jack Frost	22.1	5.24

Continued on next page.

★ 507 ★ *Continued*
Sanitary Paper Products (SIC 2676)

Top Disposable Cup Brands

Brands are ranked by sales of $424 million for the year ended January 21, 1999.

	($ mil.)	Share
Styro	$ 16.1	3.82%
Solo Ultra	9.5	2.25
Other	167.0	39.57

Source: *MMR*, May 17, 1999, p. 36, from Information Resources Inc.

★ 508 ★
Sanitary Paper Products (SIC 2676)

Top Facial Tissue Brands - 1998

Brands are ranked by total sales of $1.3 billion for the year ended February 21, 1999.

	($ mil.)	Share
Kleenex	$ 641.9	49.38%
Puffs	344.1	26.47
Scotties	63.4	4.88
Softique	19.3	1.48
Soft 'n Gentle	15.1	1.16
Marcal	11.4	0.88
Other	204.8	15.75

Source: *MMR*, May 17, 1999, p. 36, from Information Resources Inc.

★ 509 ★
Sanitary Paper Products (SIC 2676)

Top Moist Towelette Brands - 1999

Shares are shown based on sales of $632.7 million for the year ended October 10, 1999.

Pampers Baby Fresh	16.8%
Huggies Natural Care	16.1
Huggies	11.0
Huggies Sumpreme Care	8.0
Kleenex Cottonelle	6.4
Wet Ones	4.9
Luvs	4.2
Private label	21.0
Other	11.6

Source: *Chain Drug Review*, January 3, 2000, p. 48, from Information Resources Inc.

★ 510 ★
Sanitary Paper Products (SIC 2676)

Top Paper Napkin Brands - 1998

Brands are ranked by sales of $546 million for the year ended January 31, 1999.

	($ mil.)	Share
Mardi Gras	$ 80.7	14.78%
Vanity Fair	48.8	8.94
Scott	39.8	7.29
Northern	36.2	6.63
Hallmark Party Express	26.3	4.82
Sparkle	24.3	4.45
Marcal	18.4	3.37
Other	271.5	49.73

Source: *MMR*, May 17, 2000, p. 66, from Information Resources Inc.

★ 511 ★
Sanitary Paper Products (SIC 2676)

Top Paper Towel Brands - 1998

Brands are ranked by sales of $2.45 billion for the year ended February 21, 1999.

	($ mil.)	Share
Bounty	$ 980.8	40.03%
Brawny	275.8	11.26
Sparkle	188.6	7.70
Viva	157.2	6.42
Scott	155.6	6.35
Coronet	91.4	3.73
Mardi Gras	80.5	3.29
Other	520.1	21.23

Source: *MMR*, May 17, 1999, p. 66, from Information Resources Inc.

★ 512 ★
Sanitary Paper Products (SIC 2676)

Top Toilet Paper Brands - 1999

Sales are shown for the year ended October 10, 1999.

New Charmin	16.4%
Quilted Northern	12.2
Angel Soft	11.4
Kleenex Cottonelle	9.8
Other	50.2

Source: *Milwaukee Journal Sentinel*, December 5, 1999, p. 12D, from Information Resources Inc.

SIC 27 - Printing and Publishing

★ 513 ★
Printing (SIC 2700)

Printing Market by State

Print purchases is shown in billions of dollars.

	($ bil.)	Share
New York	$ 8.0	11%
California	8.0	11
Texas	4.1	6
Florida	3.9	5
Pennsylvania	3.8	5
Illinois	3.7	5
Ohio	3.3	5

Source: *Graphic Arts Monthly*, February 2000, p. 24, from Trendwatch.

★ 514 ★
Publishing (SIC 2700)

Largest Publishers/Printers - 1999

Firms are ranked by revenues in billions of dollars.

R.R. Donnelley & Sons	$ 5.9
Gannett	5.5
McGraw-Hill	3.9
Times Mirror	3.2
Tribune	3.2
Knight-Ridder	3.2
New York Times	3.1
Readers Digest Assn.	2.5
Washington Post	2.2

Source: *Fortune*, April 17, 2000, pp. I-72.

★ 515 ★
Newspapers (SIC 2711)

College Student Newspapers

Data show circulation.

The State News	30,500
Ohio State Lantern	30,000
The Minnesota Daily	25,000
The Daily Iowan	20,500
The Daily Collegian	20,300
The Purdue Exponent	19,000

Source: *Christian Science Monitor*, April 11, 2000, p. 12.

★ 516 ★
Newspapers (SIC 2711)

Largest Daily Newspapers - 1999

Circulation is shown for the six months ended September 30, 1999.

Wall Street Journal	1,752,693
USA Today	1,671,539
New York Times	1,086,293
Los Angeles Times	1,078,186
The Washington Post	763,305
New York Daily News	701,831
Chicago Tribune	626,728
Newsday	574,941
Houston Chronicle	542,414
The Dallas Morning News	490,249
Chicago Sun-Times	468,170

Source: *Chicago Tribune*, November 11, 1999, p. 3, from Audiit Bureau of Circulations.

★ 517 ★

Newspapers (SIC 2711)

Largest Newspaper Companies - 1999

Companies are ranked by revenues in billions of dollars.

Gannett	$ 5.26
Knight Ridder	3.23
Tribune	3.22
New York Times	3.13
Times Mirror	3.03
Washington Post	2.22
Dow Jones	2.00
E.W. Scripps	1.56
A.H. Belo	1.43
Media General	0.80

Source: *New York Times*, March 14, 2000, p. C17, from Bloomberg Financial Markets.

★ 518 ★

Newspapers (SIC 2711)

Largest Newspaper Groups

Gannett Co. Inc.
Knight Ridder
Tribune Co.
Advance Publications
New York Times Co.
Dow Jones & Co. Inc.
MediaNews Group Inc.
Thomson Newspapers

The largest groups in Canada and United States are ranked by circulation, in millions.

Gannett Co. Inc.	6.04
Knight Ridder	3.87
Tribune Co.	3.61
Advance Publications	2.78
New York Times Co.	2.36
Dow Jones & Co. Inc.	2.31
MediaNews Group Inc.	1.72
Thomson Newspapers	1.62

Source: *Editor & Publisher*, March 20, 2000, p. 15, from Audit Bureau of Circulations.

★ 519 ★

Newspapers (SIC 2711)

Largest Newspapers in Canada - 1999

Circulation is for the six months ended September 30, 1999.

Toronto Star	467,638
Globe and Mail	316,740
National Post	268,747
Le Journal de Montreal	258,051
Toronto Sun	239,818
The Vancouver Sun	186,448
La Presse	168,203
The Province	157,325
The Edmonton Journal	138,545

Source: *Globe and Mail*, November 26, 1999, p. B7, from Audit Bureau of Circulations and KPMG.

★ 520 ★

Newspapers (SIC 2711)

Leading Newspaper Markets

Data show the markets with the highest percentage of adult daily newspaper readers.

Wilkes-Barre/Scranton	69.5%
Hartford/New Haven	68.7
Boston	67.3
Cleveland	67.0
West Palm Beach	65.3
New York City	65.3
Providence/New Bedford	65.2

Source: *Editor & Publisher*, October 30, 1999, p. 34, from Newspaper Association of America.

★ 521 ★

Newspapers (SIC 2711)

Saturday Readership in Canada - 1999

Data show share of read yesterday for Spring 2000.

Toronto Star	44%
The Globe	11
National Post	7
Other	32

Source: *Marketing Magazine*, April 3, 2000, p. 4.

★ 522 ★
Newspapers (SIC 2711)

Top Alternative Papers - 1998

Data show circulation of giveaway newspapers, in thousands. Newspaper revenues reached $437 million in 1998.

LA Weekly	220
Creative Loafing	170
San Francisco Bay Guardian	153
Chicago Reader	137
Phoenix New Times	132
Boston Phoenix	118
New York Press	115
New York Press	115

Source: *Detroit Free Press*, September 24, 1999, p. 8E, from American Association of Alternative Newspapers.

★ 523 ★
Newspapers (SIC 2711)

Top Newspapers in New York - 1999

Data show daily circulation.

Wall Street Journal	1,792,452
New York Times	1,134,973
Daily News	729,449
Newsday	573,542
New York Post	433,774
The Star-Ledger	405,546
The Journal News	150,532
The Record	148,392

Source: *Crain's New York Business*, September 27, 1999, p. 26.

★ 524 ★
Newspapers (SIC 2711)

Top Sunday Newspapers - 1999

Circulation is for the six months ended September 30, 1999.

New York Times	1,654,531
Los Angeles Times	1,362,195
Washington Post	1,081,708
Chicago Tribune	1,005,175
Philadelphia Inquirer	820,104
New York Sunday News	790,911
Dallas Morning News	781,959
Detroit News and Free Press	768,913

Houston Chronicle	740,134
Boston Globe	730,348

Source: *Editor & Publisher*, November 13, 1999, p. 29, from Audit Bureau of Circulations.

★ 525 ★
Newspapers (SIC 2711)

Yesterday Readership in Canada - 1999

Data show share of read yesterday for Spring 2000.

Toronto Star	33%
The Globe	14
National Post	8
Other	45

Source: *Marketing Magazine*, April 3, 2000, p. 4.

★ 526 ★
Comic Books (SIC 2721)

Comic Book Market - 1998

Unit shares are for November 1998.

Marvel's	31.0%
DC Comics	28.2
Other	40.8

Source: ''The Final Word.'' Retrieved November 22, 1999 from the World Wide Web: http://www.users.ev1.net/~sherylr/1998_11/LastWord.html, from Diamond Comics Distributors.

★ 527 ★
Magazines (SIC 2721)

Most Read English-Language Magazines in Canada - 1999

Data show readership, in thousands. The numbers are reached by multiplying circulation by the average number of people who read each copy.

Reader's Digest	3,367
TV Times	2,433
Chatelaine	2,055
Canadian Living	2,023
Time	1,899

Source: Retrieved February 1, 2000 from the World Wide Web: http://www.tradeport.org/ts/countries/canada/mrr/mark0090.html, from Print Measurement Bureau.

★ 528 ★

Magazines (SIC 2721)

Most Read French-Language Magazines in Canada - 1999

Data show readership, in thousands. The numbers are reached by multiplying circulation by the average number of people who read each copy.

7 Jours	1,076
TV 7 Jours/TV Hebdo	978
T 1 Plus	674
Primeurs	671
Selection du Reader's Digest	662

Source: Retrieved February 1, 2000 from the World Wide Web: http://www.tradeport.org/ts/countries/canada/mrr/mark0090.html, from Print Measurement Bureau.

★ 529 ★

Magazines (SIC 2721)

Popular Gun Magazines

Data show circulation.

American Rifleman	1,716
Guns & Ammo	596
Shooting Times	205
Rifle & Shotgun	114

Source: *New York Times*, August 23, 1999, p. C9, from Audit Bureau of Circulations.

★ 530 ★

Magazines (SIC 2721)

Top Ad Categories for Magazines - 1999

Magazines are ranked by ad revenues in millions of dollars.

Automotive	$ 1,867.9
Direct response	1,453.8
Medicine & proprietary remedies	964.6
Computers & software	909.9
Media & advertising	868.6

Retail	$ 790.6
Financial	788.2
Public, trans, hotels & resorts	748.6
Misc. merchandise	651.6

Source: *Adweek*, March 6, 2000, p. M47, from Publishers Information Bureau and Competitive Media Reporting.

★ 531 ★

Magazines (SIC 2721)

Top Categories for Magazines - 1998

Regional interest	752
Business & industry	694
Computers & automation	605
Travel	589
Education	519
Health	494
Automotive	451

Source: "Growth of Magazines." Retrieved February 22, 2000 from the World Wide Web: http://www.magazine.org/resources/fact_sheets, from *National Directory of Magazines, 1999*, Oxbridge Communications, and Magazine Publishers of America.

★ 532 ★

Magazines (SIC 2721)

Top Magazine Publishers - 1999

Magazines are ranked by ad revenues in billions of dollars.

Time Inc.	$ 3,513.5
Conde Nast/Advance Pub.	1,305.5
Hearst Magazines	1,242.1
Hachette Filipacchi	1,023.6
Meredith Corp.	839.0
Gruner + Jahr	659.0
Parade Publications	532.9
News America Corp.	491.0
McGraw Hill	443.4
Newsweek Inc.	437.9

Source: *Adweek*, March 6, 2000, p. M47, from Publishers Information Bureau and Competitive Media Reporting.

★ 533 ★
Magazines (SIC 2721)

Top Magazines - 1999

Magazines are ranked by ad revenues in billions of dollars.

People Weekly	$ 713.9
Time	658.3
Sports Illustrated	614.0
Parade	532.8
TV Guide	491.0
Better Homes & Gardens	444.4
Business Week	443.3
Newsweek	437.9
Fortune	325.0
Forbes	320.0

Source: *Adweek*, March 6, 2000, p. M47, from Publishers Information Bureau.

★ 534 ★
Magazines (SIC 2721)

Top Teen Magazines

Data show share of advertising dollars.

Seventeen	39.5%
Teen People	25.0
Teen	18.3
YM	16.9

Source: *WWD*, October 29, 1999, p. 118, from Publishers Information Bureau.

★ 535 ★
Magazines (SIC 2721)

Top Women's Magazines in Canada

Data show circulation. Total circulation of U.S. magazines reached 2.27 million.

Chatelaine	802,714
Canadian Living	561,102
Flare	174,090
Toronto Life Fashion	125,572

Source: *Globe and Mail*, May 28, 1999, p. 1, from Telemedia Inc.

★ 536 ★
Books (SIC 2731)

Adult Book Sales - 1998

Fiction	51%
Cooking/crafts	10
Religion	10
Nonfiction	8
Psychology/recovery	6
Technology/science/education	6
Art/lit/poetry	4
Other	6

Source: *USA TODAY*, December 15, 1999, p. D1, from NPD Group, American Booksellers Association, and Book Industry Study Group.

★ 537 ★
Books (SIC 2731)

Book Industry Sales - 1999

Data are in millions of dollars.

	($mil.)	Share
Elhi (K-12)	$ 3,415.9	8.48%
High education	3,128.8	7.76
Adult hardbound	2,823.9	7.01
Adult paperbound	1,969.1	4.89
Mass market paperback	1,403.2	3.48
Book clubs	1,254.4	3.11
Religious	1,216.9	3.02
Juvenile hardbound	1,060.1	2.63
Other	24,024.2	59.62

Source: "Industry Statistics." Retrieved March 28, 2000 from the World Wide Web: http://www.publishers.org, from American Association of Publishers.

★ 538 ★
Books (SIC 2731)

Book Sales by Age

65+	16%
55-64	15
40-44	14
45-49	13
50-54	12

Continued on next page.

★ 538 ★ *Continued*
Books (SIC 2731)

Book Sales by Age

35-39	10%
30-34	9
25-29	6
Under 25	5

Source: *USA TODAY*, March 22, 2000, p. D1, from Consumer Research Study on Book Purchasing.

★ 539 ★
Books (SIC 2731)

Children's Books Sales

Fiction	46%
Coloring activity	27
Nonfiction	12
Educational	6
Religious	5
Books and tapes	2
Electronic	1
Other	1

Source: *USA TODAY*, January 5, 2000, p. D1, from NPD Group, American Booksellers Association, and Book Industry Study Group.

★ 540 ★
Books (SIC 2731)

Juvenile Book Sales by Region

Mid-Atlantic	19%
East North Central	19
Pacific	14
South Atlantic	14
West South Central	10
West North Central	7
Mountain	6

East South Central	5%
New England	2

Source: *USA TODAY*, April 12, 2000, p. D1, from NPD Group, American Booksellers Association, and Book Industry Study Group.

★ 541 ★
Books (SIC 2731)

Romance Novels by Type - 1998

According to the source, nearly 1 out of every 5 adult books sold is a romance novel. 37.9 million women age 10 and over have read at least one romance for the year ended June 1999. 57% of readers are married. Data show releases by genre.

Contemporary (set after WWI)	52%
Historical (set pre WWI)	32
Inspirational	6
Paranormal	6

Source: *Time*, March 20, 2000, p. 76, from Romance Writers Association.

★ 542 ★
Books (SIC 2731)

Top Book Publishers - 1998

Firms are ranked by revenues in billions of dollars.

Simon & Schuster	$ 2.3
Pearson	2.0
Harcourt Brace	1.8
Random House	1.7
McGraw-Hill	1.6
Thomson	1.5
Scholastic	1.2
Time Warner	1.1

Source: *Wall Street Journal*, January 12, 2000, p. B10, from Subtext.

★ 543 ★
Books (SIC 2731)

Top Children's Book Publishers - 1998

Estimated net sales are shown in millions of dollars. Popular titles included the Harry Potter series, N'Sync, Star Wars and story anthologies.

Random House	$ 197.0
Penguin Putnam	156.0
Golden Books	141.0
HarperCollins	124.0
Simon & Schuster	124.0
Scholastic	106.0
Landoll's	90.0
Disney Juvenile Publishing	85.0
DK Publishing	78.5
Hearst (Morrow/Avon)	46.0

Source: *Publishers Weekly*, September 27, 1999, p. 25.

★ 544 ★
Books (SIC 2731)

Who Controlled Hardcover Book Sales - 1999

Figures shows the company's share of the 1,530 bestseller positions during the year.

Random House Inc.	38.9%
Penguin Putnam Inc.	13.9
Simon & Schuster	13.3
HarperCollins	9.3
Time Warner	9.2
Von Holtzbrinck	4.1
Hyperion	3.9

Source: *Publishers Weekly*, January 10, 2000, p. 25.

★ 545 ★
Books (SIC 2731)

Who Controlled Paperback Book Sales - 1999

Figures shows the company's share of the 1,530 bestseller positions during the year.

Random House Inc.	33.3%
Simon & Schuster	13.3
Time Warner	13.2
HarperCollins	12.8
Penguin Putnam Inc.	12.5
Health Communications	5.0
Other	9.9

Source: *Publishers Weekly*, January 10, 2000, p. 25.

★ 546 ★
Textbooks (SIC 2731)

Math Textbook Market in Tennessee

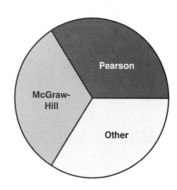

Data show share of math adoptions in the K-12 market.

Pearson	33.6%
McGraw-Hill	32.3
Other	34.1

Source: Retrieved January 18, 2000 from the World Wide Web: http://www.simbanet.com/press/headlines/em_01-03.htm, from Simba Information.

★ 547 ★

Textbooks (SIC 2731)

Math Textbook Market in Texas

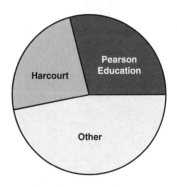

Data show share of math adoptions in the K-8 market.

Pearson Education	29.0%
Harcourt	24.2
Other	46.8

Source: Retrieved January 18, 2000 from the World Wide Web: http://www.simbanet.com/press/headlines/em_01-03.htm, from Simba Information.

★ 548 ★

Publishing (SIC 2741)

Custom Publishing Industry

The market is growing to in excess of $1 billion.

Magazines	66%
Newsletters	11
Brochures	9
Video	5
Audio	1
CD-ROM	1
Web site	1
Other	6

Source: "Major Survey Finds Custom Publishing Topping $1 Billion." Retrieved February 22, 2000 from the World Wide Web: http://www.magazine.org, from Wilkofsky Gruen Associates and Magazine Publishers of America.

★ 549 ★

Printing (SIC 2750)

Canada's Printing Market

The printing industry is the fourth largest manufacturing employer in the country with more than 75,000 workers in 3,500 establishments. Total shipments exceeded $10 billion in 1999.

Ontario	52.8%
Quebec	27.4
British Columbia	7.9
Alberta	5.5
Other	6.4

Source: "Industry Information." Retrieved December 7, 1999 from the World Wide Web: http://www.capitalnet.com/~printing/indinfo.html, from Canadian Printing Industries Association.

★ 550 ★

Printing (SIC 2750)

Free-Standing Insert Market

The $1.9 billion market is shown in percent.

Valassis Communications	50%
Other	50

Source: *Printing Impressions*, April 2000, p. 5.

★ 551 ★

Printing (SIC 2750)

Image Management Market

"Other" refers to regional participants.

Applied Graphics	14%
R.R. Donnelley	8
Big Flower	7
Wace USA	6
Schawk	5
Quad/Graphic	4
Banta Corporation	2
Other	51

Source: *Financial Times*, May 18, 2000, p. 4, from *Graphic Arts Monthly*.

★ 552 ★
Printing (SIC 2750)

Print Management Market

"Other" refers to regional participants.

R.R. Donnelley 18%
Quebecor Printing 13
World Color Press 7
Big Flower 4
Banta Corporation 4
Quad/Graphic 4
Other 50

Source: *Financial Times*, May 18, 2000, p. 4, from *Graphic Arts Monthly.*

★ 553 ★
Printing (SIC 2750)

Printing Method for Packaging - 2000

Flexographer's share of the market has been increasing steadily since 1985.

Flexo 41%
Gravure 32
Offset 27

Source: *American Ink Maker*, July 1999, p. 21, from DuPont.

★ 554 ★
Printing (SIC 2750)

Printing Process Market Shares

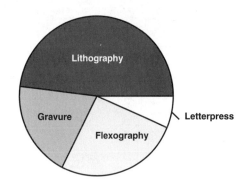

	1998	2012
Lithography	45%	37%
Gravure	18	15
Flexography	18	20
Letterpress	6	5

Source: *American Printer*, October 1999, p. 71, from PrintCom Consulting.

★ 555 ★
Printing (SIC 2750)

Top In-Plant Printers

Companies are ranked by sales in millions of dollars.

U.S. Government Printing Office . . . . $ 195.9
California Office of State Publishing 58.1
Defense Automated Printing Service 50.0
Boeing 19.1
USAA 18.1
Pitney Bowes 16.0
Cigna 16.0
University of Washington 15.8
Spartan Stores 15.1
Allstate Print Communications Center . . . 15.0

Source: "Top 50." Retrieved January 18, 2000 from the World Wide Web http://www.napco.com/ipg/top50sales.html.

★ 556 ★

Printing (SIC 2750)

Top Printing Markets - 2000

The table shows the printing potential of leading markets.

Non-newspaper publishing	$ 14.8
Telecom equip/services	14.7
Computer software	9.0
Banking/insurance	7.7
Automotive	7.1
Fashion	7.1
Real estate	6.7
Discount retailing	6.4
Medical products/pharmaceuticals	6.3
Beverages	6.3

Source: *American Printer*, December 1999, p. 39, from PB/BA International inc.

★ 557 ★

Greeting Cards (SIC 2771)

Greeting Card Market

American Greetings' share is based on a planned merger with Gibson Greetings.

Hallmark Cards	47%
American Greetings	36
Other	17

Source: *Wall Street Journal*, November 3, 1999, p. A6.

★ 558 ★

Greeting Cards (SIC 2771)

Leading Electronic Valentine Card Sites

Figures are based on a survey.

Bluemountain.com	75%
Egreetings.com	17
Americangreetings.com	16
Hallmarkconnections.com	13

Source: Retrieved February 1, 2000 from the World Wide Web: http://www.npd.com/corp/press, from NPD Group Inc.

SIC 28 - Chemicals and Allied Products

★ 559 ★
Chemicals (SIC 2800)

Additives Consumption by Industry

Data are in millions of pounds.

	(mil.)	Share
Coatings	438	41.28%
Adhesives	308	29.03
Paper coatings	166	15.65
Sealants	84	7.92
Inks	65	6.13

Source: *Industrial Paint & Powder*, October 1999, p. 8, from Kusumgar, Herfli & Growney Inc.

★ 560 ★
Chemicals (SIC 2800)

Cosmetic/Toiletry Chemical Consumption - 1999

Surfactants, specialty	20%
Silicones and polyquarterniums	20
Antimicrobials	15
UV absorbers	10
Rheology control agents	10
Emollients	10
Fixative polymers	8
Actives	7

Source: *Chemical Week*, December 8, 1999, p. 39, from Kline & Co.

★ 561 ★
Chemicals (SIC 2800)

Electronic Chemicals Market - 1998

The $3.3 billion market is shown in percent.

Gases	23%
Polymers	22
Photoresists and adjuncts	20
Semiconducting materials	12
Other	23

Source: *Chemical Week*, October 13, 1999, p. 48, from Freedonia Group.

★ 562 ★
Chemicals (SIC 2800)

Plating Chemicals Market

The market is expected to reach $1.2 billion in 2003.

Nickel	32%
Zinc	30
Copper	24
Other	14

Source: *Chemical Week*, March 8, 2000, p. 45, from Freedonia Group.

★ 563 ★
Chemicals (SIC 2800)

Top Chemical Firms - 1998

Firms are ranked by revenues in billions of dollars.

DuPont	$ 39.0
Dow	18.4
Monsanto	8.6
PPG Industries	7.5

Source: *Detroit Free Press*, August 5, 1999, p. A1, from Associated Press and *Fortune*.

★ 564 ★

Alkalies and Chlorine (SIC 2812)

Best-Selling APIs - 1999

Sales of active pharmaceutical ingredients (APIs) are shown in millions of dollars. Data are for the year ended July 1999.

Omeprazole	$ 1,988
Erythropoietin alfa	1,595
Fluoxetine	1,309
Loratadine	1,296
Atorvastatin	1,285
Lansoprazole	1,109

Source: *CMR Focus*, October 25, 1999, p. 3, from IMS Health.

★ 565 ★

Alkalies and Chlorine (SIC 2812)

Sodium Bicarbonate Demand - 1998

Data are for U.S. and Canada.

Food	32%
Agricultural feed	29
Pharma, health & beauty	9
Cleaning products	9
Chemicals	9
Other	12

Source: *Chemical Week*, June 9, 1999, p. 39, from Church & Dwight.

★ 566 ★

Alkalies and Chlorine (SIC 2812)

U.S. Chlorine Demand - 2004

Data are estimated in thousands of tons.

	(000)	Share
EDC/VCM	6,500	44.22%
Inorganic chemicals	2,500	17.01
Water treatment	650	4.42
Pulp bleaching	300	2.04
Other organics	3,500	23.81
Other	1,250	8.50

Source: *CMR Focus*, December 20, 1999, p. 8, from Consulting Resources Corp.

★ 567 ★

Inorganic Chemicals (SIC 2819)

Active Carbon Demand

Activated carbon is used as an absorbent in cleaning up liquids and gases. Sales are shown in millions of pounds. Total demand is expected to rach $573 million by 2007.

	1997	2007	Share
Granular	180	320	56.14%
Powdered	159	250	43.86

Source: *Chemical Engineering*, December 1999, p. 33, from Freedonia Group.

★ 568 ★

Inorganic Chemicals (SIC 2819)

Hydrogen Peroxide Market

Demand is shown in North America.

Pulp and paper	55%
Environmental	15
Chemicals	13
Textiles	9
Other	8

Source: *Chemical Week*, August 18, 1999, p. 37, from Consulting Resources.

★ 569 ★

Inorganic Chemicals (SIC 2819)

Sodium Chlorate Market - 1999

Shares are shown based on capacity. Data are for North America.

Eka	30%
Sterling	17
CXY	15
Finchem	7
Huron Tech	6
Elf Atochem	5
Kerr-McGee	4
Others	16

Source: *Chemical Week*, September 15, 1999, p. 37, from CXY Chemicals.

★ 570 ★

Inorganic Chemicals (SIC 2819)

Top Bromine Makers

Companies are ranked by capacity in millions of pounds.

Great Lakes	365
Albemarle	300
Ambar	30
Dow Chemical	20

Source: *CMR*, August 23, 1999, p. 37.

★ 571 ★

Plastics (SIC 2821)

ABS Resin Market

ABS stands for acrylonitrile butadiene styrene.

Transportation	26%
Appliances	25
Piping	13
Electronics	11
Other	25

Source: *CMR*, November 1, 1999, p. 41.

★ 572 ★

Plastics (SIC 2821)

Acrylic Resin Demand - 2003

Total demand is expected to reach 3.35 billion pounds.

Paints & coatings	33%
Construction	14
Plastics	11
Textiles and fibers	10
Adhesives	8
Industrial & commercial	8
Other	16

Source: *Plastics News*, January 3, 2000, p. 3, from Freedonia Group Inc.

★ 573 ★

Plastics (SIC 2821)

Largest PVC Compounders

Shares are for North America in January 2000. PVC stands for polyvinyl chloride.

Geon Co.	39%
Georgia Gulf Corp.	21
K-Bin Inc./Shintech Inc.	9
Teknor Apex Co.	8
Laporte AlphaGary	5
Other	18

Source: *Plastics News*, January 17, 2000, p. 3, from Geon Co.

★ 574 ★

Plastics (SIC 2821)

Largest PVC Producers - 1999

Data show the largest North American producers of polyvinyl chloride. Shares are based on capacity.

OxyVinyl	27%
Shintech	19
Formosa Plastics	16
Georgia Gulf	15
Borden	8
Westlake	5
CertainTeed	3
Other	7

Source: *C&EN*, January 31, 2000, p. 11, from Chemical Market Associates Inc.

★ 575 ★

Plastics (SIC 2821)

Largest Tie-layer Resin Suppliers - 1998

Shares are shown for North America.

DuPont	41%
Equistar Chemicals LP	23
Rohm and Haas Co.	21
Mitsui Petrochemical Co.	15
Other	7

Source: *Plastics News*, July 12, 1999, p. 3, from Chemical Market Resources Inc.

★ 576 ★
Plastics (SIC 2821)

PET Demand by Market - 2003

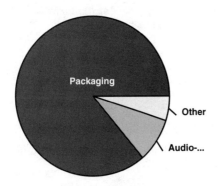

Total demand for PET (polyethylene terephthalate) is expected to reacch $6.5 billion.

Packaging	86%
Audio-visual media	9
Other	5

Source: *Plastics News*, December 20, 1999, p. 3, from Freedonia Group Inc.

★ 577 ★
Plastics (SIC 2821)

Top Compounders - 1998

Shares are estimated based on sales.

Geon Co.	10%
GE Plastics	7
M.A. Hanna Co.	5
DuPont Co.	4
Other	74

Source: *Plastics News*, July 19, 1999, p. 10, from Frost & Sullivan.

★ 578 ★
Plastics (SIC 2821)

Top Custom Rotomolders

Sales are shown in millions of dollars.

Centro Inc.	$ 54.0
Solar Plastics Inc.	29.0
Bona Plastics Inc.	27.9
Dutchland Plastics Corp.	17.5
Rotonics Manufacturing Inc.	16.5

Source: *Plastics News*, August 9, 1999, p. 14.

★ 579 ★
Plastics (SIC 2821)

Top HDPE Makers - 2000

Shares are shown based on North American capacity. HDPE stands for high-density polyethylene.

Equistar Chemicals LP	21.1%
Exxon Mobil Corp.	18.6
Dow Chemical Co./Union Carbide Corp. . . .	14.6
Phillips Petroleum Co.	11.8
Other	33.9

Source: *Plastics news*, September 6, 1999, p. 20, from CMAI and industry estimates.

★ 580 ★
Plastics (SIC 2821)

Top LDPE Makers - 2000

Shares are shown based on North American capacity. LDPE stands for low-density polyethylene.

Dow Chemical Co./Union Carbide Corp. . . .	25.6%
Equistar Chemicals LP	17.8
Exxon Mobil Corp.	11.9
Chevron Corp.	9.7
Other	35.0

Source: *Plastics News*, September 6, 1999, p. 21, from CMAI and industry estimates.

★ 581 ★
Plastics (SIC 2821)

Top LLDPE Makers - 2000

Shares are shown based on North American capacity. LLDPE stands for linear low-density polyethylene.

Dow Chemical Co./Union Carbide Corp. . . .	39.4%
Exxon Mobil Corp.	20.6
Nova Chemicals Corp.	14.9
Equistar Chemicals LP	7.8
Other	17.3

Source: *Plastics News*, September 6, 1999, p. 21, from CMAI and industry estimates.

★ 582 ★
Plastics (SIC 2821)

Top PET Makers - 2000

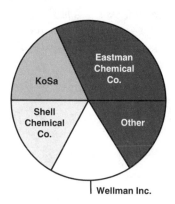

Shares are shown based on North American capacity. PET stands for polyethylene terephthalate.

Eastman Chemical Co.. . . . . 31.7%
KoSa 17.6
Shell Chemical Co. 17.4
Wellman Inc. 17.0
Other 16.3

Source: *Plastics News*, September 6, 1999, p. 24, from DeWitt & Co. and industry estimates.

★ 583 ★
Plastics (SIC 2821)

Top Polypropylene Makers - 2000

Shares are shown based on North American capacity.

Montell Polyolefins 17.8%
Fina Oil and Chemical Co. 13.8
BP Amoco/Arco 13.8
Exxon Mobil Corp. 11.4
Epsilon Products Co. 7.7
Aristech Corp. 7.1
Other 28.4

Source: *Plastics News*, September 6, 1999, p. 22, from CMAI and industry estimates.

★ 584 ★
Plastics (SIC 2821)

Top PVC Makers - 2000

Shares are shown based on North American capacity. PVC stands for polyvinyl chloride.

Oxy Vinyls LP 29.4%
Shintech Inc. 16.8
Formosa Plastics Corp. 16.4
Georgia Gulf Corp. 11.7
Other 25.7

Source: *Plastics News*, September 6, 1999, p. 23, from DeWitt & Co. and industry estimates.

★ 585 ★
Plastics (SIC 2821)

Top Rotational Molders in North America

Sales are shown in millions of dollars.

Little Tikes Co. . . . . $ 217.0
Step2 Co. 100.0
Centro Inc. 54.0
Hedstrom Corp. 53.7
Toter Inc. 51.5
Rotonics Manufacturing Inc. 47.0

Source: *Plastics News*, August 9, 1999, p. 1.

★ 586 ★
Rubber (SIC 2822)

EP Rubber Producers

Producers are ranked by capacity in thousands of metric tons per year. EP stands for ethlene-propylene.

DuPont Dow Elastomers 100
Uniroyal 95
Union Carbide 90
Exxon 85
DSM Copolymer 80
Bayer 52

Source: *CMR*, March 20, 2000, p. 4.

★ 587 ★

Rubber (SIC 2822)

Nitrile Rubber Market by End Use

Hose, belting and cable	28%
O-rings and seals	20
Molded/extruded products	15
Latex	15
Adheisives and sealants	10
Sponges	5
Other	7

Source: *CMR*, March 27, 2000, p. 45.

★ 588 ★

Rubber (SIC 2822)

Top Non-Tire Rubber Product Makers in North America

Sales are shown in millions of dollars.

Tomkins	$ 1,250.0
Goodyear	1,200.0
Mark IV Industries	975.0
Federal-Mogul	788.0
Dana Corp.	767.7
Freudenberg-NOK	720.0
Bridgestone/Firestone	600.0

Source: *Rubber & Plastics News*, July 12, 1999, p. 12.

★ 589 ★

Rubber (SIC 2822)

Top Rubber Makers in North America - 1998

Sales are shown in millions of dollars.

Goodyear	$ 7,435
Bridgestone/Firestone	5,300
Michelin North America	4,500
Cooper Tire & Rubber	1,702
Continental General Tire	1,400
Tomkins	1,250
Mark IV Industries	975
Dunlop Tire	800

Source: *Rubber & Plastics News*, July 12, 1999, p. 12.

★ 590 ★

Fibers (SIC 2823)

Nylon Filament Shipments - 1999

Data are estimated in millions of pounds.

	(mil.)	Share
Carpet face yarns	1,342	70.19%
Mechanical rubber goods	131	6.85
Broad and narrow wovens	120	6.28
Circular knits	120	6.28
Warp knit	107	5.60
Other	92	4.81

Source: *ATI*, January 2000, p. 48, from Fiber Economics Bureau.

★ 591 ★

Supplements (SIC 2833)

Largest Botanical/Dietary Supplement Makers - 1998

Companies are ranked by revenues in millions of dollars.

Nu Skin Enterprises	$ 921.6
Herbalife Intl.	899.7
Perrigo	877.6
NBTY Inc.	610.1
Rexall Sundown	590.2
Weider Nutrition Intl.	335.5
Twinlab Corp.	321.0
Nature's Sunshine	287.4
Chattem Inc.	272.8
Mannatech Inc.	168.9

Source: *CMR Focus*, November 8, 1999, p. 4, from Natural Business Communication LLC.

★ 592 ★
Supplements (SIC 2833)

Supplement Sales by Segment

Sales are shown in millions of dollars. In 1990, a total of 357 new vitamin, mineral and supplement products were introduced. In the first 10 months of 1998, 861 new products were introduced.

	1998	2003	Share
Vitamins	$ 4,160	$ 5,945	35.88%
Supplements	3,865	9,520	57.45
Minerals	855	1,105	6.67

Source: "Vitamins, Supplement & Minerals." Retrieved January 26, 2000 from the World Wide Web: http://www.exposemagazine.com.

★ 593 ★
Vitamins (SIC 2833)

Bulk Vitamin Market - 1998

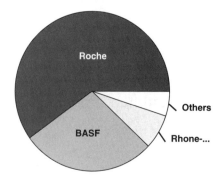

Roche	. . . .	60%
BASF	. . . .	28
Rhone-Poulenc	. . . .	7
Others	. . . .	5

Source: *New York Times*, October 10, 1999, p. 11, from company reports and court documents.

★ 594 ★
Vitamins (SIC 2833)

Leading Vitamin Markets - 1999

Sales are shown in millions of dollars in selected markets. Figures are for the year ended September 4, 1999.

New York City	. . . .	$ 81.1
Los Angeles	. . . .	. 62.2
Chicago	. . . .	. 48.1
Philadelphia	. . . .	. 43.1
Boston	. . . .	. 24.9

Source: *Grocery Headquarters*, January 2000, p. 45, from A.C. Nielsen.

★ 595 ★
Vitamins (SIC 2833)

Top Vitamin/Mineral Brands

Shares are shown based on total sales of $5.7 billion.

Spring Valley	. . . .	8%
Centrum	. . . .	8
Puritan's Pride	. . . .	4
Shaklee	. . . .	3
GNC brand	. . . .	3
One-A-Day	. . . .	3
Nature Made	. . . .	3
Private label	. . . .	17
Other .	. . . .	51

Source: Retrieved January 1, 2000 from the World Wide Web: http://www.fdcreports.com/dsmv3c1.html, from The Hartman Group: *Dietary Supplement Market View*.

★ 596 ★
Vitamins (SIC 2833)

Top Vitamin/Mineral Categories

Shares are shown based on total sales of $5.7 billion.

Multivitamins	. . . .	43%
Vitamin E .	. . . .	. 12
Calcium .	. . . .	. 10
Vitamin C	. . . .	. 8

Continued on next page.

★ 596 ★   *Continued*

Vitamins (SIC 2833)

Top Vitamin/Mineral Categories

Shares are shown based on total sales of $5.7 billion.

Children's viatmins	5%
Vitamin B complex	3
Potassium	3
Other	16

Source: Retrieved January 1, 2000 from the World Wide Web: http://www.fdcreports.com/dsmv3c1.html, from The Hartman Group: *Dietary Supplement Market View.*

★ 597 ★

Vitamins (SIC 2833)

Who Uses Vitamins in Canada

In an average week one in three Canadians use vitamins. More women then men take them, with usage highest in British Columbia.

35-49	28%
50-64	21
65+	18
25-34	18
18-24	9
12-17	6

Source: *Marketing Magazine*, August 9, 1999, p. 19, from Print Measurement Bureau.

★ 598 ★

Analgesics (SIC 2834)

Allergy/Sinus Unit Shares - 1999

Shares are shown based on unit sales for the year ended January 30, 2000.

Vicks Nyquil	16.6%
Tylenol Cold	6.2
Triaminic	5.4
Benadryl	4.8
Dimetapp	4.5
Pediacare	3.7
Vicks Dayquil	3.3
Private label	32.0
Other	23.5

Source: *Supermarket Business*, April 15, 2000, p. 130, from Information Resources Inc.

★ 599 ★

Analgesics (SIC 2834)

Best-Selling Antacids

The $1.07 billion market is shown for the year ended March 28, 1999.

	($ mil.)	Share
Pepcid	$ 223.7	21.0%
Zantac 75	168.5	15.8
Tums-Ex-An	87.4	8.2
Tagamet HB200	74.8	7.0
Tums	62.1	5.8
Rolaids	55.6	5.2

Source: *Chain Drug Review*, August 16, 1999, p. 67, from Information Resources Inc.

★ 600 ★

Analgesics (SIC 2834)

Best-Selling Anti-Itch Products - 1998

Total sales reached $323.1 million in 1998.

Cortizone-10	14.0%
Benadryl	10.4
Cortaid	7.5
Aveeno	7.4
Lanacane	3.9
Lotrimin	3.5
Gold Bond	3.0
Tinactin	2.9
Cruex	2.9
Other	55.5

Source: *Chain Drug Review*, January 4, 1999, p. 59, from Information Resources Inc.

★ 601 ★

Analgesics (SIC 2834)

Cough/Allergy/Sinus Market - 1999

Sales are for the year ended January 2, 2000.

	Share	($ mil.)
Tablets/packets	$ 1,633.1	59.84%
Liquid/powder	644.0	23.60
Throat drops	452.1	16.57

Source: ''Cough/Cold Industry Overview.'' Retrieved April 10, 2000 from the World Wide Web: http://www.exposemagazine.com, from Information Resources Inc.

★ 602 ★

Analgesics (SIC 2834)

Cough/Cold Medicine Leaders - 1998

Shares are shown for the year ended January 16, 1999.

Robitussin	13%
Nyquil	9
Sudafed	8
Alka Seltzer Plus	7
Tylenol	5
Dimetapp	5
Theraflu	4
Vicks Dayquil	3
Vicks 44	3
Triaminic	3
Private label	21
Other	19

Source: ''Cough/Cold Industry Overview.'' Retrieved January 26, 2000 from the World Wide Web: http://www.exposemagazine.com, from Information Resources Inc.

★ 603 ★

Analgesics (SIC 2834)

Cough/Cold Remedy Markets - 1999

Sales are shown in millions of dollars in selected markets. Figures are for the year ended September 4, 1999.

Los Angeles	$ 67.1
New York City	57.4
Chicago	40.6
Philadelphia	32.3
Boston	21.8

Source: *Grocery Headquarters*, January 2000, p. 45, from A.C. Nielsen.

★ 604 ★

Analgesics (SIC 2834)

Cough Medicine Market in Canada

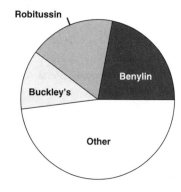

Benylin	22%
Robitussin	18
Buckley's	12
Other	48

Source: *Advertising Age*, August 2, 1999, p. 8.

★ 605 ★
Analgesics (SIC 2834)

Decongestant Eye Drop Market - 1998

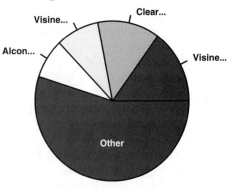

The OTC market for artificial tears posted revenues of $316 million.

Visine Decongestant	15%
Clear Eyes Decongestant	13
Visine Extra Decongestant	9
Alcon Naphcon A	8
Other	55

Source: *Medical & Healthcare Marketplace Guide*, 1999, pp. I-587.

★ 606 ★
Analgesics (SIC 2834)

Diet Pill Market - 1999

Shares are shown based on sales of $149.3 million for the year ended October 10, 1999.

Dexatrim (Chattem)	23.6%
Acutrim (Heritage)	4.8
Ultra Chroma Slim (Richardson Labs)	4.6
Great American Nutrition (Weider)	4.2
Sundown (Rexall Sundown)	3.3
Diet System 6 (Applied Nutrition)	3.3
Other	56.2

Source: *Chain Drug Review*, January 3, 2000, p. 46, from Information Resources Inc.

★ 607 ★
Analgesics (SIC 2834)

Lip Medication Market - 1999

Shares are shown based on sales of $224.9 million for the year ended October 10, 1999.

Whitehall-Robins	32.1%
Blistex	27.5
Carma Labs	8.0
Mentholatum	5.7
Bayer	3.5
Unilever HPC	2.8
Other	20.4

Source: *Chain Drug Review*, January 3, 2000, p. 48, from Information Resources Inc.

★ 608 ★
Analgesics (SIC 2834)

Liquid Cold/Allergy Relief Market - 1999

Shares are shown based on sales of $828.3 million for the year ended October 10, 1999.

Vicks NyQuil	17.8%
Tylenol	7.5
Triaminic	6.1
Dimetapp	5.9
Benadryl	5.8
Pediacare	4.2
Vicks DayQuil	2.8
Dimetapp DM	2.8
Other	47.1

Source: *Chain Drug Review*, January 3, 2000, p. 38, from Information Resources Inc.

★ 609 ★
Analgesics (SIC 2834)

Oral Pain Relief Market - 1999

Shares are shown based on sales of $133.2 million for the year ended October 10, 1999. Top producers include Whitehall-Robins, Del Pharmaceuticals, Zila Pharmaceuticals and Church & Dwight.

Arm & Hammer Dental Care	19.5%
Anbesol	17.8
Orajel	14.4
Baby Orajel	10.5
Orabase B	3.5

Continued on next page.

★ 609 ★ *Continued*
Analgesics (SIC 2834)

Oral Pain Relief Market - 1999

Shares are shown based on sales of $133.2 million for the year ended October 10, 1999. Top producers include Whitehall-Robins, Del Pharmaceuticals, Zila Pharmaceuticals and Church & Dwight.

Zilactin	2.9%
Zilactin B	2.5
Other	28.9

Source: *Chain Drug Review*, January 3, 2000, p. 60, from Information Resources Inc.

★ 610 ★
Analgesics (SIC 2834)

Self-Medication Sales

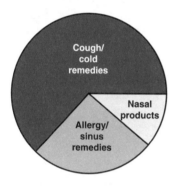

The market reached $2.5 billion in 1999. All the categories experienced healthy growth. Memphis, TN led the country with 24.7% of its population affected by colds and flu.

Cough/cold remedies	63.0%
Allergy/sinus remedies	26.3
Nasal products	10.6

Source: *MMR*, April 17, 2000, p. 43, from A.C. Nielsen.

★ 611 ★
Analgesics (SIC 2834)

Top Allergy/Sinus Remedies - 1999

Shares are for the year ended December 18, 1999.

Tylenol	21.5%
Benadryl	19.2
Nasalcrom	6.4

Sudafed	4.7%
Chlor-Trimeton	4.6
Tavist	2.2
Sinutab	2.0
Motrin	1.1
Private label	31.2
Other	3.0

Source: "Cough/Cold Industry Overview." Retrieved April 10, 2000 from the World Wide Web: http://www.exposemagazine.com, from A.C. Nielsen.

★ 612 ★
Analgesics (SIC 2834)

Top Internal Liquid Analgesic Unit Shares - 1999

Shares are shown based on unit sales for the year ended January 30, 2000.

Tylenol	34.7%
Children's Motrin	30.7
Advil	6.4
Children's Advil	4.4
Pediacare Fever	0.6
Pediacare	0.4
Private label	22.3
Other	0.5

Source: *Supermarket Business*, April 15, 2000, p. 134, from Information Resources Inc.

★ 613 ★
Analgesics (SIC 2834)

Top Laxative Brands - 1999

Shares are shown based on sales of $705 million for the year ended October 10, 1999.

Metamucil	16.3%
Citrucel	7.2
Ex-Lax	5.7
Dulcolax	5.4
Correctol	4.5
Fibercon	4.3
Senokot	3.9
Other	52.7

Source: *Chain Drug Review*, January 3, 2000, p. 48, from Information Resources Inc.

★ 614 ★

Analgesics (SIC 2834)

Top Lice Treatment Brands - 1999

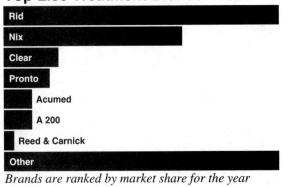

Brands are ranked by market share for the year ended July 19, 1998.

Rid	30.7%
Nix	19.9
Clear	6.0
Pronto	5.1
Acumed	3.1
A 200	2.9
Reed & Carnick	1.3
Other	31.0

Source: *MMR*, September 21, 1998, p. 47, from Information Resources Inc.

★ 615 ★

Analgesics (SIC 2834)

Top Nasal Strip Brands - 1998

Brands are ranked by market share for the year ended July 19, 1998.

Breathe Right	87.7%
Breathe Right Near Clear	11.9
Breath Right Stuffy Nose	0.2
Airmax	0.1
Breathe Fit	0.1

Source: *MMR*, September 21, 1998, p. 1, from Information Resources Inc.

★ 616 ★

Drugs (SIC 2834)

AIDS Drug Market - 1999

The AIDS drug market reached $2 billion for the year ended November 1999. Combivir refers to AZT and 3TC combination pill.

	($ mil.)	Share
Combivir	$ 385.5	19.27%
Viracept	377.7	18.89
Zerit	250.0	12.50
Crixivan	166.8	8.34
Sustiva	128.1	6.41
Other	691.9	34.60

Source: *Wall Street Journal*, February 3, 2000, p. B4, from IMS Health.

★ 617 ★

Drugs (SIC 2834)

Anti-Obesity Drug Market

Xenical	44.4%
Meridia	29.8
Adipex-P	4.5
Ionamin	3.9
Other	17.4

Source: *Advertising Age*, April 3, 2000, p. S4.

★ 618 ★

Drugs (SIC 2834)

Anti-Obesity Market in Canada - 1999

Sales are in thousands of dollars for September 1999.

	($ 000)	Share
Xenical	$ 2,206.0	85.78%
Lonamin	237.4	9.23
Tenuate Dospan	94.5	3.67
Tenuate	15.6	0.61
Sanorex	11.5	0.45
Fastin	6.8	0.26

Source: "IMS Health Reports Xenical is Canada's Leading Anti-Obesity." Retrieved April 20, 2000 from the World Wide Web: http://www.imshealth.com, from IMS Health.

★ 619 ★
Drugs (SIC 2834)
Anti-Ulcer Drug Market - 1999

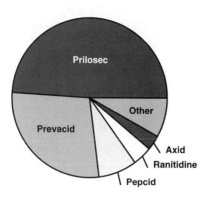

Prilosec is the best selling drug worldwide.

Prilosec 49%
Prevacid 28
Pepcid 8
Ranitidine 4
Axid 3
Other 8

Source: *Wall Street Journal*, May 23, 2000, p. B4, from
IMS Health.

★ 620 ★
Drugs (SIC 2834)
Estrogen Replacement Market

Premarin 70%
Other .30

Source: Fortune, November 22, 1999, p. 56.

★ 621 ★
Drugs (SIC 2834)
Generic Pharmaceutical Market - 1997

Mylan .12.6%
Teva 9.4
Apothecon 8.4
Watson 4.6
Other .65.0

Source: *Medical & Healthcare Marketplace Guide*, 1999,
pp. I-506, from SG Cowen Pharmaceutical Industry Pulse.

★ 622 ★
Drugs (SIC 2834)
Most Advertised Drug Products - 1999

Shares are shown based on ad expenditures.

Calcium blocking agents 6.46%
Antidepressants-other 5.11
All receptor blockers-alone 4.60
Diabetes oral 4.11
Antispasmodics-other 3.67
Cholesterol reducers/Rx 3.44
COX-2 inhibitors 2.96
Antihistimines caps & tabs 2.64
Quinolones, systemic 2.64
Other 64.37

Source: *Medical Marketing & Media*, March 2000, p. 96,
from PERQ/HCI.

★ 623 ★
Drugs (SIC 2834)
Most Advertised Drugs

*Total direct to consumer advertising is shown in
millions of dollars.*

Claritin family . . . . $ 137.3
Propecia 99.7
Viagra 93.4
Prilosec 79.5
Xenical 75.5
Zyrtec 57.0
Lipitor 55.5
Zyban 54.8

Source: "IMS Health Reports U.S. Pharmaceutical Promo-
tional Spending." Retrieved April 24, 2000 from the
World Wide Web: http://www.imshealth.com, from IMS
Health.

★ 624 ★
Drugs (SIC 2834)

Radiopharmaceutical Market Leaders - 1997

DuPont-Merck 42.0%
Nycomed-Amersham 24.0
Mallinckrodt 14.0
Fujisawa 6.2
Theragenics 4.5
Other 9.3

Source: *Medical & Healthcare Marketplace Guide*, 1999, pp. I-608.

★ 625 ★
Drugs (SIC 2834)

Retail Drug Sales in Canada - 1999

Sales are shown in millions of dollars for the year ended $4.7 billion.

	($ mil.)	Share
Cardiovascular	$ 1,147	20.07%
CNS	905	15.83
Alimentary/met.	694	12.14
Respiratory	416	7.28
Anti-infectives	313	5.48
Genito-urinary	256	4.48
Musculo-skeletal	230	4.02
Other	1,755	30.70

Source: "World Drug Purchases." Retrieved April 20, 2000 from the World Wide Web: http://www.imshealth.com, from IMS Health.

★ 626 ★
Drugs (SIC 2834)

Retail Drug Sales in North America - 1999

Sales are shown in millions of dollars for the year ended November 1999.

	($ mil.)	Share
Central nervous system	$ 18,373	21%
Cardiovascular	16,529	19
Alimentary/metabolism	13,400	15
Respiratory	8,847	10
Anti-infectives	8,806	10
Genito-urinary	5,887	7
Musculo-skeletal	4,381	5

Source: "World Drug Purchases." Retrieved April 20, 2000 from the World Wide Web: http://www.imshealth.com, from IMS Health.

★ 627 ★
Drugs (SIC 2834)

Retail Migraine Market - 1999

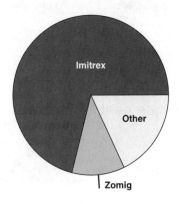

Data are for September 1999.

Imitrex 71%
Zomig 11
Other 18

Source: *Advertising Age*, September 1999, p. 4, from Scott-Levin.

★ 628 ★
Drugs (SIC 2834)

Schizophrenia Drug Market - 1999

Sales are estimated in billions of dollars.

Clozaril	$ 359
Seroquel	273
Dogmatil	129
Haldol	45
Zyprexa	2
Risperdal	1

Source: *Wall Street Journal*, August 25, 1999, p. B1, from Salomon Smith Barney.

★ 629 ★
Drugs (SIC 2834)

U.S. Glitazone Market

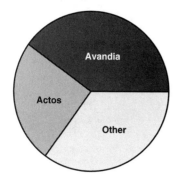

Glitazone is an insulin sensitizer.

Avandia	40%
Actos	25
Other	35

Source: *Med Ad News*, March 2000, p. 40.

★ 630 ★
Drugs (SIC 2834)

U.S. Statin Sales - 1999

Shares are as of November 1999.

Lipitor	42.1%
Zocor	30.2
Pravachol	16.8
Mevacor	5.4
Lescol	4.1

Source: *Wall Street Journal*, January 24, 2000, p. A8, from IMS Health.

★ 631 ★
Detergents (SIC 2841)

Laundry Detergent Market - 1999

The $4.7 billion market is shown in percent for the year ended November 21, 1999.

Tide	38%
Cheer	7
All	7
Wisk	6
Purex	6
Gain	6
Other	30

Source: *C&EN*, January 24, 2000, p. 42, from Information Resources Inc.

★ 632 ★
Detergents (SIC 2841)

Laundry Soap Market - 1999

Shares are shown based on a $4.7 billion market for the year ended November 1999.

Procter & Gamble	57%
Unilever	18
Dial	7
Church & Dwight	5
Colgate-Palmolive	4
USA Detergents	3
Reckitt & Benckiser	1
Huish	1
LaCorona	1
Private label	3

Source: *Chemical Week*, January 26, 2000, p. 28, from Information Resources Inc.

★ 633 ★
Detergents (SIC 2841)

Leading Detergent Markets - 1999

Sales are shown in millions of dollars in selected markets. Figures are for the year ended September 4, 1999.

New York City	$ 280.5
Los Angeles	218.2
Philadelphia	151.1
Chicago	132.3
Boston	116.8

Source: *Grocery Headquarters*, January 2000, p. 45, from A.C. Nielsen.

★ 634 ★

Detergents (SIC 2841)

Liquid Detergent Market - 1999

Shares are shown based on a $2.67 billion market for the year ended November 21, 1999.

	($ mil.)	Share
Tide	$ 872	32.5%
All	287	10.7
Purex	234	8.7
Wisk	232	8.6
Era	149	5.5
Cheer	143	5.3
Xtra	130	4.8
Arm & Hammer	90	3.3
Surf	84	3.1

Source: *Chemical Week*, January 26, 2000, p. 28, from Information Resources Inc.

★ 635 ★

Detergents (SIC 2841)

Liquid Detergent Unit Shares - 1999

Shares are shown based on 543 million units sold for the year ended October 10, 1999.

Ultra Tide	16.9%
Wisk	6.6
Xtra	6.2
All Ultra	6.0
Classic Purex	5.7
Tide Liquid	5.1

Source: *Household and Personal Products Industry*, January 2000, p. 72, from Information Resources Inc.

★ 636 ★

Detergents (SIC 2841)

Powdered Detergent Market - 1999

Shares are shown based on a $2.04 billion market for the year ended October 10, 1999.

	($ mil.)	Share
Tide	$ 749.9	36.6%
Gain	209.6	10.2
Cheer	183.4	9.0
Arm & Hammer	122.7	6.0

	($ mil.)	Share
Surf	$ 105.0	5.1%
Wisk	56.0	2.7
Ultra Surf	42.9	2.1
Private label	52.0	2.7

Source: *Household and Personal Products Industry*, January 2000, p. 72, from Information Resources Inc.

★ 637 ★

Dishwashing Detergents (SIC 2841)

Top Dish Detergent Brands - 1998

Brands are ranked by sales of $790.8 million for the year ended February 21, 1999.

	($ mil.)	Share
Dawn	$ 212.3	27.18%
Palmolive	202.5	25.92
Ajax	85.3	10.92
Joy	77.5	9.92
Ivory	45.8	5.86
Sunlight	42.7	5.47
Dawn Special Care	35.3	4.52
Other	79.7	10.20

Source: *MMR*, May 17, 1999, p. 36, from Information Resources Inc.

★ 638 ★

Dishwashing Detergents (SIC 2841)

Top Dish Detergent Makers - 1999

Shares are shown for the first quarter of the year.

P&G	48.9%
Colgate-Palmolive	38.5
Other	12.6

Source: *Advertising Age*, August 2, 1999, p. 4, from Information Resources Inc.

★ 639 ★

Dishwashing Detergents (SIC 2841)

Top Liquid Dish Detergent Brands in Canada - 1999

Shares are shown based on estimated sales of $67.6 million for the year ended January 2000.

Sunlight	38.4%
Palmolive	28.1
Ivory	9.4
Excel	1.0
Mir	0.4
Dove	0.1
Private label	22.6

Source: ''Report on Market Share.'' Retrieved June 8, 2000 from the World Wide Web: http://www. marketingmag.ca, from A.C. Nielsen MarketTrack.

★ 640 ★

Fabric Softeners (SIC 2841)

Top Fabric Softener Brands - 1999

Brands are ranked by total sales of $1.27 billion for the year ended February 21, 1999.

	($ mil.)	Share
Downy	$ 586.5	46.18%
Snuggle	202.6	15.95
Bounce	190.4	14.99
Cling Free	50.3	3.96
Nice 'n Fluffy	49.3	3.88
Final Touch	37.2	2.93
Suavitel	11.6	0.91
Other	142.1	11.19

Source: *MMR*, May 17, 1999, p. 36, from Information Resources Inc.

★ 641 ★

Soap (SIC 2841)

Leading Soap/Bath Gel Markets - 1999

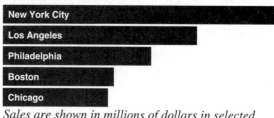

New York City
Los Angeles
Philadelphia
Boston
Chicago

Sales are shown in millions of dollars in selected markets. Figures are for the year ended September 4, 1999.

New York City	$ 94.8
Los Angeles	67.3
Philadelphia	51.0
Boston	37.7
Chicago	35.7

Source: *Grocery Headquarters*, January 2000, p. 45, from A.C. Nielsen.

★ 642 ★

Soap (SIC 2841)

Personal Soap Market - 1999

Shares are shown based on a $2.25 billion market for the year ended November 1999.

Unilever	33%
Procter & Gamble	21
Dial	15
Colgate-Palmolive	13
Kao	2
Others	16

Source: *Chemical Week*, January 26, 2000, p. 28, from Information Resources Inc.

★ 643 ★

Soap (SIC 2841)

Top Bar Soap Brands - 1998

Brands are ranked by sales of $1.39 billion for the year ended February 21, 1999.

	($ mil.)	Share
Dove	$ 272.1	19.58%
Dial	195.5	14.06
Lever 2000	137.6	9.90
Irish Spring	121.7	8.76

Continued on next page.

★ 643 ★ *Continued*
Soap (SIC 2841)

Top Bar Soap Brands - 1998

Brands are ranked by sales of $1.39 billion for the year ended February 21, 1999.

	($ mil.)	Share
Zest	$ 114.4	8.23%
Caress	93.5	6.73
Ivory	92.9	6.68
Other	362.3	26.06

Source: *MMR*, May 17, 1999, p. 66, from Information Resources Inc.

★ 644 ★
Soap (SIC 2841)

Top Bath Product Brands - 1999

Shares are shown based on sales of $188.8 million for the year ended October 10, 1999.

Vaseline Intensive Care	12.9%
Calgon	6.6
Mr. Bubble	6.5
Lander	4.6
Appearance	3.7
Sarah Michaels	3.0
Other	62.7

Source: *Chain Drug Review*, January 17, 2000, p. 15, from Information Resources Inc.

★ 645 ★
Soap (SIC 2841)

Top Liquid Soap Brands - 1999

Shares are shown based on sales of $840.3 million for the year ended October 10, 1999.

Softsoap	14.3%
Oil of Olay	10.0
Dial	9.1
Dove	7.9
Suave	6.4
Herbal Essences	5.8
Caress	5.0
Lever 2000	3.1
Other	38.4

Source: *Chain Drug Review*, January 17, 2000, p. 22, from Information Resources Inc.

★ 646 ★
Soap (SIC 2841)

Top Shower Gel Brands - 1999

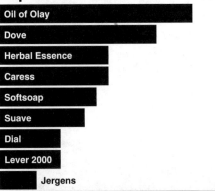

Shares are shown based on total sales of $510.9 million for the year ended November 21, 1999.

	($ mil.)	Share
Oil of Olay	$ 83.8	16.40%
Dove	67.6	13.23
Herbal Essence	47.4	9.28
Caress	47.0	9.20
Softsoap	40.2	7.87
Suave	35.3	6.91
Dial	27.4	5.36
Lever 2000	25.8	5.05
Jergens	16.7	3.27
Other	119.7	23.43

Source: *MMR*, February 7, 2000, p. 17, from Information Resources Inc.

★ 647 ★
Bleach (SIC 2842)

Chlorine Bleach Sales

Shares are shown for the third quarter of the year. Private label is the major competition.

Clorox	59.1%
Other	40.9

Source: *Advertising Age*, November 29, 1999, p. 14, from Information Resources Inc.

★ 648 ★
Cleaning Preparations (SIC 2842)

Bath/Chemical Unit Sales

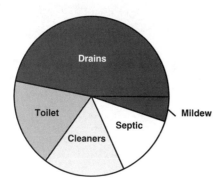

Sales are for the year ended August 1999.

Drains	47%
Toilet	18
Cleaners	17
Septic	13
Mildew	5

Source: *Do-It-Yourself Retailing*, January 2000, p. 81, from Vista Sales and Marketing.

★ 649 ★
Cleaning Preparations (SIC 2842)

Cleaning Product Sales in Canada - 1999

Sales are shown in millions of dollars for the year ended July 1999.

Laundry detergent	$ 292
Dishwashing products	115
Bathroom cleaners	24
Drain cleaners	7

Source: ''Psst Here's the Dirt on Household Cleaners.'' Retrieved February 15, 2000 from the World Wide Web: http://wwww.cdngrocer.com, from A.C. Nielsen.

★ 650 ★
Cleaning Preparations (SIC 2842)

Household Cleaning Industry - 1999

Sales are shown in millions of dollars for the year ended January 30, 2000.

All purpose cleaner/disinfectant	$ 642.6
Nonabrasive tube/tile cleaner	395.5

Toilet bowl cleaner/deodorizer	$ 377.4
Glass cleaner	301.7
Drain cleaner	205.2
Spray disinfectant	191.7
Abrasive tube/tile	138.8
Oven/appliance cleaner	67.2
Lime/rust remover	63.4

Source: *Household and Personal Products Industry*, April 2000, p. 79, from Information Resources Inc.

★ 651 ★
Cleaning Preparations (SIC 2842)

Leading Household Cleaner Markets - 1999

Sales are shown in millions of dollars in selected markets. Figures are for the year ended September 4, 1999.

New York City	$ 143.2
Los Angeles	74.1
Philadelphia	60.1
Boston	49.1
Chicago	46.6

Source: *Grocery Headquarters*, January 2000, p. 45, from A.C. Nielsen.

★ 652 ★
Cleaning Preparations (SIC 2842)

Top Bath Cleaners - 1999

Brands are ranked by total sales of $421.2 million for the year ended February 21, 1999.

	($ mil.)	Share
Tilex	$ 107.9	25.62%
Dow	58.2	13.82
Lysol	51.3	12.18
Scrub Free	31.0	7.36
Comet	18.5	4.39
Lime Away	13.8	3.28
Other	140.5	33.36

Source: *MMR*, May 17, 1999, p. 66, from Information Resources Inc.

★ 653 ★

Cleaning Preparations (SIC 2842)

Top Counter/Window Cleaners - 1998

Brands are ranked by total sales of $506.5 million for the year ended February 21, 1999.

	($ mil.)	Share
Windex	$ 174.7	34.49%
Formula 409	92.1	18.18
Fantastik	33.6	6.63
Lysol	31.4	6.20
Pine Sol	19.8	3.91
Glass Plus	19.2	3.79
Clean Up	18.8	3.71
Other	116.9	23.08

Source: *MMR*, May 17, 1999, p. 66, from Information Resources Inc.

★ 654 ★

Cleaning Preparations (SIC 2842)

Top Floor/Wall Cleaners - 1999

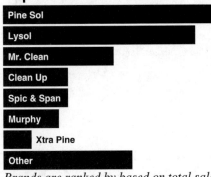

Brands are ranked by based on total sales of $398.1 million for the year ended February 21, 1999.

	($ mil.)	Share
Pine Sol	$ 120.9	30.37%
Lysol	85.4	21.45
Mr. Clean	48.3	12.13
Clean Up	27.7	6.96
Spic & Span	27.1	6.81
Murphy	22.1	5.55
Xtra Pine	11.2	2.81
Other	55.4	13.92

Source: *MMR*, May 17, 1999, p. 66, from Information Resources Inc.

★ 655 ★

Cleaning Preparations (SIC 2842)

Top Furniture Polish Brands - 1998

Shares are shown based on sales of $207 million for the year ended January 31, 1999.

	($ mil.)	Share
Pledge	$ 105.4	50.92%
Old English	31.5	15.22
Endust	23.0	11.11
Scott's Liquid Gold	11.8	5.70
Behold	5.4	2.61
Favor	5.2	2.51
Fellowes	3.4	1.64
Kleen Gard	3.3	1.59
Other	18.0	8.70

Source: *MMR*, May 17, 1999, p. 61, from Information Resources Inc.

★ 656 ★

Cleaning Preparations (SIC 2842)

Top Rug Cleaners

Market shares are shown in percent.

Reckitt & Colman	18%
Procter & Gamble	17
Rug Doctor	11
Church & Dwight	8
S.C. Johnson	8
Other	38

Source: "Household Cleaners." Retrieved March 3, 2000 from the World Wide Web: http://library.northernlight.com, from Find/SVP.

★ 657 ★

Cleaning Preparations (SIC 2842)

Top Rug/Upholstery Cleaners - 1998

Brands are ranked by sales of $543.6 million for the year ended January 31, 1999.

	($ mil.)	Share
Febreze	$ 108.1	19.89%
Resolve	75.6	13.91
Rug Doctor	55.0	10.12
Glade Potpourri	32.6	6.00

Continued on next page.

★ 657 ★ *Continued*
Cleaning Preparations (SIC 2842)

Top Rug/Upholstery Cleaners - 1998

Brands are ranked by sales of $543.6 million for the year ended January 31, 1999.

	($ mil.)	Share
Formula 409	$ 28.4	5.22%
Arm & Hammer	23.9	4.40
Bissell Carpet Care	16.7	3.07
Other	203.3	37.40

Source: *MMR*, May 17, 1999, p. 66, from Information Resources Inc.

★ 658 ★

Cleaning Preparations (SIC 2842)

Top Rug/Upholstery Cleaners - 1999

Sales reached $633.8 million for the year ended July 18, 1999.

	($ mil.)	Share
Febreze	$ 185.5	29.27%
Resolve	78.5	12.39
Rug Doctor	59.4	9.37
Glade Potpourri	33.9	5.35
Formula 409	26.9	4.24
Arm & Hammer	20.8	3.28
Woolite	16.6	2.62
Arm & Hammer Pet Fresh	16.2	2.56
Spot Shot	15.3	2.41
Other	180.7	28.51

Source: *Spray Technology & Marketing*, December 1999, p. 21, from Information Resources Inc.

★ 659 ★

Shoe Polish (SIC 2842)

Top Shoe/Vinyl Polish Brands - 1999

Shares are shown based on sales of $76.6 million for the year ended February 27, 2000.

Kiwi Shoe	51.4%
Kiwi Scuff	8.0
Kiwi Elite	5.2
Kiwi Shoe White	4.9
Camp Dry	3.9

Snow Seal	3.3%
Kiwi Twist N Shine	3.2
Kiwi Suede	3.0
Other	17.1

Source: *Supermarket Business*, May 15, 2000, p. 72, from Information Resources Inc.

★ 660 ★

Waxes (SIC 2842)

Car Wax Sales by Type

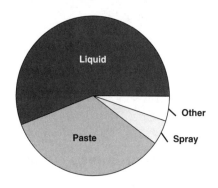

Car wax and polish sales reached $186 million at mass merchants.

Liquid	56.0%
Paste	34.0
Spray	5.2
Other	4.8

Source: *Discount Store News*, February 22, 1999, p. 25, from NPD Group.

★ 661 ★

Waxes (SIC 2842)

Popular Floor Waxes/Cleaners

An estimated 33 million people purchase floor cleaners and waxes, according to a survey. Data show the share of principal shoppers that select each brand. Armstrong's is slightly under a 4% share.

Mop & Glo	12%
Armstrong	4
Future	4
Brite	3
Other	73

Source: ''Consumer Focus: Floor Cleaners/Waxes.'' Retrieved February 29, 2000 from the World Wide Web: http://library.northernlight.com, from Find/SVP.

★ 662 ★

Baby Care (SIC 2844)

Best-Selling Baby Powder Brands - 1999

Shares are shown based on sales of $90.5 million for the year ended October 10, 1999.

Johnson's	34.7%
Johnson's Baby	24.0
Gold Bond	4.4
Mennen Baby Magic	3.7
Diaparene	1.9
Caldesene	1.9
Private label	23.1
Other	6.3

Source: *Chain Drug Review*, January 3, 2000, p. 36, from Information Resources Inc.

★ 663 ★

Baby Care (SIC 2844)

Top Baby Ointment Brands - 1999

Shares are shown based on sales of $69.8 million for the year ended October 10, 1999.

Desitin	42.6%
Balmex	16.6
A and D	10.9
Johnson's Baby	5.1
Johnson's	4.3
Other	20.5

Source: *Chain Drug Review*, January 3, 2000, p. 36, from Information Resources Inc.

★ 664 ★

Cosmetics (SIC 2844)

Color Cosmetics Market - 1998

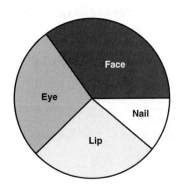

Face	35.1%
Eye	27.1
Lip	26.7
Nail	11.2

Source: Retrieved January 26, 2000 from the World Wide Web: http://www.exposemagazine.com, from Euromonitor Market Decision.

★ 665 ★

Cosmetics (SIC 2844)

Cosmetics Market Shares - 1999

Unit shares are shown for the year ended April 25, 1999.

Cover Girl	18.9%
Maybelline	17.5
Revlon	12.4
L'Oreal	8.4
Wet-n-Wild	7.9
Almay	4.5
Other	30.4

Source: *Household and Personal Products Industry*, August 1999, p. 57, from Information Resources Inc.

★ 666 ★
Cosmetics (SIC 2844)

Ethnic Cosmetics Market

Retail sales are shown in millions of dollars.

	1999	2004	Share
Hair care	$ 1,194	$ 1,318	72.90%
Cosmetics	291	372	20.58
Skin care	108	118	6.53

Source: *Advertising Age*, March 27, 2000, p. 42, from Kalorama Information.

★ 667 ★
Cosmetics (SIC 2844)

Leading Cosmetics Markets - 1999

Sales are shown in millions of dollars in selected markets. Figures are for the year ended September 4, 1999.

Chicago	$ 23.8
New York City	20.9
Los Angeles	16.4
Philadelphia	10.1
Boston	7.3

Source: *Grocery Headquarters*, January 2000, p. 45, from A.C. Nielsen.

★ 668 ★
Cosmetics (SIC 2844)

Leading Prestige Beauty Firms - 1999

Clinique Laboratories	18.3%
Estee Lauder Inc.	17.6
Lancome	12.9
Calvin Klein Cosmetics Company	4.7
Chanel Inc.	4.1

Aramis Inc.	3.5%
Ralph Lauren	3.5
Elizabeth Arden	2.7
Other	32.7

Source: *WWD*, March 2000, p. 18, from NPD Beautytrends.

★ 669 ★
Cosmetics (SIC 2844)

Prestige Color Cosmetics Market - 1999

Shares are shown for the first four months of the year.

Clinique	31.3%
Lancome	20.4
Estee Lauder	19.0
Prescriptives	5.3
Chanel	5.0
Other	19.0

Source: *WWD*, June 18, 1999, p. 8, from NPD BeautyTrends.

★ 670 ★
Cosmetics (SIC 2844)

Prestige Cosmetics Market

Unit shares are shown in percent.

Clinique	37.7%
Lancome	17.8
Estee Lauder	17.7
Prescriptives	5.1
Chanel	2.9
Other	18.8

Source: *Household and Personal Products Industry*, August 1999, p. 66, from NPD BeautyTrends.

★ 671 ★
Cosmetics (SIC 2844)

Top Cosmetics Brands - 1998

Revlon	10.6%
Clinique	10.1
Cover Girl	9.8
Maybelline	8.2
Lancome	7.1
Estee Lauder	6.0

Continued on next page.

★ 671 ★ *Continued*
Cosmetics (SIC 2844)

Top Cosmetics Brands - 1998

Almay	3.3%
Max Factor	3.0
Avon	2.8
Mary Kay	2.6
Other	36.5

Source: USA TODAY, May 27, 1999, p. 2B, from Euromonitor Market Decision.

★ 672 ★
Cosmetics (SIC 2844)

Top Cosmetics Firms - 1999

Sales are shown in millions of dollars.

Cosmair Inc.	$ 937.3
Revlon	830.0
Procter & Gamble	791.3
Dell Labs	127.1
AM Cosmetics	101.6
Bonnie Bell	80.4
Neutrogena	57.1
Estee Lauder	52.6
Bari Cosmetics	30.2
Physician's Formula Cosmetics	18.8

Source: *Investor's Business Daily*, February 7, 2000, p. A10, from company reports, Information Resources Inc., and Salomon Smith Barney.

★ 673 ★
Cosmetics (SIC 2844)

Top Eye Shadow Brands - 1999

Cover Girl
Maybelline
Revlon
L"Oreal
Almay
Jane
Other

Shares are shown for the year ended April 25, 1999.

Cover Girl	28.1%
Maybelline	26.8
Revlon	16.1
L"Oreal	13.5
Almay	4.0
Jane	2.8
Other	8.7

Source: *WWD*, June 18, 1999, p. 14, from Information Resources Inc.

★ 674 ★
Cosmetics (SIC 2844)

Top Lip Color Brands - 1999

Shares are shown for the year ended April 25, 1999.

Revlon	31.1%
L'Oreal	14.8
Maybelline	10.7
Cover Girl	8.8
Bonne Bell	6.9
Almay	6.2
Other	21.5

Source: *WWD*, June 18, 1999, p. 12, from Information Resources Inc.

★ 675 ★

Denture Needs (SIC 2844)

Best-Selling Denture Tablet Cleaners - 1999

Shares are shown based on sales of $148.5 million for the year ended October 10, 1999.

Polident	28.8%
Efferdent	24.0
Efferdent Plus	13.3
Polident Overnight	8.7
Smoker's Polident	4.3
Other	20.9

Source: *Chain Drug Review*, January 3, 2000, p. 44, from Information Resources Inc.

★ 676 ★

Denture Needs (SIC 2844)

Best-Selling Paste Denture Cleaners - 1999

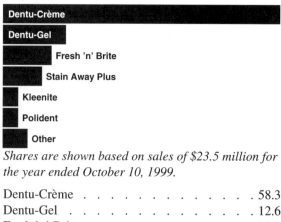

Shares are shown based on sales of $23.5 million for the year ended October 10, 1999.

Dentu-Crème	58.3%
Dentu-Gel	12.6
Fresh 'n' Brite	10.3
Stain Away Plus	7.8
Kleenite	3.3
Polident	2.9
Other	4.8

Source: *Chain Drug Review*, January 3, 2000, p. 44, from Information Resources Inc.

★ 677 ★

Denture Needs (SIC 2844)

Top Denture Adhesive Brands - 1999

Shares are shown based on sales of $224.8 million for the year ended October 10, 1999.

Fixodent	43.6%
Super Poligrip	13.4
Sea-Bond	10.7
Fixodent Free	9.4
Poligrip Free	4.9
Fixodent Fresh	4.1
Effergrip	2.7
Poligrip Ultra Fresh	2.1
Other	9.1

Source: *Chain Drug Review*, January 3, 2000, p. 44, from Information Resources Inc.

★ 678 ★

Deodorants (SIC 2844)

Deodorant Sales by Type

Sales are as of March 13, 1999. The antiperspirant market was valued at $1.6 billion. Less whitening products exhibited the largest growth rate at 165 percent.

Traditional solid	38.8%
Aerosol	14.7
Clear gel	13.3
Less whitening	12.0
Roll on	9.9
Soft solid	5.7
Clear solid	5.0
Others	0.6

Source: "Masking the Odor." Retrieved January 26, 2000 from the World Wide Web: http://www.exposemagazine.com, from A.C. Nielsen.

★ 679 ★

Deodorants (SIC 2844)

Deodorant Unit Shares - 1999

Shares are shown based on unit sales for the year ended January 30, 2000.

Degree	8.9%
Right Guard Sport	8.9
Mennen Speed Stick	8.2
Secret	7.0
Suave	6.3

Continued on next page.

★ 679 ★ *Continued*

Deodorants (SIC 2844)

Deodorant Unit Shares - 1999

Shares are shown based on unit sales for the year ended January 30, 2000.

Secret Sheer Dry	5.4%
Old Spice High Endurance	4.5
Other	50.8

Source: *Supermarket Business*, April 15, 2000, p. 130, from Information Resources Inc.

★ 680 ★

Deodorants (SIC 2844)

Top Antiperspirant Makers - 1998

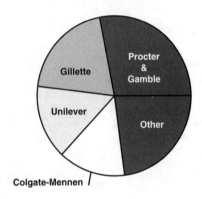

The $1.7 billion market is shown in percent.

Procter & Gamble	27.6%
Gillette	20.1
Unilever	15.4
Colgate-Mennen	14.3
Other	22.6

Source: "An Overview of Underarms." Retrieved February 22, 2000 from the World Wide Web: http://www. exposemagazine.com.

★ 681 ★

Deodorants (SIC 2844)

Top Deodorant Brands - 1999

Shares are as of March 13, 1999.

Secret	14.4%
Mennen	13.5
Right Guard	9.9
Degree	8.2
Sure	6.8

Arrid	6.2%
Old Spice	5.8
Suave	4.3
Soft & Dri	4.0
Other	26.9

Source: "Masking the Odor." Retrieved January 26, 2000 from the World Wide Web: http://www.exposemagazine. com, from A.C. Nielsen.

★ 682 ★

Eye Care (SIC 2844)

Top Eye/Lens Care Brands - 1999

Shares are shown based on sales of $1.11 billion for the year ended October 10, 1999. Top producers include CIBA Vision, Bausch & Lomb and Alcon.

ReNu	6.7%
ReNu Multi Plus	6.2
Opti-Free Express	5.9
Aosept	4.5
Opti-Free	4.2
Visine	3.3
Private label	8.6
Other	61.6

Source: *Chain Drug Review*, January 3, 2000, p. 48, from Information Resources Inc.

★ 683 ★

Foot Care (SIC 2844)

Foot Care Unit Shares - 1999

Shares are shown based on unit sales for the year ended January 30, 2000.

Dr. Scholl	33.6%
Dr. Scholl Air Pillow	8.9
Dr. Scholl Double Air Pillow	3.6
Dr. Scholl One Step	2.5
Band-Aid Corn Relief	2.0
Dr. Scholl Max. Comfort	1.9
Private label	12.1
Other	35.4

Source: *Supermarket Business*, April 15, 2000, p. 134, from Information Resources Inc.

★ 684 ★
Fragrances (SIC 2844)

Top Prestige Fragrances For Men - 1999

Shares are shown for the first four months of the year.

Tommy	6.1%
Eternity	5.9
Polo Sport	5.0
Obsession	4.7
Aqua di Gio Pour Homme	4.6
Contradiction	3.7
Pleasures	3.5
Cool Water	3.5
Other	63.0

Source: *WWD*, June 18, 1999, p. 10, from NPD BeautyTrends.

★ 685 ★
Fragrances (SIC 2844)

Top Prestige Fragrances for Women - 1999

Dollar shares are shown in percent.

Happy	5.3%
Pleasures	4.9
Beautiful	4.7
Romance	3.7
Tommy Girl	3.3
Other	78.1

Source: *Household and Personal Products Industry*, April 2000, p. 60, from NPD BeautyTrends.

★ 686 ★
Fragrances (SIC 2844)

Women's Fragrance/Gift Pack Sales - 1999

Market shares are shown in percent for the year ended January 30, 2000.

Sarah Michaels	18.1%
Calgon	7.7
Healing Garden	6.8
Body Fantasies	3.5
Body Image	2.9
Natures Preserves	2.7

San Francisco Soap	2.7%
Other	55.6

Source: *Chain Drug Review*, March 27, 2000, p. 30, from Information Resources Inc.

★ 687 ★
Hair Care (SIC 2844)

Ethnic Hair Care Market

The market had sales of $257.3 million for the year ended January 2, 2000.

	($ mil.)	Share
Chemicals	$ 81.6	36.27%
Hair dressing	41.1	18.27
Styling	38.9	17.29
Hair coloring	35.8	15.91
Conditioners	21.8	9.69
Shampoo	5.8	2.58

Source: *Household and Personal Products Industry*, April 2000, p. 92, from Information Resources Inc.

★ 688 ★
Hair Care (SIC 2844)

Ethnic Hair Care Producers - 1999

Shares are as of February 28, 1999.

Carson Products/Johnson Products	20%
Soft Sheen Products	12
Luster Products	10
African Pride/Revlon	9
Pro-Line	8
Other	41

Source: "Headed for a Fabulous Future." Retrieved January 26, 2000 from the World Wide Web: http://www.exposemagazine.com, from Information Resources Inc.

★ 689 ★

Hair Care (SIC 2844)

Hair Care Market in Canada - 1999

Market shares are shown in percent.

Pantene	9.7%
Clairol Herbal Essences	8.0
Head & Shoulders	5.5
Salon Selectives	4.5
Alberto European	4.0
Finesse	4.0
Pert	3.6
Down Under Natural	3.2
Other	57.5

Source: *Globe and Mail*, February 25, 2000, p. 1, from Unilever and A.C. Nielsen.

★ 690 ★

Hair Care (SIC 2844)

Hair Care Unit Shares - 1999

Shares are shown based on unit sales for the year ended January 30, 2000.

Pantene Pro V	10.5%
Suave	9.6
Alberto VO5	6.9
Clairol Herbal Essences	6.6
Thermasilk	6.1
Finesse	2.9
Infusium	2.4
Other	55.0

Source: *Supermarket Business*, April 15, 2000, p. 134, from Information Resources Inc.

★ 691 ★

Hair Care (SIC 2844)

Hair Category Sales

Core fashion	40%
Brushes	25
Grooming items	23
High fashion	12

Source: ''Hair Accessories Category Snap Shot.'' Retrieved February 29, 2000 from the World Wide Web: http://www.exposemagazine.com, from Information Resources Inc.

★ 692 ★

Hair Care (SIC 2844)

Hair Coloring Market

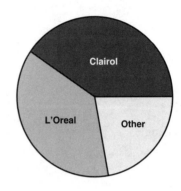

Clairol	40.3%
L'Oreal	37.3
Other	22.4

Source: *Advertising Age*, February 14, 2000, p. 16, from Information Resources Inc.

★ 693 ★

Hair Care (SIC 2844)

Hair Makeup Market - 1998

Dior Mascara Flash for Hair	79%
Other	21

Source: *WWD*, June 18, 1999, p. 12, from NPD BeautyTrends.

★ 694 ★

Hair Care (SIC 2844)

Hair Removal Market - 1999

Shares are shown based on drug store sales for the third quarter of the year.

Sally Hansen	29%
Nair	23
Surgi Cream	15
Hair Off	7
Neet	7
Lee	6

Continued on next page.

★ **694** ★ *Continued*

Hair Care (SIC 2844)

Hair Removal Market - 1999

Shares are shown based on drug store sales for the third quarter of the year.

Bikini Zone	4%
One Touch	4
Better Off	2
Other	3

Source: "Hair Today, Gone Tomorrow." Retrieved February 29, 2000 from the World Wide Web: http://www.exposemagazine.com.

★ **695** ★

Hair Care (SIC 2844)

Leading Hair Care Markets - 1999

Sales are shown in millions of dollars in selected markets. Figures are for the year ended September 4, 1999.

Los Angeles	$ 133.3
New York City	125.7
Philadelphia	61.4
Chicago	56.2
Boston	42.0

Source: *Grocery Headquarters*, January 2000, p. 45, from A.C. Nielsen.

★ **696** ★

Hair Care (SIC 2844)

Top Hair Care Vendors - 1999

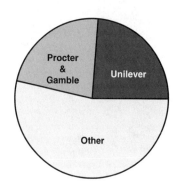

Unilever	23.9%
Procter & Gamble	22.5
Other	53.6

Source: *Brandweek*, March 27, 2000, p. 4, from A.C. Nielsen.

★ **697** ★

Hair Care (SIC 2844)

Top Hair Conditioner Brands - 1999

Shares are shown based on sales of $968.6 million for the year ended October 10, 1999.

Pantene Pro V	14.5%
Herbal Essences	8.6
Thermasilk	6.5
Infusium 23	4.4
Suave	4.2
Finesse	3.8
Alberto VO5	3.7
Frizz Ease	3.6
Other	50.7

Source: *Chain Drug Review*, January 17, 2000, p. 21, from Information Resources Inc.

★ 698 ★
Hair Care (SIC 2844)

Top Hair Relaxer Brands - 1999

Shares are as of January 3, 1999. Relaxers remain the ethnic hair care's biggest seller, with a 26% share, followed by hair dressing with a 15% share.

	($ mil.)	Share
Dark & Lovely	$ 11.8	14.2%
Soft Sheen Optimum	9.5	11.5
Johnson Gentle Treatment	6.5	7.8
African Pride	6.5	7.9
Proline Soft & Beautiful	5.8	7.0
Luster S-Curl	4.5	5.4

Source: "Headed for a Fabulous Future." Retrieved January 26, 2000 from the World Wide Web: http://www.exposemagazine.com, from Information Resources Inc.

★ 699 ★
Hair Care (SIC 2844)

Top Hair Spray/Spritzes - 1998

Shares are shown based on sales of $601.9 million for the year ended December 1998.

	($ mil.)	Share
Rave	$ 74.8	12.43%
Pantene	74.8	12.43
Clairol	45.5	7.56
Aussie	43.7	7.26
Salon Selectives	39.5	6.56
Suave	38.3	6.36
Aquanet	37.2	6.18
White Rain	29.2	4.85
Other	218.9	36.37

Source: *Chain Drug Review*, June 7, 1999, p. 85, from Information Resources Inc.

★ 700 ★
Hair Care (SIC 2844)

Top Hair Styling Brands - 1999

Shares are shown based on sales of $516.6 million for the year ended October 10, 1999.

L.A. Looks	6.8%
Pantene Pro V	5.3
Suave	5.3
Herbal Essences	4.8
Salon Selectives	4.5
Dep	3.9
Thermasilk	3.8
Finesse	2.1
Other	63.5

Source: *Chain Drug Review*, January 17, 2000, p. 21, from Information Resources Inc.

★ 701 ★
Hair Care (SIC 2844)

Top Shampoo Brands - 1999

Shares are shown based on sales for the year ended January 30, 2000.

Pantene Pro V	14.2%
Clairol Herbal Essences	7.9
Pert Plus	5.8
Head & Shoulders	5.2
Suave	5.0
Thermasilk	4.4
Finesse	2.8
Private label	3.1
Other	51.6

Source: *Supermarket Business*, April 15, 2000, p. 136, from Information Resources Inc.

★ 702 ★
Nail Care (SIC 2844)

Nail Care Market

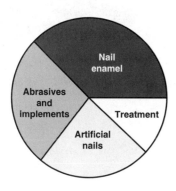

Nail enamel 38.0%
Abrasives and implements 26.9
Artificial nails 23.5
Treatment 11.6

Source: *Household and Personal Products Industry*, February 2000, p. 60, from A.C. Nielsen.

★ 703 ★
Nail Care (SIC 2844)

Top Nail Care Brands - 1999

Shares are shown for the year ended April 25, 1999.

Revlon 21.3%
Sally Hansen 19.4
Maybelline 11.1
L'Oreal 7.6
Cover Girl 5.1
Wet n Wild 4.7
Other 30.8

Source: *WWD*, June 18, 1999, p. 14, from Information Resources Inc.

★ 704 ★
Oral Care (SIC 2844)

Best-Selling Dental Floss - 1999

Shares are shown based on sales of $137.8 million for the year ended October 10, 1999.

Glide 21.7%
Reach 18.5
Reach Easy Slide 6.3
Johnson & Johnson 5.9

Reach Gentle Gum Care 5.8%
Oral-B 5.3
Reach Dentotape 4.4
Other 32.1

Source: *Chain Drug Review*, January 3, 2000, p. 43, from Information Resources Inc.

★ 705 ★
Oral Care (SIC 2844)

Best-Selling Toothpaste Brands - 1999

Total sales reached 704 million units for the year ended November 7, 1999.

	(mil.)	Share
Colgate	201.3	28.59%
Crest	190.3	27.03
Aqua Fresh	80.9	11.49
Mentadent	42.7	6.07
Arm & Hammer	28.2	4.01
Ultra Brite	21.0	2.98
Close Up	18.6	2.64
Other	121.0	17.19

Source: *Supermarket Business*, February 15, 2000, p. 86, from Information Resources Inc.

★ 706 ★
Oral Care (SIC 2844)

Leading Oral Care Markets - 1999

Sales are shown in millions of dollars in selected markets. Figures are for the year ended September 4, 1999.

New York City . . . . $ 134.3
Los Angeles 117.6
Philadelphia 65.0
Boston 54.0
Chicago 52.8

Source: *Grocery Headquarters*, January 2000, p. 45, from A.C. Nielsen.

★ 707 ★
Oral Care (SIC 2844)

Top Mouthwash Brands

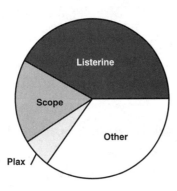

The $653 million market is shown in percent. Sales in the category have dropped 2.2% over the past three years.

Listerine	41.9%
Scope	16.6
Plax	6.2
Other	35.3

Source: *Advertising Age*, June 28, 1999, p. 8, from Information Resources Inc.

★ 708 ★

Oral Care (SIC 2844)

Top Mouthwash Unit Shares - 1999

Shares are shown based on unit sales for the year ended January 30, 2000.

Listerine	34.4%
Scope	18.8
Plax	4.8
Act	2.5
Targon	1.8
Cepacol	1.5
Act for Kids	1.0
Private label	29.0
Other	6.2

Source: *Supermarket Business*, April 15, 2000, p. 136, from Information Resources Inc.

★ 709 ★

Oral Care (SIC 2844)

Top Toothpaste Brands - 1998

Shares are shown based on sales for the year ended March 28, 1999.

Colgate	27.4%
Crest	25.6
Aqua Fresh	10.3
Mentadent	9.1
Arm & Hammer	5.6
Sensodyne	3.4
Rembrandt	3.0
Other	15.6

Source: *Supermarket Business*, September 1999, p. 134, from Information Resources Inc.

★ 710 ★

Oral Care (SIC 2844)

Top Toothpaste Brands in Canada - 1999

Shares are shown based on estimated sales of $124.2 million for the year ended January 2000.

Colgate	39.7%
Crest	26.7
Aquafresh	12.9
Sensodyne	8.4
Arm & Hammer	4.9
Close-Up	2.3
Macleans	0.9
Aim	0.8
Pepsodent	0.4
Other	3.0

Source: "Report on Market Share." Retrieved June 8, 2000 from the World Wide Web: http://www.marketingmag.ca, from *Beverage Digest*.

★ 711 ★

Oral Care (SIC 2844)

Top Toothpaste Makers - 1999

The $1.5 billion market is shown in percent.

Colgate-Palmolive	28%
Procter & Gamble	26
Other	46

Source: *Chicago Tribune*, December 8, 1999, p. 3, from Information Resources Inc.

★ 712 ★
Personal Care Products (SIC 2844)

Aromatherapy Market - 1998

Origins Salt Rub 68.2%
Other 31.8

Source: *WWD*, June 18, 1999, p. 12, from NPD
BeautyTrends.

★ 713 ★
Personal Care Products (SIC 2844)

Leading Grooming Product Markets - 1999

*Sales are shown in millions of dollars in selected
markets. Figures are for the year ended September 4,
1999.*

Los Angeles . . . . $ 13.5
New York City 12.3
Chicago 9.9
Boston 5.8
Philadelphia 5.6

Source: *Grocery Headquarters*, January 2000, p. 45, from
A.C. Nielsen.

★ 714 ★
Shaving Preparations (SIC 2844)

Best-Selling Shaving Cream Brands - 1999

*Shares are shown based on sales of $336.2 million
for the year ended October 10, 1999.*

Edge 28.5%
Skintimate 20.5
Foamy 9.4
Satin Care 9.3
Gillette Series 8.8
Colgate 8.8
Barbasol 5.5
Noxzema 2.2
Aveeno 1.4
Other 5.6

Source: *Chain Drug Review*, January 17, 2000, p. 26, from
Information Resources Inc.

★ 715 ★
Shaving Preparations (SIC 2844)

Leading Shaving Preparation Markets - 1999

*Sales are shown in millions of dollars in selected
markets. Figures are for the year ended September 4,
1999.*

New York City . . . . $ 51.6
Los Angeles 46.8
Philadelphia 27.0
Chicago 23.5
Boston 22.4

Source: *Grocery Headquarters*, January 2000, p. 45, from
A.C. Nielsen.

★ 716 ★
Skin Care (SIC 2844)

Face Moisturizer Unit Shares - 1999

*Shares are shown based on unit sales for the year
ended January 30, 2000.*

Oil of Olay 21.5%
Ponds 12.3
Oil of Olay Complete 9.7
Neutrogena Moisture 4.9
L'Oreal Plenitude Future 4.2
Oil of Olay Provital 4.0
Private label 5.4
Other 38.0

Source: *Supermarket Business*, April 15, 2000, p. 132,
from Information Resources Inc.

★ 717 ★
Skin Care (SIC 2844)

Hand/Body Lotion Unit Shares - 1999

*Shares are shown based on unit sales for the year
ended January 30, 2000.*

Vaseline Intensive Care 14.2%
Suave 10.8
Jergens 9.4
Lubriferm 4.7

Continued on next page.

★ 717 ★ *Continued*
Skin Care (SIC 2844)

Hand/Body Lotion Unit Shares - 1999

Shares are shown based on unit sales for the year ended January 30, 2000.

Nivea	3.7%
Curel	3.6
Private label	8.7
Other	44.9

Source: *Supermarket Business*, April 15, 2000, p. 134, from Information Resources Inc.

★ 718 ★

Skin Care (SIC 2844)

Prestige Skin Care Brands - 1999

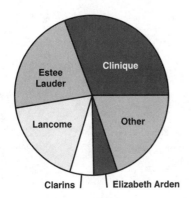

Shares are for the first four months of the year.

Clinique	30.7%
Estee Lauder	21.6
Lancome	18.2
Clarins	4.7
Elizabeth Arden	4.5
Other	20.3

Source: *WWD*, June 18, 1999, p. 8, from NPD BeautyTrends.

★ 719 ★

Skin Care (SIC 2844)

Top Face Care Brands - 1999

Shares are shown based on sales of $444.6 million for the year ended October 10, 1999.

Pond's	12.2%
Biore	7.9
Clean & Clear	6.8

Noxzema	6.3%
Oil of Olay	6.1
Biore Pore	5.3
Perfect Neutrogena	4.3
Neutrogena Deep Clean	3.8
Cetaphil	3.7
Sea Breeze	3.7
Other	39.9

Source: *Chain Drug Review*, January 17, 2000, p. 18, from Information Resources Inc.

★ 720 ★

Skin Care (SIC 2844)

Top Facial Moisturizer Brands - 1999

Shares are shown based on sales of $529.5 million for the year ended October 10, 1999.

Oil of Olay	22.6%
Pond's	8.6
Oil of Olay Complete	6.6
Neutrogena	5.9
Oil of Olay Provital	4.9
L'Oreal Plenitude Future	4.9
Oil of Olay Daily UV	4.6
Other	41.9

Source: *Chain Drug Review*, January 17, 2000, p. 18, from Information Resources Inc.

★ 721 ★

Skin Care (SIC 2844)

Top Hand/Body Lotion Brands - 1999

Shares are shown based on sales of $948.7 million for the year ended October 10, 1999.

Vaseline Intensive	13.4%
Jergens	7.7
Lubriderm	6.1
Suave	5.8
Nivea	5.2
Curel	5.0
Eucerin	4.3
Norwegian Formula	2.5
Other	50.0

Source: *Chain Drug Review*, January 17, 2000, p. 22, from Information Resources Inc.

★ 722 ★
Sun Care (SIC 2844)

Leading Sun Care Producers - 1998

Shering-Plough

Playtex

Johnson & Johnson

Tanning Research Labs

Private label

Others

Shering-Plough	10.9%
Playtex	8.3
Johnson & Johnson	7.0
Tanning Research Labs	4.7
Private label	11.0
Others	58.1

Source: Retrieved January 26, 2000 from the World Wide Web: http://www.exposemagazine.com, from Euromonitor Market Decision.

★ 723 ★
Sun Care (SIC 2844)

Self Tanning Market

	1996	1998	Share
Mass	$ 75	$ 99	77.34%
Premium	22	29	22.66

Source: *Global Cosmetic Industry*, June 1999, p. 100.

★ 724 ★
Sun Care (SIC 2844)

Sun Care Unit Shares - 1999

Shares are shown for the year ended January 2, 2000.

Banana Boat	11.0%
Coppertone	9.5
Neutrogena	6.0
Hawaiian Tropic	4.0
No Ad	4.0
Coppertone Sport	3.3
Bain de Soleil	2.5
Coppertone Water Babies	2.4
Other	57.3

Source: *Household and Personal Products Industry*, March 2000, p. 86, from Information Resources Inc.

★ 725 ★
Sun Care (SIC 2844)

Top Sun Tan Product Brands - 1999

Shares are shown based on sales of $481.5 million for the year ended October 10, 1999.

Coppertone	14.1%
Banana Boat	12.5
Neutrogena	10.1
Hawaiian Tropic	5.6
Coppertone Sport	5.2
Bain de Soleil	4.4
No-Ad	4.3
Coppertone Water Babies	3.8
Other	40.0

Source: *Chain Drug Review*, January 17, 2000, p. 26, from Information Resources Inc.

★ 726 ★
Paints and Coatings (SIC 2851)

Canadian Paints and Coatings Sales

Architectural	40.4%
Automotive	37.1
Industrial	22.6

Source: Retrieved January 1, 2000 from the World Wide Web: http://www.cdnpaint.org/english/facts/index.html.

★ 727 ★
Paints and Coatings (SIC 2851)

Coatings Industry Leaders

Shares are for the North American market.

Sherwin Williams	22%
PPG	12
DuPont	8
Valspar	8
ICI	6
RPM	5
Akzo	4
Benjamin Moore	4
Morton	4
BASF	3
Other	24

Source: *Chemical Market Reporter*, January 10, 2000, p. 18, from The Sandhills Group.

★ 728 ★

Paints and Coatings (SIC 2851)

Paint Market Leaders - 1998

Shares are shown of the $6.5 billion market in percent.

Sherwin-Williams	27%
ICI	17
PPG	10
Valspar	9
Benjamin Moore	8
Kelly Moore	5
Others	24

Source: *Chemical Week*, June 16, 1999, p. 31, from ChemQuest Group and Deutsche Bank Securities.

★ 729 ★

Paints and Coatings (SIC 2851)

Top Vehicle Colors - 1999

White	19.4%
Black	11.5
Green	11.4
Silver	11.2
Light brown	9.2
Medium/dark blue	7.4
Medium red	6.6

Source: *Christian Science Monitor*, March 15, 2000, p. 24, from DuPont Automotive.

★ 730 ★

Organic Chemicals (SIC 2865)

Bleaching Chemicals Market

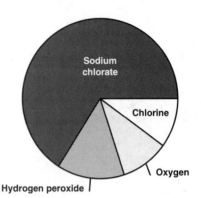

The $650 million North American market is shown in percent.

Sodium chlorate	66%
Hydrogen peroxide	14
Oxygen	10
Chlorine	10

Source: *Chemical Week*, February 2, 2000, p. 41, from Consulting Resources.

★ 731 ★

Organic Chemicals (SIC 2865)

Glycerin Consumption by Market - 1998

Personal care products	22%
Foods & beverages	22
Oral care products	17
Tobacco	12
Polyether polyols	9
Drugs	7
Other	11

Source: *C&EN*, February 14, 2000, p. 28, from *Chemicals Economics Handbook* and SRI International.

★ 732 ★

Organic Chemicals (SIC 2865)

Oral Solid Dose Formulation Market - 1999

The $550 million market is shown in percent.

Specialty binders & fillers 60%
Coatings 30
Colorants 7
Disintegrants & lubricants 3

Source: *C&EN*, November 22, 1999, p. 36, from Kline & Co.

★ 733 ★

Organic Chemicals (SIC 2865)

Organic Pigment & Dye Market

Sales are shown in millions of dollars. Organic pigments have become the largest sector of organic colorants. The use of expensive, high performance pigments is expected to boost the market.

	1998	2003	Share
Textiles	$ 737	$ 697	24.12%
Printing ink	705	924	31.97
Plastics	332	430	14.88
Paints & coatings	297	414	14.33
Other	389	425	14.71

Source: *American Ink Maker*, February 2000, p. 12, from Freedonia Group.

★ 734 ★

Organic Chemicals (SIC 2865)

U.S. Solvents Demand

Sales are in millions of pounds.

	1998	2003	Share
Hydrocarbon solvents . . .	3,336	2,920	23.53%
Alcohol solvents	3,151	3,415	27.52
Ether solvents	2,877	3,120	25.14
Ketone solvents	1,077	1,060	8.54
Ester solvents	697	835	6.73
Chlorinated solvents	596	365	2.94
Other	553	695	5.60

Source: *Industrial Paint & Powder*, October 1999, p. 10, from Freedonia Group.

★ 735 ★

Organic Chemicals (SIC 2869)

Ethylene Market by End Use

Polyethylene (LD/LLD0 . . . . 29%
Polyethylene (HD) 26
Ethylene dichloride 16
Ethylene glycol 13
Ethylebenzene 6

Source: *CMR*, January 24, 2000, p. 41.

★ 736 ★

Organic Chemicals (SIC 2869)

Fluorcarbon Use by Segment

Refrigeration and air conditioning 46%
Fluropolymer precursors 28
Foam blowing agents 20
Solvent cleansing 3

Source: *CMR*, September 11, 1999, p. 45.

★ 737 ★

Organic Chemicals (SIC 2869)

Isopropyl Alcohol Demand - 1999

Solvents 47%
Chemical derivatives 32
Household/personal care 12
Other 9

Source: *Chemical Week*, September 22, 1999, p. 61, from SRI Consulting.

★ 738 ★

Organic Chemicals (SIC 2869)

Melamine Use by Segment

Surface coatings 37%
Laminates 32
Molding compounds 7
Paper coatings 6

Source: *CMR*, July 19, 1999, p. 41.

★ 739 ★

Organic Chemicals (SIC 2869)

Sodium Hydrosulfide Market

Producers are ranked by capcity in thousands of short tons.

Jupiter Chemicals 105
PPG Industries 45
Chemical Products 20
Witco 7
Tessenderlo 4
Zeneca 3

Source: *CMR*, February 14, 2000, p. 49.

★ 740 ★

Organic Chemicals (SIC 2869)

Solvent Demand by Type

Sales are shown in millions of pounds.

	1998	2008	Share
Hydrocarbons	$ 3,336	$ 2,520	19.60%
Alcohols	3,151	3,790	29.48
Ethers	2,877	3,380	26.29
Ketones	1,077	1,045	8.13
Esters	697	980	7.62
Chlorinated	596	260	2.02
Other	553	880	6.85

Source: *Chemical Engineering*, December 1999, p. 57, from Freedonia Group.

★ 741 ★

Organic Chemicals (SIC 2869)

Sulfuric Acid Use by Segment

Fertilizers 70%
Mining 9
Petroleum alkylation 6
Inorganic chemicals/pigments 5
Pulp & paper 3

Source: *CMR*, January 10, 2000, p. 33.

★ 742 ★

Organic Chemicals (SIC 2869)

U.S. Defoamer Demand - 2004

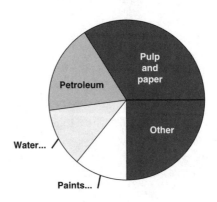

The $655 million market is shown in percent.

Pulp and paper 34%
Petroleum 18
Water treatment 12
Paints and coatings 11
Other 25

Source: *Chemical Week*, March 29, 2000, p. 44, from Freedonia Group.

★ 743 ★

Fertilizers (SIC 2870)

Mexico's Fertilizer Market - 1998

Nitrogen 70%
Phosphate 25
Potassium 5

Source: *Chemical Week*, June 16, 1999, p. 27, from Aniq.

★ 744 ★

Fertilizers (SIC 2874)

Fertilizer Sales by Type - 1998

Unit shares are shown in percent for the year ended March 1999.

Turf fertilizer 49%
A/P generic 17
Fall/winter fertilizer 17
Liq/sol powder 4

Source: *Do-It-Yourself Retailing*, July 1999, p. 74, from Vista Sales and Marketing.

★ 745 ★
Agrichemicals (SIC 2879)

Consumer Lawn and Garden Market

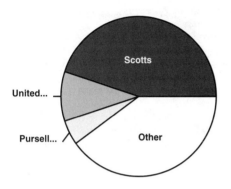

Scotts	45%
United Industries (Spectrum Brands)	10
Pursell Technologies	5
Other	40

Source: *C&EN*, April 10, 2000, p. 23.

★ 746 ★
Agrichemicals (SIC 2879)

Retail Pesticides Sales

Retail sales reached $2.2 billion.

Insecticides	73%
Herbicides	23
Fungicides	4

Source: *C&EN*, April 10, 2000, p. 23, from SRI International.

★ 747 ★
Insecticides (SIC 2879)

Indoor Pest Control Market - 1998

Brands are ranked by sales based on a total market of $183.9 million for the year ended January 31, 1999.

	($ mil.)	Share
Raid	$ 42.3	23.00%
Hot Shot	29.5	16.04
Enoz	22.4	12.18
Raid Flea Killer Plus	17.3	9.41
Black Flag	10.7	5.82
D Con Mouse Pruf 11	10.3	5.60

	($ mil.)	Share
Raid Max	$ 6.3	3.43%
Other	45.1	24.52

Source: *MMR*, May 17, 1999, p. 66, from Information Resources Inc.

★ 748 ★
Insecticides (SIC 2879)

Leading Insecticide/Repellant Markets - 1999

Sales are shown in millions of dollars in selected markets. Figures are for the year ended September 4, 1999.

Los Angeles	$ 17.6
New York City	14.5
Chicago	7.9
Philadelphia	7.3
Boston	4.4

Source: *Grocery Headquarters*, January 2000, p. 45, from A.C. Nielsen.

★ 749 ★
Insecticides (SIC 2879)

Outdoor Pest Control Market - 1998

Brands are ranked by sales based on a total market of $332.4 million for the year ended January 31, 1999.

	($ mil.)	Share
Off!	$ 49.3	14.83%
Deepwoods Off!	22.3	6.71
Raid	18.5	5.57
Eliminator	15.7	4.72
Lamplight Farms	15.2	4.57
Cutter	14.1	4.24
Off Skintastic	12.4	3.73
Other	184.9	55.63

Source: *MMR*, May 17, 1999, p. 66, from Information Resources Inc.

★ 750 ★

Insecticides (SIC 2879)

Rose/Flower Insecticide Market

The entire garden chemicals market is valued at $1.4 billion.

Ortho	75%
Other	25

Source: *National Home Center News*, March 6, 2000, p. 1.

★ 751 ★

Adhesives and Sealants (SIC 2891)

Bonding Industry in North America - 1999

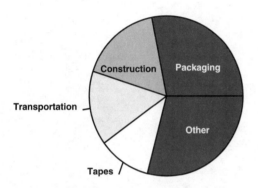

The $9.3 billion industry is shown in percent.

Packaging	28%
Construction	17
Transportation	15
Tapes	11
Other	29

Source: *Chemical Week*, March 22, 2000, p. 31, from ChemQuest.

★ 752 ★

Printing Ink (SIC 2893)

Largest Ink Makers

Sales are shown in millions of dollars.

Sun Chemical	$ 950
Flink Ink	700
INX International	333
The Alper Ink Group	180
The Ink Company	130
SICPA Securink	80

Source: *Graphic Arts Monthly*, March 1999, p. 56.

★ 753 ★

Printing Ink (SIC 2893)

Largest Printing Ink Makers

Firms are ranked by sales in millions of dollars. Data are for North America.

Sun Chemical	$ 2,500
Flint Ink Corp.	1,000
INX Intl. Ink Co.	300
Alper Group	158
The Ink Company	128
Siegwerk Inc.	80
Superior Printing Ink Co. Inc.	75
Color Converting Industries Co.	75
Wickoff Color	70
Toyo Ink	65

Source: *American Ink Maker*, October 1999, p. 16.

★ 754 ★

Printing Ink (SIC 2893)

Printing Ink Sales - 1999

Lithography	44%
Flexography	22
Gravure	17
Screen	8
Inkjet	4
Specialty	3
Letterpress	2

Source: *American Ink Maker*, February 2000, p. 40.

★ 755 ★

Air Fresheners (SIC 2899)

Top Air Freshener Brands - 1999

Brands are ranked by sales of $587.7 million for the year ended January 31, 1999.

	($ mil.)	Share
Glade Plug In	$ 122.4	20.83%
Renuzit Long Last Adjustable	78.7	13.39
Glade Potpourri	52.4	8.92
Glade Plug Ins Candle Scents	31.7	5.39
Glade Spin Fresh	30.2	5.14
Glade Candle Scents	22.4	3.81
Wizard	21.7	3.69
Other	228.2	38.83

Source: *MMR*, May 17, 1999, p. 34, from Information Resources Inc.

★ 756 ★

Antifreeze (SIC 2899)

Top Antifreeze Brands - 1999

Shares are shown based on sales of $144.8 million for the year ended February 27, 2000.

Prestone	38.4%
Zerex	6.9
Peak	6.1
Winter-Eez	3.0
Texaco	2.7
Havoline	2.0
Heet	1.9
Private label	32.8
Other	6.2

Source: *Supermarket Business*, May 15, 2000, p. 72, from Information Resources Inc.

★ 757 ★

Lubricants (SIC 2899)

Top Automotive Treatment Brands - 1999

Shares are shown based on sales of $259.5 million for the year ended February 27, 2000.

STP	17.6%
Prestone	8.7
Slick 50	7.5
Dura Lube	4.1
Gumout	3.2

Quaker State	2.8%
Restore	2.6
Private label	17.0
Other	6.5

Source: *Supermarket Business*, May 15, 2000, p. 72, from Information Resources Inc.

★ 758 ★

Salt (SIC 2899)

U.S. Salt Demand - 1998

Chemicals	47%
Deicing	25
Agriculture	5
Food	5
Industrial	5
Other	13

Source: *Chemical Week*, June 9, 1999, p. 38, from U.S. Geological Survey.

SIC 29 - Petroleum and Coal Products

★ 759 ★

Petroleum (SIC 2911)

Largest Petroleum Refiners - 1999

Firms are ranked by revenues in billions of dollars.

Exxon Mobil . . . . $ 163.8
Texaco 35.6
Chevron 32.6
USX 25.6
Conoco 20.8
Tosco 14.3
Phillips Petroleum 13.8

Source: *Fortune*, April 17, 2000, pp. I-69.

★ 760 ★

Motor Oils (SIC 2992)

Top Motor Oils - 2000

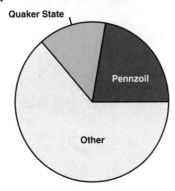

Shares are shown for the first quarter of the year.

Pennzoil 22.4%
Quaker State 14.4
Other 63.2

Source: ''Pennzoil-Quaker State Reports First Quarter.''
Retrieved May 11, 2000 from the World Wide Web: http://
www.prnewswire.com.

SIC 30 - Rubber and Misc. Plastics Products

★ 761 ★

Tires (SIC 3011)

Largest Tire Producers - 1999

Sales are shown in billions of dollars. Data are for North America.

Goodyear	$ 6.66
Bridgestone/Firestone	4.88
Michelin	4.75
Conti General	1.50
Cooper Tire	1.35

Source: *Tire Business*, August 30, 1999, p. 17.

★ 762 ★

Tires (SIC 3011)

Replacement Market for Medium Truck Tires in North America

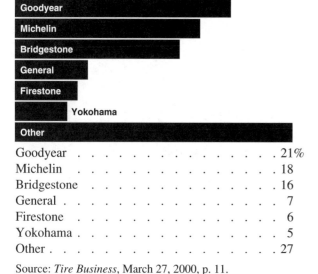

Goodyear	21%
Michelin	18
Bridgestone	16
General	7
Firestone	6
Yokohama	5
Other	27

Source: *Tire Business*, March 27, 2000, p. 11.

★ 763 ★

Tires (SIC 3011)

Tire Market - 1999

Sales are shown in millions of units. OE stands for original equipment.

	(mil.)	Share
Aftermarket auto	191.0	67.09%
OE auto	61.0	21.43
Aftermarket light truck	17.2	6.04
OE light truck	8.5	2.99
OE medium truck	7.0	2.46

Source: *Rubber & Plastics News*, December 6, 1999, p. 3, from Rubber Manufacturers Association Tire Market Analysis Committee.

★ 764 ★

Tires (SIC 3011)

Top Passenger Tire Makers in North America - 1999

The replacement market in the U.S. and Canada is shown in percent.

Goodyear	16%
Michelin	11
Firestone	10
B.F. Goodrich	6
Uniroyal	5
General	5
Cooper	5
Bridgestone	5
Other	37

Source: *Tire Business*, February 28, 2000, p. 12.

★ 765 ★

Tires (SIC 3011)

Top Tire Makers in North America - 1999

The $22.5 billion market in the U.S. and Canada are shown in percent.

Goodyear	28.0%
Bridgestone/Firestone	23.1
Michelin/Uniroyal/Goodrich	22.7
Continental General Tire	6.9
Cooper	6.2
Others	13.1

Source: *Tire Business*, February 28, 2000, p. 12.

★ 766 ★

Tires (SIC 3011)

Top Tire Producing States

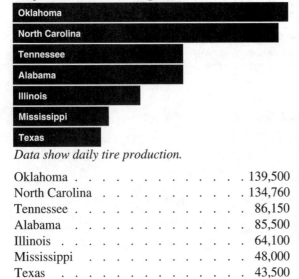

Data show daily tire production.

Oklahoma	139,500
North Carolina	134,760
Tennessee	86,150
Alabama	85,500
Illinois	64,100
Mississippi	48,000
Texas	43,500

Source: *Tire Business*, February 28, 2000, p. 13, from Rubber Manufacturers Association.

★ 767 ★

Athletic Footwear (SIC 3021)

Basketball Shoe Market - 2000

Shares are for the first quarter. Nike's market share ranks first for cleated shoes (56.6%), second for aerobic shoes (22.7%) and casual shoes (12.0), and third among court/fitness shoes (16.3%).

Nike	65.5%
Other	34.5

Source: "Athletic Footwear Market Share Report Announced." Retrieved April 10, 2000 from the World Wide Web: http://www.businesswire.com, from SportsTrend. Info.

★ 768 ★

Athletic Footwear (SIC 3021)

Canada's Sports Shoe Sales - 1998

Data show estimated retail sales in thousands of dollars.

	($ 000)	Share
Athletic shoes/sneakers	$ 901,000	63.32%
Golf	111,000	7.80
Soccer	48,000	3.37
Baseball/softball	32,000	2.25
Court	26,000	1.83
Curling	22,000	1.55
Bowling	18,000	1.26
Other	265,000	18.62

Source: Retrieved January 21, 2000 from the World Wide Web: http://strategis.ic.gc.ca/SSG, from Industry Canada.

★ 769 ★

Athletic Footwear (SIC 3021)

Sports Shoe Market

Shares are estimated for the first quarter of each year.

	1Q 1999	1Q 2000
Nike	48.9%	39.2%
Adidas	16.9	15.1
Reebok	10.9	10.9
New Balance	3.7	9.4
K-Swiss	3.1	3.6
Timberland	2.1	2.9
Asics	1.5	2.1

Continued on next page.

★ 769 ★ *Continued*
Athletic Footwear (SIC 3021)

Sports Shoe Market

Shares are estimated for the first quarter of each year.

	1Q 1999	1Q 2000
Saucony	0.9%	1.4%
Skechers	0.9	1.4

Source: "Athletic Footwear Market Share Report Announced." Retrieved April 10, 2000 from the World Wide Web: http://www.businesswire.com, from SportsTrend. Info.

★ 770 ★
Athletic Footwear (SIC 3021)

Sports Shoe Market - 2000

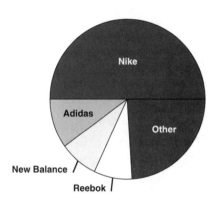

Shares are estimated.

Nike	50%
Adidas	10
New Balance	8
Reebok	8
Other	24

Source: *New York Times*, December 11, 1999, p. B4, from First Security Van Kasper.

★ 771 ★
Athletic Footwear (SIC 3021)

Sports Shoe Sales by Segment - 1999

Retail sales are shown in billions of dollars for the first six months of the year. Data are based on a survey of 120,000 households.

	($ mil.)	Share
Women's	$ 3.13	48.83%
Men's	2.50	39.00
Junior's	0.51	7.96
Not reported	0.18	2.81
Infant's	0.09	1.40

Source: Retrieved January 1, 2000 from the World Wide Web: http://www.sportlink.com/press_room/1999_releases/afa99-004.html, from NPD Group Inc.

★ 772 ★
Athletic Footwear (SIC 3021)

Sports Shoe Sales by Type - 1999

Total sales reached $6.2 billion for the first six months of the year.

Running	$ 1,170
Cross training	927
Basketball	808
Athleisure	792
Walking	630
Tennis	446
Hiking	376
Aerobic	173
Baseball/softball	115

Source: Retrieved January 1, 2000 from the World Wide Web: http://www.sportlink.com/press_room/1999_releases/afa99-004.html, from NPD Group Inc. and Athletic Footwear Association.

★ 773 ★

Athletic Footwear (SIC 3021)

Top Men's Sports Shoe Brands - 1998

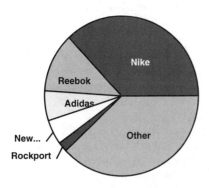

Dollar shares are shown in percent.

Nike 37%
Reebok 12
Adidas 6
New Balance 5
Rockport 2
Other 38

Source: "Athletic Footwear Sales Decline for 1998."
Retrieved December 2, 1999 from the World Wide Web:
http://www.npd.com, from NPD Group Inc.

★ 774 ★

Athletic Footwear (SIC 3021)

Top Sports Shoe Brands for Juniors - 1998

Dollar shares are shown in percent. Juniors refers to ages 4-11.

Nike 39%
Reebok 9
Adidas 6
Fila 3
Converse 3
Other 40

Source: "Athletic Footwear Sales Decline for 1998."
Retrieved December 2, 1999 from the World Wide Web:
http://www.npd.com.

★ 775 ★

Athletic Footwear (SIC 3021)

Top Women's Sports Shoe Brands - 1998

Nike 29%
Reebok 16
Adidas 6
New Balance 5
Easy Spirit 5
Other 39

Source: "Athletic Footwear Sales Decline for 1998."
Retrieved December 2, 1999 from the World Wide Web:
http://www.npd.com, from NPD Group Inc.

★ 776 ★

Abrasives (SIC 3052)

Top Markets for Abrasives in the South- Atlantic

Sales are shown in millions of dollars.

Wood household furniture . . . . $ 32.7
Ship building & repairing 21.7
Millwork 16.3
Upholstered household furniture 16.2
Boat building & repairing 11.6

Source: *Industrial Distribution*, December 1999, p. 119.

★ 777 ★

Abrasives (SIC 3052)

Top Markets for Hoses/Fittings in Northeast Coastal

Sales are shown in millions of dollars.

Aircraft engines & engine parts . . . . . $ 29.5
Ship building & repairing 11.9
Machine tools (metal cutting) 5.7
Machine tools (accessories) 4.6
Industrial machinery 4.1

Source: *Industrial Distribution*, December 1999, p. 119.

★ 778 ★
Belts and Hoses (SIC 3052)

Rubber Belting Sales - 2002

Bar chart labeled: Motor vehicles; Appliances and office equipment; Industrial machinery & equipment; Off-road equipment; Non-automotive transportation equipment; Other

Sales are estimated in millions of dollars.

Motor vehicles	$ 875
Appliances and office equipment	360
Industrial machinery & equipment	185
Off-road equipment	160
Non-automotive transportation equipment	110
Other	90

Source: *Plastics News*, June 14, 1999, p. 13, from Freedonia Group Inc.

★ 779 ★
Belts and Hoses (SIC 3052)

Rubber Hose Sales - 2002

Sales are estimated in millions of dollars.

Motor vehicles	$ 990
Appliances & office equipment	340
Industrial machinery & equipment	305
Off-road equipment	200
Non-automotive transportation equipment	175
Other markets	90

Source: *Rubber & Plastics News*, June 14, 1999, p. 13, from Freedonia Group Inc.

★ 780 ★
Belts and Hoses (SIC 3052)

Top Belting Markets for Northeast Central States

Sales are shown in millions of dollars.

Plumbing, heating & air conditioning	$ 10.6
Engineering services	9.4
Electrical work	7.1
Grocery stores	7.0
Blast furnaces & steel mills	5.3

Source: *Industrial Distribution*, September 1999, p. 73, from Industrial Market Information.

★ 781 ★
Belts and Hoses (SIC 3052)

Top Belting Markets in the South-Atlantic States

Sales are shown in millions of dollars.

Plumbing, heating & air conditioning	$ 13.1
Electrical work	10.7
Grocery stores	9.6
Engineering services	8.8
Nonresidential construction	5.4

Source: *Industrial Distribution*, September 1999, p. 73, from Industrial Market Information Inc.

★ 782 ★
Belts and Hoses (SIC 3052)

Top Markets for Hoses/Fittings for Mid- Atlantic States

Sales are shown in millions of dollars.

Pulp mills	$ 24.4
Plumbing, heating & air conditioning	16.4
Petroleum refining	10.3
Pharmaceutical preparations	10.2
Industrial organic chemicals	6.4

Source: *Industrial Distribution*, January 2000, p. 119.

★ 783 ★
Belts and Hoses (SIC 3052)

Top Markets for Hoses/Fittings in the Southwest Central

Sales are shown in millions of dollars.

Petroleum refining	$ 31.7
Plumbing, heating & air conditioning	13.6
Industrial organic chemicals	12.2
Industrial inorganic chemicals	9.9
Heavy construction	9.3

Source: *Industrial Distribution*, January 2000, p. 119.

★ 784 ★
Gaskets and Seals (SIC 3053)

Gaskets and Seals Demand

Data are in millions of dollars.

	1998 ($ mil.)	2003 ($ mil.)	Share
Seals	$ 3,020	$ 3,980	54.78%
Gaskets	2,525	3,285	45.22

Source: *Design News*, April 17, 2000, p. 44, from Freedonia Group.

★ 785 ★
Plastic Pipe (SIC 3084)

Plastic Pipe Demand

Demand is shown by market.

Potable water	28%
Sewer	26
Waste and vent	15
Conduit	11
Gas, oil	6
Irrigation	6
Other	8

Source: *Investor's Business Daily*, May 19, 2000, p. A9, from Freedonia Group and company reports.

★ 786 ★
Plastic Pipe (SIC 3084)

Plastic Pipe Market

The market share is estimated.

Tyco	60%
Other	40

Source: *Wall Street Journal*, February 15, 2000, p. A1.

★ 787 ★
Plastic Pipe (SIC 3084)

Top Pipe/Profile/Tube Extruders

Sales are estimated in millions of dollars.

Royal Group Technologies Ltd.	$ 690
CertaiNTeed Corp.	594
J-M Manufacturing Co. Inc.	490
Alcoa Building Products	430
Standard Products Co.	330
North American Pipe Corp.	320
Owens Corning	317

Source: *Plastics News*, June 21, 1999, p. 1.

★ 788 ★
Plastic Bottles (SIC 3085)

PET Bottle Market

The market for polyethylene terephthalate bottles reached 2.7 million metric tons.

Two liter soft-drink bottles	32%
Single service soft-drink bottles	17
Food containers	13
Fruit juices and tea bottles	11
Health care and cosmetic packaging	6
One liter soft-drink bottles	4
Water bottles	4
Thermoformed cups	3
Liquor bottles	2
Other	8

Source: *Chemical Week*, March 22, 2000, p. 43, from Lehman Brothers.

★ 789 ★
Plastic Foam (SIC 3086)

Foamed Plastic Demand - 2003

Urethanes	54%
Polystyrene	26
Other	20

Source: *Plastics News*, August 2, 1999, p. 3, from Freedonia Group Inc.

★ 790 ★
Baby Bottle Liners (SIC 3089)

Disposable Baby Bottle Liner Market

Playtex Drop-Ins 84%
Other 16

Source: *Fortune*, March 20, 2000, p. 48.

★ 791 ★
Condoms (SIC 3089)

Best-Selling Condom Brands - 1999

Trojan
Trojan Enz
Durex
LifeStyles
Kling Tite Natural Lamb
Conceptrol
Encare
Trojan Magnum
Other

Shares are shown based on sales of $268.8 million for the year ended October 10, 1999.

Trojan 30.3%
Trojan Enz 18.5
Durex 14.2
LifeStyles 11.4
Kling Tite Natural Lamb 3.5
Conceptrol 3.4
Encare 2.0
Trojan Magnum 2.0
Other 14.7

Source: *Chain Drug Review*, January 3, 2000, p. 40, from Information Resources Inc.

★ 792 ★
Condoms (SIC 3089)

Condom Market in Canada

Ansell Healthcare Products Inc. 11%
Johnson & Johnson 9
Other 80

Source: *Rubber & Plastics News*, May 1, 2000, p. 1.

★ 793 ★
Condoms (SIC 3089)

Condom Market Leaders - 1999

Market shares are shown for the 36 weeks ended June 5, 1999.

Trojan 60.0%
Durex 14.7
Life Styles 14.0
Other 11.3

Source: *Advertising Age*, July 5, 1999, p. 12, from A.C. Nielsen.

★ 794 ★
Condoms (SIC 3089)

Condom Sales by Type

Carter-Wallace has an estimated 65% of the market.

	1999	2002
Latex	91.8%	81.0%
Synthetic	4.7	17.5
Natural	3.5	1.5

Source: *Urethane Technology*, December 1999, p. 34, from Frost & Sullivan.

★ 795 ★
Diaper Pails (SIC 3089)

Diaper Pail Market

Dollar shares are shown in percent.

Diaper Genie 82%
Other 18

Source: Retrieved January 1, 2000 from the World Wide Web: http://www.playtexproductsinc.com/investor/pressrel.

★ 796 ★
Plastic Hangers (SIC 3089)

Plastic Garment Hanger Market

The market share is estimated between 70-80%. Tyco controls the market through its hanger arm A&E Products Group. A&E claims it has 30% of the entire hanger market, which includes those that display shoes, socks, blankets, towels and swatches.

Tyco International 70%
Other 30

Source: *Wall Street Journal*, February 15, 2000, p. A1.

★ 797 ★
Plastics (SIC 3089)

Cap and Closure Demand

	1998	2003	Share
Beverages	$ 1,174	$ 1,655	39.08%
Food	1,026	1,204	28.43
Other	1,160	1,376	32.49

Source: *Injection Molding*, November 1999, p. 66, from Freedonia Group.

★ 798 ★
Plastics (SIC 3089)

Plasticware Market by Segment - 1998

Sales are shown at department stores and mass merchants.

Beverageware 76%
Dinnerware 24

Source: *HFN*, September 13, 1999, p. 10.

★ 799 ★
Rubber and Plastic Products (SIC 3089)

Largest Rubber/Plastic Firms - 1999

Firms are ranked by revenues in billions of dollars.

Goodyear Tire . . . . $ 12.8
PACTIV 2.9
Sealed Air 2.8
M.A. Hanna 2.3
Mark IV Industries 2.3
Cooper Tire & Rubber 2.1
Gencorp. 1.7
Carlisle 1.6

Source: *Fortune*, April 17, 2000, pp. I-72.

★ 800 ★
Vinyl Siding (SIC 3089)

Top Vinyl Siding Makers - 1998

Sales are estimated in millions of dollars.

CertainTeed Corp. . . . . $ 433
Alcoa Building Products 430
Owens Corning 317
Jannock Vinyl Group 230
Variform Inc. 193
Royal Group Technologies Ltd. 110
Crane Plastics Co. 100

Source: *Plastics News*, June 21, 1999, p. 42.

SIC 31 - Leather and Leather Products

★ 801 ★
Leather Goods (SIC 3100)

Leather Goods Market In Canada

Luggage 30.8%
Handbags 25.8
Personal leathergoods 16.1
Backpacks 15.5
Business cases 11.8

Source: ''Equiping Your Students.'' Retrieved December 2, 1999 from the World Wide Web: http://www.llha.org/info.htm.

★ 802 ★
Footwear (SIC 3140)

Golf Shoe Market

Market shares are shown in percent.

Footjoy Worldwide 50%
Other 50

Source: Retrieved January 14, 2000 from the World Wide Web: http://www.amcity.com/triad/stories/1999/11/01/story6.html.

★ 803 ★
Footwear (SIC 3140)

Men's Wholesale Footwear Market

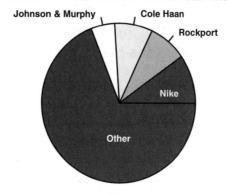

Nike 10.0%
Rockport 8.3
Cole Haan 8.0
Johnson & Murphy 4.7
Other 69.0

Source: *Footwear News*, March 20, 2000, p. 21, from NPD Group.

★ 804 ★
Footwear (SIC 3140)

Women's Wholesale Footwear Market

Easy Spirit 9.1%
Nine West 5.7
Nike 5.0
Enzo 3.9
Other 76.3

Source: *Footwear News*, March 20, 2000, p. 21, from NPD Group.

★ 805 ★
Luggage (SIC 3161)

Luggage Sales in Canada - 1998

Uprights (non carryon)	40%
Carry on with wheels	26
Carryon without wheels	23
Garment bags	11

Source: "Equiping Your Students." Retrieved December 2, 1999 from the World Wide Web: http://www.llha.org/info.htm.

★ 806 ★
Handbags (SIC 3171)

Purse Sales in Canada by Type

Flapover	35.8%
Organizer	22.5
Totes	20.9
Sling	9.1
Mama	6.6
Other	5.1

Source: "Equiping Your Students." Retrieved December 2, 1999 from the World Wide Web: http://www.llha.org/info.htm.

★ 807 ★
Handbags (SIC 3171)

Women's Handbag Sales by Material

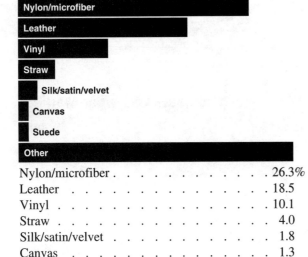

Nylon/microfiber	26.3%
Leather	18.5
Vinyl	10.1
Straw	4.0
Silk/satin/velvet	1.8
Canvas	1.3
Suede	1.0
Other	31.1

Source: *WWD*, April 24, 2000, p. 14.

★ 808 ★
Handbags (SIC 3171)

Women's Handbag Sales by Type

Tote	20.4%
Shopper	17.5
Top flap	12.8
Top zip	8.8
Hobo	8.1
Backpack	4.7
Messenger/school	4.2
Shoulder bag	4.0
Other	18.1

Source: *WWD*, April 24, 2000, p. 14.

★ 809 ★
Dayplanners (SIC 3172)

Dayplanner Sales in Canada

Leather	76.6%
Vinyl	18.2
Polyester	5.2

Source: "Equiping Your Students." Retrieved December 2, 1999 from the World Wide Web: http://www.llha.org/info.htm.

★ 810 ★
Briefcases (SIC 3199)

Soft Sided Attache Sales in Canada

Soft sided cases represent 87.5% of total business case sales.

Leather	68.9%
Polyester	16.0
Vinyl	15.1

Source: "Equiping Your Students." Retrieved December 2, 1999 from the World Wide Web: http://www.llha.org/info.htm.

SIC 32 - Stone, Clay, and Glass Products

★ 811 ★
Crystal (SIC 3229)

Crystal Market by Segment - 1998

Giftware 69%
Stemware 23
Barware 8

Source: *HFN*, September 13, 1999, p. 1.

★ 812 ★
Glassware (SIC 3229)

Glassware Market by Segment - 1998

Beverageware 42%
Serveware 25
Ovenware 15
Decorative accessories 12
Storageware 6

Source: *HFN*, September 13, 1999, p. 1.

★ 813 ★
Tabletop Items (SIC 3229)

U.S. Tabletop Market - 1998

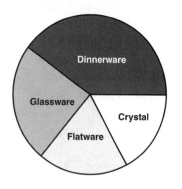

Dinnerware 40%
Glassware 24
Flatware 19
Crystal 17

Source: *HFN*, September 13, 1999, p. 3.

★ 814 ★
Cement (SIC 3241)

Ready-Mixed Concrete Market - 2000

Data are in thousands of cubic yards.

	(000)	Share
Public construction	215,417	50.23%
Residential buildings	114,431	26.68
Nonresidential buildings	98,985	23.08

Source: *Concrete Construction*, October 1999, p. 16.

★ 815 ★

Cement (SIC 3241)

Top Cement Makers

Production is shown in millions of tons per year.

Holnam/St. Lawrence Cement 12.23
Southdown/Medusa Cement & Kosmos	
Cement 9.97
Lafarge 8.08
Ash Grove Cement/North Texas Cement . . 6.37
Lehigh Portland Cement/Calaveras & Texas	
Lehigh 6.13

Source: *Financial Times*, September 7, 1999, p. 18, from *Global Cement Report* and British Cement Association.

★ 816 ★

Ceramics (SIC 3250)

Advanced Ceramic Components Market - 2003

Data are estimated in millions of dollars.

	($ mil.)	Share
Electronic ceramics	$ 7,414	67.71%
Chemical processing,		
environmental related	1,840	16.80
Ceramic coatings	1,056	9.64
Structural ceramics	640	5.84

Source: *American Ceramic Society Bulletin*, October 1999, p. 25, from Business Communications Co. Inc.

★ 817 ★

Ceramics (SIC 3250)

Ceramic Market by Segment - 1997

The market was valued at $36.5 billion.

Glass 44.0%
Advanced ceramics 19.0
Cement 12.0
Whitewares 12.0
Refractories 6.5
Structural clays 4.0
Abrasives 2.0
Other 0.5

Source: *Chemical Engineering*, July 1999, p. 53, from American Ceramics Society.

★ 818 ★

Refractories (SIC 3250)

Refractory Product Demand

Sales are shown in millions of dollars.

	1998	2003	Share
Bricks and shapes	$ 1,415	$ 1,615	58.73%
Monolithics and other . . .	1,010	1,135	41.27

Source: *American Ceramic Society Bulletin*, November 1999, p. 16, from Freedonia Group Inc.

SIC 33 - Primary Metal Industries

★ 819 ★
Metals (SIC 3300)

Largest Metals Companies in North America - 1998

Firms are ranked by metal sales in billions of dollars.

Alcoa Inc.	$ 11.9
Alcan Aluminum Ltd.	7.0
U.S. Steel Group of CSX Corp.	6.1
Reynolds Metals Co.	4.8
Bethlehem Steel Corp.	4.4
LTV Corp.	4.2
Nucor Corp.	4.1
Noranda Inc.	3.1
National Steel Corp.	2.8

Source: *American Metal Market*, June 11, 1999, p. 4A.

★ 820 ★
Metals (SIC 3300)

Largest Metals Firms - 1999

Firms are ranked by revenues in billions of dollars.

Alcoa	$ 16.4
Reynolds Metals	4.7
AK Steel Holding	4.2
LTV	4.1
Nucor	4.0
Bethlehem Steel	3.9

Allegheny Technologies	$ 3.4
Phelps Dodge	3.1

Source: *Fortune*, April 17, 2000, pp. I-69.

★ 821 ★
Steel (SIC 3312)

Cold Rolling Steel

Cold-rolling capacity has increased 20% from 1997-2000.

Traditional mills	84%
Independent processors	6
Mini-mills	6
Strip converters	3
End/users/manufacturers	1

Source: *American Metal Market*, September 14, 1999, p. 12A, from MSI estimates.

★ 822 ★
Steel (SIC 3312)

Steel Product Shipments - 1999

Shipments are as of October 1999.

Steel service centers and distributors	20.1%
Automotive	15.1
Construction and contractors	14.0
Containers, packaging and shipping materials	3.6
Electrical equipment	2.2
Other	45.0

Source: *AISE Steel Technology*, February 2000, p. 28.

★ 823 ★

Steel (SIC 3312)

U.S. Steel Market - 1998

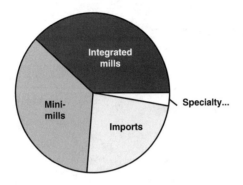

Integrated mills	41.6%
Mini-mills	39.0
Imports	26.3
Specialty steel	3.1

Source: *American Metal Market*, August 10, 1999, p. 14A, from American Iron and Steel Institute.

★ 824 ★

Steel Pipe (SIC 3317)

U.S. Thin-Wall Steel Pipe

The market share is estimated.

Tyco	70%
Other	30

Source: *Wall Street Journal*, February 15, 2000, p. A1.

★ 825 ★

Aluminum (SIC 3334)

Aluminum Market in North America

Alcoa
APA
Other

Alcoa	35%
APA	20
Other	45

Source: *The Economist*, August 14, 1999, p. 54.

★ 826 ★

Aluminum (SIC 3334)

Largest Aluminum Firms

Firms are ranked by average annual capacity.

Alcoa	3,138
Alcan	1,681
Reynolds	1,118
Billton	886
Pechiney	828
Hydro	745
Comalco	659
Aluminium Bahrain	537

Source: *Wall Street Journal*, August 12, 1999, p. B4, from CRU International.

★ 827 ★

Aluminum (SIC 3334)

U.S. Aluminum Distributor Shipments

Data are in millions of pounds.

	1998	2000	Share
Sheet	$ 1,513	$ 1,735	68.39%
Rod, bar & wire	291	325	12.81
Extruded shapes	240	257	10.13
Plate	240	220	8.67

Source: *American Metal Market*, January 20, 2000, p. 7A, from Scott & Stringfellow.

★ 828 ★

Aluminum (SIC 3334)

U.S. Aluminum Use - 1998

	(mil.)	Share
Transportaion	7.16	30.89%
Containers and packaging	5.01	21.61
Building and construction	3.07	13.24
Exports	2.78	11.99
Consumer durables	1.60	6.90
Electrical	1.57	6.77
Other	1.99	8.58

Source: *New York Times*, August 12, 1999, p. C8, from Aluminum Association.

★ 829 ★

Cobalt (SIC 3339)

U.S. Cobalt Use - 1999

Consumption is estimated in metric tons.

	mt	Share
Superalloys	4,000	47.48%
Cemented carbides	850	10.09
Other chemical	800	9.50
Catalysts	775	9.20
Magnetics	750	8.90
Salts and dryers	600	7.12
Steels	150	1.78
Other	500	5.93

Source: *Engineering & Mining Journal*, March 20, 2000, p. 20.

★ 830 ★

Superalloys (SIC 3339)

How Superalloys Are Used - 1999

Nickel/iron/cobalt	59%
Titanium	35
Others	4

Source: *American Metal Market*, August 24, 1999, p. 2A, from Resource Strategis.

★ 831 ★

Copper (SIC 3351)

Copper Consumption by End Use - 1997

Electrical	61%
Corrosion resistance	20
Heat transfer	11
Structural	6
Aesthetic	2

Source: "Top 10 Copper Markets." Retrieved April 10, 2000 from the World Wide Web: http://marketdata.copper. org/graphs/e97.html, from Copper Development Association.

★ 832 ★

Copper (SIC 3351)

Copper Metal Use

Building construction	42%
Electric/electronic products	25
Transportation equipment	13
Industrial machinery	11
Consumer products	9

Source: *Purchasing*, March 9, 2000, p. 40B.

★ 833 ★

Copper (SIC 3351)

Top Copper Markets - 1997

Total pounds reached 8.3 billion pounds.

	(mil.)	Share
Building wire	1,351	15.94%
Plumbing & heating	1,195	14.10
Power utilities	694	8.19
Air conditioning & commercial refrigerator	692	8.17
Automotive electrical	667	7.87
Telecommunications	622	7.34
In-plant equipment	518	6.11
Other	2,736	32.28

Source: "Top 10 Copper Markets." Retrieved April 10, 2000 from the World Wide Web: http://marketdata.copper. org/graphs/e97.html, from Copper Development Association.

★ 834 ★

Copper (SIC 3351)

Top Copper Markets - 1998

Building wiring	16.6%
Plumbing & heating	13.8
Telecommunications	8.6
Power utilities	8.6
Air conditioning & commercial refrigeration	8.5
Other	43.9

Source: *American Metal Market*, August 17, 1999, p. 8A, from Copper Development Association.

★ 835 ★
Aluminum Foil (SIC 3353)

Top Aluminum Foil Brands

Brands are ranked by sales of $453.1 million for the year ended January 21, 1999.

	($ mil.)	Share
Reynolds Wrap	$ 263.2	58.10%
Reynolds Diamond	24.4	5.39
Reynolds Wrappers	3.8	0.84
Wonder Foil	0.5	0.11
Arrow Budget Buy	0.1	0.02
Other	161.0	35.54

Source: *MMR*, May 17, 1999, p. 36, from Information Resources Inc.

★ 836 ★
Aluminum Foil Pans (SIC 3353)

Top Disposable Aluminum Foil Pan Brands - 1999

Shares are shown based on sales of $231.7 million for the year ended February 27, 2000.

EZ Foil	53.1%
Handi Foil	18.9
Durable	7.1
EZ Elegance	7.0
Handi Foil Cook N Carry	4.2
Dur O Peg Handle Ware	1.4
Fancifoil	1.4
Private label	2.1
Other	4.8

Source: *Supermarket Business*, May 15, 2000, p. 70, from Information Resources Inc.

★ 837 ★
Titanium (SIC 3356)

Titanium Shipments by End Use - 1999

Data are estimated.

Commercial aerospace	54%
Industrial	19
Military aerospace	19
Consumer	8

Source: *American Metal Market*, October 20, 1999, p. 8A, from RTI International Metals Inc.

SIC 34 - Fabricated Metal Products

★ 838 ★

Cutlery (SIC 3421)

Travel Knife Market

Swiss Army 75%
Other 25

Source: *WWD Fairchild 100 Supplement*, January 2000, p. 56.

★ 839 ★

Razor Blades (SIC 3421)

Disposable Razor Blade Unit Shares - 1999

Shares are shown based on unit sales for the year ended January 30, 2000.

Bic 16.6%
Schick Slim Twin 13.0
Gillette Good News 9.5
Gillette Good News Plus 9.1
Gillette Custom Plus 8.2
Gillette Daisy Plus 5.7
Bic Plus 4.1
Other 33.8

Source: *Supermarket Business*, April 15, 2000, p. 132, from Information Resources Inc.

★ 840 ★

Razor Blades (SIC 3421)

Permanent Razor Sales - 1999

Sales are for the year ended November 7, 1999.

	($ mil.)	Share
Gillette Mach 3	$ 65.5	40.76%
Gillette Sensor Excel	10.7	6.66
Other	84.5	52.58

Source: *Supermarket News*, December 13, 1999, p. 41, from Information Resources Inc.

★ 841 ★

Razor Blades (SIC 3421)

Razor Blade Refill Market - 1999

| Gillette Sensor for Women |
| Gillette Sensor Excel |
| Schick Silk Effects |
| Personal Touch |

Sales are shown for the year ended October 10, 1999.

Gillette Sensor for Women . . . . $ 43.9
Gillette Sensor Excel 41.4
Schick Silk Effects 40.5
Personal Touch (Schick) 17.3

Source: *Wall Street Journal*, December 2, 1999, p. B8, from Information Resources Inc.

★ 842 ★

Razor Blades (SIC 3421)

Top Disposable Razor Brands - 1999

Shares are for the year ended October 10, 1999. Top producers are Warner-Lambert, Gillette, and Bic.

Schick Slim Twin 14.8%
Good News 12.4
Custom Plus 12.0
Good News Plus 11.7
Bic 10.7
Daisy Plus 7.1
Custom Plus for Women 4.2
Other 27.1

Source: *Chain Drug Review*, January 17, 2000, p. 24, from Information Resources Inc.

★ 843 ★
Locksets (SIC 3429)

Lockset Sales by Type - 1999

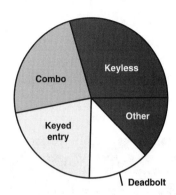

Dollar shares are for the hardware/home improvement channel for the year ended May 1999.

Keyless	30%
Combo	24
Keyed entry	22
Deadbolt	13
Other	13

Source: *Do-It-Yourself Retailing*, October 1999, p. 84, from Vista Sales and Marketing.

★ 844 ★
Locksets (SIC 3429)

Padlock Sales by Price

Dollar shares are shown for the hardware/home improvement channel for the year ended May 1999.

$12.00+	40%
$6.00-$8.99	24
$3.00-5.99	20
$9.00-$11.99	13
$3.00	3

Source: *Do-It-Yourself Retailing*, October 1999, p. 85, from Vista Sales and Marketing.

★ 845 ★
Titanium (SIC 3463)

Titanium Wrought Shipments - 1999

Data are in thousands of tons.

	(000)	Share
Commercial aerospace	13.4	45.27%
Core industries	7.0	23.65
Emerging industries	4.7	15.88
Military aerospace	4.5	15.20

Source: *JOM*, June 1999, p. 40.

★ 846 ★
Guns (SIC 3484)

Largest Sources of Guns - 1998

Data show the number of handgun imports by country.

Austria	170,240
Brazil	133,270
Germany	107,232
Italy	41,071

Source: *Washington Post*, June 28, 1999, p. A1, from U.S. Bureau of the Census.

★ 847 ★
Piping (SIC 3498)

Power Plant-Piping Market

Shaw	70%
Other	30

Source: *Investor's Business Daily*, April 10, 2000, p. A12.

★ 848 ★
Powdered Materials (SIC 3499)

Nanostructured Materials Market

	1998	2003	Share
Particles	$ 64	$ 149	96.13%
Coatings	2	6	3.87

Source: *Ceramic Bulletin*, September 1999, p. 23, from Business Communications Co.

SIC 35 - Industry Machinery and Equipment

★ 849 ★

Industrial Machinery (SIC 3500)

Largest Farm/Industrial Equipment Makers - 1999

Firms are ranked by revenues in billions of dollars.

Caterpillar	$ 19.7
Deere	11.7
Ingersoll-Rand	8.5
American Standard	7.2
Cummins Engine	6.6
Parker Hannifin	4.9
Baker Hughes	4.9
ITT Industries	4.6

Source: *Fortune*, April 17, 2000, pp. I-69.

★ 850 ★

Farm Equipment (SIC 3523)

Combine Market in North America - 1998

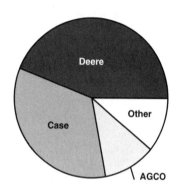

Shares are shown in percent.

Deere	44%
Case	34
AGCO	11
Other	11

Source: *Farm Journal*, July/August 1998, p. 33, from Stark's Research.

★ 851 ★

Farm Equipment (SIC 3523)

Retail Tractor and Combine Sales - 2000

Data are forecast as of January 2000.

	Units
2 wheel drive, under 40 PTO hp	75,333
2 wheel drive, 40 to 100 PTO hp	45,175
100 PTO hp and over	15,389
4 wheel drive tractors	2,841

Source: *Wallace's Farmer*, April 2000, p. 9, from Equipment Manufacturers Institute.

185

★ 852 ★

Farm Equipment (SIC 3523)

Tractor Market in North America

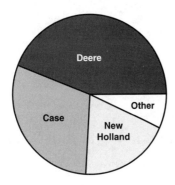

Shares are shown for two-wheeldrive tractors, 100 hp and over.

Deere	44%
Case	30
New Holland	19
Other	7

Source: *Farm Journal*, July/August 1999, p. 33, from Stark's Research.

★ 853 ★

Farm Equipment (SIC 3523)

Two-Wheel Drive Tractor Leaders - 1998

Shares refer to two-wheel-drive tractors, 40 hp to 99 hp. Data refer to North America.

Deere	32%
New Holland	29
Case	16
Massey-Fergusson	14
Kubota	6
AGCO	2
Others	1

Source: *Farm Journal*, July/August 1999, p. 33, from Stark's Research.

★ 854 ★

Lawn & Garden Equipment (SIC 3524)

Lawn & Garden Sales - 1999

Sales are shown in millions of dollars.

	($ mil.)	Share
Containers, all types	$ 1,102	19%
Lawn decorations	754	13
Water features	638	11
Gift items	580	10
Outdoor lighting	464	8
Sprayers	406	7
Weed barriers	290	5
Lawn edging	232	4
Gloves	232	4
Play equipment	232	4
Other	870	15

Source: *Nursery Retailer*, February/March 2000, p. 74.

★ 855 ★

Lawn & Garden Equipment (SIC 3524)

Lawn & Garden Sales by State - 1999

Total sales reached $44.2 billion.

California	10.3%
New York	8.1
Texas	6.1
Pennyslvania	5.3
Ohio	5.2
Illinois	5.1
Michigan	4.2
Other	55.7

Source: *Nursery Retailer*, February/March 2000, p. 74.

★ 856 ★

Lawn & Garden Equipment (SIC 3524)

Lawn Mower Shipments

Value of shipments are shown in billions of dollars.

	1997	2000	Share
Riding	$ 1.8	$ 2.4	64.86%
Nonriding	1.2	1.3	35.14

Source: *USA TODAY*, October 12, 1999, p. B1, from Freedonia Group.

★ 857 ★

Lawn & Garden Equipment (SIC 3524)

Riding Gas Mower Market - 1998

Shares are shown based on shipments.

American Yard Products 21%
Murray 17
MTD 16
John Deere 9
Others 37

Source: *Appliance Manufacturer*, April 1999, p. 21.

★ 858 ★

Lawn & Garden Equipment (SIC 3524)

Top Leafblower Makers - 1998

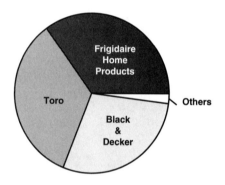

Shares are shown based on shipments. Data refer to handheld, electric models.

Frigidaire Home Products 35%
Toro 34
Black & Decker 29
Others 2

Source: *Appliance Manufacturer*, April 1999, p. 21.

★ 859 ★

Lawn & Garden Equipment (SIC 3524)

Top Snowblower Makers - 1998

Shares are shown based on shipments.

MTD 23%
Toro 22
American Yard Products 15
Murray 12
Ariens 6
Other 22

Source: *Appliance Manufacturer*, April 1999, p. 21.

★ 860 ★

Lawn & Garden Equipment (SIC 3524)

Top String Trimmer Makers - 1998

Shares are shown based on shipments.

Frigidaire Home Products 44%
Toro 27
Black & Decker 24
Ryobi 3
Others 2

Source: *Appliance Manufacturer*, April 1999, p. 21.

★ 861 ★

Lawn & Garden Equipment (SIC 3524)

Walk-Behind Mower Market

Shares are shown based on shipments.

American Yard Products 23%
Murray 21
MTD Products 19
Toro 9
Other 28

Source: *Appliance Manufacturer*, April 1999, p. 21.

★ 862 ★
Conveyors (SIC 3535)

Conveyor Market in Northeast Central States

Sales are in millions of dollars.

U.S. Postal Service . . . . $ 54.4
Concrete work 43.5
Blast furnaces & steel mills 39.8
Plastics products 37.9
Construction machinery 36.5

Source: *Industrial Distribution*, March 2000, p. 77, from Industrial Market Information.

★ 863 ★
Conveyors (SIC 3535)

Conveyor Market in South-Atlantic States

Sales are in millions of dollars.

U.S. Postal Service . . . . $ 62.6
Highway & street construction 58.8
Concrete work 46.9
Nonresidential construction 30.4
Paper mills 26.2

Source: *Industrial Distribution*, March 2000, p. 77, from Industrial Market Information.

★ 864 ★
Water Filter Equipment (SIC 3556)

Point of Use Water Equipment Sales

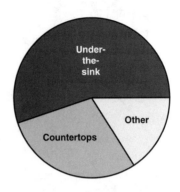

The market has annual revenues of $235.5 million.

Under-the-sink 55%
Countertops 29
Other 16

Source: "Consumer Concerns Drive Water Treatment Market." Retrieved April 24, 2000 from the World Wide Web: http://www.pmmag.com, from Frost & Sullivan.

★ 865 ★
Plastics Machinery (SIC 3559)

Plastics Machinery Sales

Sales are shown in millions of dollars.

	1998	2003	Share
Injection molding	$ 1,105	$ 1,465	60.79%
Blow molding	370	505	20.95
Extrusion	335	440	18.26

Source: *Modern Plastics*, September 1999, p. 14, from Freedonia Group.

★ 866 ★
Packaging Machinery (SIC 3565)

Packaging Machinery Shipments - 1998

Total shipments reached $4.18 billion.

Conveying, feeding, orienting machinery . . . 21.1%
Coding, printing, stamping machinery 12.2
Case tray forming, packing, sealing
  machinery 8.3
Palletizing machinery 7.9
Labeling machinery 6.9

Continued on next page.

★ 866 ★ *Continued*
Packaging Machinery (SIC 3565)

Packaging Machinery Shipments - 1998

Total shipments reached $4.18 billion.

Inspecting, checkweighting machinery 5.5%
Form/fill/seal machinery 4.7
Cartoning and coupon placing machinery . . . 4.7
Other 28.7

Source: "5th Annual Packaging Machinery Outlook Study." Retrieved April 20, 2000 from the World Wide Web: http://www.packaging-technology.org, from PMMI.

★ 867 ★
Packaging Machinery (SIC 3565)

Packaging Machinery Shipments in Canada - 1998

Total shipments reached $229.8 million.

Conveying, feeding machinery 19.6%
Palletizing machinery 18.2
Cartoning machinery 7.9
Bottle line machinery 4.4
Labeling machinery 2.9
Other 47.0

Source: "5th Annual Packaging Machinery Outlook Study." Retrieved April 20, 2000 from the World Wide Web: http://www.packaging-technology.org, from PMMI.

★ 868 ★
Power Equipment (SIC 3568)

Small-Scale Power Systems - 2003

Sales are shown in millions of dollars.

	($ mil.)	Share
Microturbine	$ 8,500	50.28%
Combustion turbine	3,990	23.60
Engine/generator set	3,322	19.65
Fuel cell	1,094	6.47

Source: *American Ceramic Society Bulletin*, August 1999, p. 41, from Business Communications Co.

★ 869 ★
Sprinklers (SIC 3569)

U.S. Sprinkler Market

The market share is estimated.

Tyco 50%
Other 50

Source: *Wall Street Journal*, February 15, 2000, p. A1.

★ 870 ★
Computers (SIC 3571)

Handheld Companion Market

Market shares are shown in percent.

PalmOS 42%
Windows CE 27
Sharp OS 9
Psion 8
Others 14

Source: *Infoworld*, May 31, 1999, p. 29, from International Data Corp.

★ 871 ★
Computers (SIC 3571)

Handheld Companion Market - 2003

Shares are estimated by operating system.

Palm 53.8%
Windows CE 46.1
Other 1.1

Source: *Wall Street Journal*, September 20, 1999, p. R20, from International Data Corp.

★ 872 ★
Computers (SIC 3571)

Handheld Computer Market

Data show the source of mobile computers.

Reseller 29%
Retailer 25
Vendor 23
Catalog, mail order 19
Systems integrator, consultant 4

Source: *Informationweek*, June 23, 1999, p. 57.

★ 873 ★
Computers (SIC 3571)

Notebook Market Leaders - 1999

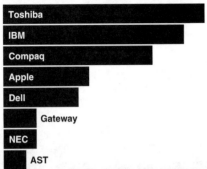

Shares are for the first quarter of the year.

Toshiba	19.2%
IBM	17.4
Compaq	14.0
Apple	7.9
Dell	7.1
Gateway	3.4
NEC	3.2
AST	1.8
Other	26.0

Source: Retrieved January 4, 2000 from the World Wide Web: http://www.infotechtrends.com, from *Mobile Computing* and ZD Market Intelligence.

★ 874 ★

Computers (SIC 3571)

Palmtop Market Leaders - 1998

Shares are shown based on shipments.

3Com	56%
Sharp	20
Hewlett-Packard	6
Philips	5
Psion	4
Other	11

Source: *Fortune*, July 5, 1999, p. 122, from Dataquest Inc.

★ 875 ★

Computers (SIC 3571)

PC Market - 3rd Quarter 1999

Market shares are shown in percent.

Compaq	12.8%
Dell	10.8
IBM	7.6
Hewlett-Packard	6.2
Gateway	4.3
Others	58.3

Source: *New York Times*, October 25, 1999, p. C4, from Dataquest Inc.

★ 876 ★

Computers (SIC 3571)

PC Market in Canada - 1999

Shares are shown based on estimated revenues of $7. 46 billion for the year ended December 31, 1999.

Compaq	16.9%
IBM	16.2
Dell	15.3
Hewlett-Packard	5.2
Toshiba	5.2
Apple	3.5
Packard Bell NEC	2.1
Other	35.6

Source: "Report on Market Share." Retrieved June 8, 2000 from the World Wide Web: http://www. marketingmag.ca, from The Yankee Group in Canada.

★ 877 ★

Computers (SIC 3571)

PC Market Leaders - 1999

Market shares are shown in percent.

Dell	17.1%
Compaq	15.3
Gateway	9.3
Hewlett-Packard	8.2
IBM	7.6
Others	42.5

Source: *Detroit Free Press*, November 4, 1999, p. C1, from Dataquest Inc.

★ 878 ★

Computers (SIC 3571)

PC Market Leaders - 2000

Shares are for the first quarter of the year.

	(000)	Share
Dell	1,860	16.8%
Compaq	1,820	16.4
Hewlett-Packard	1,393	12.6
Gateway	1,023	9.2
eMachines	535	4.8
Apple	486	4.4
IBM	445	4.0
Others	3,512	31.7

Source: *Wall Street Journal*, April 24, 2000, p. A3, from Dataquest Inc.

★ 879 ★

Computers (SIC 3571)

PC Market Shares

Compaq	16.8%
Dell	16.4
IBM	8.4
Gateway	8.4
Hewlett-Packard	8.2
Others	41.8

Source: *Los Angeles Times*, August 13, 1999, p. C4, from Bloomberg News and Dataquest Inc.

★ 880 ★

Computers (SIC 3571)

Personal Digital Assistant Market - 1999

Data are for December 1999.

3Com	84.9%
Casio	7.0
Hewlett-Packard	4.1
Compaq	1.0
IBM	0.9
Other	2.1

Source: ''NPD INTELECT Reports Year End Data for PDA Category.'' Retrieved March 8, 2000 the World Wide Web: http://www.npd.com/corp/press, from NPD INTELECT.

★ 881 ★

Computers (SIC 3571)

Retail Desktop Market

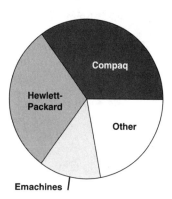

Unit shares are for December 1999.

Compaq	34.5%
Hewlett-Packard	30.4
Emachines	13.4
Other	21.7

Source: ''Retail Desktop Sales End 1999 on a Sour Note.'' Retrieved January 25, 2000 from the World Wide Web: http://www.pcdata.com/press.

★ 882 ★

Computers (SIC 3571)

Retail PC Market

Hewlett-Packard	35.0%
Compaq	29.2
Emachines	13.5
IBM	11.1
Others	11.2

Source: *Investor's Business Daily*, October 5, 1999, p. A7, from ZD Infobeads.

★ 883 ★

Computers (SIC 3571)

Small Business PC Market - 1999

Market shares are shown for the first quarter of the year.

Dell	19.7%
IBM	10.7
Compaq	10.0
Acer	5.5
Toshiba	5.5
Hewlett-Packard	5.0
Other	48.6

Source: "Dell Expands U.S. Small Biz PC Lead." Retrieved December 8, 1999 from the World Wide Web: http://www.msnbc.com/news/277856.asp, from International Data Corp.

★ 884 ★

Computers (SIC 3571)

Thin Client Market - 1998

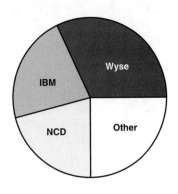

Wyse	31.8%
IBM	22.1
NCD	20.9
Other	25.2

Source: *VAR Business*, August 30, 1999, p. 27, from International Data Corp.

★ 885 ★

Computers (SIC 3571)

U.S. Palmtop Market

	1998	2003
PalmOS	73%	54%
Windows CE	14	39
Others	13	7

Source: *Network World*, October 18, 1999, p. 60, from International Data Corp.

★ 886 ★

Workstations (SIC 3571)

Unix Workstation Market - 1999

Shares are shown based on shipments of third quarter 1999.

	Units	Share
Sun	47,930	64%
HP	10,638	14
IBM	6,921	9
SGI	5,306	7
Compaq	2,062	3
Other	1,300	2

Source: "Sun Remains Number 1 in the World." Retrieved January 11, 2000 from the World Wide Web: http://www.idc.com, from International Data Corp.

★ 887 ★

Workstations (SIC 3571)

Windows NT Workstation Market - 1999

Shares are shown based on shipments of third quarter 1999.

	Units	Share
Dell	49,592	37%
HP	29,673	22
Compaq	19,025	14
IBM	13,975	10
Other	21,291	16

Source: "Sun Remains Number 1 in the World." Retrieved January 11, 2000 from the World Wide Web: http://www.idc.com, from International Data Corp.

★ 888 ★
Computer Data Storage (SIC 3572)
ATA RAID Controller Market

Unit shares are shown for the host-based UDMA RAID (redundant array of independent drives) array. This is a combination of high-performance ATA drives with the data protection and added performance made by RAID arrays.

Promise Technology 90%
Other 10

Source: "Promise Technology Attains 90% Unit Share." Retrieved April 10, 2000 from the World Wide Web: http://www.internetwire.com, from Dataquest Inc.

★ 889 ★
Computer Data Storage (SIC 3572)
CD/DVD-ROM Drive Market Leaders

LGE 15%
Toshiba 13
Panasonic 11
TEAC 10
Samsung 7
Acer 6
Sony 6
Other 31

Source: *E-Media Professional*, August 1999, p. 15, from International Data Corp.

★ 890 ★
Computer Data Storage (SIC 3572)
CD-R Market Shares

ATAPI 74%
SCSI 23
Other 3

Source: *E-Media Professional*, February 2000, p. 12, from Santa Clara Consulting.

★ 891 ★
Computer Data Storage (SIC 3572)
Computer Storage Market

Shares are based on a survey.

EMC 36%
IBM 28
Compaq 16
HP/Hitachi 10
StorageTek 6
Others 4

Source: *Investor's Business Daily*, April 5, 2000, p. A6, from Merrill Lynch.

★ 892 ★
Computer Data Storage (SIC 3572)
Enterprise Storage Market

EMC 51.0%
IBM 27.4
Hitachi 18.1
Amdahl 3.5

Source: *Windows NT Magazine*, October 1999, p. 17, from International Data Corp.

★ 893 ★
Computer Data Storage (SIC 3572)
RAID Market Shares

EMC 35%
IBM 22
Compaq 9
Hitachi Data Systems 7
Hewlett-Packard 6
Other 21

Source: *Windows NT Magazine*, October 1999, p. 14, from Dataquest Inc. and Gartner Group.

★ 894 ★

Computer Data Storage (SIC 3572)

Rewritable Disc Drive Market - 1999

Shares are shown for the second quarter of the year.

Sony	27%
Philips	24
Ricoh	10
Yamaha	9
Teac	7
Others	23

Source: *Investor's Business Daily*, November 3, 1999, p. A6, from International Data Corp. and DiskTrend Inc.

★ 895 ★

Computer Data Storage (SIC 3572)

Storage Market by Segment - 2002

Server attached storage	55%
Storage area networks	28
Network attached storage	17

Source: Retrieved January 4, 2000 from the World Wide Web: http://www.infotechtrends.com, from *Federal Computer Week*.

★ 896 ★

Computer Data Storage (SIC 3572)

Top Hard Drive Vendors - 1999

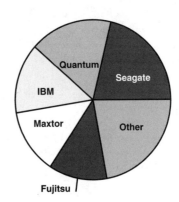

Seagate	21.0%
Quantum	17.1
IBM	14.1
Maxtor	13.3
Fujitsu	12.3
Other	22.2

Source: *Computer Reseller News*, February 28, 2000, p. 73, from TrendFocus.

★ 897 ★

Computer Data Storage (SIC 3572)

Zip Drive Sales

Iomega	75%
Imation	9
Other	16

Source: *Brandweek*, December 13, 1999, p. 13, from Disk/Trend.

★ 898 ★
Computer Hardware (SIC 3577)

Computer Hardware Market for the Government

The top providers are shown based on federal contracts.

Unisys Corp.	7.29%
IBM Corp.	5.26
Lockheed Martin Corp.	5.23
Dell Computer Corp.	4.13
Compaq Computer Corp.	3.71
Other	74.38

Source: *Government Executive*, Annual 1999, p. 48.

★ 899 ★
Computer Hardware (SIC 3577)

Computer Monitor Market by Color Depth

Data include both home and work, based on real-time analysis of net surfers at 650,000 web sites.

16-bit	54.0%
32-bit	22.7
24-bit	12.4
8-bit	10.5
4-bit	0.3
2-bit	0.1

Source: *Industry Standard*, March 20, 2000, p. 184, from mycomputer.com.

★ 900 ★
Computer Hardware (SIC 3577)

Computer Product Sales - 1999

Total sales through retail, online and mail order channels reached an estimated $36.5 billion. Digital cameras were one of the fastest growing segments.

Desktop computers/servers	25.4%
Printers/supplies	20.9
Portable PCs	15.9
Data storage	9.7
Displays	8.2
Networking products	5.4

Multimedia	3.8%
Accessories	3.4
Computer memory	3.1
Other	4.2

Source: Retrieved February 1, 2000 from the World Wide Web: http://www.pcdata.com/press, from PC Data.

★ 901 ★
Computer Hardware (SIC 3577)

Largest Computer Peripheral Firms - 1999

Firms are ranked by revenues in billions of dollars.

Seagate Technology	$ 6.8
EMC	6.7
Quantum	4.9
Lexmark International	3.4
Maxtor	2.4
Storage Technology	2.3

Source: *Fortune*, April 17, 2000, pp. I-58.

★ 902 ★
Computer Hardware (SIC 3577)

Projector Device Industry

The audio-visual market still has 80% of the market. Data show market share of sales shown through computer distributors.

In Focus	56.2%
Proxima	17.4
Epson	8.4
Sony	4.7
Other	13.3

Source: "In Focus Continues It's Dominance." Retrieved January 13, 2000 from the World Wide Web: http://www.amcity.com/portland/stories, from TFC.NET.

★ 903 ★

Computer Hardware (SIC 3577)

Top Scanner Makers - 1999

Shares are shown for the first nine months of the year.

Hewlett-Packard	24%
Umax Technologies	22
Visioneer	18
Microtek	12
Mustek	6
Others	18

Source: *Investor's Business Daily*, October 20, 1999, p. A8, from PC Data Inc.

★ 904 ★

Computer Printers (SIC 3577)

Color Page Printer Market - 1999

Data are for the first six months of the year.

Hewlett-Packard	55.1%
Tektronix	26.7
Lexmark	5.4
Minolta	4.0
QMS	2.8
Others	6.0

Source: *Computer Reseller News*, November 1, 1999, p. 91, from Dataquest Inc.

★ 905 ★

Computer Printers (SIC 3577)

Desktop Laser Printer Market - 1998

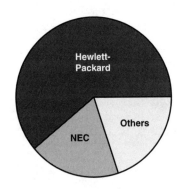

Shares are shown based on shipments.

Hewlett-Packard	61%
NEC	19
Others	20

Source: *Appliance*, September 1999, p. 78.

★ 906 ★

Computer Printers (SIC 3577)

Ink Jet Printer Market - 1999

Hewlett-Packard	49%
Canon	16
Epson	15
Lexmark	13
Other	7

Source: Retrieved March 8, 2000 from the World Wide Web: http://www.gartnergroup.com/dq/static/about/press, from Dataquest Inc.

★ 907 ★

Computer Printers (SIC 3577)

Serial Dot Matrix Market - 1998

Epson	29.9%
Okidata	25.0
Panasonic	17.0
Other	28.1

Source: *Appliance*, September 1999, p. 78, from International Data Corp.

★ 908 ★
Automated Teller Machines (SIC 3578)

ATM Market Shares - 1999

Total shipments reached 46,458 units in 1999. Off—premise ATM makers are taking a greater share of the market.

	Units	Share
Diebold	9,900	21.31%
Triton	9,445	20.33
NCR	9,243	19.90
Other	17,870	38.46

Source: *Bank Network News*, February 29, 2000, p. 1.

★ 909 ★
Computer Services (SIC 3578)

Computer Services Market - 1997

Data are in billions of dollars. The market includes data processing, programming and computer maintenance.

California	$ 13.6
New York	7.0
New Jersey	6.0
Texas	5.5
Illinois	5.1
Florida	4.1
Massachusetts	3.9

Source: *Crain's New York Business*, July 5, 1999, p. 32, from NYC Comptroller.

★ 910 ★
POS Terminals (SIC 3579)

POS Terminal Market - 1999

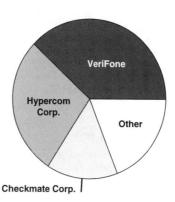

POS terminal makers shipped 1.63 million units in United States and Canada.

VeriFone	38.0%
Hypercom Corp.	28.2
Checkmate Corp.	15.3
Other	18.5

Source: *Bank Network News*, February 29, 2000, pp. I-3.

★ 911 ★
Postage Machines (SIC 3579)

Postage Machine Market

Pitney Bowes	85%
Other	15

Source: *Business Week Frontier*, September 1999, p. F16.

★ 912 ★
Printer Drums (SIC 3579)

Laser-Printer Cartridge Drum Industry

Floturn Inc.	70%
Other	30

Source: *Wall Street Journal*, January 18, 2000, p. 2B.

★ 913 ★
Heating and Cooling (SIC 3585)

Air Conditioner Market - 1998

Shares are shown based on shipments.

Fedders	25%
Electrolux (Frigidaire)	21
Whirlpool	18
Goodman/Amana	7
LG Electronics/Goldstar	7
Other	21

Source: *Appliance*, September 1999, p. 76.

★ 914 ★
Heating and Cooling (SIC 3585)

Electric Room Heater Market - 1998

Shares are shown based on estimated shipments.

Holmes	40%
Honeywell/Duracraft	15
Rival (Patton)	13
Arvin (HeatStream)	9
Other	23

Source: *Appliance Manufacturer*, April 1999, p. 20.

★ 915 ★
Heating and Cooling (SIC 3585)

Foodservice Refrigerator/Freezer Market

Shares are shown based on shipments.

True	34%
Beverage Air	21
Delfield	8
Traulsen	8
Hobart	6
Victory	6
Other	17

Source: *Appliance Manufacturer*, April 1999, p. 23.

★ 916 ★
Heating and Cooling (SIC 3585)

Gas Water Heater Market - 1998

Shares are shown based on estimated shipments.

Rheem	31%
State	23
American	17
A.O. Smith	15
Bradford White	14

Source: *Appliance Manufacturer*, April 1999, p. 20.

★ 917 ★
Heating and Cooling (SIC 3585)

Icemaker Leaders - 1998

Shares are shown based on shipments.

Manitowac	38%
Hoshizaki	24
Scotsman	20
Welbilt (Mile High)	9
Cornelius	5
Crystal Tips	4

Source: *Appliance Manufacturer*, April 1999, p. 23.

★ 918 ★
Heating and Cooling (SIC 3585)

Leading Room Air Conditioner Makers - 1999

Shares are shown based on domestic shipments.

Fedders	16.0%
Kenmore	13.8
Whirlpool	12.9
GE	11.0
Frigidaire	7.3
Goldstar	5.4
Other	43.6

Source: *HFN*, March 27, 2000, p. 89, from Association of Home Appliance Manufacturers.

★ 919 ★
Heating and Cooling (SIC 3585)
Top Central Air Makers - 1998

Shares are estimated based on shipments.

United Technologies 21%
Goodman 17
American Standard 13
Rheem 12
Lennox 10
Other 27

Source: *Appliance Manufacturer*, April 1999, p. 20.

★ 920 ★
Heating and Cooling (SIC 3585)
Top Dehumidifier Makers - 1998

Shares are shown based on shipments.

Whirlpool 35%
Electrolux (Frigidaire) 33
Fedders 10
W.C. Wood 8
Other 14

Source: *Appliance*, September 1999, p. 76.

★ 921 ★
Heating and Cooling (SIC 3585)
Top Gas Residential Furnace Makers - 1998

Shares are shown based on estimated shipments.

United Technologies 23%
Goodman 17
Lennox 13
Rheem 12
Other 35

Source: *Appliance Manufacturer*, April 1999, p. 20.

★ 922 ★
Heating and Cooling (SIC 3585)
Top Room Air Conditoner Brands - 1998

Kenmore 17%
Fedders 17
Whirlpool 12
GE 7
White Westinghouse 6
Frigidaire 5
Amana 5
Other 31

Source: *Discount Store News*, August 9, 1999, p. 25, from IMR Continuing Consumer Survey.

★ 923 ★
Heating and Cooling (SIC 3585)
Unitary/Heat Pump Market - 1998

Shares are shown based on shipments.

Carrier 22%
Goodman 17
Trane 13
Rheem 12
Other 36

Source: *Appliance*, September 1999, p. 76.

★ 924 ★

Gas Pumps (SIC 3586)

Gas Pump Market

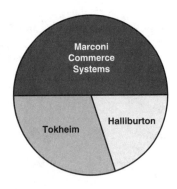

Shares are estimated.

Marconi Commerce Systems 50%
Tokheim 30
Halliburton 20

Source: *Wall Street Journal*, February 18, 2000, p. 4B, from *National Petroleum News*, Herbst Lazar Bell, Petroleum Equipment Institute, and companies.

★ 925 ★

Water Filters (SIC 3589)

Water Filter Market

Shares are shown for the year ended July 18, 1999.

Brita 66%
PUR 21
Other 13

Source: *Wall Street Journal*, August 27, 1999, p. B2, from Information Resources Inc.

★ 926 ★

Motors (SIC 3594)

Fractional Horsepower Motor Demand

Sales are shown in millions of dollars.

	1998	2003	Share
Light vehicles	$ 3,010	$ 3,500	33.64%
Industrial machinery & others	1,855	2,315	22.25
Appliances & durables . . .	1,270	1,500	14.42
Heating & cooling	1,265	1,540	14.80
Computer & office	1,195	1,550	14.90

Source: *Appliance*, August 1999, p. 19, from Freedonia Group.

SIC 36 - Electronic and Other Electric Equipment

★ 927 ★

Electronics (SIC 3600)

Factory Electronics Sales - 1999

Sales are shown in millions of dollars for the first six months of the year.

	($ mil.)	Share
Electronic components	$ 72,528	29.73%
Computers & peripherals	45,638	18.71
Telecommunications	41,595	17.05
Industrial electronics	17,876	7.33
Defense communications	15,644	6.41
Electromedical equipment	6,577	2.70
Consumer electronics	4,352	1.78
Other	39,739	16.29

Source: *Electronic Packaging & Production*, September 1999, p. 8, from U.S. Department of Commerce and EIA Market Research.

★ 928 ★

Motion Control Instruments (SIC 3625)

Motion Control Market - 2000

Data are for North America.

Standalone controllers and drives	42.3%
PC-bus boards	38.5
PLCs	9.8
Non-PC bus	5.5

Source: *Design News*, July 19, 1999, p. 62, from ARC.

★ 929 ★

Cooking Equipment (SIC 3631)

Electric Range Market

Shares are shown based on shipments.

GE	43%
Whirlpool	21
Maytag	18
Electrolux	11
Other	7

Source: *Appliance*, September 1999, p. 77.

★ 930 ★

Cooking Equipment (SIC 3631)

Leading Gas Range Makers - 1999

Shares are shown based on domestic shipments.

Kenmore	17.7%
GE/Profile	16.4
Whirlpool	11.8
Maytag	9.7
Magic Chef	7.1
Tappan	6.6
Other	30.7

Source: *HFN*, March 27, 2000, p. 89, from Association of Home Appliance Manufacturers.

★ 931 ★
Cooking Equipment (SIC 3631)

Leading Microwave Makers - 1999

Shares are shown based on domestic shipments.

Sharp	28.6%
GE/Profile	13.8
Kenmore	11.5
Panasonic	9.6
Whirlpool	6.5
Samsung	5.8
Other	24.2

Source: *HFN*, March 27, 2000, p. 89, from Association of Home Appliance Manufacturers.

★ 932 ★
Cooking Equipment (SIC 3631)

Microwave Oven Market - 1998

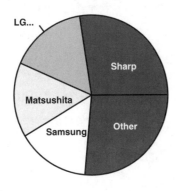

Shares are shown based on shipments.

Sharp	29%
LG Electronics/Goldstar	17
Matsushita	16
Samsung	16
Other	28

Source: *Appliance*, September 1999, p. 77.

★ 933 ★
Cooking Equipment (SIC 3631)

Outdoor Grill Market - 1998

Shares are shown based on unit shipments.

Bradley	36%
Sunbeam Outdoor Products	32
Ducane	4
Thermos/Structo	4
Weber-Stephen	4
Others	20

Source: *Appliance*, September 1999, p. 77.

★ 934 ★
Cooking Equipment (SIC 3631)

Top Deep Fryer Brands - 1999

Shares are for the first half of the year.

Presto	66%
Dazey	15
Sunbeam	4
Rival	3
T-Fal	2
Others	10

Source: "NPD Reports Fryer Sales Sizzle." Retrieved December 2, 1999 from the World Wide Web: http://www.intelectmt.com/corp/intelectmt/press, from NPD Intelect.

★ 935 ★
Cooking Equipment (SIC 3631)

Top Range Hood Makers - 1998

Shares are estimated based on shipments.

Broan/Nutone	69%
Rangaire	16
Other	15

Source: *Appliance Manufacturer*, April 1999, p. 19.

★ 936 ★
Freezers (SIC 3632)

Top Freezer Makers - 1998

Shares are shown based on shipments.

Electrolux (Frigidaire)	68%
W.C. Wood	31
Sanyo	1

Source: *Appliance*, September 1999, p. 77.

★ 937 ★
Refrigerators (SIC 3632)

Compact Refrigerator Market - 1998

Shares are shown based on shipments. Market includes compact, built-in and undercounter models.

U-Line	61%
Marvel Industries	29
Sub-Zero Freezer	9
Others	1

Source: *Appliance*, September 1999, p. 77.

★ 938 ★
Refrigerators (SIC 3632)

Top Refrigerator Makers - 1998

GEA	
Whirlpool	
Electrolux	
Maytag	
Goodman	

Shares are shown bsed on shipments.

GEA	36%
Whirlpool	28
Electrolux	16
Maytag	13
Goodman	7

Source: *Appliance Manufacturer*, April 1999, p. 19.

★ 939 ★
Laundry Equipment (SIC 3633)

Electric Dryer Market

Shares are shown based on shipments.

Whirlpool	55%
GE	18
Maytag	16
Electrolux (Frigiadaire)	6
Goodman (Speed Queen)	5

Source: *Appliance*, September 1999, p. 77.

★ 940 ★
Laundry Equipment (SIC 3633)

Leading Automatic Washer Makers - 1999

Shares are shown based on domestic shipments.

Kennmore	27.9%
Maytag	20.5
Whirlpool	19.3
GE/Profile	11.1
Frigidaire	6.8
Amana	3.5
Other	10.9

Source: *HFN*, March 27, 2000, p. 89, from Association of Home Appliance Manufacturers.

★ 941 ★
Laundry Equipment (SIC 3633)

Top Dryer Makers - 1998

Shares are estimated based on shipments. Figures are for both electric and gas.

Whirlpool	51%
Maytag	19
GEA	17
Electrolux	8
Goodman	5

Source: *Appliance Manufacturer*, April 1999, p. 19.

★ 942 ★

Laundry Equipment (SIC 3633)

Top Washer Makers - 1998

Shares are shown based on unit shipments.

Whirlpool	53%
Maytag	21
GE	15
Other	11

Source: *Appliance*, September 1999, p. 77.

★ 943 ★

Household Appliances (SIC 3634)

Largest Air Purifier Makers - 1998

Shares are shown based on estimated shipments.

Holmes	38%
Honeywell	19
Rival (Bionaire)	10
Duracraft	8
Sunbeam	6
Hunter	4
Others	15

Source: *Appliance Manufacturer*, April 1999, p. 20.

★ 944 ★

Household Appliances (SIC 3634)

Small Electrics Market - 1998

Hamilton Beach/Proctor-Silex	40.6%
Black & Decker	15.9
Sunbeam-Oster	8.0
Signature Brands USA	5.8
Rival	4.1
Appliance Corp.	3.3
Toastmaster	3.0

Braun	2.4%
Other	25.2

Source: *Appliance Manufacturer*, April 1999, p. 22.

★ 945 ★

Household Appliances (SIC 3634)

Standalone Mixer Market - 1999

Shares are for the first 10 months of the year.

KitchenAid	83%
Other	17

Source: *Advertising Age*, December 13, 1999, p. 4, from NPD Intelect.

★ 946 ★

Household Appliances (SIC 3634)

Top Blender Makers - 1998

Shares are shown based on estimated shipments.

Hamilton Beach/Proctor Silex	55%
Sunbeam-Oster	28
Braun	6
Appliance Corp. (Betty Crocker)	5
Others	6

Source: *Appliance Manufacturer*, April 1999, p. 20.

★ 947 ★

Household Appliances (SIC 3634)

Top Breadmaker Producers - 1998

Shares are shown based on shipments.

West Bend	20%
Oster/Sunbeam	16
Regal	16
Appliance Corp.	15
Toastermaster	10
Other	23

Source: *Appliance*, September 1999, p. 78.

★ 948 ★
Household Appliances (SIC 3634)

Top Can Opener Makers - 1998

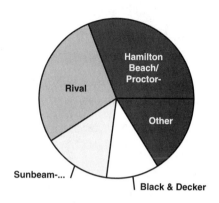

Hamilton Beach/Proctor-Silex	31%
Rival	28
Sunbeam-Oster	14
Black & Decker	11
Other	16

Source: *Appliance Manufacturer*, April 1999, p. 21.

★ 949 ★
Household Appliances (SIC 3634)

Top Drip Coffeemaker Producers - 1998

Shares are shown based on shipments.

Hamilton Beach/Proctor-Silex	30%
Signature Brands USA	28
Black & Decker	11
Appliance Corp. (Betty Crocker)	7
Braun	7
Krups	6
Others	11

Source: *Appliance Manufacturer*, April 1999, p. 21.

★ 950 ★
Household Appliances (SIC 3634)

Top Electric Knive Makers - 1998

Shares are shown based on shipments.

Hamilton Beach/Proctor-Silex	38%
Black & Decker	28
Toastmaster	17
Other	17

Source: *Appliance*, September 1999, p. 78.

★ 951 ★
Household Appliances (SIC 3634)

Top Food Chopper Makers - 1998

Shares are shown based on shipments.

Black & Decker	35%
Hamilton Beach/Proctor-Silex	18
Cuisinart	13
Toastmaster	12
Other	22

Source: *Appliance*, September 1999, p. 78.

★ 952 ★
Household Appliances (SIC 3634)

Top Food Processor Makers - 1998

Shares are shown based on shipments.

Hamilton Beach/Proctor-Silex	44%
Cuisinart	20
Black & Decker	9
Sunbeam-Oster	5
KitchenAid	5
Braun	5
Others	12

Source: *Appliance Manufacturer*, April 1999, p. 22.

★ 953 ★

Household Appliances (SIC 3634)

Top Hand Mixer Makers - 1998

Hamilton Beach/Proctor Silex
Black & Decker
Oster/Sunbeam
West Bend
KitchenAid
Rival
Other

Shares are shown based on shipments.

Hamilton Beach/Proctor Silex	36%
Black & Decker	13
Oster/Sunbeam	12
West Bend	7
KitchenAid	5
Rival	5
Other	22

Source: *Appliance*, September 1999, p. 78.

★ 954 ★

Household Appliances (SIC 3634)

Top Humidifer Makers - 1998

Shares are shown based on estimated shipments.

Holmes	44%
Honeywell/Duracraft	30
Rival (Bionaire)	8
Other	18

Source: *Appliance Manufacturer*, April 1999, p. 20.

★ 955 ★

Household Appliances (SIC 3634)

Top Iron Makers - 1998

Shares are shown based on shipments.

Black & Decker	35%
Hamilton Beach/Proctor Silex	33
Oster/Sunbeam	13
Rowenta	7
Other	12

Source: *Appliance*, September 1999, p. 78.

★ 956 ★

Household Appliances (SIC 3634)

Top Percolator Makers

Shares are shown based on shipments.

Appliance Corp. (Betty Crocker, Welbilt)	40%
Regal Ware	31
West Bend	15
Other	14

Source: *Appliance Manufacturer*, April 1999, p. 22.

★ 957 ★

Household Appliances (SIC 3634)

Top Rice Cooker Producers - 1998

Shares are shown based on shipments.

Black & Decker	34%
Aroma Manufacturing	17
Oster/Sunbeam	15
Rival	10
Other	24

Source: *Appliance*, September 1999, p. 78.

★ 958 ★

Household Appliances (SIC 3634)

Top Toaster Makers - 1998

Shares are shown based on shipments.

Hamilton Beach/Procotr-Silex	60%
Toastmaster	17
Rival	5
Black & Decker	2
Appliance Corp (Betty Crocker)	2
Others	14

Source: *Appliance Manufacturer*, April 1999, p. 22.

★ 959 ★

Household Appliances (SIC 3634)

Top Waffle Iron Makers - 1998

Shares are shown based on shipments.

Salton	27%
Hamilton Beach/Proctor-Silex	15
Oster-Sunbeam	10
Other	48

Source: *Appliance*, September 1999, p. 78.

★ 960 ★

Personal Care Appliances (SIC 3634)

Curling Iron Market - 1998

Helen of Troy	41%
Conair	38
Windmere	9
Belson	4
Others	8

Source: *Appliance*, September 1999, p. 77.

★ 961 ★

Personal Care Appliances (SIC 3634)

Electric Toothbrush Market

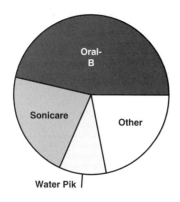

The $229 million market is shown in percent. Braun makes Oral-B; Optiva Corp. makes Sonicare; Teledyne makes Water Pik.

	($ mil.)	Share
Oral-B	$ 107.5	46.94%
Sonicare	49.6	21.66
Water Pik	22.2	9.69
Other	49.7	21.70

Source: *Advertising Age*, April 3, 2000, p. 10, from Information Resources Inc.

★ 962 ★

Personal Care Appliances (SIC 3634)

Hair Dryer Market

Shares are shown based on shipments. Figures are for the hand-held market.

Conair	40%
Helen of Troy	30
Windmere	11
Remington	2
Other	17

Source: *Appliance Manufacturer*, April 1999, p. 21.

★ 963 ★

Personal Care Appliances (SIC 3634)

Hair Setter Market - 1998

Shares are shown based on shipments.

Conair	42%
Helen of Troy	22
Remington/Clairol	20
Others	16

Source: *Appliance*, September 1999, p. 77.

★ 964 ★

Personal Care Appliances (SIC 3634)

Lighted Make-Up Mirror Market - 1998

Shares are shown based on shipments.

Conair	37%
Windmere	17
Revlon	15
Hartman	15
Other	13

Source: *Appliance*, September 1999, p. 77.

★ 965 ★

Personal Care Appliances (SIC 3634)

Men's Shaver Market

Shares are shown based on shipments.

Norelco	55%
Remington	22
Braun	15
Wahl	5
Matsushita	3

Source: *Appliance Manufacturer*, April 1999, p. 21.

★ 966 ★

Personal Care Appliances (SIC 3634)

Women's Shaver Market - 1998

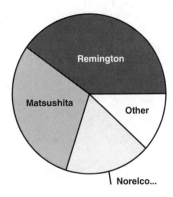

Shares are shown based on shipments.

Remington	40%
Matsushita (Panasonic)	30
Norelco Consumer Products	18
Other	12

Source: *Appliance*, September 1999, p. 77.

★ 967 ★

Floor Care Equipment (SIC 3635)

Top Extractor Makers - 1998

Shares are shown based on shipments.

Hoover	55%
Bissell	38
Eureka	4
Others	3

Source: *Appliance Manufacturer*, April 1999, p. 21.

★ 968 ★

Floor Care Equipment (SIC 3635)

Top Floor Polishers - 1998

Shares are shown based on shipments.

Hoover	70%
Thorne Electric	20
Electrolux	10

Source: *Appliance Manufacturer*, April 1999, p. 21.

★ 969 ★

Vacuum Cleaners (SIC 3635)

Hand-Held Vacuum Cleaner Market - 1998

Shares are shown based on shipments.

Royal	43%
Black & Decker	25
Hoover	14
Bissell	6
Other	12

Source: *Appliance Manufacturer*, April 1999, p. 21.

★ 970 ★

Vacuum Cleaners (SIC 3635)

Vacuum Cleaner Market - 1998

Shares are shown based on shipments.

Hoover	34%
Eureka	27
Royal	13
Matsushita	9
Other	17

Source: *Appliance*, September 1999, p. 76.

★ 971 ★

Vacuum Cleaners (SIC 3635)

Vacuum Cleaner Sales - 1998

A total of 16.3 milion units were sold for the year. Sales are shown by type.

Uprights	45.3%
Stick vacs	19.9
Hand vacs	17.1
Extractors	9.3
Wet/dry	5.9
Canisters	2.5

Source: *Discount Store News*, May 24, 1999, p. D1, from Vacuum Cleaner Manufacturers Association.

★ 972 ★

Vacuum Cleaners (SIC 3635)

Wet/Dry Vac Market - 1998

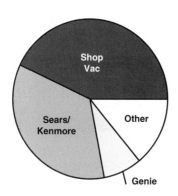

Shares are shown based on shipments.

Shop Vac	43%
Sears/Kenmore	35
Genie	8
Other	14

Source: *Appliance*, September 1999, p. 76.

★ 973 ★

Dishwashers (SIC 3639)

Top Dishwasher Makers - 1998

Market shares are shown based on shipments.

Whirlpool	39%
GEA	37
Maytag	18
Electrolux	6

Source: *Appliance Manufacturer*, April 1999, p. 19.

★ 974 ★

Dishwashers (SIC 3639)

Top Dishwasher Makers - 1999

Shares are shown based on domestic shipments.

Kenmore	24.6%
Maytag	18.8
Whirlpool	16.0
GE/Profile	14.5
Figidaire	8.2
KitchenAid	8.0
Other	9.9

Source: *HFN*, March 27, 2000, p. 89, from Association of Home Appliance Manufacturers.

★ 975 ★

Garbage Disposals (SIC 3639)

Garbage Disposal Market - 1998

Shares are shown based on shipments.

In-Sink-Erator	77%
Anaheim Manufacturing	22
Others	1

Source: *Appliance*, September 1999, p. 77.

★ 976 ★

Trash Compactors (SIC 3639)

Top Compactor Makers - 1998

Shares are estimated based on shipments.

Whirlpool	89%
Broan	11

Source: *Appliance Manufacturer*, April 1999, p. 1.

★ 977 ★

Light Bulbs (SIC 3641)

Incandescent Bulb Sales - 1999

Sales are shown for the year ended May 1999.

A19	46%
Decorative	12
Incandescent reflectors	8
Appliance	6
Incandescent par	4
Globe	3
Other	21

Source: *Do-It-Yourself Retailing*, September 1999, p. 104, from Vista Sales and Marketing.

★ 978 ★

Light Bulbs (SIC 3641)

Top Light Bulb Brands - 1999

The $1.05 billion market is shown in percent for the year ended January 2, 2000.

GE Lighting	66.0%
GE Miser	6.0
Sylvania	4.9
GE Long Life	2.0
Phillips	1.7
GE Kitchen/Bath	0.9
Light of America	0.8
Private label	8.8
Other	8.9

Source: *Supermarket Business*, March 15, 2000, p. 85, from Information Resources Inc.

★ 979 ★

Light Bulbs (SIC 3641)

Top Light Bulb Makers - 1999

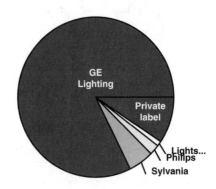

The $1.05 billion market is shown in percent for the year ended January 2, 2000.

	($ mil.)	Share
GE Lighting	$ 827.9	78.6%
Sylvania	56.8	5.4
Philips	19.9	1.9
Lights of America	7.9	0.8
Private label	92.3	8.8

Source: *Supermarket Business*, March 15, 2000, p. 85, from Information Resources Inc.

★ 980 ★

Consumer Electronics (SIC 3651)

Consumer Electronics Leaders - 1998

Shares are shown based on shipments.

Sony	22.4%
Thomson	13.0
Matsushita	9.9
NAP	9.2
Pioneer	6.2
Other	39.3

Source: *Appliance Manufacturer*, April 1999, p. 22.

★ 981 ★

Consumer Electronics (SIC 3651)

DVD Player Market in Canada - 1999

Shares are shown based on sales of 274,000 units for the year ended March 31, 2000.

Pioneer	22.3%
Toshiba	20.6

Continued on next page.

★ 981 ★ *Continued*

Consumer Electronics (SIC 3651)

DVD Player Market in Canada - 1999

Shares are shown based on sales of 274,000 units for the year ended March 31, 2000.

Sony	18.3%
Panasonic	13.5
RCA/Proscan	9.0
JVC	5.2
Hitachi	3.1
Samsung	2.4
Others	5.6

Source: ''Report on Market Share.'' Retrieved June 8, 2000 from the World Wide Web: http://www.marketingmag.ca, from industry sources.

★ 982 ★

Consumer Electronics (SIC 3651)

Healthcare Dictation Market

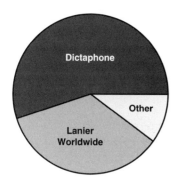

Dictaphone	55%
Lanier Worldwide	35
Other	10

Source: *New York Times*, December 27, 1999, p. C3, from APS Financial Corporation and company reports.

★ 983 ★

Consumer Electronics (SIC 3651)

Top Camcorder Makers - 1998

Shares are shown based on shipments.

Sony	33%
Thomson	20
JVC	15
Matsushita	15
Other	17

Source: *Appliance*, September 1999, p. 76.

★ 984 ★

Consumer Electronics (SIC 3651)

Top CD Player Makers - 1998

Shares are shown based on shipments.

Sony	36%
Pioneer	13
Matsushita	11
Kenwood	8
Sanyo Fisher	7
NAP	6
JVC	6
Others	13

Source: *Appliance Manufacturer*, April 1999, p. 22.

★ 985 ★

Consumer Electronics (SIC 3651)

Top CD Player Producers

Shares are shown based on shipments.

Sony	26%
N.A.P.	18
Pioneer	11
Matsushita	10
Other	35

Source: *Appliance*, September 1999, p. 76.

★ 986 ★

Consumer Electronics (SIC 3651)

Top Digital Camcorder Makers - 1999

Sony	67.5%
JVC	22.2
Canon	4.8
Pansonic	4.5
Sharp	1.0

Source: "NPD Intelect Sees Digital Imaging Going Main-stream." Retrieved May 1, 2000 from the World Wide Web: http://www.intelectmt.com, from NPD Intelect.

★ 987 ★

Consumer Electronics (SIC 3651)

Top VCR Makers - 1998

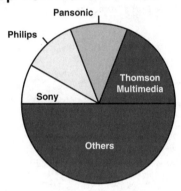

Thomson Multimedia	19%
Pansonic	12
Philips	11
Sony	8
Others	50

Source: *Investor's Business Daily*, December 20, 1999, p. A10, from company reports, CG Gowen, and Consumer Electronics Association.

★ 988 ★

Consumer Electronics (SIC 3651)

Top VCR Producers - 1998

Shares are shown based on shipments.

Thomson	18%
NAP	12
Matsushita	12
Emerson	7
Sony	6

LG Electronics (Zenith)	6%
JVC	6
Fisher	5
Sanyo Fisher	5
Others	23

Source: *Appliance Manufacturer*, April 1999, p. 22.

★ 989 ★

Consumer Electronics (SIC 3651)

TV Set Market - 1999

Market shares are shown for the third quarter of the year.

Philips/Magnavox	12.5%
Sanyo	12.0
RCA	12.0
Zenith	9.0
Sony	8.2
Panasonic	7.2
Sharp	7.1
Toshiba	5.3
Other	26.7

Source: *Wall Street Journal*, August 10, 1999, p. B6, from Intelect/NPD Group.

★ 990 ★

Consumer Electronics (SIC 3651)

TV Set Market - 30-35 Inches

2.15 million units were sold for the year ended June 1998.

Sony	19.0%
RCA	16.8
Toshiba	13.0
Zenith	10.1
Panasonic	7.9
Other	33.2

Source: Retrieved January 26, 2000 from the World Wide Web: http://www.hkeia.com/E-news/enewsdec/colorTV. htm, from *Twice* and Scout Report American.

★ 991 ★

Consumer Electronics (SIC 3651)

TV Set Market - Over 39 Inches

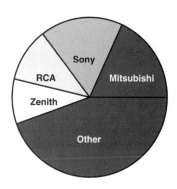

500,000 units were sold for the year ended June 1998.

Mitsubishi	19.6%
Sony	19.1
RCA	12.2
Zenith	10.0
Other	49.1

Source: Retrieved January 26, 2000 from the World Wide Web: http://www.hkeia.com/E-news/enewsdec/colorTV. htm, from *Twice* and Scout Report American.

★ 992 ★

Consumer Electronics (SIC 3651)

TV Set Market - Under 18 Inches

Total sales reached $405.1 million, their highest since 1996. Data show selected shares.

Orion	11.0%
Magnavox	10.7
Sony	8.1
Other	70.2

Source: Retrieved January 26, 2000 from the World Wide Web: http://www.hkeia.com/E-news/enewsdec/colorTV. htm, from *Twice* and Scout Report American.

★ 993 ★

Prerecorded Music (SIC 3652)

Album Sales by Genre - 1999

Sales are shown in millions of units for January 1, 1999 - January 2, 2000.

R&B	175.3
Alternative	120.9

Rap	87.6
Country	69.3
Christian/gospel	46.8
Soundtrack	41.6
Metal	29.7
Latin	22.2
Jazz	19.5
Classical	17.3
New age	5.8

Source: Retrieved February 17, 2000 from the World Wide Web: http://library.northernlight.com, from Soundscan.

★ 994 ★

Prerecorded Music (SIC 3652)

Best-Selling Albums - 1999

Sales are shown in millions of units.

Millennium	9.4
...Baby One More Time	8.4
Ricky Martin	6.0
Come On Over	5.6
Significant Other	5.0
Supernatural	4.7
Devil Without A Cause	4.3
Fanmail	4.2
Christina Aguilera	3.7
Wide Open Spaces	3.5

Source: *Billboard*, January 22, 2000, p. 63, from Soundscan.

★ 995 ★

Prerecorded Music (SIC 3652)

Best-Selling R&B/Hip Hop Albums - 1999

Sales are shown in millions of units.

Fanmail	4.2
Juvenile	3.3
The Slim Shady LP	2.8
The Miseducation of Lauryn Hill	2.7
Rainbow	2.1
Dr. Dre 2001	1.9

Source: *Rolling Stone*, February 17, 2000, p. 63, from Soundscan.

★ 996 ★
Prerecorded Music (SIC 3652)

Best-Selling Rock Albums - 1999

Sales are shown in millions of units.

Significant Other	4.9
Supernatural, ...	4.7
Devil Without A Cause, ...	4.3
Americana	2.9
Astra Lounge	2.5
Enema of the State	2.4

Source: *Rolling Stone*, February 17, 2000, p. 63, from Soundscan.

★ 997 ★
Prerecorded Music (SIC 3652)

Best-Selling Summer Singles

Sales are shown in thousands of units for May 23 - August 15, 1999.

"Genie in a Bottle" by Christina Aguilera . .	1,230
"If You Had My Love" by J. Lopez	1,078
"Bills, Bills, Bills" by Destiny's Child . . .	849
"Last Kiss" by Pearl Jam	769
"Fortunate" by Maxwell	563

Source: *Entertainment Weekly*, September 3, 1999, p. 26, from Soundscan.

★ 998 ★
Prerecorded Music (SIC 3652)

Christian Music Market

Integrity Incorporated ranked No. 1 among praise and worship companies and No. 2 among all companies producing Christian music. Its listed share refers to the praise and worship, non-artist-title category.

Integrity	58%
Other	42

Source: "Integrity Expands Market Share." Retrieved February 24, 2000 from the World Wide Web: http://library.northernlight.com, from Sounscan.

★ 999 ★
Prerecorded Music (SIC 3652)

Country Music Distributors - 1999

Market shares are shown in percent.

Universal	28.5%
WEA	21.5
Sony	18.1
BMG	17.3
EMD	9.5
Indies	5.2

Source: *Billboard*, January 22, 2000, p. 57, from Soundscan.

★ 1000 ★
Prerecorded Music (SIC 3652)

Hispanic Music Sales - 1997

Shipments are shown in millions of dollars.

	($ mil.)	Share
CDs	$ 344.7	70.26%
Cassettes	144.6	29.47
Music videos	1.3	0.26

Source: "Hispanic Record Sales." Retrieved November 1, 1999 from the World Wide Web: http://www.riaa.com/stats/sthrs.htm, from Recording Industry Association of America.

★ 1001 ★
Prerecorded Music (SIC 3652)

Internet Album Sales - 1999

Sales are shown in millions of units for January 1, 1999 - January 2, 2000.

	(mil.)	Share
Albums	754.8	50.00%
CDs	648.1	42.93
Cassettes	105.1	6.96
Other	1.6	0.11

Source: Retrieved February 17, 2000 from the World Wide Web: http://library.northernlight.com, from Soundscan.

★ 1002 ★
Prerecorded Music (SIC 3652)
Music Leaders - 1999

Unit shares are shown for the first six months of the year.

Universal	27%
Independents	17
Warner Music	17
Sony	16
BMG	14
EMI	10

Source: *USA TODAY*, August 25, 1999, p. 2B, from Soundscan via Merrill Lynch.

★ 1003 ★
Prerecorded Music (SIC 3652)
Music Market in Canada - 1999

Shares are shown based on sales of 64 million units for the year ended December 31, 1999.

Universal Music	27.2%
Sony	18.6
Warner Music	14.3
EMI	13.2
BMG	12.4
Others	14.3

Source: "Report on Market Share." Retrieved June 8, 2000 from the World Wide Web: http://www. marketingmag.ca, from HMV Canada.

★ 1004 ★
Prerecorded Music (SIC 3652)
Music Sales by Age - 1998

45+ years	18.1%
15-19 years	15.8
35-39 years	12.6
20-24 years	12.2
30-34 years	11.4
25-29 years	11.4

10-14 years	9.1%
40-44 years	8.3

Source: *Discount Merchandiser*, August 1999, p. 68, from Recording Industry Association of America.

★ 1005 ★
Prerecorded Music (SIC 3652)
Music Sales by Format - 1998

CDs	74.8%
Cassettes	14.8
Singles (all types)	6.8
Music videos	1.0
Vinyl LPs	0.7

Source: *Discount Merchandiser*, August 1999, p. 68, from Recording Industry Association of America.

★ 1006 ★
Prerecorded Music (SIC 3652)
Music Sales by Segment - 1998

Rock	25.7%
Country	14.1
R&B	12.8
Pop	10.0
Rap	9.7
Gospel	6.3
Other	16.5

Source: *Discount Merchandiser*, August 1999, p. 68, from Recording Industry Association of America.

★ 1007 ★
Prerecorded Music (SIC 3652)
R&B Music Distributors - 1999

Market shares are shown in percent.

Universal	38.4%
BMG	17.3
Sony	16.2
EMD	11.1
WEA	8.8
Indies	8.1

Source: *Billboard*, January 22, 2000, p. 57, from Soundscan.

★ 1008 ★

Prerecorded Music (SIC 3652)

Record Market Sales - 1998

Sales are shown in millions of units. The industry had 5.7% net unit increase in sales from 1997 to 1998, with the industry reaching an estimated value of $14 bilion.

	Units	Share
CDs	847.0	77.80%
Cassettes	158.5	14.56
CD single units	56.0	5.14
Music videos	27.2	2.50

Source: "U.S. Record Sales." Retrieved November 30, 1999 from the World Wide Web: http://www.riaa.com/stats/stusrs.htm, from Recording Industry Association of America.

★ 1009 ★

Prerecorded Music (SIC 3652)

Singles Music Distributors - 1999

Market shares are shown in percent.

BMG	27.7%
Sony	22.2
Universal	17.9
WEA	15.0
Indies	8.3
EMD	8.1

Source: *Billboard*, January 22, 2000, p. 57, from Soundscan.

★ 1010 ★

Fax Machines (SIC 3661)

Fax Machine Market - 1998

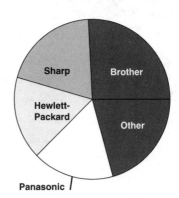

Shares are shown based on shipments.

Brother	25.8%
Sharp	19.8
Hewlett-Packard	17.3
Panasonic	16.6
Other	20.5

Source: *Appliance*, September 1999, p. 78, from Dataquest Inc.

★ 1011 ★

Fax Machines (SIC 3661)

High-End Plain Paper Fax Market - 1998

Market shares are shown in percent.

Sharp	45.3%
Canon	43.9
Muratec	6.1
Menolta	1.8
Other	0.9

Source: "Market Share Information." Retrieved November 9, 1999 from the World Wide Web: http://www.sharp-usa.com, from Dataquest.

★ 1012 ★

Fax Machines (SIC 3661)

Laser Facsimile Machine Market

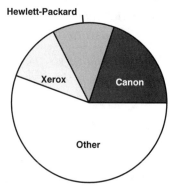

Shares are shown based on unit shipments.

Canon	19.9%
Hewlett-Packard	12.7
Xerox	11.6
Other	55.8

Source: ''Final IDC Reports Canon No. 1.'' Retrieved May 15, 2000 from the World Wide Web: http://www.businesswire.net, from International Data Corp.

★ 1013 ★

Fax Machines (SIC 3661)

Top Teletype/Fax Machine Providers to Government

The top providers are ranked by share of total contracts.

Meridian One Corp.	28.50%
Fax Plus Inc.	17.66
Ricoh Corp.	13.63
Northrop Grumman Corp.	3.87
Datametrics Corp.	3.41
Other	32.93

Source: *Government Executive*, 1999, p. 112.

★ 1014 ★

Fax Machines (SIC 3661)

Workgroup Multifunctional Fax Market - 1998

Market shares are shown in percent.

Sharp	32.0%
Xerox	25.2
Canon	14.9
Jetfax	7.4
Lanier	4.5
Pitney Bowles	3.3

Source: ''Market Share Information.'' Retrieved November 9, 1999 from the World Wide Web: http://www.sharp-usa.com, from Dataquest.

★ 1015 ★

Modems (SIC 3661)

Cable Modem Market - 1999

Shares are shown for the third quarter of the year.

Motorola	37.2%
Arris Interactive/Nortel	12.6
Com21	9.6
Terayon	8.2
General Instrument	7.1
Other	25.3

Source: *Investor's Business Daily*, December 28, 1999, p. A6, from Dataquest Inc.

★ 1016 ★

Modems (SIC 3661)

Modem Market Shares

Data are as of October 1998.

28.8K/33.6K bps	38.9%
56.6K bps	17.0
14.4K bps	15.6
9.6K bps and slower	3.1
Other	16.0

Source: Retrieved January 4, 2000 from the World Wide Web: http://www.infotechtrends.com, from *Computer Retail Week* and Media Metrix.

★ 1017 ★
Telephones (SIC 3661)

Cordless Phone Market

Shares are shown based on shipments.

AT&T/Lucent 22%
GE 14
Sony 12
Bellsouth 10
Other 41

Source: *Appliance*, September 1999, p. 76.

★ 1018 ★
Cellular Phones (SIC 3663)

Top Cell Phone Markets

Data show the share of adults living in a household with a cell phone.

Chicago, IL 55.3%
Charlotte, NC 54.0
Detroit, MI 51.3
Greensboro/Winston-Salem, NC 50.5
St. Louis, MO 50.1
Atlanta, GA 48.3
Austin, TX 48.0

Source: *Detroiter*, January 2000, p. 6, from Scarborough Research.

★ 1019 ★
Cellular Phones (SIC 3663)

Top Cellular Phone Makers - 1999

Shares of the digital handset market are shown for the first quarter of the year.

Nokia 32.4%
Qualcomm 14.8
Ericsson 12.7
Motorola 11.2
Audiovox 7.4
Samsung 6.7
Sony 6.6
Mitsubishi 2.3

Source: *RCR*, July 5, 1999, p. 1, from Dataquest Inc.

★ 1020 ★
Cellular Phones (SIC 3663)

Wireless Handset Market - 1999

Data are for the second quarter of the year.

Digital 77.8%
Analog 22.2

Source: *Investor's Business Daily*, October 8, 1999, p. A6, from Dataquest Inc.

★ 1021 ★
Cellular Phones (SIC 3663)

Wireless Phone Makers - 1999

Unit shares are shown in percent.

Nokia 34.5%
Motorola 23.1
Qualcomm 12.0
Other 30.4

Source: *Twice*, February 7, 2000, p. 19, from Strategis Group.

★ 1022 ★
Pagers (SIC 3663)

Pager Market by Segment - 2002

Numeric 61.4%
Two-way or 1.5 . . . . 19.3
Voice 9.9
Alphanumeric 9.8

Source: *Los Angeles Times*, November 11, 1999, p. C1, from Personal Communications Industry Association and Yankee Group.

★ 1023 ★
Calling Cards (SIC 3669)

Prepaid Calling Card Market

Consumers 75%
Business travelers 10
College students 8
Mobile Workforce 6

Source: Retrieved January 4, 2000 from the World Wide Web: http://www.infotechtrends.com, from *Telecommunications* and Frost & Sullivan.

★ 1024 ★
Castings (SIC 3669)

U.S. Metal Casting Shipments - 2000

Shipments are in thousands of tons.

	(000)	Share
Gray iron	5,441	39.29%
Ductile iron	4,095	29.57
Aluminum	1,905	13.75
Steel	1,353	9.77
Zinc	345	2.49
Copper-base	301	2.17
Malleable iron	165	1.19
Other	245	1.77

Source: *Modern Casting*, January 2000, p. 30.

★ 1025 ★
Information Devices (SIC 3669)

Industrial Asset Monitoring

The market for devices to monitor industrial assets is estimated to be 160 million units.

Fixed asset monitoring	35%
Messaging	25
Mobile asset monitoring	10
Other	30

Source: *Investor's Business Daily*, April 17, 2000, p. A8, from Obcomm Global LP.

★ 1026 ★
Networking Equipment (SIC 3669)

Access Concentrator Market - 1999

Data are for the first quarter.

Ascend	31%
Cisco	30
3Com	24
Other	15

Source: *Business Communications Review*, July 1999, p. 8, from Cahenrs In-Stat Group.

★ 1027 ★
Networking Equipment (SIC 3669)

ASP Industry

Shares are shown by number of contacts.

Usi	36%
Breakaway	16
Oracle	9
Corio	9
FutureLink	7
Other	23

Source: *VAR Business*, February 21, 2000, p. 16, from Internet Research Group.

★ 1028 ★
Networking Equipment (SIC 3669)

ATM LAN Switch Market Leaders

Fore Systems	32.9%
Cisco	27.6
Nortel	13.3
Others	26.2

Source: *Business Communications Review*, October 1999, p. 8, from Cahners In-Stat Group.

★ 1029 ★
Networking Equipment (SIC 3669)
ATM Switch Makers - 1998

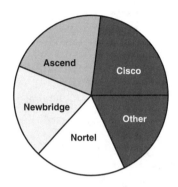

Cisco	23%
Ascend	21
Newbridge	19
Nortel	19
Other	18

Source: *Investor's Business Daily*, June 28, 1999, p. A6, from International Data Corp.

★ 1030 ★
Networking Equipment (SIC 3669)
ATM WAN Switch Market Leaders

Lucent	36%
Cisco	23
Nortel	12
Other	29

Source: *Business Communications Review*, October 1999, p. 8, from Cahners In-Stat Group.

★ 1031 ★
Networking Equipment (SIC 3669)
Broadband Access - 2004

High-speed Internet connections are expected to reach 24 million subscribers by 2004.

Cable modems	47%
Digital subscriber lines	45
Satellite/wireless	8

Source: *Investor's Business Daily*, December 9, 1999, p. A6, from Parks Associates.

★ 1032 ★
Networking Equipment (SIC 3669)
Core Device Market

Shares are shown based on revenues.

Cisco	46%
Lucent	31
Fore	10
Juniper	7
Nortel	3
NEC	3

Source: *Telephony*, April 3, 2000, p. 8, from RHK.

★ 1033 ★
Networking Equipment (SIC 3669)
Core Switch and Router Device Market in North America - 1999

Shares are for the second half of the year. The study defines a core device as a product that functions at the center of the network and performs high-speed forwarding.

Cisco	48%
Lucent	27
Juniper Networks	9
Other	16

Source: "New Study by RHK Shows Cisco Secure Top Billing." Retrieved April 24, 2000 from the World Wide Web: http://www.businesswire.com, from RHK Inc.

★ 1034 ★
Networking Equipment (SIC 3669)
Digital Loop Carrier Market - 1999

Alcatel	28%
Lucent	20
Nortel	20
RelTec	14
Advanced Fibre	10
Other	8

Source: *Investor's Business Daily*, November 24, 1999, p. A10, from RHK.

★ 1035 ★

Networking Equipment (SIC 3669)

DSL Equipment Market Shares

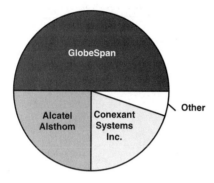

Shares are shown in percent. Digital subscriber lines in the United States grew sevenfold from the first quarter of 1999 to the fourth quarter.

GlobeSpan 50%
Alcatel Alsthom 25
Conexant Systems Inc. 20
Other 5

Source: *Investor's Business Daily*, April 11, 2000, p. A12.

★ 1036 ★

Networking Equipment (SIC 3669)

Fiber Optic Network Gear Industry - 2000

In 1999, the access products segment had a 97% share, with optical switching gear holding the balance.

Long-haul products 50%
Metropolitan-area networks 23
Optical switching gear 23
Access products 4

Source: *Investor's Business Daily*, May 3, 2000, p. A6, from Aberdeen Group.

★ 1037 ★

Networking Equipment (SIC 3669)

Fibre Channel Switch Market - 1999

Shares are shown for the estimated $83.1 million market.

Brocade 78.0%
McData 8.5
Ancor 4.0
Vixel 2.8
Other 6.7

Source: *Investor's Business Daily*, September 3, 1999, p. A8, from International Data Corp., Morgan Keegan & Co., and First Call.

★ 1038 ★

Networking Equipment (SIC 3669)

Internet Backbone Market

Shares are shown based on revenues.

MCI WorldCom 38%
GTE/BBN 15
AT&T 11
Sprint 9
Cable & Wireless 6
Others 21

Source: *Telephony*, March 27, 2000, p. 38, from Sanford C. Bernstein & Co.

★ 1039 ★

Networking Equipment (SIC 3669)

Multimedia Projection Market

InFocus 21%
Proxima 10

Source: *The Business Journal of Portland*, March 13, 2000, p. 1.

★ 1040 ★

Networking Equipment (SIC 3669)

Multiservice Switch Unit Shipments - 1999

Cisco	25.6%
Nortel	24.4
Lucent	21.6
Newbridge	14.5
Others	13.9

Source: *Telephony*, March 27, 2000, p. 24, from Dell'Oro Group.

★ 1041 ★

Networking Equipment (SIC 3669)

Networking Equipment Market by End User

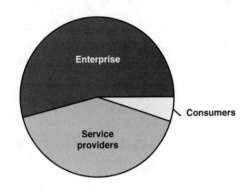

	1998	2002
Enterprise	68%	54%
Service providers	29	41
Consumers	3	5

Source: Retrieved January 4, 2000 from the World Wide Web: http://www.infotechtrends.com, from *Telecommunications* and Forrester Research.

★ 1042 ★

Networking Equipment (SIC 3669)

Networking Leaders - 1999

First quarter market shares are shown in the IP and IP PBX segment. IP stands for internet protocol. PBX stands for private branch exchange.

Cisco	6.91%
3Com	5.42
Intel	5.35
Ascend	5.30
Hewlett-Packard	5.08
Cabletron	4.52
Other	67.42

Source: *Computer Reseller News*, July 19, 1999, p. 109, from Technology Business Research Inc's Network Business Quarterly.

★ 1043 ★

Networking Equipment (SIC 3669)

Node Shipments for Home Networking

	1999	2004
Phone line	63%	49%
RF	22	38
Ethernet	11	1
Power line	4	12

Source: *Wireless Week*, June 28, 1999, p. 48, from Allied Business Intelligence Inc.

★ 1044 ★

Networking Equipment (SIC 3669)

PBX Market by Server Base - 1998

Data are for North America. PBX stands for private branch exchange.

AltiGen	41%
Picazzo	33
IBM/NetPhone	10
Interactive Intelligence	7
Others	9

Source: Retrieved January 20, 2000 from the World Wide Web: http://www.mcas.com/Altigen2.htm, from Frost & Sullivan.

★ 1045 ★

Networking Equipment (SIC 3669)

PBX Shipments - 1999

A total of 8 million private branch exchanges were shipped during the year. Market revenues, including installation and wiring, were about $5 billion.

New system 64%
Upgrade add-ons 20
Basic add-ons 16

Source: *Business Communications Review*, January 2000, p. 43, from TEQ Consult Group.

★ 1046 ★

Networking Equipment (SIC 3669)

SONET/SDH Multiplexer Market Shares

Shares are shown for the third quarter of the year. SONET stands for synchronous optical network. SDH stands for synchronous digital hierarchy.

Nortel 42%
Lucent 30
Other 28

Source: "SONET/SDH Multiplexer Market Grew 16% in 3Q99." Retrieved February 4, 2000 from the World Wide Web: http://library.northernlight.com, from Dell'Oro Group.

★ 1047 ★

Networking Equipment (SIC 3669)

Top Hub Vendors - 1998

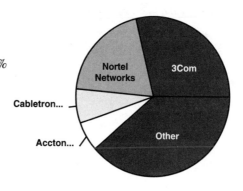

3Com 29.2%
Nortel Networks 19.6
Cabletron Systems 6.5
Accton Technology 5.7
Other 39.0

Source: *VAR Business*, August 16, 1999, p. 40, from Dataquest Inc.

★ 1048 ★

Networking Equipment (SIC 3669)

Top Internet Backbone Companies - 1999

Firms are ranked by Internet-related revenues in millions of dollars.

MCI WorldCom . . . . $ 3,538
AT&T 1,206
GTE Internetworking 1,004
Sprint 600
Cable and Wireless 320
Qwest 300
PSINet 289

Source: *New York Times*, March 13, 2000, p. C1, from *Boardwatch* and International Data Corp.

★ 1049 ★

Networking Equipment (SIC 3669)

Top Port Vendors - 1999

Market shares are shown for the first six months of the year.

Extreme Networks	21.4%
Cabletron Systems	20.4
Nortel Networks	18.6
Cisco Systems	9.5
Alcatel/Xylan	7.1
Foundry	6.1
Other	16.9

Source: *Investor's Business Daily*, September 15, 1999, p. A18, from Dell'Oro Group.

★ 1050 ★

Networking Equipment (SIC 3669)

Wireless Gear Market

Market shares are shown in percent.

Ericsson	33%
Motorola	12
Lucent	12
Nortel	11
Other	32

Source: *Investor's Business Daily*, April 5, 2000, p. A6, from Ericsson and PaineWebber.

★ 1051 ★

Networking Equipment (SIC 3669)

Wireless Phone Location Sector

The market refers to the ability of consumers to access "location relevant" information from the Internet from a digital phone.

XYPoint	80%
Other	20

Source: "XYPOINT Takes 80% Market Share in U.S." Retrieved May 5, 2000 from the World Wide Web: http://www.businesswire.com.

★ 1052 ★

Satellites (SIC 3669)

Military Satellite Market

Data are for 1999-2008.

Reconnaissance and surveillance	27%
Technology development	24
Navigation	17
Communications	16
Early warning	14
Meterological and earth resources	2

Source: *Aerospace America*, June 1999, p. 24.

★ 1053 ★

Smart Cards (SIC 3669)

Smart Card Market - 1999

Market shares are shown in percent.

Gemplus	47%
Schlumberger	29
Oberthur	17
Other	7

Source: *Los Angeles Times*, February 28, 2000, p. C5, from The Nilson Report and company reports.

★ 1054 ★

Smart Cards (SIC 3669)

Smart Card Market - 2003

Sales are estimated in millions of dollars.

	($ mil.)	Share
Automatic ID and security	$ 450	33.33%
Transaction processing	350	25.93
Communications	155	11.48
Government	150	11.11
Other	245	18.15

Source: *Electronic Design*, June 28, 1999, p. 80A.

★ 1055 ★

Telecommunications Equipment (SIC 3669)

Customer Premise Equipment - 1998

The call center market share is by new and add-on agent shipments.

Lucent	35.8%
Nortel	30.7
Siemens	7.1

Continued on next page.

★ 1055 ★ *Continued*

Telecommunications Equipment (SIC 3669)

Customer Premise Equipment - 1998

The call center market share is by new and add-on agent shipments.

Aspect	6.5%
NEC	4.8
Rockwell	4.0
Mitel	3.4
Other	7.7

Source: *Computer Reseller News*, October 18, 1999, p. 121, from The Pelorus Group.

★ 1056 ★

Telecommunications Equipment (SIC 3669)

Top Amplifier Makers - 1998

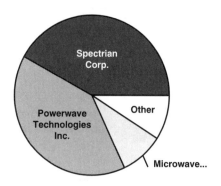

Market shares are shown in percent.

Spectrian Corp.	42%
Powerwave Technologies Inc.	40
Microwave Power Co.	9
Other	9

Source: *Investor's Business Daily*, July 8, 1999, p. A10.

★ 1057 ★

Telecommunications Equipment (SIC 3669)

Videoconferencing Market in Canada

PictureTel	60%
Other	40

Source: Retrieved January 1, 2000 from the World Wide Web: http://www.tradeport.org/ts/countries/canada.

★ 1058 ★

Wire Boards (SIC 3672)

Printed Wire Board Market

The market is shown in percent.

Computers	31%
Communications	30
Industrial	10
Instrument	9
Automotive	9
Other	11

Source: *Chemical Market Reporter*, July 5, 1999, p. 20, from BT Alex Brown and Institute for Interconnecting & Packaging Electronic Circuits.

★ 1059 ★

Microprocessors (SIC 3674)

Digital Signal Processing Market - 1998

Shares are shown in percent.

TI	47.1%
Lucent	28.1
Motorola	12.8
Analog Devices	8.6
Others	3.4

Source: *Wall Street Journal*, June 25, 1999, p. B4, from Forward Concepts.

★ 1060 ★

Microprocessors (SIC 3674)

High-Ended Processor Market - 1999

Shares are estimated.

ARM	25.5%
68000	19.9
Hitachi SH	11.0
LSI MIPS	7.9
NEC MIPS	6.8
Intel	4.4
Other	18.4
Other MIPS	6.1

Source: *Computer Reseller News*, January 10, 2000, p. 8, from Semico Research Corp.

★ 1061 ★

Microprocessors (SIC 3674)

PC Processor Market - 1999

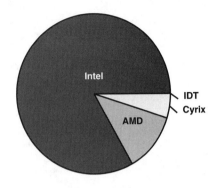

Unit shares are shown for the second quarter of the year.

Intel	82.5%
AMD	12.1
Cyrix	4.9
IDT	0.4

Source: *USA TODAY*, September 14, 1999, p. 3B, from Cahners MicroDesign Resources.

★ 1062 ★

Microprocessors (SIC 3674)

Specialty Communications Memory Suppliers - 1998

Integrated Device	53%
Cypress Semi	16
Toshiba	13
Motorola	9
Other	9

Source: *Investor's Business Daily*, February 1, 2000, p. A10, from company reports, Prudential Volpe Technology Group, and Cahners In-Stat group.

★ 1063 ★

Microprocessors (SIC 3674)

Standard Processing Market - 1999

Shares are estimated.

Intel	74.9%
AMD	12.8
Motorola PowerPC	2.8
IBM PowerPC	1.3
Other	3.2

Source: *Computer Reseller News*, January 10, 2000, p. 8, from Semico Research Corp.

★ 1064 ★

Microprocessors (SIC 3674)

Top Microprocessor Makers - 1998

Intel	79.6%
AMD	5.8
National (Cyrix)	1.1
IDT	0.6
Other	12.9

Source: *Investor's Business Daily*, August 2, 1999, p. A6, from Dataquest Inc.

★ 1065 ★

Semiconductors (SIC 3674)

Largest Semiconductor Firms - 1999

The semiconductor firms are ranked by revenues in billions of dollars.

Intel	$ 29.3
Texas Instruments	9.4
Advanced Micro Devices	2.8
LSI Logic	2.0
Amkor Technology	1.9
National Semiconductor	1.9
Analog Devices	1.4

Source: *Fortune*, April 17, 2000, pp. I-72.

★ 1066 ★
Semiconductors (SIC 3674)

Top Semiconductor Makers - 1998

Companies are ranked by sales in millions of dollars.

Intel	$ 22,800
Texas Instruments	6,500
Motorola	5,880
IBM	4,900
Lucent	2,750
AMD	2,473

Source: *AAII Journal*, July 1999, p. 6, from IC Insights.

★ 1067 ★
Liquid Crystal Displays (SIC 3679)

Flat Panel Market - 1999

The market for laptop PCs is shown for the second quarter of the year.

Samsung	20%
LG LCD	16
Sharp	14
Toshiba	10
Hitachi	9
Sanyo	8
Other	23

Source: *Investor's Business Daily*, July 29, 1999, p. A6, from Techno Systems Research Co.

★ 1068 ★
Liquid Crystal Displays (SIC 3679)

Liquid Crystal Display Leaders - 1999

Shares are shown based on third quarter revenues. Figures are for North America.

NEC	26.8%
Viewsonic	12.7
IBM	7.3
Dell	6.7
HP	6.1
Other	40.6

Source: Retrieved February 10, 2000 from the World Wide Web: http://www.displaysearch.com/english/e_releases. html.

★ 1069 ★
Liquid Crystal Displays (SIC 3679)

Liquid Crystal Displays - 1999

Unit shares are shown based on shipments.

Viewsonic	15.2%
NEC	14.3
Dell	7.9
IBM	7.1
Compaq	5.6
Hewlett-Packard	5.5
Others	44.4

Source: *Investor's Business Daily*, October 11, 1999, p. A6, from DisplaySearch.

★ 1070 ★
Batteries (SIC 3691)

Alkaline Battery Sales - 1999

Data are as of June 1999.

Duracell	50.2%
Energizer	31.2
Rayovac	10.3
Other	8.3

Source: *The Boston Globe*, July 25, 1999, p. G1, from Duracell, A.C. Nielsen, and Gillette Co.

★ 1071 ★
Batteries (SIC 3691)

Battery Market Sales

Sales in the battery and battery-related markets are shown in millions of dollars.

	1998	2003	Share
Portable batteries	$ 3,500	$ 4,445	41.04%
Large/advanced batteries . .	2,500	3,673	33.91
Battery control technology .	1,000	1,400	12.93
Fuel cells	355	1,313	12.12

Source: *Power Engineering*, July 1999, p. 5, from Business Communications Company Inc.

★ 1072 ★
Batteries (SIC 3691)

Best-Selling Battery Brands - 1999

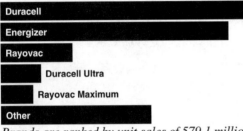

Brands are ranked by unit sales of 579.1 million for the year ended November 7, 1999.

	(mil.)	Share
Duracell	200.0	34.54%
Energizer	166.5	28.75
Rayovac	50.5	8.72
Duracell Ultra	27.1	4.68
Rayovac Maximum	24.4	4.21
Other	110.6	19.10

Source: *MMR*, January 24, 2000, p. 18, from Information Resources Inc.

★ 1073 ★
Batteries (SIC 3691)

U.S. Battery Sales - 1998

Sales are shown in millions of dollars. The market is valued at $5.6 billion. Button cell refers to hearing aids and watches.

	($ mil.)	Share
General batteries	$ 2,884	50.96%
Specialty	1,347	23.80
Button cell	648	11.45
Industrial	410	7.25
OEM	267	4.72
Government	103	1.82

Source: Retrieved January 26, 2000 from the World Wide Web: http://www.exposemagazine.com, from A.C. Nielsen, Vista, and NPE Group.

★ 1074 ★
Recording Media (SIC 3695)

Top Blank Audio/Video Brands - 1999

Shares are shown based on sales of $620 million for the year ended February 27, 2000.

Sony	12.0%
RCA	9.9
Maxwell HGX Gold	5.3
Fuji	5.3
Maxell GX Silver	5.0
TDK D	3.7
TDK Revue	3.6
Maxell	3.0
Other	52.2

Source: *Supermarket Business*, May 15, 2000, p. 80, from Information Resources Inc.

★ 1075 ★
Electronic Voice Products (SIC 3699)

Electronic Voice Products - 1999

Data show sales.

Interactive voice response	72%
Voice generation	24
Voice recognition	4

Source: *Investor's Business Daily*, October 27, 1999, p. A6, from Computer Economics Inc.

★ 1076 ★

Microdevices (SIC 3699)

Microdevice Market by Segment - 2004

Data show estimated sales in billions of dollars.

	2000 ($ bil.)	2004 ($ bil.)	Share
Information technology and peripherals	$ 8.7	$ 13.4	43.93%
Medical & biochemical . .	2.4	7.4	24.26
Automotive	1.3	2.3	7.54
Industrial and automation	1.2	1.9	6.23
Environmental monitoring	0.5	1.8	5.90
Telecommunications . . .	0.1	3.7	12.13

Source: *New York Times*, May 8, 2000, p. D1, from Roger Grace Associates.

SIC 37 - Transportation Equipment

★ 1077 ★
Autos (SIC 3711)

Auto Market Leaders - 1999

GM 29.4%
Ford 25.1
DaimlerChrysler 16.7
Toyota 8.7
Honda 6.4
Nissan 4.0
Volkswagen 2.2
Others 7.5

Source: *Detroit News*, January 6, 2000, p. 9A, from Autodata Inc.

★ 1078 ★
Autos (SIC 3711)

Auto Market Leaders in Canada - 1999

Total sales were 806,400 vehicles.

	Units	Share
GM	259,674	32.20%
Honda	104,427	12.95
Toyota	94,214	11.68
Ford	87,830	10.89

	Units	Share
Chrysler	84,616	10.49%
Volkswagen	46,883	5.81
Mazda	31,955	3.96
Other	96,801	12.00

Source: *Globe and Mail*, January 5, 2000, p. A3.

★ 1079 ★
Autos (SIC 3711)

Best-Selling Cars - 1999

Data are as of November 30, 1999.

Toyota Camry 418,000
Honda Accord 373,000
Ford Taurus 339,000
Honda Civic 296,000
Ford Escort 255,000

Source: *Time*, January 1, 2000, p. 4, from WARDS AutoInfoBank.

★ 1080 ★
Autos (SIC 3711)

Best-Selling Cars in Canada - 1999

Shares are shown based on sales of 806,506 units for the year ended December 31, 1999.

Honda Civic 7.2%
GM Chevrolet Cavalier 6.3
GM Pontiac Sunfire 5.8
Toyota Corolla 5.2
Chrysler Neon 3.6
Ford Taurus 3.3
Chrysler Intrepid 3.2

Continued on next page.

★ 1080 ★ *Continued*
Autos (SIC 3711)

Best-Selling Cars in Canada - 1999

Shares are shown based on sales of 806,506 units for the year ended December 31, 1999.

Mazda Protégé	3.1%
GM Pontiac Grand Am	3.1
GM Chevrolet Malibu	3.1
Others	56.1

Source: "Report on Market Share." Retrieved June 8, 2000 from the World Wide Web: http://www. marketingmag.ca, from *Canadian Auto World*.

★ 1081 ★
Autos (SIC 3711)

Best-Selling Minivans in Canada - 1999

Shares are shown based on sales of 251,673 units for the year ended December 31, 1999.

Chrysler Dodge Caravan	29.4%
Ford Windstar	22.1
GM FWD Minivans	20.1
GM Chevrolet/GMC Astro/Safari	7.2
Toyota Sienna	6.3
Chrysler Plymouth Voyager	6.2
Honda Odyssey	5.0
Mazda MVP	1.8
Other	2.9

Source: "Report on Market Share." Retrieved June 8, 2000 from the World Wide Web: http://www. marketingmag.ca, from *Canadian Auto World*.

★ 1082 ★
Autos (SIC 3711)

Best-Selling Pickup Truck in Canada - 1999

Shares are shown based on sales of 233,812 units for the year ended December 31, 1999.

Ford F-series	34.1%
GM Chevrolet/GMC Silverado/Sierra	33.7
Chrysler Dodge Ram	12.9
Chrysler Dodge Dakota	6.2
GM Chevrolet/GMC S10/Sonoma	4.8
Ford Ranger	4.0
Mazda B Series	2.0

Toyota Tacoma	1.1%
Other	2.1

Source: "Report on Market Share." Retrieved June 8, 2000 from the World Wide Web: http://www. marketingmag.ca, from *Canadian Auto World*.

★ 1083 ★
Autos (SIC 3711)

Best-Selling Sport Utility Vehicles in Canada - 1999

Shares are shown based on sales of 233,812 units for the year ended December 31, 1999.

Ford Explorer	13.9%
GM Chevrolet/GMC Blazer/Jimmy	13.3
Chrysler Jeep Grand Cherokee	10.6
Honda CRV	8.1
Nissan Pathfinder	5.6
GM Chevrolet/GMC Tahoe/Yukon	5.2
Chrysler Dodge Durango	4.5
Toyota 4Runner	4.2
Ford Expedition	4.1
Chrysler Jeep Cherokee	3.5
Other	27.0

Source: "Report on Market Share." Retrieved June 8, 2000 from the World Wide Web: http://www. marketingmag.ca, from *Canadian Auto World*.

★ 1084 ★
Autos (SIC 3711)

Best-Selling Vehicles in Canada - 1999

Chevrolet Cavalier	27,691
Honda Civic	26,922
Pontiac Sunfire	24,231
Toyota Corolla	21,335
Ford Taurus	16,156
Chevrolet Malibu	13,137
Mazda Protégé	13,083
Pontiac Grand Am	13,077

Source: *Toronto Star*, July 21, 1999, p. D1.

★ 1085 ★
Autos (SIC 3711)

Car Salvaging Market

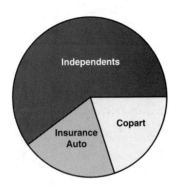

The $3 billion industry is estimated in percent.

Independents	60%
Insurance Auto	20
Copart	20

Source: *Investor's Business Daily*, July 22, 1999, p. A10.

★ 1086 ★
Autos (SIC 3711)

Electric Car Sales

	1998	1999
Ford	440	404
Toyota	359	255
GM	258	166

Source: *Wall Street Journal*, March 28, 2000, p. B4, from Electric Vehicle Association of the Americas.

★ 1087 ★
Autos (SIC 3711)

Light Truck Leaders - 1998

GM	29.2%
Ford	27.8
Daimler-Chrysler	22.1
Toyota	7.9
Nissan	4.3
Honda	3.3

Source: *New York Times*, September 3, 1999, p. C2, from Ward's Auto InfoBank.

★ 1088 ★
Autos (SIC 3711)

Light Truck Sales in Canada - 1999

Total sales were 696,995 vehicles.

	Units	Share
GM	217,248	31.17%
Ford	194,623	27.92
Chrysler	180,201	25.85
Toyota	35,651	5.11
Honda	26,976	3.87
Other	42,296	6.07

Source: *Globe and Mail*, January 5, 2000, p. A3.

★ 1089 ★
Autos (SIC 3711)

Luxury Car Market in Canada - 1998

Volvo 700+	18.4%
BMW	15.7
Cadillac	13.5
Mercedes Benz	12.9
Lincoln	6.8
Other	32.7

Source: *Globe and Mail*, July 5, 1999, p. B1, from DesRoisies Automotive Consultants.

★ 1090 ★
Autos (SIC 3711)

Luxury Car Sales - 1999

Sales are shown for the year ended November 1999.

Mercedes-Benz	170,319
Lexus	169,025
Cadillac	161,941
Lincoln	159,996
BMW	141,876
Acura	107,972
Volvo	104,530
Infiniti	64,836
Audi	59,480
Jaguar	30,093

Source: *New York Times*, December 12, 1999, p. 50.

★ 1091 ★
Autos (SIC 3711)

Most Advertised Vehicles - 1998

Ad spending is shown in millions of dollars.

Jeep Grand Cherokee . . . . $ 136.3
Dodge Intrepid 125.4
Toyota Camry 112.9
Honda Accord 108.5
Dodge Caravan 100.6

Source: *Aftermarket Business*, June 1999, p. 6.

★ 1092 ★
Autos (SIC 3711)

Transmission Sales in North America - 1998

Data are for North America.

Automatic 83%
Manual 17

Source: *Automotive Industries*, November 1999, p. 15.

★ 1093 ★
Autos (SIC 3711)

U.S. Minivan Market - 1999

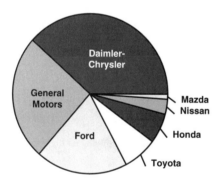

Daimler-Chrysler 37.6%
General Motors 25.2
Ford 19.4
Toyota 7.4
Honda 5.8
Nissan 3.3
Mazda 1.2

Source: *Wall Street Journal*, January 11, 2000, p. 4B, from Autodata Corp.

★ 1094 ★
Autos (SIC 3711)

U.S. Sales by Model - 1999

Middle car 26.26%
Pickups 19.20
Sport utility 19.11
Small car 11.88
Vans 10.40
Luxury car 8.65
Large car 4.31
Commercial chassis 0.19

Source: *Ward's Dealer Busienss*, May 1999, p. 20.

★ 1095 ★
Luxury Coaches (SIC 3713)

Luxury Coach Sales in Ontario

Prevost/MCI 95%
Other 5

Source: Retrieved January 1, 2000 from the World Wide Web: http://www.tradeport.org/ts/countries/canada/mrr/mark0025.html.

★ 1096 ★
Trucks (SIC 3713)

Class 8 Truck Market

Freightliner 30.7%
Navistar 18.4
Mack 12.8
Volvo 11.5
Kenworth 10.7
Peterbilt 10.1
Other 5.8

Source: *CCJ*, July 1999, p. 41.

★ 1097 ★

Trucks (SIC 3713)

Light Truck Sales - 1999

Shares are shown through August 1999.

Mid-size SUV	10.6%
Full-size SUV	3.5
Mini SUV	2.6
Luxury SUV	1.3
Other	82.0

Source: *Washington Post*, September 25, 1999, p. E1, from J.D. Power & Associates.

★ 1098 ★

Auto Parts (SIC 3714)

Cylinder Head Market in North America

There has been a dramatic shift in the industry from iron to aluminum. Aluminum's market share is expected to increase from 72% in 1998 to 94% in 2006.

Teksid	21%
Nemak	17
Other	72

Source: *Mexico Business*, March 2000, p. 13.

★ 1099 ★

Auto Parts (SIC 3714)

Leading Truck Engine Producers - 1999

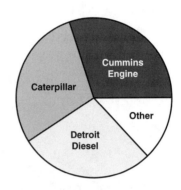

Cummins Engine	30.4%
Caterpillar	29.0
Detroit Diesel	27.5
Other	13.1

Source: *Wall Street Journal*, March 13, 2000, p. B6, from company and Baseline.

★ 1100 ★

Auto Parts (SIC 3714)

Seat Module Market - 2000

The $7 billion North American market is shown in percent.

Lear	44.29%
Johnson Controls	37.14
Magna	5.70
Visteon	3.90
Other	9.00

Source: *Automotive Industries*, January 2000, p. 50.

★ 1101 ★

Trailers (SIC 3715)

Truck Trailer Market - 1998

Wabash National	18.4%
Great Dane	13.1
Utility	8.2
Trailmobile	7.3
Hyundai	5.5
Stoughton	4.6
Strick Trailers	4.3

Continued on next page.

★ **1101** ★ *Continued*

Trailers (SIC 3715)

Truck Trailer Market - 1998

Pines Trailer	4.0%
Lufkin	2.4
Other	32.2

Source: *CCJ*, July 1999, p. 41, from Polk Co.

★ **1102** ★

Aircraft (SIC 3721)

Top Aircraft Providers to Government

The top providers of aircraft to the Department of Defense are ranked by share of total contracts.

Boeing Co.	34.18%
Lockheed Martin Corp.	18.93
United Technologies Corp.	8.76
General Electric Co.	4.83
Northrop Grumman Corp.	4.77
Other	28.53

Source: *Government Executive*, Annual 1999, p. 97.

★ **1103** ★

Helicopters (SIC 3721)

Top Helicopter Providers to Government

The top providers to the Department of Defense are ranked by share of total contracts.

Boeing Co.	39.13%
United Technologies Corp.	37.48
Textron Inc.	15.30
Allied-Signal Inc.	2.08
Other	6.01

Source: *Government Executive*, Annual 1999, p. 98.

★ **1104** ★

Aircraft Parts (SIC 3724)

Aircraft Engine Providers With Government

The top providers of aircraft engines to the Department of Defense are ranked by share of total contracts.

United Technologies Corp.	33.07%
General Electric Co.	29.57
Rolls Royce PLC	7.33
Allied-Signal	4.74
Northrop Grumman	3.69
Other	21.60

Source: *Government Executive*, Annual 1999, p. 98.

★ **1105** ★

Boats (SIC 3731)

Boat Market Leaders - 1999

The marine industry is defined as fiberglass and aluminum boats, minus personal watercraft. The industry sold 331,382 units. Fiberglass had 60.6% of boat sales.

Brunswick Marine	11.8%
Genmar Industries	9.5
Outboard Marine Corp.	9.1
Tracker Marine	8.2
Godfrey Marine	3.1
Alumacraft Boat Co.	3.0
Smoker-Craft	2.9
Yamaha Motor Corp.	2.9
Other	49.5

Source: ''Statistical Survey Releases Boating Industry Sales.'' Retrieved April 3, 2000 from the World Wide Web: http://library.northernlight.com, from Statistical Surveys.

★ 1106 ★
Railway Cars (SIC 3743)

Railcar Deliveries - 2000

Data are estimated.

Total covered hopper	16
Tank	10
Total gondola	9
Total flat car	7
Total open hopper	6
Boxcar	2

Source: *Railway Age*, July 1999, p. 32, from American Rail Car Institute and Economic Planning Associates.

★ 1107 ★
Bicycles (SIC 3751)

26 inch Bike Market

Market shares are shown by style.

	1998	1999
Rigid	64%	53%
Suspension	30	41
Cruiser	5	6

Source: *Bicycle Retailer & Industry News*, February 1, 2000, p. 1, from BPSA.

★ 1108 ★
Bicycles (SIC 3751)

Bicycle Sales in Canada - 1997

Total bike sales reached $420.7 million in 1997. With accessories, the figure jumps to $512.5 million. The table shows the best-selling types, in millions of dollars.

	($ mil.)	Share
Adult mountain	$ 254.5	60.52%
Adult road	46.6	11.08
Juvenile mountain	35.0	8.32
Adult hybrid	34.9	8.30
Juvenile road	26.2	6.23
Adult other	18.1	4.30
Adult racing	3.2	0.76
Juvenile racing	2.0	0.48

Source: "General Statistics." Retrieved December 3, 1999 from the World Wide Web: http://www.btac.org/english/activities/mediastats.htm, from Bicycle Trade Association of Canada.

★ 1109 ★
Bicycles (SIC 3751)

Retail Bike Sales - 1999

Unit shares are shown in percent.

Youth	30.7%
Mountain, no suspension	23.7
Mountain, front suspension	18.6
Hybrid cross	10.7
Comfort	8.2
Mountain, full suspension	2.6
Road/700c	2.5
Other	3.0

Source: *Bicycle Retailer and Industry News*, April 1, 2000, p. 1, from National Bicycle Dealers Association.

★ 1110 ★
Bicycles (SIC 3751)

Youth Bike Sales - 1999

Sales are shown for the first quarter of the year.

Mountain bikes	48.20%
Hybrid/cross bikes	9.50
Comfort bikes	6.25
Road	2.80
Cruiser	2.60
Tandems	0.20

Source: "Youth Bikes - Hot!" Retrieved November 22, 1999 from the World Wide Web: http://www.nbda.com/youth.htm, from National Bicycle Dealers Association.

★ 1111 ★
Dirtbikes (SIC 3751)

Top Dirtbike Brands - 1999

Shares are shown based on estimated sales of 137,875 units through September 1999.

Honda	39.43%
Yamaha	29.40
Kawasaki	14.18
Suzuki	10.24
KTM	6.14
Othe	0.61

Source: *Dealernews*, January 2000, p. 78.

★ 1112 ★

Motorcycles (SIC 3751)

U.S. Motorcycle Market - 1999

Harley-Davidson	27.82%
Honda	23.11
Yamaha	18.15
Kawasaki	12.40
Suzuki	12.07
Other	6.45

Source: *Dealernews*, October 1999, p. 80.

★ 1113 ★

Electric Scooters (SIC 3799)

Electric Scooter Market

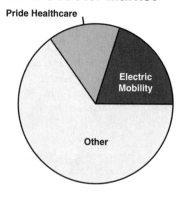

Electric Mobility	20%
Pride Healthcare	15
Other	65

Source: Retrieved January 13, 2000 from the World Wide Web: http://www.amcity.com/philadelphia/stories/1999/06/28/focus5.html.

★ 1114 ★

Personal Watercraft (SIC 3799)

Personal Watercraft Leaders - 1999

The industry had sales of 94,308 units.

Bombardier	35.4%
Yamaha	24.9
Kawasaki	15.7
Polaris	6.2
Arctic Cat	4.9
Other	12.9

Source: "Statistical Survey Releases Boating Industry Sales." Retrieved April 3, 2000 from the World Wide Web: http://library.northernlight.com, from Statistical Surveys.

SIC 38 - Instruments and Related Products

★ 1115 ★
Laboratory Instruments (SIC 3821)
AA Spectrometer Market

Market shares are shown based on units. Figures are based on a survey of scientists who now use the product.

PerkinElmer Inc. 50.11%
Varian Analytical Instruments 16.93
Shimadzu Corp. 11.21
Other 11.75

Source: *American Laboratory*, January 2000, p. 35.

★ 1116 ★
Laboratory Instruments (SIC 3821)
Blood Gas Analyzer Market

Market shares are shown based on units. Figures are based on a survey of scientists who now use the product.

Chiron Diagnostics (Ciba Corning) 21.29%
Instrumentation Laboratory 17.42
Radiometer 16.77
AVL 12.90
Other 31.62

Source: *American Clinical Laboratory*, July 1999, p. 29.

★ 1117 ★
Laboratory Instruments (SIC 3821)
Cell Culture Equipment Market

Over 60,000 life science researchers use HPLC equipment, spending over $100 million on instruments and media.

New Brunswick 36.5%
Lebline 22.0
Bellco 10.1
Other 31.4

Source: "Cell & Tissue Markets Showing Healthy Growth." Retrieved January 13, 2000 from the World Wide Web: http://www.phortech.com/97cell.htm, from Phortech International.

★ 1118 ★
Laboratory Instruments (SIC 3821)
Cell Culture Equipment Sales

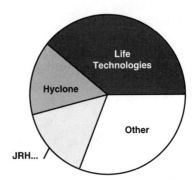

The market for cell culture media, serum and reagents reached $395 million in 1999.

Life Technologies 39%
Hyclone 15
JRH Biosciencces 15
Other 31

Source: *Medical & Healthcare Marketplace Guide*, 1999, pp. I-251.

★ 1119 ★
Laboratory Instruments (SIC 3821)
Chemical Analyzer Market

Market shares are shown based on units. Figures are based on a survey of scientists who now use the product.

Abbott	16.59%
Beckman	14.63
Boehringer Mannheim/Hitachi	8.73
bioMerieeux Vitek	8.52
Other	68.12

Source: *American Clinical Laboratory*, July 1999, p. 29.

★ 1120 ★
Laboratory Instruments (SIC 3821)
Coagulation Analyzer Market

Market shares are shown based on units. Figures are based on a survey of scientists who now use the product.

Coulter/Il	15.96%
Beckston Dickinson	15.49
Sigma (Amelung)	12.68
Dade International	11.74
Other	44.13

Source: *American Clinical Laboratory*, July 1999, p. 29.

★ 1121 ★
Laboratory Instruments (SIC 3821)
Cytokine Supplier Market

R&D Systems	23.4%
Sigma	12.5
BRL	10.7
Genzyme	8.2
Other	45.2

Source: Retrieved January 13, 2000 from the World Wide Web: http://www.phortech.com/98cytok.htm, from Phortech International.

★ 1122 ★
Laboratory Instruments (SIC 3821)
Electrolyte Analyzer Market

Market shares are shown based on units. Figures are based on a survey of scientists who now use the product.

Beckman	34.46%
AVL	10.14
Chiron Diagnostics (Ciba Corning)	10.14
Other	45.26

Source: *American Clinical Laboratory*, July 1999, p. 29.

★ 1123 ★
Laboratory Instruments (SIC 3821)
Flow Cytometer Market

Market shares are shown based on units. Figures are based on a survey of scientists who now use the product.

Becton Dickinson	49.11%
Beckman (Coulter)	25.00
Bio-Rad Diagnostic Group	16.07
Ortho	4.46
Other	5.36

Source: *American Clinical Laboratory*, July 1999, p. 31.

★ 1124 ★
Laboratory Instruments (SIC 3821)
Fume Hood Market

Market shares are shown based on units. Figures are based on a survey of scientists who now use the product.

Labconco Corp.	25.19%
Duralab Equipment Corp.	9.41
Airclean Systems Inc.	8.65
Kewaunee Scientific Corp.	6.87
Other	49.98

Source: *American Laboratory*, January 2000, p. 35.

★ 1125 ★

Laboratory Instruments (SIC 3821)

Hematology Analyzer Market

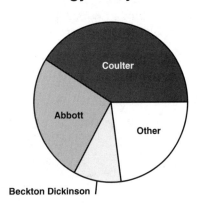

Market shares are shown based on units. Figures are based on a survey of scientists who now use the product.

Coulter	40.53%
Abbott	26.32
Beckton Dickinson	10.00
Other	23.15

Source: *American Clinical Laboratory*, July 1999, p. 30.

★ 1126 ★

Laboratory Instruments (SIC 3821)

High Performance Liquid Chromatography Market

Over 43,000 life science researchers use HPLC equipment, spending over $250 million on instruments and columns.

Waters	27.50%
Hewlett-Packard	27.35
Thermo Sep	7.83
Others	37.32

Source: "Undercurrents and Riptides Trap the Unwary." Retrieved January 13, 2000 from the World Wide Web: http://www.phortech.com/98hplc.htm, from Phortech International.

★ 1127 ★

Laboratory Instruments (SIC 3821)

Histriology Slide Stainer Market

Market shares are shown based on units. Figures are based on a survey of scientists who now use the product.

Leica	20.45%
Carl Zeiss	18.18
Shandon-Lipshaw	13.64
Hacker Instruments	9.09
Other	38.64

Source: *American Clinical Laboratory*, July 1999, p. 30.

★ 1128 ★

Laboratory Instruments (SIC 3821)

Immunoassay Analyzer Market

Market shares are shown based on units. Figures are based on a survey of scientists who now use the product.

Abbott	27.07%
bioMerieux Vitek	10.53
Beckman	8.52
Bio-Rad Diagnostic Group	7.02
Other	46.86

Source: *American Clinical Laboratory*, July 1999, p. 30.

★ 1129 ★

Laboratory Instruments (SIC 3821)

Ion Specific Electrode Market

Market shares are shown based on units. Figures are based on a survey of scientists who now use the product.

Orion	37.92%
Corning Inc.	26.04
Cole Parmer	10.00
Hach Co.	7.29
Other	18.75

Source: *American Laboratory*, January 2000, p. 35.

★ 1130 ★

Laboratory Instruments (SIC 3821)

Lab Rheometer Market

Market shares are shown based on units. Figures are based on a survey of scientists who now use the product.

Brookfield Engineering Labs	32.06%
TA Instruments	13.74
Rheometrics Inc.	11.45
Other	42.75

Source: *American Laboratory*, January 2000, p. 35.

★ 1131 ★

Laboratory Instruments (SIC 3821)

Laboratory Balance Market

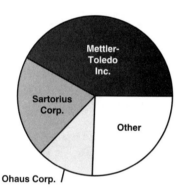

Market shares are shown based on units. Figures are based on a survey of scientists who now use the product.

Mettler-Toledo Inc.	42.88%
Sartorius Corp.	20.92
Ohaus Corp.	11.50
Other	25.70

Source: *American Laboratory*, January 2000, p. 35.

★ 1132 ★

Laboratory Instruments (SIC 3821)

Laboratory Furnace Market

Market shares are shown based on units. Figures are based on a survey of scientists who now use the product.

Barnstead Thermolyne	39.04%
Lindberg Blue M	25.50
Applied Test Systems Inc.	11.95
Other	23.51

Source: *American Laboratory*, January 2000, p. 35.

★ 1133 ★

Laboratory Instruments (SIC 3821)

Laboratory Washer Market

Market shares are shown based on units. Figures are based on a survey of scientists who now use the product.

Labconco	41.18%
Meile	17.65
Hotpack	11.31
Other	29.86

Source: *American Laboratory*, January 2000, p. 35.

★ 1134 ★

Laboratory Instruments (SIC 3821)

Leading Centrifuge Makers

Market shares are shown based on units. Figures are based on a survey of scientists who now use the product.

Beckman	29.53%
Sorvall (Kendro)	20.71
Brinkmann/Eppendorf	10.59
IEC	10.11
Other	29.06

Source: *American Clinical Laboratory*, July 1999, p. 31.

★ 1135 ★

Laboratory Instruments (SIC 3821)

Leading Incubator Makers

Market shares are shown based on units. Figures are based on a survey of scientists who now use the product.

Forma	20.85%
Lab-Line	20.09
Revco Scientific Inc.	12.24
Precision Scientific	11.48
Other	35.38

Source: *American Clinical Laboratory*, July 1999, p. 30.

★ 1136 ★

Laboratory Instruments (SIC 3821)

Leading Titrator Makers

Market shares are shown based on units. Figures are based on a survey of scientists who now use the product.

Brinkmann Inst./Metrohm	55.09%
Mettler-Toledo Inc.	16.47
Orion	13.47
Other	14.97

Source: *American Laboratory*, January 2000, p. 35.

★ 1137 ★

Laboratory Instruments (SIC 3821)

Leading Water Bath Makers

Market shares are shown based on units. Figures are based on a survey of scientists who now use the product.

Barnstead/Thermolyne	35.71%
Brinkmann Inst./Lauda	30.88
Neslab Instruments Inc.	11.06
Other	22.35

Source: *American Laboratory*, January 2000, p. 35.

★ 1138 ★

Laboratory Instruments (SIC 3821)

Microbiology Analyzer Market

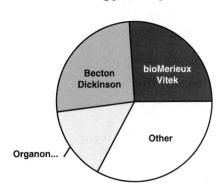

Market shares are shown based on units. Figures are based on a survey of scientists who now use the product.

bioMerieux Vitek	26.32%
Becton Dickinson	25.75
Organon Teknika Corp.	14.85
Other	33.08

Source: *American Clinical Laboratory*, July 1999, p. 30.

★ 1139 ★

Laboratory Instruments (SIC 3821)

Microwave Digestion System Market

Market shares are shown based on units. Figures are based on a survey of scientists who now use the product.

CEM Corp.	49.58%
OL Analytical	10.08
A.I. Scientific	8.40
Milestone Inc.	7.56
Other	24.38

Source: *American Laboratory*, January 2000, p. 35.

★ 1140 ★

Laboratory Instruments (SIC 3821)

Top Microscope Makers

Market shares are shown based on units. Figures are based on a survey of scientists who now use the product.

Olympus America	32.40%
Nikon	30.53
Carl Zeiss	19.94
Leica	11.21
Other	5.92

Source: *American Clinical Laboratory*, July 1999, p. 30.

★ 1141 ★

Laboratory Instruments (SIC 3821)

Water Purification Equipment Market

Market shares are shown based on units. Figures are based on a survey of scientists who now use the product.

Millipore Corp.	55.12%
Barnstead/Thermolyne	20.79
U.S. Filter	9.24
Other	14.85

Source: *American Laboratory*, January 2000, p. 35.

★ 1142 ★

Monitoring Equipment (SIC 3822)

Air Monitoring Equipment Sales

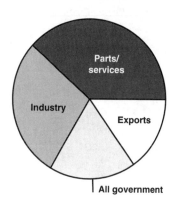

Sales are shown in millions of dollars.

	1998	2003	Share
Parts/services	$ 576	$ 810.9	38.48%
Industry	420	588.6	27.93
All government	320	388.0	18.41
Exports	200	320.1	15.19

Source: *American Ceramic Society Bulletin*, July 1999, p. 28, from Business Communications Co.

★ 1143 ★

Monitoring Equipment (SIC 3822)

Temperature Transmitter Shipments - 1999

High tier	36%
Analog	22
Smart	20
Programmable	17
Low-cost	5

Source: *InTech*, March 2000, p. 28.

★ 1144 ★
Pollution Control Equipment (SIC 3822)

Air Pollution Control Market

The fastest growing market is membranes and separations.

	1999 ($ mil.)	2004 ($ mil.)	Share
Filtration systems . .	$ 1,020.1	$ 1,297.1	30.12%
Scrubbers/strippers . . .	876.7	1,021.3	23.72
Oxidizers	866.4	1,241.1	28.82
Absorbent systems . . .	306.0	408.1	9.48
Energy recovery	122.0	166.4	3.86
Membranes/separations .	92.7	134.8	3.13
Novel technologies . . .	25.3	37.7	0.88

Source: *Power Engineering*, March 2000, p. 12, from Business Communications Co. Inc.

★ 1145 ★
Sensing Systems (SIC 3826)

Intelligent Sensing Systems

Data are in millions of dollars.

	1998	2003	Share
Electronic noses	$ 14	$ 20	46.51%
Vision chips	8	21	48.84
Artificial tongues	0	2	4.65

Source: *American Ceramic Society Bulletin*, September 1999, p. 29, from Business Communications Co.

★ 1146 ★
Medical Devices (SIC 3841)

Blood Testing Market

Immucor	54%
Johnson & Johnson	46

Source: *Atlanta Business Chronicle*, July 12, 1999, p. 1.

★ 1147 ★
Medical Devices (SIC 3841)

Bradycardia Market Leaders

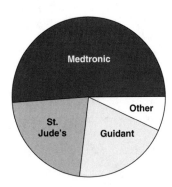

Bradycardia is an abnormally low heart rate.

Medtronic	51%
St. Jude's	22
Guidant	20
Other	7

Source: Retrieved May 25, 2000 from the World Wide Web: http://www.ahcpub.com.

★ 1148 ★
Medical Devices (SIC 3841)

Insulin Pump Market

MiniMed	75%
Other	25

Source: "Alternative Delivery Systems." Retrieved May 25, 2000 from the World Wide Web: http://www.ahcpub.com.

★ 1149 ★
Medical Devices (SIC 3841)

Tachycardia Market Leaders

Medtronic	50%
Guidant	40
St. Jude	10

Source: Retrieved May 25, 2000 from the World Wide Web: http://www.ahcpub.com.

★ 1150 ★
First Aid Needs (SIC 3842)

Adhesive Bandage Market in Canada

Shares are estimated.

Band-Aid/Elastoplast 65%
Other 35

Source: *Marketing Magazine*, December 13, 1999, p. 12.

★ 1151 ★
First Aid Needs (SIC 3842)

First Aid Unit Shares - 1999

Shares are shown based on unit sales for the year ended January 30, 2000. Shares are for tape, bandages, gauze and cotton.

Band-Aid 23.0%
Johnson & Johnson 14.9
3M Active Strips 3.8
Curad First Aid 3.1
Band-Aid Sport Strip 2.6
3M Comfort Strip 2.1
3M Nexcare 2.0
Private label 18.7
Other 29.8

Source: *Supermarket Business*, April 15, 2000, p. 132, from Information Resources Inc.

★ 1152 ★
First Aid Needs (SIC 3842)

Top Antiseptic Brands - 1999

Total sales of first aid accessories reached $464.6 million for the year ended March 28, 1999.

Neosporin Plus . . . . $ 47.7
Neosporin 43.2
Solarcaine 13.3
Betadine 12.6
B-D 9.5
Polysporin 9.2
Fruit of the Earth 7.7
Campho Phonique 7.6

Source: "Trends in First Aid." Retrieved January 26, 2000 from the World Wide Web: http://www.exposemagazine. com, from Information Resources Inc.

★ 1153 ★
First Aid Needs (SIC 3842)

Top Bandage Brands - 1999

Sales are shown in millions of dollars for the year ended March 28, 1999.

Band-Aid . . . . $ 109.2
Johnson & Johnson 74.9
3M Active Strips 16.5
Curad 12.4
Band-Aid Sport 12.2
3M Comfort Strips 12.2
Johnson & Johnson Kling 10.4
3M Nexcare 10.2
3M 10.0

Source: "Trends in First Aid." Retrieved January 26, 2000 from the World Wide Web: http://www.exposemagazine. com, from Information Resources Inc.

★ 1154 ★
Medical Products (SIC 3842)

Surgeons Glove Sales - 1998

Unit sales are shown.

Powdered 76.6%
Powder free 15.8
Specialty 5.2
Nonlatex 2.1

Source: *OR Manager*, June 1999, p. 11, from IMS Health.

★ 1155 ★
Surgical Implants (SIC 3842)

Breast Implant Market

According to the source, Inamed and Mentor are the two survivors of a market once dominated by Dow Corning, Baxter, 3M Corp. and Bristol-Myers Squibb. The number of women receiving breast augmentation fell from 100,000 to less than 30,000 by 1992.

Inamed 50%
Mentor Corp. 35
Other 15

Source: *Investor's Business Daily*, December 1, 1999, p. A10.

★ 1156 ★

Surgical Implants (SIC 3842)

Human Heart Valve Market

Cryolife is the largest for-profit supplier of frozen human tissue. The company has shipped nearly 31,000 heart valves.

CryoLife	80%
Other	20

Source: *Forbes*, November 2, 1999, p. 214.

★ 1157 ★

Surgical Implants (SIC 3842)

Spinal Implant Market - 1999

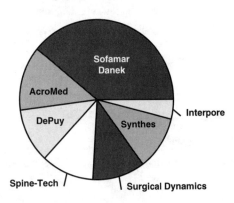

Spinal fusion is a $700 million market.

Sofamar Danek	39%
AcroMed	13
DePuy	11
Spine-Tech	11
Surgical Dynamics	11
Synthes	11
Interpore	4

Source: *Investor's Business Daily*, February 2, 2000, from company reports.

★ 1158 ★

Surgical Implants (SIC 3842)

Stent Market Leaders - 2000

Shares are estimated for the second quarter of the year.

	1Q 2000	2Q 2000
Guidant	46%	43%
Medtronic	31	29
Boston Scientific	17	22
Other	6	6

Source: *Investor's Business Daily*, June 2, 2000, p. 1, from Bank of America Securities.

★ 1159 ★

Surgical Instruments (SIC 3842)

Custom Kit and Tray Market

Custom procedure trays cut time needed, costs and risks of disease transmission. Kits and trays generated estimated revenues of $1.02 billion.

Allegiance	52%	0%
Maxxim	29	0
DeRoyal	6	0
Medline	4	0
Others	9	0

Source: *Medical & Healthcare Marketplace Guide*, 1999, from Wachovia Securities and Dorland's Biomedical Database.

★ 1160 ★

Surgical Instruments (SIC 3842)

Gynecology Endoscopy Market

Market shares are shown in percent.

Olympus	29%
Circon/Maxxim	26
Storz	25
Wolf	18
Other	11

Source: *Medical & Healthcare Marketplace Guide*, 2000, pp. I-825.

★ 1161 ★

Surgical Instruments (SIC 3842)

Urology Endoscopy Market

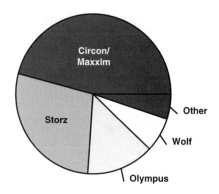

Market shares are shown in percent.

Circon/Maxxim 46%
Storz 28
Olympus 14
Wolf 7
Other 5

Source: *Medical & Healthcare Marketplace Guide*, 1999, pp. I-825.

★ 1162 ★

Dental Equipment (SIC 3843)

Dental Supply Market

The $3.5 billion dental supply market is shown in percent.

Henry Schein Inc. 31%
Patterson 27
Other 42

Source: *Forbes*, January 24, 2000, p. 96.

★ 1163 ★

Radiology (SIC 3844)

Leading Radiology Advertisers - 1999

Data show share of ad expenditures.

Siemens Medical Systems Inc. 3.86%
GE Medical Systems 3.61
Nycomed Amersham Inc. 3.26
Kodak 3.09
Bracco Diagnostics 3.00
Picker International 2.73

Philip Medical System 2.49%
Other 77.96

Source: *Medical Marketing & Media*, April 2000, p. 68, from PERQ/HCI Journal Ad Review.

★ 1164 ★

Lasers (SIC 3845)

Medical Laser Market

Data refer to Nd: YAG cosmetic and refractive market.

Coherent 33%
Nidek 15
Alcon 11
Other 41

Source: *Medical Laser Insight*, July 1999, p. 3, from American Society for Cataract and Refractive Surgery.

★ 1165 ★

Contact Lenses (SIC 3851)

Soft Contact Lens Market - 1998

Market shares are shown based on new fits/refits.

Vistakon 26.0%
CIBA Vision 21.0
Bausch & Lomb 15.0
Wesley Jessen 15.0
Ocular Sciences 12.0
Cooper Vision 5.5
Sunsoft 2.0
Specialty Ultravision 1.0
Other 2.5

Source: *Medical & Healthcare Marketplace Guide*, 1999, pp. I-837.

★ 1166 ★

Ophthalmology Products (SIC 3851)

Laser Vision Correction Market

Nidek's share is estimated at 10-12%.

Visx 80%
Nidek 12
Other 8

Source: *East Bay Business Times*, May 9, 2000, p. 1.

★ 1167 ★

Ophthalmology Products (SIC 3851)

Leading Ophthalmology Advertsiers - 1999

Data show share of ad expenditures.

Allergan Inc.	7.40%
Alcon Laboratories Inc.	6.16
Merck	5.35
Pharmacia & Upjohn Inc.	3.67
Bausch & Lomb Surgical	3.20
Allergan Pharmaceuticals	2.95
Bausch & Lomb Pharmaceutical Products	2.62
Other	68.65

Source: *Medical Marketing & Media*, April 2000, p. 68, from PERQ/HCI.

★ 1168 ★

Ophthalmology Products (SIC 3851)

Leading Optometry Advertisers - 1999

Data show share of ad expenditures.

Transitions Optical	2.74%
Luxottica Group	2.69
Johnson & Johnson	2.67
Marchon Eyewear	2.59
Safilo Group	2.11
Wesley-Jessen	2.09
Sola Optical USA	1.93
Other	83.18

Source: *Medical Marketing & Media*, April 2000, p. 68, from PERQ/HCI Journal Ad Review.

★ 1169 ★

Ophthalmology Products (SIC 3851)

Most Advertised Ophthalmology Products - 1999

Data show share of ad expenditures.

Alphagen	3.46%
Cosopt	2.97
Xalatan Solution	2.71
Acular and Acular PF	1.67

Bausch & Lomb Surgical Ad	1.50%
Ocuflux	1.48
Ciloxan	1.41
Other	84.80

Source: *Medical Marketing & Media*, April 2000, p. 68, from PERQ/HCI.

★ 1170 ★

Cameras (SIC 3861)

Camera Sales by Type

	1998	1999
Film	74%	64%
Digital	26	36

Source: *Investor's Business Daily*, April 11, 2000, p. 1, from NPD Intelect.

★ 1171 ★

Cameras (SIC 3861)

Digital Camera Unit Shares - 2000

Retail shares are shown as of February 2000.

Sony	33.1%
Eastman Kodak	21.2
Hewlett-Packard	10.1
Olympus	9.3
Polaroid	5.5
Agfa	3.4
Canon	3.1
Toshiba	3.0
IXLA Limited	2.9
Nikon	2.3
Other	6.2

Source: *New York Times*, March 27, 2000, p. C1, from International Data Corp. and PC Data.

★ 1172 ★
Cameras (SIC 3861)

Dollar Camera Sales

Dollar shares are shown in percent.

35mm lens shutter	50.6%
APS lens shutter	21.7
35mm SLR	21.2
Instant	4.3
APS SLR	1.3
110	1.0

Source: *Discount Merchandiser*, January 2000, p. 3, from Photo Marketing Association International.

★ 1173 ★
Cameras (SIC 3861)

Entry-Level Digital Camera Market

Polaroid	38%
KB Gear	35
Other	27

Source: "KB Gear Leads 199 Sales." Retrieved March 24, 2000 from the World Wide Web: http://library. northernlight.com, from International Data Corp.

★ 1174 ★
Cameras (SIC 3861)

Top Digital Camera Makers - 1999

Market shares are shown for July 1999.

Sony	50%
Kodak	14
Creative Labs	12
Olympus	11
Hewlett-Packard	4
Other	9

Source: *PC Magazine*, November 16, 1999, p. 12, from Ziff-Davis.

★ 1175 ★
Cameras (SIC 3861)

Top Single-Use Camera Vendors - 1999

Brands are ranked by total sales of $720.9 million for the year ended December 5, 1999.

	($ mil.)	Share
Eastman Kodak	$ 439.4	60.95%
Fuji Photo Film	144.3	20.02
Jazz Photo	17.7	2.46
Polaroid	11.2	1.55
Other	108.3	15.02

Source: *MMR*, February 7, 2000, p. 18, from Information Resources Inc.

★ 1176 ★
Cameras (SIC 3861)

Unit Camera Sales - 1998

35mm lens shutter	56.0%
Advanced photo system	18.5
Instant	11.9
110	8.0
355mm SLR	5.3
Advanced photo system SLR	0.3

Source: *Supermarket Business*, January 15, 2000, p. 95, from Photo Marketing Association International.

★ 1177 ★
Copiers (SIC 3861)

Analog Copier Market

The $5.6 billion market is shown in percent.

Canon	38%
Xerox	27
Others	35

Source: *Forbes*, March 20, 2000, p. I54, from International Data Corp., Dataquest, and PaineWebber.

★ 1178 ★
Copiers (SIC 3861)

Black & White Laser Printer Market

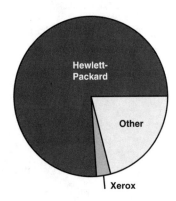

The $4.6 billion market is shown in percent.

Hewlett-Packard 76%
Xerox 3
Other 21

Source: *Forbes*, March 20, 2000, p. I54, from International Data Corp., Dataquest, and PaineWebber.

★ 1179 ★
Copiers (SIC 3861)

Copier Market by Segment

	(000)	Share
Digital connected	793	47.09%
Digital standalone	513	30.46
Analog	378	22.45

Source: *Purchasing*, January 13, 2000, p. 129, from CAP Ventures.

★ 1180 ★
Copiers (SIC 3861)

Digital Stand-Alone Copier Market

The $2.2 billion market is shown in percent.

Xerox 32%
Canon 18
Other 50

Source: *Forbes*, March 20, 2000, p. I54, from International Data Corp., Dataquest, and PaineWebber.

★ 1181 ★
Imaging (SIC 3861)

Positron Emission Tomography Market

CTI/Siemens 75%
Other 25

Source: "Siemens and CTI Inc." Retrieved April 20, 2000 from the World Wide Web: http://library.northernlight.com.

★ 1182 ★
Photographic Film (SIC 3861)

35-mm Market Leaders

Eastman Kodak 69%
Other 31

Source: *Forbes*, May 29, 2000, p. 62.

★ 1183 ★
Photographic Film (SIC 3861)

Top Film Brands - 1999

Shares are shown based on sales of $1.6 billion for the year ended February 27, 2000.

Kodak Gold 21.7%
Polaroid Platinum 600 . . . . 17.5
Kodak Gold Max 16.0
Fuji 10.1
Kodak Adantix 8.8
Kodak Kodacolor Gold 3.1
Kodak 2.8
Private label 4.9
Other 15.1

Source: *Supermarket Business*, May 15, 2000, p. 80, from Information Resources Inc.

★ 1184 ★

Photographic Film (SIC 3861)

Top Photo Brands - 1999

Shares are shown based on total sales of $1.68 billion for the year ended December 5, 1999.

	($ mil.)	Share
Eastman Kodak	$ 986.6	58.73%
Polaroid	390.5	23.24
Fuji Photo Film	212.3	12.64
Konishiroku Photo (Konica)	0.6	0.04
Other	90.0	5.36

Source: *MMR*, February 7, 2000, p. 17, from Information Resources Inc.

SIC 39 - Miscellaneous Manufacturing Industries

★ 1185 ★

Flatware (SIC 3914)

U.S. Flatware Market

Oneida 65%
Other 35

Source: *HFN*, March 7, 2000, p. 39.

★ 1186 ★

Musical Instruments (SIC 3931)

Music Product Sales by State

Sales are shown in billions of dollars.

California . . . . $ 1,033.0
New York 564.1
Texas 527.4
Florida 458.7
Illinois 351.9
Pennyslvania 257.3
Ohio 255.4
Michigan 243.7
New Jersey 239.7
Maryland 239.0

Source: *Music Trades*, August 1999, p. 179.

★ 1187 ★

Toys and Games (SIC 3940)

Top Toy Brands - 1999

Traditional toy brands are ranked by share of dollar sales.

Barbie 6.5%
Hot Wheels 2.3
Star Wars 2.3
Lego: Basic/Themed/Freestyle 2.2
Furby 1.9
Crayola 1.5
Sesame Street 1.4
Winnie the Pooh 1.1
Power Rangers 0.9
WWF 0.9
Other 79.0

Source: *Playthings*, March 2000, p. 24, from NPD Group TRSTS.

★ 1188 ★

Dolls (SIC 3942)

Action Figure Market - 1999

Shares are for the first 11 months of the year.

Hasbro 48.3%
Bandai America 13.6
Toy Biz 11.5
Jakks Pacific 10.0
Mattel 3.5
Other 13.2

Source: *Playthings*, February 2000, p. 14, from NPD Group.

★ 1189 ★
Dolls (SIC 3942)

Collectible Dolls/Plush Toy Producers - 1998

Data show revenues in millions of dollars.

Enesco	$ 451
Russ Berrie	271
Department 56	243
Boyds	198

Source: *Investor's Business Daily*, August 6, 1999, p. A6, from Merrill Lynch and U.S. Census Bureau.

★ 1190 ★
Dolls (SIC 3942)

Doll Sales by Segment - 1998

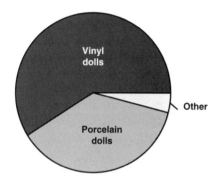

Dolls remain the second largest collectibles category after figurines. An estimated 11.3 million adults collect dolls.

	($ mil.)	Share
Vinyl dolls	$ 972	58.59%
Porcelain dolls	617	37.19
Other	70	4.22

Source: "Collectible Doll Market Maturing." Retrieved January 20, 2000 from the World Wide Web: http://www.unitymarketingonline.com, from Unity Marketing.

★ 1191 ★
Dolls (SIC 3942)

Fashion Doll Sales

	1997	1999
Barbie	96%	79%
Other	4	21

Source: *New York Times*, April 1, 2000, p. C1, from Gerard Klauer Mattison & Company.

★ 1192 ★
Dolls (SIC 3942)

Large Doll Makers - 2000

Shares are shown for January 2000.

Hong Kong	17.3%
Mattel	15.6
Gi-Go Toys Factory	12.2
Toy Biz	9.2
Unimax	8.5
Goldberger Doll	7.0
Others	30.2

Source: *Playthings*, April 2000, p. 20, from NPD's TRSTS.

★ 1193 ★
Dolls (SIC 3942)

Mini Doll Makers - 2000

Shares are shown for January 2000.

Empire Interactive	12.3%
Mattel	11.0
Toy Biz	9.2
Arco	9.1
Ohio Art	8.1
Other	50.3

Source: *Playthings*, April 2000, p. 20, from NPD's TRSTS.

★ 1194 ★
Dolls (SIC 3942)

Wrestling Action Figure Market - 1999

Jakks	55%
Marvel's	45

Source: *Investor's Business Daily*, October 19, 1999, p. A10, from NPD Group.

★ 1195 ★

Toys and Games (SIC 3944)

Pinball Machine Market - 1999

Global pinball sales have fallen from 100,000 units in 1992 to 10,000 units in 1999. The market is expected to be maintained by sticking to classic designs and cafe and cinema installations, rather than arcades.

WMS	75%
Other	25

Source: *The Economist*, March 11, 2000, p. 72.

★ 1196 ★

Toys and Games (SIC 3944)

Sports Activity Market

Shares are as of May 1999.

Hedstrom	10.1%
General Sportscraft	9.4
Wham-O	7.8
OddzOn	7.4
Hasbro	6.5
Franklin Sports	6.3
Regent Sports	5.2
Other	47.3

Source: *Playthings*, August 1999, p. 18, from NPD TRSTS Report.

★ 1197 ★

Toys and Games (SIC 3944)

Top Licensed Properties

Dollar shares are shown in percent.

Barbie	6.2%
Star Wars	5.5
Lego	2.5
Furby	2.4
Hot Wheels	2.2
Pokemon	2.0
Nascar	1.8
Winnie the Pooh	1.7
Nickelodeon	1.3
Power Rangers	1.3
Super Soaker	1.3
Other	71.8

Source: *Brandweek*, October 18, 1999, p. 18, from NPD Group.

★ 1198 ★

Toys and Games (SIC 3944)

Water/Pool/Sand Toy Market - 1999

Shares are as of May 1999.

Intex	35.9%
General Foam Plastic	9.4
Aqua Leisure	7.9
Kidpower	4.8
Tony Trading	4.8
Florida Pool Products	3.0
Wellington Leisure	2.3
Other	31.9

Source: *Playthings*, August 1999, p. 18, from NPD TRSTS Report.

★ 1199 ★

Video Games (SIC 3944)

Best Selling Video Games 1994-1999

Data show unit sales.

Myst and Raven	5.60
Doom and sequels	4.27
MS Flight Sim Games	3.95
Warcraft	2.95
Monopoly	1.98

Source: *Forbes*, October 18, 1999, p. I60, from PC Data Inc.

★ 1200 ★

Video Games (SIC 3944)

Game Machine Market - 2000

Shares are for February 2000.

Sony	52%
Nintendo	33
Sega	15

Source: *Wall Street Journal*, April 4, 2000, p. B4, from NPD Group.

★ 1201 ★
Video Games (SIC 3944)

Handheld Game Players

The battery-powered device market is shown in percent. The entire electronic game market is valued at $13 billion.

Gameboy 99.8%
Other 0.2

Source: *Forbes*, May 1, 2000, p. 90.

★ 1202 ★
Video Games (SIC 3944)

Leading Video Game Publishers

Nintendo	
Sony	
Electronic Arts	
Midway	
Acclaim	
Other	

Shares are shown based on revenues.

Nintendo 25.5%
Sony 17.3
Electronic Arts 11.6
Midway 5.1
Acclaim 4.7
Other 35.8

Source: "Console, PC Games Industry Sales Top $7.4B in 1999." Retrieved February 4, 2000 from the World Wide Web: http://www.pcdata.com, from PC Data.

★ 1203 ★
Video Games (SIC 3944)

PC Games Unit Sales - 1998

Strategy 24.9%
Adventure 17.6
Sports 17.0
Action 15.7
Flight/war sim 10.3
Racing 5.9
Other 8.9

Source: "The State of the PC Game Market." Retrieved February 23, 2000 from the World Wide Web: http://www.dfcint.com/game-article, from NPD Group.

★ 1204 ★
Video Games (SIC 3944)

Video Console Market - 1999

The $7 billion market is shown in percent.

Sony PlayStation 43%
Nintendo 64 26
Nintendo Game Boy 18
Sega Dreamcast 11
Others 2

Source: *Investor's Business Daily*, March 7, 2000, p. A1.

★ 1205 ★
Video Games (SIC 3944)

Video Game Console Leaders - 1999

Shares are for the first quarter.

Sony PlayStation 66.3%
Nintendo 64 . . . . 33.4
Sega Saturn 0.3

Source: *Investor's Business Daily*, May 25, 1999, p. A6, from NPD Group.

★ 1206 ★
Video Games (SIC 3944)

Video Game Industry - 1999

Shares are shown based on console, hand-held and software sales.

Nintendo 47%
Sony 44
Sega 9

Source: *Investor's Business Daily*, February 4, 2000, p. A6, from NPD Group Inc.

★ 1207 ★
Video Games (SIC 3944)

Video Game Software Market - 1999

Shares are for the fourth quarter.

Sony 64.3%
Nintendo 28.6
Sega 7.1

Source: *Wall Street Journal*, January 13, 2000, p. B4, from NPD Group.

★ 1208 ★

Video Games (SIC 3944)

Wrestling Video Games

WCW	71%
WWF	21
Other	8

Source: *Investor's Business Daily*, October 19, 1999, p. A10, from NPD Group.

★ 1209 ★

Exercise Equipment (SIC 3949)

Exercise Equipment Sales in Canada - 1998

Data show estimated retail sales in thousands of dollars.

	($ 000)	Share
Treadmills	$ 119,000	43.59%
Multipurpose home gyms	31,000	11.36
Stationary/exercise bikes	19,000	6.96
Barbells	14,000	5.13
Rowing machines	6,000	2.20
Aerobic stepups	5,000	1.83
X-country ski-exerciser	5,000	1.83
Other	74,000	27.11

Source: Retrieved January 21, 2000 from the World Wide Web: http://strategis.ic.gc.ca/SSG, from Industry Canada.

★ 1210 ★

Sporting Goods (SIC 3949)

Bicycle Helmet Market

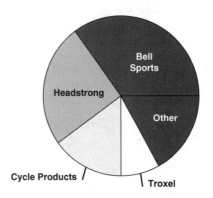

Data are estimated.

	(000)	Share
Bell Sports	4,500	34.62%
Headstrong	3,300	25.38
Cycle Products	2,000	15.38
Troxel	1,000	7.69
Other	2,200	16.92

Source: "Some Helmet Manufacturers." Retrieved November 30, 1999 from the World Wide Web: http://www.bhsi.org/webdocs/manufacs.htm, from Headstrong Group.

★ 1211 ★

Sporting Goods (SIC 3949)

Camping Equipment Sales in Canada - 1998

Data show estimated sales in thousands of dollars.

	($ 000)	Share
Tents, 3+ men	$ 60,000	31.91%
Sleeping bags	33,000	17.55
Tents, 1-2 men	20,000	10.64
Camp stoves	16,000	8.51
Backpacks	11,000	5.85
Ice chests	9,000	4.79
Lanterns	3,000	1.60
Jus/coolers	2,000	1.06
Other	34,000	18.09

Source: Retrieved January 21, 2000 from the World Wide Web: http://strategis.ic.gc.ca/SSG, from Industry Canada.

★ **1212** ★

Sporting Goods (SIC 3949)

Field Sports Market in Canada - 1998

Data show estimated unit sales, in thousands.

	($ 000)	Share
Soccer balls	318	40.15%
Basketballs	244	30.81
Volleyballs	106	13.38
Lacross equipment, protective . . .	33	4.17
Football equipment	27	3.41
Footballs	27	3.41
Lacross sticks	23	2.90
Backboard/hoop/net sets	14	1.77

Source: Retrieved January 21, 2000 from the World Wide Web: http://strategis.ic.gc.ca/SSG, from Industry Canada.

★ **1213** ★

Sporting Goods (SIC 3949)

Fishing Equipment Sales in Canada - 1998

Data show estimated retail sales in thousands of dollars.

	($ 000)	Share
Lures	$ 41,000	32.8%
Rod/reel combo	22,000	17.6
Rod only	16,000	12.8
Reel only	10,000	8.0
Tackle boxes	6,000	4.8
Lines	6,000	4.8
Hooks	3,000	2.4
Other	21,000	16.8

Source: Retrieved January 21, 2000 from the World Wide Web: http://strategis.ic.gc.ca/SSG, from Industry Canada.

★ **1214** ★

Sporting Goods (SIC 3949)

Golf Ball Market

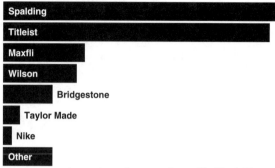

Shares are shown based on number of balls sold.

Spalding	34.0%
Titleist	32.6
Maxfli	10.0
Wilson	9.0
Bridgestone	5.5
Taylor Made	1.7
Nike	1.1
Other	6.1

Source: *Wall Street Journal*, June 15, 2000, p. A10.

★ **1215** ★

Sporting Goods (SIC 3949)

Golf Equipment Market

Shares are shown in percent.

Callaway	30%
Titleist	15
Wilson	6
Other	49

Source: *Crain's Chicago Business*, February 28, 2000, p. 4.

★ 1216 ★

Sporting Goods (SIC 3949)

Golf Equipment Sales - 1999

*Sales are shown in millions of dollars for the first 11
months of the year.*

	($ mil.)	Share
Woods	$ 532.8	32.79%
Golf balls	475.9	29.29
Irons	408.4	25.13
Putters	147.7	9.09
Wedges	60.1	3.70

Source: *Sports Business Journal*, February 7, 2000, p. 25,
from Golf Datatech.

★ 1217 ★

Sporting Goods (SIC 3949)

Golf Product Unit Sales

*Data are based on second quarter sales at golf spe-
cialty shops.*

	Units	Share
Irons	2,400,000	48.01%
Woods	941,160	18.83
Footwear	801,550	16.04
Putters	591,060	11.82
Wedges	264,860	5.30

Source: *Golfweek*, August 14, 2000, p. 22, from Datatech.

★ 1218 ★

Sporting Goods (SIC 3949)

Golf Wedge Makers

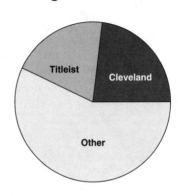

Cleveland	23.0%
Titleist	19.9
Other	57.1

Source: *Golfweek*, August 14, 1999, p. 20.

★ 1219 ★

Sporting Goods (SIC 3949)

Hockey Equipment Sales in Canada - 1998

Sales are shown in percent.

	($ 000)	Share
Sticks, ice	$ 33,000	33.33%
Protective equipment, ice	26,000	26.26
Ice hockey helmets	15,000	15.15
Ice hockey gloves	14,000	14.14
Other	11,000	11.11

Source: Retrieved January 21, 2000 from the World Wide
Web: http://strategis.ic.gc.ca/SSG, from Industry Canada.

★ 1220 ★
Sporting Goods (SIC 3949)

Ice Skate Sales in Canada - 1998

Data show estimated retail sales in thousands of dollars.

	($ 000)	Share
Hockey skates	$ 111,000	73.03%
Figures skates	37,000	24.34
Speed skates	4,000	2.63

Source: Retrieved January 21, 2000 from the World Wide Web: http://strategis.ic.gc.ca/SSG, from Industry Canada.

★ 1221 ★
Sporting Goods (SIC 3949)

Outdoor Sports Industry - 1999

Firms are ranked by projected sales in millions of dollars.

Coleman	$ 480
The North Face	280
JanSport	180
American Camper	180
American Recreation	150

Source: "Top 10." Retrieved May 16, 2000 from the World Wide Web: http://www.sgblink.com.

★ 1222 ★
Sporting Goods (SIC 3949)

Ski Equipment Sales

Sales are shown in millions of dollars.

	1997	1999	Share
Down-hill ski equipment .	$ 722.7	$ 739.3	74.61%
Snowboard equipment . . .	135.6	183.5	18.52
Cross-country equipment . .	69.4	68.1	6.87

Source: *Christian Science Monitor*, November 30, 1999, p. 20.

★ 1223 ★
Sporting Goods (SIC 3949)

Sporting Goods Market - 1998

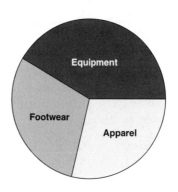

Equipment	42.0%
Footwear	29.5
Apparel	28.5

Source: *Discount Store News*, July 12, 1999, p. 27, from National Sporting Goods Association.

★ 1224 ★
Sporting Goods (SIC 3949)

Sporting Goods Market in Canada

The market reached an estimated $5.3 billion for July 1998 - June 1999.

	($ bil.)	Share
Sporting goods equipment	$ 2.62	49.25%
Sports footwear	1.39	26.13
Sports clothing	1.31	24.62

Source: "Industry Status Report." Retrieved May 16, 2000 from the World Wide Web: http://www.csga.ca/industry/report.html.

★ 1225 ★
Sporting Goods (SIC 3949)

Sporting Goods Market in Canada - 1998

Data show estimated sales in thousands of dollars.

Sports footwear	$ 1,431,000
Sports clothing	1,372,000
Bicycles/bicycle equipment	579,000
Golf equipment	413,000
Exercise equipment	276,000
Camping equipment	201,000

Continued on next page.

★ 1225 ★ *Continued*
Sporting Goods (SIC 3949)

Sporting Goods Market in Canada - 1998

Data show estimated sales in thousands of dollars.

Ice hockey/figure/speed skates . . . . . $ 151,000
In-line skates 149,000

Source: Retrieved January 21, 2000 from the World Wide Web: http://strategis.ic.gc.ca/SSG, from Industry Canada.

★ 1226 ★
Sporting Goods (SIC 3949)

Team Sports Industry - 1999

Firms are ranked by projected sales in millions of dollars.

Rawlings . . . . $ 165.0
Wilson 157.1
Easton 143.0
Spalding 141.0
Franklin 110.2

Source: "Top 10." Retrieved May 16, 2000 from the World Wide Web: http://www.sgblink.com.

★ 1227 ★
Sporting Goods (SIC 3949)

Tennis Racket Market

The company had a 15% share in 1986.

Wilson 50%
Other 50

Source: *Forbes*, April 17, 2000, p. I44.

★ 1228 ★
Sporting Goods (SIC 3949)

Top In-line Skating Cities - 1997

Data show thousands of participants.

New York City 1,924
Los Angeles 1,570
Detroit 859
Minneapolis/St. Paul 716
San Francisco 626
Cleveland 594
Chicago 534

Source: "In-line Skating Industry Facts." Retrieved November 30, 1999 from the World Wide Web: http://www.rollerblade.com, from Rollerblade Inc.

★ 1229 ★
Sporting Goods (SIC 3949)

Top In-line Skating States - 1997

Data show thousands of participants.

California 3,188
Texas 2,014
New York 1,776
Michigan 1,549
Florida 1,511
Ohio 1,511
Pennyslvania 1,315

Source: "In-line Skating Industry Facts." Retrieved November 30, 1999 from the World Wide Web: http://www.rollerblade.com, from Rollerblade Inc.

★ 1230 ★
Sporting Goods (SIC 3949)

Top Sports Equipment Firms - 1999

Companies are ranked by estimated sales in millions of dollars.

Adidas-Salomon . . . . $ 844.0
Spalding 445.1
Nike 312.2
Riddell 210.5
Rawlings 167.3
Wilson 157.1
Easton 143.0
Hillerich & Bradsby 112.0
Franklin 110.2

Source: *Sports Business Journal*, February 7, 2000, p. 29, from *Sporting Goods Business*.

★ 1231 ★

Sporting Goods (SIC 3949)

Wood Bat Market

The market is valued at $15 million.

H&B 65%
Other 35

Source: *U.S. News & World Report*, November 1, 1999, p. 60.

★ 1232 ★

Writing Instruments (SIC 3950)

Writing Instrument Market - 1998

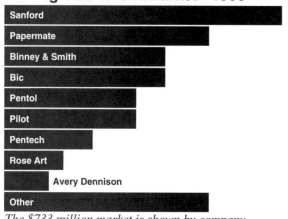

Sanford
Papermate
Binney & Smith
Bic
Pentol
Pilot
Pentech
Rose Art
Avery Dennison
Other

The $733 million market is shown by company.

Sanford 18.8%
Papermate 14.3
Binney & Smith 11.4
Bic 11.1
Pentol 8.8
Pilot 8.8
Pentech 5.8
Rose Art 4.1
Avery Dennison 3.1
Other 13.8

Source: *Discount Store News*, February 22, 1999, p. 41, from A.C. Nielsen.

★ 1233 ★

Writing Instruments (SIC 3950)

Writing Instrument Shipments

Shipments are shown in millions of units.

	(000)
Ballpoint pens, nonrefillable	2,320
Pencils, cased	2,135

	(000)
Ballpoint pens, refillable	1,303
Markers & highlighters	759
Markers & pens, coloring	564
Pens, roller	454
Mechanical pens	400
Porous point pens	170
Fountain pens	14

Source: Retrieved January 1, 2000 from the World Wide Web: http://www.wima.org/industry/i-07indstatinfor/ 97stats.html.

★ 1234 ★

Fasteners (SIC 3965)

Fastener Demand by Type

Data are in billions of dollars.

	($ bil.)	($ bil.)	Share
Standard	$ 7.83	$ 9.4	89.52%
Aerospace	0.86	1.1	10.48

Source: *Assembly*, November 1999, p. 16, from Freedonia Group.

★ 1235 ★

Brushes (SIC 3991)

Industrial Brush Market in the Mid-Atlantic States

Sales are shown in millions of dollars.

Building maintenance services . . . . . . $ 5.6
Medical and surgical hospitals 4.6
Elementary/secondary schools 4.3
Eating places 4.3
Grocery stores 2.0

Source: *Industrial Distribution*, July 1999, p. 73, from Industrial Market Information Inc.

★ 1236 ★
Brushes (SIC 3991)

Industrial Brush Market in the Pacific Coast

Sales are shown in millions of dollars.

Eating places	$ 5.4
Building maintenance services	5.3
Elementary/secondary schools	3.5
Medical & surgical hospitals	3.1
Grocery stores	1.7

Source: *Industrial Distribution*, July 1999, p. 73, from Industrial Market Information Inc.

★ 1237 ★
Mops and Brooms (SIC 3991)

Top Mop/Broom Brands - 1999

Shares are shown based on sales of $856.8 million for the year ended February 27, 2000.

Swiffer	17.7%
Pledge Grab It	7.5
Quickie	5.9
Rubbermaid	5.3
Libman	3.9
Roll O Matic	2.3
O Cedar 2000	2.0
Other	55.4

Source: *Supermarket Business*, May 15, 2000, p. 70, from Information Resources Inc.

★ 1238 ★
Flooring (SIC 3996)

Laminate Floor Market

An estimated 38 firms occupy the $500 million market.

Perstorp/Wilsonart/Formica	65%
Other	35

Source: *Floor Focus*, April 1999, p. 1.

★ 1239 ★
Flooring (SIC 3996)

Resilient Floor Covering

Sales are shown in millions of dollars.

	1996	1998	Share
Vinyl sheet & floor tile	$ 1,819.1	$ 1,981.5	72.69%
Rubber flooring	637.5	744.3	27.31

Source: *Floor Covering Weekly*, November 1999, p. 1.

★ 1240 ★
Arts and Crafts (SIC 3999)

Arts and Crafts Market

Dollar shares are shown in percent.

Binney & Smith	20.2%
Rose Art	10.9
Flying Colors	3.3
Fiskars	2.9
Lisa Frank	2.4
Mattel	2.4
Others	57.9

Source: *Playthings*, September 1999, p. 18, from NPD TRSTS Report.

★ 1241 ★
Baby Care (SIC 3999)

Top Baby Care/Accessory Brands - 1999

Shares are shown based on sales of $388.8 million for the year ended February 27, 2000.

Safety 1st	17.2%
Cosco	10.2
Diaper Genie	8.7
Fisher Price	6.6
First Years	6.1

Continued on next page.

★ 1241 ★ *Continued*
Baby Care (SIC 3999)

Top Baby Care/Accessory Brands - 1999

Shares are shown based on sales of $388.8 million for the year ended February 27, 2000.

Gerico	5.5%
Century Baby Care	5.4
Other	40.3

Source: *Supermarket Business*, May 15, 2000, p. 80, from Information Resources Inc.

★ 1242 ★
Baby Care (SIC 3999)

Top Nursing/Feeding Accessory Brands - 1999

Shares are shown based on sales of $443.6 million for the year ended February 27, 2000.

Playtex	18.4%
Gerber	8.6
Evenflo	5.2
Playtex Spill Proof	5.1
Luv N Care	5.0
Playtex Drop Ins	4.7
Evenflo Natural Mother	4.1
Zak	2.9
Other	46.0

Source: *Supermarket Business*, May 15, 2000, p. 84, from Information Resources Inc.

★ 1243 ★
Candles (SIC 3999)

Leading Candle/Incense/Accessories Markets - 1999

Sales are shown in millions of dollars in selected markets. Figures are for the year ended September 4, 1999.

New York City	$ 22.0
Los Angeles	21.2
Chicago	10.9
Philadelphia	9.8
Boston	9.1

Source: *Grocery Headquarters*, January 2000, p. 45, from A.C. Nielsen.

★ 1244 ★
Candles (SIC 3999)

Top Candle Brands - 1999

Shares are shown based on sales of $882 million for the year ended February 27, 2000.

Glade Candle Scents	13.8%
Candle Lite	11.1
Fragrance De Lite	5.4
Ambria	5.1
Mood Makers	4.6
Renuzit Longlast	3.5
Colony	3.2
American Greetings	2.4
Reeds	2.0
Other	48.9

Source: *Supermarket Business*, May 15, 2000, p. 84, from Information Resources Inc.

★ 1245 ★
Charcoal (SIC 3999)

Leading Charcoal/Log/Accessory Markets - 1999

Sales are shown in millions of dollars in selected markets. Figures are for the year ended September 4, 1999.

Los Angeles	$ 32.6
New York City	16.7
Chicago	12.4
Boston	8.0
Philadelphia	7.8

Source: *Grocery Headquarters*, January 2000, p. 45, from A.C. Nielsen.

★ 1246 ★
Christmas Items (SIC 3999)

U.S. Christmas Item Imports - 1999

Imports are shown in millions of dollars as of October 31, 1999. China is the leading source of imports.

Ornaments	$ 866
Related holiday items	363
Artificial trees	160
Nativity sets	47

Source: *USA TODAY*, December 23, 1999, p. 3B, from U. S. Census Bureau.

★ 1247 ★

Hair Accessories (SIC 3999)

Top Hair Accessory Brands - 1999

Shares are shown based on sales of $790 million for the year ended October 10, 1999.

Goody	24.3%
Scunci	11.7
Vidal Sassoon	8.6
Seventeen	4.5
Cosmopolitan	3.0
Ace	2.9
Wilhold	2.8
Goody Classic	2.3
Conair	2.1
Other	37.8

Source: *Chain Drug Review*, January 17, 2000, p. 21, from Information Resources Inc.

★ 1248 ★

Kitty Litter (SIC 3999)

Top Kitty Litter Brands - 1998

Brands are ranked by sales of $803.1 million for the year ended January 21, 1999.

	($ mil.)	Share
Scoop Away	$ 99.8	12.43%
Fresh Step Scoop	71.1	8.85
Fresh Step	66.3	8.26
Tidy Cat Scoop MC	48.7	6.06
Jonny Cat	43.6	5.43
ARM & Hammer Super Scoop	41.1	5.12
Tidy Cat	31.2	3.88
Tidy Scoop	30.5	3.80
Other	370.8	46.17

Source: *MMR*, May 17, 1999, p. 36, from Information Resources Inc.

★ 1249 ★

Lunch Boxes (SIC 3999)

Lunch Box Sales

Data show share of the $50 million soft- and hardsided licensed lunch box sector. The entire lunch box and portable cooler segment generated sales of $470 million.

Thermos Co.	80%
Other	20

Source: *Crain's Chicago Business*, November 8, 1999, p. 4.

★ 1250 ★

Permanent Magnets (SIC 3999)

Permanent Magnet Sales

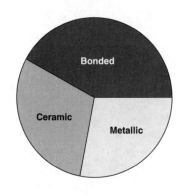

Sales are shown in millions of dollars.

	1999	2004	Share
Bonded	$ 285	$ 445	41.67%
Ceramic	252	320	29.96
Metallic	207	303	28.37

Source: *Ceramic Bulletin*, January 2000, p. 27, from Business Communications Co.

★ 1251 ★

Pet Products (SIC 3999)

Natural/Organic Pet Product Market

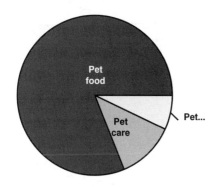

Sales are shown in millions of dollars at natural product stores. Figures are for the year ended April 1999.

	($ mil.)	Share
Pet food	$ 30.9	81.53%
Pet care	4.5	11.87
Pet supplies	2.5	6.60

Source: *Grocery Headquarters*, October 1999, p. 87, from SPINS and A.C. Nielsen.

★ 1252 ★

Shoe Store Sizers (SIC 3999)

Shoe Store Sizer Market

Brannock Device Co.	80%
Other	20

Source: *Forbes*, May 29, 2000, p. 62.

SIC 40 - Railroad Transportation

★ 1253 ★

Railroads (SIC 4011)

Largest Railroad Firms - 1999

Union Pacific	
CSX	
Burlington No. Santa Fe	
Norfolk Southern	
	Kansas City So. Inds.

Firms are ranked by revenues in billions of dollars.

Union Pacific	$ 11.2
CSX	10.8
Burlington No. Santa Fe	9.1
Norfolk Southern	5.1
Kansas City So. Inds.	1.6

Source: *Fortune*, April 17, 2000, pp. I-72.

★ 1254 ★

Railroads (SIC 4011)

Railroad Market Shares - 1998

UP	32%
CP	15
CSX	14
BNSF	13
CN	9
NS	9
IC	5
KCS	3

Source: *Chemical Week*, September 22, 1999, p. 31, from American Association of Railroads.

SIC 41 - Local and Interurban Passenger Transit

★ 1255 ★
Bus Companies (SIC 4111)

Largest Private Bus Companies in the U.S. and Canada

Companies are ranked by total number of buses.

Laidlaw Transit Services/Greyhound Lines	6,049
Coach USA Inc.	5,800
Travelways	1,042
Academy Bus Tours Inc.	689
Pacific Western Transportation Ltd.	437
Martz Group	405
Liberty Lines	392
Queens Surface Corp.	321
Holland America Line-Westours Inc.	297

Source: ''Statistics.'' Retrieved April 20, 2000 from the World Wide Web: http://www.transit-center.com.

★ 1256 ★
Bus Companies (SIC 4111)

Largest Transit Bus Agencies in the U.S. and Canada

Companies are ranked by size of fleet.

MTA New York City Transit	4,172
New Jersey Transit Corp.	2,931
Los Angeles County MTA	2,200
Chicago Transit Authority	1,877
Montreal Urban Community Transit Corp.	1,686
Toronto Transit Commission	1,608
Washington Metropolitan Area Transit	1,411
Metropolitan Transit Authority of Harris County (TX)	1,371
Southeastern Pennsylvania Transportation Authority	1,319

Source: ''Statistics.'' Retrieved April 20, 2000 from the World Wide Web: http://www.transit-center.com.

★ 1257 ★
Rail Companies (SIC 4111)

Largest Rail Agencies

Companies are ranked by cost of projects, in millions.

Amtrak	$ 5,400
Mass. Bay Transportation Authority	2,800
Metro-Dade Transit Agency	2,731
Bay Area Rapid Transit District	2,645
Central Puget Sound Regional Transit Authority	2,400
MTA New York City Transit	2,356
San Francisco Municipal Railway	2,200
Orange County Transportation Authority	1,917
Treno Urbano	1,718

Source: ''Statistics.'' Retrieved April 20, 2000 from the World Wide Web: http://www.transit-center.com.

★ 1258 ★
Limousine Services (SIC 4119)

Limo Market in Las Vegas, NV

Data are estimated.

Bell Transportation	90%
Other	10

Source: *Limousine & Chauffered Transportation*, August 1999, p. 51.

★ 1259 ★
Limousine Services (SIC 4119)

Top Markets for Limo Services - 1998

Data show share of revenues, based on a survey.

Corporate work 24%
Airport transfers 22
Weddings 20
Other 34

Source: Retrieved January 18, 2000 from the World Wide
Web: http://www.limousinecentral.com/noflash/operate1.
cfn.

SIC 42 - Trucking and Warehousing

★ 1260 ★

Trucking (SIC 4210)

Largest Bulk Transporters - 1998

Firms are ranked by revenues in millions of dollars.

Quality Distribution	$ 620.2
Trimac Transportation	443.4
Matlack	238.9
Initial DSI Transports	156.2
Kenan Transport	138.0
Greendyke	124.7
Bilkmatic Transport	123.1
Dewy	121.4
Tankstar USA	114.3

Source: *CMR Focus*, November 22, 1999, p. 11, from *Modern Bulk Transporter*.

★ 1261 ★

Trucking (SIC 4210)

Largest Car Hauling Firms - 1998

Firms are ranked by revenues in millions of dollars.

Allied Systems	$ 726.7
Leaseway Motorcar Trpt.	191.3
Cassens Transport Co.	183.6

Source: *CCJ*, August 1999, p. 48.

★ 1262 ★

Trucking (SIC 4210)

Largest Household Goods Firms - 1998

United Van Lines
Allied Van Lines Inc.
Atlas Van Lines Inc.
Mayflower Transit
Bekins Van Lines

Firms are ranked by revenues in millions of dollars.

United Van Lines	$ 756.6
Allied Van Lines Inc.	491.3
Atlas Van Lines Inc.	385.9
Mayflower Transit	316.6
Bekins Van Lines	220.7

Source: *CCJ*, August 1999, p. 48.

★ 1263 ★

Trucking (SIC 4210)

Largest Refrigerated Good Firms - 1998

Firms are ranked by revenues in millions of dollars.

FFE Transportation Services	$ 257.1
KLLM Inc.	228.9
Simon Transportation	193.5
Stevens Transport Inc.	169.5
Midwest Coast Transport	128.1

Source: *CCJ*, August 1999, p. 48.

★ 1264 ★

Trucking (SIC 4210)

Largest Top Tank Truck Carriers - 1998

Firms are ranked by revenues in millions of dollars.

Quality Distribution	$ 620
Trimac Transportation	443
Matlack Systems	239
Initial DSI Transports	156
Kenan Transport	138
Groendyke Transport	125
Bulkamatic Transport	123
Dewey Corp.	121

Source: *Chemical Week*, September 22, 1999, p. 37, from *Modern Bulk Transporter*.

★ 1265 ★

Trucking (SIC 4210)

Largest Trucking Firms - 1998

Firms are ranked by revenues in millions of dollars.

United Parcel Services	$ 17.0
Schneider National Carriers	2.7
Roadway Express Inc.	2.5
Yellow Freight Systems	2.4
C F Motor Freight	2.1
J.B. Hunt Transport Inc.	1.8
Roadway Package Systems	1.8
Con-Way Trans. Services	1.5
Ryder Integrated Logistics	1.3

Source: *CCJ*, August 1999, p. 48.

★ 1266 ★

Package Delivery Services (SIC 4215)

Holiday Shipping Market - 1998

Data show who handled the business, based on a survey of 491 Internet retailers.

UPS	55%
U.S. Postal Service	32
Federal Express	10
Other	3

Source: *Detroit Free Press*, August 9, 1999, p. 6F, from Zona Research Inc.

★ 1267 ★

Package Delivery Services (SIC 4215)

Internet Shipping Market

UPS	55%
Other	45

Source: "United Parcel Service Opens Stores." Retrieved March 24, 2000 from the World Wide Web: http://library.northernlight.com.

★ 1268 ★

Package Delivery Services (SIC 4215)

Ontime Package Delivery Market

UPS	55%
Federal Express	25
Other	20

Source: *Fortune*, February 7, 2000, p. 104.

★ 1269 ★

Shipping (SIC 4215)

Enterprise Shipping Market

E-Stamp had recently ventured past its Internet postage service into such fields as mailing, shipping and supplies. It has launched into strategic alliances with some companies, such as Kewill Electronic Commerce, a multi-carrier shipping leader.

Kewill Electronic Commerce	70%
Other	30

Source: "E-Stamp Corp. Announces First Quarter 2000 Results." Retrieved April 24, 2000 from the World Wide Web: http://www.businesswire.com.

SIC 44 - Water Transportation

★ 1270 ★

Shipping (SIC 4412)

Largest Container Carriers

Data are in thousands of twenty-foot equivalent units.

Sea-Land Service	1,376.8
Evergreen	1,298.0
Maersk Line	1,064.9
Hanjin Shipping Co.	902.3
APL Ltd.	895.5
China Ocean Shipping	657.5
Hyundai Merchant Marine	637.1
P&O Nedlloyd	551.8
NYK Line	527.0

Source: *Journal of Commerce*, January 29, 1999, p. 14, from *U.S. Global Container Report* by PIERS.

★ 1271 ★

Shipping (SIC 4412)

Top South-bound Commodities

Data show the top commodities hauled south.
Figures are estimated revenues in millions of dollars.

Road motor vehicles, parts and accessories	$ 325.5
Wood fabricated materials	234.0
Paper and paperboard	219.7
Furniture and fixtures	138.6
Iron, steel and alloys	115.2
End products	88.5
Food, food materials, food preparations	87.8

Source: *Motor Truck*, October 1999, p. 48, from *Trucking in Canada* and Statistics Canada.

★ 1272 ★

Ports (SIC 4419)

Largest Container Ports - 1998

Market shares are shown in percent.

Long Beach	34.9%
Los Angeles	28.9
Other	36.2

Source: *Journal of Commerce*, April 14, 1999, p. A1.

SIC 45 - Transportation by Air

★ 1273 ★
Airlines (SIC 4512)
Airline Market - 2000

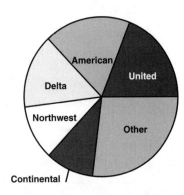

Shares are for January 2000.

United	19%
American	18
Delta	15
Northwest	11
Continental	10
Other	27

Source: *USA TODAY*, March 2, 2000, p. B1, from *Aviation Daily*.

★ 1274 ★
Airlines (SIC 4512)
Airline Market in Atlanta, GA

Shares are shown in percent.

Delta	75.3%
Other	24.7

Source: *Wall Street Journal*, June 8, 2000, p. A16, from Salomon Smith Barney "2000 Hub Factbook".

★ 1275 ★
Airlines (SIC 4512)
Airline Market in Boston, MA

Shares are shown in percent.

US Airways	23.0%
Delta	22.1
American	14.9
Other	40.0

Source: *Wall Street Journal*, June 8, 2000, p. A16, from Salomon Smith Barney "2000 Hub Factbook".

★ 1276 ★
Airlines (SIC 4512)
Airline Market in Canada

The $12 billion domestic airline industry is shown in percent.

Air Canada	80%
Charter airlines	14
WestJet Airlines	5
Others	1

Source: *Wall Street Journal*, April 24, 2000, p. A26, from Air Transport Association of Canada.

★ 1277 ★
Airlines (SIC 4512)
Airline Market in Columbus, OH

Shares are shown in percent.

America West	23.2%
US Airways	16.7
Delta	16.0
Other	44.1

Source: *Wall Street Journal*, June 8, 2000, p. A16, from Salomon Smith Barney "2000 Hub Factbook".

★ 1278 ★
Airlines (SIC 4512)

Airline Market in Los Angeles, CA

Shares are shown in percent.

United 26.9%
American 12.1
Southwest 11.6
Other 49.4

Source: *Wall Street Journal*, June 8, 2000, p. A16, from
Salomon Smith Barney ''2000 Hub Factbook''.

★ 1279 ★
Airlines (SIC 4512)

Airline Market in Minneapolis, MN

Data are for June 1999.

Northwest 80.5%
United 3.8
American 2.7
Delta 2.6
Sun Country 2.3
TWA 1.5
Continental 1.5
Others 5.1

Source: *New York Times*, August 25, 1999, p. C1, from
Salomon Smith Barney and Minneapolis-St. Paul Metropolitan Airports Commission.

★ 1280 ★
Airlines (SIC 4512)

Airline Market Leaders - 1999

Market shares are shown in percent.

United 19.2%
American 17.2
Delta 16.1
Continental 8.9
USAirways 6.4
Southwest 5.6
Other 26.6

Source: *Forbes*, March 6, 2000, p. 53, from Air Transport
Association.

★ 1281 ★
Airlines (SIC 4512)

Airport Market in Charlotte, NC

Market shares are shown in percent.

US Airways 80.7%
United 1.0
Other 19.3

Source: *Wall Street Journal*, May 25, 2000, p. A16, from
Aviation Daily.

★ 1282 ★
Airlines (SIC 4512)

Airport Market in Philadelphia, PA

Market shares are shown in percent.

US Airways 60.2%
United 5.4
Other 34.4

Source: *Wall Street Journal*, May 25, 2000, p. A16, from
Aviation Daily.

★ 1283 ★

Airlines (SIC 4512)

Airport Market in Pittsburgh, PA

Market shares are shown in percent.

US Airways	74.7%
United	1.7
Other	23.6

Source: *Wall Street Journal*, May 25, 2000, p. A16, from *Aviation Daily*.

★ 1284 ★

Airlines (SIC 4512)

Canada's Airline Market

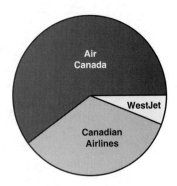

Data are for September 1999.

Air Canada	60%
Canadian Airlines	34
WestJet	6

Source: *Globe and Mail*, October 19, 1999, p. B1.

★ 1285 ★

Airlines (SIC 4512)

Fractional Ownership Market

Executive Jet

Other

Shares are shown in percent. This refers to owners buying a portion of a plane and receiving a proportional amount of air time.

Executive Jet	75%
Other	25

Source: *Time*, September 13, 1999, p. 49.

★ 1286 ★

Airlines (SIC 4512)

Largest Airline Firms - 1999

Firms are ranked by revenues in billions of dollars.

AMR	$ 20.2
UAL	18.0
Delta Air Lines	14.7
Northwest Airlines	10.2
Continental Airlines	8.6
US Airways Group	8.5
Southwest Airlines	4.7

Source: *Fortune*, April 17, 2000, pp. I-63.

★ 1287 ★

Air Cargo (SIC 4513)

Air Cargo Leaders - 1999

Shares are shown for the first three months of the year.

United	25.1%
Northwest	18.6
American	17.5
Delta	16.1
Continental	8.1
US Airways	4.8
Other	9.8

Source: *Air Cargo World*, June 1999, p. 63, from company reports.

★ 1288 ★

Air Cargo (SIC 4513)

Air Cargo Market

Shares are shown based on shipments.

USPS	44.7%
Federal Express	25.6
UPS	15.6
Airborne Express	11.3
DHL	1.1
Emery	0.2
BAX Global	0.1
Others	1.5

Source: *Traffic World*, August 23, 1999, p. 41, from The Colography Group.

★ 1289 ★
Air Cargo (SIC 4513)

Dallas-Ft. Worth Intl. Airport Market

A total of 528,851 tons transported for the first seven months of the year.

United Parcel Service	131,126
Federal Express	72,275
Emery Worldwide	47,339
Express One	18,892
China Airlines	13,418

Source: *American Shipper*, November 1999, p. 95.

★ 1290 ★
Air Cargo (SIC 4513)

Largest Air Exporters

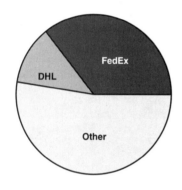

FedEx	35.5%
DHL	12.0
Other	52.5

Source: *USA TODAY*, October 20, 1999, p. 3B, from Colography Group.

★ 1291 ★
Air Cargo (SIC 4513)

Top Air Couriers to Government

The top providers are ranked by share of total contracts.

Worldcorp. Inc.	39.69%
Federal Express Corp.	25.53
Flight International Inc.	9.20
Canadian Commercial Corp.	4.07
Other	21.51

Source: *Government Executive*, 1999, p. 112.

★ 1292 ★
Airports (SIC 4581)

Baltimore - Los Angeles Route Shares

Market shares are shown in percent.

US Airways	64.3%
United	35.7

Source: *USA TODAY*, May 30, 2000, p. 3B, from BACK Information Services.

★ 1293 ★
Airports (SIC 4581)

Boston - Washington Dulles Route Shares

Market shares are shown in percent.

United	63.4%
US Airways	36.6

Source: *USA TODAY*, May 30, 2000, p. 3B, from BACK Information Services.

★ 1294 ★
Airports (SIC 4581)

Denver Airport Market Shares

UAL	69.94%
Delta	5.08
AMR	4.83
Continental	3.89
Other	16.26

Source: "Market Share Survey." Retrieved January 20, 2000 from the World Wide Web: http://www.activemedia-guide.com/mrksurvey.htm, from U.S. Business Reporter.

★ 1295 ★

Airports (SIC 4581)

Eastern Air Market

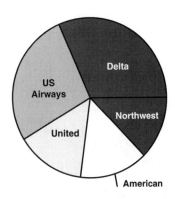

Shares are shown based on passengers for the year ended September 30, 1999.

Delta	45.7	22.0%
US Airways	39.7	19.1
United	21.2	10.2
American	20.6	9.9
Northwest	18.5	8.9

Source: *USA TODAY*, May 30, 2000, p. 3B, from Global Aviation Associates.

★ 1296 ★

Airports (SIC 4581)

Kennedy Airport Market Shares

AMR	32.33%
TWA	22.51
Delta	19.15
United	10.94
Other	15.07

Source: "Market Share Survey." Retrieved January 20, 2000 from the World Wide Web: http://www.activmedia-guide.com/mrksurvey.htm.

★ 1297 ★

Airports (SIC 4581)

Philadelphia - San Francisco Route Shares

Market shares are shown in percent.

US Airways	58.9%
United	41.1

Source: *USA TODAY*, May 30, 2000, p. 3B, from BACK Information Services.

★ 1298 ★

Airports (SIC 4581)

Pittsburgh - Chicago O'Hare Route Shares

Market shares are shown in percent.

US Airways	47.4%
United	37.4
Other	15.2

Source: *USA TODAY*, May 30, 2000, p. 3B, from BACK Information Services.

★ 1299 ★

Airports (SIC 4581)

Salt Lake City Airport Market Shares

Delta	69.36%
Southwest	13.21
Other	17.43

Source: "Market Share Survey." Retrieved January 20, 2000 from the World Wide Web: http://www.activemedia-guide.com/mrksurvey.htm, from U.S. Business Reporter.

SIC 46 - Pipelines, Except Natural Gas

★ 1300 ★
Pipelines (SIC 4610)

Largest Pipelines - 1999

Firms are ranked by revenues in billions of dollars.

Enron	$ 40.1
Dynegy	15.4
El Paso Energy	10.5
Williams	8.3
Kinder Morgan	5.9

Source: *Fortune*, April 17, 2000, pp. I-70.

SIC 47 - Transportation Services

★ 1301 ★
Tourism (SIC 4720)

How Tourists Spend Money

Annual spending is shown in billions of dollars.

Transportation	$ 154.4
Foodservice	93.2
Lodging	67.4
Entertainment/recreation	39.2

Source: *Michigan Retailer*, July/August 1999, p. 1, from Travel Industry Association of America.

★ 1302 ★
Tourism (SIC 4720)

Online Travel Market - 2003

The market is projected to reach $29 billion.

Air fare	36.0%
Hotels	33.8
Tours	16.3
Cruises	8.5
Rental cars	5.4

Source: *Investor's Business Daily*, March 17, 2000, p. A8, from Forrester Research Inc.

★ 1303 ★
Tourism (SIC 4720)

Popular Destinations for Gay Travelers

Data are for the last three years.

San Francisco, CA	49%
New York City, NY	47
Los Angeles, CA	44
Miami, FL	34
Palm Springs, FL	31
Key West, FL	27
Caribbean	27

Source: *USA TODAY*, March 30, 2000, p. D1, from *Travel Weekly*.

★ 1304 ★
Tourism (SIC 4720)

Top U.S. Travel Markets

Data show the top air travel markets to and from the United States, based on scheduled passengers. Figures are for the year ended September 30, 1998.

Canada	8.8
Mexico	6.3
United Kingdom	5.2
Japan	5.1

Continued on next page.

★ 1304 ★ *Continued*
Tourism (SIC 4720)

Top U.S. Travel Markets

Data show the top air travel markets to and from the United States, based on scheduled passengers. Figures are for the year ended September 30, 1998.

Germany 3.3
France 2.5
Bahamas 1.7
Italy 1.6

Source: *USA TODAY*, August 31, 1999, p. 10B, from Air Transport Association.

★ 1305 ★

Tourism (SIC 4720)

Tourism Spending by State

Total spending is expected to reach $524.4 million for 1998-99.

Illinois . . . . $ 40.1
Hawaii 37.9
Texas 29.4
Florida 27.2
Pennsylvania 23.0
Massachusetts 21.3
New York 18.7

Source: *Brandweek*, October 4, 1999, p. 50.

★ 1306 ★
Cruise Lines (SIC 4724)

Cruise Line Market

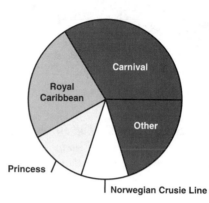

Market shares are shown by capacity in percent for North America.

Carnival 34%
Royal Caribbean 24
Princess 12
Norwegian Crusie Line 10
Other 20

Source: *Wall Street Journal*, December 2, 1999, p. A3, from Deutsche Bank and Alexander Brown.

★ 1307 ★
Cruise Lines (SIC 4724)

Cruise Line Market Leaders

Shaes are shown based on capacity.

Carnival Cruise Lines 18.33%
Royal Caribbean 15.12
Princess Cruises 10.18
Holland America Line 8.92
Norwegan Cruise Lines 8.15
Celebrity Cruises 6.23
Costa Cruises 5.68
Premier Cruises Lines 3.93
Other 23.46

Source: Retrieved January 18, 2000 from the World Wide Web: http://www.cruisetrade.com/berthcap.html.

★ 1308 ★

Travel Agencies (SIC 4724)

Leading Online Travel Agencies

Offline, travel agents still sell 75% of all airline tickets; 22% of tickets are sold directly to the public. Market shares for online agencies are shown in percent.

Travelocity.com	39%
Expedia.com	26
Priceline.com	11
GetThere.com	8
Hotel Reservations Work	4
Other	12

Source: *Industry Standard*, April 17, 2000, p. 106, from PhocusWright and Jupiter Communications.

SIC 48 - Communications

★ 1309 ★
Cellular Services (SIC 4812)

Cellular Service Leaders - 1999

Shares are for the first quarter of the year.

SBC 13%
Vodafone Airtouch 11
Bell Atlantic 9
GTE 7
Others 60

Source: *New York Times*, November 13, 1999, p. B2, from Yankee Group.

★ 1310 ★
Paging Services (SIC 4812)

Paging Service Revenues

Data are in millions of dollars.

	1999	2004	Share
One-way	$ 4,251	$ 2,755	46.93%
Advanced messaging . . .	176	3,115	53.07

Source: Retrieved January 13, 2000 from the World Wide Web: http://strategisgroup.com/press/pubs/uspage99.html.

★ 1311 ★
Telecommunications (SIC 4812)

Internet Telephony Market

Data show share of minutes routed over the Internet.

Net2Phone 18%
AT&T Jens 9
AlphaNet 8
Qwest 6

CalTech 6%
VIP Calling 5
Delta/Three 5
Other 43

Source: *Investor's Business Daily*, September 16, 1999, p. A10, from company reports and Bear, Stearns & Co.

★ 1312 ★
Telecommunications (SIC 4812)

Long-Distance Phone Services (Data) in Canada - 1999

Shares are shown based on estimated sales of $2.9 billion for the year ended December 31, 1999.

Bell Canada 50%
Telus 18
AT&T Canada 15
Sprint Canada 5
Aliant 3
Others 9

Source: "Report on Market Share." Retrieved June 8, 2000 from the World Wide Web: http://www.marketingmag.ca, from The Yankee Group in Canada.

★ 1313 ★

Telecommunications (SIC 4812)

Long-Distance Phone Services (Voice) in Canada - 1999

Shares are shown based on estimated revenues of $2. 9 billion for the year ended December 31, 1999.

Bell Canada	34%
Telus	22
Sprint Canada	18
AT&T Canada	6
Aliant	5
Other	15

Source: "Report on Market Share." Retrieved June 8, 2000 from the World Wide Web: http://www. marketingmag.ca, from The Yankee Group in Canada.

★ 1314 ★

Telecommunications (SIC 4812)

Telecom Market in Canada - 1999

Total revenues reached $21.7 billion.

Local	41%
Long-distance voice	31
Mobile	18
Long-distance data	10

Source: *Marketing Magazine*, July 5, 1999, p. 15, from Yankee Group in Canada.

★ 1315 ★

Wireless Services (SIC 4812)

Digital PCS Market in Canada - 1999

Rogers AT&T

Microcell Telecom

Clearnet Communications

Bell Mobility

Telus Mobility

Other

Shares are shown based on 2.93 million subscribers for the year ended December 31, 1999.

Rogers AT&T	33.1%
Microcell Telecom	22.3
Clearnet Communications	20.9
Bell Mobility	15.0
Telus Mobility	6.1
Other	2.6

Source: "Report on Market Share." Retrieved June 8, 2000 from the World Wide Web: http://www. marketingmag.ca, from The Yankee Group in Canada.

★ 1316 ★

Wireless Services (SIC 4812)

Largest Wireless Firms

Data are in millions of subscribers.

Bell Atlantic	23.0
AT&T	12.2
SBC	11.2
Sprint PCS	6.0
Alltel	5.8
BellSouth	5.3

Source: *Wall Street Journal*, March 1, 2000, p. A3.

★ 1317 ★
Wireless Services (SIC 4812)

Largest Wireless Networks

Data show millions of subscribers.

AT&T Wireless	10.2
Vodafone Airtouch	9.0
SBC Wireless	7.2
Bell Atlantic Mobile	6.4
Bellsouth Mobile	5.0
GTE	4.9
AllTel	4.2

Source: *Financial Times*, September 14, 1999, p. 20.

★ 1318 ★
Wireless Services (SIC 4812)

Leading Wireless Service Providers

Data show millions of subscribers.

Bell Atlantic/Vodafone Airtouch	20.0
AT&T Corp.	11.5
Sprint Corp.	4.0
Nextel Communications Corp.	3.5

Source: *Computerworld*, September 27, 1999, p. 29.

★ 1319 ★
Wireless Services (SIC 4812)

Packet/Cell-Based Services Market - 1998

Shares are estimated based on revenues. According to the report, frame relay dominates the market, and its share of the market is expected to increase.

AT&T	33%
Sprint	25
WorldCom/MCI/Compuserve Network	23
Other	19

Source: "AT&T Overtakes Sprint as Leader in Packet/Cell-Based Services." Retrieved November 19, 1999 from the World Wide Web: http://www.idc.com.

★ 1320 ★
Wireless Services (SIC 4812)

U.S. Wireless Market

Data show millions of subscribers.

	(mil.)	Share
Verizon	24.5	28.16%
SBC/BellSouth	16.2	18.62
AT&T	12.2	14.02
Sprint PCS	5.9	6.78
Alltel	5.8	6.67
Nextel	4.5	5.17
Others	17.9	20.57

Source: *Telephony*, April 10, 2000, p. 8, from The Yankee Group.

★ 1321 ★
Wireless Services (SIC 4812)

Wireless Market in Los Angeles, CA

Shares are shown based on subscribers.

AirTouch Cellular	37%
AT&T Wireless	29
Pacific Bell Wireless	15
Sprint PCS	12
Nextel	3
Other	4

Source: *Wireless Week*, September 27, 1999, p. 14, from Telephia.

★ 1322 ★
Wireless Services (SIC 4812)

Wireless Market in Mexico

Telcel has 5.2 million customers as of December 1999 and is the only provider with national coverage.

Telcel	70%
Other	30

Source: "Ericcson and Telcel to Lead Mass Market Mobile in Mexico." Retrieved April 17, 2000 from the World Wide Web: http://www.businesswire.com.

★ 1323 ★

Wireless Services (SIC 4812)

Wireless Market in North America

Data show millions of users. TDMA stands for time division multiple access. CDMA stands for code division multiple access. GSM stands for global system for multiple access.

Analog	51.43
TDMA	15.58
CDMA	15.53
GSM	6.82
ESMR	4.48

Source: *Wired*, March 2000, p. 104, from International Telecommunication Union and The Yankee Group.

★ 1324 ★

Wireless Services (SIC 4812)

Wireless Services - 2003

The market is estimated.

Cellular	63%
Paging	31
Other	6

Source: *Investor's Business Daily*, July 1, 1999, p. A6, from International Data Corp.

★ 1325 ★

Wireless Services (SIC 4812)

Wireless Services Market in Canada

Rogers AT&T Wireless	27%
Bell Mobility	21
Microcell	20
Clearnet	15
Telus Mobility	10
Others	7

Source: *Globe and Mail*, March 31, 2000, p. E3, from Yankee Group.

★ 1326 ★

Telephone Services (SIC 4813)

Federal Network & Telecom Service Vendors - 1998

Data show estimated shares.

AT&T	24%
Sprint	14
MCI WorldCom	7
TRW	5
GTE	4
Lockheed Martin	3
US West	3
Other	40

Source: *Washington Technology*, May 1, 2000, p. 1, from Input.

★ 1327 ★

Telephone Services (SIC 4813)

Long Distance Leaders - 1998

Data show revenues in billions of dollars.

AT&T	$ 40.67
MCI WorldCom	24.13
Sprint	9.91
Qwest	2.26
Teleglobe	1.88

Source: *Wall Street Journal*, September 27, 1999, p. A4, from FCC.

★ 1328 ★

Telephone Services (SIC 4813)

Long Distance Market

AT&T	56%
MCI WorldCom	11
Sprint	6
Other	27

Source: *Detroit Free Press*, August 31, 1999, p. D1, from Associated Press.

★ 1329 ★

Telephone Services (SIC 4813)

Long Distance Revenues - 1998

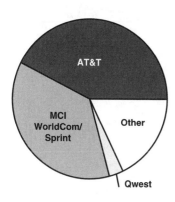

Shares are for a post MCI and Sprint merger.

AT&T	.43.0%
MCI WorldCom/Sprint	.37.0
Qwest	.2.5
Other	.17.5

Source: *Telephony*, April 10, 2000, p. 30, from Communications Workers of America.

★ 1330 ★

Electronic Billing (SIC 4822)

Largest U.S. Billers

Monthly volume is shown in millions of dollars.

Credit cards	$ 306
Utilities	.175
Retail	.169
Insurance	.90
Telephones	.90
Oil cards	.80
Cable	.60
Cellular	.34

Source: *US Banker*, October 1999, p. 51, from Mitchell Madison Group.

★ 1331 ★

Electronic Commerce (SIC 4822)

Business E-Commerce Market

Other includes marketing and advertising research, finance reporting, and recruiting.

Business-to-business	.39%
Business-to-consumer	.29
Other	.32

Source: *KM World*, May 2000, p. 1.

★ 1332 ★

Electronic Commerce (SIC 4822)

Business-to-Business Commerce Sales

Travel/entertainment	.29%
Financial services	.26
Computers and software	.17
Books, music and video	.8
Other	.20

Source: *CIO Enterprise*, September 15, 1999, p. 14, from Ernst & Young.

★ 1333 ★

Electronic Commerce (SIC 4822)

Internet Online Sales - 1999

The $14.9 billion market is shown in percent.

Computer hardware and software	.36.2%
Travel	.28.2
Books	.8.7
Apparel and footwear	.6.0
Music	.2.0
Other	.18.9

Source: *New York Times*, September 30, 1999, p. C25, from Media Metrix and Jupiter Communications.

★ 1334 ★

Electronic Commerce (SIC 4822)

Leading Computer Hardware/ Software Retailers

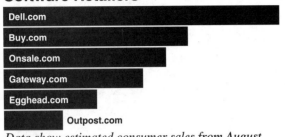

Data show estimated consumer sales from August 1998 - July 1999. Figures are in millions of dollars.

Dell.com	$ 600
Buy.com	400
Onsale.com	350
Gateway.com	300
Egghead.com	200
Outpost.com	125

Source: *Stores*, September 1999, p. V3.

★ 1335 ★

Electronic Commerce (SIC 4822)

Leading Internet Retailers

Data show estimated consumer sales from August 1998 - July 1999. Figures are in millions of dollars.

eBay.com	$ 1,300
Amazon.com	1,000
Dell.com	600
Buy.com	400
OnSale.com	350
Gateway.com	300
Egghead.com	200
CDnow.com	175
barnesandnoble.com	175

Source: *Stores*, September 1999, p. V3.

★ 1336 ★

Electronic Commerce (SIC 4822)

Leading Music Retailers

Data show estimated consumer sales from August 1998 - July 1999. Figures are in millions of dollars.

CDNow.com	$ 175
ColumbiaHouse.com	110
BMGMusicService.com	90

Source: *Stores*, September 1999, p. V3.

★ 1337 ★

Electronic Commerce (SIC 4822)

Online Business Market Sizes - 1999

Data are in billions of dollars.

Financial	$ 7.3
Corporate travel	5.0
Professional	4.4
Administrative support	3.9
Telecommunications	1.5

Source: *Business 2.0*, January 2000, p. 179, from Forrester Research.

★ 1338 ★

Electronic Commerce (SIC 4822)

Online Sales - 1998

Data show estimated sales in millions of dollars.

Travel	$ 3,073
Computer hardware	1,090
Software	665
Books	630
Apparel	530
Food and beverage	235
Health and beauty	213
Flowers	212

Source: *Investor's Business Daily*, July 7, 1999, p. A4, from Goolsbee and Zittrain and Forrester Research.

★ 1339 ★

Electronic Commerce (SIC 4822)

Online Sales - 1999

Retail revenues are shown in millions of dollars.

Leisure travel	$ 7,798
Computer hardware	2,404

Continued on next page.

★ 1339 ★ *Continued*
Electronic Commerce (SIC 4822)

Online Sales - 1999

Retail revenues are shown in millions of dollars.

Books	$ 1,166
Software	1,147
General apparel	878
Food and beverage	513
Health and beauty	509
Consumer electronics	411
Flowers	374
Music	374
Clothing accessories	362

Source: *Wired*, November 1999, p. 122, from Forrester Research.

★ 1340 ★
Electronic Commerce (SIC 4822)

Online Sales - 2001

Sales are shown in billions of dollars.

	($ bi.)	Share
Computing and electronics	$ 229.1	45.91%
Utilities	62.9	12.61
Motor vehicles	53.2	10.66
Petrochemicals	48.0	9.62
Aerospace and defense	25.6	5.13
Shipping and warehouse	15.4	3.09
Paper and office products	14.3	2.87
Consumer goods	12.7	2.55
Other	37.8	7.58

Source: *Chemical Engineering*, July 1999, p. 26, from Forrester Research Inc.

★ 1341 ★
Electronic Commerce (SIC 4822)

Online Sales - 2002

Sales are estimated in millions of dollars.

Travel	$ 12,802.1
Computer hardware	6,434.1
Grocery	3,661.0
Books	3,529.2
Software	2,844.5
Clothes and accessories	2,379.1
Music	1,590.6
Consumer electronics	792.5

Source: *New York Times*, September 10, 1999, p. C18, from Jupiter Communications.

★ 1342 ★
Electronic Commerce (SIC 4822)

Online Sales - 2003

Spending is shown in billions of dollars.

Groceries	$ 7.5
Apparel	6.7
Books	4.9
Music	2.6
Electronics	2.1
Toys	1.6
Housewares	1.5
Videos	1.1

Source: *Inc.*, November 1999, p. 9, from Jupiter Communications.

★ 1343 ★
Electronic Commerce (SIC 4822)

Online Spending by Gender

Total spending is expected to increase from $7.8 billion to $53 billion.

	1998	2002
Men	67%	49%
Women	34	51

Source: *Time*, December 13, 1999, p. 4, from Jupiter Communications.

★ 1344 ★
Electronic Commerce (SIC 4822)

Online Targeted Advertising

The table shows the market shares, by year, of online marketplaces in targeted industries.

2003	17.2%
2002	9.7
2001	5.3
2000	2.7
1999	0.3

Source: *BtoB*, April 10, 2000, p. 18, from Frank Lynn & Associates Inc.

★ 1345 ★
Electronic Commerce (SIC 4822)

Popular Online Grocers

Data show number of customers.

Peapod	90,000
NetGrocer	60,000
HomeGrocer.com	50,000
Webvan Group	25,000

Source: *Industry Standard*, November 22, 1999, p. 194.

★ 1346 ★
Electronic Commerce (SIC 4822)

Popular Online Items for College Students

College students are expected to spend $1.3 billion online. Data show the most popular items.

Books	20%
Software	16
Clothing	15
Music	13
Movies and videos	11
Other	25

Source: *Industry Standard*, February 7, 2000, p. 158, from Cyber Dialogue.

★ 1347 ★
Electronic Commerce (SIC 4822)

Popular Online Purchases in Canada

Computer software	15.7%
Music	12.7
Books	11.4
Computer hardware	8.9
Online banking	8.0
Video	4.4
Gifts	3.7
Tickets	3.7
Apparel, accessories, shoes	3.5
Travel	3.3
Other	24.7

Source: *Globe and Mail*, September 16, 1999, p. T4, from J.C. Williams Group.

★ 1348 ★
Electronic Commerce (SIC 4822)

Top E-Commerce States

Sales are shown in billions of dollars.

California	$ 5.9
Texas	3.2
New York	3.1
Florida	2.3
Illinois	2.2

Source: "IDC Map Plots Consumer Internet Commerce." Retrieved March 14, 2000 from the World Wide Web: http://www.idc.com, from International Data Corp.

★ 1349 ★
Electronic Commerce (SIC 4822)

Top Toy Sites

Online toy sales grew from $45 million in 1998 to $425 million in 1999.

amazon.com	26%
etoys.com	19
toysrus.com	12
kbkids.com	10
smarterkids.com	7

Continued on next page.

★ 1349 ★ *Continued*

Electronic Commerce (SIC 4822)

Top Toy Sites

Online toy sales grew from $45 million in 1998 to $425 million in 1999.

toysmart.com	2%
toytime.com	2
wal-mart.com	2
Other	2

Source: "Report Shows Tenfold Increase in 1999." Retrieved March 16, 2000 from the World Wide Web: http://www.npd.com/corp/press, from NPD Online Research.

★ 1350 ★

Electronic Publishing (SIC 4822)

Web/Online Services Market

Data show revenues in billions of dollars. The business/professional segments include brokerage, financial, new/research, legal/tax/public records, credit marketing and vertical markets.

	1998	2003	Share
Business/professional	$ 27.9	$ 52.5	75.21%
Internet service providers	6.2	17.3	24.79

Source: "Web/Online Information Market Forecast to Hit $40B." Retrieved January 6, 2000 from the World Wide Web: http://www.simbanet.com/press, from Simba Information.

★ 1351 ★

Internet (SIC 4822)

How People Spend Time Online

Data show share of hours spent online at home and work in May 1999.

America Online	38.7%
Microsoft	4.4
Yahoo	4.3
Juno	2.8
Ebay	2.0
Others	47.8

Source: *New York Times*, July 4, 1999, p. 1, from Media Metrix.

★ 1352 ★

Internet (SIC 4822)

Internet Use at Work

Data show share of people who use the Web at work.

Washington D.C.	39.5%
Austin, TX	36.8
San Jose, CA	34.6
Seattle, WA	32.5
San Francisco, CA	32.1
Dallas, TX	30.6
Oakland, CA	30.0

Source: *Yahoo! Internet Life*, March 2000, p. I25, from Census Bureau and Bureau of Labor Statistics.

★ 1353 ★

Internet (SIC 4822)

Leading Apparel Sites

Figures indicate average daily unique visitors for the week ending December 5, 1999.

Eddiebauer.com	77,000
Landsend.com	73,000
Victoriassecret.com	59,000

Source: *Time*, December 27, 1999, p. 88, from Media Metrix.

★ 1354 ★

Internet (SIC 4822)

Leading Finance Sites

Data show number of unique visitors in December 1999.

MarketWatch.com	3,214,000
Fool.com	2,066,000
CNNfn.com	1,187,000
TheStreet.com	908,000
Bloomberg.com	899,000
SmartMoney.com	833,000
CNBC.com	699,000

Source: *New York Times*, February 17, 2000, p. C11, from Media Metrix.

★ 1355 ★
Internet (SIC 4822)

Leading Government Sites - 1999

Data show thousands of visitors in December 1999.

www.nasa.gov	2,295
ww.usps.gov	2,294
www.ca.gov	1,303
www.nih.gov	1,264
www.noaa.gov	1,235
www.fedworld.gov	1,019
www.ustreas.gov	1,011

Source: *PC Magazine*, April 7, 2000, p. 84, from Media Metrix.

★ 1356 ★
Internet (SIC 4822)

Leading Health Sites

Figures indicate average daily unique visitors for the week ending December 5, 1999.

Discoveryhealth.com	68,000
Planetrx.com	53,000
Mothernature.com	52,000

Source: *Time*, December 27, 1999, p. 88, from Media Metrix.

★ 1357 ★
Internet (SIC 4822)

Leading Music Information Sites - 1999

Data show revenues in millions of dollars for the first six months of the year.

MTV.com	$ 9.9
Launch.com	4.7
UBL.com	3.7
MP3.com	2.6
Tunes.com	1.4

Source: *Forbes*, November 15, 1999, p. 78, from Media Metrix and company documents.

★ 1358 ★
Internet (SIC 4822)

Leading Toy Sites

Figures indicate average daily unique visitors for the week ending December 5, 1999.

eToys.com	384,000
Toysrus.com	314,000
Kbkids.com	237,000

Source: *Time*, December 27, 1999, p. 88, from Media Metrix.

★ 1359 ★
Internet (SIC 4822)

Online Auction Categories - 2000

Data show millions of dollars in sales for the first two months of the year.

Baseball cards	$ 15.6
Rolex	14.2
Pokemon cards	6.1
Beanies	5.4
Portable computers	5.3
Digital cameras	4.0
Barbie	3.6
Sports memorabilia	2.5
Camcorders	2.0

Source: *USA TODAY*, April 4, 2000, p. 3D, from WorthGuide.com.

★ 1360 ★
Internet (SIC 4822)

Online Auction Market

Ebay	70%
Other	30

Source: *Forbes*, November 29, 1999, p. 54.

★ 1361 ★
Internet (SIC 4822)
Online Bill Payment

Data show U.S. households in 1999. Electronic bill payment has numerous advantages. The savings in paper and postage for billers is estimated to pass $2 billion over the next few years. People should find it so convenient the number of online bill payers should jump from 1.3 million households to 10 million by 2002.

Not online 66%
Online, not banking 26
Banking, not bill payment 6
Bill payment 2

Source: *Global Finance*, January 2000, p. 50, from Towers Group, Forrester Research, and Deloitte Research.

★ 1362 ★
Internet (SIC 4822)
Pay to View Online Market

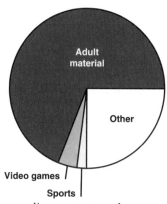

The pay online content market was valued at $1.4 billion.

Adult material 69%
Video games 4
Sports 2
Other 25

Source: *U.S. News & World Report*, March 27, 2000, p. 38.

★ 1363 ★
Internet (SIC 4822)
Popular Internet Brands

Data show the percentage of Americans who recognize each brand.

Amazon.com 60.1%
Priceline.com 55.4
Ebay 46.4
E*Trade 43.8
Etoys 26.2
Hotjobs.com 26.0
Monster.com 24.1
Autobytel.com 22.6
CDNow 20.2
Reel.com 19.4

Source: *Wired*, December 1999, p. 140, from Opinion Research Corporation International.

★ 1364 ★
Internet (SIC 4822)
Popular Online Cities

Data show percentage of adults online.

Washington D.C. 59.9%
San Francisco 56.1
Austin, TX 55.5
Seattle/Tacoma, WA 53.3
Salt Lake City, Utah 50.0
Dallas/Fort Worth, TX 49.6
Denver, CO 49.0

Source: *USA TODAY*, October 20, 1999, p. 10D, from Scarborough Research.

★ 1365 ★
Internet (SIC 4822)
Popular Online Games

Data show millions of players for December 1999. According to a new study, 61% of computer users play games on their PCs.

Interplay Solitaire 20.7
Microsoft Freecell 17.1
Microsoft Entertainment Pack 12.4
Microsoft Hearts Network 9.1
Microsoft Minesweeper 7.9
Nvision Design Elf Bowling 7.6
Microsoft Solitaire 3.2

Continued on next page.

Internet (SIC 4822)

Popular Online Games

Data show millions of players for December 1999. According to a new study, 61% of computer users play games on their PCs.

Microsoft Golf	2.6
Slingo	1.9

Source: *USA TODAY*, March 7, 2000, p. 3D, from Media Metrix.

★ 1366 ★
Internet (SIC 4822)

Time Spent Online - 1999

Share of time spent online in May 1999. AOLers typically spent 52 minutes online in 1999.

America Online	38.7%
Microsoft	4.4
Yahoo	4.3
Juno	2.8
eBay	2.0
Other	47.8

Source: *Infoworld*, March 27, 2000, p. 20, from Gartner Group.

★ 1367 ★
Internet (SIC 4822)

Top Online Textbook Sites

| ecampus.com |
| BigWords.com |
| VarsityBooks |
| efollett.com |
| Textbooks.com |

Data show the top sites for 18-34 year olds.

ecampus.com	28%
BigWords.com	24
VarsityBooks	24
efollett.com	15
Textbooks.com	9

Source: "ecampus.com is the Leading Online Textbook Site." Retrieved March 13, 2000 from the World Wide Web: http://library.northernlight.com, from PC Data.

★ 1368 ★
Internet (SIC 4822)

Top Retail Sites on the Web

Data show estimated sales in millions of dollars.

Ebay.com	$ 1,300
Amazon.com	1,100
Dell.com	500
Buy.com	350
OnSale.com	300
Gateway.com	250
Egghead.com	150

Source: *Investor's Business Daily*, September 20, 1999, p. A6, from National Retail Federation.

★ 1369 ★
Internet (SIC 4822)

Top Sports Sites Online

Data show thousands of unique visitors in December 1999.

Fasonly Network	9.7
ESPN.com	4.9
Sportsline.com	3.8
NFL.com	2.8
CNNSI.com	1.9
NBA.com	1.0

Source: *Sports Business Journal*, January 31, 2000, p. 19.

★ 1370 ★
Internet (SIC 4822)

Top Websites at Home

Data show millions of unique visitors.

Yahoo.com	26.7
AOL.com	23.8
Msn.com	23.5
Microsoft.com	15.5
Geocities.com	15.3

Source: *Business 2.0*, January 2000, p. 36, from Media Metrix.

★ 1371 ★
Internet (SIC 4822)

Top Websites at Work

Data show millions of unique visitors.

Yahoo.com	11.9
Msn.com	9.8
Microsoft.com	8.1
Netscape.com	8.0
AOL.com	7.8

Source: *Business 2.0*, January 2000, p. 36, from Media Metrix.

★ 1372 ★
Internet (SIC 4822)

Web Hosting Market - 1999

Shares are shown based on revenues.

Exodus	9.3%
Verio (NTT)	7.5
Global Crossing	5.9
Qwest	3.9
AT&T	3.2
PSINet	1.8
Other	68.4

Source: *Forbes*, June 12, 2000, p. 232, from International Data Corp.

★ 1373 ★
Internet (SIC 4822)

What Teenage Boys Do Online

Research	71%
Send/receive e-mail	59
Download	58
Browse	57
Chat	41
Play games	32
Check out stuff to buy	28

Source: *Advertising Age*, February 14, 2000, p. 38, from Teen Research Unlimited.

★ 1374 ★
Online Services (SIC 4822)

Largest Instant-Messaging Services

Data show millions of registered users.

America Online Instant Messanger	45
America Online ICQ	40
Tribal Voice PowWow	5
Microsoft MSN Messenger	2

Source: *Wall Street Journal*, September 7, 1999, p. B6, from companies.

★ 1375 ★
Online Services (SIC 4822)

Leading Paid/Free Internet Service Providers - 1999

Shares are shown for the fourth quarter of the year, in thousands. There were an estimated 101 million households in 1998; 41.5 million had only paid ISPs; 2 million had only free ISPs; 1.4 million had paid for and free ISPs.

	(000)	Share
America Online/CompuServe	18,300	39.62%
MindSpring/EarthLink	3,100	6.71
Microsoft Corp.'s MSN	2,100	4.55
AT&T WorldNet	1,600	3.46
NetZero	1,500	3.25
Prodigy	1,130	2.45
Freeinternet.com	1,040	2.25
Microsoft WebTV	800	1.73
@Home	800	1.73
Altavista.Co	750	1.62
Other	15,071	32.63

Source: *Advertising Age*, March 27, 2000, p. 57, from Jupiter Communications.

★ 1376 ★

Online Services (SIC 4822)

Top Internet Providers for Home Businesses

America Online	35%
Local providers	29
MSN	9
Local phone co.	7
AT&T	5
Compuserve	4

Source: *Wall Street Journal*, July 22, 1999, p. B8, from Ziff-Davis InfoBeads.

★ 1377 ★

Online Services (SIC 4822)

Top Online Services in Canada - 1999

Shares are shown based on estimated 3.29 million subscribers for the year ended December 31, 1999.

Sympatico	18.3%
Telus Planet + BCTel Sympatico	9.1
Rogers@Home	5.7
Shaw@Home	5.6
Sprint Canada	5.6
AOL Canada	4.6
PSINet Ltd.	4.3
Videotron	4.1
Other	42.7

Source: "Report on Market Share." Retrieved June 8, 2000 from the World Wide Web: http://www.marketingmag.ca, from The Yankee Group in Canada.

★ 1378 ★

Radio Broadcasting (SIC 4832)

Largest Radio Firms

Data show revenues in billions of dollars.

AMFM	$ 1,856.7
Infinity Broadcasting	1,667.5
Clear Channel	1,223.1
ABC Radio	355.6
Entercom Comm.	311.8
Cox Radio	284.5
Hispanic Broadcasting	187.1

Source: *Broadcasting & Cable*, August 30, 1999, p. 26.

★ 1379 ★

Radio Broadcasting (SIC 4832)

Largest Webcasting Stations

Arbitron's report is the first on 236 radio stations that are streaming their signal on the web. These 236 stations, however, only account for an estimated 12% of the Webcasting universe. Data show October 1999 listeners.

KFAN-FM (Texas)	83,900
KPIG-FM (California)	70,200
KCDU-FM (California)	66,300
KHYI-FM (Texas)	56,700
KLAQ-FM (Texas)	55,700
WKPO-FM (Wisconsin)	39,000

Source: *Mediaweek*, December 13, 1999, p. 8, from Arbitron Infostream.

★ 1380 ★

Radio Broadcasting (SIC 4832)

Private Radio Users - 1998

Business	61%
Ste/local govt	19
Public safety	10
Transportation	6
Utilities	4

Source: Retrieved January 13, 2000 from the World Wide Web: http://www.strategisgroup.com/press/pubs/radio.html, from Strategis Group.

★ 1381 ★

Radio Broadcasting (SIC 4832)

Radio Listenership in Canada - 1999

Data show share of listeners for Spring 1999. Figures are based on a 12+ audience, all week.

Standard	8.4%
Telemedia	8.1
CHUM	7.1
WIC	6.9
Rogers	6.4
Radiomutuel	4.4
Shaw	4.4
Other	54.3

Source: *Marketing Magazine*, July 12, 1999, p. 11, from BBM Bureau of Measurement and Integrated Media Sales.

★ 1382 ★

Radio Broadcasting (SIC 4832)

Radio Listening in Canada - 1998

Data are for Fall 1998.

Adult contemporary	24.8%
Country	13.0
Golden oldies/rock	12.6
Talk	11.5
Contemporary	10.2
Canadian Broadcasting Corp.	9.5
Album-oriented rock	4.1
U.S. stations	3.4
Other	10.9

Source: *Globe and Mail*, July 23, 1999, p. B1, from Statistics Canada.

★ 1383 ★

Radio Broadcasting (SIC 4832)

Radio Market in Atlanta, GA

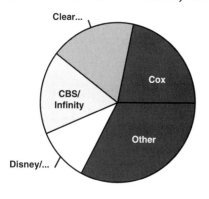

Shares are shown based on revenues.

Cox	21.9%
Clear Channel/Jacor	17.8
CBS/Infinity	17.0
Disney/ABC	10.5
Other	32.8

Source: *Mediaweek*, September 27, 1999, p. 28, from *Duncan's Radio Market Guide, 1999.*

★ 1384 ★

Radio Broadcasting (SIC 4832)

Radio Market in Atlanta, GA

AMFM	36.8%
CBS/Infinity	36.3
Renda Broadcasting	6.7
Steel City Media	6.5
ABC/Disney	5.9
Other	7.8

Source: *Mediaweek*, October 4, 1999, p. 30, from *Duncan's Radio Market Guide, 1999.*

★ 1385 ★

Radio Broadcasting (SIC 4832)

Radio Market in Boston, MA

Data show who controls the Boston market.

Infinity Broadcasting	42.1%
Greater Media	17.3
Entercom	16.5
AMFM	15.2
Other	8.9

Source: *Mediaweek*, December 13, 1999, p. 30, from Arbitron.

★ 1386 ★

Radio Broadcasting (SIC 4832)

Radio Market in Columbus, Ohio

Shares are shown based on ownership.

Clear Channel	40.7%
Infinity Broadcasting	15.8
Saga Communications	14.8
North American Broadcasting	9.2
Blue Chip Broadcasting	5.7
Radio Ohio	5.6

Source: *Mediaweek*, March 20, 2000, p. 28, from BIA Research.

★ 1387 ★
Radio Broadcasting (SIC 4832)

Radio Market in Memphis, TN

Shares are shown based on ownership.

Clear Channel	38.2%
Barnstable Broadcasting	20.6
Entercom	19.2
Raycom Media	9.4
Other	12.6

Source: *Mediaweek*, March 27, 2000, p. 26, from BIA Research.

★ 1388 ★
Radio Broadcasting (SIC 4832)

Radio Market in Miami/Ft. Lauderdale, FL

Shares are shown based on ownership.

Clear Channel	23.6%
Beasley Broadcasting	18.1
Cox Radio	16.7
Hispanic Broadcasting	14.2
Spanish Broadcasting	10.5
Jefferson-Pilot	9.5
Other	7.4

Source: *Mediaweek*, April 3, 2000, p. 28, from BIA Research.

★ 1389 ★
Radio Broadcasting (SIC 4832)

Radio Market in San Diego, CA

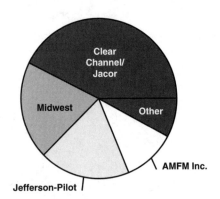

Shares are shown based on revenues

Clear Channel/Jacor	42.5%
Midwest	19.6
Jefferson-Pilot	18.9
AMFM Inc.	11.3
Other	7.7

Source: *Mediaweek*, September 20, 1999, p. 22, from *Duncan's Radio Market Guide, 1999.*

★ 1390 ★
Radio Broadcasting (SIC 4832)

Radio Market in Tampa Bay, FL

Clear Channel Communications	44.3%
Infinity Broadcasting	29.9
Cox Radio	18.3
Mega Communications	2.6
WGUL FM Inc.	1.1
Other	3.8

Source: *Mediaweek*, October 18, 1999, p. 26, from BIA Research.

★ 1391 ★
Radio Broadcasting (SIC 4832)

Top Radio Companies

Data show number of stations.

Clear Channel	512
Cox Radio	484
AMFM	443
Cumulus	248
Infinity	163
Citadel	118
Entercom	85

Source: *Investor's Business Daily*, October 5, 1999, p. 1.

★ 1392 ★
Radio Broadcasting (SIC 4832)

Top Radio Formats in Canada - 1999

Data show share of listeners for the top 12 markets in Spring 1999.

Adult contemporary	28.6%
News/talk	23.0
Contemporary hit radio	15.9
Album oriented rock	7.6
Classical	6.6
Country	5.6
Gold	3.9
Classic rock	2.8
Full service	2.2
Other	3.7

Source: *Marketing Magazine*, July 12, 1999, p. 20, from BBM Bureau of Measurement and Integrated Media Sales.

★ 1393 ★
Radio Broadcasting (SIC 4832)

Top Radio Networks

Data show revenue per station, in millions of dollars.

Infinity	$ 10.3
Emmis	9.9
Bonneville	8.5
Disney/ABC	8.2
Greater Media	7.8
Jefferson	6.6
Susquehanna	6.3

Source: *Investor's Business Daily*, November 15, 1999, p. A10, from PaineWebber and *Who Owns What*.

★ 1394 ★
Television Broadcasting (SIC 4833)

Broadcast Ad Revenues - 1999

Revenues are shown in billions of dollars.

	($ bil.)	Share
NBC	$ 4.66	31.1%
ABC	3.78	25.3
CBS	3.23	21.6
Fox	2.27	15.2

Source: *Electronic Media*, May 1, 2000, p. 26, from Competitive Media Reporting.

★ 1395 ★
Television Broadcasting (SIC 4833)

Popular TV Networks

Data show millions of viewers for the season so far.

NBC	14.1
CBS	13.1
ABC	12.1
Fox	9.0
WB	4.3
UPN	3.9

Source: *Entertainment Weekly*, December 3, 1999, p. 37.

★ 1396 ★
Television Broadcasting (SIC 4833)

Prime Time Leaders 1998-99

Ad-supported cable	34.7%
NBC affiliates	12.3
CBS affiliates	12.2
ABC affiliates	11.2
Other TV	29.6

Source: *Broadcasting & Cable*, December 6, 1999, p. C3, from *NHI Quarterly*.

★ 1397 ★
Television Broadcasting (SIC 4833)

Spanish-Language TV Market

Univision 88%
Other 12

Source: *Investor's Business Daily*, December 9, 1999, p. A10.

★ 1398 ★
Television Broadcasting (SIC 4833)

Spanish Television Market

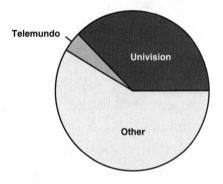

Shares are for the 1998-99 season.

Univision 37.4%
Telemundo 4.3
Other 58.3

Source: *Wall Street Journal*, September 20, 1999, p. B1, from Nielsen Media Research.

★ 1399 ★
Television Broadcasting (SIC 4833)

Top TV Networks - 1999

Data show estimated revenues in billions of dollars.

ABC . . . . $ 3.4
CBS 3.3
NBC 3.3
QVC 2.4
ESPN 1.8
Fox 1.7
HBO 1.6
HSN 1.1

Source: *Broadcasting & Cable*, December 13, 1999, p. 31, from Paul Kagan Associates and Wall Street analysts.

★ 1400 ★
Cable Broadcasting (SIC 4841)

Children's TV Market - 1999

Market shares are shown in perent.

Nickelodeon 42.5%
Cartoon Network 29.5
Other 28.0

Source: *Electronic Media*, November 15, 1999, p. 1A.

★ 1401 ★
Cable Broadcasting (SIC 4841)

Largest Multichannel Video Providers

Firms are ranked by millions of subscribers as of January 2000.

AT&T 14.6
Time Warner Cable 12.6
Comcast 8.2
DirecTV 8.1
Charter Communications 6.1
Cox Communications 6.0
Adelphia Communications 5.6
EchoStar 3.4
Cablevision 3.1

Source: *New York Times*, February 27, 2000, p. 10, from Hughes Electronics, EchoStar, and The Yankee Group.

★ 1402 ★
Cable Broadcasting (SIC 4841)

Top Cable Broadcasters in Canada

Data show thousands of estimated subscribers. Figures are based on a series of planned mergers in the industry.

Rogers & Videotron 3,700
Shaw 1,800
Cogeco 835
Moffat 383

Source: *Globe and Mail*, February 8, 2000, p. B12.

★ 1403 ★

Cable Broadcasting (SIC 4841)

Top Cable Firms - 1998

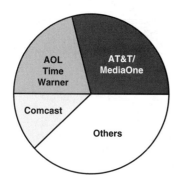

Data show millions of homes.

	(mil.)	Share
AT&T/MediaOne	27.9	29.37%
AOL Time Warner	20.0	21.05
Comcast	11.0	11.58
Others	36.1	38.00

Source: *Wall Street Journal*, January 12, 2000, p. B10, from Kinetic Strategies.

★ 1404 ★

Satellite Broadcasting (SIC 4841)

Leading Satellite Broadcasters

Data show millions of subscribers.

DirecTV 7.7
EchoStar 3.0
C-band broadcast 1.6

Source: *New York Times*, November 26, 1999, p. C6, from Satellite Broadcasting and Communications Association.

★ 1405 ★

Satellite Broadcasting (SIC 4841)

Satellite TV Market - 1999

Shares are for August 1999.

DirecTV 45%
Echostar 24
Primestar 16
C-band 15

Source: *USA TODAY*, November 26, 1999, p. 3B, from Skyreport.com.

SIC 49 - Electric, Gas, and Sanitary Services

★ 1406 ★

Energy (SIC 4900)

How Energy is Consumed

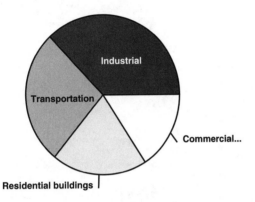

Industrial	37%
Transportation	27
Residential buildings	20
Commercial buildings	16

Source: *HPAC Engineering*, January 2000, p. 136.

★ 1407 ★

Utilities (SIC 4911)

Electric Power Generation in Pennsylvania/ New Jersey/ Maryland

Coal	42%
Nuclear	34
Natural gas	3
Hydro	2
Oil	2
Other	19

Source: *International Water Power & Dam Construction*, September 1999, p. 29.

★ 1408 ★

Utilities (SIC 4911)

Largest Power Marketers - 1999

Shares are for the second quarter of the year.

Enron Power & Subs	15.8%
PG&E Energy Trading	9.9
Aquila Energy	9.3
Southern Co. Energy & Subs	8.1
Duke Energy & Subs	4.1
Reliant Energy & Subs	3.9
Other	48.9

Source: *Financial Times*, December 8, 1999, p. 2, from *Power Markets Week*.

★ 1409 ★

Utilities (SIC 4911)

Largest Power Purchasers - 1999

Data are in megawatt-hours for the first quarter.

Enron Power Marketing	78.08
Southern Company Energy Marketing	38.34
Aquila Power Corp.	29.09
PG&E Energy Trading & Marketing	28.46
Duke Energy Trading & Marketing	20.14
LG&E Energy Marketing	15.60
PacifiCorp. Power Marketing	11.80
Entergy Power Marketing Corp.	10.79
Tractabel Energy Marketing	9.82

Source: *Power Engineering*, August 1999, p. 16, from RDI and PMA.

★ 1410 ★

Utilities (SIC 4911)

Largest Utilities - 1999

The largest gas and electric utilities are ranked by revenues in billions of dollars.

Duke Energy	$ 21.7
PG&E Corp.	20.8
Utilicorp. United	18.6
Texas Utilities	17.1
Reliant Energy	15.3
Southern	11.5
Edison International	9.6
Entergy	8.7
Vista	7.9

Source: *Fortune*, April 17, 2000, pp. I-75.

★ 1411 ★

Pipelines (SIC 4922)

Leading Gas Pipelines - 1999

Data show the number of gas pipeline operated.

GPM Gas Corp.	28,000
Northern Natural Gas Co.	16,613
Tennessee Gas Pipeline Co.	14,537
Columbia Gas Transmission Co.	13,459
Natural Gas Pipeline Co. of America	11,902
Tejas Energy Co.	11,891
ANR Pipeline Co.	10,599
Transcontinental Gas Pipe Lien Corp.	10,562
El Paso Natural Gas Co.	9,870
PG&E Texas Pipeline	9,758

Source: *Pipeline & Gas Journal*, November 1999, p. 53.

★ 1412 ★

Pipelines (SIC 4922)

Top Gas Distribution Utilities - 1999

Data show millions of customers.

Southern California Gas Co.	4.90
Pacific Gas & Electric Co.	3.73
Nicor Gas	1.91
Consolidated Natural Gas Co. Dist.	1.88
Public Service Electric & Gas Co.	1.55
Consumers Energy Co.	1.53
Atlanta Gas Light Co.	1.45
Reliant Energy Entex	1.44

Oneok Inc.	1.42
TXU Gas Company	1.37

Source: *Pipeline & Gas Journal*, November 1999, p. 45.

★ 1413 ★

Utilities (SIC 4922)

Largest Electricity Marketers - 1998

Data are in millions of megawatt hours.

Enron Corp.	399.0
Southern Co.	185.5
Aquila Power	121.0
Dynegy	120.4
Entergy Corp.	98.0
Duke Energy	96.7
LG&E Corp.	91.9

Source: *Atlanta Journal-Constitution*, June 26, 1999, p. D12, from MegaWattDaily, Federal Energy Regulatory Commission, and Southern Co.

★ 1414 ★

Water Services (SIC 4941)

Largest Water Companies - 1999

Companies are ranked by estimated revenues in millions of dollars.

American Water Works	$ 1,300
United Water Resources	520
Philadelphia Suburban	300
California Water	200
Etown	150
San Jose Water	120
Indianapolis Water	120

Source: *Wall Street Journal*, August 24, 1999, p. A13, from Suez Lyonnaise des Eaux.

★ 1415 ★
Water Treatment (SIC 4941)

Advanced Bulk Water Treatment-2000

Technologies such as reverse osmosis are expected to become more popular as seawater desalinization becomes a viable method of providing fresh water.

	($ mil.)	Share
Membrane-based	$ 420	47.67%
Sorption	400	45.40
Distillation	61	6.92

Source: *Water Engineering & Management*, January 2000, p. 9, from Business Communications Co.

★ 1416 ★
Water Treatment (SIC 4941)

Water Treatment Services - 1999

The $1.5 billion market is shown in percent.

Suez	30%
Hercules	27
Drew	5
ChemTreat	2
Other	36

Source: *Chemical Week*, May 3, 2000, p. 25.

★ 1417 ★
Landfills (SIC 4953)

Landfill Ownership - 1998

Waste Management Inc.

USA Waste Systems Inc.

Browning-Ferris Industries Inc.

Allied Waste Industries Inc.

Republic Services Inc.

Other

Approximately 64% of the market is owned by the public sector.

Waste Management Inc.	15%
USA Waste Systems Inc.	8
Browning-Ferris Industries Inc.	7
Allied Waste Industries Inc.	5
Republic Services Inc.	2
Other	63

Source: *Waste News*, May 1, 2000, p. 1.

★ 1418 ★
Trash Collection (SIC 4953)

Largest Trash Collection Firms - 1998

Firms are ranked by revenues in millions of dollars.

Waste Management Inc.	$ 12,703.0
Browning-Ferris	4,745.7
Allied Waste Industries	1,575.6
Republic Services Inc.	1,369.0
Norcal Waste Systems Inc.	335.0
Superior Services Inc.	319.7
Recycling Industries Inc.	250.0
Rumpke Consolidated Companies Inc. . .	240.6
Eastern Environmental Inc.	187.0
Waste Industries Inc.	171.0

Source: *Waste Age*, September 1999, p. 53.

★ 1419 ★
Trash Collection (SIC 4953)

Waste Disposal Market in North America

The market is valued at $35-40 billion.

	($ bil.)
Allied Waste	$ 10
Browning Ferris	7
Other	23

Source: *Waste News*, March 15, 1999, p. 1.

★ 1420 ★
Trash Collection (SIC 4953)

Waste Disposal Market in Vancouver, BC

Canadian Waste Services Inc.'s share is estimated.

Canadian Waste Services Inc.	60%
BFI	30
Other	10

Source: *Waste Age*, April 26, 1999, p. 10.

SIC 50 - Wholesale Trade - Durable Goods

★ 1421 ★
Wholesale Trade - Office Products (SIC 5040)

Largest Office Supply Chains - 1998

Chains are ranked by sales in millions of dollars.

Office Depot	$ 5,129
Staples	4,867
OfficeMax	4,338
Arvey Paper & Supplies	99

Source: *Discount Store News*, August 9, 1999, p. 50.

★ 1422 ★
Wholesale Trade - Office Products (SIC 5044)

Office Product Sales

Office superstores	20%
Discount stores	16
Specialty retailers	6
Wholesalers/distributors/mass	5
Wholesale trade	5
Drug stores	4
Food stores	3
Other	41

Source: *MMR*, November 15, 1999, p. 28.

★ 1423 ★
Wholesale Trade - Electronics (SIC 5060)

Top Electronics Wholesalers in North America

Firms are ranked by revenues in bilions of dollars.

Arrow Electronics	$ 5.3
Avnet	4.8
Veba Electronics	2.1
Pioneer Standard	2.1
Future Electronics	1.8
Marshall Industries	1.7

Source: *Electronic Business*, April 1999, p. 23.

★ 1424 ★
Wholesale Trade - Exercise Equipment (SIC 5091)

Exercise Equipment Sales - 1998

Data show manufacturer sales in millions of dollars. Figures are wholesale. Total home use sales increased from $2.68 billion in 1997 to $2.79 billion in 1998. Institutional sales bring the entire market to $3.3 billion.

	($ mil.)	Share
Treadmills	$ 830	29.70%
Aerobic riders	300	10.73
X-country ski machines	260	9.30
Home gyms	240	8.59
Stationary bikes	190	6.80
Free weights	135	4.83
Benches	125	4.47
Abdominal trainers	115	4.11

Continued on next page.

★ 1424 ★ *Continued*

Wholesale Trade - Exercise Equipment (SIC 5091)

Exercise Equipment Sales - 1998

Data show manufacturer sales in millions of dollars. Figures are wholesale. Total home use sales increased from $2.68 billion in 1997 to $2.79 billion in 1998. Institutional sales bring the entire market to $3.3 billion.

	($ mil.)	Share
Stair-climbing machines	$ 100	3.58%
Other	500	17.89

Source: "Home Market Soft: Institutional Market Robust." Retrieved December 2, 1999 from the World Wide Web: http://www.sportlink.com, from Fitness Products Council and Sporting Goods Manufacturers Association.

SIC 51 - Wholesale Trade - Nondurable Goods

★ 1425 ★
Wholesale Trade - Food (SIC 5140)
Largest Broadline Distributors

Sales are shown in millions of dollars.

Sysco Corp.	$ 16.1
Alliant Foodservice	6.1
U.S. Foodservice	5.8
PYA/Monarch Inc.	2.7
Performance Food Group	1.8
Gordon Food Service	1.6

Source: *ID*, March 1999, p. 47.

★ 1426 ★
Wholesale Trade - Chemicals (SIC 5160)
Leading Chemicals Distributors - 1999

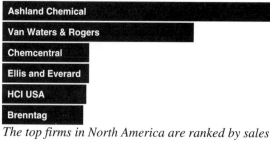

The top firms in North America are ranked by sales in millions of dollars.

Ashland Chemical	$ 2,900
Van Waters & Rogers	2,000
Chemcentral	900
Ellis and Everard	900
HCI USA	872
Brenntag	840

Source: *CMR*, April 17, 2000, p. 11.

★ 1427 ★
Wholesale Trade - Beverages (SIC 5180)
Largest Wine and Spirits Wholesalers - 1999

Southern Wine & Spirits of America	11.8%
Charmer Industries/Sunbelt Beverage	6.8
National Distributing	5.7
Young's Market	4.5
Glazer's Wholesale Distributors	4.5
Other	66.7

Source: *Wall Street Journal*, October 4, 1999, p. A8, from Impact Newsletter and Wine Institute.

SIC 52 - Building Materials and Garden Supplies

★ 1428 ★
Home Improvement Stores (SIC 5211)

Kitchen Cabinet Sales

Distributor	31.0%
Dealers	29.1
Home centers	20.4
Builders	18.4
Direct	1.0
Other	0.1

Source: *Wood Digest*, October 1999, p. 34.

★ 1429 ★
Home Improvement Stores (SIC 5231)

Top Home Center Stores - 1997

Other	70.6%
Menard's	2.5
Hechinger's	2.9
Lowe's	7.1
Home Depot	16.9

Source: *Financial Times*, June 29, 1999, p. 18, from companies.

★ 1430 ★
Home Improvement Stores (SIC 5231)

Top Home Center Stores - 1998

Chains are ranked by sales in billions of dollars.

Home Depot	$ 30.2
Lowe's	12.2
Menard	4.0
Hechinger/Builders Square	3.4
Payless Cashways	1.9
84 Lumber	1.6

HomeBase	$ 1.4
Carolina Holdings	1.4
Sears/Orchard Supply	1.3
Eagle Hardware	1.0

Source: *Stores*, July 1999, p. S14.

★ 1431 ★
Paint Stores (SIC 5231)

Leading Paint/Home Décor Retailers - 1998

Data show sales in millions of dollars. Shares of the group are shown based on sales of 8.04 billion by the top 50 firms.

	Sales ($ mil.)	% of Group
Sherwin-Williams	$ 2,786.0	34.69%
ICI Paints	1,590.0	19.80
Dal Tile Corp.	751.8	9.36
Kelly-Moore Paint	290.0	3.61
Duron Paints & Wallcoverings	285.0	3.55
Dunn Edwards Corp.	243.0	3.03
M.A. Bruder & Sons	228.0	2.84
Porter Paints	195.0	2.43
Frazee Industries	145.0	1.81
Diamond Vogel Paint	128.0	1.59
Other	1,390.2	17.31

Source: *National Home Center News*, May 24, 1999, p. 117.

★ 1432 ★

Hardware Stores (SIC 5251)

Top Hardware Chains in Canada - 1998

Shares are shown based on estimated sales of $23.4 billion for the year ended December 31, 1998.

Canadian Tire	20.3%
Home Hardware	12.2
Home Depot Canada	10.6
Rona	8.3
Revy Home Centres	3.4
Reno Depot	2.5
Cashway	1.5
Kent Building Supplies	1.5
Others	40.2

Source: "Report on Market Share." Retrieved June 8, 2000 from the World Wide Web: http://www. marketingmag.ca, from *Hardware Merchandising.*

★ 1433 ★

Hardware Stores (SIC 5251)

Top Hardware Co-ops - 1998

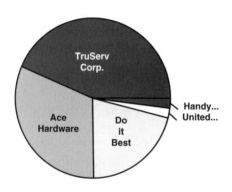

Market shares are shown in percent.

TruServ Corp.	44.3%
Ace Hardware	31.7
Do it Best	21.1
United Hardware Distributing	1.5
Handy Hardware	1.5

Source: *National Home Center News*, June 21, 1999, p. 36.

★ 1434 ★

Hardware Stores (SIC 5251)

Top Hardware Stores in Milwaukee, MN

True Value	16%
Home Depot	15
Builders Square	13
Farm & Fleet	13
Other	43

Source: *National Home Center News*, May 3, 1999, p. 9.

★ 1435 ★

Retailing - Nursery Products (SIC 5261)

Lawn and Soil Fertilizer Sales

Sales are shown for the year ended September 4, 1999.

Mass	89.0%
Food stores	6.4
Drug	4.5

Source: *Grocery Headquarters*, December 1999, p. 44, from A.C. Nielsen.

SIC 53 - General Merchandise Stores

★ 1436 ★
Retailing (SIC 5300)

Largest Retailers

Firms are ranked by estimated annual sales in billions of dollars.

Wal-Mart	$ 95.3
Kmart	33.6
Home Depot	30.2
Costco Companies	23.8
Target	23.0
SAM's Club	22.8
Lowe's Companies	12.2
Toys R Us	11.2
Best Buy	10.0
Meijer's	9.1

Source: *Discount Merchandiser*, July 1999, p. 50.

★ 1437 ★
Retailing (SIC 5300)

Retail Market by Segment

The top 100 retailers generated revenues of $891.6 billion.

Supermarkets	23.9%
Discount stores	14.8
Hard line stores	10.8
Drug stores	7.3
Department stores	7.1
Supercenters	6.4
Warehouse wholesale clubs	6.3
Home centers	6.1
Other	17.3

Source: *Chain Store Age*, August 1999, p. 3A.

★ 1438 ★
Retailing (SIC 5300)

Top Retailers - 1998

The top retailers are ranked by revenues in billions of dollars.

Wal-Mart	$ 137.6
Sears, Roebuck & Co.	41.3
Kmart	33.6
Dayton Hudson	30.9
J.C. Penney	30.6
Home Depot	30.2
Kroger	28.2
Safeway	24.4
Costco	24.2
American Stores	19.8

Source: *Chain Store Age*, August 1999, p. 3A.

★ 1439 ★
Retailing (SIC 5300)

Where We Holiday Shop - 1999

Figures are based on a survey.

Discount dept. stores	80%
Catalogs	42
Traditional dept. stores	41
Internet	10

Source: *New York Times*, November 24, 1999, p. C1, from U.S. Department of Commerce and Deloitte & Touche survey.

★ 1440 ★
Department Stores (SIC 5311)

Top Department Stores - 1998

Chains are ranked by sales in billions of dollars.

Sears	$ 33.5
J.C. Penney	19.3
Federated	15.8

Continued on next page.

★ 1440 ★ *Continued*
Department Stores (SIC 5311)

Top Department Stores - 1998

Chains are ranked by sales in billions of dollars.

May	$ 13.0
Dillard	8.0
Saks	6.2
Nordstrom	5.0
Mervyn's	4.1
Montgomery Ward	3.6
Kohl's	3.6

Source: *Stores*, July 1999, p. S14.

★ 1441 ★
Department Stores (SIC 5311)

Top Department Stores in Canada - 1999

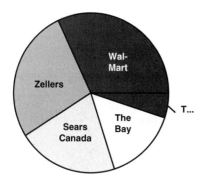

Shares are shown based on estimated sales of $17.9 billion for the year ended December 31, 1999.

Wal-Mart	32.1%
Zellers	27.3
Sears Canada	20.5
The Bay	14.8
T Eaton Co.	5.3

Source: "Report on Market Share." Retrieved June 8, 2000 from the World Wide Web: http://www.marketingmag.ca, from Kubas Consultants.

★ 1442 ★
Convenience Stores (SIC 5331)

Largest Convenience Stores in North America - 1999

Data show number of outlets. Equilon and Motiva were formed last year when Shell Oil, Texaco Inc. and Saudi Aramco joined assets.

Equilon Enterprises LLC and Motiva Enterprises LLC	6,530
7-Eleven Inc.	6,307
Mobil Corp.	3,630
Tosco Corp.	3,099
BP Amoco	3,000
Chevron Corp.	2,700
Ultramar Diamond Shamrock Corp.	2,634
Speedway Superamerica LLC	2,283
Alimentation Couche-Tard Inc.	1,329
The Pantry Inc.	1,202

Source: *Convenience Store News*, August 1999, p. 77.

★ 1443 ★
Discount Merchandising (SIC 5331)

Discount Club Market in Boston, MA

Market shares are shown in percent.

Costco	48.3%
BJs	41.4
Sam's Club	10.3

Source: *DSN Supercenter & Club Business*, March 15, 1999, p. 1.

★ 1444 ★
Discount Merchandising (SIC 5331)

Discount Club Market in Boston, MA - 1999

Costco	52.1%
Other	47.9

Source: *DSN Supercenter & Club Business*, March 13, 2000, p. 1.

★ 1445 ★
Discount Merchandising (SIC 5331)

Discount Club Market in Florida

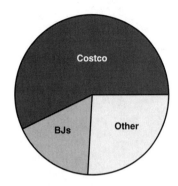

Market shares are shown in percent.

Costco	56.7%
BJs	17.0
Other	26.3

Source: *DSN Supercenter & Club Business*, October 25, 1999, p. 1.

★ 1446 ★
Discount Merchandising (SIC 5331)

Discount Club Market in Ohio - 1998

The market is valued at $1.2 -$1.3 billion.

Sam's Club	91.3%
BJ's	8.7

Source: *DSN Supercenter & Club Business*, April 12, 1999, p. 1, from *Supermerchants Market Guide, 1998.*

★ 1447 ★
Discount Merchandising (SIC 5331)

Discount Club Market in Ohio - 2000

Retail sales of clubs and supercenters reached $5.9 billion.

Meijer	40.6%
Sam's Club	19.5
Wal-Mart Supercenters	13.1
Super Kmart	11.7
Big Bear Plus	6.3
Biggs	5.1
Other	3.7

Source: *DSN Supercenter & Club Business*, April 10, 2000, p. 1, from *Supermerchants Market Guide, 1998.*

★ 1448 ★
Discount Merchandising (SIC 5331)

Discount Club Market in Virginia - 1998

The market is valued at $1.2 -$1.3 billion.

Costco	60.4%
Sam's Club	28.9
BJ's	10.7

Source: *DSN Supercenter & Club Business*, May 10, 1999, p. 1, from *Supermerchants Market Guide, 1998.*

★ 1449 ★
Discount Merchandising (SIC 5331)

Discount Club Market in Washington

Market shares are shown in percent.

Costco	94.9%
Sam's Club	5.1

Source: *DSN Supercenter & Club Business*, June 14, 1999, p. 1.

★ 1450 ★
Discount Merchandising (SIC 5331)

Discount Club Market in Washington D.C./ Baltimore

Market shares are shown in percent.

Costco	50.0%
Sam's Club	29.1
BJ's	20.9

Source: *DSN Supercenter & Club Business*, February 7, 2000, p. 1.

★ 1451 ★
Discount Merchandising (SIC 5331)

Discount Store Market in California - 1998

The membership club market is worth $8.8 billion, the largest in the country.

Costco	91.5%
Sam's Clubs	8.5

Source: *DSN Supercenter & Club Business*, October 11, 1999, p. 1, from *Supermerchants Market Guide, 1998.*

★ 1452 ★
Discount Merchandising (SIC 5331)

Discount Store Market in Colorado - 1999

Wal-Mart	71.9%
Super Kmart	19.5
Biggs	8.6

Source: *DSN Supercenter & Club Business*, April 26, 1999, p. 1, from *Supermerchants Market Guide, 1998.*

★ 1453 ★
Discount Merchandising (SIC 5331)

Largest Supercenter Chains - 1998

Chains are ranked by sales in millions of dollars.

Wal-Mart Supercenter	$ 36,595
Fred Meyer	14,878
Meijer	8,268
Super Kmart Centers	4,565
Fedco	650

Source: *Discount Store News*, August 9, 1999, p. 50.

★ 1454 ★
Discount Merchandising (SIC 5331)

Supercenter Market in Chicago, IL - 1998

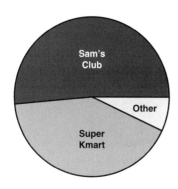

The market is shown in percent.

Sam's Club	51.5%
Super Kmart	41.6
Other	6.9

Source: *DSN Supercenter & Club Business*, January 11, 1999, p. 1, from *Supermerchants Market Guide, 1998.*

★ 1455 ★
Discount Merchandising (SIC 5331)

Supercenter Market in Detroit, MI - 1999

Meijer	77.4%
Super Kmart	22.6

Source: *DSN Supercenter & Club Business*, January 24, 2000, p. 1, from *Supermerchants Market Guide, 1998.*

★ 1456 ★
Discount Merchandising (SIC 5331)

Supercenter Market in Missouri - 1999

Wal-Mart Supercenter	79.4%
Other	20.6

Source: *DSN Supercenter & Club Business*, March 27, 2000, p. 1.

★ 1457 ★
Discount Merchandising (SIC 5331)

Supercenter Market in Ohio - 1998

The market is valued at $4.0-$4.4 billion.

Meijer	56.2%
Super Kmart	14.7
Wal-Mart	14.0
Big Bear Plus	8.6
Biggs	6.5
Other	10.0

Source: *DSN Supercenter & Club Business*, April 12, 1999, p. 1, from *Supermerchants Market Guide, 1998.*

★ 1458 ★
Discount Merchandising (SIC 5331)

Supercenter Market in Phoenix, AZ - 1999

Costco	44.4%
Fred Meyer	37.7
Sam's	17.9

Source: *DSN Supercenter & Club Business*, February 28, 2000, p. 1, from *Supermerchants Market Guide, 1998.*

★ 1459 ★

Discount Merchandising (SIC 5331)

Top Discount Stores - 1998

Chains are ranked by sales in billions of dollars.

Wal-Mart	$ 95.3
Kmart	33.6
Costco	24.2
Target	23.0
Sam's Club	22.8
Meijer	7.0
Consolidated Stores	4.1
BJ's Wholesale Club	3.4
Dollar General	3.2

Source: *Stores*, July 1999, p. S17.

SIC 54 - Food Stores

★ 1460 ★
Grocery Stores (SIC 5411)

Grocery Market in Atlanta, GA

Kroger	34.02%
Publix	24.34
Winn-Dixie	8.38
Ingles	6.61
Cub Foods	5.17
Wal-Mart	3.80
Harry's Farmers Market	2.65
Harris Teeter	2.43
Other	12.60

Source: ''Winn-Dixie Sales Slip in Atlanta Grocery War.'' Retrieved April 10, 2000 from the World Wide Web: http://library.northernlight.com, from Shelby Report.

★ 1461 ★
Grocery Stores (SIC 5411)

Grocery Market in Baltimore, MN

The supermarket industry reached $3.91 billion.

Giant	45.00%
Metro	9.54
Safeway Food & Drug	8.83
Valu Food Inc.	2.20

Source: Retrieved January 13, 2000 from the World Wide Web: http://www.amcity.com/sanantonio/stories/1999/12/20/story2.html, from *Food World*.

★ 1462 ★
Grocery Stores (SIC 5411)

Grocery Market in Colorado - 1999

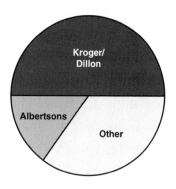

Kroger/Dillon	50%
Albertsons	15
Other	35

Source: *DSN Supercenter & Club Business*, April 26, 1999, p. 1, from *Supermerchants Market Guide, 1998*.

★ 1463 ★
Grocery Stores (SIC 5411)

Grocery Market in Dallas/Ft. Worth, TX

Albertson's	18.5%
Tom Thumb	12.3
Kroger	12.2
Brookshire Grocery Co.	11.4
Other	45.6

Source: *Progressive Grocer*, September 1999, p. 11, from Trade Dimensions.

★ 1464 ★
Grocery Stores (SIC 5411)

Grocery Market in Dallas, TX

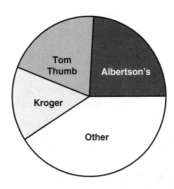

Albertson's 23.5%
Tom Thumb 20.4
Kroger 15.2
Other 40.9

Source: "Internet Supermarket Web Sites." Retrieved May 1, 2000 from the World Wide Web: http://library.northernlight.com, from *Market Scope*.

★ 1465 ★
Grocery Stores (SIC 5411)

Grocery Market in Houston, TX

Grocers Supply Co. 24.9%
Kroger 24.8
Randalls 15.2
H.E. Butt 13.6
Other 21.5

Source: *Progressive Grocer*, September 1999, p. 11, from Trade Dimensions.

★ 1466 ★
Grocery Stores (SIC 5411)

Grocery Market in Lockport, NY

Tops Markets 72%
Wegmans 4
Other 24

Source: Retrieved January 13, 2000 from the World Wide Web: http://www.amcity.com/buffalo/stories/1999/05/17/newscolumn1.html, from Goldhaber Research Associates.

★ 1467 ★
Grocery Stores (SIC 5411)

Grocery Market in New Jersey

Wakefern 13%
Pathmark/Edwards 11
A&P 9
Grand Union 7
Other 60

Source: *Business News New Jersey*, June 21, 1999, p. 6.

★ 1468 ★
Grocery Stores (SIC 5411)

Grocery Market in New York

ShopRite 18.9%
A&P 12.3
Other 68.8

Source: *Crain's New York Business*, June 28, 1999, p. 3, from *Griffin's Modern Grocer*.

★ 1469 ★
Grocery Stores (SIC 5411)

Grocery Market in Ontario

Market shares are shown in percent.

Loblaws 34.5%
A&P 16.2
Agora 9.9
Metro/Loeb 2.8
Other channel 26.1
Other grocery 10.5

Source: *Toronto Star*, August 13, 1999, p. E3, from A.C. Nielsen.

★ 1470 ★
Grocery Stores (SIC 5411)
Grocery Market in Tampa Bay, FL

Marketshares are shown for the quarter ending October 31, 1999.

Publix 40%
Kash N' Karry 18
Other 42

Source: "Winn-Dixie Struggles." Retrieved May 5, 2000 from the World Wide Web: http://library.northernlight.com.

★ 1471 ★
Grocery Stores (SIC 5411)
Grocery Market Leaders in Austin, TX

Shares are shown based on number of outlets.

H.E. Butt 60.6%
Albertson's 12.9
Randalls 11.5
Wal-Mart Supercenters 5.5
Fiesta Mart 1.6
Mass Marketing Inc. 1.6

Source: *Supermarket Business*, April 15, 2000, p. 51, from Trade Dimensions.

★ 1472 ★
Grocery Stores (SIC 5411)
Grocery Market Leaders in Milwaukee, WI

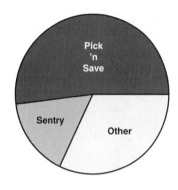

Pick 'n Save 52%
Sentry 16
Other 32

Source: Retrieved May 1, 2000 from the World Wide Web: http://library.northernlight.com.

★ 1473 ★
Grocery Stores (SIC 5411)
Grocery Store in Detroit, MI

Shares are shown based on number of outlets.

A&P 24.4%
Kroger 22.5
Meijer 10.5
IGA 3.2
Super Kmart 3.1
VO5 Group Stores 2.2
VG's Food Centers 2.1
Other 32.0

Source: *Supermarket Business*, May 15, 2000, p. 32, from Trade Dimensions.

★ 1474 ★
Grocery Stores (SIC 5411)

Grocery Store Market in Western New York

Top Markets 58%
Wegmans 27
Other 15

Source: Retrieved January 13, 2000 from the World Wide Web: http://www.amcity.com/buffalo/stories/1999/05/17/newscolumn1.html, from Goldhaber Research Associates.

★ 1475 ★
Grocery Stores (SIC 5411)

Largest Supermarkets

Data show number of stores.

Wal-Mart 3,599
Albertson's 2,468
Kroger 2,200
Safeway 1,656

Source: *Cincinnati Enquirer*, December 5, 1999, p. E1.

★ 1476 ★
Grocery Stores (SIC 5411)

Top Supermarkets - 1998

	($ bil.)	Share
Kroger	$ 43.1	10.4%
Albertson's	36.0	8.7
Safeway	27.3	6.6
Ahold USA	23.4	5.6
Winn-Dixie	13.9	3.4
Delhaize America	13.5	3.3
Publix	12.1	2.9

Source: *Feedstuffs*, August 23, 1999, p. 4, from Food Institute.

★ 1477 ★
Retailing - Food (SIC 5411)

Natural Food Retailers

Sales are shown in millions of dollars.

Whole Foods . . . . $ 1,560
Wild Oats 542

Source: *Supermarket News*, November 8, 1999, p. 1.

★ 1478 ★
Retailing - Meat (SIC 5421)

Where Chicken is Purchased

Retail grocery stores 54.0%
Fast-food restaurants 27.6
Other restaurants/foodservice 18.4

Source: *Pork*, April 2000, p. 13, from National Chicken Council.

★ 1479 ★
Retailing - Confectionery (SIC 5441)

Where Candy is Purchased in Canada - 1999

Sales are shown for the year ended March 27, 1999.

Convenience stores 25.6%
Grocery stores 20.1
Mass merchandisers/warehouse 18.7
Drug stores 16.8
Other 18.8

Source: *The Manufacturing Confectioner*, January 2000, p. 8, from A.C. Nielsen MarketTrack.

★ 1480 ★

Bakeries (SIC 5461)

Popular Bakery Items

According to a survey, sales for big bakeries are increasing while decreasing for small ones. Median annual sales were $371,000.

Cakes, custom decorated 18%
Donuts, yeast-raised 13
Breads/rolls 11

Source: Retrieved January 1, 2000 from the World Wide Web: http://www.aibonline.org/SERICES/.e/ StatisticsAndTrends, from *Modern Baking*.

★ 1481 ★

Bakeries (SIC 5461)

Who Sells Bread

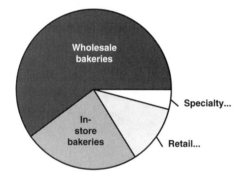

Sales are shown in billions of dollars.

Wholesale bakeries . . . . $ 6.90   59.68%
In-store bakeries 2.70   23.84
Retail bakeries 1.40   11.99
Specialty bread stores 0.51   4.40

Source: Retrieved January 1, 2000 from the World Wide Web: http://www.aibonline.org/SERVICES/.e/ StatisticsAndTrends, from U.S. Department of Commerce.

★ 1482 ★

Retailing - Bagels (SIC 5461)

Bagel Sales by Outlet

There are an estimated 2,000 retail bagel shops with the bulk of them located in New York, New Jersey, California and Florida.

Retail shops 38%
Instore bakeries 26
Foodservice 19
Frozen wholesale 10
Fresh wholesale 6
Refrigerated wholesale 1

Source: Retrieved January 1, 2000 from the World Wide Web: http://www.aibonline.org/SERVICES/Online/ StatisticsAndTrends.

SIC 55 - Automotive Dealers and Service Stations

★ 1483 ★
Auto Dealerships (SIC 5511)

Auto Dealership Market

Data show number of dealerships and share of market.

	Outlets	Share
GM	7,700	29.6%
Daimler-Chrysler	4,452	16.9
Ford	4,208	25.0

Source: *Wall Street Journal*, September 29, 1999, p. A3, from Autodata Corp.

★ 1484 ★
Auto Dealerships (SIC 5511)

Top Car Dealer Groups - 1999

Data show new retail units.

AutoNation Inc.	468,981
Asbury Automotive Group	102,000
United Auto Group Inc.	93,259
V.T. Inc.	80,445
Sonic Automotive Inc.	74,065
Hendrick Automotive Group	61,861
Group 1 Automotive Inc.	60,384
Bill Heard Enterprises Inc.	34,714
Planet Automotive	31,511

Source: *Automotive News*, May 1, 2000, p. 54.

★ 1485 ★
Retailing - Auto Supplies (SIC 5531)

Auto Battery Sales

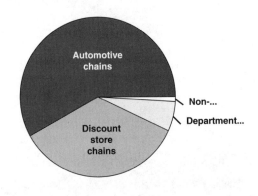

Automotive chains	58%
Discount store chains	35
Department store chains	6
Non-automotive chains	1

Source: *Aftermarket Business*, April 2000, p. 72.

★ 1486 ★
Retailing - Auto Supplies (SIC 5531)

Motor Oil Sales

Sales are shown for the year ended September 4, 1999.

Mass	83.5%
Food	12.8
Drug stores	3.7

Source: *Grocery Headquarters*, December 1999, p. 44, from A.C. Nielsen.

★ 1487 ★

Retailing - Auto Supplies (SIC 5531)

Running Board Sales

Automotive chains	74%
Discount store chains	24
Non-automotive chains	1
Department store chains	1

Source: *Aftermarket Business*, April 2000, p. 72.

★ 1488 ★

Tire Dealerships (SIC 5531)

Largest Tire Retailers in Canada

Data show number of outlets. The top 15 stores account for more than 40 percent of the estimated 40,000 retail tire outlets in the country.

Canadian Tire	430
OK Tire Stores	203
Kal Tire	149
President Tire Canada	128
Tirecraft Auto Centers	127
Wal-Mart	124
Fountain Tire	113
Firestone Tire & Auto	80
Unimax Tire Ltd.	75
Sears Auto Centres	67

Source: *Tire Business*, January 17, 2000, p. 12.

★ 1489 ★

Tire Dealerships (SIC 5531)

Top Tire Dealerships - 1999

The top companies in the U.S. and Canada are ranked by commercial sales in millions of dollars.

Treadco Inc.	$ 186.6
Les Schwab Tire Centers	169.8
Kal Tire	157.0
Purcell Tire & Rubber Co.	116.0
Parkhouse Tire Co.	89.0
Pomps Tire Service Inc.	89.0
Bauer Built Inc.	85.0
Cross-Midwest Tire	80.0
Snider Tire Inc.	66.0

Source: *Tire Business*, March 27, 2000, p. 15.

★ 1490 ★

Gas Stations (SIC 5541)

Largest Gas Station Chains

Data show number of branded retail outlets.

BP Amoco	15,500
CITGO	15,079
Motiva	14,200
ExxonMobil	13,500
Equilon	9,400
Chevron	8,126
Tosco	6,267
Phillips	5,916

Source: *National Petroleum News*, January 2000, p. 36, from *1999 NPN Market Facts*.

SIC 56 - Apparel and Accessory Stores

★ 1491 ★

Apparel Stores (SIC 5600)

Largest Off-Price Apparel Chains - 1998

Chains are ranked by sales in millions of dollars.

T.J. Maxx/Marshalls	$ 7,817
Ross Stores	2,182
Burlington Coat Factory	1,796
Goody's Family Clothing	1,091
Stein Mart	898
Kids R Us	779
The Men's Wearhouse	768
Dress Barn	598
Filene's Basement	589
Loehmann's	432

Source: *Discount Store News*, August 9, 1999, p. 45.

★ 1492 ★

Apparel Stores (SIC 5600)

Top Apparel Stores - 1998

Chains are ranked by sales in billions of dollars.

Limited	$ 9.1
TJX	7.3
Gap	6.5
Venator	4.0
Intimate Brands	3.6
Ross Stores	1.9
Burlington Coat	1.7
American Retail Group	1.3
Spiegel/Eddie Bauer	1.3

Source: *Stores*, July 1999, p. S14.

★ 1493 ★

Apparel Stores (SIC 5611)

Top Retailers for Boy's Apparel in Canada - 1998

Market shares are shown in percent.

Sears	19.2%
Zellers	11.6
Wal-Mart	9.9
The Bay	5.4
Eaton's	4.1
Northern Getaway	3.5
SAAN	3.1
Bi-Way	2.2
K-Mart	2.1
Other	38.9

Source: "Men's and Boy's Apparel." Retrieved March 14, 2000 from the World Wide Web: http://www.tradeport.org/ts/countries.

★ 1494 ★

Apparel Stores (SIC 5611)

Top Retailers for Men's Apparel in Canada - 1998

Market shares are shown in percent.

Sears	11.2%
The Bay	9.5
Zellers	7.1
Eaton's	6.1
Moores	4.3
Wal-Mart	4.2
Mark's Work Warehouse	3.9
Harry Rosen	2.0
Costco/Price Club	2.0
Other	50.3

Source: "Men's and Boy's Apparel." Retrieved March 14, 2000 from the World Wide Web: http://www.tradeport.org/ts/countries.

★ 1495 ★
Retailing - Apparel (SIC 5611)
Men's Jeans Sales

Sales are for the year ended November 1999.

Discount stores	27.5%
Chain stores	26.2
Specialty stores	18.6
Department stores	12.0
Factory outlets	5.9
Direct mail	2.6
Off price	2.5
Other	4.7

Source: *Discount Store News*, February 7, 2000, p. A9.

★ 1496 ★
Retailing - Apparel (SIC 5621)
Girl's Jeans Sales

Sales are for the year ended November 1999.

Discount stores	35.3%
Chain stores	22.7
Specialty stores	20.0
Department stores	9.1
Off price	6.2
Factory outlets	4.1
Other	2.6

Source: *Discount Store News*, February 7, 2000, p. A9.

★ 1497 ★
Retailing - Apparel (SIC 5621)
Women's Jeans Sales, Age 14-24

Unit sales are shown for July 1998 - June 1999.

Specialty/sporting	40.3%
Discount stores	23.5
Chain stores	15.7
Department stores	10.7
Off-price	3.3
Factory outlet	3.1
Direct mail	1.3
Other	2.3

Source: *WWD*, July 1999, p. 12, from NPD Group.

★ 1498 ★
Retailing - Apparel (SIC 5621)
Women's Jeans Sales, Age 25-44

Unit sales are shown for July 1998 - June 1999.

Discount stores	37.0%
Specialty/sporting	24.8
Chain stores	18.1
Department stores	6.4
Factory outlet	4.0
Direct mail	3.5

Source: *WWD*, October 7, 1999, p. 12, from NPD Group.

★ 1499 ★
Retailing - Apparel (SIC 5632)
Canada's Sports Apparel Sales - 1998

Sales are shown in percent.

Sporting goods stores	31.8%
Department stores	15.5
Shoe stores	13.6
Discount stores	9.8
Other	29.3

Source: Retrieved January 21, 2000 from the World Wide Web: http://strategis.ic.gc.ca/SSG, from Industry Canada.

★ 1500 ★
Retailing - Apparel (SIC 5632)
Retail Panty Hose/Nylon Market

The $269 million market is shown for the year ended Janaury 3, 1999.

Mass	46.2%
Food	29.4
Drug stores	24.4

Source: *Supermarket News*, May 17, 1999, p. 79, from A. C. Nielsen.

★ 1501 ★

Retailing - Apparel (SIC 5632)

Sports Apparel Sales

Data show estimated sales.

Discount stores	26.5%
Chain stores	15.2
Sporting goods	14.7
Dept. stores	12.6
Specialty	9.3

Source: Retrieved January 1, 2000 from the World Wide Web: http://www.sportlink.com/1998_research, from NPD Group.

★ 1502 ★

Retailing - Apparel (SIC 5632)

Women's Apparel Accessory Sales by Outlet - 1999

Sales are from October 1998 - September 1999.

Department stores	29%
Specialty stores	18
Discount stores	15
Major chains	12
Off-price	8
Factory outlets	7
Direct mail	6
Other	5

Source: *Footwear News*, November 29, 1999, p. 13, from NPD American Shoppers Panel.

★ 1503 ★

Retailing - Apparel (SIC 5651)

Men's and Women's Outerwear Sales - 1998

Dept. store	15%
Off-price/factory	13
Chains	12
Spec. chains	11
Dir. Mail	10
Disc.	10

Source: *WWD*, August 24, 1999, p. 5.

★ 1504 ★

Shoe Stores (SIC 5661)

Sports Shoe Sales in Canada - 1998

Department stores

Sporting goods stores

Athletic specialty stores

Discount stores

Other

Sales are shown in percent.

Department stores	25.1%
Sporting goods stores	17.6
Athletic specialty stores	13.4
Discount stores	13.4
Other	30.5

Source: Retrieved January 21, 2000 from the World Wide Web: http://strategis.ic.gc.ca/SSG, from Industry Canada.

SIC 57 - Furniture and Homefurnishings Stores

★ 1505 ★
Retailing - Floorcoverings (SIC 5713)

Floor Covering Leaders

Data show selected retailers ranked by sales of residential flooring. Figures are in millions of dollars.

Home Depot	$ 1,500
Lowe's	545
Coleman Floor	108
Floors Inc.	97
Wisenbaker Builder Srvices	61
Carpet Barn	48
Arvada Hardwood	46
Builders Showcase	30
Payless Cashways	28
Pergament	28

Source: *Floor Covering Weekly*, May 1999, p. 1.

★ 1506 ★
Retailing - Floorcoverings (SIC 5713)

Floorcovering Market by Segment - 1999

The estimated market is expected to reach $33.7 billion.

	($ bil.)	Share
Flooring stores	$ 15.90	47.13%
Flooring contractors	5.90	17.49
Tile contractors	3.30	9.78
Building materials	3.00	8.89
OEM/direct non-retail	2.20	6.52
Department stores	1.20	3.56
Furniture	0.98	2.90
Paint & wallpaper stores	0.56	1.66
Other retail	0.70	2.07

Source: *Floor Focus*, November 1999, p. 1.

★ 1507 ★
Retailing - Upholstery (SIC 5714)

Retail Upholstery Sales - 1999

Total retail sales reached $21.9 billion.

Furniture stores & furniture chains	69%
Department stores & chains	20
Specialty stores	6
Other	5

Source: *HFN*, March 13, 2000, p. 34.

★ 1508 ★
Retailing - Wallcoverings (SIC 5714)

Wall Covering Sales - 1998

Discount stores
Department stores
Catalogs
Sears/Montgomery Ward
Other

Total window treatment sales reached $3.7 billion in 1999, a jump from $3.5 billion in 1998.

Discount stores	31%
Department stores	20
Catalogs	17
Sears/Montgomery Ward	10
Other	22

Source: *Home Textiles Today 2000 Business Annual Supplement*, Annual, p. 64.

★ 1509 ★

Retailing - Homefurnishings (SIC 5719)

Bath Towel Sales - 1999

Total retail sales reached $1.9 billion.

Mass merchants & clubs	49%
Department stores & chains	23
Specialty stores	14
Catalogs	3
Other	11

Source: *HFN*, March 13, 2000, p. 34.

★ 1510 ★

Retailing - Homefurnishings (SIC 5719)

Bed Pillow Sales by Outlet

Market is shown in percent.

Mass merchant	43%
National chains	19
Specialty stores	13
Dept. stores	11
Catalogs	8
Other	6

Source: *HFN*, November 8, 1999, p. 10.

★ 1511 ★

Retailing - Homefurnishings (SIC 5719)

Case Goods Sales - 1999

Total retail sales reached $26.1 billion.

Furniture stores & furniture chains	75.5%
Department stores	15.0
Mass merchants & clubs	4.0
Specialty stores	3.5
Other	2.0

Source: *HFN*, March 13, 2000, p. 34.

★ 1512 ★

Retailing - Homefurnishings (SIC 5719)

Comforter Sales by Outlet

Market is shown in percent.

Dept. stores	32%
Specialty stores	21
Catalogs	20
Mass merchants & clubs	11
National chains	8
Other	8

Source: *HFN*, November 8, 1999, p. 10.

★ 1513 ★

Retailing - Homefurnishings (SIC 5719)

Largest Bedding Retailers

Sales are shown in millions of dollars.

Heiling-Meyers	$ 439.1
Federated Stores	250.0
Select Comfort	246.3
Sleepy's	144.4
Home Life	110.5

Source: *HFN*, November 8, 1999, p. 10.

★ 1514 ★

Retailing - Homefurnishings (SIC 5719)

Largest Bedding Stores - 1998

Sales are shown in millions of dollars.

Mattress Discounters	$ 238.6
Select Comfort	215.0
Sleepy's	152.0
Mattress Giant	100.0
Mattress Firm	96.7
Dial-A-Mattress	80.0
Rockaway Bedding	70.0

Source: *Furniture Today*, August 23, 1999, p. 18.

★ **1515** ★

Retailing - Homefurnishings (SIC 5719)

Metal Cookware Sales - 1999

Total retail sales reached $1.89 billion.

Mass merchants & clubs	50%
Specialty stores	30
Department stores & chains	18
Drugstores/supermarkets	1
Other	2

Source: *HFN*, March 13, 2000, p. 51.

★ **1516** ★

Retailing - Homefurnishings (SIC 5719)

Metal Glassware Sales - 1999

Mass merchants

Specialty stores

Department stores

Other

Total retail sales reached $1.12 billion.

Mass merchants	56%
Specialty stores	25
Department stores	15
Other	4

Source: *HFN*, March 13, 2000, p. 51.

★ **1517** ★

Retailing - Homefurnishings (SIC 5719)

Portable Lamp Sales - 1999

Total retail sales reached $1.6 billion.

Lighting & specialty stores	47%
Home improvement chains	41
Furniture stores/furniture chains	5
Mass merchants & clubs	4
National chains	3

Source: *HFN*, March 13, 2000, p. 51.

★ **1518** ★

Retailing - Homefurnishings (SIC 5719)

Retail Bedding Sales - 1999

Department includes J.C. Penney.

Discount stores	35%
Department stores	23
Specialty chains	17
Catalogs	12
Sears, Wards	7
Warehouse clubs	3
Home improvement	1
Online retailing	1
Single-unit specialty stores	1

Source: *Home Textiles Today*, March 13, 2000, p. 12.

★ **1519** ★

Retailing - Homefurnishings (SIC 5719)

Retail Clock Sales - 1999

Total retail sales reached $585.7 million.

Mass merchant & clubs	50%
Specialty stores	20
Catalogs	12
Department stores & chains	8
Drugstores & supermarkets	4
Other	6

Source: *HFN*, March 13, 2000, p. 36.

★ **1520** ★

Retailing - Homefurnishings (SIC 5719)

Retail Crystal Sales - 1999

Department stores	54%
Specialty stores	36
Catalogs	7
Other	3

Source: *HFN*, March 13, 2000, p. 46.

★ 1521 ★
Retailing - Homefurnishings (SIC 5719)

Retail Glassware Sales - 1999

Mass merchants & clubs	56%
Specialty stores	25
Department stores	15
Other	4

Source: *HFN*, March 13, 2000, p. 46.

★ 1522 ★
Retailing - Homefurnishings (SIC 5719)

Retail Houseware/Dinnerware Sales - 1999

Mass merchant & clubs	61%
Specialty stores	22
Department stores	11
Chains	2
Supermarkets & drugstores	2
Other	2

Source: *HFN*, March 13, 2000, p. 46.

★ 1523 ★
Retailing - Homefurnishings (SIC 5719)

Retail Sterling Flatware Sales - 1999

Specialty stores	42%
Department stores & Chains	39
Catalogs	18
Other	1

Source: *HFN*, March 13, 2000, p. 46.

★ 1524 ★
Retailing - Homefurnishings (SIC 5719)

Retail Tabletop Sales - 1998

Mass merchants	33%
Dept. stores/chains	29
Specialty stores	28
Catalogs	5
Other	5

Source: *HFN*, September 13, 1999, p. 3.

★ 1525 ★
Retailing - Appliances (SIC 5722)

Household Appliance Accessory Sales

Sales are shown for the year ended September 4, 1999.

Mass	70.9%
Drug stores	21.0
Food stores	4.7

Source: *Grocery Headquarters*, December 1999, p. 44, from A.C. Nielsen.

★ 1526 ★
Retailing - Appliances (SIC 5722)

Retail Appliance Sales - 1999

Total retail sales reached $4.7 billion.

Appliance/electronic stores	52%
Chains	37
Home improvement centers	8
Mass merchants & clubs	3

Source: *HFN*, March 13, 2000, p. 57.

★ 1527 ★
Retailing - Appliances (SIC 5722)

Room Air Conditoner Sales - 1998

Sears	17%
Appliance/TV Store	15
Wal-Mart	12
Home Depot	6
Lowe's	6
Other	44

Source: *Discount Store News*, August 9, 1999, p. 25, from IMR Continuing Consumer Survey.

★ 1528 ★
Retailing - Electronics (SIC 5731)

Retail Audio/Video Sales - 1999

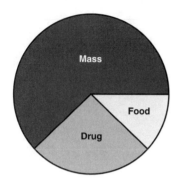

Shares are shown based on sales of $620 million for the year ended February 27, 2000.

	($ mil.)	Share
Mass	$ 386.3	62.24%
Drug	158.4	25.52
Food	76.0	12.24

Source: *Supermarket Business*, May 15, 2000, p. 80, from Information Resources Inc.

★ 1529 ★
Retailing - Computers (SIC 5734)

Computer Sales by Outlet - 1999

Shares are for the second quarter.

Consumer electronics stores	42.3%
PC superstores	40.0
Office superstores	17.7

Source: *Investor's Business Daily*, September 3, 1999, p. A6, from Ziff Davis Inc.'s Storeboard.

★ 1530 ★
Retailing - Music (SIC 5735)

Music Sales by Outlet - 1998

Record stores	50.8%
Tape/record clubs	9.0
Mail order	2.9
Internet	1.1
Other stores	34.4

Source: *Discount Merchandiser*, August 1999, p. 68, from Recording Industry Association of America.

★ 1531 ★
Retailing - Music (SIC 5735)

Online Music Market

Online sales are expected to increase from $200 million 1998 to $3 billion in 2001.

Amazon.com	40%
CDNow	20
Other	40

Source: "Gomez Advisors Releases Music Video Report." Retrieved March 28, 2000 from the World Wide Web: http://www.gomez.com, from Gomez Advisors.

★ 1532 ★
Retailing - Music (SIC 5735)

Top Music Retailers in Canada - 1999

Shares are shown based on estimated sales of $1.4 billion for the year ended December 31, 1999.

HMV	19.7%
Music World	10.5
A&B Sound	7.3
Future Shop	4.6
Archambault Musique	3.9
Sam the Record Man	3.3
Tower Records	1.0
Virgin Records	1.0
Other	48.7

Source: "Report on Market Share." Retrieved June 8, 2000 from the World Wide Web: http://www.marketingmag.ca, from HMV Canada.

★ 1533 ★
Retailing - Music (SIC 5735)

Where College Students Buy Records

Traditional stores	55%
Online	28
Music clubs	12
Second hand stores	4
Other	1

Source: *Wall Street Journal*, November 15, 1999, p. B8, from Cyber Dialogue and Web Noize survey.

★ 1534 ★

Musical Product Stores (SIC 5736)

Largest Music Retailers - 1998

Data show number of stores.

Music Go Round	52
Guitar Center Inc.	48
Fletcher Music Centers	34
Brook Mays/H&H	27
Music & Arts	25
Schmitt Music Company	24
Sam Ash Music Corp.	24
MARS Inc.	22
Daddy's Junky Music	19

Source: *Music Trades*, August 1999, p. 110.

★ 1535 ★

Musical Product Stores (SIC 5736)

Music Stores by State - 1999

There were 8,531 stores.

	No.
California	997
New York	517
Texas	457
Florida	442
Pennsylvania	415
Illinois	390
Ohio	366
Other	4,947

Source: *MMR*, July 1999, p. 58.

★ 1536 ★

Musical Product Stores (SIC 5736)

Top Music Retailers - 1998

Companies are ranked by estimated revenues in millions of dollars. Total sales of the top 200 companies reached $2.8 billion and had a 44.2% market share.

Guitar Center Inc.	$ 391.7
Sam Ash Music Group	230.0
MARS Inc.	114.0
Musicians Friend	98.0
Brook Mays/H&H	78.0
Hermes Music	60.4
Schmitt Music Company	59.2
Washington Music Center	47.6
Fletcher Music Centers	$ 47.6
J.W. Pepper	44.0
Thoroughbred Music	43.0
Full Compass	41.0
Sweetwater Sound Inc.	39.0

Source: *Music Trades*, August 1999, p. 98.

SIC 58 - Eating and Drinking Places

★ 1537 ★

Foodservice (SIC 5812)

Canada's Foodservice Industry

Workplace	
Leisure	
Education	
Health care	
Travel	
Other	

Revenues from institutional foodservice reached C$ 2.27 billion. With leisure, travel and vending added in, the market grows to C$3.7 billion.

Workplace	37.8%
Leisure	24.8
Education	16.1
Health care	16.0
Travel	0.9
Other	4.4

Source: *Nation's Restaurant News*, January 17, 2000, p. 44, from Canadian Restaurant & Foodservice Association.

★ 1538 ★

Foodservice (SIC 5812)

Foodservice Puchases - 1999

Data are in billions of dollars.

B&I	$ 11.9
Schools	5.9
Colleges	3.8
Hospitals	3.5
Nursing homes	2.7

Source: *Food Management*, November 1999, p. 14, from Technomic Inc.

★ 1539 ★

Foodservice (SIC 5812)

Foodservice Purchases

Data show the leading purchases of restaurants based on a survey.

Meat	23%
Poultry	14
Fish/seafood	11
Fruits/vegetables	11
Beverages, nonalcoholic	8
Dairy products	8
Other	25

Source: *Restaurants and Institutions*, November 1, 1999, p. 86.

★ 1540 ★

Foodservice (SIC 5812)

Largest Business/Industry Dining Services

The top firms are ranked by food and beverage sales in millions of dollars.

Motorola Hospitality Group	$ 14.0
Abbott Laboratories	5.0
Aetna Life & Casualty	4.0
Corning Inc.	3.5
The Limited	3.0

Source: *Restaurants & Institutions*, September 15, 1999, p. 96.

★ 1541 ★
Foodservice (SIC 5812)

Largest Contract Management Firms - 1998

The top firms in North America are ranked by food and beverage sales in millions of dollars.

Sodexho Marriott Services	$ 4,160
Aramark	3,700
Compass Group	2,300
Delaware North Companies	1,300
The Wood Co.	470
Volume Services America	406
Guckenheimer Enterprises	265

Source: *Restaurants and Institutions*, September 15, 1999, p. 72.

★ 1542 ★
Foodservice (SIC 5812)

Largest Corrections Operations - 1998

The top firms are ranked by food and beverage sales in millions of dollars.

California Dept. Of Corrections	$ 145.0
Federal Bureau of Prisons	87.2
Texas Dept. of Criminal Justice	70.0
New Jersey Dept. of Corrections	60.0
New York State Dept. of Corrections	53.0

Source: *Restaurants and Institutions*, September 15, 1999, p. 106.

★ 1543 ★
Foodservice (SIC 5812)

Largest Military Foodservice Providers

The top firms are ranked by food and beverage sales in millions of dollars.

U.S. Army Center of Excellence, Subsistence	$ 439.0
Naval Supply Systems Command-Support	251.7
Army and Air Force Exchange Service	166.0
U.S. Air Force APF Food Operations	91.5
U.S. Marine Corps.	75.8

Source: *Restaurants and Institutions*, September 15, 1999, p. 102.

★ 1544 ★
Foodservice (SIC 5812)

Top Food Contractors

Companies are ranked by managed volume in billions of dollars.

Sodexho Marriott Services	$ 6.60
Aramark	4.90
Compass Group North America	2.60
Delaware North Companies	1.30
Morrison Management Specialists	0.72
The Wood Co.	0.50
Ogden Entertainment Group	0.40

Source: *Food Management*, April 2000, p. 30.

★ 1545 ★
Foodservice (SIC 5812)

Top Self-Operated Health Care Firms

The top firms are ranked by food and beverage sales in millions of dollars.

Florida Hospital	$ 8.0
Mt. Sinai NYU Health	7.0
Continuum Health Partners	6.6
Massachusetts General Hospital	6.0
Baptist Memorial Hospital	5.7

Source: *Restaurants and Institutions*, September 15, 1999, p. 80.

★ 1546 ★
Resaurants (SIC 5812)

Top Independent Restaurants - 1999

Restaurants are ranked by food & beverage sales in billions of dollars.

Windows on the World	$ 34.9
Tavern on the Green	34.4
Bob Chinn's Crab House	22.3
Sparks Steakhouse	21.4
Joe's Stone Crab	20.4
21 Club	18.2
The Four Seasons	16.2
Fulton's Crab House	15.6

Source: *Restaurants & Institutions*, April 1, 2000, p. 44.

★ 1547 ★

Restaurants (SIC 5812)

Burger Market Leaders

Total category sales reached $60.26 billion.

McDonald's	$ 35.9
Burger King	10.3
Wendy's	5.5
Hardee's	2.4
Sonic Drive-Ins	1.3

Source: *Restaurants and Institutions*, July 15, 1999, p. 8.

★ 1548 ★

Restaurants (SIC 5812)

Burger Market Leaders - 1998

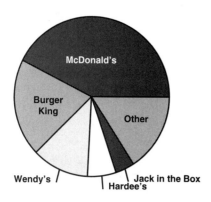

Figures are estimated.

McDonald's	43%
Burger King	20
Wendy's	12
Hardee's	6
Jack in the Box	4
Other	16

Source: *Forbes*, November 1, 1999, p. 222, from Technomic Inc.

★ 1549 ★

Restaurants (SIC 5812)

Cafeteria Chain Leaders

Total category sales reached $2.09 billion.

Old Country Buffet	$ 554.0
Luby's	509.0
Hometown Buffet	295.0
Piccadilly Cafterias	288.0
Furr's Family Dining	187.3

Source: *Restaurants and Institutions*, July 15, 1999, p. 10.

★ 1550 ★

Restaurants (SIC 5812)

Chicken Chain Leaders

Total category sales reached $12.15 billion.

KFC	$ 8,446.0
Popeye's	982.0
Chick-fil-A	798.6
Church's Chicken	755.1
Bojangles	249.9
El Pollo Loco	246.0

Source: *Restaurants and Institutions*, July 15, 1999, p. 9.

★ 1551 ★

Restaurants (SIC 5812)

Chicken Product Sales in Restaurants

Data show the popular forms of chicken products.

Grilled	41%
Fried	34
Baked	14
Other	11

Source: *Broiler Industry*, October 1999, p. 31, from Food Research Institute Inc. and FlavorTrak Database of Resturant Menus.

★ 1552 ★
Restaurants (SIC 5812)

Eating Place Sales in Mid-Atlantic - 2000

Sales are estimated in millions of dollars.

	($ mil.)	Share
New York	$ 14,262.2	37.85%
Pennsylvania	9,864.1	26.18
New Jersey	6,226.3	16.52
Maryland	5,272.6	13.99
Washington D.C.	1,156.7	3.07
Delaware	896.2	2.38

Source: *Nation's Restaurant News*, January 3, 2000, p. 62, from National Restaurant Association.

★ 1553 ★
Restaurants (SIC 5812)

Eating Place Sales in Midwest - 2000

Sales are estimated in millions of dollars.

	($ mil.)	Share
Ohio	$ 13,326.0	22.12%
Illinois	12,267.2	20.36
Michigan	10,007.4	16.61
Indiana	6,221.5	10.33
Missouri	5,968.8	9.91
Wisconsin	5,255.5	8.72
Minnesota	4,510.1	7.49
Iowa	2,683.0	4.45

Source: *Nation's Restaurant News*, January 3, 2000, p. 62, from National Restaurant Association.

★ 1554 ★
Restaurants (SIC 5812)

Eating Place Sales in New England - 2000

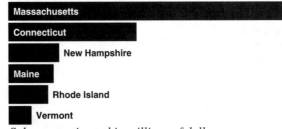

Sales are estimated in millions of dollars.

	($ mil.)	Share
Massachusetts	$ 6,257.9	49.60%
Connecticut	2,889.5	22.90
New Hampshire	1,147.2	9.09
Maine	1,002.6	7.95
Rhode Island	837.7	6.64
Vermont	483.1	3.83

Source: *Nation's Restaurant News*, January 3, 2000, p. 62, from National Restaurant Association.

★ 1555 ★
Restaurants (SIC 5812)

Eating Place Sales in Southeast - 2000

Sales are estimated in millions of dollars.

	($ mil.)	Share
Florida	$ 18,333.0	32.09%
Georgia	8,772.9	15.35
North Carolina	8,672.7	15.18
Virginia	7,576.4	13.26
Tennessee	5,607.1	9.81
Louisiana	4,110.5	7.19
South Carolina	4,063.4	7.11

Source: *Nation's Restaurant News*, January 3, 2000, p. 62, from National Restaurant Association.

★ 1556 ★
Restaurants (SIC 5812)
Family Dining Leaders

Total category sales reached $14.3 billion.

Denny's	$ 1,960.0
Waffle House	1,064.0
International House of Pancakes	1,040.3
Shoney's	1,021.0
Cracker Barrel Old Country Store	1,004.9
Boston Market	950.0
Perkins Family Restaurants	776.0

Source: *Restaurants and Institutions*, July 15, 1999, p. 8.

★ 1557 ★
Restaurants (SIC 5812)
Fast-Food Market in Mexico

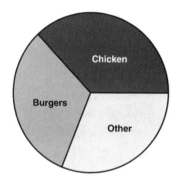

Mexicans spend $500 million annually on fast food.

Chicken	37%
Burgers	32
Other	31

Source: *Market Latin America*, January 2000, p. 6.

★ 1558 ★
Restaurants (SIC 5812)
Italian Chain Leaders

Total category sales reached $3.9 billion.

The Olive Garden	$ 1,380.0
Sbarro	511.0
Romano's Macaroni Grill	350.2
Fazoli's	322.8
Pizzeria Uno Chicago Bar & Grill	280.2
Mazzio's Pizza	157.0

Source: *Restaurants and Institutions*, July 15, 1999, p. 10.

★ 1559 ★
Restaurants (SIC 5812)
Mexican Chain Leaders

Total category sales reached $7.7 billion.

Taco Bell	$ 5,000.0
Del Taco	280.0
Don Pablo's	270.4
Chi-Chi's	243.7
Chevy's Mexican Restaurants	223.5

Source: *Restaurants and Institutions*, July 15, 1999, p. 10.

★ 1560 ★
Restaurants (SIC 5812)
Pizza Restaurant Market - 1998

Pizza Hut	21.4%
Domino's	11.3
Little Caesars	7.4
Papa John's	5.2
Others	54.7

Source: *Detroit News*, October 24, 1999, p. B1, from Technomic Inc.

★ 1561 ★
Restaurants (SIC 5812)

Sandwich Chain Leaders

Total category sales reached $9.6 billion.

Subway Sandwiches & Salads	$ 3,454.0
Arby's	2,200.0
Blimpie Subs & Salads	441.0
Schlotzsky's Deli	348.5
Einstein Bros. Bagels	292.9
A&W Restaurants	278.0
Au Bon Pain	213.0

Source: *Restaurants and Institutions*, July 15, 1999, p. 9.

★ 1562 ★
Restaurants (SIC 5812)

Seafood Chain Leaders

Total category sales reached $4.07 billion.

Red Lobster	$ 1,810.0
Long John Silver's	828.0
Captain D's	478.7
Joe's Crab Shack	223.0
Landry's Seafood Restaurants	114.0
Shells Seafood Restaurants	94.0

Source: *Restaurants and Institutions*, July 15, 1999, p. 10.

★ 1563 ★
Restaurants (SIC 5812)

Steak/Barbeque Chain Leaders

Total category sales reached $8.07 billion.

Outback Steakhouse	$ 1,522.0
Golden Corral	864.0
Ponderosa/Bonanza	730.2
Ryan's Family Steak House	675.0
Lone Star Steakhouse & Saloon	566.0
Sizzler	462.0

Source: *Restaurants and Institutions*, July 15, 1999, p. 9.

★ 1564 ★
Restaurants (SIC 5812)

Sweet/Snack Chain Leaders

Total category sales reached $10.51 billion.

Dairy Queen	$ 2,698
Dunkin Donuts	2,258
Starbucks Coffee	936
Tim Hortons	895
TCBY	824
Baskin Robbins	824

Source: *Restaurants and Institutions*, July 15, 1999, p. 9.

★ 1565 ★
Restaurants (SIC 5812)

Top Chicken Chains - 1998

Market shares are shown based on aggregate sales in this source's annual top 100 list.

KFC	57.08%
Boston Market	12.62
Popeyes	11.45
Chick-fil-A	10.42
Churchs Chicken	8.43

Source: *Nation's Restaurant News*, June 28, 1999, p. 144.

★ 1566 ★
Restaurants (SIC 5812)

Top Dinner House Chains - 1998

Market shares are shown based on aggregate sales in this source's annual top 100 list.

Applebee's Neighborhood Grill & Bar	16.73%
Red Loster	15.91
Olive Garden	12.27
Outback Steakhouse	11.92
Chili's Grill & Bar	11.32
T.G.I.Friday's	9.19
Other	22.66

Source: *Nation's Restaurant News*, June 28, 1999, p. 118.

★ 1567 ★
Restaurants (SIC 5812)

Top Family Chains - 1998

*Market shares are shown based on aggregate sales
in this source's annual top 100 list.*

Denny's	21.99%
Shoney's	11.43
Cracker Barrel Old Country Store	11.23
International House of Pancakes	11.15
Other	44.20

Source: *Nation's Restaurant News*, June 28, 1999, p. 144.

★ 1568 ★
Restaurants (SIC 5812)

Top Fast-Food Chains in Canada

*Shares are shown based on estimated sales of $10.0
billion for the year ended December 31, 1998.*

McDonald's	19.1%
Cara Operations	12.5
Tricon Global Restaurants	11.7
Subway Franchise Systems	4.3
Burger King	3.6
S R Acquisitions	3.5
Wendy's Restaurants	3.5
A&W Food Services	3.4
Dairy Queen Canada	3.0
Les Rotisseries	2.1
Other	33.0

Source: ''Report on Market Share.'' Retrieved June 8,
2000 from the World Wide Web: http://www.
marketingmag.ca, from *Foodservice & Hospitality Magazine*.

★ 1569 ★
Restaurants (SIC 5812)

Top Grill Buffet Chains - 1998

*Market shares are shown based on aggregate sales
in this source's annual top 100 list.*

Golden Corral	32.13%
Ryan's Family Steak House	25.10
Ponderosa Steakhouse	19.71
Western Sizzlin'	11.71
Sizzler	11.34

Source: *Nation's Restaurant News*, June 28, 1999, p. 118.

★ 1570 ★
Restaurants (SIC 5812)

Top Sandwich Chains - 1998

*Market shares are shown based on aggregate sales
in this source's annual top 100 list.*

McDonald's	34.79%
Burger King	15.83
Taco Bell	9.60
Wendy's	9.59
Subway	5.95
Hardee's	4.60
Arby's	3.99
Dairy Queen	3.87
Other	11.78

Source: *Nation's Restaurant News*, June 28, 1999, p. 118.

★ 1571 ★
Coffee Houses (SIC 5813)

Top Coffee Chains in Canada - 1998

*Shares are shown based on estimated sales of $2.2
billion for the year ended December 31, 1998.*

TDL Group	58.8%
The Second Cup	12.6
Allied Domecq Retailing	6.2
Coffee Time Donut	5.4
Country Style Food Services	4.8
Starbucks Coffee	4.8
mmmmuffins Canada	2.4
Timothy's World Coffee	1.8
Other	3.2

Source: ''Report on Market Share.'' Retrieved June 8,
2000 from the World Wide Web: http://www.
marketingmag.ca, from *Foodservice and Hospitality Magazine*.

SIC 59 - Miscellaneous Retail

★ 1572 ★
Drug Stores (SIC 5912)

Beauty Sales in the New York City Area

Data show the share of beauty care sales in the New York Metropolitan area.

Duane Reade	27.8%
CVS	19.1
Rite Aid	17.1
Eckerd/Genovese	12.8
Other	23.2

Source: *WWD*, January 21, 2000, p. 10.

★ 1573 ★
Drug Stores (SIC 5912)

Drug Store Market in Boston, MA

CVS	51%
Other	49

Source: *Chain Drug Review*, June 7, 1999, p. 326.

★ 1574 ★
Drug Stores (SIC 5912)

Drug Store Market in Florida - 1998

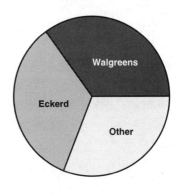

Market shares are shown in percent.

Walgreens	35%
Eckerd	34
Other	31

Source: *Chain Drug Review*, June 7, 1999, p. 335.

★ 1575 ★
Drug Stores (SIC 5912)

Drug Store Market in Grand Rapids/ Muskegon/ Holland, MI

This is the 73th largest drug store market in the country.

Walgreens	34%
Rite Aid Corp.	30
Other	36

Source: *Chain Drug Review*, November 8, 1999, p. 3.

★ **1576** ★
Drug Stores (SIC 5912)
Drug Store Market in Memphis, TN

Walgreen's	. . . . 49%
USA Drug	 16
Rite Aid	 14
Other	 21

Source: Retrieved January 13, 2000 from the World Wide Web: http://www.amcity.com/memphis/stories/1999/11/08/story3.html, from *Chain Drug Review*.

★ **1577** ★
Drug Stores (SIC 5912)
Drug Store Market in Nashville, TN

Walgreen's	. . . . 26%
CVS	 23
Other	 51

Source: Retrieved January 13, 2000 from the World Wide Web: http://www.amcity.com/memphis/stories/1999/11/08/story3.html.

★ **1578** ★
Drug Stores (SIC 5912)
Drug Store Market in Northern TX

Shares are estimated.

Eckerd	. . . . 30%
Albertson's	 14
Drug Emporium	 8
Walgreen	 8
Other	 40

Source: Retrieved January 13, 2000 from the World Wide Web: http://www.amcity.com/dallas/stories/1999/11/08/story1.html, from *Drug Store Market Guide*.

★ **1579** ★
Drug Stores (SIC 5912)
Drug Store Market in Tampa/St. Petersburg/ Clearwater, FL

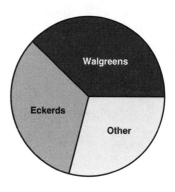

This is the 13th largest drug store market in the country.

Walgreens	. . . . 38%
Eckerds	 33
Other	 29

Source: *Chain Drug Review*, November 8, 1999, p. 3.

★ **1580** ★
Drug Stores (SIC 5912)
Top Drug Stores - 1998

Chains are ranked by sales in billions of dollars.

Walgreen	. . . . $ 15.3
CVS	. . . . 15.2
Rite Aid	. . . . 12.7
Eckerd	. . . . 10.3
American Stores	. . . . 6.3
Longs	. . . . 3.2
General Nutrition	. . . . 1.4
Medicine Shoppe	. . . . 1.3
Phar-Mor	. . . . 1.1

Source: *Stores*, July 1999, p. S12.

★ 1581 ★
Retailing - Drugs (SIC 5912)

How the Elderly Pay for Drugs

An estimated 68.8% of senior citizens have coverage.

No coverage 31.2%
Employer-sponsored 30.7
Individually purchased 10.5
Medicaid 10.5
Medicare HMO 8.2
Switched during year 7.3
Other 1.6

Source: *American Medical News*, April 10, 2000, p. 8, from Congressional Research Service.

★ 1582 ★
Retailing - Drugs (SIC 5912)

OTC Medication Sales - 1998

OTC stands for over-the-counter. Data are in billions of dollars.

Traditional chains . . . . $ 9.4
Mass merchandiser 9.2
Food stores 8.9
Independents 1.3

Source: Retrieved January 1, 2000 from the World Wide Web: http://www.nacds.org/industry/table4.html.

★ 1583 ★
Retailing - Drugs (SIC 5912)

Retail Pharmacy Sales - 1999

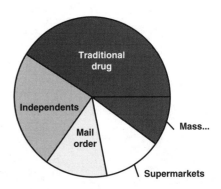

Total sales are expected to reach $121.6 billion.

Traditional drug 41.0%
Independents 24.4
Mail order 12.6
Supermarkets 11.7
Mass merchandisers 10.2

Source: Retrieved January 1, 2000 from the World Wide Web: http://www.nacds.org/news/releases, from National Association of Chain Drug Stores.

★ 1584 ★
Retailing - Drugs (SIC 5912)

Retail Prescription Drug Market - 1998

Traditional chains 40.3%
Independents 25.7
Mail order 12.8
Supermarkets 11.1
Mass merchandisers 10.1

Source: Retrieved January 1, 2000 from the World Wide Web: http://www.nacds.org/industry/table1.html, from IMS Health and NACDS.

★ 1585 ★
Retailing - Exercise Equipment (SIC 5941)
Canada's Exercise Equipment Sales

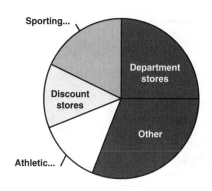

Sales are shown in percent.

Department stores	25.1%
Sporting goods stores	17.6
Discount stores	13.4
Athletic specialty stores	13.4
Other	30.5

Source: Retrieved January 21, 2000 from the World Wide Web: http://strategis.ic.gc.ca/SSG, from Industry Canada.

★ 1586 ★
Retailing - Sporting Goods (SIC 5941)
Canada's Ice Skates Sales - 1998

Sales are shown by outlet.

Sporting goods stores	59.0%
Discount stores	9.0
Athletic specialty stores	5.4
Department stores	4.2
Shoe stores	1.3
Other	21.1

Source: Retrieved January 21, 2000 from the World Wide Web: http://strategis.ic.gc.ca/SSG, from Industry Canada.

★ 1587 ★
Retailing - Sporting Goods (SIC 5941)
Canada's Sporting Goods Sales - 1998

Data show estimated sales in thousands of dollars.

Sporting goods stores	31.6%
Athletic specialty stores	14.6
Footwear specialty stores	11.3
Department stores	10.9
Discount stores	9.9
Other	32.8

Source: Retrieved January 21, 2000 from the World Wide Web: http://strategis.ic.gc.ca/SSG, from Industry Canada.

★ 1588 ★
Retailing - Sporting Goods (SIC 5941)
Largest Sporting Good Chains - 1998

The top 10 chains had 12.7% of the $45.8 billion market. Figures are in millions of dollars.

The Sports Authority	$ 1,600
Champs (Venator)	718
Gart Sports/Sportmart	658
Dick's	580
Academy	499
Big 5	491
Jumbo Sports	362
Modell's	360
Oshman's	309
Galyan's	220

Source: *New York Times*, November 28, 1999, p. 4, from National Sporting Goods Association.

★ 1589 ★
Retailing - Sporting Goods (SIC 5941)
Sporting Goods Sales in Canada - 1999

The market reached an estimated $5.3 billion for July 1998 - June 1999.

Canadian Tire	7.8%
Sears	7.0
Sports Experts	6.2
Zellers	4.4
Sport Chek	4.0
Wal-Mart	3.9

Continued on next page.

★ 1589 ★ *Continued*
Retailing - Sporting Goods (SIC 5941)

Sporting Goods Sales in Canada - 1999

The market reached an estimated $5.3 billion for July 1998 - June 1999.

The Bay	2.7%
Other	64.0

Source: ''Industry Status Report.'' Retrieved May 16, 2000 from the World Wide Web: http://www.csga.ca/industry/report.html.

★ 1590 ★
Retailing - Books (SIC 5942)

Adult Book Sales - 1998

Bookstores, large chain	25%
Book clubs	18
Bookstores, small chain/indep.	17
Mass merchandisers	6
Wholesale/price club	6
Mail order	5
Food/drug stores	4
Discount stores	3
Used bookstores	3
Internet	2
Multimedia	1
Other	10

Source: *USA TODAY*, December 8, 1999, p. D1, from NPD Group, American Booksellers Association, and Book Industry Study Group.

★ 1591 ★
Retailing - Books (SIC 5942)

Book Sales by Outlet

Total sales reached $26 billion.

Chain bookstores	26.3%
Independents	22.1
Book clubs	17.6
Discount stores	8.3
Warehouse clubs	6.1
Food/drug stores	3.8
Other	15.8

Source: *Investor's Business Daily*, September 1, 1999, p. A10, from company reports, Granite Financial Group, and First Call.

★ 1592 ★
Retailing - Books (SIC 5942)

Online Book Sales - 1999

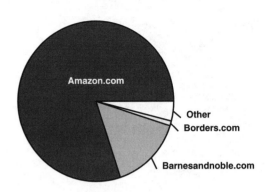

The $1.6 billion online market is shown in percent.

Amazon.com	80%
Barnesandnoble.com	15
Borders.com	1
Other	4

Source: *Business Week*, April 3, 2000, p. 75, from Gomez Advisors.

★ 1593 ★
Retailing - Books (SIC 5942)

Top Book Stores - 1999

Sales are shown in millions of dollars. The top 4 firms have 50% of retail sales.

Barnes & Noble	$ 3,006.0
Borders Group	2,590.4
Books-A-Million	347.9
Crown Books	216.8

Source: *Publishers Weekly*, March 27, 2000, p. 13.

★ 1594 ★
Retailing - General Merchandise (SIC 5943)

Retail Marker Sales

Sales are shown for the year ended September 4, 1999.

Mass	57.8%
Drug stores	25.4
Food stores	16.8

Source: *Grocery Headquarters*, December 1999, p. 44, from A.C. Nielsen.

★ 1595 ★
Retailing - Office Products (SIC 5943)

Personal Planners and Binder Sales

Sales are shown for the year ended September 4, 1999.

Mass	70.9%
Drug stores	21.0
Food stores	9.0

Source: *Grocery Headquarters*, December 1999, p. 44, from A.C. Nielsen.

★ 1596 ★
Retailing - Writing Instruments (SIC 5943)

Retail Writing Instrument Sales - 1998

The $733 million market is shown in percent.

Mass	54.6%
Drug	28.2
Food	17.1

Source: *Discount Store News*, February 22, 1999, p. 41, from A.C. Nielsen.

★ 1597 ★
Retailing - Hobby Stores (SIC 5945)

Artist/Hobby Supply Stores Sales

Sales are shown for the year ended September 4, 1999.

Mass	72.2%
Drug stores	17.6
Food	10.2

Source: *Grocery Headquarters*, December 1999, p. 44, from A.C. Nielsen.

★ 1598 ★
Retailing - Toys (SIC 5945)

Building Set Sales - 1998

Total sales reached 50.4 million units, worth $605.9 million.

Discount stores	59%
National toy chains	22
Dept. stores	2
Variety	2
Other	15

Source: *Playthings*, August 1999, p. 32.

★ 1599 ★
Retailing - Toys (SIC 5945)

Scientific Toy Sales - 1998

Total sales reached 11.5 million units, worth $134.3 million.

Discount stores	29%
National toy chains	16
All other toy stores	13
Variety	7
Dept stores	5
Other	30

Source: *Playthings*, August 1999, p. 32.

★ 1600 ★
Retailing - Toys (SIC 5945)

Top Toy Retailers - 1998

Shares are shown in percent.

Wal-Mart	17.4%
Toys R Us	16.8
Kmart	8.0
Target	6.9
KB Toys/Toy Works	4.9
J.C. Penney	1.6
Ames	1.3
Meijer	1.2
Hills	1.1
Sears	1.1
Other	39.7

Source: "Industry Statistics." Retrieved November 1, 1999 from the World Wide Web: http://www.toy-tma.org/STATISTICS/is-table3.html, from Toy Market Index.

★ 1601 ★
Retailing - Toys (SIC 5945)

Top Toy Retailers - 1999

Data show estimated market shares.

Wal-mart	17.4%
Toys R Us	15.6
Kmart	7.2
Target	6.8
KB Toys/Toy Works	5.1
Ames	1.6
J.C. Penney	1.2
Hallmark	1.1

Continued on next page.

★ 1601 ★ *Continued*
Retailing - Toys (SIC 5945)

Top Toy Retailers - 1999

Data show estimated market shares.

Meijer	1.0%
Other	43.0

Source: "Industry Statistics." Retrieved May 2, 2000 from the World Wide Web: http://www.toy-tma.com, from NPD Toy Market Index Service.

★ 1602 ★

Retailing - Photography Supplies (SIC 5946)

Amateur Photo Market - 1998

Photo processing	42.0%
Film sales	19.4
Conventional cameras	10.7
Digital imaging products/services	8.2
Portrait studio	4.6
Photo accessories	4.0
Frames	3.1
Albums	2.6
Other	5.2

Source: *Supermarket Business*, January 15, 2000, p. 95, from Photo Marketing Association International.

★ 1603 ★

Retailing - Photography Supplies (SIC 5946)

Single-Use Camera Sales - 1999

Distribution is based on total sales of $720.9 million for the year ended December 5, 1999.

Drug stores	38.0%
Discounters	36.3
Supermarkets	25.7

Source: *MMR*, February 7, 2000, p. 18, from Information Resources Inc.

★ 1604 ★

Retailing - Photography Supplies (SIC 5946)

Where Cameras Are Purchased

Discount stores	50.5%
Camera stores	12.9
Mail order	5.8
Drug stores	4.9
Catalog showrooms	4.6
Other	21.3

Source: *Discount Merchandiser*, January 2000, p. 3, from Photo Marketing Association International.

★ 1605 ★

Mail Order (SIC 5961)

Nutrition Mail Order Sales - 1998

$40 million in dietary supplements were sold online in 1998. Total consumer supplements sales reached $13.6 billion.

Printed catalog and direct mail	88%
TV and radio ads	8
Internet	4

Source: "1998 Internet Sales of Supplements Hits $40M." Retrieved October 5, 1999 from the World Wide Web: http://www.nbj.net/news7.htm, from *Nutrition Business Journal*.

★ 1606 ★

Mail Order (SIC 5961)

Top Areas for Catalog Shopping

Data show the markets with the most households that shop by mail.

Juneau, Alaska	81%
Fairbanks, Alaska	71
Charlottesville, VA	65
Anchorage, Alaska	65
Presque Isle, Maine	64
Burlington, VT-Plattsburgh, NY	64
Marquette, Michigan	62

Source: *USA TODAY*, March 8, 2000, p. B1, from Polk.

★ 1607 ★
Mail Order (SIC 5961)

Top Catalogers

Firms are ranked by sales in millions of dollars.

Dell Computer Corp.	$ 18.2
International Business Machines Corp.	5.5
J.C. Penney Co.	3.9
Office Depot	2.6
Micro Warehouse	2.2
Henry Schein	1.9
CDW Computer Centers	1.7
Fingerhut Cos.	1.6
Global Directmail	1.4
Spiegel	1.3

Source: Retrieved May 12, 2000 from the World Wide Web: http://www.catalogagemag.com.

★ 1608 ★
Vending Machines (SIC 5962)

Best-Selling Vended Drinks

Dollar shares are shown for the year ended April 18, 1999.

Coke Classic 12-oz	13.47%
Pepsi Cola 12-oz.	11.88
Mountain Dew 12-oz	6.77
Dr. Pepper Original 12-oz.	6.68
Diet Coke 12-oz.	6.65
Coke Classic 20-oz	5.75
Diet Pepsi 12-oz.	4.62
Sprite Original 12-oz.	3.33
Other	40.85

Source: *Automatic Merchandiser*, July 1999, p. 12.

★ 1609 ★
Vending Machines (SIC 5962)

Best-Selling Vended Snacks/Candies

Dollar shares are shown for the year ended April 18, 1999.

Snicker's Original 2-oz.	4.99%
M&M Peanut 1.74-oz.	3.80
Reese's Peanut Butter Cups 1.6-oz.	2.53
Twix Bar 2-oz.	1.80
Original Fritos 1.25 oz.	1.79
Lay's Regular Potato Chips 1-oz.	1.69
M&M Plain 1.69-oz.	1.61

Hershey Almond Bar 1.45 oz.	1.59%
Other	80.20

Source: *Automatic Merchandiser*, July 1999, p. 12.

★ 1610 ★
Vending Machines (SIC 5962)

Vended Hot Drink Sales - 1998

The $2.8 billion market is shown in percent.

Coffee	76.0%
Decaffinated coffee	11.5
Hot chocolate	10.0
Tea	1.5
Soup	1.0
Novelty flavored beverages	0.5

Source: *Vending Times Census of the Industry Issue*, 1999, p. 10.

★ 1611 ★
Vending Machines (SIC 5962)

Vending Machine Market - 1998

The $34.8 billion market is shown in percent.

Cold drinks (can)	41.6%
Packaged confections/snacks	18.7
Hot drinks	8.1
All-purpose vender food	7.1
Cold drinks (cup)	6.2
Cold drinks (bottled)	5.7
Cigarettes/cigars	3.6

Source: *Vending Times Census of the Industry Issue*, 1999, p. 10.

★ 1612 ★
Retailing - Propane (SIC 5983)

Largest Propane Retailers - 1999

Marketers are ranked by fiscal year sales in millons of gallons.

Ferrellgas Partners	960.0%
AmeriGas Partners	783.2
Cenex Propane Partners	627.1
Surburban Propane Partners	524.2
Columbia Propane Corp.	242.5
Cornerstone Propane Partners	235.6
Heritage Propane Partners	190.0

Continued on next page.

★ 1612 ★ *Continued*

Retailing - Propane (SIC 5983)

Largest Propane Retailers - 1999

Marketers are ranked by fiscal year sales in millons of gallons.

Level Propane Gases Inc.	105.0%
Star Gas Propane	99.4

Source: *LP/GAS*, January 2000, p. 22.

★ 1613 ★

Retailing - Flowers (SIC 5992)

Flower Industry - 1999

The estimated $15 billion market is shown by segment.

	No.	Share
Retail florist shops	27,341	38.07%
Supermarkets with floral depts.	23,000	32.03
Retail nurseries, lawn & garden supply stores	10,857	15.12
Growers	9,666	13.46
Wholesalers	950	1.32

Source: "Facts & Figures." Retrieved February 11, 2000 from the World Wide Web: http://www.aboutflowers.com/industrysnapshot.com.

★ 1614 ★

Retailing - Flowers (SIC 5992)

Popular Valentine's Day Sales

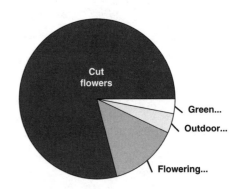

The entire floral industry is valued at $15 billion. Of the cut flowers purchased, 47% are roses.

Cut flowers	79%
Flowering houseplants	14
Outdoor plants	4
Green plants	3

Source: *Washington Post*, February 12, 2000, p. E1.

★ 1615 ★

Retailing - Tobacco (SIC 5993)

Smokeshops by State

The number of smokeshops fell from 6,745 in 1997 to 5,204 in 1998. After several years of rapid growth industry analysts saw the year as one of correction for the specialty tobacco industry.

	No.	Share
California	599	11.51%
New York	514	9.88
Florida	371	7.13
Pennsylvania	295	5.67
Texas	272	5.23
New Jersey	250	4.80
Other	2,903	55.78

Source: "Change of Pace." Retrieved June 1, 2000 from the World Wide Web: http://www.gosmokeshop.com/0899/report.htm.

★ 1616 ★
Retailing - Tobacco (SIC 5993)

Where People Purchase Tobacco

Retail store	93%
Mail order	5
Website	1
Other	1

Source: Retrieved February 11, 2000 from the World Wide Web: http://www.gosmokeshop.com.

★ 1617 ★
Optical Goods Stores (SIC 5995)

Largest Optical Goods Retailers - 1997

Companies are ranked by domestic sales in millions of dollars.

Cole Vision	$ 997.0
LensCrafters	955.0
Eye Care Centers of America	240.4
Wal-Mart Corp.	235.6
National Vision Associates Ltd.	182.3
Consolidated Vision Group Inc.	180.0
Sterling Vision	160.0
U.S. Vision	125.0
Costco Wholesale	105.0
D.O.C. Optics	98.0

Source: *20 20 Magazine*, April 1999, p. 1.

★ 1618 ★
Optical Goods Stores (SIC 5995)

Retail Optical Sales

Spectacle lenses/lens treatments	50.0%
Frames	33.3
Contact lenses	12.0
Piano sunglasses/clips	4.8

Source: *20 20 Magazine*, February 2000, p. 1.

★ 1619 ★
Optical Goods Stores (SIC 5995)

Retail Sunglasses Sales - 1998

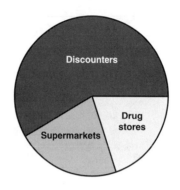

The $517 million market is shown in percent.

Discounters	59.0%
Supermarkets	21.5
Drug stores	19.5

Source: *MMR*, September 20, 1999, p. 86, from *Today's Optical*.

★ 1620 ★
Retailing - Baby Food (SIC 5999)

Baby Food Sales

Supermarkets	91.3%
Mass merchandisers	7.0
Drug Stores	1.7

Source: *Progressive Grocer*, July 1999, p. AD, from Information Resources Inc.

★ 1621 ★
Retailing - Batteries (SIC 5999)

Battery Sales by Outlet - 1999

Brands are ranked by unit sales of 579.1 million for the year ended November 7, 1999.

Discounters	48.4%
Supermarkets	26.4
Drug stores	25.2

Source: *MMR*, January 24, 2000, p. 18, from Information Resources Inc.

★ 1622 ★
Retailing - Batteries (SIC 5999)
Retail Battery Sales - 1998

Sales are shown in percent.

Mass	41%
Food stores	19
Drug stores	18
Warehouse clubs	9
Hardware/home centers	8
Other	5

Source: ''All Charged Up About Batteries.'' Retrieved January 26, 2000 from the World Wide Web: http://www.exposemagazine.com, from A.C. Nielsen, Vista, and NPE Group.

★ 1623 ★
Retailing - Cleaners (SIC 5999)
Floor/Wall Cleaner Sales - 1999

Distribution is based on total sales of $398.1 million for the year ended February 21, 1999.

Supermarkets	62.4%
Discounters	33.8
Drug stores	3.8

Source: *MMR*, May 17, 1999, p. 66, from Information Resources Inc.

★ 1624 ★
Retailing - Cleaners (SIC 5999)
Furniture Polish Sales - 1998

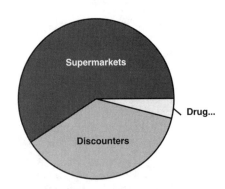

Distribution is based on total sales of $207.7 million for the year ended February 21, 1999.

Supermarkets	58.5%
Discounters	37.1
Drug stores	4.4

Source: *MMR*, May 17, 1999, p. 66, from Information Resources Inc.

★ 1625 ★
Retailing - Cleaners (SIC 5999)
Rug/Upholstery Cleaner Sales - 1998

Distribution is based on sales of $543.6 million for the year ended January 31, 1999.

Supermarkets	49.1%
Discounters	44.8
Drug stores	6.1

Source: *MMR*, May 17, 1999, p. 66, from Information Resources Inc.

★ 1626 ★
Retailing - Cosmetics (SIC 5999)
Nail Polish Sales

The market is shown for the year ended September 4, 1999.

Drug stores	47.2%
Mass	40.3
Food stores	12.6

Source: *Grocery Headquarters*, December 1999, p. 39, from A.C. Nielsen.

★ 1627 ★
Retailing - Cosmetics (SIC 5999)

Where Canadians Shop for Cosmetics - 1999

Data show the top specialty stores in Canada, based on a survey.

Arbors Drug Mart/Pharmaprix	39%
Jean Coutu Pharmacy	12
The Body Shop	11
London Drugs	8
Pharma Plus Drugmart	5

Source: *Marketing Magazine*, March 18, 2000, p. 15, from *J.C. Williams Group National Retail Report*.

★ 1628 ★
Retailing - Cosmetics (SIC 5999)

Where Internet Users Buy Cosmetics - 1999

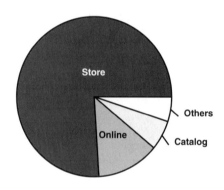

Store	76%
Online	13
Catalog	6
Others	5

Source: *Investor's Business Daily*, November 19, 1999, p. A6, from NPD Group Inc.

★ 1629 ★
Retailing - Drugs (SIC 5999)

Retail Antacid Sales

The $1.07 billion market is shown for the year ended March 28, 1999.

Discounters	34.0%
Drug stores	33.4
Food stores	32.6

Source: *Chain Drug Review*, August 16, 1999, p. 67, from Information Resources Inc.

★ 1630 ★
Retailing - First Aid Needs (SIC 5999)

Adhesive Bandage Sales

The market is shown for the year ended September 4, 1999.

Food stores	37.6%
Drug stores	34.6
Mass	27.8

Source: *Grocery Headquarters*, December 1999, p. 39, from A.C. Nielsen.

★ 1631 ★
Retailing - First Aid Needs (SIC 5999)

Retail Bandage Brands - 1999

Sales are shown in percent for the year ended March 28, 1999.

Drug stores	44.2%
Supermarkets	30.5
Discounters	25.3

Source: "Trends in First Aid." Retrieved January 26, 2000 from the World Wide Web: http://www.exposemagazine. com, from Information Resources Inc.

★ 1632 ★

Retailing - First Aid Needs (SIC 5999)

Retail First Aid Sales - 1999

Shares are shown based on unit sales for the year ended January 30, 2000.

	($ mil.)	Share
Drug stores	$ 172.4	44.84%
Food	109.2	28.40
Mass	102.9	26.76

Source: *Supermarket Business*, April 15, 2000, p. 132, from Information Resources Inc.

★ 1633 ★

Retailing - Food (SIC 5999)

Meal Replacement Bar Sales

The $206 million market is shown in percent.

Food stores	67%
Drug stores	20
Mass retailer	13

Source: *Discount Store News*, February 7, 2000, p. 53, from A.C. Nielsen.

★ 1634 ★

Retailing - Food (SIC 5999)

Retail Cookie Sales - 1999

Sales are shown for the year ended January 30, 2000.

	($ mil.)	Share
Supermarkets	$ 3,658.2	81.38%
Mass	712.4	15.85
Drug stores	124.8	2.78

Source: *Baking Business*, April 2000, p. 1, from Information Resources Inc.

★ 1635 ★

Retailing - General Merchandise (SIC 5999)

Cleaning Tool/Mop/Broom Sales

The $220 million market is shown for the year ended January 3, 1999.

Mass	56.7%
Food	35.2
Drug	8.1

Source: *Supermarket News*, May 17, 1999, p. 80, from Information Resources Inc.

★ 1636 ★

Retailing - General Merchandise (SIC 5999)

Fabric Softener Sales - 1998

Distribution is based on sales of $1.27 billion for the year ended February 21, 1999.

Supermarkets	56.9%
Discounters	39.8
Drug stores	3.3

Source: *MMR*, May 17, 1999, p. 66, from Information Resources Inc.

★ 1637 ★

Retailing - General Merchandise (SIC 5999)

Light Bulb Sales - 1999

Distribution is shown based on sales of $1.04 billion for the year ended January 31, 1999.

Discount stores	48.5%
Supermarkets	41.9
Drug stores	9.6

Source: *MMR*, May 17, 2000, p. 66, from Information Resources Inc.

★ 1638 ★

Retailing - General Merchandise (SIC 5999)

Prerecorded Video Sales

Sales are shown for the year ended September 4, 1999.

Mass	80.5%
Food stores	12.3
Drug stores	7.2

Source: *Grocery Headquarters*, December 1999, p. 44, from A.C. Nielsen.

★ 1639 ★

Retailing - General Merchandise (SIC 5999)

Retail Film Sales

Sales are shown for the year ended September 4, 1999.

Mass	42.1%
Drug stores	35.5
Food stores	22.3

Source: *Grocery Headquarters*, December 1999, p. 44, from A.C. Nielsen.

★ 1640 ★

Retailing - General Merchandise (SIC 5999)

Retail Scissor Sales

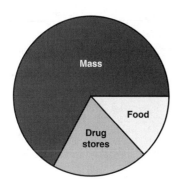

Sales are shown for the year ended September 4, 1999.

Mass 67.1%
Drug stores 20.2
Food 12.7

Source: *Grocery Headquarters*, December 1999, p. 44, from A.C. Nielsen.

★ 1641 ★

Retailing - General Merchandise (SIC 5999)

Storage/Space Management Product Sales

Sales are shown for the year ended September 4, 1999.

Mass 87.7%
Drug stores 6.8
Food stores 5.5

Source: *Grocery Headquarters*, December 1999, p. 44, from A.C. Nielsen.

★ 1642 ★

Retailing - General Merchandise (SIC 5999)

Water Purifier/Filter Sales

Sales are shown for the year ended September 4, 1999.

Mass 63.6%
Food stores 20.8
Drug 15.6

Source: *Grocery Headquarters*, December 1999, p. 44, from A.C. Nielsen.

★ 1643 ★

Retailing - Hair Care Products (SIC 5999)

Retail Hair Coloring Sales - 1999

Retail sales reached $1.31 billion.

Drug stores 42%
Mass merchants 38
Grocery 20

Source: *C&EN*, March 20, 2000, p. 16, from Information Resources Inc.

★ 1644 ★

Retailing - Hair Care Products (SIC 5999)

Retail Hair Spray Sales - 1999

Retail sales reached $590 million.

Mass merchant 45%
Grocery 32
Drug stores 23

Source: *C&EN*, March 20, 2000, p. 16, from Information Resources Inc.

★ 1645 ★

Retailing - Hair Care Products (SIC 5999)

Retail Shampoo Sales

The market is shown for the year ended September 4, 1999.

Food stores 39.8%
Mass 39.2
Drug stores 21.0

Source: *Grocery Headquarters*, December 1999, p. 39, from A.C. Nielsen.

★ 1646 ★

Retailing - Hair Care Products (SIC 5999)

Retail Shampoo Sales - 1999

Retail sales reached $1.74 billion.

Mass merchants 43%
Grocery 38
Drug stores 19

Source: *C&EN*, March 20, 2000, p. 16, from Information Resources Inc.

★ 1647 ★

Retailing - Homefurnishings (SIC 5999)

As Seen on TV Product Sales

The "as seen on TV" market has reached sales of $800 million in 1998. The category was once considered novelty items by many mass market retailers. Chains often experiment with occasional promotion and holiday displays.

Discount stores 78%
Drug stores 16
Supermarkets 5

Source: *MMR*, February 18, 2000, p. 30.

★ 1648 ★

Retailing - Insecticides (SIC 5999)

Pest Control Market - 1998

Distribution is based on sales of $183.9 million for the year ended January 31, 1999.

Discounters 45.2%
Supermarkets 42.8
Drug stores 1.2

Source: *MMR*, May 17, 1999, p. 66, from Information Resources Inc.

★ 1649 ★

Retailing - Natural Products (SIC 5999)

Natural Product Sales

Distribution is shown based on sales of $14 billion in food, supplements and personal care products.

Natural food stores/health food chains 63%
Mass merchandisers 37

Source: Retrieved January 1, 2000 from the World Wide Web: http://www.nbj.net/news5.htm.

★ 1650 ★

Retailing - Oral Care Products (SIC 5999)

Retail Toothbrush Sales

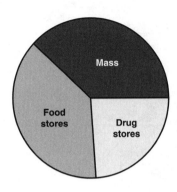

The market is shown for the year ended September 4, 1999.

Mass 38.0%
Food stores 37.6
Drug stores 24.4

Source: *Grocery Headquarters*, December 1999, p. 39, from A.C. Nielsen.

★ 1651 ★

Retailing - Oral Care Products (SIC 5999)

Retail Toothpaste Sales

The market is shown for the year ended September 4, 1999.

Food stores 46.3%
Mass 34.5
Drug stores 19.1

Source: *Grocery Headquarters*, December 1999, p. 39, from A.C. Nielsen.

★ 1652 ★

Retailing - Paper Products (SIC 5999)

Disposable Cup Sales

Distribution is shown based on sales of $424 million for the year ended January 21, 1999.

Supermarkets 70.4%
Discounters 25.0
Drug stores 4.6

Source: *MMR*, May 17, 1999, p. 36, from Information Resources Inc.

★ 1653 ★

Retailing - Paper Products (SIC 5999)

Paper Napkin Sales - 1998

Distribution is shown based on sales of $546 million for the year ended January 31, 1999.

Supermarkets	75.4%
Discounters	21.3
Drug stores	3.3

Source: *MMR*, May 17, 2000, p. 66, from Information Resources Inc.

★ 1654 ★

Retailing - Paper Products (SIC 5999)

Paper Towel Sales - 1998

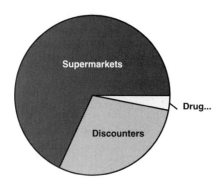

Distribution is shown based on sales of $2.45 billion for the year ended February 21, 1999.

Supermarkets	68.1%
Discounters	28.5
Drug stores	3.4

Source: *MMR*, May 17, 1999, p. 66, from Information Resources Inc.

★ 1655 ★

Retailing - Personal Care Products (SIC 5999)

Analgesic Chest Rub Sales

The market is shown for the year ended September 4, 1999.

Drug stores	49.8%
Food stores	26.9
Mass	23.3

Source: *Grocery Headquarters*, December 1999, p. 39, from A.C. Nielsen.

★ 1656 ★

Retailing - Personal Care Products (SIC 5999)

Cough Syrup/Tablet Sales

The market is shown for the year ended September 4, 1999.

Drug stores	48.6%
Food stores	34.6
Mass	16.8

Source: *Grocery Headquarters*, December 1999, p. 39, from A.C. Nielsen.

★ 1657 ★

Retailing - Personal Care Products (SIC 5999)

Denture Adhesive Sales - 1999

Shares are shown based on sales of $224.8 million for the year ended October 10, 1999.

Chain drug stores	33%
Discount stores	33
Food/drug	27
Supermarkets	5
Independent drug stores	2

Source: *Chain Drug Review*, January 3, 2000, p. 44, from Information Resources Inc. and Rachers Press.

★ 1658 ★

Retailing - Personal Care Products (SIC 5999)

Diabetes Test Kit Sales - 1999

Shares are shown based on sales of $588.1 million.

Chain drug stores	61%
Discount stores	23
Independent drug stores	8
Food/drug	5
Supermarkets	3

Source: *Chain Drug Review*, January 3, 2000, p. 43, from Rachers Press.

★ 1659 ★
Retailing - Personal Care Products (SIC 5999)

Disposable Razor Sales

The market is shown for the year ended September 4, 1999.

Food stores	39.2%
Mass	38.4
Drug stores	22.4

Source: *Grocery Headquarters*, December 1999, p. 39, from A.C. Nielsen.

★ 1660 ★
Retailing - Personal Care Products (SIC 5999)

Foot Care Medication Sales

Sales are shown in percent. The market for foot care products, including devices and medications, is worth $615 million. Foot medication sales reached $282.5 million.

Drug stores	43.4%
Mass	32.2
Food retailers	24.4

Source: *Supermarket News*, July 26, 1999, p. 43, from Information Resources Inc.

★ 1661 ★
Retailing - Personal Care Products (SIC 5999)

Hand/Body Lotion Sales - 1999

Distribution is shown based on sales of $948.7 million for the year ended October 10, 1999.

Chain drug stores	36%
Discount stores	35
Food/drug combination stores	24
Supermarkets	3
Independent drug stores	1

Source: *Chain Drug Review*, January 17, 2000, p. 26, from Information Resources Inc. and Rachers Press.

★ 1662 ★
Retailing - Personal Care Products (SIC 5999)

Headache Remedy Sales

The market is shown for the year ended September 4, 1999.

Food stores	37.4%
Drug stores	34.0
Mass	28.6

Source: *Grocery Headquarters*, December 1999, p. 39, from A.C. Nielsen.

★ 1663 ★
Retailing - Personal Care Products (SIC 5999)

Liquid Cold/Allergy Relief Sales - 1999

Shares are shown based on sales of $828.3 million for the year ended October 10, 1999.

Chain drug stores	36%
Food/drug	29
Discount stores	24
Supermarkets	10
Independent drug stores	1

Source: *Chain Drug Review*, January 3, 2000, p. 38, from Rachers Press.

★ 1664 ★
Retailing - Personal Care Products (SIC 5999)

Liquid Soap Sales

Discounters 47.9%
Supermarkets 36.6
Drug stores 15.5

Source: "A Modern Soap Story." Retrieved February 29, 2000 from the World Wide Web: http://www.exposemagazine.com, from Information Resources Inc.

★ 1665 ★
Retailing - Personal Care Products (SIC 5999)

Liquid Soap Sales - 1999

Shares are shown based on sales of $840.3 million for the year ended October 10, 1999.

Discount stores 39%
Food/drug 34
Chain drug stores 14
Supermarkets 12
Independent drug stores 1

Source: *Chain Drug Review*, January 17, 2000, p. 22, from Rachers Press and Information Resources Inc.

★ 1666 ★
Retailing - Personal Care Products (SIC 5999)

Retail Antacid Sales

The market is shown for the year ended September 4, 1999.

Food stores 35.7%
Drug stores 33.0
Mass 31.4

Source: *Grocery Headquarters*, December 1999, p. 39, from A.C. Nielsen.

★ 1667 ★
Retailing - Personal Care Products (SIC 5999)

Retail Cough Drop Sales

The $519.5 million market is shown in percent.

Chain drug stores 42%
Food/drug combo 21
Discount 18
Supermarkets 13
Independent drug stores 6

Source: *Chain Drug Review*, January 4, 1999, p. 39, from Information Resources Inc.

★ 1668 ★
Retailing - Personal Care Products (SIC 5999)

Retail Dedorant Sales

The market is shown for the year ended September 4, 1999.

Food stores 39.8%
Mass 39.0
Drug stores 21.3

Source: *Grocery Headquarters*, December 1999, p. 39, from A.C. Nielsen.

★ 1669 ★
Retailing - Personal Care Products (SIC 5999)

Retail Eye Care Product Sales

Sales are for the year ended January 31, 1999.

Discounters 39.0%
Drug stores 35.6
Food stores 25.4

Source: *Chain Drug Review*, April 12, 1999, p. 20, from Information Resources Inc.

★ 1670 ★
Retailing - Personal Care Products (SIC 5999)

Retail Laxative Sales

The market is shown for the year ended September 4, 1999.

Drug stores 47.2%
Mass 27.8
Food stores 25.0

Source: *Grocery Headquarters*, December 1999, p. 39, from A.C. Nielsen.

★ 1671 ★

Retailing - Personal Care Products (SIC 5999)

Retail Razor Blade Sales

The total razor market - permanent and disposable razor and blades - reached $1.51 billion for the year ended November 7, 1999.

Mass 40.8%
Supermarkets 33.7
Drug stores 25.5

Source: *Supermarket News*, December 13, 1999, p. 41, from Information Resources Inc.

★ 1672 ★

Retailing - Personal Care Products (SIC 5999)

Retail Urinary Continence Product Sales

The $541.2 million market is shown for the year ended March 28, 1999.

	($ mil.)	Share
Drug stores	$ 251.8	46.53%
Mass	170.1	31.43
Supermarkets	119.3	22.04

Source: *Supermarket News*, May 31, 1999, p. 31, from Information Resources Inc.

★ 1673 ★

Retailing - Personal Care Products (SIC 5999)

Sanitary Napkin Sales

The market is shown for the year ended September 4, 1999.

Food stores 42.4%
Mass 34.7
Drug stores 22.9

Source: *Grocery Headquarters*, December 1999, p. 39, from A.C. Nielsen.

★ 1674 ★

Retailing - Personal Care Products (SIC 5999)

Shower Gel Sales - 1999

Distribution is based on total sales of $510.9 million for the year ended November 21, 1999.

Discounters 50.4%
Supermarkets 31.1
Drug stores 18.5

Source: *MMR*, February 7, 2000, p. 22, from Information Resources Inc.

★ 1675 ★

Retailing - Personal Care Products (SIC 5999)

Sinus Remedy Sales

The market is shown for the year ended September 4, 1999.

Drug stores 36.3%
Food stores 35.7
Mass 28.0

Source: *Grocery Headquarters*, December 1999, p. 39, from A.C. Nielsen.

★ 1676 ★

Retailing - Personal Care Products (SIC 5999)

Tampon Sales by Outlet - 1998

Food stores 42.7%
Discount stores 33.1
Drug stores 24.2

Source: *Chain Drug Review*, February 1, 1999, p. 53.

★ 1677 ★
Retailing - Pet Food (SIC 5999)
Cat Food Sales - 1998

Distribution is based on sales of $1.21 billion for the year ended January 21, 1999.

Supermarkets	82.8%
Discounters	15.8
Drug stores	1.4

Source: *MMR*, May 17, 1999, p. 36, from Information Resources Inc.

★ 1678 ★
Retailing - Pet Food (SIC 5999)
Dry Dog Food Sales - 1998

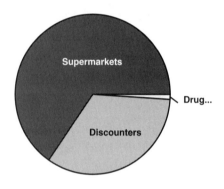

Distribution is shown based on total sales of $2.43 billion for the year ended January 1, 1999.

Supermarkets	65.8%
Discounters	33.6
Drug stores	0.6

Source: *MMR*, May 17, 1999, p. 61, from Information Resources Inc.

★ 1679 ★
Retailing - Pet Food (SIC 5999)
Pet Food Sales in Canada - 1997

Grocery stores	50.9%
Pet stores	32.8
Mass merchandisers	6.5
Warehouse clubs	3.9
Other	5.9

Source: Retrieved January 18, 2000 from the World Wide Web: http://www.bizlink.com, from A.C. Nielsen and *Food in Canada*.

★ 1680 ★
Retailing - Vitamins (SIC 5999)
Vitamin Sales by Outlet - 1999

Distribution is based on sales of $802.7 million for the year ended March 28, 1999.

Drug stores	39.1%
Discounters	31.8
Supermarkets	29.1

Source: *MMR*, May 17, 2000, p. 62, from Information Resources Inc.

SIC 60 - Depository Institutions

★ 1681 ★
Banking (SIC 6020)

Banking Market in Hamilton County, Ohio

Market shares are shown in percent.

Fifth Third Bank 28.6%
First Southwestern Bank 28.4
Other 43.0

Source: "Provident Regains Top Spot." Retrieved January 13, 2000 from the World Wide Web: http://www.amcity.com/cincinnati/stories.

★ 1682 ★
Banking (SIC 6020)

Banking Market Shares in Mexico

Banamex 39%
Bancomer 25
Banamex 20
Serfin 13
Santander 5

Source: "Banamex-Bancomer Merger Would Result in 39% Share." Retrieved May 5, 2000 from the World Wide Web: http://library.northernlight.com, from InfoLatina S.A. de C.V.

★ 1683 ★
Banking (SIC 6020)

Financial Guarantee Market

MBIA 29.3%
AMBAC 26.8
FSA 22.2
FGIC 21.7

Source: *Business Insurance*, January 31, 2000, p. 1, from Fitch IBCA.

★ 1684 ★
Banking (SIC 6020)

Internet Banking Market

Market shares are shown in percent.

Wells Fargo 14.14%
Bank of America 9.55
Citigroup 4.82
Bank One 4.01
First Union 2.96
BankBoston 2.53
Washington Mutual 2.29
Other 59.70

Source: *Wall Street Journal*, January 21, 2000, p. C1, from Gomez Advisors Inc.

★ 1685 ★
Banking (SIC 6020)

Largest Online Banks

Data show thousands of customers.

Wells Fargo 1,500
Bank of America 1,250
First Union 900
Citibank 750
Chase Manhattan 575
Bank One 500

Source: *US Banker*, October 1999, p. 26.

★ 1686 ★
Banking (SIC 6020)

Top Banking Companies

Firms are ranked by net income in millions of dollars.

Citicorp.	$ 2,162
NationsBank Corp.	1,905
The Chase Manhattan Corp.	1,799
BankAmerica Corp.	1,725
Banc One Corp.	1,036

Source: *Banking Strategies*, September/October 1999, p. 16.

★ 1687 ★
Banking (SIC 6020)

Top Banks in Boston, MA

Market shares are shown in percent.

Fleet Financial	37.45%
State Street	12.94
Citizens Financial	4.72
UST	4.29
Mellon Bank	3.61
Other	36.99

Source: *Financial Times*, June 22, 1999, p. 29, from SNL Securities.

★ 1688 ★
Banking (SIC 6020)

Top Banks in Canada

Assets are shown as of July 31, 1999.

Royal Bank of Canada	$ 189.29
Canadian Imperial Bank of Commerce	177.77
Bank of Nova Scotia	154.42
Bank of Montreal	152.94
Toronto Dominion Bank	151.09

Source: *Wall Street Journal*, October 28, 1999, p. C16.

★ 1689 ★
Banking (SIC 6020)

Top Banks in Canada - 1999

Shares are shown based on $924.4 million for the year ended October 31, 1999.

Royal Bank of Canada	20.3%
CIBC	17.3
Bank of Montreal	17.2
Scotiabank	16.9
Toronto Dominion Bank	15.2
National Bank of Canada	5.4
Laurentian Bank of Canada	1.1
Other	6.7

Source: "Report on Market Share." Retrieved June 8, 2000 from the World Wide Web: http://www.marketingmag.ca, from Canadian Bankers Association.

★ 1690 ★
Banking (SIC 6020)

Top Banks in Maryland - 1999

Shares are shown based on deposits.

Bank of America	16.28%
Allfirst Bank (Baltimore)	11.73
Crestar Bank	8.62
Chevy Chase	7.10
First Union	6.89
Other	49.38

Source: *Baltimore Business Journal*, February 7, 2000, p. 1.

★ 1691 ★
Banking (SIC 6020)

Top Banks in Massachusetts

Market shares are shown in percent.

Fleet Financial	35.75%
State Street	10.60
Citizens Financial	3.89
UST	3.51
Mellon Bank	2.95
Other	53.30

Source: *Financial Times*, June 22, 1999, p. 29, from SNL Securities.

★ 1692 ★

Banking (SIC 6020)

Top Banks in Mexico - 1998

Assets are shown in billions of dollars as of December 31, 1998.

Bancomer	$ 25.6
Banamex	25.5
Serfin	16.7
Bital	10.4
Santander Mexicano	7.8
Banorte	7.5
Bilbao Viscaya	7.0

Source: *MB*, July/August 1998, p. 36, from National Banking and Securities Commission.

★ 1693 ★

Banking (SIC 6020)

Top Banks in New England

Market shares are shown based on $243.1 billion in deposits.

FleetBoston	26.2%
Citizens Financial Group	7.7
State Street	5.3
Soverign Bancorp.	4.9
Peoples Heritage Financial	4.5
Other	51.4

Source: *Wall Street Journal*, April 10, 2000, p. B4, from SNL Securities.

★ 1694 ★

Banking (SIC 6020)

Top Banks in New York

Market shares are shown based on $421.6 billion in deposits.

Chase Manhattan	23.0%
Citigroup	10.5
HSBC Holdings	8.3
Bank of New York	5.4
FleetBoston	4.2
Other	48.6

Source: *Wall Street Journal*, April 10, 2000, p. B4, from SNL Securities.

★ 1695 ★

Banking (SIC 6020)

Top Banks in New York City

Market shares are shown based on $250.3 billion in deposits.

Chase Manhatttan	31.0%
Citigroup	14.5
HSBC Holdings	7.1
Deutsche Bank	6.7
Bank of New York	5.9
Other	34.8

Source: *Wall Street Journal*, April 10, 2000, p. B4, from SNL Securities.

★ 1696 ★

Banking (SIC 6020)

Top Banks in Rhode Island

Market shares are shown in percent.

Fleeet Financial	59.03%
Citizens Financial	27.08
Washington Trust Bancorp.	3.22
Bank of Rhode Island	2.66
Bank of Newport	2.20
Other	5.81

Source: *Financial Times*, June 22, 1999, p. 29, from SNL Securities.

★ 1697 ★

Banking (SIC 6022)

Leading States by Bank Assets

Assets are shown in billions of dollars.

New York	$ 1,179
North Carolina	599
California	492
Illinois	281
Ohio	254

Source: *US Banker*, June 1999, p. 12, from Sheshunoff Information Services.

★ 1698 ★

Banking (SIC 6029)

Leading Community Banks in the Northeast

Banks are ranked by asset size in billions of dollars.

State Bank of Long Island	$ 803.8
Bank of Newport	618.0
Wilber National Bank (NY)	570.3
Bar Harbor Banking & Trust	425.3
Commercial NB/West Co. (PA)	328.7
FNB of St. Mary's	305.9
Swineford National Bank (PA)	259.0

Source: *ABA Banking Journal*, September 1999, p. 18.

★ 1699 ★

Banking (SIC 6029)

Leading Midwest Community Banks

Banks are ranked by asset size in billions of dollars.

Empire Bank (MO)	$ 526.7
Security National Bank (IA)	485.4
Iowa State B&T Co.	366.8
First National Bank (IA)	326.0
Bank of Blue Valley (KA)	277.2
Goodhue County National (MN)	274.0

Source: *ABA Banking Journal*, September 1999, p. 18.

★ 1700 ★

Banking (SIC 6081)

Foreign Banks in the United States - 1999

Data show total assets in billions of dollars as of September 1999.

Japan	$ 213.6
Germany	209.2
France	163.6
Canada	125.0
United Kingdom	88.5
Netherlands	88.3
Switzerland	56.1
Italy	26.3

Source: *The Banker*, March 2000, p. 67, from Federal Reserve Bank.

★ 1701 ★

Money Transfers (SIC 6099)

Money Transfer Market

Western Union	81%
Other	19

Source: *Forbes*, May 29, 2000, p. 62.

SIC 61 - Nondepository Institutions

★ 1702 ★
Credit Cards (SIC 6141)

Credit Card Market - 1999

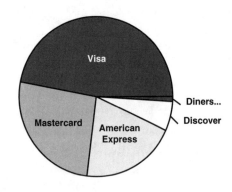

Shares are for midyear.

Visa 47.0%
Mastercard 25.6
American Express 20.2
Discover 6.0
Diners Club 1.3

Source: *Newsweek*, October 4, 1999, p. 55, from Nilson Report.

★ 1703 ★
Credit Cards (SIC 6141)

Online Credit Card Market - 1998

Reports suggest that one out of every six credit cards will have been obtained online, with Net-sourced credit lines nearing $22 billion. Data show who controlled the market for four million online applications last year.

NextCard/First USA 50%
Other 50

Source: *Cards International*, April 15, 1999, p. 12.

★ 1704 ★
Credit Cards (SIC 6141)

Who Controls E-Commerce Transactions

First USA 25%
American Express 16
Discover Card 10
Other 49

Source: *Card Fax*, September 20, 1999, p. 1.

★ 1705 ★
Business Credit (SIC 6150)

Home Equity Line of Credit Market

The market segment is based on 700 homeowners.

Rejectors 65%
Ex-holders 19
Prospects 9
Active holders 3
Inactive holders 3
Unclassified 1

Source: *US Banker*, November 1999, p. 18, from Synergistics.

★ 1706 ★
Mortgage Loans (SIC 6162)

Largest Residential Originators - 1999

Market shares are shown for the first six months of the year.

Chase Manhattan Mortgage 7.92%
Norwest Mortgage Inc. 7.12
Countrywide Credit Industries Inc. 6.59
Bank of America Mortgage 5.32
Washington Mutual Bank 3.00
Other 70.05

Source: *US Banker*, October 1999, p. 74, from Database Products Group.

★ 1707 ★

Mortgage Loans (SIC 6162)

Largest Residential Servicers - 1999

Market shares are shown for the first six months of the year.

Bank of America Mortgage	6.02%
Norwest Mortgage Inc.	5.90
Chase Manhattan Mortgage	5.21
Countrywide Credit Industries Inc.	5.06
HomeSide Lending Inc.	3.13
Other	74.68

Source: *US Banker*, October 1999, p. 76, from Database Products Group.

★ 1708 ★

Mortgage Loans (SIC 6162)

Low/Moderate Income Loan Providers - 1997

Market shares are shown in percent.

Green Tree Financial	4.41%
Norwest Mortgage	2.90
Countrywide Home Loans	2.65
The Money Store	2.16
Bank of America	2.07
Chase Manhattan Mortgage	1.41
North American Mortgage Co.	1.26
Other	83.14

Source: *Builder Online*, July 1999, p. 152, from PCI Services.

★ 1709 ★

Mortgage Loans (SIC 6162)

Mortgage Market in Louisiana

Hibernia National Bank

Countrywide Home Loans Inc.

Bank One

Northwest Mortgage Inc.

Real Estate Financing Inc.

Standard Federal Bank

North American Mortgage Company

Other

Shares are shown based on loan volume.

Hibernia National Bank	14.3%
Countrywide Home Loans Inc.	5.3
Bank One	3.6
Northwest Mortgage Inc.	2.9
Real Estate Financing Inc.	2.9
Standard Federal Bank	2.5
North American Mortgage Company	2.5
Other	66.0

Source: "Hibernia Leads Louisiana in Mortgage Market." Retrieved December 13, 1999 from the World Wide Web: http://library.northernlight.com, from *MMS Market Share Report*.

★ 1710 ★

Loan Arrangers (SIC 6163)

Commercial Loan Market in Mexico

Bancomer	30%
Banamex	20
Other	50

Source: *Mexico Monthly Business*, April 1999, p. 5.

★ 1711 ★

Loan Arrangers (SIC 6163)

Largest Construction/Land Development Banks

Sales are shown in billions of dollars.

Bank of America (NC)	$ 14.8
US Bank (Minneapolis)	5.2
Wells Fargo & Co. (San Francisco)	5.0
First Union Bank (NC)	4.1
KeyBank (Cleveland)	3.9
Southtrust Bank (Alabama)	3.9

Source: *US Banker*, November 1999, p. 74, from Sheshunoff Information Services.

★ 1712 ★

Loan Arrangers (SIC 6163)

Top Subprime Loan Underwriters - 1999

Lehman Brothers	18.0%
Bear, Stearns	12.6
Greenwich Capital Markets	12.1
Bank of America Securities	11.9
Merrill Lynch	10.8
Prudential Securities	9.8
Residential Funding	5.6
Salomon Smith Barney	3.8
Other	15.4

Source: *New York Times*, March 15, 2000, p. C13, from *Inside MBS and ABS*.

SIC 62 - Security and Commodity Brokers

★ 1713 ★

Annuities (SIC 6211)

Equity-Indexed Annnuity Market

Provider shares are shown in percent.

Fidelity & Guaranty Life Insurance	21.64%
Conseco Inc.	15.92
Jackson National Life Insurance Co.	11.43
American Equity Investment Life Insurance Co.	9.09
Other	41.92

Source: *Best's Review*, August 1999, p. 22, from The Advantage Group.

★ 1714 ★

Annuities (SIC 6211)

Largest Variable Annuity Contracts - 1999

Contracts are ranked in billions of dollars through the third quarter of the year.

TIAA-CREF Retirement Annuity	$ 6.51
Hartford Director	5.22
VALIC Portfolio Director	4.24
SunAmerica Polaris/Polaris II	2.52
Prudential Discovery Select	2.44
Equitable Accumulator	2.41
Hartford Putnam Capital Manager	2.27

Source: *Advisor Today*, January 2000, p. 20, from *VARDS Report*.

★ 1715 ★

Brokerages (SIC 6211)

Largest Trading Firms

Firms are ranked by number of branches.

Bright Trading	30
All-Tech Investment	24
Cornerstone Securities	21
On-Line Investment	15
Momentum Securities	9

Source: *USA TODAY*, August 3, 1999, p. 3B.

★ 1716 ★

Investment Banking (SIC 6211)

401(K) Asset Holders - 1998

Data show estimated market shares.

Mutual fund companies	42%
Insurance companies	22
Banks	20
Other managers	14

Source: *Best's Review*, January 2000, p. 13, from Spectrem Group.

★ 1717 ★

Investment Banking (SIC 6211)

Largest Managers of Enhanced Domestic Indexed Equity

Firms are ranked by millions of dollars.

TIAA-CREF	$ 81
Barclays Global Investors	21
Dimensional Fund Advisors	15
PIMCO	14
UBS Brinson	5
TradeStreet	4
Prudential Insurance	4
American Express	4

Source: *Pensions & Investments*, May 17, 1999, p. 50.

★ 1718 ★

Mutual Funds (SIC 6211)

Mutual Fund Market in Canada - 2000

Shares are shown based on $413.5 million for the year ended March 31, 2000.

Investors Group	10.4%
Royal Mutual Funds	8.3
Mackenzie Financial	8.0
Fidelity Investments Canada	7.7
TD Asset Management	7.1
Trimark Investment Management	6.0
CI Mutual Funds	5.6
CIBC Securities	5.5
Other	41.4

Source: "Report on Market Share." Retrieved June 8, 2000 from the World Wide Web: http://www. marketingmag.ca, from Canadian Bankers Association.

★ 1719 ★

Mutual Funds (SIC 6211)

Who Sells Mutual Funds - 1998

Data are estimated.

Brokerages	61%
Financial planners	22
Banks	9
Insurance companies	8

Source: *New York Times*, January 23, 2000, p. 13, from Cerulli Associates and Limra International.

★ 1720 ★

Underwriting (SIC 6211)

Leading Debt and Equity Underwriters - 1999

Market shares are shown in percent.

Merrill Lynch	15.9%
Salomon Smith Barney	12.6
Morgan Stanley Dean Witter	10.3
Goldman, Sachs	9.4
Credit Suisse First Boston	8.4
Lehman Brothers	7.8
Chase Manhattan	5.8
Other	39.8

Source: *New York Times*, January 3, 2000, p. C18, from Thomson Financial and Securities Data.

★ 1721 ★

Underwriting (SIC 6211)

Leading IPO Underwriters - 1999

Market shares are shown in percent. IPO stands for initial public offering.

Goldman, Sachs	21.2%
Morgan Stanley Dean Witter	20.2
Merrill Lynch	11.3
Credit Suisse First Boston	8.6
Donaldson, Lufkin & Jenrette	5.6
Lehman Brothers	4.2
J.P. Morgan	4.0
Other	24.9

Source: *New York Times*, January 3, 2000, p. C18, from Thomson Financial and Securities Data.

★ 1722 ★

Underwriting (SIC 6211)

Stock and Bond Underwriting - 2000

Shares are for the first quarter.

Merrill Lynch	14.3%
Salomon Smith Barney	12.4
Morgan Stanley Dean Wittter	11.1
Goldman Sachs	9.7
Credit Suisse First Boston	9.5
Other	43.0

Source: *Financial Times*, April 3, 2000, p. 20, from Thompson Financial and Securities Data.

★ 1723 ★
Underwriting (SIC 6211)

Top Bank Underwriters - 1999

Shares are for the first six months of the year, full credit given to book manager.

Salomon Smith Barney	17.9%
Chase Manhattan Corp.	16.5
Banc of America Securities	8.9
Credit Suisse First Boston	5.9
Other	50.8

Source: *US Banker*, August 1999, p. 55, from Thomson Financial Securities Data.

★ 1724 ★
Venture Capital (SIC 6211)

Largest Venture Capital Firms - 1999

Companies are ranked by assets under management in billions of dollars.

Chase Capital Partners	$ 10.0
Warburg Pincus Ventures	7.0
Patricof & Company Ventures	5.5
Sandler Capital Management	2.0
Sprout Group	1.7
Invesco Private Capital	1.3
21st Century Communications	1.0
Venrock Associates	0.9

Source: *New York Times*, February 7, 2000, p. C1, from Venture One.

★ 1725 ★
Venture Capital (SIC 6211)

Largest Venture Capital Industries in New York - 1998

Investments are in millions of dollars.

Software and information	$ 249.8
Communications	174.9
Business services	77.9
Health care	66.2
Industrial	37.3
Biotechnology	29.6
Pharmaceuticals	27.1

Source: *Crain's New York Business*, July 5, 1999, p. 36, from Pricewaterhousecoopers.

★ 1726 ★
Venture Capital (SIC 6211)

Venture Capital Investment in New England - 1999

Data are for the second quarter.

Communications	34.2%
Software/information	29.6
Consumer	10.4
Business services	5.5
Medical instruments/devices	4.4
Other	15.9

Source: *The Boston Globe*, August 15, 1999, p. G1, from PriceWaterhouse.

★ 1727 ★
Annuities (SIC 6231)

Who Sells Individual Annuities - 1998

Data are estimated.

Insurance agents	46%
Brokerages	27
Banks	14
Internet/phone/mail	9
Others	4

Source: *New York Times*, January 23, 2000, p. 13, from Cerulli Associates and Limra International.

★ 1728 ★
Brokerages (SIC 6231)

Online Brokerage Accounts

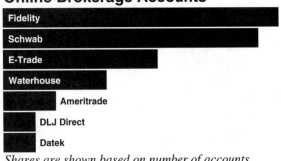

Shares are shown based on number of accounts.

	No.	Share
Fidelity	3,466	26.7%
Schwab	3,300	25.4
E-Trade	1,881	14.5
Waterhouse	1,300	10.0
Ameritrade	686	5.3
DLJ Direct	347	2.7
Datek	340	2.6

Source: *Investor's Business Daily*, February 18, 2000, p. B1, from U.S. Bancorp Piper Jaffray.

★ 1729 ★
Brokerages (SIC 6231)

Online Brokerage Market Shares - 1998

Shares are shown based on trades per day for the fourth quarter of the year.

Schwab	28%
Waterhouse	12
E*Trade	12
Fidelity	10
Datek	10
Ameritrade	8
Other	20

Source: *AAII Journal*, May 1999, p. 28, from Piper Jaffray.

★ 1730 ★
Brokerages (SIC 6231)

Online Brokerage Market Shares - 1999

Shares are shown based on average daily trades for the third quarter.

Charles Schwab	18.4%
E*Trade	14.7
Waterhouse	12.4
Datek	11.3
Fidelity	9.9
Ameritrade	9.5
Brown & Co.	4.3
DLJ Direct	3.6
Other	15.9

Source: *Financial Times*, November 23, 1999, p. 21, from company reports and Hambrecht & Quist.

★ 1731 ★
Brokerages (SIC 6231)

Online Brokerages - 1999

Shares are shown based on average daily trades for the first quarter of the year.

Schwab	27.9%
E*Trade	13.3
Waterhouse	11.7
Datek	10.1
Fidelity	10.1
Ameritrade	8.3
Other	18.6

Source: *New York Times*, June 2, 1999, p. C26, from U.S. Bancorp Piper Jaffray.

★ 1732 ★
Securities Exchanges (SIC 6231)
ECNs and Nasdaqs

Data show electronic communication networks percent of Nasdaq share volume. Data are as of June 1999.

Instinet	13.38%
Island	4.35
REDIBook	0.80
Tradebook	0.69
Archipelago	0.61
Others	80.00
Others	0.21

Source: *Fortune*, November 22, 1999, p. 256, from Salomon Smith Barney.

★ 1733 ★
Securities Exchanges (SIC 6231)
Largest ECNs - 1999

Electronic communication networks are ranked by share of trade volume.

Instinet	48.8%
Island	19.5
TradeBook	11.4
Archipelago	8.1
RediBook	5.9
Brut	3.6
Strike	2.0

Source: *Risk*, November 1999, p. 9.

★ 1734 ★
Securities Exchanges (SIC 6231)
Online Stock Distribution - 1999

The top online distributors of stock to Web investors, based on value of deals led or comanaged. Shares exceed 100% because credit is given to co-managers on the same deals.

WIT Capital	39.8%
DLJdirect	32.0
E*Offering	16.5
Charles Schwab	7.8
W.R. Hambrecht	3.9
Fidelity Capital Markets	3.9

Source: *Wall Street Journal*, January 26, 2000, p. C1, from CommScan.

★ 1735 ★
Securities Exchanges (SIC 6231)
Where NYSE Stocks Trade - 1999

Data show trading volume in NYSE-listed shares at each market, in trillions.

NYSE	204.06
NASD	20.80
Chicago	10.47
Pacific	4.16
Boston	4.02
Cincinnati	2.26
Philadelphia	1.64

Source: *Wall Street Journal*, April 7, 2000, p. C1, from NYSE.

SIC 63 - Insurance Carriers

★ 1736 ★
Insurance (SIC 6300)

Durable Wholesale Goods Insurance Market

Data show estimated premiums in millions of dollars. Total premiums represent 4.3% of total commercial premiums written.

	($ mil.)	Share
Northeast	$ 1,368.6	25.26%
West	1,172.0	21.63
Southeast	1,071.8	19.78
Midwest	1,018.4	18.79
Southwest	788.3	14.55

Source: *Rough Notes*, August 1999, p. 78, from IMR Corp.

★ 1737 ★
Insurance (SIC 6300)

Food Processor Insurance Market

West
Midwest
Southwest
Northeast
Southeast

Data show estimated premiums in millions of dollars. Total premiums represent 1.3% of total commercial premiums written. There are 19,936 food processors in the United States, employing about 1.53 million people.

	($ mil.)	Share
West	$ 390.7	23.62%
Midwest	326.6	19.75
Southwest	322.1	19.48
Northeast	316.7	19.15
Southeast	297.8	18.01

Source: *Rough Notes*, August 1999, p. 78, from IMR Corp.

★ 1738 ★
Insurance (SIC 6300)

Largest Accident and Health Reinsurers - 1998

Shares are shown based on reinsurance assumed from non-affiliates. Data are for North America.

Swiss Re Life Amer/Life Re	15.0%
Lincoln Re	13.5
Cologne Life Re	11.8
Sun Life Assur.	8.5
Transamer. Occid.	6.3
RGA Reinsurance	6.3
Reassur of Hannover	5.6
Other	33.0

Source: *Best's Review*, September 1999, p. 25, from A.M. Best & Co.

★ 1739 ★
Insurance (SIC 6300)

Largest Business Insurance Agencies in Michigan

Companies are ranked by revenues in millions of dollars.

Meadowbrook Insurance Group Inc.	$ 60.2
Marsh USA Inc.	38.5
Aon Risk Services Inc. of Michigan	27.0
Willis Corroon Corp. of Michigan	23.5
Kelter-Thorner Inc.	17.3

Source: *Crain's Detroit Business*, September 27, 1999, p. 16.

★ 1740 ★

Insurance (SIC 6300)

Largest Case Management Service Providers

Firms are ranked by revenues in millions of dollars.

Intracorp	$ 304.0
Concentra Managed Care Inc.	146.0
CorVel Corp.	109.0
Crawford & Co.	72.5
Genex Services Inc.	70.0
CORE Inc.	47.2
National Healthcare Resources Inc.	29.0

Source: *Business Insurance*, January 24, 2000, p. 19.

★ 1741 ★

Insurance (SIC 6300)

Largest Reinsurers - 1999

Firms are ranked by net premiums written for the first six months of the year. Total premiums reached $10.323 billion.

Employers Re	$ 1,680.6
American Re	1,394.9
General Re	1,233.1
Berkshire Hathaway	685.0
Transatlantic Re/Putnam Re	583.4
Everest Re	521.3
Zurich Reins.	482.6
Swiss Re America	457.2
Hartford Re Co.	392.1

Source: *Business Insurance*, September 6, 1999, p. 6, from Reinsurance Association of America.

★ 1742 ★

Life Insurance (SIC 6311)

Leading Life Reinsurers - 1998

Shares are shown based on reinsurance assumed amount in force.

Swiss Re Group	14.9%
RGA Reinsurance	11.3
Transamer Occid	9.6
Lincoln National	9.3
Employers Re Group	7.8
Secur Life Denver	7.1
Other	40.0

Source: *Best's Review*, August 1999, p. 49, from A.M. Best & Co.

★ 1743 ★

Life Insurance (SIC 6311)

Variable Life Distribution

Distribution is shown based on single premium products.

Stockbrokers/wirehouses	44%
Independent brokers/dealers	32
Career/controlled agents	16
Stockbrokers/regional firms	5
Banks/credit unions	2
Direct	1

Source: *National Underwriter*, March 13, 2000, p. 1, from Tillinghast-Towers Perrin.

★ 1744 ★

Life Insurance (SIC 6311)

Variable Life Market - 1999

Shares are shown based on year-end assets.

	1997	1999
The Prudential	24.33%	10.60%
John Hancock	10.24	9.85
Pacific Life	7.03	8.44
AEGON	6.94	10.37
Provident	5.46	5.22
Nationwide	3.36	4.71
Other	42.64	60.81

Source: *Advisor Today*, April 2000, p. 26, from VARDS Report.

★ 1745 ★

Life Insurance (SIC 6311)

Who Sells Life Insurance - 1998

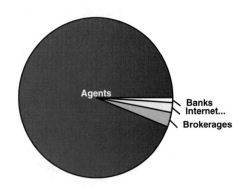

Data are estimated.

Agents	94%
Brokerages	3
Internet, phone and mail	2
Banks	1

Source: *New York Times*, January 23, 2000, p. 13, from Cerulli Associates and Limra International.

★ 1746 ★

Auto Insurance (SIC 6321)

Auto Insurance Market in California

Market shares are shown in percent.

State Farm Group	13.8%
Farmers Ins Group	13.0
Other	73.2

Source: *Best's Review*, October 1999, p. 44, from A.M. Best & Co.

★ 1747 ★

Auto Insurance (SIC 6321)

Auto Insurance Market in Canada - 1999

Shares are shown based on $10.4 billion for the year ended December 31, 1999.

ING Canada	10.1%
CGU Group Canada	8.4
Royal & Sunalliance Canada	6.6
Co-operators General	5.8
State Farm Insurance	5.5
Economical Insurance Group	4.8

AXA Canada	4.4%
Wawanesa Mutual Insurance	3.7
Other	50.7

Source: "Report on Market Share." Retrieved June 8, 2000 from the World Wide Web: http://www. marketingmag.ca, from *Canadian Insurance*.

★ 1748 ★

Auto Insurance (SIC 6321)

Auto Insurance Market in Massachusetts

Market shares are shown in percent.

Commerce Group Inc.	20.2%
Arbella Ins. Group	13.1
Other	66.7

Source: *Best's Review*, October 1999, p. 44, from A.M. Best & Co.

★ 1749 ★

Auto Insurance (SIC 6321)

Auto Insurance Market in North Carolina

Market shares are shown in percent. Figures are for the private passenger market.

Nationwide Group	18.7%
State Farm Group	14.7
Other	66.6

Source: *Best's Review*, October 1999, p. 44, from A.M. Best & Co.

★ 1750 ★

Auto Insurance (SIC 6321)

Auto Insurance Market in Pennsylvania

Market shares are shown in percent.

State Farm Group	17.5%
Erie Ins Group	13.3
Other	69.2

Source: *Best's Review*, October 1999, p. 44, from A.M. Best & Co.

★ 1751 ★
Auto Insurance (SIC 6321)

Auto Insurance Market in Tennessee

Market shares are shown in percent. Figures are for the auto liability market.

State Farm Group	20.1%
Tennessee Frmrs Cos.	13.4
Other	66.5

Source: *Best's Review*, October 1999, p. 44, from A.M. Best & Co.

★ 1752 ★
Auto Insurance (SIC 6321)

Auto Insurance Market in Vermont

Market shares are shown in percent. Figures are for the commercial auto market.

W R Berkley Corp. Group	9.1%
GRE Ins Group	8.0
Other	82.9

Source: *Best's Review*, October 1999, p. 44, from A.M. Best & Co.

★ 1753 ★
Auto Insurance (SIC 6321)

Auto Insurance Market in Wisconsin

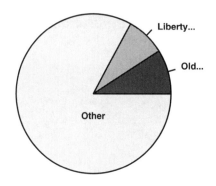

Liberty...

Old...

Other

Market shares are shown in percent. Figures are for the commercial auto market.

Old Republic General Group	8.6%
Liberty Mutual Ins Cos.	8.1
Other	83.3

Source: *Best's Review*, October 1999, p. 44, from A.M. Best & Co.

★ 1754 ★
Auto Insurance (SIC 6321)

Auto Liability Insurance Market

Market shares are shown in percent.

State Farm	16.7%
Allstate Ins Group	10.6
Farmers Ins. Group	5.1
Nationwide Group	4.1
Progressive Group	4.0
Berkshire Hathaway	3.1
Travelers PC Group	2.5
USAA Group	2.4
Other	51.5

Source: *Best's Review*, October 1999, p. 44, from A.M. Best & Co.

★ 1755 ★
Auto Insurance (SIC 6321)

Largest Auto Insurance Writers - 1998

Shares are shown based on total premiums of $18.3 billion.

CNA Ins Companies	5.4%
Travelers PC Group	4.6
Zurich US Group	4.3
Liberty Mutual Ins. Cos.	4.1
St. Paul Companies	3.9
State Farm Group	3.7
CGU Group	3.1
Old Republic Gen Group	2.7
Reliance Ins group	2.6
Amer Inter Group	2.6
Other	63.0

Source: *Best's Review*, July 1999, p. 33, from A.M. Best & Co.

★ 1756 ★
Auto Insurance (SIC 6321)

Largest Private Passenger Auto Insurance Writers - 1998

Shares are shown based on total premiums of $117.6 billion.

State Farm Group	19.7%
Allstate Ins Group	12.4
Farmers Ins. Group	5.9
Nationwide Group	4.3

Continued on next page.

★ 1756 ★ *Continued*

Auto Insurance (SIC 6321)

Largest Private Passenger Auto Insurance Writers - 1998

Shares are shown based on total premiums of $117.6 billion.

Progressive Group	4.2%
Berkshire Hathaway	3.5
USAA Group	3.0
Amer Family Ins Group	1.9
Travelers PC Group	1.9
Other	43.2

Source: *Best's Review*, July 1999, p. 33, from A.M. Best & Co.

★ 1757 ★

Auto Insurance (SIC 6321)

Leading Auto Insurance Writers - 1998

Shares are shown based on total premiums of $135.9 billion.

State Farm Group	17.6%
Allstate Ins Group	11.0
Farmers Ins Group	5.2
Nationwide Group	4.0
Progressive Group	3.9
Berkshire Hathaway	3.1
USAA Group	2.6
Travelers PC Group	2.3
Liberty Mut Ins Cos.	2.1
Other	48.2

Source: *Best's Review*, July 1999, p. 34.

★ 1758 ★

Health Insurance (SIC 6321)

Dread Disease Policy Writing

Companies are ranked by net premiums written in millions of dollars.

American Family Life Assur.	$ 4,392.0
Conseco Health Insurance Co.	266.1
Liberty National Life Ins. Co.	115.2
Allstate Life Ins. Co.	108.7
Conseco Senior Health Ins. Co.	74.1
Life Investors Ins. Co. of America	61.2

Source: *Best's Review*, July 1999, p. 84, from A.M. Best Co.

★ 1759 ★

Health Insurance (SIC 6321)

Federal Employee Health Insurance Market - 1998

Market shares are shown based on total directly written premiums of $668.8 million.

Antherm Group	70.8%
BC/BS SC Group	29.2

Source: *Best's Review*, July 1999, p. 32.

★ 1760 ★

Health Insurance (SIC 6321)

Largest Life/Health Insurance Firms - 1998

Firms are ranked by premium income in millions of dollars.

Metropolitan Life Ins co.	$ 22.7
Prudential Ins Co of America	15.5
Principal Life Insurance Co.	14.1
Lincoln National Life	13.4
Connecticut General Life	12.7
Nationwide Life Insurance Co.	12.5
Equitable Life	9.4
Anchor National	8.8

Source: *National Underwriter*, July 26, 1999, p. 23.

★ 1761 ★

Long-Term Care Insurance (SIC 6321)

Individual Long-Term Care Market - 1998

Shares are shown based on net premiums.

General Electric Capital Assurance	21.40%
American Travellers	13.83
American Family Life	11.26
Bankers Life & Casualty	9.70
Travelers Insurance	7.67
John Hancock Mutual Life	5.50
Other	30.64

Source: *Best's Review*, March 2000, p. 104, from A.M. Best & Co.

★ 1762 ★

Health Plans (SIC 6324)

Health Plan Enrollments - 1999

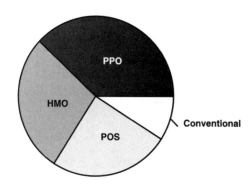

PPO	38%
HMO	28
POS	25
Conventional	9

Source: *H&HN*, November 1999, p. 66, from Kaiser/HRET Survey of Employer-Sponsored Health Benefits.

★ 1763 ★

Health Plans (SIC 6324)

Health Plans in Philadelphia - 1998

Aetna	52%
Independence Blue Cross	40
Cigna	3
Prudential	2
QualMed	2
Other	1

Source: *Best's Review*, July 1999, p. 72, from Pennsylvania Department of Health Bureau of Managed Care.

★ 1764 ★

Health Plans (SIC 6324)

HMO Enrollment by State

Data show share as a percent of insured population.

Massachusetts	51.6%
California	48.8
Delaware	48.8
Oregon	48.8
Maryland	44.0
Tennessee	38.0
Colorado	37.7
New York	37.6

Source: *Modern Physician*, March 2000, p. 50, from Inter-Study Publications.

★ 1765 ★

Health Plans (SIC 6324)

HMO Market in Massachusetts

Data are as of July 1, 1998.

Harvard Pilgrim	39.9%
Tufts Health Plan	21.5
HMO Blue	21.2
Others	17.4

Source: *Modern Physician*, February 2000, p. 64, from Interstudy.

★ 1766 ★
Health Plans (SIC 6324)

Largest Health Care Firms - 1999

Firms are ranked by revenues in billions of dollars.

Aetna	$ 26.4
Cigna	20.6
UnitedHealth Group	19.5
Columbia/HCA Healthcare	16.6
Tenet Healthcare	10.8

Source: *Fortune*, April 17, 2000, pp. I-69.

★ 1767 ★
Health Plans (SIC 6324)

Largest Health Plans in California - 1999

Data show membership, in millions.

Kaiser Foundation	6.0
Blue Cross of California	3.7
PacifiCare	2.3
Health Net	2.1
Blue Shield of California	2.0

Source: *Los Angeles Times*, March 3, 2000, p. C1, from Bloomberg News, California Department of Corporations, and company reports.

★ 1768 ★
Financial Insurance (SIC 6331)

Financial Guaranty Writers - 1998

Shares are shown based on total premiums of $1.1 billion.

MBIA Group	43.1%
Financial Sec Asr Group	23.2
Other	33.7

Source: *Best's Review*, July 1999, p. 32.

★ 1769 ★
Fire Insurance (SIC 6331)

Leading Fire Insurance Writers

Allianz of America	6.2%
Amer Intern Group	6.0
Travelers PC Group	4.2
Zurich US Group	4.0
Arkwright Ins Group	3.7

St. Paul Companies	3.5%
Protection Mut Ins	2.7
Nationwide Group	2.3
Other	32.6

Source: *Best's Review*, December 1999, p. 46, from A.M. Best & Co.

★ 1770 ★
Fire Insurance (SIC 6331)

Leading Fire Insurance Writers in California

Farmers Ins Group	11.3%
Allianz of America	8.5
Other	80.2

Source: *Best's Review*, December 1999, p. 45, from A.M. Best & Co.

★ 1771 ★
Homeowners Insurance (SIC 6331)

Homeowners Insurance Market in North Carolina

Total directly written premiums reached $770.6 million in 1998.

State Farm	18.81%
Nationwide Group	18.17
North Carolina Farm Bureau	12.02
Allstate Insurane	10.32
Travelers PC Group	4.30
Other	36.38

Source: *Best's Review*, November 1999, p. 32, from A.M. Best & Co.

★ 1772 ★
Homeowners Insurance (SIC 6331)

Homeowners Market in Alaska

Market shares are shown in percent.

State Farm Group	40.4%
Allstate Ins Group	28.5
Other	31.1

Source: *Best's Review*, August 1999, p. 77.

★ 1773 ★

Homeowners Insurance (SIC 6331)

Homeowners Market in Delaware

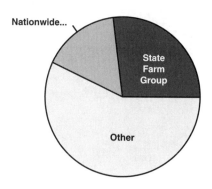

Market shares are shown in percent.

State Farm Group	26.8%
Nationwide Group	16.4
Other	56.8

Source: *Best's Review*, August 1999, p. 77, from A.M. Best & Co.

★ 1774 ★

Homeowners Insurance (SIC 6331)

Homeowners Market in Iowa

Market shares are shown in percent.

State Farm Group	23.4%
Nationwide Group	14.6
Other	62.0

Source: *Best's Review*, August 1999, p. 77, from A.M. Best & Co.

★ 1775 ★

Product Insurance (SIC 6331)

Aircraft Insurance Writers - 1999

Shares are shown based on total premiums of $1.1 billion.

Amer Intern Group	15.8%
HCC Ins Holdings Group	12.0
Other	72.2

Source: *Best's Review*, July 1999, p. 32, from A.M. Best & Co.

★ 1776 ★

Product Insurance (SIC 6331)

Boiler and Machinery Insurance Writers - 1998

Market shares are shown based on total premiums of $675.3 million.

Hartford Steam Group	21.9%
Chubb Group of Ins Cos.	10.4
Other	67.7

Source: *Best's Review*, July 1999, p. 32.

★ 1777 ★

Product Insurance (SIC 6331)

Product Liability Market in Hawaii

Market shares are shown in percent.

CNA Ins Companies	37.2%
TIG Holdings	17.0
Other	45.8

Source: *Best's Review*, August 1999, p. 79, from A.M. Best & Co.

★ 1778 ★

Product Insurance (SIC 6331)

Product Liability Market in Kansas

Market shares are shown in percent.

Travel Air Ins Co.	36.2%
St. Paul Companies	9.1
Other	54.7

Source: *Best's Review*, August 1999, p. 79, from A.M. Best & Co.

★ 1779 ★

Product Insurance (SIC 6331)

Product Liability Market in Michigan

Market shares are shown in percent.

Chrysler Ins Co.	48.4%
Dorinco Reins Co.	26.2
Other	25.4

Source: *Best's Review*, August 1999, p. 79, from A.M. Best & Co.

★ 1780 ★
Product Insurance (SIC 6331)

Product Liability Market in Rhode Island

Market shares are shown in percent.

Allianz of America	32.7%
Chubb Group of Ins Cos.	14.7
Other	52.6

Source: *Best's Review*, August 1999, p. 79, from A.M. Best & Co.

★ 1781 ★
Property Insurance (SIC 6331)

Directors-and Officers Liability Market

Shares are shown based on premium volume.

AIG	29%
Chubb Exec. Risk	23
Lloyd's of London	14
Aegis	7
CAN	4
Other	23

Source: *Best's Review*, April 2000, p. 107, from Tillinghast-Towers Perrin.

★ 1782 ★
Property Insurance (SIC 6331)

Homeowners Insurance Market - 1998

Market shares are shown in percent.

State Farm Group	22.7%
Allstate Ins. Group	11.5

Farmers Ins. Group	7.0%
Nationwide Group	4.2
Travelers PC Group	3.6
USAA Group	3.4
SAFECO Ins Cos.	2.3
Chubb Group of Ins Cos.	2.2
Amer Family Ins Group	1.9
Other	41.2

Source: *Best's Review*, September 1999, p. 60.

★ 1783 ★
Property Insurance (SIC 6331)

Property/Casualty Insurance Market in Canada - 1999

Shares are shown based on $20 billion for the year ended December 31, 1999.

ING Canada	9.4%
CGU Group Canada	8.2
Co-operators Group	7.0
Royal & Sunalliance Canada	6.5
AXA Canada	4.7
Economical Insurance Group	4.1
State Farm Insurance	3.7
Wawanesa Mutual Insurance	3.2
Liberty Mutual Group	3.1
Lloyd's Underwriters	2.6
Other	47.5

Source: "Report on Market Share." Retrieved June 8, 2000 from the World Wide Web: http://www.marketingmag.ca, from *Canadian Insurance*.

★ 1784 ★
Workers Comp Insurance (SIC 6331)

Leading Worker's Compensation Writers - 1998

Shares are shown based on total premiums of $28.8 billion.

Liberty Mut Ins Cos.	9.9%
CNA Ins Companies	6.1
Amer Intern Group	4.9
Travelers PC Group	4.6
Kemper Ins Cos.	4.5

Continued on next page.

★ 1784 ★ *Continued*

Workers Comp Insurance (SIC 6331)

Leading Worker's Compensation Writers - 1998

Shares are shown based on total premiums of $28.8 billion.

State Comp Fund Cal	4.2%
Hartford Ins Group	3.8
Fremont General Group	2.9
Other	59.1

Source: *Best's Review*, July 1999, p. 37.

★ 1785 ★

Disaster Insurance (SIC 6351)

Commercial Multiple Peril Market in California

Market shares are shown in percent.

Allianz of America	11.6%
Farmers Ins Group	9.7
Other	78.7

Source: *Best's Review*, August 1999, p. 76.

★ 1786 ★

Disaster Insurance (SIC 6351)

Commercial Multiple Peril Market in Louisiana

Market shares are shown in percent.

CNA Ins Companies	12.2%
Travelers PC Group	10.4
Other	77.4

Source: *Best's Review*, August 1999, p. 76.

★ 1787 ★

Disaster Insurance (SIC 6351)

Commercial Multiple Peril Market in Maine

Market shares are shown in percent.

CGU Group	26.2%
Allmerica P&C Cos.	16.1
Other	57.7

Source: *Best's Review*, August 1999, p. 76.

★ 1788 ★

Disaster Insurance (SIC 6351)

Earthquake Insurance Writers - 1998

Shares are shown based on total premiums of $738.1 million.

State Farm Group	20.3%
SAFECO Ins Cos.	5.7
Other	74.0

Source: *Best's Review*, July 1999, p. 32.

★ 1789 ★

Malpractice Insurance (SIC 6351)

Leading Medical Malpractice Writers - 1998

Shares are shown based on total premiums of $6 billion.

St. Paul Companies	6.1%
MLMIC Group	5.5
CNA Ins Companies	5.2
Doctors' Co. Ins Group	4.6
Health Care Indemn	4.6
GE Global Ins Group	4.0
Amer Intern Group	3.7
Medical Int-In Ex Group	3.5
MMI Companies Group	3.5
PHICO Group	3.5
Other	55.8

Source: *Best's Review*, July 1999, p. 37, from A.M. Best & Co.

★ 1790 ★

Malpractice Insurance (SIC 6351)

Medical Malpractice Market in Colorado

Market shares are shown in percent.

COPIC Group	46.9%
Doctors Co Ins Group	14.1
Other	39.0

Source: *Best's Review*, August 1999, p. 79, from A.M. Best & Co.

★ 1791 ★

Malpractice Insurance (SIC 6351)

Medical Malpractice Market in Iowa

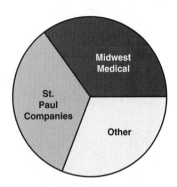

Market shares are shown in percent.

Midwest Medical	35.0%
St. Paul Companies	34.2
Other	30.8

Source: *Best's Review*, August 1999, p. 79, from A.M. Best & Co.

★ 1792 ★

Malpractice Insurance (SIC 6351)

Medical Malpractice Market in Massachusetts

Market shares are shown in percent.

ProMutual Group	69.8%
HUM Group	3.3
Other	26.9

Source: *Best's Review*, August 1999, p. 79, from A.M. Best & Co.

★ 1793 ★

Malpractice Insurance (SIC 6351)

Medical Malpractice Market in New Jersey

Market shares are shown in percent.

Medical Int-In Ex Gr	41.3%
Princeton Ins Cos.	34.7
Other	24.0

Source: *Best's Review*, August 1999, p. 79, from A.M. Best & Co.

★ 1794 ★

Malpractice Insurance (SIC 6351)

Medical Malpractice Market in South Carolina

Market shares are shown in percent.

MMI Companies Group	26.9%
St. Paul Companies	22.5
Other	50.6

Source: *Best's Review*, August 1999, p. 79, from A.M. Best & Co.

★ 1795 ★

Surety Insurance (SIC 6351)

Commerical Multiple Peril Writers - 1998

Shares are shown based on total premiums of $21.1 billion.

Travelers PC Group	7.0%
CNA Ins. Companies	6.7
Hartford Ins Group	4.7
State Farm Group	4.4
Allianz of America	4.3
CGU Group	4.2
Chubb Group of Ins Cos.	4.1
St. Paul Companies	3.7
Other	60.9

Source: *Best's Review*, July 1999, p. 36.

★ 1796 ★

Surety Insurance (SIC 6351)

Liability Insurance Writers - 1998

Shares are shown based on total premiums of $25.1 billion. Market refers to products not covered under usual liability markets.

Amer Intern Group	20.1%
Chubb Group of Ins Cos.	5.9
CAN Ins Companies	4.9
Zurich US Group	4.6
Reliance Ins Group	4.1
Travelers PC Group	3.5
St. Paul Companies	3.4
Allianz of America	2.9
Other	50.6

Source: *Best's Review*, July 1999, p. 36, from A.M. Best & Co.

SIC 64 - Insurance Agents, Brokers, and Service

★ 1797 ★

Insurance Brokers (SIC 6411)

Largest Insurance Brokers - 1998

Companies are ranked by revenues in millions of dollars.

Marsh & McLennan	$ 3,350
Aon Group Inc.	2,286
Willis Corroon Group	630
Arthur J. Gallagher & Co.	471
USI Insurance Services Corp.	327
Acordia Inc.	306
Hilb, Rogal & Hamilton Co.	172

Source: *Best's Review*, October 1999, p. 99, from Hales & Co.

SIC 65 - Real Estate

★ 1798 ★
Office Space (SIC 6512)

Largest Office Developers in Baltimore, MD Area

Market shares are shown in percent.

The Rouse Co. Inc.	5.0%
MIE Properties Inc.	3.5
Manekin LLC	3.2
Merritt Properties LLC	2.9
Dickinson-Heffner Inc.	2.1
Hill Management Services Inc.	1.7
Nottingham Properties Inc.	1.6
Trammell Crow Company	1.6
Other	64.0

Source: *Baltimore Business Journal*, March 2000, p. 19.

★ 1799 ★
Shopping Centers (SIC 6512)

Top Shopping Center Owners

Companies are ranked by millions of gross leasable area.

Simon Property Group	136.0
General Growth Properties	71.5
Westfield Holdings Ltd.	60.8
Kimco Realty Corp.	60.6
The Richard E. Jacobs Group Inc.	40.3
Developers Diversified Realty Corp.	40.3
New Plan Excel Realty Trust	37.3
The Macerich Co.	35.0
Benderson Development Co. Inc.	33.2

Source: *Shopping Center World*, August 1999, p. B2.

★ 1800 ★
Apartments (SIC 6513)

Largest Apartment Owners

Owners are ranked by number of units with ownership interest.

Almco	240,540
Equity Research	228,504
Related Capital	148,080
Lend Lease	113,744
Whitehall Street	105,000
Boston Capital	102,564

Source: *National Real Estate Investor*, March 2000, p. 2, from National Multi Housing Council.

★ 1801 ★
Real Estate (SIC 6531)

Condo and Co-Op Sales - 1999

Sales of existing condos and co-ops reached 677,000 units.

South	289,000
West	190,000
Northeast	117,000
Midwest	81,000

Source: *Realtor Magazine*, April 2000, p. 17, from National Association of Realtors Economic Research.

★ 1802 ★
Real Estate (SIC 6531)

Largest Real Estate Brokerages

Sales are shown in billions of dollars.

NRT Inc.	$ 84.1
Weichert Realtors	16.1
Long & Foster Real Estate Inc.	10.5
Windermere	8.5
Coldwell Banker Residential Brokerage	7.2
Prudential California Realty	7.1
Arvida Realty Services	5.9

Source: *Wall Street Journal*, August 6, 1999, p. B8, from National Relocation & Real Estate.

★ 1803 ★
Real Estate (SIC 6531)

Largest Real Estate Brokerages in New York City, NY - 1999

Sales are shown in millions of dollars.

Douglas Elliman	$ 2,200.3
Corcoran Group	2,000.0
Brown Harris Stevens	1,320.0
Halstead Property	1,048.0
Bellmarc Realty	882.0

Source: *Crain's New York Business*, March 6, 2000, p. 30.

★ 1804 ★
Real Estate (SIC 6531)

Largest Real Estate Firms - 1999

Firms are ranked by revenues in billions of dollars.

Equity Office Properties	$ 1.9
Simon Property Group	1.8
Equity Res. Properties	1.7
Del Webb	1.4

Source: *Fortune*, April 17, 2000, pp. I-72.

★ 1805 ★
Real Estate (SIC 6531)

Top Home Sellers in Washington State - 1999

Shares are for representing buyers, based on number of transactions.

Windermere	33%
John L. Scott	17
Coldwell Banker	15
Re/Max	4
Prudential	4
Other	27

Source: "1999 Market Share by Company." Retrieved April 18, 2000 from the World Wide Web: http://www.meierteam.com.

SIC 67 - Holding and Other Investment Offices

★ 1806 ★

Trusts (SIC 6730)

Largest Trusts - 1998

Institutions are ranked by total discretionary assets in billions of dollars.

State Street Bank & Trust Co. . . . . . . $ 454.2
Barclays Global Investors 429.8
Bankers Trust Co. 299.5
The Northern Trust Co. 189.9
PNC Bank 189.6
Chase Manhattan Bank 155.9
The Bank of New York 114.9
Morgan Guaranty Trust Co. of N.Y. 110.5

Source: *U.S. Banker*, February 2000, p. 50.

★ 1807 ★

Franchising (SIC 6794)

Largest Franchise Companies

Data are in units.

McDonald's Corp. 18,361
7-Eleven Inc. 13,819
Subway Sandwiches and Salads 13,300
Burger King Corp. 7,495
Pizza Hut Inc. 7,200
Jani-King International Inc. 6,700
Cendant Corp. 5,600
International Dairy Queen Inc. 5,347

Source: *Investor's Business Daily*, July 30, 1999, p. 1, from International Franchise Association.

SIC 70 - Hotels and Other Lodging Places

★ 1808 ★
Hotels (SIC 7011)

Largest Economy Hotel Chains

Data show number of rooms.

Days Inn of America	163,761
Ramada Ltd.	131,731
Super 8	98,286
Motel 6	84,273
Howard Johnson	55,953
Economy Lodge	45,886

Source: Retrieved February 1, 2000 from the World Wide Web: http://www.activemedia-guide.com/mrk_3835.htm, from U.S. Business Reporter.

★ 1809 ★
Hotels (SIC 7011)

Largest Hotel Companies

Companies are ranked by number of guestrooms.

Cendant Corp.	543
Bass Hotels & Resorts	453
Marriott International	339
Choice Hotels International	327
Best Western International	306
Starwood Hotels & Resorts Worldwide	213
Promus Hotel Corp.	198

Source: *Hotel & Motel Management*, September 20, 1999, p. 42.

★ 1810 ★
Hotels (SIC 7011)

Largest Highway/Airport Hotels

The top hotels are ranked by sales per room.

Ameristar Casino Hotel	$ 109
Apple Farm	98
Hanover Inn At Darmouth	83
Malibu Beach Inn	69
Sheraton At Woodbridge Pl.	67

Source: *Lodging Hospitality*, August 1999, p. 43.

★ 1811 ★
Hotels (SIC 7011)

Largest Hotel Markets

Data show number of rooms.

Las Vegas	105,800
Orlando	87,200
Los Angeles-Long Beach	79,100
Atlanta	70,300
Chicago	69,400
Washington D.C.	68,500
New York City	65,800

Source: Retrieved January 20, 2000 from the World Wide WebL: http://www.actovemedia-guide.com/mrk_3835.htm, from *Hotel & Motel Management*.

★ 1812 ★
Hotels (SIC 7011)

Leading Economy Lodging Chains - 1999

Chains are ranked by number of guestrooms as of December 1, 1999.

Days Inns of America 165,000
Super 8 Motels 114,304
Motel 6 86,227
Travelodge Hotels 47,168
Econo Lodge 45,055
Red Roof Inns 37,325
Extended Stay America Efficiency
   Studios 25,124
Homestead Village Guest Studios 19,595

Source: *Hotel & Motel Management*, February 7, 2000, p. 31, from Smith Travel Research.

★ 1813 ★
Hotels (SIC 7011)

Lodging Industry Revenues - 1998

Rooms 71.7%
Food & beverage 21.8
Minor operated dept. 2.8
Telecommunications 2.2
Rentals & other 1.5

Source: *USA TODAY*, June 29, 1999, p. 1B, from Smith Travel Research.

★ 1814 ★
Hotels (SIC 7011)

Popular Resorts

The top resorts are ranked by sales per room.

La Jolla Beach & Tennis Club . . . . . . $ 305
The Boulders 223
Barton Creek Resort 198
Pollard Brook Resort 190
Ponte Vedra Inn/Club 165

Source: *Lodging Hospitality*, August 1999, p. 35.

★ 1815 ★
Hotels (SIC 7011)

Top Hotel Management Companies

Companies are ranked by total rooms managed.

Starwood Hotels & Resorts 99
Wyndham International 74
Meristar Hotels & Resorts 45
Interstate Hotels Corp. 31
Bristol Hotels & Reosrts 30
Prime Hospitality 27
Lodgian 25

Source: *Lodging Hospitality*, August 1999, p. 51.

★ 1816 ★
Hotels (SIC 7011)

Top Hotel Management Firms - 1999

Firms are ranked by rooms managed.

MeriStar Hotels & Resorts 47,046
Westmont Hospitality 34,769
Interstate Hotels Corp. 29,379
Bristol Hotels & Resorts 29,228
Prime Hospitality Corp. 27,839
Lodgian 25,000
Tharaldson Enterprises 21,179

Source: *Hotel & Motel Management*, March 20, 2000, p. 33.

SIC 72 - Personal Services

★ 1817 ★

Funeral Services (SIC 7261)

Cremation Rates by State - 1997

Data show states with the highest rates.

Hawaii	57.6%
Nevada	55.2
Washington	53.8
Arizona	50.2
Alaska	49.9

Source: *USA TODAY*, October 8, 1999, p. 2A, from Cremation Association of North America.

SIC 73 - Business Services

★ 1818 ★

Advertising (SIC 7310)

Largest Business-to-Business Advertisers

Firms are ranked by spending in billions of dollars.

IBM Corp.	$ 293.4
AT&T Corp.	288.6
Microsoft Corp.	207.3
First Union Corp.	172.0
American Express Co.	168.3
SBC Communications	155.6
MCI WorldCom	137.8
Compaq Computer Corp.	136.0
Sprint Corp.	130.3
Bell Atlantic	123.4

Source: *Business Marketing*, December 1999, p. 26.

★ 1819 ★

Advertising (SIC 7310)

Largest Magazine Advertisers - 1999

Shares are shown based on ad dollars as of September 1999.

Time Inc.	20.7%
Conde Nast	7.7
Hearst	7.4
Others	64.2

Source: *Wall Street Journal*, January 12, 2000, p. B10, from Kinetic Strategies.

★ 1820 ★

Advertising (SIC 7310)

Largest Online Ad Spenders

Spending is shown in millions of dollars.

E-Trade	$ 89.0
Value Online stores	46.5
Charles Schwab	40.9
Snip.com	38.1
Ameritrade	36.4

Source: *Investor's Business Daily*, December 29, 1999, p. A9, from Competitve Media Reporting and McCann Erickson.

★ 1821 ★

Advertising (SIC 7310)

Newspaper Ad Spending

Spending is shown in billions of dollars.

	1999
Retail	$ 21.5
Classfied	18.6
National	6.4

Source: *Editor & Publisher*, November 13, 1999, p. 56, from Verona, Suhler & Associates, Wilkofsky Gruen Associates, and Newspaper Association of America.

★ 1822 ★
Advertising (SIC 7310)
Top Ad Categories in Canada - 1998

Spending is shown in millions of dollars.

Retailing	$ 953.5
Automotive	753.8
Business equipment & services	521.6
Food	395.6
Financial services & insurance services	388.0
Entertainment	314.8
Local automotive dealers	266.6
Travel & transportation	249.3
Restaurants, catering, nightclubs	199.3

Source: *Marketing Magazine*, September 27, 1999, p. 44, from A.C. Nielsen.

★ 1823 ★
Advertising (SIC 7310)
Top Ad Industries in Radio - 1999

Data are estimated in millions of dollars.

Retail	$ 425
Telecom	302
Media	256
Automotive	210
Internet	197

Source: *Industry Standard*, November 15, 1999, p. 72, from Radio Advertising Bureau and Robertson Stephens.

★ 1824 ★
Advertising (SIC 7312)
Outdoor Ad Markets - 1998

Data show estimated revenues by type of media.

	($ mil.)	Share
Billboards, large	$ 1,596	36.2%
Billboards, medium size	962	21.8
In-store ads	459	10.4
Sports arenas	320	7.2
Transit ads	300	6.8
Bus shelters	250	5.7
Billboards, small	$ 168	3.8%
Airport ads	93	2.1
Mall ads	39	0.9
Other	39	0.9

Source: *Inc.*, March 2000, p. 23, from Outdoor Services Inc.

★ 1825 ★
Advertising (SIC 7319)
Digital Advertisement Insertion

Seachange makes servers and software that store TV commercials digitally then sends those ads onto millions of TV screens at a set time. This niche market started in 1993.

SeaChange	75%
Other	25

Source: *Investor's Business Daily*, December 28, 1999, p. A9.

★ 1826 ★
Advertising (SIC 7319)
Health Care Communications Market

Shares are shown based on gross income. The 1999 market was valued at $1.77 trillion.

CommonHealth	9.1%
Nelson Communications Inc.	7.6
Lowe Healthcare Worldwide	7.2
Healthworld Corp.	6.8
Torre Lazur Healthcare Group	6.5
Sudler & Hennessey	5.5
Grey Healthcare Group Inc.	5.4
Other	51.9

Source: *Med Ad News*, April 2000, p. 18.

★ 1827 ★
Advertising (SIC 7319)

Largest Advertisers - 1998

Sales are shown in millions of dollars.

General Motors	$ 2.1
Procter & Gamble	1.7
DaimlerChrysler	1.4
Philip Morris	1.3
Ford Motor	1.0

Source: *Cincinnati Enquirer*, August 1, 1999, p. E1, from Competitive Media Reporting.

★ 1828 ★
Advertising (SIC 7319)

Largest Business Publication Advertisers - 1998

Spending is shown in millions of dollars.

IBM	$ 102.4
Microsoft Corp.	94.2
Compaq	78.7
Dell Computer	65.5
Hewlett-Packard Co.	56.9
Micron Technology	51.0
Gateway	45.2
Computer Associates	42.9

Source: *Business Marketing*, December 1999, p. 32, from Competitive Media Reporting.

★ 1829 ★
Advertising (SIC 7319)

Largest Cable Advertisers - 1999

Spending is shown in millions of dollars.

Procter & Gamble Co.	$ 275.2
MCI WorldCom	248.0
General Motors Corp.	245.7
Philip Morris Cos.	152.1
Johnson & Johnson	125.6
AT&T Corp.	112.4
Diageo	106.0
Sony Corp.	103.6
Sprint Corp.	103.6

Source: *Advertising Age*, April 10, 2000, p. S36, from Competitive Media Reporting.

★ 1830 ★
Advertising (SIC 7319)

Largest Cable Advertising Categories - 1999

Spending is shown in millions of dollars.

	($ mil.)	Share
Automotive	$ 787.4	16.05%
Financial	648.6	13.22
Pharmaceutical	578.5	11.79
Retailing	517.0	10.54
Telecommunications	508.9	10.37
Direct response companies	465.5	9.49
Other	1,399.2	28.53

Source: *Advertising Age*, April 10, 2000, p. S36, from Competitive Media Reporting.

★ 1831 ★
Advertising (SIC 7319)

Largest Consumer Publication Advertisers - 1998

Spending is shown in millions of dollars.

Microsoft Corp.	$ 57.5
IBM	50.8
AT&T Corp.	33.8
Hewlett-Packard	31.3
American Express	27.9
State Farm Mutual Auto	26.6
Compaq Computer	25.0
Canon	19.9

Source: *Business Marketing*, December 1999, p. 32, from Competitive Media Reporting.

★ 1832 ★
Advertising (SIC 7319)

Largest Dot-Com Ad Spenders - 1999

Spending is shown in millions of dollars. Most-dot-com dollars were spent on TV advertising.

E*Trade	$ 88.9
Value American Store	46.5
Charles Schwab	40.8
Snap.com	38.0
Ameritrade Brokerage	36.0
AT&T Business Network	32.8
America Online	30.0
Monster.com	20.6

Source: *Business 2.0*, March 2000, p. 24, from Competitive Media Reporting.

★ 1833 ★
Advertising (SIC 7319)

Leading Pharmacy Advertisers - 1999

Data show share of ad expenditures.

Pfizer Laboratories	6.84%
AstraZeneca	4.10
Schering Corporation	3.39
Searle Pharmaceuticals	2.55
Wyeth-Ayerst	2.36
Roxane Laboratories Inc.	2.27
ESI Lederle Inc.	2.23
Other	76.26

Source: *Medical Marketing & Media*, April 2000, p. 68, from PERQ/HCI Journal Ad Review.

★ 1834 ★
Advertising (SIC 7319)

Top Newspapers for Dot-Com Advertising - 1999

Revenues are for the first nine months of the year.

Wall Street Journal	$ 91,744.2
USA TODAY	39,802.5
New York Times	17,113.2
Chicago Tribune	6,770.7
Los Angeles Times	6,605.0
The Washington Post	4,811.0
San Francisco Chronicle	4,131.9

Source: *Editor & Publisher*, January 3, 2000, p. 26, from Competitive Media Reporting.

★ 1835 ★
Advertising (SIC 7319)

Web Advertising Spending - 1999

Spending is shown in percent.

Search/new media content	24%
Computer-related/technique	24
Consumer/retail	12
Financial services	10
Telecom	6
Other	24

Source: Retrieved January 11, 2000 from the World Wide Web: http://www.emarketer.com/estats/.

★ 1836 ★
Advertising (SIC 7319)

Where Internet Firms Advertise

Data are in millions of dollars for the year to date November.

Internet	$ 1,699.5
Network television	556.8
Magazines	495.9
Cable TV	396.3
Spot television	325.7
National newspapers	250.7
National spot radio	248.4
Newspapers	106.6
Network radio	62.1

Source: *Industry Standard*, March 13, 2000, p. 284, from Competitive Media Reporting.

★ 1837 ★
Collection Agencies (SIC 7322)

Top Collection Agencies - 1998

Firms are ranked by commercial volume in billions of dollars.

Dun & Bradstreet Corp.	$ 7.6
GC Services Ltd. Partnership	3.7
Vengroff, Williams & Associates	3.2
Outsourcing Solutions Inc.	2.5
NCO Group Fort	1.8
IntelliRisk Management Corp.	1.1
Creditors Multisystems Inc.	1.0

Source: *Credit Collections News*, November 1999, p. 1, from *Credit Collections Directory*.

★ 1838 ★
Direct Marketing (SIC 7331)

B-to-B Direct Marketing Sales - 1999

Sales are shown in billions of dollars.

Business services	$ 124.8
Insurance carriers/agents	53.4
Real estate	45.4
Wholesale trade	32.3
Printing & publishing	28.8
Industrial machinery & equipment	27.5
Professional services	27.1
Chemicals/allied products	27.0
Communications	24.1

Source: *BtoB*, April 24, 2000, p. 16, from Direct Marketing Association.

★ 1839 ★
Photocopying Services (SIC 7334)

Largest Speedy Printers

Sir Speedy
Kwik Copy
PIP
American Speedy
AlphaGraphics
Insty-Print
ProForma
Other

Shares are shown based on franchises.

Sir Speedy	18%
Kwik Copy	18
PIP	11
American Speedy	9
AlphaGraphics	7
Insty-Print	6
ProForma	6
Other	25

Source: *American Printer*, June 1999, p. 87, from GAMIS.

★ 1840 ★
Temp Agencies (SIC 7363)

Largest Temp Agencies

Market shares are shown in percent. Adecco and Olsten are planning to merge.

Manpower	4.8%
Adecco	4.2
Interim Services/Norrell Corp.	4.0
Kelly Services	3.7
Olsten	3.1
CDI	2.4
Robert Half Intl.	2.1
Other	75.7

Source: *Wall Street Journal*, August 19, 1999, p. C1, from Staffing Industry Analysts Inc.

★ 1841 ★
Temp Agencies (SIC 7363)

Largest Temp Help Firms - 1999

The largest temp firms are ranked by revenues in billions of dollars.

Manpower	$ 9.7
Olsten	4.9
Kelly Services	4.2
Interim Services	3.1
Volt Info. Sciences	2.1
Robert Half Intl.	2.0
Modis Professional Services	1.9

Source: *Fortune*, April 17, 2000, pp. I-74.

★ 1842 ★
Temp Agencies (SIC 7363)

Top Staffing Firms in Detroit, MI - 1998

Firms are ranked by revenues in millions of dollars.

Kelly Services	$ 4,092.0
Manpower Metro Detroit	113.0
The Bartech Group	76.5
TAC Automotive Group	75.0
Arcadia Services	64.0
Robert Half International	60.4
Adecco Employment	49.0

Source: *Crain's Detroit Business*, November 29, 1999, p. 15.

★ 1843 ★
Software (SIC 7372)

2D Plant Design Market

Shares are estimated for 1999.

Autodesk	33.3%
Bentley	23.9
Intergraph	23.1
Rebis	3.5
Dassault Systemes	3.3

Source: *Chemical Engineering*, July 1999, p. 109.

★ 1844 ★
Software (SIC 7372)

3D Plant Design/Visualization Market

Shares are estimated.

Intergraph	56.4%
Cadcentre	17.7
Rebis	6.4
Bentley	3.8
Dassault Systemes	3.3
Other	12.4

Source: *Chemical Engineering*, July 1999, p. 109.

★ 1845 ★
Software (SIC 7372)

CAD/CAM/CAE Market Leaders - 1999

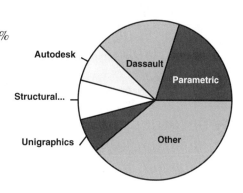

Shares are estimated. CAD/CAM/CAE stands for computer aided design, manufacturing and engineering.

Parametric	20.0%
Dassault	18.3
Autodesk	8.1
Structural Dynamics	7.6
Unigraphics	6.7
Other	39.3

Source: *Investor's Business Daily*, July 23, 1999, p. A7, from company reports and Jackson Partners & Associates.

★ 1846 ★
Software (SIC 7372)

Computer Animation Production System Shares

Computer animation revenues reached $20 billion in 1998.

PC	37.3%
NT	35.4
Unix	15.5
Mac	11.9

Source: *Computer Graphics World*, October 1999, p. 26, from *The Ronicarelli Report on the Computer Animation Industry, 1998*.

★ 1847 ★
Software (SIC 7372)

CRM Software Leaders - 1998

CRM stands for customer relationship management.

Siebel	14.5%
Vantive	6.0
Clarify	4.8
Trilogy	4.6
Baan	4.6
Oracle	2.2
Other	63.3

Source: *Investor's Business Daily*, December 17, 1999, p. A6, from International Data Corp.

★ 1848 ★
Software (SIC 7372)

CRM Software/Services Market

CRM stands for customer relationship management.

Siebel	19%
Oracle	10
Clarify	6
Vantive	5
Other	60

Source: *Informationweek*, February 14, 2000, p. 88, from AMR Research.

★ 1849 ★
Software (SIC 7372)

Data Solution Market - 1997

Sales are shown in millions of dollars.

IBM	$ 2,400
Oracle	800
NCR	750
Hewlett-Packard	750
Compaq	700

Source: *Washington Technology*, August 2, 1999, p. 34, from Palo Alto Management Group.

★ 1850 ★
Software (SIC 7372)

Database Market Leaders - 1998

IBM	32.3%
Oracle	29.3
Microsoft	10.2
Informix	4.4
Sybase	3.5
Other	20.3

Source: Retrieved January 4, 2000 from the World Wide Web: http://www.infotechtrends.com, from *Smart Reseller*.

★ 1851 ★
Software (SIC 7372)

Document Technology Software Revenues

Banking & finance	24%
Manufacturing	16
Insurance & pensions	14
Public sector	11
Telecoms	8
Other	18

Source: *Inform*, June 1999, p. 20, from Strategy Partners International.

★ 1852 ★
Software (SIC 7372)

E-Commerce Application Market - 1998

Shares are shown based on revenues.

Netscape ECXpert suite	9.4%
BroadVision	8.1
Ariba	5.6
Oracle	5.6
Open Market	5.2
Intershop	2.9
IBM	2.8

Continued on next page.

★ 1852 ★ *Continued*
Software (SIC 7372)

E-Commerce Application Market - 1998

Shares are shown based on revenues.

Sterling Commerce	2.7%
Intelysis	2.4
Interworld	2.4
Other	52.9

Source: *Infoworld*, March 15, 1999, p. 53, from International Data Corp.

★ 1853 ★
Software (SIC 7372)

E Verification Language Market

The program is an effort to promote aid in inter-operability between third-party verification solutions by allowing Verisity partners to develop tools using the e language.

LicenseE	77%
Other	23

Source: "Verisity Openly Licenses Its No 1 Language." Retrieved May 5, 2000 from the World Wide Web: http://www.businesswire.com.

★ 1854 ★
Software (SIC 7372)

Enterprise Messaging Software - 1999

Lotus Notes	31%
Microsoft	28
Other	41

Source: Retrieved January 1, 2000 from the World Wide Web: http://businessjournal.netscape.co. erymarket+share&offerIDNETCENTER, from Radicati Group.

★ 1855 ★
Software (SIC 7372)

Enterprise Network Browers

Internet Explorer	59%
Netscape Navigator	41

Source: Retrieved January 4, 2000 from the World Wide Web: http://www.infotechtrends.com, from *Network World* and Zona Research.

★ 1856 ★
Software (SIC 7372)

ERP Software Leaders

ERP stands for enterprise resources planning.

SAP	41.9%
Datasul	7.6
Baan	5.5
J.D. Edwards	4.8
SSA	4.4
PeopleSoft	3.4
Oracle	3.0
Others	29.4

Source: *Latin Trade*, August 1999, p. 65, from International Data Corp.

★ 1857 ★
Software (SIC 7372)

ERP Software Market - 2000

ERP stands for enterprise resource planning.

Oracle	29.0%
SAP	18.0
PeopleSoft	15.0
J.D. Edwards	12.5
Others	25.5

Source: *Infoworld*, October 4, 1999, p. 12, from AMR Research Inc.

★ 1858 ★

Software (SIC 7372)

Game Software Market

The entertainment software market is still largely controlled by men: 69% of consoles and 62% of PCs are by men. The table shows market revenues in billions of dollars.

	1997	2000	Share
Video game console software	$ 2.80	$ 3.69	62.54%
CD-ROMs	1.86	2.10	35.59
Online games	0.05	0.11	1.86

Source: *Communications of the ACM*, January 2000, p. 44, from Veronis, Suhler & Associates and SRI Consulting.

★ 1859 ★

Software (SIC 7372)

Internet Call Answering Machine Industry

Data show estimated shares of the market. According to the source, out of the 54 million U.S. homes with PCs, more than in million homes will use the software. The market is expected to grow 38% annually.

CallWave	55%
Other	45

Source: "CallWave's Internet Answering Machine Leads." Retrieved May 18, 2000 from the World Wide Web: http://www.businesswire.net.

★ 1860 ★

Software (SIC 7372)

IP-ACD Industry

IP-ACD stands for Internet Protocol Automatic Call Distributor.

CosmoCom	50%
PakNetX	25
Other	25

Source: "CosmoCom Takes 50% of IP-ACD Market." Retrieved May 23, 2000 from the World Wide Web: http://www.yahoo.com, from Frost & Sullivan.

★ 1861 ★

Software (SIC 7372)

Java Development Market - 1998

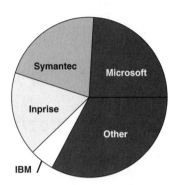

Microsoft	24%
Symantec	21
Inprise	17
IBM	5
Other	33

Source: Retrieved January 4, 2000 from the World Wide Web: http://www.infotechtrends.com, from *Interactive Week* and International Data Corp.

★ 1862 ★

Software (SIC 7372)

Largest Business Software Publishers - 1999

Microsoft	41.0%
Symantec	11.6
Adobe	8.1
Other	39.3

Source: "Business, Finance Led '99 Software Sales." Retrieved March 27, 2000 from the World Wide Web: http://www.pcdata.com, from PC Data.

★ 1863 ★
Software (SIC 7372)

Largest Computer Software Firms - 1999

Firms are ranked by revenues in billions of dollars.

Microsoft . . . . $ 19.7
Oracle 8.8
Computer Associates 5.2
Compuware 1.6
PeopleSoft 1.4
BMC Software 1.3

Source: *Fortune*, April 17, 2000, pp. I-58.

★ 1864 ★
Software (SIC 7372)

Largest Education Software Publishers - 1999

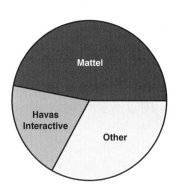

Mattel 47%
Havas Interactive 20
Other 33

Source: "Business, Finance Led '99 Software Sales."
Retrieved March 27, 2000 from the World Wide Web:
http://www.pcdata.com, from PC Data.

★ 1865 ★
Software (SIC 7372)

Largest Entertainment Software Publishers - 1999

Havas Interactive 16%
Electronic Arts 14
Hasbro Interactive 12
Other 58

Source: "Business, Finance Led '99 Software Sales."
Retrieved March 27, 2000 from the World Wide Web:
http://www.pcdata.com, from PC Data.

★ 1866 ★
Software (SIC 7372)

Largest Finance Software Publishers - 1999

Accounting software increased 36% in revenues.

Intuit 81%
Block Financial 7
Peachtree 4
Other 8

Source: "Business, Finance Led '99 Software Sales."
Retrieved March 27, 2000 from the World Wide Web:
http://www.pcdata.com, from PC Data.

★ 1867 ★
Software (SIC 7372)

Largest Personal Productivity Software Publishers - 1999

Mattel 43.0%
Microsoft 16.5
Other 40.5

Source: "Business, Finance Led '99 Software Sales."
Retrieved March 27, 2000 from the World Wide Web:
http://www.pcdata.com, from PC Data.

★ 1868 ★
Software (SIC 7372)

Largest Reference Software Publishers - 1999

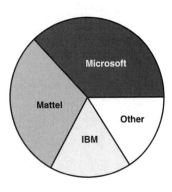

Encyclopedias made up nearly 70% of reference software revenues.

Microsoft	37%
Mattel	30
IBM	17
Other	16

Source: "Business, Finance Led '99 Software Sales." Retrieved March 27, 2000 from the World Wide Web: http://www.pcdata.com, from PC Data.

★ 1869 ★
Software (SIC 7372)

Largest Software Publishers - 1999

Microsoft	23.6%
Mattel	12.0
Other	64.4

Source: "Business, Finance Led '99 Software Sales." Retrieved March 27, 2000 from the World Wide Web: http://www.pcdata.com, from PC Data.

★ 1870 ★
Software (SIC 7372)

Leading PC Game Publishers

Shares are shown based on units.

Havas Interactive	16.8%
Electronic Arts	13.1
Hasbro Interactive	12.5
Other	57.6

Source: "Console, PC Games Industry Sales Top $7.4B in 1999." Retrieved February 4, 2000 from the World Wide Web: http://www.pcdata.com, from PC Data.

★ 1871 ★
Software (SIC 7372)

Linux Retail Market - 2000

Shares are for February 2000.

Red Hat	40.4%
Macmillan	19.6
Corel	19.3
S.U.S.E.	7.1
TurboLinux	4.1
Caldera	3.0

Source: "Corel Linux Market Share Grows." Retrieved April 3, 2000 from the World Wide Web: http://library.northernlight.com, from PC Data.

★ 1872 ★
Software (SIC 7372)

Media Player Market

Shares are for the month of November 1999.

	Users (mil.)
Real Network's RealPlayer	8.9%
Apple Computer's Quick Time	5.4
Microsoft's Windows Media Player	2.4

Source: *New York Times*, March 15, 2000, p. C2, from Nilesen NetRatings.

★ 1873 ★

Software (SIC 7372)

Messaging Software For Service Providers - 1999

The total market reached $69.5 million.

Sendmail	64%
Software.com	19
Sun-Netscape Alliance	10
Other	7

Source: Retrieved January 1, 2000 from the World Wide Web: http://businessjournal.netscape.co. erymarket+share&offerIDNETCENTER, from Radicati Group.

★ 1874 ★

Software (SIC 7372)

Mid-Range Video Editing Software

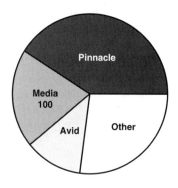

Pinnacle	41%
Media 100	20
Avid	12
Other	27

Source: "Market Spotlight on Digital Video Editing Systems." Retrieved March 13, 2000 from the World Wide Web: http://www.digitalmedia.com.

★ 1875 ★

Software (SIC 7372)

Mobile Database Market - 1998

Sybase SQL Anywhere	55%
Oracle Lite	20
Progress	7
Centura	6
Interprise/Interbase	5
Others	7

Source: *Computer Reseller News*, February 28, 2000, p. 1, from Dataquest Inc.

★ 1876 ★

Software (SIC 7372)

Office Software Leaders

Corel has less than 1% of the market.

Microsoft	92%
Lotus	7
Other	1

Source: *Investor's Business Daily*, June 7, 1999, p. A6, from Giga Information Group.

★ 1877 ★

Software (SIC 7372)

OLAP Market Shares - 1999

The market is valued at $2.4 billion, which is expected to reach $4.0 billion by 2001.

Hyperion	24.1%
Oracle	11.4
Cognos	11.1
Microstrategy	10.1
Business Objects	5.3
Microsoft	4.4
Other	33.6

Source: *ENT*, February 23, 2000, p. 33, from *The OLAP Report*.

★ 1878 ★

Software (SIC 7372)

Operating System Sales - 1999

Windows NT	38%
Linux	25
NetWare	19
Unix	15
Other	3

Source: *Computerworld*, January 31, 2000, p. 16, from International Data Corp.

★ 1879 ★

Software (SIC 7372)

Personal Finance Software

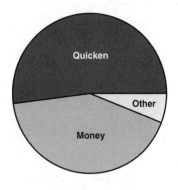

Data are as of June 30, 1999.

	(mil.)	Share
Quicken	13.0	52%
Money	10.5	42
Other	1.4	6

Source: *USA TODAY*, September 10, 1999, p. 3B, from Media Metrix.

★ 1880 ★

Software (SIC 7372)

Professional Animation Software

Discreet	44%
Newtek	26
Alias/Wavefront	9
Avid	9
Maxon	6
Electric Image	3
Nichimen	2

Source: "Market Spotlight on Digital Video Editing Systems." Retrieved March 13, 2000 from the World Wide Web: http://www.digitalmedia.com.

★ 1881 ★

Software (SIC 7372)

Server Market Share - 1999

Shares are shown based on revenues.

Unix	53%
Windows NT	30
Linux	1
Other	16

Source: *Investor's Business Daily*, March 6, 2000, p. A8, from Dataquest Inc., International Data Corp., and Merrill Lynch & Co.

★ 1882 ★

Software (SIC 7372)

Server Operating Systems

Windows NT	38.3%
NetWare	22.8
Unix	18.8
Linux	15.8
Other	4.3

Source: *Investor's Business Daily*, September 24, 1999, p. A6, from International Data Corp.

★ **1883** ★

Software (SIC 7372)

Server Software Shipments - 1998

Windows NT	38.3%
NetWare	22.8
Linux	15.8
Other	18.8

Source: *Upside*, September 1999, p. 82, from International Data Corp.

★ **1884** ★

Software (SIC 7372)

Signal Integrity Software

According to the source, signal integrity analysis involves analyzing the connection between signal lines and PCBs or multi-chip modules.

ViewLogic	69%
Other	31

Source: Retrieved January 1, 2000 from the World Wide Web: http://ftp.viewlogic.com/pr/1999/dataquest.html.

★ **1885** ★

Software (SIC 7372)

Software Ratings

Data show the ratings by the Entertainment Software Rating Board on more than 5,000 titles. The industry had sales of $6.7 billion in 1998.

Everybody	70%
Teen	19
Mature (17+)	7
Early childhood	3
Adults only	1

Source: *USA TODAY*, June 23, 1999, p. D1.

★ **1886** ★

Software (SIC 7372)

Speech Recognition Market in Canada

Data are estimated.

Dragon Systems	45%
IBM	40
L&H	25

Source: *National Trade Data Bank*, STAT-USA, May 1, 1999, from U.S. Dept. of Commerce.

★ **1887** ★

Software (SIC 7372)

Speech Recognition Software

Closely	48%
L&H	36
IBM	15
Other	11

Source: *Wall Street Journal*, March 28, 2000, p. B9.

★ **1888** ★

Software (SIC 7372)

Storage Management Software - 1999

The $4.2 billion market is shown by company.

EMC	18.2%
IBM	17.3
Computer Associates	16.4
Veritas	12.1
BMC Software	5.6
Others	30.4

Source: *Investor's Business Daily*, April 14, 2000, p. A4, from Gartner Group.

★ **1889** ★

Software (SIC 7372)

Streaming Video Technology

RealNetworks	85%
Other	15

Source: ''RealNetworks Market Share Well Earned.'' Retrieved December 13, 1999 From the World Wide Web: http://home.zdnet.co.desk/talkback.

★ 1890 ★
Software (SIC 7372)

Supply Chain Executive Market

EXE Technologies	5%
McHugh Software	5
Manhattan Associates	3
Catalyst International	2
Optum	2
HK Systems	2
Kewill Logistics	2
TRW (LES Div.)	2
Provia Software	2
Other	75

Source: *Transportation & Distribution*, January 2000, p. 40, from AMR Research.

★ 1891 ★
Software (SIC 7372)

Top Computer Service/Software Providers to Government

The top providers are shown based on share of total contracts.

Lockheed Martin Corp.	6.94%
Computer Sciences Corp.	5.00
Unisys Corp.	4.39
Sciences Applications Intl Corp.	3.08
Northrop Grumman Corp.	2.58
Other	78.01

Source: *Government Executive*, 9, p. 46.

★ 1892 ★
Software (SIC 7372)

Vertical Application Device Market

Shares are by operating system.

	1999	2002
MS-DOS	63.6%	57%
Windows 3x/9x	12.2	6
Windows CE	2.1	9
Windows NT	1.9	7
Other	20.2	21

Source: *Network World*, October 18, 1999, p. 60, from International Data Corp.

★ 1893 ★
Software (SIC 7372)

Web Browser Market - 1998

Microsoft	53%
Netscape	47

Source: *USA TODAY*, November 8, 1999, p. 2B, from Gartner Group.

★ 1894 ★
Software (SIC 7372)

Web Browser Market - 2000

Shares are for February 2000. Data are based on re-al-time analysis of home and work net surfers at 650,000 web siters.

Internet Explorer 5.0	51%
Internet Explorer 4.0	20
Internet Explorer 3.0	10
Netscape 4.5	9
Netscape 4.0	6
America Online	3
Netscape 3.0	1

Source: *Industry Standard*, March 20, 2000, p. 185, from mycomputer.com.

★ 1895 ★
Software (SIC 7372)

Web Browser Market in Canada - 1997

Netscape	68%
Other	32

Source: "Drive-Thru Stats." Retrieved December 16, 1999 from the World Wide Web: http://www.prophead.net/drive.htm.

★ 1896 ★

Software (SIC 7372)

Web Development Tool Vendors

Market shares are shown of sales for business applications.

Microsoft	61.4%
JavaSoft	21.6
Oracle	5.4
Inprise (Borland)	4.7
Allaire	1.9
Symantec	1.0
Other	4.0

Source: Retrieved January 1, 2000 from the World Wide Web: http://www.ziffdavis.com/news/docs98/1005-5.htm, from CI Technology Database.

★ 1897 ★

Software (SIC 7372)

Web Surfers Operating System Use

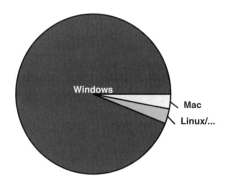

Data show the operating system used by web surfers.

Windows	94%
Linux/Unix/other	3
Mac	3

Source: *PC Computing*, August 1999, p. 72, from Statmarket.

★ 1898 ★

Integrated Systems (SIC 7373)

Largest Systems Integrators for Government

Market shares are shown based on government contracts.

Lockheed Martin Corp.	9.49%
Litton Industries Inc.	5.32
Computer Sciences Corp.	5.08
Science Applications Intl. Corp.	4.86
Unisys Corp.	3.89
Other	71.36

Source: *Government Executive*, Annual 1999, p. 48.

★ 1899 ★

Networks (SIC 7373)

Linux Server Market - 1999

Shares are for the fourth quarter of the year.

Compaq	25%
IBM	10
Hewlett-Packard	7
Dell	7
VA Linux Systems	5
Other	46

Source: "IDC Rate VA Linux Systems." Retrieved April 24, 2000 from the World Wide Web: http://www. businesswire.com, from International Data Corp.

★ 1900 ★

Networks (SIC 7373)

Midrange Server Market

Midrange servers cost $100,000 to $1 million.

IBM	26.8%
HP	21.5
Sun	17.4
Compaq	6.5
Siemens	6.1
Other	21.1

Source: *Investor's Business Daily*, March 30, 2000, p. A8, from International Data Corp.

★ 1901 ★

Networks (SIC 7373)

PC Server Market - 1999

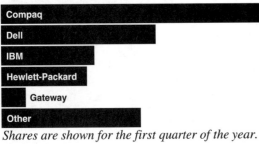

Shares are shown for the first quarter of the year.

Compaq	35.5%
Dell	20.0
IBM	11.6
Hewlett-Packard	11.2
Gateway	3.0
Other	18.0

Source: *Network World*, October 11, 1999, p. 17, from International Data Corp.

★ 1902 ★

Networks (SIC 7373)

Top Server Vendors - 1998

Shares are shown based on revenues.

IBM	29.1%
Hewlett-Packard	16.4
Sun	13.1
Compaq	11.3
Dell	5.8
Other	24.3

Source: *Computer Reseller News*, July 26, 1999, p. 12, from Dataquest Inc.

★ 1903 ★

Computer Services (SIC 7375)

Network Consulting/Integration Market

The top 10 vendors account for only 48% of the market.

IBM	12%
EDS	8
Other	80

Source: "IBM's Global Services Unit Dominates Network Market." Retrieved April 17, 2000 from the World Wide Web: http://www.businesswire.com, from International Data Corp.

★ 1904 ★

Information Technology (SIC 7375)

Leading IT Health Companies

Firms are ranked by revenues in millions of dollars.

McKesson/HBOC	$ 1,745.1
SMS Corp.	1,135.4
EDS	1,100.0
Science Applications International Corp. . .	440.0
NDC Health Information Services	357.5
CSC Healthcare Group	348.0
Cemer Corp.	330.9
IDX Systems Corp.	321.7

Source: *Healthcare Informatics*, June 1999, p. 52.

★ 1905 ★

Computer Services (SIC 7378)

Largest Computer and Data Service Firms - 1999

Firms are ranked by revenues in billions of dollars.

Electronic Data Systems	$ 18.5
Computer Sciences	7.6
Unisys	7.5
First Data	5.5
Automatic Data Proc.	5.5
Science Applications Intl.	5.2
America Online	4.7
Comdisco	4.1

Source: *Fortune*, April 17, 2000, pp. I-58.

★ 1906 ★
Security Services (SIC 7380)

Security Product/Service Revenues - 2000

Manufacturers/distributors includes estimated value of shipments and service revenues.

	($ bil.)	Share
Manufacturers/distributors	$ 37.2	36.08%
Guard companies	21.5	20.85
Proprietary security	16.0	15.52
Alarm companies	14.0	13.58
Private investigations	4.6	4.46
Armored cars	1.3	1.26
Consultants/engineers	1.0	0.97
Others	7.5	7.27

Source: *Security Magazine*, February 2000, p. 14, from Security Group, Hallcrest Division, and *Security Industry Association Update*.

★ 1907 ★
Security Services (SIC 7382)

Home Security Market Leaders - 1998

ADT
SecurityLink
Protection One
Brink's

Firms are ranked by revenue in millions of dollars.

ADT	$ 1,000
SecurityLink	482
Protection One	421
Brink's	204

Source: *Advertising Age*, September 13, 1999, p. 8.

★ 1908 ★
Photofinishing (SIC 7384)

Where Film is Developed

Today, nearly 35% of all photofinishing rolls are processed in an hour.

Mass	34.8%
Drug stores	24.2
Supermarkets	13.6
Stand-alone mini-labs	11.8

Source: *Supermarket Business*, September 1999, p. 5, from Photo Marketing Association.

★ 1909 ★
Mergers & Acquisitions (SIC 7389)

Auto Industry Mergers in North America - 1999

Data show the number of acquisitions for the third quarter of the year.

	No.	Share
Suppliers	39	38.61%
Dealers	20	19.80
Retail parts	17	16.83
Heavy-duty	14	13.86
Automakers	1	0.99
Other	10	9.90

Source: *Crain's Detroit Business*, November 8, 1999, p. 1, from First Union Securities Inc.

★ 1910 ★
Mergers & Acquisitions (SIC 7389)

Top Health Deals

Deals are shown in millions of dollars. Acquirers are shown in parentheses.

MetraHealth (United HealthCare)	$ 2,290
Health Systems International (Foundation Health)	1,502
Prudential Healthcare (Aetna)	1,060
NYLCare Health Plans (Aetna)	1,050
Value Health (Columbia/HCA Healthcare) . .	1,007

Source: *Business & Health*, October 1999, p. 48, from Thomson Financial Securities Data.

★ 1911 ★
Mergers & Acquisitions (SIC 7389)

Top Internet Mergers

Data show value of deal in billions of dollars. Acquirers are shown in parentheses.

Time Warner (America Online)	$ 181,941
Bay Networks (Nortel)	9,009
WebMD (Healtheon)	7,865
USWeb/CKS (Whittman-Hart)	7,220
Excite (AtHome)	5,925
IBM's Global Network (AT&T)	5,000
Broadcast.com (Yahoo)	4,733

Source: *Industry Standard*, January 24, 2000, p. 185.

★ 1912 ★

Training (SIC 7389)

Computer Training

Data show how computer-delivered training is done.

CD-ROM 28%
Online via Internet/Web 26
Via computer by some other means 21
Diskette 17
Online internal computer network 8

Source: *Cincinnati Enquirer*, August 1, 1999, p. E4.

★ 1913 ★

Training (SIC 7389)

U.S. Training Market - 1999

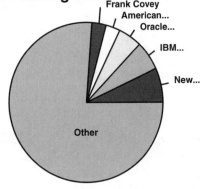

The top 20 firms had 53.8% of the market.

New Horizons 7.3%
IBM Learning Services 5.7
Oracle University 4.6
American Management Association 2.8
Frank Covey 2.5
Other 77.1

Source: Retrieved March 28, 2000 from the World Wide
Web: http://www.simbanet.com/press/headlines, from
Simba Information.

★ 1914 ★

Weight Loss Centers (SIC 7389)

Diet Center Market

Weight Watchers share has been placed elsewhere at 36% of the market.

Weight Watchers 51%
Jenny Craig 24
Nutri/System 12
Other 13

Source: Retrieved January 1, 2000 from the World Wide
Web: http://www.findexonline.com.

SIC 75 - Auto Repair, Services, and Parking

★ 1915 ★

Auto Rental (SIC 7514)

Car Rental Fleets - 1998

Data show average fleet size, in thousands.

Enterprise	368
Hertz	255
Avis	205
National	140
Budget	131
Alamo	130
Dollar	65

Source: *USA TODAY*, October 28, 1999, p. 3B, from *Auto Rental News Factbook, 1999*.

★ 1916 ★

Auto Repair Services (SIC 7530)

Auto Repair Part Use

Data show the types of parts used to repair collision-dmaged vehicles.

OEM parts	72%
Non-certified generic parts	14
CAPA-certified parts	10
Recycled/salvaged parts	10

Source: *Auto Body Repair News*, April 2000, p. 1, from Automotive Recyclers Association.

★ 1917 ★

Auto Repair Services (SIC 7530)

Brake Replacement Sales

Automotive chains	75%
Discount store chains	17
Department store chains	7
Non-automotive chains	1

Source: *Aftermarket Business*, April 2000, p. 52.

★ 1918 ★

Retreading Shops (SIC 7534)

Leading Passenger/Light Truck Tire Retreaders in North America - 1998

Companies are ranked by millions of pounds per year.

Les Schwab Tire Centers Inc.	2.30
Goodyear	1.70
Eastern Tire Service Ltd.	1.30
Ray Carr Tires Inc.	1.09
White's Tire Service of Wilson Inc.	0.97
Retreads Unlimited Inc.	0.81
Mt. Morris Tire Service Inc.	0.80

Source: *Tire Business*, June 7, 1999, p. 12.

★ 1919 ★

Retreading Shops (SIC 7534)

Leading Tire Retreaders in North America - 1998

Companies are ranked by millions of pounds per year. Data are medium and heavy truck tires.

Goodyear	39.65
Tire Distribution Systems/Bandag	23.30
Treadco Inc.	15.50
Tire Centers Inc.	13.10
Bridgestone/Firestone Inc.	11.80
Les Schwab Tire Centers	6.94
Premier Bandag Inc.	6.90
Purcell Tire & Rubber Co.	6.50

Source: *Tire Business*, June 7, 1999, p. 12.

SIC 78 - Motion Pictures

Motion Pictures (SIC 7812)

DVD Market Sales

Warner Bros.	30.5%
Buena Vista (Disney)	20.7
Universal	13.2
Columbia Tristar	8.4
Parmount	6.9
Fox Video	6.5
Others	13.8

Source: *USA TODAY*, April 20, 2000, p. 3B, from Adams Media Research.

Motion Pictures (SIC 7812)

Top DVD Firms - 1999

Shares are shown based on sales as of November 14, 1999.

Warner Home Video	29.6%
Universal Home Video	11.2
Buena Vista	10.9
Columbia	10.7
Paramount Home Video	7.7
Fox	5.4
MGM	4.7
Other	19.8

Source: *Los Angeles Times*, November 24, 1999, p. C6, from VideoScan.

Motion Pictures (SIC 7812)

Top Movies - 1999

Data show box office grosses in millions of dollars as of December 19, 1999.

Star Wars: Epsiode I - The Phantom Menace	$ 429.9
The Sixth Sense	275.2
Austin Powers: The Spy Who Shagged Me	205.4
Toy Story 2	179.7
The Matrix	171.4
Tarzan	170.9
Big Daddy	163.5
The Mummy	155.3
Runaway Bride	151.8
The Blair Witch Project	140.5

Source: *Detroit Free Press*, December 28, 1999, p. 6E.

★ 1923 ★

Video Tapes (SIC 7812)

Exercise Video Market - 1999

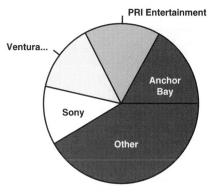

Shares are year-to-date as of January 30, 2000.

Anchor Bay	.16.9%
PRI Entertainment	16.2
Ventura Distribution	13.7
Sony	.11.5
Other	.41.7

Source: *Los Angeles Times*, February 16, 2000, p. C8, from VideoScan.

★ 1924 ★

Video Tapes (SIC 7812)

Top Exercise Video Vendors - 1999

Shares are shown for the year ended August 15, 1999.

Ventura Distribution	.40.2%
Anchor Bay	12.9
PPI Entertainment	11.2
Living Arts	9.0
Sony Music/Sony Wonder	7.0
BMG Video	4.6
Other	15.1

Source: *Los Angeles Times*, August 25, 1999, p. 8, from VideoScan.

★ 1925 ★

Film Distribution (SIC 7822)

Specialized Film Market - 2000

Limited release market shares are for January 3 - April 2, 2000.

Buena Vista	.40.8%
Sony Classics	.11.2
Fox Searchlight	8.3
USA	7.7
IMAX	4.3
Destination Cinema	4.1
Miramax	4.0
Lions Gate	2.3
Artisan	2.1
New Line	2.1
Other	.13.1

Source: *Variety*, April 10, 2000, p. 20, from A.C. Nielsen and Entertainment Data Inc.

★ 1926 ★

Film Distribution (SIC 7829)

Film Distribution Market - 1999

Buena Vista	.17.0%
Warner Bros.	14.2
Universal	.12.7
Paramount	.11.6
20th Century Fox	10.8
Sony	8.6
Dreamworks SKG	4.4
Miramax	4.3
Other	.16.4

Source: *Entertainment Weekly*, February 4, 2000, p. 34, from *Hollywood Reporter*.

★ 1927 ★

Film Distribution (SIC 7829)

Science Fiction Market - 1999

The domestic box office for science fiction films reached $768 million in 1999, as of March 5, 2000.

Fox	.58%
WB	22
Others	20

Source: *Variety*, March 13, 2000, p. 12, from Entertainment Data Inc.

★ 1928 ★

Movie Theaters (SIC 7832)

Imax Theaters in North America

*Data show screens in the United States and Canada.
There are more than 200 Imax screens worldwide.*

United States 100
Canada 25

Source: *Wall Street Journal*, December 10, 1999, p. A15.

★ 1929 ★

Movie Theaters (SIC 7832)

Largest Movie Theaters

Data show number of screens.

Carmike Cinemas 2,658
AMC Entertainment 2,607
Loews Cineplex Entertainment 1,972
GC Companies 1,067

Source: *New York Times*, July 12, 1999, p. C2, from
Bloomberg Financial Markets and National Association of
Theater Owners.

★ 1930 ★

Video Tape Rental (SIC 7841)

Most-Rented Videos - 1998

Data show revenues in millions of dollars.

As Good As It Gets . . . . $ 64.23
Air Force One 61.34
Conspiracy Theory 56.72
U.S. Marshals 52.02
Good Will Hunting 51.73
Devil's Advocate 50.99
Kiss The Girls 49.19
The Wedding Singer 48.10

Source: Retrieved December 3, 1999 from the World Wide
Web: http://www.vsda.org/news/top100of1998.html.

★ 1931 ★

Video Tape Rental (SIC 7841)

Video Rental Store Market

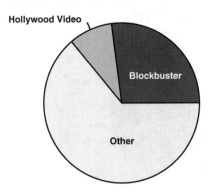

"Other" refers to independents.

Blockbuster 27%
Hollywood Video 9
Other 64

Source: Retrieved January 13, 2000 from the World Wide
Web: http://www.amcity.com/sanfrancisco/stories/1999/
05/31/story2.html.

★ 1932 ★

Video Tape Rental (SIC 7841)

Video Tape Rental in Canada - 1999

*Shares are shown based on estimated sales of $1.9
billion for the year ended December 31, 1999.*

Blockbuster Entertainment 16.4%
Rogers Video 7.9
Le Superclub Videotron 3.5
Video Update 3.2
Jumbo Video 2.3
Others 66.7

Source: "Report on Market Share." Retrieved June 8,
2000 from the World Wide Web: http://www.
marketingmag.ca, from industry sources.

SIC 79 - Amusement and Recreation Services

★ 1933 ★
Operas (SIC 7922)

Most Performed Operas

In North America 8 million people attended the opera in 1998-1999. Shows are ranked by number of productions.

Madama Butterfly	21
Don Giovanni	16
La Boheme	15
Rigoletto	12
La Traviata	11
Aida	11
Die Zauberflote	9
Die Fledermaus	9
Cosi Fan Tuti	9
Carmen	9

Source: *Time*, November 29, 1999, p. 6, from Opera America.

★ 1934 ★
Theatrical Entertainment (SIC 7922)

Broadway Shows - 1999

Data show the types of productions at Christmas 1999. No new plays were produced during this period; 12 were produced in 1979 and 8 in 1989. Other includes reviews, solo performances, and limited engagements.

	No.	Share
New musicals	20	68.97%
Musical revivals	4	13.79
Play revivals	3	10.34
Other	2	6.90

Source: *New York Times*, December 28, 1999, p. B1.

★ 1935 ★
Sports (SIC 7941)

Leading Basketball Teams

Teams are ranked by current value in millions of dollars. See the source for details.

New York Knicks	$ 334
Chicago Bulls	307
Los Angeles Lakers	282
Portland Trail Blazers	257
Phoenix Suns	239
Philadelphia 76ers	231

Continued on next page.

★ 1935 ★ *Continued*

Sports (SIC 7941)

Leading Basketball Teams

Teams are ranked by current value in millions of dollars. See the source for details.

Detroit Pistons	$ 226
Utah Jazz	215

Source: *Forbes*, December 13, 1999, p. 100.

★ 1936 ★

Sports (SIC 7941)

Leading Hockey Teams

Teams are ranked by current value in millions of dollars. See the source for details.

New York Rangers	$ 236
Philadelphia Flyers	211
Boston Bruins	197
Detroit Red Wings	194
Chicago Blackhawks	185
Montreal Canadians	175
Florida Panthers	163
Colorado Avalanche	160

Source: *Forbes*, December 13, 1999, p. 100.

★ 1937 ★

Sports (SIC 7941)

Popular Sports for Women

Data show millions of participants.

Exercise walking	13.6
Working out with equipment	9.6
Aerobic walking	9.0
Swimming	8.5
Bowling	7.5

Source: *Men's Fitness*, September 1999, p. 28, from National Sporting Goods Association.

★ 1938 ★

Sports (SIC 7941)

Top NFL Teams

Teams are ranked by current value in millions of dollars.

Dallas Cowboys	$ 663
Washington Redskins	607
Tampa Bay Buccaneers	502
Carolina Panthers	488
New England Patriots	460
Miami Dolphins	446
Denver Broncos	427

Source: *Forbes*, September 20, 1999, p. 177.

★ 1939 ★

Golf Courses (SIC 7992)

Public Courses by State

Michigan	783
Florida	724
California	641
New York	609
Ohio	600
Texas	557
Illinois	517

Source: *Detroiter*, October 1999, p. 9, from National Golf Foundation.

★ 1940 ★

Corporate Sponsorship (SIC 7999)

Corporate Sponsorship - 1998

Spending reached $6.8 billion.

Sports	67%
Entertainment tours/attractions	10
Festivals and fairs	9
Causes	8
Arts	6

Source: *New York Times*, July 16, 1999, p. C1, from *IEG Sponsorship Report*.

★ 1941 ★
Gambling (SIC 7999)

Casino Visits by Region

North Central 30%
West 26
South 25
Northeast 19

Source: *Financial Times*, January 9, 2000, p. 2, from
Harrah's Entertainment and INFO Research.

★ 1942 ★
Gambling (SIC 7999)

Largest Riverboat Casinos in Indiana

Casinos are ranked by revenue in millions of dollars.

Argosy . . . . $ 256.5
Empress 194.4
Harrah's 172.1
Blue Chip 134.6
Caesars 131.1
Grand Victoria 120.3

Source: *Cincinnati Enquirer*, December 5, 1999, p. E1,
from Indiana Gambling Commission.

★ 1943 ★
Gambling (SIC 7999)

Riverboat Gambling in Kansas - 2000

Data are for January 2000.

Station Casino Kansas City 34.5%
Harrah's 31.4
Argosy Riverside 18.7
Flamingo Hilton 15.2

Source: *Kansas City Star*, February 12, 2000, p. C1.

★ 1944 ★
Ski Resorts (SIC 7999)

Ski Resort Market

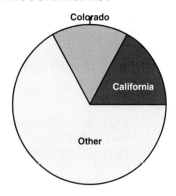

*Market shares are for overnight ski trips, based on a
survey.*

California 17.1%
Colorado 16.2
Other 66.7

Source: *New York Times*, November 20, 1999, p. A7, from
Colorado Ski Country USA.

★ 1945 ★
Tourist Attractions (SIC 7999)

Largest Tourist Attractions Near Pittsburgh, PA

Data show number of visitors.

Kennywood 1,380,000
Pittsburgh Zoo 764,989
Andy Warhol Museum 64,806

Source: *Pittburgh Post-Gazette*, October 31, 1999, p. C1.

★ 1946 ★

Training (SIC 7999)

Training Market - 2000

The corporate training market is expected to reach $10 billion in 2001. IT training companies specialize in computer skills; soft skill trainers specialize in leadership and management skills.

IT training companies 61%
Soft skills trainers 39

Source: ''Simba Predicts Corporate Training Market.'' Retrieved November 1, 1999 from the World Wide Web: http://www.simbanet.com/press, from Simba Information.

★ 1947 ★

Training (SIC 7999)

Training Market - 2003

The market is expected to reach $9.4 billion by 2003.

Traditional instructor led 51%
Technology based 46
Text based 3

Source: *Investor's Business Daily*, December 2, 1999, p. A10, from International Data Corp.

SIC 80 - Health Services

★ 1948 ★
Health Care (SIC 8000)

Alternative Medicine Sales - 1997

Sales are shown in billions of dollars.

Chiropractic services	$ 8,000
Massage therapists	4,000
Chinese medicine and acupuncture	3,900
Homeopathy	560

Source: "CAM a $27B Market." Retrieved October 5, 1999 from the World Wide Web: http://www.nbj.net/news8.htm, from *Nutrition Business Journal*.

★ 1949 ★
Health Care (SIC 8000)

Stress Management Industry

Revenues are shown in millions of dollars.

	1996	2000
Mental health counselors	$ 6,727	$ 6,990
Psychotherapy clinics	3,424	3,570
Individual counselors	3,293	3,420
Massage therapy/clinics	1,870	2,900
Individual services	1,293	2,000
Stress management centers	623	775
Massage centers	577	900
Biofeedback therapy counsel	420	523
Retail clinics	203	252

Source: *Medical & Healthcare Marketplace Guide*, 1999, pp. I-1007.

★ 1950 ★
Surgery (SIC 8000)

Popular Cosmetic Surgery for Women - 1998

Data show number of procedures.

Liposuction	152,290
Breast augmentation	132,378
Eyelid surgery	104,437
Face lift	64,987
Chemical peel	62,715

Source: *USA TODAY*, November 1, 1999, p. 7A, from American Society of Plastic and Reconstructive Surgeons.

★ 1951 ★
Physicians (SIC 8011)

Physican Organization Sales - 1999

The number of mergers & acquisitions involving medical practices has fallen to its lowest level in four years.

PPM	42.1%
Multispecialty practice	23.8
IPA	14.4
Remaining single-specialty practices	2.3
Orthopedics	1.8
Other	2.0

Source: *Modern Physician*, April 2000, p. 20, from *The Physician Medical Group Acquisition Report*.

★ 1952 ★
Nursing Homes (SIC 8050)

Largest Nursing Home Chains

Data show number of beds.

Beverly Enterprises	62,293
Mariner Post-Acute Network	49,656
HCR Manor Care	47,138

Continued on next page.

★ 1952 ★ *Continued*

Nursing Homes (SIC 8050)

Largest Nursing Home Chains

Data show number of beds.

Sun Healthcare Group	44,941
Integrated Health Services	44,302
Vencor	38,362
Genesis Health Centures	35,016
Life Care Centers of America	26,989

Source: *Provider*, July 1999, p. 56.

★ 1953 ★

Senior Housing (SIC 8050)

Senior Housing Construction - 1999

CCRC stands for continued care retirement community.

Assisted living	68%
Congregate	17
CCRCs	8
Senior apartments	7

Source: *Contemporary Long Term Care*, September 1999, p. 42.

★ 1954 ★

Assited Living Chains (SIC 8052)

Largest Assisted Living Chains - 1998

Companies are ranked by total assisted living beds as of December 31, 1998.

Alterra Healthcare Corp.	15,003
Emeritus Assisted Living	11,900
Marriott Senior Living Services	9,675
ARV Assisted Living	7,512
CareMatrix Corp.	7,345
Atria Senior Quarters	6,703
HCR Manor Care	5,752
Capital Senior Living	5,655
Sunrise Assitred Living	5,623

Source: *Provider*, July 1999, p. 52.

★ 1955 ★

Hospitals (SIC 8060)

Tampa Bay's Hospital Market

Shares are shown based on number of beds.

St. Joseph's Hospitals	6.41%
Tampa General Hospital	6.36
Lakeland Regional Medical Center	6.18
Sarasota Memorial Health Care System	6.13
Morton Plant Hospital	5.06
Bay Pines VA Medical Center	4.51
Other	65.40

Source: *Tampa Bay Business Journal*, December 1999, p. 20, from American Health Care Association.

★ 1956 ★

Home Health Care (SIC 8082)

Home Health Care Market - 1998

Olsten Health Services	4.0%
Apria Healthcare	3.6
Integrated Health Services	2.1
Other	90.3

Source: *Medical & Healthcare Marketplace Guide*, 1999, pp. I-956.

SIC 81 - Legal Services

★ 1957 ★

Legal Services (SIC 8111)

Largest Law Firms

| Skadden, Arps, Slate Meagher & Flom |
| Baker & Mckenzie |
| Jones, Day, Reavis & Pogue |

Data show gross fees in millions of dollars.

Skadden, Arps, Slate Meagher & Flom . . . $ 555
Baker & Mckenzie   510
Jones, Day, Reavis & Pogue 330

Source: *Financial Times*, January 1, 2000, p. 5, from *The Legal Business 100* and *American Lawyer 100*.

SIC 82 - Educational Services

★ 1958 ★

Schools (SIC 8211)

Largest Public School Enrollments

Total public school enrollments reached 46.8 million.

California	5.8
Texas	3.9
New York	2.9
Florida	2.3
Illinois	2.0
Ohio	1.8
Pennyslvania	1.8
Michigan	1.7

Source: *AS&U*, January 2000, p. 14, from National Center for Education Statistics.

★ 1959 ★

Universities (SIC 8221)

Largest College/University Enrollments

Data show total enrollment, in thousands.

California	1,959.9
New York	1,029.5
Texas	969.2
Illinois	726.1
Florida	658.2
Pennsylvania	588.1
Michigan	549.7
Ohio	537.7

Source: *AS&U*, January 2000, p. 14, from National Center for Education Statistics.

★ 1960 ★

Universities (SIC 8221)

Top Universities by R&D Funding

Funding is shown in millions of dollars.

Johns Hopkins University	$ 752.9
Stanford University	342.4
University of Washington	336.7
MIT	310.7
University of California, San Diego	262.3
Harvard University	251.8
University of Pennsylvania	247.9

Source: *Wired*, April 2000, p. 89, from Arbitron.

★ 1961 ★

Libraries (SIC 8231)

Largest Public Libraries

New York City
Queens, New York
Cincinnati and Hamilton County, Ohio
Chicago
Free Library of Philadelphia
County of Los Angeles
Carnegie Library of Pittsburgh
Boston

Data show millions of volumes.

New York City	11.4
Queens, New York	9.2
Cincinnati and Hamilton County, Ohio	8.6
Chicago	8.1
Free Library of Philadelphia	7.9
County of Los Angeles	7.4
Carnegie Library of Pittsburgh	6.6
Boston	6.6

Source: *Christian Science Monitor*, January 4, 2000, p. 12, from *Top 10 of Everything 2000*.

★ 1962 ★

Libraries (SIC 8231)

Public Library Spending

Libraries are expected to spend $977.2 million on materials in 1999.

Books	$ 766.4
Periodicals	134.2
Audiovisuals	38.6
Microfiche/film	19.2
Bindings	18.8

Source: *USA TODAY*, November 24, 1999, p. D1, from Book Industry Study Group.

★ 1963 ★

Libraries (SIC 8231)

Top Library Funders

| New York |
| Illinois |
| Pennsylvania |
| California |
| Massachusetts |

States are ranked by millions of dollars invested in libraries.

New York	$ 97.5
Illinois	63.2
Pennsylvania	43.8
California	42.8
Massachusetts	42.6

Source: *USA TODAY*, May 15, 2000, p. A1, from National Center for Education Statistics.

SIC 83 - Social Services

★ 1964 ★
Child Care (SIC 8351)

Child Care Centers in Canada

Independent, non-profit 31%
Proprietorship, for profit 14
Corporation, for profit 10
Govt sponsored, non-profit 7
Community sponsored, non-profit 7
Religious, non-profit 6
Other 25

Source: *Child Care Information Exchange*, March 2000, p. 10, from Lero.

★ 1965 ★
Child Care (SIC 8351)

Largest For-Profit Child Care Organizations

Data show capacity in North America.

KinderCare Learning Centers 145,100
La Peitiee Academy 108,000
Children's World Learning Centers . . . 77,551
Childtime Learning Centers 37,678
Bright Horizons Family Solutions Inc. . . 37,500
Knowledge Learning Corporation 30,411
Nobel Education Dynamics Inc. 26,000
Childcare Network Inc. 12,832
New Horizons Child Care 12,000

Source: *Child Care Information Exchange*, January 2000, p. 21.

★ 1966 ★
Charities (SIC 8399)

Charitable Contributions in 1998

Data are in billions of dollars.

Religion . . . . $ 76
Education 25
Foundations . . . . $ 17
Health 17
Human services 16
Arts/humanities 11
Public/social benefits 11
Environment/wildlife 5

Source: *USA TODAY*, June 29, 1999, p. A1, from AAFRC Trust for Philanthropy and Giving USA.

★ 1967 ★
Charities (SIC 8399)

Largest Charities - 1998

Institutions are ranked by income in millions of dollars.

The National Council of YMCAs . . . $ 3,248.7
Catholic Charities USA 2,309.0
Salvation Army 2,078.2
American Red Cross 2,057.8
Goodwill Industries International 1,503.7
Shriners Hospitals for Children 1,493.6
The Arc 1,261.8
Fidelity Investments Charitable Gift Fund . 695.3
Boy Scouts of America 648.9
YWCA of the USA 629.9

Source: *Christian Science Monitor*, December 6, 1999, p. 18, from *NonProfit Times* and *Chronicle of Philanthopy*.

★ 1968 ★
Charities (SIC 8399)

Largest Corporate Givers

Figures are for millions of dollars.

Merck . . . . $ 221.0
Johnson & Johnson 176.2
Pfizer 123.9
Eli Lilly 121.4

Continued on next page.

★ 1968 ★ *Continued*
Charities (SIC 8399)

Largest Corporate Givers

Figures are for millions of dollars.

IBM	$ 116.1
Microsoft	104.7
Intel	101.0
Bank of America	91.5
Procter & Gamble	73.2

Source: *Business Week*, January 24, 2000, p. 8, from The Taft Group.

★ 1969 ★
Charities (SIC 8399)

Largest Private Foundations

Firms are ranked by assets in billions of dollars.

Bill & Melinda Gates Foundation	$ 17.1
David and Lucille Packard Foundation	13.0
Ford Foundation	11.4
Lilly Endowment	11.1
Robert Wood Johnson Foundation	8.1
W.K. Kellogg Foundation	6.2
Pew Charitable Trusts	4.8

Source: *The Chronicle of Philanthropy*, August 26, 1999, p. 8.

★ 1970 ★
Charities (SIC 8399)

Who Gave to Charities in 1998

Individuals	77.3%
Foundations	9.8
Bequests	7.8
Corporations	5.1

Source: *Christian Science Monitor*, December 6, 1999, p. 14, from Giving USA and AAFRC Trust for Philanthropy.

★ 1971 ★
Charities (SIC 8399)

Who Received Donations in 1998

Religion	43.6%
Education	14.1
Foundations	9.7
Health	9.7

Human services	9.2%
Public/society	6.2
Arts	6.0
Other	4.2

Source: *Christian Science Monitor*, December 6, 1999, p. 14, from Giving USA and AAFRC Trust for Philanthropy.

SIC 84 - Museums, Botanical, Zoological Gardens

★ 1972 ★

Museums (SIC 8412)

Largest Museum Shows

Data show attendance, in thousands. A Century of Progress was held at The Art Institute; Rodin Discovered was held at National Gallery of Art; The Mona Lisa exhibit was held at the Metropolitan Museum.

A Century of Progress 1,500
Rodin Rediscovered 1,100
The Mona Lisa 1,100
Matisse: A Retrospective 940
Monet in the 20th Century 566

Source: *Business Week*, November 1, 1999, p. 8, from *Official Museum Directory* and museum staffs.

★ 1973 ★

Museums (SIC 8412)

Museums by Type

There are an estimated 15,000 libraries in the United States. Museums get an average of 865 million visitors a year and over half charge no admission.

Hisory museums 29.4%
Historic site 24.5
Art museum 14.8
General museum 8.6
Natural history museum/nature center 6.7
Specialized museum 5.7
Arboreteums/botanical gardens 3.9
Science museum 2.2
Other 3.2

Source: *New York Times*, April 19, 2000, p. 20, from American Association of Museums and American Museum of Natural History.

★ 1974 ★

Museums (SIC 8412)

New Museums Established 1998-2000

Specialized 14
History 10
Science 9
Art 7
Children's 6
Natural history 4
Aquarium 3
General 2

Source: *New York Times*, April 19, 2000, p. 20, from American Association of Museums and American Museum of Natural History.

★ 1975 ★

Gardens (SIC 8422)

Public Gardens by City

New York City, NY 1,906
Newark, NJ 1,318
Minneapolis, MN 536
Boston, MA 148

Source: *Garden Design*, July 1999, p. 30, from American Community Gardening Association.

SIC 86 - Membership Organizations

★ 1976 ★

Membership Organizations (SIC 8611)

Horse Group Memberships - 1999

Data are estimated, in thousands.

American Horse Shows Association 71,000
U.S. Dressage Federation 41,000
U.S. Trotting Association 28,500
U.S. Pony Clubs 12,750
National Cutting Horse Association . . . 12,000
U.S. Combined Training Association . . . 12,000

Source: *Equus*, November 1999, p. 265.

★ 1977 ★

Fan Clubs (SIC 8641)

Top Fan Clubs on Yahoo

Data show the membership on Yahoo's web site.

Hanson 21
'N Sync Official Club 6
South Park 4
Just Justin Timberlake 3
DX Suck It 2
The Original WWF Fan Club 2
Simpsons Uncovered Fan Club 2
Brittany Spears Unofficial Club 2

Source: *Industry Standard*, August 2, 1999, p. 92, from Yahoo.

SIC 87 - Engineering and Management Services

★ 1978 ★

Engineering Services (SIC 8711)

Canada's Consulting/Engineering Industry

More than 60% of engineering fees are generated by firms in Ontario and Quebec. Ontario is the focus of structural, mechanical and electrical building services. Quebec is in power and mining.

Primary resources processing 26%
Environmental 14
Building services 13
Power generation 11
Transportation 11
Municipal 9
Other 16

Source: *National Trade Data Bank,* STAT-USA, November 1, 1999.

★ 1979 ★

Engineering Services (SIC 8711)

Leading Engineering Firms

Firms are ranked by revenues in millions of dollars.

Fluor Daniel Inc. . . . . $ 288.32
Dames & Moore Inc. 229.00
BE&K Inc. 182.40
Day & Zimmermann International Inc. . . . 150.67
Raytheon Engineers & Constructors 122.38
Bechtel Group Inc. 109.41
Simons Engineering Inc. 64.90

Source: *Building Design & Construction,* July 1999, p. 4.

★ 1980 ★

Architectural Services (SIC 8712)

Canada's Architectural Industry

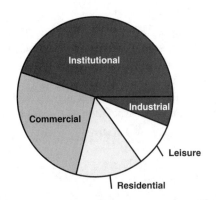

The industry generated nearly $599.6 million in direct revenues.

Institutional 45%
Commercial 26
Residential 14
Leisure 9
Industrial 6

Source: *National Trade Data Bank,* STAT-USA, November 1, 1999.

★ 1981 ★

Architectural Services (SIC 8712)

Leading Architects

Firms are ranked by revenues in millions of dollars.

Gensler . . . . $ 165.0
NBBJ 65.0
The Hillier Group 47.8
Zimmer Gunsul Frasca Partnership 35.0
Callison Architecture 34.4
Thompson, Ventulett, Stainback &
    Associates 30.9

Source: *Building Design & Construction,* July 1999, p. 4.

★ 1982 ★

Deisgn Firms (SIC 8712)

Largest Educational Facility Design Firms

Einhorn Yaffee Prescott

Shepley Bulfinch Richardson and Abbott

The Hillier Group

CBT/Childs Bertman Tseckares

Leo A Daly

Firms are ranked by design fees in millions of dollars.

Einhorn Yaffee Prescott	$ 7.5
Shepley Bulfinch Richardson and Abbott . . .	3.6
The Hillier Group	2.8
CBT/Childs Bertman Tseckares	2.6
Leo A Daly	2.3

Source: *Interior Design*, January 2000, p. 78.

★ 1983 ★

Design Firms (SIC 8712)

Largest Communications Industry Design Firms

Firms are ranked by design fees in thousands of dollars.

Gensler	$ 5.5
The Hillier Group	2.8
Mancini-Duffy	2.3
DBI Architects	2.0
RNL Design	2.0

Source: *Interior Design*, January 2000, p. 78.

★ 1984 ★

Design Firms (SIC 8712)

Largest Corporate/Office Design Firms

Firms are ranked by design fees in millions of dollars.

Gensler	$ 49.5
Hellmuth, Obata & Kassabaum	29.9
The Phillips Group	18.0
SpAce	16.0
Workplace Design Group	13.1

Source: *Interior Design*, January 2000, p. 78.

★ 1985 ★

Design Firms (SIC 8712)

Largest Medical Institution Design Firms

Firms are ranked by design fees in millions of dollars.

Perkins & Will	$ 5.2
Granary Associates	4.8
HKS	4.3
Loebl Schlossman & Hacki/Hague Ricahrds . .	3.0
NBBJ	3.0

Source: *Interior Design*, January 2000, p. 78.

★ 1986 ★

Design Firms (SIC 8712)

Largest Museum/Gallery Design Firms

Firms are ranked by design fees in thousands of dollars.

Gensler	$ 1,100
Skidmore, Owings & Merrill	1,029
Hellmuth, Obata & Kassabaum	393
TVS Interiors	347
RMW Architecture & Design	217

Source: *Interior Design*, January 2000, p. 78.

★ 1987 ★

Design Firms (SIC 8712)

Leading Retail Design Firms - 1999

Firms are ranked by store design fees in millions of dollars.

Callison Architecture Inc.	$ 36.3
Pavlik Design Team	31.7
Retail Planning Associates	21.5
Gensler	19.1
FRCH Design Worldwide	17.2
Carter & Burgess	16.1
Little & Associates Architects	16.0
Fitch	15.5
Entolo	11.4
Design Forum	11.0

Source: *VM + SD*, February 2000, p. 18.

★ 1988 ★
Design Firms (SIC 8712)

Top Educational Building Designers - 1998

Firms are ranked by design revenues in millions of dollars.

Jacobs Sverdrup	$ 38.0
URS Grenier Woodward-Clyde	35.7
DLR Group Inc.	31.0
Fanning/Howey Assocaites Inc.	30.8
SHW Group Inc.	20.3
HMC Group	19.5
Heery International Inc.	16.1

Source: *ENR*, July 1999, p. 46.

★ 1989 ★
Design Firms (SIC 8712)

Top Entertainment Building Designers - 1998

Firms are ranked by design revenues in millions of dollars.

Gould Evans Affiliates	$ 15.9
Hellmuth, Obata + Kassabaum	11.8
Parsons Corp.	11.1
Holmes & Narver	9.0
Gensler	7.9
Daniel, Mann, Johnson & Mendenhall	7.0

Source: *ENR*, July 1999, p. 46.

★ 1990 ★
Design Firms (SIC 8712)

Top Hotel/Motel/Convention Center Designers - 1998

Firms are ranked by design revenues in millions of dollars.

Smallwood, Reynolds, Stewart, Stewart & Associates	$ 15.6
RTKL Associates Inc.	15.4
Hellmuth, Obata + Kassabaum	14.8
Knutson Construction Co.	13.0
Brennan Beer Gorman/Architects	12.7
Parsons Brinckerhoff Inc.	11.6

Source: *ENR*, July 1999, p. 46.

★ 1991 ★
Design Firms (SIC 8712)

Top Manufacturing Facility Designers - 1998

Firms are ranked by design revenues in millions of dollars.

CH2M Hill Cos. Ltd.	$ 113.3
Lockwood Greene Engineers Inc.	98.8
General Physics Corp.	63.6
Dames & Moore Group	48.6
Morrison Knudsen Corp.	46.0
Lester B. Knight & Associates Inc.	39.7

Source: *ENR*, July 1999, p. 46.

★ 1992 ★
Design Firms (SIC 8712)

Top Petroleum Facility Designers - 1998

Firms are ranked by design revenues in millions of dollars.

Kellogg Brown & Root	$ 848.0
ABB Lummus Global Inc.	704.6
Foster Wheeler Corp.	508.5
Fluor Daniel Inc.	504.0
Bechtel Group Inc.	428.0
Parsons Corp.	301.2
Jacobs Sverdrup	282.0

Source: *ENR*, July 1999, p. 46.

★ 1993 ★
Design Firms (SIC 8712)

Top Warehouse Designers - 1998

Firms are ranked by design revenues in millions of dollars.

Parsons Brinckerhoff Inc.	$ 11.5
Carter & Burgess Inc.	10.1
URS Grenier Woodward-Clyde	7.9
Giffels Associates Inc.	7.9
Parsons Corp.	7.3
Earth Tech Inc.	7.0

Source: *ENR*, July 1999, p. 46.

★ **1994** ★

Accounting Services (SIC 8721)

Leading Accounting Firms - 1998

PricewaterhouseCoopers	
Ernst & Young	
Deloitte & Touche	
KPMG	
Arthur Andersen LLP	

Firms are ranked by fee income in billions of dollars.

PricewaterhouseCoopers	$ 5.85
Ernst & Young	5.54
Deloitte & Touche	4.70
KPMG	3.80
Arthur Andersen LLP	2.75

Source: *The Accountant*, May 1999, p. 17, from *International Accounting Bulletin*.

★ **1995** ★

Accounting Services (SIC 8721)

Leading Accounting Firms in Canada

Firms are ranked by fee income in millions of Canadian dollars.

PricewaterhouseCoopers	720.0
KPMG	688.5
Deloitte & Touche	669.0
Ernsy & Young	575.0
Grant Thornton Canada	214.4

Source: *Accountancy International*, May 1999, p. 11.

★ **1996** ★

Accounting Services (SIC 8721)

Leading Accounting Firms in Canada - 1998

Firms are ranked by fee income in millions of Canadian dollars.

PriceWaterhouseCoopers	741.1
KPMG LLP	688.5
Deloitte & Touche	669.0
Ernst & Young	531.0
Grant Thornton Canada	214.4
Arthur Andersen	165.0

Source: *The Accountant*, July 1999, p. 14, from *International Accounting Bulletin*.

★ **1997** ★

Accounting Services (SIC 8721)

Top Accounting Firms in the Midwest States - 1998

Firms are ranked by revenues in millions of dollars.

Baird Kurtz & Dobson	$ 98.0
Larson Allen Weishair & Co.	59.1
Eide Bailly	33.5
Rubin, Brown, Gornstein & Co.	18.7
Kennedy & Coe	18.2
Lurie, Besikof, Lapidus & Co.	13.0

Source: *Practical Accountant*, April 1999, p. S12.

★ **1998** ★

Accounting Services (SIC 8721)

Top Accounting Firms in the Mountain States - 1998

Firms are ranked by revenues in millions of dollars.

Heinz & Associates	$ 12.5
Galusha, Higgins and Galusha	11.0
Ehrhardt Keefe Steiner & Hottman	10.5
Anderson ZurMuehlen & Co.	7.9
Gelfond Hochstadt Pangburn & Co.	6.5
Brock & Company	5.8

Source: *Practical Accountant*, April 1999, p. S12.

★ **1999** ★

Noncommercial Research (SIC 8733)

DOE Weapons Labs

Data show funding in billions of dollars.

Sandia	$ 1.29
Lawrence Livermore	1.25
Los Alamos	1.24

Source: *C&EN*, December 6, 1999, p. 27, from Department of Energy.

★ 2000 ★

Medical Testing (SIC 8734)

Independent Medical Testing Market in California

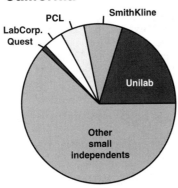

The California medical lab market is valued at $4 billion.

Unilab	20%
SmithKline	8
PCL	5
LabCorp.	4
Quest	1
Other small independents	62

Source: *Sacremento Business Journal*, April 30, 1999, p. 26.

★ 2001 ★

Construction Management (SIC 8741)

Leading Construction Managers

Firms are ranked by revenues in millions of dollars.

Bovis Inc.	$ 2,493.70
Gilbane Building Co.	2,065.94
Heery International Inc.	1,275.00
Tishman Construction Corp.	1,005.48
Parsons Brinckerhoff	950.00
3D/International	944.09
H&N/McClier	800.90

Source: *Building Design & Construction*, July 1999, p. 4.

★ 2002 ★

Construction Management (SIC 8741)

Leading Construction Managmeent For- Fee Firms

Firms are ranked by fees in millions of dollars.

Parsons Corp.	$ 850.4
Bechtel Group Inc.	729.0
Kellogg Brown & Root	669.0
Foster Wheeler Corp.	479.0
Jacobs Sverdrup	365.0
Fluor Daniel Inc.	362.0
CH2M Hill Inc.	343.7

Source: *ENR*, June 14, 1999, p. 54.

★ 2003 ★

Public Relations Services (SIC 8743)

Largest PR Firms in St. Louis, MO - 1998

Companies are ranked by local income in thousands of dollars.

Fleishman-Hillard	$ 40,349
Shandwick International	4,045
Kupper Parker Communciations	2,557
The Standing Partnership	1,276
The Vandiver Group	874

Source: *PR Week*, August 23, 1999, p. 17, from Council of Public Relations Firms.

★ 2004 ★

Public Relations Services (SIC 8743)

Top PR Agencies in New Jersey - 1998

Companies are ranked by income.

The MRR Group	$ 9,200,519
Gillespie	1,892,049
Star/Rosen PR	1,066,000
Danlee Public Relations	896,000
Torre Lazur/Weber PR	470,000

Source: *PR Week*, November 22, 1999, p. 25.

★ 2005 ★

Public Relations Services (SIC 8743)

Top PR Firms in Keystone, PA - 1998

Companies are ranked by income in millions of dollars.

Ketchum PR 7.7
BSMG (The Tierney Group) 6.3
Burson-Marsteller 4.8
Dorland Sweeney Jones 2.9
Earle Palmer Brown PR 2.1

Source: *PR Week*, December 20, 1999, p. 27.

★ 2006 ★

Public Relations Services (SIC 8743)

Top PR Firms in San Francisco, CA

Firms are ranked by fee income in millions of dollars.

Fleishman-Hillard . . . . $ 19,201
Hill & Knowlton 16,743
Burson-Marsteller 16,528
Ketchum 15,594
GCI Group 12,170
Niehaus Ryan Wong 9,527
Access Communications 9,069
Golin/Harris 7,730
Alexander Ogilvy 7,420

Source: *PR Week*, May 22, 2000, p. 21.

★ 2007 ★

Public Relations Services (SIC 8743)

Top PR Firms in Washington D.C. - 1998

Firms are ranked by revenues in millions of dollars.

Burson-Marsteller . . . . $ 32.9
Hill & Knowlton 27.0
Fleishman-Hilliard 19.6
Ketchum 18.9
Porter Novelli 17.5
Ogilvy PR Worldwide 16.2
Powell Tate 15.7

Source: *New York Times*, November 16, 1999, p. C1, from *O'Dwyer's Directory of Public Relations Firms.*

★ 2008 ★

Human Resource Consulting (SIC 8748)

Largest Benefits Consultants - 1999

Firms are ranked by estimated revenues in millions of dollars.

Hewitt Associates . . . . $ 904.6
Towers Perrin 685.8
William M. Mercer Cos. 660.0
PricewaterhouseCoopers 499.7
Watson Wyatt Worldwide 388.3
Aon Consulting Worldwide 328.3
Buck Consultants Inc. 288.0

Source: *Business Insurance*, December 13, 1999, p. 4.

SIC 92 - Justice, Public Order, and Safety

★ 2009 ★

Prisons (SIC 9223)

Prisoners by State

California 124,813
New York 69,529
Florida 65,117
Ohio 47,116
Michigan 41,625

Source: *New York Times*, November 30, 1999, p. A20,
from Florida House of Representatives.

SIC 94 - Administration of Human Resources

★ 2010 ★

Health Department (SIC 9431)

Top Contractors with Health/Human Services

The leading contractors are ranked by market shares of total contracts.

James Management Corp.	5.94%
Science Applications Intl. Corp.	4.24
Westat Inc.	4.24
Research Triangle Institute	1.89
Other	83.64

Source: *Government Executive*, Annual 1999, p. 93.

★ 2011 ★

Veterans Affairs (SIC 9451)

Top Contractors with the Veterans Affairs Dept.

The top contractors are ranked by market shares of contracts.

Amerisource Distribution Corp.	11.70%
Compaq Computer Corp.	2.63
Bindley Western Industries	2.23
McKesson Corp.	1.38
General Electric Co.	1.36
Other	80.70

Source: *Government Executive*, Annual 1999, p. 94.

SIC 95 - Environmental Quality and Housing

★ 2012 ★

Environmental Services (SIC 9510)

Leading Environmental Firms - 1998

Firms are ranked by revenues derived from providing environmental products and services to companies. Data are in millions of dollars.

U.S. Filter Corp.	$ 4,608.0
Bechtel Group Inc.	2,597.9
Foster Wheeler Corp.	1,373.0
The IT Group	1,295.0
URS Group	1,090.0
CH2M Hill Inc.	1,017.0
ICF Kaiser International Inc.	985.2
Fluor Daniel Inc.	818.7
EARTH TECH	720.0
Black & Veatch	640.0

Source: *ENR*, July 5, 1999, p. 52.

SIC 96 - Administration of Economic Programs

★ 2013 ★

Transportation Department (SIC 9621)

Top Contractors with the Transportation Dept.

The leading contractors are ranked by market shares of total contracts.

Raytheon Co.	9.04%
IBM Corp.	5.52
Lockheed Martin Corp.	4.42
Computer Sciences Corp.	2.57
Marinette Marine Corp.	2.23
Other	76.22

Source: *Government Executive*, Annual 1999, p. 94.

★ 2014 ★

Transportation Department (SIC 9621)

Transportation Infrastructure Spending - 2002

Government and private transportation spending has been increasing steadily since the passage of the Transportation Equity Act for the 21st Century in 1998. Spending is shown in billions of dollars.

	($ bil.)	Share
Highway	$ 104.9	55.01%
Transit	33.9	17.78
Air	25.5	13.37
Private	17.4	9.12
Water	8.1	4.25
Rail	0.9	0.47

Source: *Traffic World*, October 18, 1999, p. 21, from American Road & Transportation Builders Association.

★ 2015 ★

Agricultural Department (SIC 9641)

Top Contractors with the Agriculture Dept.

The leading contractors are ranked by market shares of total contracts.

ConAgra Inc.	5.19%
IBM Corp.	4.73
Continental Grain Co.	4.45
Cargill Inc.	3.55
Cal Western Packaging Corp.	3.43
Other	78.65

Source: *Government Executive*, Annual 1999, p. 93.

★ 2016 ★

Defense (SIC 9661)

Top NASA Contractors

Total spending reached $9.8 billion.

Boeing	16.9%
United Space Alliance	13.4
Lockheed Martin	10.7
Thiokol	4.3
Other	54.7

Source: *Wired*, February 2000, p. 84.

SOURCE INDEX

This index is divided into *primary sources* and *original sources*. Primary sources are the publications where the market shares were found. Original sources are sources cited in the primary sources. Numbers following the sources are entry numbers, arranged sequentially; the first number refers to the first appearance of the source in *Market Share Reporter*. All told, 1025 organizations are listed.

Primary Sources

"1998 Internet Sales of Supplements Hits $40M." Retrieved October 5, 1999 from the World Wide Web: http://www.nbj.net/news7.htm, 1605

"1999 Market Share by Company." Retrieved April 18, 2000 from the World Wide Web: http://www.meierteam.com, 1805

"1999 UDM Top 50." Retrieved January 21, 2000 from the World Wide Web: http://www.fdmmag.com/top50.htm, 479

20 20 Magazine, 1617-1618

"5th Annual Packaging Machinery Outlook Study." Retrieved April 20, 2000 from the World Wide Web: http://www.packaging-technology.org, 866-867

"A Modern Soap Story." Retrieved February 29, 2000 from the World Wide Web: http://www.exposemagazine.com, 1664

AAII Journal, 1066, 1729

ABA Banking Journal, 1698-1699

"About the Industry." Retrieved February 29, 2000 from the World Wide Web: http://www.sleepproducts.org, 483

Accountancy International, 1995

The Accountant, 1994, 1996

Advertising Age, 177, 183, 211, 233, 250, 277, 327, 332, 380, 419, 423, 428, 604, 617, 627, 638, 647, 666, 692, 707, 793, 945, 961, 1373, 1375, 1829-1830, 1907

Advisor Today, 1714, 1744

Adweek, 530, 532-533

Aerospace America, 1052

Aftermarket Business, 1091, 1485, 1487, 1917

Ag Lender, 84

Air Cargo World, 1287

AISE Steel Technology, 822

"Alberta Potato Industry." Retrieved July 21, 1999 from the World Wide Web: http://www.cadvision.com/Home_Pages, 38

"All Charged Up About Batteries." Retrieved January 26, 2000 from the World Wide Web: http://www.exposemagazine.com, 1622

"Alternative Delivery Systems." Retrieved May 25, 2000 from the World Wide Web: http://www.ahcpub.com, 1148

American Ceramic Society Bulletin, 816, 818, 868, 1142, 1145

American Clinical Laboratory, 1116, 1119-1120, 1122-1123, 1125, 1127-1128, 1134-1135, 1138, 1140

American Ink Maker, 553, 733, 753-754

American Laboratory, 1115, 1124, 1129-1133, 1136-1137, 1139, 1141

American Medical News, 1581

American Metal Market, 819, 821, 823, 827, 830, 834, 837

American Printer, 554, 556, 1839

American Shipper, 1289

"An Inside Look at Housewares." Retrieved January 26, 2000 from the World Wide Web: http://www.exposemagazine.com, 11

"An Overview of Underarms." Retrieved February 22, 2000 from the World Wide Web: http://www.exposemagazine.com, 680

Appliance, 905, 907, 913, 920, 923, 926, 929, 932-933, 936-937, 939, 942, 947, 950-951, 953, 955, 957, 959-960, 963-964, 966, 970, 972, 975, 983, 985, 1010, 1017

Appliance Manufacturer, 857-861, 914-917, 919, 921, 935, 938, 941, 943-944, 946, 948-949, 952, 954, 956, 958, 962, 965, 967-969, 973, 976, 980, 984, 988

AS&U, 1958-1959

Assembly, 24, 1234

"AT&T Overtakes Sprint as Leader in Packet/Cell-Based Services." Retrieved November 19, 1999 from the World Wide Web: http://www.idc.com, 1319

"Athletic Apparel Market Share Report." Retrieved May 1, 2000 from the World Wide Web: http://www.businesswire.com, 445, 449, 451

"Athletic Footwear Market Share Report Announced." Retrieved April 10, 2000 from the World Wide Web: http://www.businesswire.com, 767, 769

"Athletic Footwear Sales Decline for 1998." Retrieved December 2, 1999 from the World Wide Web: http://www.npd.com, 773-775

ATI, 590

Atlanta Business Chronicle, 1146

Atlanta Journal-Constitution, 370, 1413

"Aurora Foods Completes Lender's Bagles." Retrieved May 2, 2000 from the World Wide Web: http://www.aurorafoods.com, 264

Auto Body Repair News, 1916

Automatic Merchandiser, 1608-1609

Automotive Industries, 1092, 1100

Automotive News, 1484

AVG, 39-42

Baking Business, 274, 1634

Baltimore Business Journal, 1690, 1798

"Banamex-Bancomer Merger Would Result in 39% Share." Retrieved May 5, 2000 from the World Wide Web: http://library.northernlight.com, 1682

Bank Network News, 908, 910

The Banker, 1700

Banking Strategies, 1686

Best's Review, 1713, 1716, 1738, 1742, 1746, 1748-1759, 1761, 1763, 1768-1782, 1784-1797

Beverage Digest, 366, 379

Beverage Industry, 198, 333, 335, 342, 345, 363-365, 373-374

Beverage World, 334, 340, 368, 377

Beverage World 2000 Databank, 344, 362

Bicycle Retailer & Industry News, 1107, 1109

Billboard, 994, 999, 1007, 1009

Bobbin, 454

The Boston Globe, 1070, 1726

Brandweek, 146, 210, 369, 431, 696, 897, 1197, 1305

Brill's Content, 14

Broadcasting & Cable, 1378, 1396, 1399

Broiler Industry, 1, 1551

BtoB, 1344, 1838

Builder, 102, 112, 114, 475

Builder Online, 1708

Building Design & Construction, 115, 1979, 1981, 2001

Building Material Dealer, 128-129

"Business, Finance Led '99 Software Sales." Retrieved March 27, 2000 from the World Wide Web: http://www.pcdata.com, 1862, 1864-1869

Business 2.0, 1337, 1370-1371, 1832

Business & Health, 1910

Business Communications Review, 1026, 1028, 1030, 1045

Business Insurance, 1683, 1740-1741, 2008

The Business Journal of Portland, 1039

Business Marketing, 1818, 1828, 1831

Business News New Jersey, 1467

Business Week, 1592, 1968, 1972

Business Week Frontier, 911

C&EN, 574, 631, 731-732, 745-746, 1643-1644, 1646, 1999

"CallWave's Internet Answering Machine Leads." Retrieved May 18, 2000 from the World Wide Web: http://www.businesswire.net, 1859

"CAM a $27B Market." Retrieved October 5, 1999 from the World Wide Web: http://www.nbj.net/news8.htm, 1948

"Campbell Soup Reports Disappointing Earnings." Retrieved May 30, 2000 from the World Wide Web: http://www.library.northernlight.com, 191

Canadian Grocer, 254

Candy Business, 307

Card Fax, 1704

Cards International, 1703

CCJ, 1096, 1101, 1261-1263, 1265

"Cell & Tissue Markets Showing Healthy Growth." Retrieved January 13, 2000 from the World Wide Web: http://www.phortech.com/97cell.htm, 1117

Ceramic Bulletin, 848, 1250

Cereal Foods World, 139

Chain Drug Review, 10, 286, 426, 494, 496-497, 509, 599-600, 606-609, 613, 644-645, 662-663, 675-677, 682, 686, 697, 699-700, 704, 714, 719-721, 725, 791, 842, 1247, 1573-1575, 1579, 1629, 1657-1658, 1661, 1663, 1665, 1667, 1669, 1676

Chain Store Age, 1437-1438

"Change of Pace." Retrieved June 1, 2000 from the World Wide Web: http://www.gosmokeshop.com/0899/report.htm, 1615

Chemical Engineering, 567, 740, 817, 1340, 1843-1844

Chemical Week, 560-562, 565, 568-569, 632, 634, 642, 728, 730, 737, 742-743, 751, 758, 788, 1254, 1264, 1416

Chicago Tribune, 202, 279, 516, 711

Child Care Information Exchange, 1964-1965

Christian Science Monitor, 76, 515, 729, 1222, 1961, 1967, 1970-1971

The Chronicle of Philanthropy, 1969

"Cider." Retrieved January 25, 2000 from the World Wide Web: http://www.beveragebusiness.com/art%2Darch/99estes10.html, 349

Cincinnati Enquirer, 1475, 1827, 1912, 1942

CIO Enterprise, 1332

CMR, 137, 570-571, 586-587, 727, 735-736, 738-739, 741, 1058, 1426

CMR Focus, 564, 566, 591, 1260

"Collectible Doll Market Maturing." Retrieved January 20, 2000 from the World Wide Web: http://www.unitymarketingonline.com, 1190

Communications of the ACM, 1858

Computer Graphics World, 1846

Milling & Baking News, 240

Milwaukee Journal Sentinel, 512

Mining Engineering, 91

MMR, 165, 190, 257-258, 330, 393-394, 492, 504, 507-508, 510-511, 610, 614-615, 637, 640, 643, 646, 652-655, 657, 747, 749, 755, 835, 1072, 1175, 1184, 1248, 1422, 1535, 1603, 1619, 1621, 1623-1625, 1636-1637, 1647-1648, 1652-1654, 1674, 1677-1678, 1680

Modern Casting, 1024

Modern Materials Handling, 473

Modern Physician, 1764-1765, 1951

Modern Plastics, 18, 865

Motor Truck, 1271

Music Trades, 1186, 1534, 1536

National Home Center News, 85, 750, 1431, 1433-1434

National Petroleum News, 1490

National Real Estate Investor, 1800

National Trade Data Bank, STAT-USA, 1886, 1978, 1980

National Underwriter, 1743, 1760

Nation's Restaurant News, 1537, 1552-1555, 1565-1567, 1569-1570

Network World, 885, 1892, 1901

"New Beverage Marketing Report Surveys Beverage Market." Retrieved April 26, 2000 from the World Wide Web: http://ww.just-drinks.com, 336

"New Study by RHK Shows Cisco Secure Top Billing." Retrieved April 24, 2000 from the World Wide Web: http://www.businesswire.com, 1033

New York Times, 4, 6, 8, 43, 53, 64, 66, 93, 187, 396, 517, 529, 593, 770, 828, 875, 982, 1048, 1076, 1087, 1090, 1171, 1191, 1279, 1309, 1333, 1341, 1351, 1354, 1401, 1404, 1439, 1588, 1712, 1719-1721, 1724, 1727, 1731, 1745, 1872, 1929, 1934, 1940, 1944, 1973-1974, 2007, 2009

Newsweek, 1702

Nonwovens Industry, 493

"NPD HomeTrak Reports Almost $2B in RTA Sales." Retrieved April 24, 2000 from the World Wide Web: http://www.businesswire.com, 480

"NPD INTELECT Reports Year End Data for PDA Category." Retrieved March 8, 2000 the World Wide Web: http://www.npd.com/corp/press, 880

"NPD Intelect Sees Digital Imaging Going Mainstream." Retrieved May 1, 2000 from the World Wide Web: http://www.intelectmt.com, 986

"NPD Reports Fryer Sales Sizzle." Retrieved December 2, 1999 from the World Wide Web: http://www.intelectmt.com/corp/intelectmt/press, 934

"NPD Reports U.S. Apparel Sales." Retrieved February 29, 2000 from the World Wide Web: http://library.northernlight.com, 443

Nursery Retailer, 63, 854-855

OR Manager, 1154

PC Computing, 1897

PC Magazine, 1174, 1355

"Pennzoil-Quaker State Reports First Quarter." Retrieved May 11, 2000 from the World Wide Web: http://www.prnewswire.com, 760

Pensions & Investments, 1717

"Pet Food Market." Retrieved September 21, 1999 from the World Wide Web: http://atn-riae.agr.ca/public/htmldocs/e2124.htm, 251

Pet Product News, 255

"Phosphate Rock." Retrieved April 10, 2000 from the World Wide Web: http://www.flaphos.org/Facts97.html, 100

Pipeline & Gas Journal, 1411-1412

Pit & Quarry, 97, 99

Pittsburgh Post-Gazette, 1945

Plastics News, 17, 19, 21, 572-573, 575-585, 778, 787, 789, 800

Playthings, 1187-1188, 1192-1193, 1196, 1198, 1240, 1598-1599

Pork, 65, 1478

Poultry & Egg Marketing, 150

Power Engineering, 1071, 1144, 1409

PR Week, 2003-2006

Practical Accountant, 1997-1998

Prepared Foods, 133

Printing Impressions, 550

Professional Candy Buyer, 298-299

Progressive Grocer, 185, 192, 194, 215, 247, 385, 417, 421, 1463, 1465, 1620

"Promise Technology Attains 90% Unit Share." Retrived April 10, 2000 from the World Wide Web: http://www.internetwire.com, 888

"PROMO 100." Retrieved November 11, 1999 from the World Wide Web: http://www.promomagazine/Magazines/Promo, 22

"Provident Regains Top Spot." Retrieved January 13, 2000 from the World Wide Web: http://www.amcity.com/cincinnati/stories, 1681

Provider, 1952, 1954

"Psst Here's the Dirt on Household Cleaners." Retrieved February 15, 2000 from the World Wide Web: http://wwww.cdngrocer.com, 649

Publishers Weekly, 543-545, 1593

Pulp & Paper, 487-488, 490-491

Purchasing, 832, 1179

Railway Age, 1106

RCR, 1019

"RealNetworks Market Share Well Earned." Retrieved December 13, 1999 From the World Wide Web: http://home.zdnet.co.desk/talkback, 1889

Retrieved January 11, 2000 from the World Wide Web: http://www.gosmokeshop.com, 430, 1616

Retrieved January 11, 2000 from the World Wide Web: http://www.library.northernlight.com, 195

Retrieved January 13, 2000 from the World Wide Web: http://strategisgroup.com/press/pubs/uspage99.html, 1310

Retrieved January 13, 2000 from the World Wide Web: http://www.amcity.com/sanantonio/stories/1999/12/20/story2.html, 338

Retrieved January 13, 2000 from the World Wide Web: http://www.amcity.com/philadelphia/stories/1999/06/28/focus5.html, 1113

Retrieved January 13, 2000 from the World Wide Web: http://www.amcity.com/sanantonio/stories/1999/12/20/story2.html, 1461

Retrieved January 13, 2000 from the World Wide Web: http://www.amcity.com/buffalo/stories/1999/05/17/newscolumn1.html, 1466, 1474

Retrieved January 13, 2000 from the World Wide Web: http://www.amcity.com/memphis/stories/1999/11/08/story3.html, 1576-1577

Retrieved January 13, 2000 from the World Wide Web: http://www.amcity.com/dallas/stories/1999/11/08/story1.html, 1578

Retrieved January 13, 2000 from the World Wide Web: http://www.amcity.com/sanfrancisco/stories/1999/05/31/story2.html, 1931

Retrieved January 13, 2000 from the World Wide Web: http://www.phortech.com/98cytok.htm, 1121

Retrieved January 13, 2000 from the World Wide Web: http://www.strategisgroup.com/press/pubs/radio.html, 1380

Retrieved January 14, 2000 from the World Wide Web: http://www.amcity.com/triad/stories/1999/11/01/story6.html, 802

Retrieved January 17, 2000 from the World Wide Web: http://library.northernlight.com, 993, 1001

Retrieved January 17, 2000 from the World Wide Web: http://www.store.yahoo.com/nbj/aninov99.html, 15

Retrieved January 18, 2000 from the World Wide Web: http://www.bizlink.com, 371, 1679

Retrieved January 18, 2000 from the World Wide Web: http://www.cruisetrade.com/berthcap.html, 1307

Retrieved January 18, 2000 from the World Wide Web: http://www.limousinecentral.com/noflash/operate1.cfn, 1259

Retrieved January 18, 2000 from the World Wide Web: http://www.nass.usda.gov/fl/misc/98aqua14.htm, 80

Retrieved January 18, 2000 from the World Wide Web: http://www.simbanet.com/press/headlines/em_01-03.htm, 546-547

Retrieved January 20, 2000 from the World Wide Web: http://www.activemedia-guide.com/prem_icecream.htm, 175

Retrieved January 20, 2000 from the World Wide Web: http://www.mcas.com/Altigen2.htm, 1044

Retrieved January 20, 2000 from the World Wide WebL: http://www.actovemedia-guide.com/mrk_3835.htm, 1811

Retrieved January 21, 2000 from the World Wide Web: http://strategis.ic.gc.ca/SSG, 444, 768, 1209, 1211-1213, 1219-1220, 1225, 1499, 1504, 1585-1587

Retrieved January 26, 2000 from the World Wide Web: http://www.exposemagazine.com, 664, 722, 1073

Retrieved January 26, 2000 from the World Wide Web: http://www.hkeia.com/E-news/enewsdec/colorTV.htm, 990-992

Retrieved March 1, 2000 from the World Wide Web: http://library.northernlight.com, 1472

Retrieved March 1, 2000 from the World Wide Web: http://www.ahcpub.com, 1147, 1149

Retrieved March 1, 2000 from the World Wide Web: http://www.catalogagemag.com, 1607

Retrieved March 1, 2000 from the World Wide Web: http://www.gartnergroup.com/dq/static/about/press, 906

Retrieved March 1, 2000 from the World Wide Web: http://www.husa.com/annualreport/home.html, 209

Retrieved March 1, 2000 from the World Wide Web: http://www.retailmerchandising.net, 325

Retrieved March 1, 2000 from the World Wide Web: http://www.simbanet.com/press/headlines, 1913

Rice Journal, 33

Risk, 1733

Rock Products, 98

Rolling Stone, 995-996

Rough Notes, 1736-1737

Rubber & Plastics News, 588-589, 763, 779, 792

Sacremento Business Journal, 2000

''Salad Dessing and Sauce Trends.'' Retrieved January 11, 2000 from the World Wide Web: http://www.dressings-sauces.org/trends.html, 142

Security Magazine, 1906

The Shepard, 68

Shopping Center World, 1799

''Siemens and CTI Inc.'' Retrieved April 20, 2000 from the World Wide Web: http://library.northernlight.com, 1181

''Simba Predicts Corporate Training Market.'' Retrieved November 1, 1999 from the World Wide Web: http://www.simbanet.com/press, 1946

Snack Food & Wholesale Bakery, 138, 159-160, 162-164, 170, 182, 205-207, 231-232, 234, 265, 269, 273, 278, 283, 300, 302-303, 322, 329, 395, 397, 399, 401-402, 404-407, 409-410

''Soft Drink Sales Increased 0.6% in 1999.'' Retrieved April 13, 2000 from the World Wide Web: http://www.just-drinks.com, 383

Ward's Dealer Busienss, 1094

Washington Post, 189, 429, 846, 1097, 1614

Washington Technology, 1326, 1849

Waste Age, 23, 1418, 1420

Waste News, 1417, 1419

Water Engineering & Management, 1415

WATT PoultryUSA, 70

''Web/Online Information Market Forecast to Hit $40B.''
 Retrieved January 6, 2000 from the World Wide Web:
 http://www.simbanet.com/press, 1350

Windows NT Magazine, 892-893

Wines & Vines, 48, 348

''Winn-Dixie Sales Slip in Atlanta Grocery War.''
 Retrieved April 10, 2000 from the World Wide Web:
 http://library.northernlight.com, 1460

''Winn-Dixie Struggles.'' Retrieved May 5, 2000 from
 the World Wide Web: http://library.northernlight.com,
 1470

Wired, 25-26, 1323, 1339, 1363, 1960, 2016

Wireless Week, 1043, 1321

Wood & Wood Products, 471-472, 485

Wood Digest, 29-30, 1428

Wood Digest - Industry Trends Report, 122

Wood Technology, 468-470

''World Drug Purchases.'' Retrieved April 20, 2000 from
 the World Wide Web: http://www.imshealth.com,
 625-626

World Oil, 94-96

WWD, 455, 459-460, 534, 668-669, 673-674, 684, 693,
 703, 712, 718, 807-808, 1497-1498, 1503, 1572

WWD Fairchild 100 Supplement, 437, 838

''XYPOINT Takes 80% Market Share in U.S.''
 Retrieved May 5, 2000 from the World Wide Web:
 http://www.businesswire.com, 1051

Yahoo! Internet Life, 1352

''Youth Bikes - Hot!'' Retrieved November 22, 1999
 from the World Wide Web: http://www.nbda.com/
 youth.htm, 1110

Original Sources

PLACE NAMES INDEX

This index shows countries, political entities, states and provinces, regions within countries, parks, airports, and cities. The numbers that follow listings are entry numbers; they are arranged sequentially so that the first mention of a place is listed first. The index shows references to more than 170 places.

Place Names Index

PRODUCTS, SERVICES, NAMES, AND ISSUES INDEX

This index shows, in alphabetical order, references to products, services, personal names, and issues covered in *Market Share Reporter*, 11th Edition. More than 1,870 terms are included. Terms include subjects not readily categorized as products and services, including such subjects as *crime* and *welfare*. The numbers that follow each term refer to entry numbers and are arranged sequentially so that the first mention is listed first.

Flooring contractors, 1506

Flooring stores, 1506

Florists, 1613

Flour, 242, 247

Flowers, 56-62, 750, 1338-1339

Flowers, cut, 1614

Flurocarbons, 736

Fluropolymer precursors, 736

Foam blowing agents, 736

Food, 7, 35, 74, 133-142, 146, 149, 153, 156-159, 161-164
168, 191, 212, 216, 218-220, 222, 224-226, 231, 233,
236-241, 243-245, 250, 259-260, 263-265, 269, 272,
278-279, 281-282, 284, 315, 328-329, 387-389, 412-413
415-416, 424, 565, 731, 758, 1271, 1425, 1486, 1500,
1551, 1597, 1611, 1635, 1640, 1649, 1822

Food, breakfast, 226

Food, canned, 385

Food, ethnic, 424

Food, hand-held, 222

Food, health, 139

Food, natural, 15, 1477

Food, organic, 82

Food and beverages, 1338-1339

Food and drug stores, 1590-1591, 1657-1658, 1661, 1663,
1665, 1667

Food choppers, 951

Food containers, 788

Food preparations, 417, 421

Food processors, 952

Food stores, 1422, 1594-1595, 1622, 1626, 1629-1630,
1633, 1638-1639, 1641-1642, 1645, 1650-1651,
1655-1656, 1659-1660, 1662, 1666, 1668-1670, 1673

Foodservice, 1301, 1482, 1537-1545

Foodservice, business, 1538

Foot care products, 683, 1660

Football, 1938

Football equipment, 1212

Footballs, 1212

Footwear, 768, 771-772, 796, 802-804, 1217, 1223

Footwear, athletic, 767, 769-770, 773-775

Footwear, basketball, 767

Footwear, cleated, 767

Forks, 1523

Form/fill/seal machinery, 866

Formulations, 732

Foundations, 1966, 1969

Fountain pens, 1233

Fractional ownership industry, 1285

Fragrances, 684-686

Frame relay, 1319

Frames, 1602, 1618

Franchising, 1807

Frankfurters, refrigerated, 147

Franks, cocktail, refrigerated, 147

Free-standing inserts (advertising), 550

Freezers, 936

French fries, 225

Freshwater fish, 20

Frozen bakery products, 272, 282

Frozen desserts, 167, 169, 171, 176

Frozen dinners, 221, 230, 238

Frozen food industry, 149, 166, 216-218, 221-228,
230-232, 234-235, 238, 240-241, 281-284, 387-389, 412

Frozen yogurt, 169, 173

Fruit, 32, 45-48, 52-55, 1539

Fruit, canned, 192

Fruit, citrus, 32

Fruit, dried, 205-206

Fruit, frozen, 219

Fruit, mixed, 192

Fruit roll-ups, 401

Fuel cells, 868, 1071

Fume hoods, 1124

Functional food industry, 139

Funeral services, 1817

Fungicides, 746

Furnaces, 921

Furniture, 11, 467, 478-482, 1271, 1506

Furniture, bedroom, 480-481

Furniture, entertainment, 480

Furniture, office, 480

Furniture, wood, 776

Furniture polish, 655, 1624

Furniture stores, 1507, 1511, 1517

Galleries, 1986

Gambling, 1941-1943

Garages, 27

Garbage, 1418

Garbage disposals, 975

Gardening, 85

Gardens, 1973, 1975

Garment bags, 805

Gas pumps, 924

Gas stations, 1490

Gases, 561

Gaskets, 784

Gauze, 1151

Gays and Lesbians, 1303

Gelatin, 417

Gift wrap, ribbons, bows, 10

Gifts, 686, 811, 854, 1347

Gin, 351-352

Girdles, 436

Glass, 17-19, 817

Glass cleaner, 650

Glasses, 811-813, 1516, 1521

Products, Services, Names, and Issues Index

Products, Services, Names, and Issues Index

COMPANY INDEX

The more than 3,260 companies and institutions in this book are indexed here in alphabetical order. Numbers following the terms are entry numbers. They are arranged sequentially; the first entry number refers to the first mention of the company in *Market Share Reporter*. Although most organizations appear only once, some entities are referred to under abbreviations in the sources and these have not always been expanded.

@Home, 1375
20th Century Fox, 1926
21 Club, 1546
21st Century Communications, 1724
3Com, 874, 1026, 1042, 1047
3D/International, 2001
3M Corp., 1155
7-Eleven Inc., 1442, 1807
84 Lumber, 1430
A-1, 419
A&A Spice & Food, 420
A&B Sound, 1532
A&E Products Group, 796
A&P, 1467-1469, 1473
A&W, 379
A&W Food Services, 1568
A&W Restaurants, 1561
A. Duda & Sons Inc., 41
ABB Lummus Global Inc., 1992
Abbott, 1119, 1125, 1128, 1540
ABC, 1378, 1384, 1394-1396, 1399
Aberfoyle, 361
Abitibi-Consolidated, 489-490
Academy (retailer), 1588
Academy Bus Tours Inc., 1255
Access Communications, 2006
Acclaim, 1202
Accton Technology, 1047
Ace Hardware, 1433
Acer, 883, 889
Acordia Inc., 1797
Acousti Engineering Co. of Florida, 125
AcroMed, 1157
A.D. Makepeace Co., 46
Adams, 326
Adecco Employment, 1840, 1842
Adelphia Communications, 1401
Adidas, 445, 449, 451, 769-770
Adidas-Salomon, 1230
Adobe, 1862

ADT, 1907
Advance Publications, 518
Advanced Fibre, 1034
Advanced Micro Devices, 1065
Aegis, 1781
AEGON, 1744
Aetna, 1540, 1763, 1766, 1910
African Pride, 688
AGCO, 850, 853
Agfa, 1171
Agilink Foods, 218
Agora, 1469
AGRA Foundations Inc., 131
Agrilink Foods, 219
Agripac Inc., 219
A.H. Belo, 517
Ahold USA, 1476
A.I. Scientific, 1139
AIG, 1781
Air Canada, 1276, 1284
Airborne Express, 1288
Airclean Systems Inc., 1124
AirTouch Cellular, 1321
AK Steel Holding, 820
Akzo, 727
Alain Pinel, Realtors, 111
Alamo, 1915
Albemarle, 570
Alberto Culver, 420
Albertson's, 1462-1464, 1471, 1475-1476, 1578
Alcatel Alsthom, 1034-1035, 1049
Alcoa, 819-820, 825-826
Alcoa Building Products, 787, 800
Alcon Laboratories Inc., 682, 1164, 1167
Alcone Marketing, 22
Alexander Ogilvy, 2006
Alexandria Moulding, 485
Aliant, 1312-1313
Alias/Wavefront, 1880
Alimentation Couche-Tard Inc., 1442

Aqua Leisure, 1198
Aquafina, 361
Aquila Energy, 1408
Aquila Power Corp., 1409, 1413
Aramark, 1541, 1544
Aramis Inc., 668
Arbella Ins. Group, 1748
Arbors Drug Mart/Pharmaprix, 1627
Arby's, 1561, 1570
The Arc, 1967
Arcadia Services, 1842
Archambault Musique, 1532
Archer Daniels Midland, 135
Archipelago, 1732-1733
Arco, 92-93, 1193
Arctic Cat, 1114
Area Erectors, 130
Argosy Riverside, 1942-1943
Ariba, 1852
Ariens, 859
Aristech Corp., 583
Arkwright Ins Group, 1769
Armstrong World Inds., 3
Army and Air Force Exchange Service, 1543
Aroma Manufacturing, 957
Arris Interactive/Nortel, 1015
Arrow Electronics, 1423
Arthur Andersen LLP, 1994, 1996
Arthur J. Gallagher & Co., 1797
Arthur Shuster, 116
Artisan, 1925
ARV Assisted Living, 1954
Arvada, 1505
Arvey Paper & Supplies, 1421
Arvida Realty Services, 1802
Arvin (HeatStream), 914
Asarco, 90
Asbury Automotive Group, 1484
Ascend, 1026, 1029, 1042
Ascher Brothers Co. Inc., 123
Ash Grove Cement/North Texas Cement, 815
Ashland Chemical, 1426
Ashley Furniture Industries, 478-479
Asics, 769
Aspect, 1055
AST, 873
AstraZeneca, 1833
AT&T, 1017, 1038, 1048, 1316, 1318-1320, 1326-1329,
    1372, 1376, 1401, 1818, 1829, 1831
AT&T Business Network, 1832
AT&T Canada, 1312-1313
AT&T Jens, 1311
AT&T/MediaOne, 1403

AT&T Wireless, 1317, 1321
AT&T WorldNet, 1375
Athome, 1911
Atlanta Gas Light Co., 1412
Atlantic Blueberry Co., 46
Atlas Van Lines Inc., 1262
Atria Senior Quarters, 1954
Au Bon Pain, 1561
Audiovox, 1019
Autobytel.com, 1363
Autodesk, 1843, 1845
Automatic Data Proc., 1905
AutoNation Inc., 1484
Avalotis Corp., 123
Avery Dennison, 1232
Avid, 1874, 1880
Avis, 1915
AVL, 1116, 1122
Avnet, 1423
AvoMex, 208
AXA Canada, 1747, 1783
Axor Group Inc., 119
Baan, 1847, 1856
Bachman, 159, 409
Baird & Warner Inc., 105
Baird Kurtz & Dobson, 1997
Baker & Mckenzie, 1957
Baker Hughes, 849
Banamex, 1682, 1692, 1710
Banc One Corp., 1686
Bancomer, 1682, 1692, 1710
Band-Aid, 1150
Bandai America, 1188
Bank of America, 1684-1685, 1690, 1708, 1711, 1968
Bank of America Mortgage, 1706-1707
Bank of America Securities, 1712
Bank of Blue Valley (KA), 1699
Bank of Montreal, 1688-1689
Bank of New York, 1694-1695, 1806
Bank of Newport, 1696, 1698
Bank of Nova Scotia, 1688
Bank of Rhode Island, 1696
Bank One, 1684-1685, 1709
BankAmerica Corp., 1686
BankBoston, 1684
Bankers Life & Casualty, 1761
Bankers Trust Co., 1806
The Banko Family, 340
Banorte, 1692
Banta Corporation, 551-552
Baptist Memorial Hospital, 1545
Bar Harbor Banking & Trust, 1698
Barclays Global Investors, 1717, 1806

Company Index

Company Index

Company Index

Company Index

Rowenta, 955
Roxane Laboratories Inc., 1833
Royal, 969-970
Royal & Sunalliance Canada, 1747, 1783
Royal Bank of Canada, 1688-1689
Royal Caribbean, 1306-1307
Royal Crown, 370
Royal Group Technologies Ltd., 787, 800
Royal Mutual Funds, 1718
RPM, 727
R.R. Donnelley, 514, 551-552
RSI Home Products, 471
RTKL Associates, 116, 1990
Rubin, Brown, Gornstein & Co., 1997
Rug Doctor, 656
Rumpke Consolidated Companies Inc., 1418
Russ Berrie, 1189
Russell Athletic, 445, 451
Russell Stover, 308, 324
R.W. DuBose & Son, 54
Ryan Homes, 106
Ryan Incorporated Central, 131
Ryan's Family Steak House, 1563, 1569
Ryder Integrated Logistics, 1265
The Ryland Group, 112, 114
Ryobi, 860
S&P Industries, 344
S R Acquisitions, 1568
SAAN, 1493
SAFECO Ins Cos., 1782, 1788
Safeway, 1438, 1461, 1475-1476
Safeway Stores - Dairy Division, 178
Safilo Group, 1168
Saga Communications, 1386
St. Joseph's Hospitals, 1955
St. Jude's, 1147, 1149
St. Paul Companies, 1755, 1769, 1778, 1789, 1791,
   1794-1796
Sakata Farms Inc., 40
Saks, 1440
Salomon Smith Barney, 1712, 1720, 1722
Salton, 959
Salvation Army, 1967
Sam Ash Music, 1534, 1536
Sam the Record Man, 1532
Sam's Club, 1436, 1443, 1446-1451, 1454, 1458-1459
Samsung, 889, 931, 981, 1019, 1067
San Francisco Municipal Railway, 1257
San Jose Water, 1414
Sanderson Farms, 70, 150
Sandia, 1999
Sandler Capital Management, 1724
Sanford, 1232

Santander, 1682
Santander Mexicano, 1692
Sanwa Bank California, 84
Sanyo, 936, 984, 988-989, 1067
SAP, 1856-1857
Sappi Fine Paper, 491
Saputo Group, 152
Sara Lee Corp., 133, 135-137
Sara Lee Foods, 75, 259
Sara Lee Sock Co., 439
Sarasota Memorial Health Care System, 1955
Sargento Foods Inc., 229
Sartorius Corp., 1131
SASCO Group, 124
Saucony, 769
Sauder, 478
Sbarro, 1558
SBC, 1309, 1316-1317, 1320, 1818
S.C. Johnson, 656
Schawk, 551
Scheid Vineyards, 47
Schering Corporation, 1833
Schlotzsky's Deli, 1561
Schlumberger, 1053
Schmitt Music Company, 1534, 1536
Schneider National Carriers, 1265
Scholastic, 542-543
Schreiber Foods Inc., 152-153
Schuff Steel Inc., 130
Schwab, 1728-1729, 1731
Schwan's Sales Enterprise, 229, 241
Schwan's Sales Enterprises, 228
Science Applications Intl Corp., 1891
Science Applications Intl. Corp., 1898, 1904-1905, 2010
Scotiabank, 1689
Scotsman, 917
Scott Co. of California, 127
Scotts, 745
Sea-Land Service, 1270
Seaboard Corporation, 64, 67
SeaChange, 1825
Seagate Technology, 896, 901
The Seagram Company Ltd., 13, 134, 333-334
Seagram's, 370, 383
Sealed Air, 799
Searle Pharmaceuticals, 1833
Sears, 972, 1438, 1440, 1493-1494, 1508, 1518, 1527,
   1589, 1600
Sears Auto Centres, 1488
Sears Canada, 1441
Sears/Orchard Supply, 1430
The Second Cup, 1571
Security Life Denver, 1742

Company Index

Company Index

Company Index

BRANDS INDEX

This index shows more than 1,570 brands—including names of periodicals, television programs, popular movies, and other "brand-equivalent" names. Each brand name is followed by one or more numerals; these are entry numbers; they are arranged sequentially, with the first mention of the brand shown first.

Brands Index

505

Brands Index

Sudafed, 602, 611
Sun-Maid, 206-207
Sun-Rype, 203
Sunbeam, 934
Sunbelt, 314
Sundown, 606
Sunkist, 330, 401
Sunlight, 637, 639
Sunmark Shock Tarts, 304
Sunrise, 181
Sunshine Cheez-It, 278
Sunshine Cheez It Party Mixes, 410
Sunshine Cheez It Snack Mixes, 410
Super Poligrip, 677
Super Soaker, 1197
Supernatural, 994, 996
Sure, 681
Sure Care, 501
Surf, 634, 636
Surgi Cream, 694
Sustiva, 616
Suzuki, 1111
Swanson, 233
Sweet Breath, 286
Sweet N Low, 298
Sweet Tarts, 304
Swiffer, 1237
Swiss Miss, 170
Sylvania, 978
T 1 Plus, 528
T-Fal, 934
Taco Bell, 424
Tagamet HB200, 599
Tampax, 493-494, 496
Targon, 708
Tartan, 492
Tarzan, 1922
Taster's Choice Original, 393
Tastykake, 269
Tavist, 611
TDK D, 1074
TDK Revue, 1074
Tecate, 345
Teen, 534
Teen People, 534
Tenuate, 618
Tenuate Dospan, 618
Texaco, 756
T.G.I. Friday's, 232
Theraflu, 602
Thermasilk, 16, 690, 697, 700-701
Thibault, 155
Thomas', 265

Three Musketeers, 319
Tia Rosa, 424
Tic Tac, 287
Tide, 631, 634, 636
Tide Liquid, 635
Tidy Cat, 1248
Tidy Cat Scoop MC, 1248
Tidy Scoop, 1248
Tilex, 652
Time, 527, 533
Tina, 223
Tinactin, 600
Toadally Snax, 404
Tombstone, 236, 239-240
Tommy, 684
Tommy Girl, 685
Tommy Hilfiger, 6
Tony's, 236, 239-240
Tootsie Roll Pops, 294, 300-301
Topps Push Pop, 304
Topps Ring Pop, 304
Toronto Life Fashion, 535
Toronto Star, 519, 521, 525
Toronto Sun, 519
Tostitos, 399
Total Kamchatka, 356
Totino's, 231, 239-240
Totino's Pizza Rolls, 231
Toy Story 2, 1922
Toyota 4Runner, 1083
Toyota Camry, 1079, 1091
Toyota Corolla, 1080, 1084
Toyota Sienna, 1081
Toyota Tacoma, 1082
Triaminic, 598, 602, 608
Tribal Voice PowWow, 1374
Trojan, 791, 793
Trojan Enz, 791
Trojan Magnum, 791
Trolli, 299
Tropicana, 201-202
Tums, 599
Tums-Ex-An, 599
Turkey Hill, 169
TV 7 Jours/TV Hebdo, 528
TV Guide, 533
TV Times, 527
Twix, 319
Twix Bar 2-oz., 1609
Tylenol, 602, 608, 611-612
Tylenol Cold, 598
Tyson, 149
Ultra Brite, 705

Brands Index

APPENDIX I

SIC COVERAGE

This appendix lists the Standard Industrial Classification codes (SICs) included in *Market Share Reporter*. Page numbers are shown following each SIC category; the page shown indicates the first occurrence of an SIC. *NEC* stands for not elsewhere classified.

Appendix: SIC Nomenclature

Appendix: SIC Nomenclature

SIC TO NAICS CONVERSION GUIDE

AGRICULTURE, FORESTRY, & FISHING

0111 Wheat
NAICS 11114   Wheat Farming
0112 Rice
NAICS 11116   Rice Farming
0115 Corn
NAICS 11115   Corn Farming
0116 Soybeans
NAICS 11111   Soybean Farming
0119 Cash Grains, nec
NAICS 11113   Dry Pea & Bean Farming
NAICS 11112   Oilseed Farming
NAICS 11115   Corn Farming
NAICS 111191 Oilseed & Grain Combination Farming
NAICS 111199 All Other Grain Farming
0131 Cotton
NAICS 11192   Cotton Farming
0132 Tobacco
NAICS 11191   Tobacco Farming
0133 Sugarcane & Sugar Beets
NAICS 111991 Sugar Beet Farming
NAICS 11193   Sugarcane Farming
0134 Irish Potatoes
NAICS 111211 Potato Farming
0139 Field Crops, Except Cash Grains, nec
NAICS 11194   Hay Farming
NAICS 111992 Peanut Farming
NAICS 111219 Other Vegetable & Melon Farming
NAICS 111998 All Other Miscellaneous Crop Farming
0161 Vegetables & Melons
NAICS 111219 Other Vegetable & Melon Farming
0171 Berry Crops
NAICS 111333 Strawberry Farming
NAICS 111334 Berry Farming
0172 Grapes
NAICS 111332 Grape Vineyards
0173 Tree Nuts
NAICS 111335 Tree Nut Farming
0174 Citrus Fruits
NAICS 11131   Orange Groves
NAICS 11132   Citrus Groves
0175 Deciduous Tree Fruits
NAICS 111331 Apple Orchards
NAICS 111339 Other Noncitrus Fruit Farming
0179 Fruits & Tree Nuts, nec
NAICS 111336 Fruit & Tree Nut Combination Farming
NAICS 111339 Other Noncitrus Fruit Farming
0181 Ornamental Floriculture & Nursery Products
NAICS 111422 Floriculture Production
NAICS 111421 Nursery & Tree Production
0182 Food Crops Grown under Cover
NAICS 111411 Mushroom Production
NAICS 111419 Other Food Crops Grown under Cover
0191 General Farms, Primarily Crop
NAICS 111998 All Other Miscellaneous Crop Farming
0211 Beef Cattle Feedlots
NAICS 112112 Cattle Feedlots
0212 Beef Cattle, Except Feedlots
NAICS 112111 Beef Cattle Ranching & Farming

0213 Hogs
NAICS 11221   Hog & Pig Farming
0214 Sheep & Goats
NAICS 11241   Sheep Farming
NAICS 11242   Goat Farming
0219 General Livestock, Except Dairy & Poultry
NAICS 11299   All Other Animal Production
0241 Dairy Farms
NAICS 112111 Beef Cattle Ranching & Farming
NAICS 11212   Dairy Cattle & Milk Production
0251 Broiler, Fryers, & Roaster Chickens
NAICS 11232   Broilers & Other Meat-type Chicken
                     Production
0252 Chicken Eggs
NAICS 11231   Chicken Egg Production
0253 Turkey & Turkey Eggs
NAICS 11233   Turkey Production
0254 Poultry Hatcheries
NAICS 11234   Poultry Hatcheries
0259 Poultry & Eggs, nec
NAICS 11239   Other Poultry Production
0271 Fur-bearing Animals & Rabbits
NAICS 11293   Fur-bearing Animal & Rabbit Production
0272 Horses & Other Equines
NAICS 11292   Horse & Other Equine Production
0273 Animal Aquaculture
NAICS 112511 Finfish Farming & Fish Hatcheries
NAICS 112512 Shellfish Farming
NAICS 112519 Other Animal Aquaculture
0279 Animal Specialities, nec
NAICS 11291   Apiculture
NAICS 11299   All Other Animal Production
0291 General Farms, Primarily Livestock & Animal Specialties
NAICS 11299   All Other Animal Production
0711 Soil Preparation Services
NAICS 115112 Soil Preparation, Planting & Cultivating
0721 Crop Planting, Cultivating & Protecting
NAICS 48122   Nonscheduled Speciality Air Transportation
NAICS 115112 Soil Preparation, Planting & Cultivating
0722 Crop Harvesting, Primarily by Machine
NAICS 115113 Crop Harvesting, Primarily by Machine
0723 Crop Preparation Services for Market, Except Cotton Ginning
NAICS 115114 Postharvest Crop Activities
0724 Cotton Ginning
NAICS 115111 Cotton Ginning
0741 Veterinary Service for Livestock
NAICS 54194   Veterinary Services
0742 Veterinary Services for Animal Specialties
NAICS 54194   Veterinary Services
0751 Livestock Services, Except Veterinary
NAICS 311611 Animal Slaughtering
NAICS 11521   Support Activities for Animal Production
0752 Animal Specialty Services, Except Veterinary
NAICS 11521   Support Activities for Animal Production
NAICS 81291   Pet Care Services
0761 Farm Labor Contractors & Crew Leaders
NAICS 115115 Farm Labor Contractors & Crew Leaders
0762 Farm Management Services
NAICS 115116 Farm Management Services
0781 Landscape Counseling & Planning
NAICS 54169   Other Scientific & Technical Consulting
                     Services
NAICS 54132   Landscape Architectural Services

0782 Lawn & Garden Services
　NAICS 56173　Landscaping Services
0783 Ornamental Shrub & Tree Services
　NAICS 56173　Landscaping Services
0811 Timber Tracts
　NAICS 111421 Nursery & Tree Production
　NAICS 11311　Timber Tract Operations
0831 Forest Nurseries & Gathering of Forest Products
　NAICS 111998 All Other Miscellaneous Crop
　NAICS 11321　Forest Nurseries & Gathering of Forest
　　　　　　　Products
0851 Forestry Services
　NAICS 11531　Support Activities for Forestry
0912 Finfish
　NAICS 114111 Finfish Fishing
0913 Shellfish
　NAICS 114112 Shellfish Fishing
0919 Miscellaneous Marine Products
　NAICS 114119 Other Marine Fishing
　NAICS 111998 All Other Miscellaneous Crop Farming
0921 Fish Hatcheries & Preserves
　NAICS 112511 Finfish Farming & Fish Hatcheries
　NAICS 112512 Shellfish Farming
0971 Hunting, Trapping, & Game Propagation
　NAICS 11421　Hunting & Trapping

MINING INDUSTRIES

1011 Iron Ores
　NAICS 21221　Iron Ore Mining
1021 Copper Ores
　NAICS 212234 Copper Ore & Nickel Ore Mining
1031 Lead & Zinc Ores
　NAICS 212231 Lead Ore & Zinc Ore Mining
1041 Gold Ores
　NAICS 212221 Gold Ore Mining
1044 Silver Ores
　NAICS 212222 Silver Ore Mining
1061 Ferroalloy Ores, Except Vanadium
　NAICS 212234 Copper Ore & Nickel Ore Mining
　NAICS 212299 Other Metal Ore Mining
1081 Metal Mining Services
　NAICS 213115 Support Activities for Metal Mining
　NAICS 54136　Geophysical Surveying & Mapping Services
1094 Uranium-radium-vanadium Ores
　NAICS 212291 Uranium-radium-vanadium Ore Mining
1099 Miscellaneous Metal Ores, nec
　NAICS 212299 Other Metal Ore Mining
1221 Bituminous Coal & Lignite Surface Mining
　NAICS 212111 Bituminous Coal & Lignite Surface Mining
1222 Bituminous Coal Underground Mining
　NAICS 212112 Bituminous Coal Underground Mining
1231 Anthracite Mining
　NAICS 212113 Anthracite Mining
1241 Coal Mining Services
　NAICS 213114 Support Activities for Coal Mining
1311 Crude Petroleum & Natural Gas
　NAICS 211111 Crude Petroleum & Natural Gas Extraction
1321 Natural Gas Liquids
　NAICS 211112 Natural Gas Liquid Extraction
1381 Drilling Oil & Gas Wells
　NAICS 213111 Drilling Oil & Gas Wells

1382 Oil & Gas Field Exploration Services
　NAICS 48122　Nonscheduled Speciality Air Transportation
　NAICS 54136　Geophysical Surveying & Mapping Services
　NAICS 213112 Support Activities for Oil & Gas Field
　　　　　　　Operations
1389 Oil & Gas Field Services, nec
　NAICS 213113 Other Oil & Gas Field Support Activities
1411 Dimension Stone
　NAICS 212311 Dimension Stone Mining & Quarry
1422 Crushed & Broken Limestone
　NAICS 212312 Crushed & Broken Limestone Mining &
　　　　　　　Quarrying
1423 Crushed & Broken Granite
　NAICS 212313 Crushed & Broken Granite Mining &
　　　　　　　Quarrying
1429 Crushed & Broken Stone, nec
　NAICS 212319 Other Crushed & Broken Stone Mining &
　　　　　　　Quarrying
1442 Construction Sand & Gravel
　NAICS 212321 Construction Sand & Gravel Mining
1446 Industrial Sand
　NAICS 212322 Industrial Sand Mining
1455 Kaolin & Ball Clay
　NAICS 212324 Kaolin & Ball Clay Mining
1459 Clay, Ceramic, & Refractory Minerals, nec
　NAICS 212325 Clay & Ceramic & Refractory Minerals Mining
1474 Potash, Soda, & Borate Minerals
　NAICS 212391 Potash, Soda, & Borate Mineral Mining
1475 Phosphate Rock
　NAICS 212392 Phosphate Rock Mining
1479 Chemical & Fertilizer Mineral Mining, nec
　NAICS 212393 Other Chemical & Fertilizer Mineral Mining
1481 Nonmetallic Minerals Services Except Fuels
　NAICS 213116 Support Activities for Non-metallic Minerals
　NAICS 54136　Geophysical Surveying & Mapping Services
1499 Miscellaneous Nonmetallic Minerals, Except Fuels
　NAICS 212319 Other Crushed & Broken Stone Mining or
　　　　　　　Quarrying
　NAICS 212399 All Other Non-metallic Mineral Mining

CONSTRUCTION INDUSTRIES

1521 General Contractors-single-family Houses
　NAICS 23321　Single Family Housing Construction
1522 General Contractors-residential Buildings, Other than
　　Single-family
　NAICS 23332　Commercial & Institutional Building
　　　　　　　Construction
　NAICS 23322　Multifamily Housing Construction
1531 Operative Builders
　NAICS 23321　Single Family Housing Construction
　NAICS 23322　Multifamily Housing Construction
　NAICS 23331　Manufacturing & Industrial Building
　　　　　　　Construction
　NAICS 23332　Commercial & Institutional Building
　　　　　　　Construction
1541 General Contractors-industrial Buildings & Warehouses
　NAICS 23332　Commercial & Institutional Building
　　　　　　　Construction
　NAICS 23331　Manufacturing & Industrial Building
　　　　　　　Construction

1542 General Contractors-nonresidential Buildings, Other than Industrial Buildings & Warehouses
NAICS 23332   Commercial & Institutional Building Construction
1611 Highway & Street Construction, Except Elevated Highways
NAICS 23411   Highway & Street Construction
1622 Bridge, Tunnel, & Elevated Highway Construction
NAICS 23412   Bridge & Tunnel Construction
1623 Water, Sewer, Pipeline, & Communications & Power Line Construction
NAICS 23491   Water, Sewer & Pipeline Construction
NAICS 23492   Power & Communication Transmission Line Construction
1629 Heavy Construction, nec
NAICS 23493   Industrial Nonbuilding Structure Construction
NAICS 23499   All Other Heavy Construction
1711 Plumbing, Heating, & Air-conditioning
NAICS 23511   Plumbing, Heating & Air-conditioning Contractors
1721 Painting & Paper Hanging
NAICS 23521   Painting & Wall Covering Contractors
1731 Electrical Work
NAICS 561621 Security Systems Services
NAICS 23531   Electrical Contractors
1741 Masonry, Stone Setting & Other Stone Work
NAICS 23541   Masonry & Stone Contractors
1742 Plastering, Drywall, Acoustical & Insulation Work
NAICS 23542   Drywall, Plastering, Acoustical & Insulation Contractors
1743 Terrazzo, Tile, Marble, & Mosaic Work
NAICS 23542   Drywall, Plastering, Acoustical & Insulation Contractors
NAICS 23543   Tile, Marble, Terrazzo & Mosaic Contractors
1751 Carpentry Work
NAICS 23551   Carpentry Contractors
1752 Floor Laying & Other Floor Work, nec
NAICS 23552   Floor Laying & Other Floor Contractors
1761 Roofing, Siding, & Sheet Metal Work
NAICS 23561   Roofing, Siding, & Sheet Metal Contractors
1771 Concrete Work
NAICS 23542   Drywall, Plastering, Acoustical & Insulation Contractors
NAICS 23571   Concrete Contractors
1781 Water Well Drilling
NAICS 23581   Water Well Drilling Contractors
1791 Structural Steel Erection
NAICS 23591   Structural Steel Erection Contractors
1793 Glass & Glazing Work
NAICS 23592   Glass & Glazing Contractors
1794 Excavation Work
NAICS 23593   Excavation Contractors
1795 Wrecking & Demolition Work
NAICS 23594   Wrecking & Demolition Contractors
1796 Installation or Erection of Building Equipment, nec
NAICS 23595   Building Equipment & Other Machinery Installation Contractors
1799 Special Trade Contractors, nec
NAICS 23521   Painting & Wall Covering Contractors
NAICS 23592   Glass & Glazing Contractors
NAICS 56291   Remediation Services
NAICS 23599   All Other Special Trade Contractors

FOOD & KINDRED PRODUCTS

2011 Meat Packing Plants
NAICS 311611 Animal Slaughtering
2013 Sausages & Other Prepared Meats
NAICS 311612 Meat Processed from Carcasses
2015 Poultry Slaughtering & Processing
NAICS 311615 Poultry Processing
NAICS 311999 All Other Miscellaneous Food Manufacturing
2021 Creamery Butter
NAICS 311512 Creamery Butter Manufacturing
2022 Natural, Processed, & Imitation Cheese
NAICS 311513 Cheese Manufacturing
2023 Dry, Condensed, & Evaporated Dairy Products
NAICS 311514 Dry, Condensed, & Evaporated Milk Manufacturing
2024 Ice Cream & Frozen Desserts
NAICS 31152   Ice Cream & Frozen Dessert Manufacturing
2026 Fluid Milk
NAICS 311511 Fluid Milk Manufacturing
2032 Canned Specialties
NAICS 311422 Specialty Canning
NAICS 311999 All Other Miscellaneous Food Manufacturing
2033 Canned Fruits, Vegetables, Preserves, Jams, & Jellies
NAICS 311421 Fruit & Vegetable Canning
2034 Dried & Dehydrated Fruits, Vegetables, & Soup Mixes
NAICS 311423 Dried & Dehydrated Food Manufacturing
NAICS 311211 Flour Milling
2035 Pickled Fruits & Vegetables, Vegetables Sauces & Seasonings, & Salad Dressings
NAICS 311421 Fruit & Vegetable Canning
NAICS 311941 Mayonnaise, Dressing, & Other Prepared Sauce Manufacturing
2037 Frozen Fruits, Fruit Juices, & Vegetables
NAICS 311411 Frozen Fruit, Juice, & Vegetable Processing
2038 Frozen Specialties, nec
NAICS 311412 Frozen Specialty Food Manufacturing
2041 Flour & Other Grain Mill Products
NAICS 311211 Flour Milling
2043 Cereal Breakfast Foods
NAICS 31192   Coffee & Tea Manufacturing
NAICS 31123   Breakfast Cereal Manufacturing
2044 Rice Milling
NAICS 311212 Rice Milling
2045 Prepared Flour Mixes & Doughs
NAICS 311822 Flour Mixes & Dough Manufacturing from Purchased Flour
2046 Wet Corn Milling
NAICS 311221 Wet Corn Milling
2047 Dog & Cat Food
NAICS 311111 Dog & Cat Food Manufacturing
2048 Prepared Feed & Feed Ingredients for Animals & Fowls, Except Dogs & Cats
NAICS 311611 Animal Slaughtering
NAICS 311119 Other Animal Food Manufacturing
2051 Bread & Other Bakery Products, Except Cookies & Crackers
NAICS 311812 Commercial Bakeries
2052 Cookies & Crackers
NAICS 311821 Cookie & Cracker Manufacturing
NAICS 311919 Other Snack Food Manufacturing
NAICS 311812 Commercial Bakeries

Appendix: SIC/NAICS Conversion

529

2053 Frozen Bakery Products, Except Bread
NAICS 311813 Frozen Bakery Product Manufacturing
2061 Cane Sugar, Except Refining
NAICS 311311 Sugarcane Mills
2062 Cane Sugar Refining
NAICS 311312 Cane Sugar Refining
2063 Beet Sugar
NAICS 311313 Beet Sugar Manufacturing
2064 Candy & Other Confectionery Products
NAICS 31133   Confectionery Manufacturing from Purchased
Chocolate
NAICS 31134   Non-chocolate Confectionery Manufacturing
2066 Chocolate & Cocoa Products
NAICS 31132   Chocolate & Confectionery Manufacturing from
Cacao Beans
2067 Chewing Gum
NAICS 31134   Non-chocolate Confectionery Manufacturing
2068 Salted & Roasted Nuts & Seeds
NAICS 311911 Roasted Nuts & Peanut Butter Manufacturing
2074 Cottonseed Oil Mills
NAICS 311223 Other Oilseed Processing
NAICS 311225 Fats & Oils Refining & Blending
2075 Soybean Oil Mills
NAICS 311222 Soybean Processing
NAICS 311225 Fats & Oils Refining & Blending
2076 Vegetable Oil Mills, Except Corn, Cottonseed, & Soybeans
NAICS 311223 Other Oilseed Processing
NAICS 311225 Fats & Oils Refining & Blending
2077 Animal & Marine Fats & Oils
NAICS 311613 Rendering & Meat By-product Processing
NAICS 311711 Seafood Canning
NAICS 311712 Fresh & Frozen Seafood Processing
NAICS 311225 Edible Fats & Oils Manufacturing
**2079 Shortening, Table Oils, Margarine, & Other Edible Fats &
Oils, nec**
NAICS 311225 Edible Fats & Oils Manufacturing
NAICS 311222 Soybean Processing
NAICS 311223 Other Oilseed Processing
2082 Malt Beverages
NAICS 31212   Breweries
2083 Malt
NAICS 311213 Malt Manufacturing
2084 Wines, Brandy, & Brandy Spirits
NAICS 31213   Wineries
2085 Distilled & Blended Liquors
NAICS 31214   Distilleries
2086 Bottled & Canned Soft Drinks & Carbonated Waters
NAICS 312111 Soft Drink Manufacturing
NAICS 312112 Bottled Water Manufacturing
2087 Flavoring Extracts & Flavoring Syrups nec
NAICS 31193   Flavoring Syrup & Concentrate Manufacturing
NAICS 311942 Spice & Extract Manufacturing
NAICS 311999 All Other Miscellaneous Food Manufacturing
2091 Canned & Cured Fish & Seafood
NAICS 311711 Seafood Canning
2092 Prepared Fresh or Frozen Fish & Seafoods
NAICS 311712 Fresh & Frozen Seafood Processing
2095 Roasted Coffee
NAICS 31192   Coffee & Tea Manufacturing
NAICS 311942 Spice & Extract Manufacturing
2096 Potato Chips, Corn Chips, & Similar Snacks
NAICS 311919 Other Snack Food Manufacturing

2097 Manufactured Ice
NAICS 312113 Ice Manufacturing
2098 Macaroni, Spaghetti, Vermicelli, & Noodles
NAICS 311823 Pasta Manufacturing
2099 Food Preparations, nec
NAICS 311423 Dried & Dehydrated Food Manufacturing
NAICS 111998 All Other Miscellaneous Crop Farming
NAICS 31134   Non-chocolate Confectionery Manufacturing
NAICS 311911 Roasted Nuts & Peanut Butter Manufacturing
NAICS 311991 Perishable Prepared Food Manufacturing
NAICS 31183   Tortilla Manufacturing
NAICS 31192   Coffee & Tea Manufacturing
NAICS 311941 Mayonnaise, Dressing, & Other Prepared Sauce
Manufacturing
NAICS 311942 Spice & Extract Manufacturing
NAICS 311999 All Other Miscellaneous Food Manufacturing

TOBACCO PRODUCTS

2111 Cigarettes
NAICS 312221 Cigarette Manufacturing
2121 Cigars
NAICS 312229 Other Tobacco Product Manufacturing
2131 Chewing & Smoking Tobacco & Snuff
NAICS 312229 Other Tobacco Product Manufacturing
2141 Tobacco Stemming & Redrying
NAICS 312229 Other Tobacco Product Manufacturing
NAICS 31221   Tobacco Stemming & Redrying

TEXTILE MILL PRODUCTS

2211 Broadwoven Fabric Mills, Cotton
NAICS 31321   Broadwoven Fabric Mills
2221 Broadwoven Fabric Mills, Manmade Fiber & Silk
NAICS 31321   Broadwoven Fabric Mills
2231 Broadwoven Fabric Mills, Wool
NAICS 31321   Broadwoven Fabric Mills
NAICS 313311 Broadwoven Fabric Finishing Mills
NAICS 313312 Textile & Fabric Finishing Mills
**2241 Narrow Fabric & Other Smallware Mills: Cotton, Wool,
Silk, & Manmade Fiber**
NAICS 313221 Narrow Fabric Mills
2251 Women's Full-length & Knee-length Hosiery, Except Socks
NAICS 315111 Sheer Hosiery Mills
2252 Hosiery, nec
NAICS 315111 Sheer Hosiery Mills
NAICS 315119 Other Hosiery & Sock Mills
2253 Knit Outerwear Mills
NAICS 315191 Outerwear Knitting Mills
2254 Knit Underwear & Nightwear Mills
NAICS 315192 Underwear & Nightwear Knitting Mills
2257 Weft Knit Fabric Mills
NAICS 313241 Weft Knit Fabric Mills
NAICS 313312 Textile & Fabric Finishing Mills
2258 Lace & Warp Knit Fabric Mills
NAICS 313249 Other Knit Fabric & Lace Mills
NAICS 313312 Textile & Fabric Finishing Mills
2259 Knitting Mills, nec
NAICS 315191 Outerwear Knitting Mills
NAICS 315192 Underwear & Nightwear Knitting Mills
NAICS 313241 Weft Knit Fabric Mills
NAICS 313249 Other Knit Fabric & Lace Mills

2261 Finishers of Broadwoven Fabrics of Cotton
NAICS 313311 Broadwoven Fabric Finishing Mills
2262 Finishers of Broadwoven Fabrics of Manmade Fiber & Silk
NAICS 313311 Broadwoven Fabric Finishing Mills
2269 Finishers of Textiles, nec
NAICS 313311 Broadwoven Fabric Finishing Mills
NAICS 313312 Textile & Fabric Finishing Mills
2273 Carpets & Rugs
NAICS 31411 Carpet & Rug Mills
2281 Yarn Spinning Mills
NAICS 313111 Yarn Spinning Mills
2282 Yarn Texturizing, Throwing, Twisting, & Winding Mills
NAICS 313112 Yarn Texturing, Throwing & Twisting Mills
NAICS 313312 Textile & Fabric Finishing Mills
2284 Thread Mills
NAICS 313113 Thread Mills
NAICS 313312 Textile & Fabric Finishing Mills
2295 Coated Fabrics, Not Rubberized
NAICS 31332 Fabric Coating Mills
2296 Tire Cord & Fabrics
NAICS 314992 Tire Cord & Tire Fabric Mills
2297 Nonwoven Fabrics
NAICS 31323 Nonwoven Fabric Mills
2298 Cordage & Twine
NAICS 314991 Rope, Cordage & Twine Mills
2299 Textile Goods, nec
NAICS 31321 Broadwoven Fabric Mills
NAICS 31323 Nonwoven Fabric Mills
NAICS 313312 Textile & Fabric Finishing Mills
NAICS 313221 Narrow Fabric Mills
NAICS 313113 Thread Mills
NAICS 313111 Yarn Spinning Mills
NAICS 314999 All Other Miscellaneous Textile Product Mills

APPAREL & OTHER FINISHED PRODUCTS MADE FROM FABRICS & SIMILAR MATERIALS

2311 Men's & Boys' Suits, Coats & Overcoats
NAICS 315211 Men's & Boys' Cut & Sew Apparel Contractors
NAICS 315222 Men's & Boys' Cut & Sew Suit, Coat, & Overcoat Manufacturing
2321 Men's & Boys' Shirts, Except Work Shirts
NAICS 315211 Men's & Boys' Cut & Sew Apparel Contractors
NAICS 315223 Men's & Boys' Cut & Sew Shirt, Manufacturing
2322 Men's & Boys' Underwear & Nightwear
NAICS 315211 Men's & Boys' Cut & Sew Apparel Contractors
NAICS 315221 Men's & Boys' Cut & Sew Underwear & Nightwear Manufacturing
2323 Men's & Boys' Neckwear
NAICS 315993 Men's & Boys' Neckwear Manufacturing
2325 Men's & Boys' Trousers & Slacks
NAICS 315211 Men's & Boys' Cut & Sew Apparel Contractors
NAICS 315224 Men's & Boys' Cut & Sew Trouser, Slack, & Jean Manufacturing
2326 Men's & Boys' Work Clothing
NAICS 315211 Men's & Boys' Cut & Sew Apparel Contractors
NAICS 315225 Men's & Boys' Cut & Sew Work Clothing Manufacturing
2329 Men's & Boys' Clothing, nec
NAICS 315211 Men's & Boys' Cut & Sew Apparel Contractors

NAICS 315228 Men's & Boys' Cut & Sew Other Outerwear Manufacturing
NAICS 315299 All Other Cut & Sew Apparel Manufacturing
2331 Women's, Misses', & Juniors' Blouses & Shirts
NAICS 315212 Women's & Girls' Cut & Sew Apparel Contractors
NAICS 315232 Women's & Girls' Cut & Sew Blouse & Shirt Manufacturing
2335 Women's, Misses' & Junior's Dresses
NAICS 315212 Women's & Girls' Cut & Sew Apparel Contractors
NAICS 315233 Women's & Girls' Cut & Sew Dress Manufacturing
2337 Women's, Misses' & Juniors' Suits, Skirts & Coats
NAICS 315212 Women's & Girls' Cut & Sew Apparel Contractors
NAICS 315234 Women's & Girls' Cut & Sew Suit, Coat, Tailored Jacket, & Skirt Manufacturing
2339 Women's, Misses' & Juniors' Outerwear, nec
NAICS 315999 Other Apparel Accessories & Other Apparel Manufacturing
NAICS 315212 Women's & Girls' Cut & Sew Apparel Contractors
NAICS 315299 All Other Cut & Sew Apparel Manufacturing
NAICS 315238 Women's & Girls' Cut & Sew Other Outerwear Manufacturing
2341 Women's, Misses, Children's, & Infants' Underwear & Nightwear
NAICS 315212 Women's & Girls' Cut & Sew Apparel Contractors
NAICS 315211 Men's & Boys' Cut & Sew Apparel Contractors
NAICS 315231 Women's & Girls' Cut & Sew Lingerie, Loungewear, & Nightwear Manufacturing
NAICS 315221 Men's & Boys' Cut & Sew Underwear & Nightwear Manufacturing
NAICS 315291 Infants' Cut & Sew Apparel Manufacturing
2342 Brassieres, Girdles, & Allied Garments
NAICS 315212 Women's & Girls' Cut & Sew Apparel Contractors
NAICS 315231 Women's & Girls' Cut & Sew Lingerie, Loungewear, & Nightwear Manufacturing
2353 Hats, Caps, & Millinery
NAICS 315991 Hat, Cap, & Millinery Manufacturing
2361 Girls', Children's & Infants' Dresses, Blouses & Shirts
NAICS 315291 Infants' Cut & Sew Apparel Manufacturing
NAICS 315223 Men's & Boys' Cut & Sew Shirt, Manufacturing
NAICS 315211 Men's & Boys' Cut & Sew Apparel Contractors
NAICS 315232 Women's & Girls' Cut & Sew Blouse & Shirt Manufacturing
NAICS 315233 Women's & Girls' Cut & Sew Dress Manufacturing
NAICS 315212 Women's & Girls' Cut & Sew Apparel Contractors
2369 Girls', Children's & Infants' Outerwear, nec
NAICS 315291 Infants' Cut & Sew Apparel Manufacturing
NAICS 315222 Men's & Boys' Cut & Sew Suit, Coat, & Overcoat Manufacturing
NAICS 315224 Men's & Boys' Cut & Sew Trouser, Slack, & Jean Manufacturing
NAICS 315228 Men's & Boys' Cut & Sew Other Outerwear Manufacturing
NAICS 315221 Men's & Boys' Cut & Sew Underwear & Nightwear Manufacturing
NAICS 315211 Men's & Boys' Cut & Sew Apparel Contractors

NAICS 315234 Women's & Girls' Cut & Sew Suit, Coat, Tailored Jacket, & Skirt Manufacturing

NAICS 315238 Women's & Girls' Cut & Sew Other Outerwear Manufacturing

NAICS 315231 Women's & Girls' Cut & Sew Lingerie, Loungewear, & Nightwear Manufacturing

NAICS 315212 Women's & Girls' Cut & Sew Apparel Contractors

2371 Fur Goods

NAICS 315292 Fur & Leather Apparel Manufacturing

2381 Dress & Work Gloves, Except Knit & All-leather

NAICS 315992 Glove & Mitten Manufacturing

2384 Robes & Dressing Gowns

NAICS 315231 Women's & Girls' Cut & Sew Lingerie, Loungewear, & Nightwear Manufacturing

NAICS 315221 Men's & Boys' Cut & Sew Underwear & Nightwear Manufacturing

NAICS 315211 Men's & Boys' Cut & Sew Apparel Contractors

NAICS 315212 Women's & Girls' Cut & Sew Apparel Contractors

2385 Waterproof Outerwear

NAICS 315222 Men's & Boys' Cut & Sew Suit, Coat, & Overcoat Manufacturing

NAICS 315234 Women's & Girls' Cut & Sew Suit, Coat, Tailored Jacket, & Skirt Manufacturing

NAICS 315228 Men's & Boys' Cut & Sew Other Outerwear Manufacturing

NAICS 315238 Women's & Girls' Cut & Sew Other Outerwear Manufacturing

NAICS 315291 Infants' Cut & Sew Apparel Manufacturing

NAICS 315999 Other Apparel Accessories & Other Apparel Manufacturing

NAICS 315211 Men's & Boys' Cut & Sew Apparel Contractors

NAICS 315212 Women's & Girls' Cut & Sew Apparel Contractors

2386 Leather & Sheep-lined Clothing

NAICS 315292 Fur & Leather Apparel Manufacturing

2387 Apparel Belts

NAICS 315999 Other Apparel Accessories & Other Apparel Manufacturing

2389 Apparel & Accessories, nec

NAICS 315999 Other Apparel Accessories & Other Apparel Manufacturing

NAICS 315299 All Other Cut & Sew Apparel Manufacturing

NAICS 315231 Women's & Girls' Cut & Sew Lingerie, Loungewear, & Nightwear Manufacturing

NAICS 315212 Women's & Girls' Cut & Sew Apparel Contractors

NAICS 315211 Mens' & Boys' Cut & Sew Apparel Contractors

2391 Curtains & Draperies

NAICS 314121 Curtain & Drapery Mills

2392 Housefurnishings, Except Curtains & Draperies

NAICS 314911 Textile Bag Mills

NAICS 339994 Broom, Brush & Mop Manufacturing

NAICS 314129 Other Household Textile Product Mills

2393 Textile Bags

NAICS 314911 Textile Bag Mills

2394 Canvas & Related Products

NAICS 314912 Canvas & Related Product Mills

2395 Pleating, Decorative & Novelty Stitching, & Tucking for the Trade

NAICS 314999 All Other Miscellaneous Textile Product Mills

NAICS 315211 Mens' & Boys' Cut & Sew Apparel Contractors

NAICS 315212 Women's & Girls' Cut & Sew Apparel Contractors

2396 Automotive Trimmings, Apparel Findings, & Related Products

NAICS 33636 Motor Vehicle Fabric Accessories & Seat Manufacturing

NAICS 315999 Other Apparel Accessories, & Other Apparel Manufacturing

NAICS 323113 Commercial Screen Printing

NAICS 314999 All Other Miscellaneous Textile Product Mills

2397 Schiffli Machine Embroideries

NAICS 313222 Schiffli Machine Embroidery

2399 Fabricated Textile Products, nec

NAICS 33636 Motor Vehicle Fabric Accessories & Seat Manufacturing

NAICS 315999 Other Apparel Accessories & Other Apparel Manufacturing

NAICS 314999 All Other Miscellaneous Textile Product Mills

LUMBER & WOOD PRODUCTS, EXCEPT FURNITURE

2411 Logging

NAICS 11331 Logging

2421 Sawmills & Planing Mills, General

NAICS 321913 Softwood Cut Stock, Resawing Lumber, & Planing

NAICS 321113 Sawmills

NAICS 321914 Other Millwork

NAICS 321999 All Other Miscellaneous Wood Product Manufacturing

2426 Hardwood Dimension & Flooring Mills

NAICS 321914 Other Millwork

NAICS 321999 All Other Miscellaneous Wood Product Manufacturing

NAICS 337139 Other Wood Furniture Manufacturing

NAICS 321912 Hardwood Dimension Mills

2429 Special Product Sawmills, nec

NAICS 321113 Sawmills

NAICS 321913 Softwood Cut Stock, Resawing Lumber, & Planing

NAICS 321999 All Other Miscellaneous Wood Product Manufacturing

2431 Millwork

NAICS 321911 Wood Window & Door Manufacturing

NAICS 321914 Other Millwork

2434 Wood Kitchen Cabinets

NAICS 337131 Wood Kitchen Cabinet & Counter Top Manufacturing

2435 Hardwood Veneer & Plywood

NAICS 321211 Hardwood Veneer & Plywood Manufacturing

2436 Softwood Veneer & Plywood

NAICS 321212 Softwood Veneer & Plywood Manufacturing

2439 Structural Wood Members, nec

NAICS 321913 Softwood Cut Stock, Resawing Lumber, & Planing

NAICS 321214 Truss Manufacturing

NAICS 321213 Engineered Wood Member Manufacturing

2441 Nailed & Lock Corner Wood Boxes & Shook

NAICS 32192 Wood Container & Pallet Manufacturing

2448 Wood Pallets & Skids

NAICS 32192 Wood Container & Pallet Manufacturing

2449 Wood Containers, nec
  NAICS 32192   Wood Container & Pallet Manufacturing
2451 Mobile Homes
  NAICS 321991 Manufactured Home Manufacturing
2452 Prefabricated Wood Buildings & Components
  NAICS 321992 Prefabricated Wood Building Manufacturing
2491 Wood Preserving
  NAICS 321114 Wood Preservation
2493 Reconstituted Wood Products
  NAICS 321219 Reconstituted Wood Product Manufacturing
2499 Wood Products, nec
  NAICS 339999 All Other Miscellaneous Manufacturing
  NAICS 337139 Other Wood Furniture Manufacturing
  NAICS 337148 Other Nonwood Furniture Manufacturing
  NAICS 32192   Wood Container & Pallet Manufacturing
  NAICS 321999 All Other Miscellaneous Wood Product
       Manufacturing

FURNITURE & FIXTURES

2511 Wood Household Furniture, Except Upholstered
  NAICS 337122 Wood Household Furniture Manufacturing
2512 Wood Household Furniture, Upholstered
  NAICS 337121 Upholstered Household Furniture
       Manufacturing
2514 Metal Household Furniture
  NAICS 337124 Metal Household Furniture Manufacturing
2515 Mattresses, Foundations, & Convertible Beds
  NAICS 33791   Mattress Manufacturing
  NAICS 337132 Upholstered Wood Household Furniture
       Manufacturing
**2517 Wood Television, Radio, Phonograph & Sewing Machine
  Cabinets**
  NAICS 337139 Other Wood Furniture Manufacturing
2519 Household Furniture, nec
  NAICS 337143 Household Furniture (except Wood & Metal)
       Manufacturing
2521 Wood Office Furniture
  NAICS 337134 Wood Office Furniture Manufacturing
2522 Office Furniture, Except Wood
  NAICS 337141 Nonwood Office Furniture Manufacturing
2531 Public Building & Related Furniture
  NAICS 33636   Motor Vehicle Fabric Accessories & Seat
       Manufacturing
  NAICS 337139 Other Wood Furniture Manufacturing
  NAICS 337148 Other Nonwood Furniture Manufacturing
  NAICS 339942 Lead Pencil & Art Good Manufacturing
**2541 Wood Office & Store Fixtures, Partitions, Shelving, &
  Lockers**
  NAICS 337131 Wood Kitchen Cabinet & Counter Top
       Manufacturing
  NAICS 337135 Custom Architectural Woodwork, Millwork, &
       Fixtures
  NAICS 337139 Other Wood Furniture Manufacturing
**2542 Office & Store Fixtures, Partitions Shelving, & Lockers,
  Except Wood**
  NAICS 337145 Nonwood Showcase, Partition, Shelving, &
       Locker Manufacturing
2591 Drapery Hardware & Window Blinds & Shades
  NAICS 33792   Blind & Shade Manufacturing
2599 Furniture & Fixtures, nec
  NAICS 339113 Surgical Appliance & Supplies Manufacturing
  NAICS 337139 Other Wood Furniture Manufacturing

  NAICS 337148 Other Nonwood Furniture Manufacturing

PAPER & ALLIED PRODUCTS

2611 Pulp Mills
  NAICS 32211   Pulp Mills
  NAICS 322121 Paper Mills
  NAICS 32213   Paperboard Mills
2621 Paper Mills
  NAICS 322121 Paper Mills
  NAICS 322122 Newsprint Mills
2631 Paperboard Mills
  NAICS 32213   Paperboard Mills
2652 Setup Paperboard Boxes
  NAICS 322213 Setup Paperboard Box Manufacturing
2653 Corrugated & Solid Fiber Boxes
  NAICS 322211 Corrugated & Solid Fiber Box Manufacturing
2655 Fiber Cans, Tubes, Drums, & Similar Products
  NAICS 322214 Fiber Can, Tube, Drum, & Similar Products
       Manufacturing
2656 Sanitary Food Containers, Except Folding
  NAICS 322215 Non-folding Sanitary Food Container
       Manufacturing
2657 Folding Paperboard Boxes, Including Sanitary
  NAICS 322212 Folding Paperboard Box Manufacturing
2671 Packaging Paper & Plastics Film, Coated & Laminated
  NAICS 322221 Coated & Laminated Packaging Paper &
       Plastics Film Manufacturing
  NAICS 326112 Unsupported Plastics Packaging Film & Sheet
       Manufacturing
2672 Coated & Laminated Paper, nec
  NAICS 322222 Coated & Laminated Paper Manufacturing
2673 Plastics, Foil, & Coated Paper Bags
  NAICS 322223 Plastics, Foil, & Coated Paper Bag
       Manufacturing
  NAICS 326111 Unsupported Plastics Bag Manufacturing
2674 Uncoated Paper & Multiwall Bags
  NAICS 322224 Uncoated Paper & Multiwall Bag
       Manufacturing
2675 Die-cut Paper & Paperboard & Cardboard
  NAICS 322231 Die-cut Paper & Paperboard Office Supplies
       Manufacturing
  NAICS 322292 Surface-coated Paperboard Manufacturing
  NAICS 322298 All Other Converted Paper Product
       Manufacturing
2676 Sanitary Paper Products
  NAICS 322291 Sanitary Paper Product Manufacturing
2677 Envelopes
  NAICS 322232 Envelope Manufacturing
2678 Stationery, Tablets, & Related Products
  NAICS 322233 Stationery, Tablet, & Related Product
       Manufacturing
2679 Converted Paper & Paperboard Products, nec
  NAICS 322215 Non-folding Sanitary Food Container
       Manufacturing
  NAICS 322222 Coated & Laminated Paper Manufacturing
  NAICS 322231 Die-cut Paper & Paperboard Office Supplies
       Manufacturing
  NAICS 322298 All Other Converted Paper Product
       Manufacturing

PRINTING, PUBLISHING, & ALLIED INDUSTRIES

2711 Newspapers: Publishing, or Publishing & Printing
NAICS 51111   Newspaper Publishers
2721 Periodicals: Publishing, or Publishing & Printing
NAICS 51112   Periodical Publishers
2731 Books: Publishing, or Publishing & Printing
NAICS 51223   Music Publishers
NAICS 51113   Book Publishers
2732 Book Printing
NAICS 323117 Book Printing
2741 Miscellaneous Publishing
NAICS 51114   Database & Directory Publishers
NAICS 51223   Music Publishers
NAICS 511199 All Other Publishers
2752 Commercial Printing, Lithographic
NAICS 323114 Quick Printing
NAICS 323110 Commercial Lithographic Printing
2754 Commercial Printing, Gravure
NAICS 323111 Commercial Gravure Printing
2759 Commercial Printing, nec
NAICS 323113 Commercial Screen Printing
NAICS 323112 Commercial Flexographic Printing
NAICS 323114 Quick Printing
NAICS 323115 Digital Printing
NAICS 323119 Other Commercial Printing
2761 Manifold Business Forms
NAICS 323116 Manifold Business Form Printing
2771 Greeting Cards
NAICS 323110 Commercial Lithographic Printing
NAICS 323111 Commercial Gravure Printing
NAICS 323112 Commercial Flexographic Printing
NAICS 323113 Commercial Screen Printing
NAICS 323119 Other Commercial Printing
NAICS 511191 Greeting Card Publishers
2782 Blankbooks, Loose-leaf Binders & Devices
NAICS 323110 Commercial Lithographic Printing
NAICS 323111 Commercial Gravure Printing
NAICS 323112 Commercial Flexographic Printing
NAICS 323113 Commercial Screen Printing
NAICS 323119 Other Commercial Printing
NAICS 323118 Blankbook, Loose-leaf Binder & Device
   Manufacturing
2789 Bookbinding & Related Work
NAICS 323121 Tradebinding & Related Work
2791 Typesetting
NAICS 323122 Prepress Services
2796 Platemaking & Related Services
NAICS 323122 Prepress Services

CHEMICALS & ALLIED PRODUCTS

2812 Alkalies & Chlorine
NAICS 325181 Alkalies & Chlorine Manufacturing
2813 Industrial Gases
NAICS 32512   Industrial Gas Manufacturing
2816 Inorganic Pigments
NAICS 325131 Inorganic Dye & Pigment Manufacturing
NAICS 325182 Carbon Black Manufacturing
2819 Industrial Inorganic Chemicals, nec
NAICS 325998 All Other Miscellaneous Chemical Product
   Manufacturing

NAICS 331311 Alumina Refining
NAICS 325131 Inorganic Dye & Pigment Manufacturing
NAICS 325188 All Other Basic Inorganic Chemical
   Manufacturing
2821 Plastics Material Synthetic Resins, & Nonvulcanizable Elastomers
NAICS 325211 Plastics Material & Resin Manufacturing
2822 Synthetic Rubber
NAICS 325212 Synthetic Rubber Manufacturing
2823 Cellulosic Manmade Fibers
NAICS 325221 Cellulosic Manmade Fiber Manufacturing
2824 Manmade Organic Fibers, Except Cellulosic
NAICS 325222 Noncellulosic Organic Fiber Manufacturing
2833 Medicinal Chemicals & Botanical Products
NAICS 325411 Medicinal & Botanical Manufacturing
2834 Pharmaceutical Preparations
NAICS 325412 Pharmaceutical Preparation Manufacturing
2835 In Vitro & in Vivo Diagnostic Substances
NAICS 325412 Pharmaceutical Preparation Manufacturing
NAICS 325413 In-vitro Diagnostic Substance Manufacturing
2836 Biological Products, Except Diagnostic Substances
NAICS 325414 Biological Product Manufacturing
2841 Soaps & Other Detergents, Except Speciality Cleaners
NAICS 325611 Soap & Other Detergent Manufacturing
2842 Speciality Cleaning, Polishing, & Sanitary Preparations
NAICS 325612 Polish & Other Sanitation Good Manufacturing
2843 Surface Active Agents, Finishing Agents, Sulfonated Oils, & Assistants
NAICS 325613 Surface Active Agent Manufacturing
2844 Perfumes, Cosmetics, & Other Toilet Preparations
NAICS 32562   Toilet Preparation Manufacturing
NAICS 325611 Soap & Other Detergent Manufacturing
2851 Paints, Varnishes, Lacquers, Enamels, & Allied Products
NAICS 32551   Paint & Coating Manufacturing
2861 Gum & Wood Chemicals
NAICS 325191 Gum & Wood Chemical Manufacturing
2865 Cyclic Organic Crudes & Intermediates, & Organic Dyes & Pigments
NAICS 32511   Petrochemical Manufacturing
NAICS 325132 Organic Dye & Pigment Manufacturing
NAICS 325192 Cyclic Crude & Intermediate Manufacturing
2869 Industrial Organic Chemicals, nec
NAICS 32511   Petrochemical Manufacturing
NAICS 325188 All Other Inorganic Chemical Manufacturing
NAICS 325193 Ethyl Alcohol Manufacturing
NAICS 32512   Industrial Gas Manufacturing
NAICS 325199 All Other Basic Organic Chemical
   Manufacturing
2873 Nitrogenous Fertilizers
NAICS 325311 Nitrogenous Fertilizer Manufacturing
2874 Phosphatic Fertilizers
NAICS 325312 Phosphatic Fertilizer Manufacturing
2875 Fertilizers, Mixing Only
NAICS 325314 Fertilizer Manufacturing
2879 Pesticides & Agricultural Chemicals, nec
NAICS 32532   Pesticide & Other Agricultural Chemical
   Manufacturing
2891 Adhesives & Sealants
NAICS 32552   Adhesive & Sealant Manufacturing
2892 Explosives
NAICS 32592   Explosives Manufacturing
2893 Printing Ink
NAICS 32591   Printing Ink Manufacturing

2895 Carbon Black
NAICS 325182 Carbon Black Manufacturing
2899 Chemicals & Chemical Preparations, nec
NAICS 32551   Paint & Coating Manufacturing
NAICS 311942 Spice & Extract Manufacturing
NAICS 325199 All Other Basic Organic Chemical
Manufacturing
NAICS 325998 All Other Miscellaneous Chemical Product
Manufacturing

PETROLEUM REFINING & RELATED INDUSTRIES

2911 Petroleum Refining
NAICS 32411   Petroleum Refineries
2951 Asphalt Paving Mixtures & Blocks
NAICS 324121 Asphalt Paving Mixture & Block Manufacturing
2952 Asphalt Felts & Coatings
NAICS 324122 Asphalt Shingle & Coating Materials
Manufacturing
2992 Lubricating Oils & Greases
NAICS 324191 Petroleum Lubricating Oil & Grease
Manufacturing 2999

RUBBER & MISCELLANEOUS PLASTICS PRODUCTS

3011 Tires & Inner Tubes
NAICS 326211 Tire Manufacturing
3021 Rubber & Plastics Footwear
NAICS 316211 Rubber & Plastics Footwear Manufacturing
3052 Rubber & Plastics Hose & Belting
NAICS 32622   Rubber & Plastics Hoses & Belting
Manufacturing
3053 Gaskets, Packing, & Sealing Devices
NAICS 339991 Gasket, Packing, & Sealing Device
Manufacturing
3061 Molded, Extruded, & Lathe-cut Mechanical Rubber Products
NAICS 326291 Rubber Product Manufacturing for Mechanical
Use
3069 Fabricated Rubber Products, nec
NAICS 31332   Fabric Coating Mills
NAICS 326192 Resilient Floor Covering Manufacturing
NAICS 326299 All Other Rubber Product Manufacturing
3081 Unsupported Plastics Film & Sheet
NAICS 326113 Unsupported Plastics Film & Sheet
Manufacturing
3082 Unsupported Plastics Profile Shapes
NAICS 326121 Unsupported Plastics Profile Shape
Manufacturing
3083 Laminated Plastics Plate, Sheet, & Profile Shapes
NAICS 32613   Laminated Plastics Plate, Sheet, & Shape
Manufacturing
3084 Plastic Pipe
NAICS 326122 Plastic Pipe & Pipe Fitting Manufacturing
3085 Plastics Bottles
NAICS 32616   Plastics Bottle Manufacturing
3086 Plastics Foam Products
NAICS 32615   Urethane & Other Foam Product
Manufacturing
NAICS 32614   Polystyrene Foam Product Manufacturing

3087 Custom Compounding of Purchased Plastics Resins
NAICS 325991 Custom Compounding of Purchased Resin
3088 Plastics Plumbing Fixtures
NAICS 326191 Plastics Plumbing Fixtures Manufacturing
3089 Plastics Products, nec
NAICS 326122 Plastics Pipe & Pipe Fitting Manufacturing
NAICS 326121 Unsupported Plastics Profile Shape
Manufacturing
NAICS 326199 All Other Plastics Product Manufacturing

LEATHER & LEATHER PRODUCTS

3111 Leather Tanning & Finishing
NAICS 31611   Leather & Hide Tanning & Finishing
3131 Boot & Shoe Cut Stock & Findings
NAICS 321999 All Other Miscellaneous Wood Product
Manufacturing
NAICS 339993 Fastener, Button, Needle, & Pin Manufacturing
NAICS 316999 All Other Leather Good Manufacturing
3142 House Slippers
NAICS 316212 House Slipper Manufacturing
3143 Men's Footwear, Except Athletic
NAICS 316213 Men's Footwear Manufacturing
3144 Women's Footwear, Except Athletic
NAICS 316214 Women's Footwear Manufacturing
3149 Footwear, Except Rubber, nec
NAICS 316219 Other Footwear Manufacturing
3151 Leather Gloves & Mittens
NAICS 315992 Glove & Mitten Manufacturing
3161 Luggage
NAICS 316991 Luggage Manufacturing
3171 Women's Handbags & Purses
NAICS 316992 Women's Handbag & Purse Manufacturing
3172 Personal Leather Goods, Except Women's Handbags & Purses
NAICS 316993 Personal Leather Good Manufacturing
3199 Leather Goods, nec
NAICS 316999 All Other Leather Good Manufacturing

STONE, CLAY, GLASS, & CONCRETE PRODUCTS

3211 Flat Glass
NAICS 327211 Flat Glass Manufacturing
3221 Glass Containers
NAICS 327213 Glass Container Manufacturing
3229 Pressed & Blown Glass & Glassware, nec
NAICS 327212 Other Pressed & Blown Glass & Glassware
Manufacturing
3231 Glass Products, Made of Purchased Glass
NAICS 327215 Glass Product Manufacturing Made of
Purchased Glass
3241 Cement, Hydraulic
NAICS 32731   Hydraulic Cement Manufacturing
3251 Brick & Structural Clay Tile
NAICS 327121 Brick & Structural Clay Tile Manufacturing
3253 Ceramic Wall & Floor Tile
NAICS 327122 Ceramic Wall & Floor Tile Manufacturing
3255 Clay Refractories
NAICS 327124 Clay Refractory Manufacturing

3259 Structural Clay Products, nec
NAICS 327123 Other Structural Clay Product Manufacturing
3261 Vitreous China Plumbing Fixtures & China & Earthenware Fittings & Bathroom Accessories
NAICS 327111 Vitreous China Plumbing Fixture & China & Earthenware Fittings & Bathroom Accessories Manufacturing
3262 Vitreous China Table & Kitchen Articles
NAICS 327112 Vitreous China, Fine Earthenware & Other Pottery Product Manufacturing
3263 Fine Earthenware Table & Kitchen Articles
NAICS 327112 Vitreous China, Fine Earthenware & Other Pottery Product Manufacturing
3264 Porcelain Electrical Supplies
NAICS 327113 Porcelain Electrical Supply Manufacturing
3269 Pottery Products, nec
NAICS 327112 Vitreous China, Fine Earthenware, & Other Pottery Product Manufacturing
3271 Concrete Block & Brick
NAICS 327331 Concrete Block & Brick Manufacturing
3272 Concrete Products, Except Block & Brick
NAICS 327999 All Other Miscellaneous Nonmetallic Mineral Product Manufacturing
NAICS 327332 Concrete Pipe Manufacturing
NAICS 32739 Other Concrete Product Manufacturing
3273 Ready-mixed Concrete
NAICS 32732 Ready-mix Concrete Manufacturing
3274 Lime
NAICS 32741 Lime Manufacturing
3275 Gypsum Products
NAICS 32742 Gypsum & Gypsum Product Manufacturing
3281 Cut Stone & Stone Products
NAICS 327991 Cut Stone & Stone Product Manufacturing
3291 Abrasive Products
NAICS 332999 All Other Miscellaneous Fabricated Metal Product Manufacturing
NAICS 32791 Abrasive Product Manufacturing
3292 Asbestos Products
NAICS 33634 Motor Vehicle Brake System Manufacturing
NAICS 327999 All Other Miscellaneous Nonmetallic Mineral Product Manufacturing
3295 Minerals & Earths, Ground or Otherwise Treated
NAICS 327992 Ground or Treated Mineral & Earth Manufacturing
3296 Mineral Wool
NAICS 327993 Mineral Wool Manufacturing
3297 Nonclay Refractories
NAICS 327125 Nonclay Refractory Manufacturing
3299 Nonmetallic Mineral Products, nec
NAICS 32742 Gypsum & Gypsum Product Manufacturing
NAICS 327999 All Other Miscellaneous Nonmetallic Mineral Product Manufacturing

PRIMARY METALS INDUSTRIES

3312 Steel Works, Blast Furnaces , & Rolling Mills
NAICS 324199 All Other Petroleum & Coal Products Manufacturing
NAICS 331111 Iron & Steel Mills
3313 Electrometallurgical Products, Except Steel
NAICS 331112 Electrometallurgical Ferroalloy Product Manufacturing

NAICS 331492 Secondary Smelting, Refining, & Alloying of Nonferrous Metals
3315 Steel Wiredrawing & Steel Nails & Spikes
NAICS 331222 Steel Wire Drawing
NAICS 332618 Other Fabricated Wire Product Manufacturing
3316 Cold-rolled Steel Sheet, Strip, & Bars
NAICS 331221 Cold-rolled Steel Shape Manufacturing
3317 Steel Pipe & Tubes
NAICS 33121 Iron & Steel Pipes & Tubes Manufacturing from Purchased Steel
3321 Gray & Ductile Iron Foundries
NAICS 331511 Iron Foundries
3322 Malleable Iron Foundries
NAICS 331511 Iron Foundries
3324 Steel Investment Foundries
NAICS 331512 Steel Investment Foundries
3325 Steel Foundries, nec
NAICS 331513 Steel Foundries
3331 Primary Smelting & Refining of Copper
NAICS 331411 Primary Smelting & Refining of Copper
3334 Primary Production of Aluminum
NAICS 331312 Primary Aluminum Production
3339 Primary Smelting & Refining of Nonferrous Metals, Except Copper & Aluminum
NAICS 331419 Primary Smelting & Refining of Nonferrous Metals
3341 Secondary Smelting & Refining of Nonferrous Metals
NAICS 331314 Secondary Smelting & Alloying of Aluminum
NAICS 331423 Secondary Smelting, Refining, & Alloying of Copper
NAICS 331492 Secondary Smelting, Refining, & Alloying of Nonferrous Metals
3351 Rolling, Drawing, & Extruding of Copper
NAICS 331421 Copper Rolling, Drawing, & Extruding
3353 Aluminum Sheet, Plate, & Foil
NAICS 331315 Aluminum Sheet, Plate, & Foil Manufacturing
3354 Aluminum Extruded Products
NAICS 331316 Aluminum Extruded Product Manufacturing
3355 Aluminum Rolling & Drawing, nec
NAICS 331319 Other Aluminum Rolling & Drawing,
3356 Rolling, Drawing, & Extruding of Nonferrous Metals, Except Copper & Aluminum
NAICS 331491 Nonferrous Metal Rolling. Drawing, & Extruding
3357 Drawing & Insulating of Nonferrous Wire
NAICS 331319 Other Aluminum Rolling & Drawing
NAICS 331422 Copper Wire Drawing
NAICS 331491 Nonferrous Metal Rolling, Drawing, & Extruding
NAICS 335921 Fiber Optic Cable Manufacturing
NAICS 335929 Other Communication & Energy Wire Manufacturing
3363 Aluminum Die-castings
NAICS 331521 Aluminum Die-castings
3364 Nonferrous Die-castings, Except Aluminum
NAICS 331522 Nonferrous Die-castings
3365 Aluminum Foundries
NAICS 331524 Aluminum Foundries
3366 Copper Foundries
NAICS 331525 Copper Foundries
3369 Nonferrous Foundries, Except Aluminum & Copper
NAICS 331528 Other Nonferrous Foundries

3398 Metal Heat Treating
NAICS 332811 Metal Heat Treating
3399 Primary Metal Products, nec
NAICS 331111 Iron & Steel Mills
NAICS 331314 Secondary Smelting & Alloying of Aluminum
NAICS 331423 Secondary Smelting, Refining & Alloying of Copper
NAICS 331492 Secondary Smelting, Refining, & Alloying of Nonferrous Metals
NAICS 332618 Other Fabricated Wire Product Manufacturing
NAICS 332813 Electroplating, Plating, Polishing, Anodizing, & Coloring

FABRICATED METAL PRODUCTS, EXCEPT MACHINERY & TRANSPORTATION EQUIPMENT

3411 Metal Cans
NAICS 332431 Metal Can Manufacturing
3412 Metal Shipping Barrels, Drums, Kegs & Pails
NAICS 332439 Other Metal Container Manufacturing
3421 Cutlery
NAICS 332211 Cutlery & Flatware Manufacturing
3423 Hand & Edge Tools, Except Machine Tools & Handsaws
NAICS 332212 Hand & Edge Tool Manufacturing
3425 Saw Blades & Handsaws
NAICS 332213 Saw Blade & Handsaw Manufacturing
3429 Hardware, nec
NAICS 332439 Other Metal Container Manufacturing
NAICS 332919 Other Metal Valve & Pipe Fitting Manufacturing
NAICS 33251　Hardware Manufacturing
3431 Enameled Iron & Metal Sanitary Ware
NAICS 332998 Enameled Iron & Metal Sanitary Ware Manufacturing
3432 Plumbing Fixture Fittings & Trim
NAICS 332913 Plumbing Fixture Fitting & Trim Manufacturing
NAICS 332999 All Other Miscellaneous Fabricated Metal Product Manufacturing
3433 Heating Equipment, Except Electric & Warm Air Furnaces
NAICS 333414 Heating Equipment Manufacturing
3441 Fabricated Structural Metal
NAICS 332312 Fabricated Structural Metal Manufacturing
3442 Metal Doors, Sash, Frames, Molding, & Trim Manufacturing
NAICS 332321 Metal Window & Door Manufacturing
3443 Fabricated Plate Work
NAICS 332313 Plate Work Manufacturing
NAICS 33241　Power Boiler & Heat Exchanger Manufacturing
NAICS 33242　Metal Tank Manufacturing
NAICS 333415 Air-conditioning & Warm Air Heating Equipment & Commercial & Industrial Refrigeration Equipment Manufacturing
3444 Sheet Metal Work
NAICS 332322 Sheet Metal Work Manufacturing
NAICS 332439 Other Metal Container Manufacturing
3446 Architectural & Ornamental Metal Work
NAICS 332323 Ornamental & Architectural Metal Work Manufacturing
3448 Prefabricated Metal Buildings & Components
NAICS 332311 Prefabricated Metal Building & Component Manufacturing

3449 Miscellaneous Structural Metal Work
NAICS 332114 Custom Roll Forming
NAICS 332312 Fabricated Structural Metal Manufacturing
NAICS 332321 Metal Window & Door Manufacturing
NAICS 332323 Ornamental & Architectural Metal Work Manufacturing
3451 Screw Machine Products
NAICS 332721 Precision Turned Product Manufacturing
3452 Bolts, Nuts, Screws, Rivets, & Washers
NAICS 332722 Bolt, Nut, Screw, Rivet, & Washer Manufacturing
3462 Iron & Steel Forgings
NAICS 332111 Iron & Steel Forging
3463 Nonferrous Forgings
NAICS 332112 Nonferrous Forging
3465 Automotive Stamping
NAICS 33637　Motor Vehicle Metal Stamping
3466 Crowns & Closures
NAICS 332115 Crown & Closure Manufacturing
3469 Metal Stamping, nec
NAICS 339911 Jewelry Manufacturing
NAICS 332116 Metal Stamping
NAICS 332214 Kitchen Utensil, Pot & Pan Manufacturing
3471 Electroplating, Plating, Polishing, Anodizing, & Coloring
NAICS 332813 Electroplating, Plating, Polishing, Anodizing, & Coloring
3479 Coating, Engraving, & Allied Services, nec
NAICS 339914 Costume Jewelry & Novelty Manufacturing
NAICS 339911 Jewelry Manufacturing
NAICS 339912 Silverware & Plated Ware Manufacturing
NAICS 332812 Metal Coating, Engraving , & Allied Services to Manufacturers
3482 Small Arms Ammunition
NAICS 332992 Small Arms Ammunition Manufacturing
3483 Ammunition, Except for Small Arms
NAICS 332993 Ammunition Manufacturing
3484 Small Arms
NAICS 332994 Small Arms Manufacturing
3489 Ordnance & Accessories, nec
NAICS 332995 Other Ordnance & Accessories Manufacturing
3491
3492 Fluid Power Valves & Hose Fittings
NAICS 332912 Fluid Power Valve & Hose Fitting Manufacturing
3493 Steel Springs, Except Wire
NAICS 332611 Steel Spring Manufacturing
3494 Valves & Pipe Fittings, nec
NAICS 332919 Other Metal Valve & Pipe Fitting Manufacturing
NAICS 332999 All Other Miscellaneous Fabricated Metal Product Manufacturing
3495 Wire Springs
NAICS 332612 Wire Spring Manufacturing
NAICS 334518 Watch, Clock, & Part Manufacturing
3496 Miscellaneous Fabricated Wire Products
NAICS 332618 Other Fabricated Wire Product Manufacturing
3497 Metal Foil & Leaf
NAICS 322225 Laminated Aluminum Foil Manufacturing for Flexible Packaging Uses
NAICS 332999 All Other Miscellaneous Fabricated Metal Product Manufacturing
3498 Fabricated Pipe & Pipe Fittings
NAICS 332996 Fabricated Pipe & Pipe Fitting Manufacturing

3499 Fabricated Metal Products, nec
NAICS 337148 Other Nonwood Furniture Manufacturing
NAICS 332117 Powder Metallurgy Part Manufacturing
NAICS 332439 Other Metal Container Manufacturing
NAICS 33251 Hardware Manufacturing
NAICS 332919 Other Metal Valve & Pipe Fitting
Manufacturing
NAICS 339914 Costume Jewelry & Novelty Manufacturing
NAICS 332999 All Other Miscellaneous Fabricated Metal
Product Manufacturing

INDUSTRIAL & COMMERCIAL MACHINERY & COMPUTER EQUIPMENT

3511 Steam, Gas, & Hydraulic Turbines, & Turbine Generator Set Units
NAICS 333611 Turbine & Turbine Generator Set Unit
Manufacturing
3519 Internal Combustion Engines, nec
NAICS 336399 All Other Motor Vehicle Parts Manufacturing
NAICS 333618 Other Engine Equipment Manufacturing
3523 Farm Machinery & Equipment
NAICS 333111 Farm Machinery & Equipment Manufacturing
NAICS 332323 Ornamental & Architectural Metal Work
Manufacturing
NAICS 332212 Hand & Edge Tool Manufacturing
NAICS 333922 Conveyor & Conveying Equipment
Manufacturing
3524 Lawn & Garden Tractors & Home Lawn & Garden Equipment
NAICS 333112 Lawn & Garden Tractor & Home Lawn &
Garden Equipment Manufacturing
NAICS 332212 Hand & Edge Tool Manufacturing
3531 Construction Machinery & Equipment
NAICS 33651 Railroad Rolling Stock Manufacturing
NAICS 333923 Overhead Traveling Crane, Hoist, & Monorail
System Manufacturing
NAICS 33312 Construction Machinery Manufacturing
3532 Mining Machinery & Equipment, Except Oil & Gas Field Machinery & Equipment
NAICS 333131 Mining Machinery & Equipment Manufacturing
3533 Oil & Gas Field Machinery & Equipment
NAICS 333132 Oil & Gas Field Machinery & Equipment
Manufacturing
3534 Elevators & Moving Stairways
NAICS 333921 Elevator & Moving Stairway Manufacturing
3535 Conveyors & Conveying Equipment
NAICS 333922 Conveyor & Conveying Equipment
Manufacturing
3536 Overhead Traveling Cranes, Hoists & Monorail Systems
NAICS 333923 Overhead Traveling Crane, Hoist & Monorail
System Manufacturing
3537 Industrial Trucks, Tractors, Trailers, & Stackers
NAICS 333924 Industrial Truck, Tractor, Trailer, & Stacker
Machinery Manufacturing
NAICS 332999 All Other Miscellaneous Fabricated Metal
Product Manufacturing
NAICS 332439 Other Metal Container Manufacturing
3541 Machine Tools, Metal Cutting Type
NAICS 333512 Machine Tool Manufacturing
3542 Machine Tools, Metal Forming Type
NAICS 333513 Machine Tool Manufacturing

3543 Industrial Patterns
NAICS 332997 Industrial Pattern Manufacturing
3544 Special Dies & Tools, Die Sets, Jigs & Fixtures, & Industrial Molds
NAICS 333514 Special Die & Tool, Die Set, Jig, & Fixture
Manufacturing
NAICS 333511 Industrial Mold Manufacturing
3545 Cutting Tools, Machine Tool Accessories, & Machinists' Precision Measuring Devices
NAICS 333515 Cutting Tool & Machine Tool Accessory
Manufacturing
NAICS 332212 Hand & Edge Tool Manufacturing
3546 Power-driven Handtools
NAICS 333991 Power-driven Hand Tool Manufacturing
3547 Rolling Mill Machinery & Equipment
NAICS 333516 Rolling Mill Machinery & Equipment
Manufacturing
3548 Electric & Gas Welding & Soldering Equipment
NAICS 333992 Welding & Soldering Equipment Manufacturing
NAICS 335311 Power, Distribution, & Specialty Transformer
Manufacturing
3549 Metalworking Machinery, nec
NAICS 333518 Other Metalworking Machinery Manufacturing
3552
3553 Woodworking Machinery
NAICS 33321 Sawmill & Woodworking Machinery
Manufacturing
3554 Paper Industries Machinery
NAICS 333291 Paper Industry Machinery Manufacturing
3555 Printing Trades Machinery & Equipment
NAICS 333293 Printing Machinery & Equipment
Manufacturing
3556 Food Products Machinery
NAICS 333294 Food Product Machinery Manufacturing
3559 Special Industry Machinery, nec
NAICS 33322 Rubber & Plastics Industry Machinery
Manufacturing
NAICS 333319 Other Commercial & Service Industry
Machinery Manufacturing
NAICS 333295 Semiconductor Manufacturing Machinery
NAICS 333298 All Other Industrial Machinery Manufacturing
3561 Pumps & Pumping Equipment
NAICS 333911 Pump & Pumping Equipment Manufacturing
3562 Ball & Roller Bearings
NAICS 332991 Ball & Roller Bearing Manufacturing
3563 Air & Gas Compressors
NAICS 333912 Air & Gas Compressor Manufacturing
3564 Industrial & Commercial Fans & Blowers & Air Purification Equipment
NAICS 333411 Air Purification Equipment Manufacturing
NAICS 333412 Industrial & Commercial Fan & Blower
Manufacturing
3565 Packaging Machinery
NAICS 333993 Packaging Machinery Manufacturing
3566 Speed Changers, Industrial High-speed Drives, & Gears
NAICS 333612 Speed Changer, Industrial High-speed Drive, &
Gear Manufacturing
3567 Industrial Process Furnaces & Ovens
NAICS 333994 Industrial Process Furnace & Oven
Manufacturing
3568 Mechanical Power Transmission Equipment, nec
NAICS 333613 Mechanical Power Transmission Equipment
Manufacturing

3569 General Industrial Machinery & Equipment, nec
NAICS 333999 All Other General Purpose Machinery Manufacturing

3571 Electronic Computers
NAICS 334111 Electronic Computer Manufacturing

3572 Computer Storage Devices
NAICS 334112 Computer Storage Device Manufacturing

3575 Computer Terminals
NAICS 334113 Computer Terminal Manufacturing

3577 Computer Peripheral Equipment, nec
NAICS 334119 Other Computer Peripheral Equipment Manufacturing

3578 Calculating & Accounting Machines, Except Electronic Computers
NAICS 334119 Other Computer Peripheral Equipment Manufacturing
NAICS 333313 Office Machinery Manufacturing

3579 Office Machines, nec
NAICS 339942 Lead Pencil & Art Good Manufacturing
NAICS 334518 Watch, Clock, & Part Manufacturing
NAICS 333313 Office Machinery Manufacturing

3581 Automatic Vending Machines
NAICS 333311 Automatic Vending Machine Manufacturing

3582 Commercial Laundry, Drycleaning, & Pressing Machines
NAICS 333312 Commercial Laundry, Drycleaning, & Pressing Machine Manufacturing

3585 Air-conditioning & Warm Air Heating Equipment & Commercial & Industrial Refrigeration Equipment
NAICS 336391 Motor Vehicle Air Conditioning Manufacturing
NAICS 333415 Air Conditioning & Warm Air Heating Equipment & Commercial & Industrial Refrigeration Equipment Manufacturing

3586 Measuring & Dispensing Pumps
NAICS 333913 Measuring & Dispensing Pump Manufacturing

3589 Service Industry Machinery, nec
NAICS 333319 Other Commercial and Service Industry Machinery Manufacturing

3592 Carburetors, Pistons, Piston Rings & Valves
NAICS 336311 Carburetor, Piston, Piston Ring & Valve Manufacturing

3593 Fluid Power Cylinders & Actuators
NAICS 333995 Fluid Power Cylinder & Actuator Manufacturing

3594 Fluid Power Pumps & Motors
NAICS 333996 Fluid Power Pump & Motor Manufacturing

3596 Scales & Balances, Except Laboratory
NAICS 333997 Scale & Balance Manufacturing

3599 Industrial & Commercial Machinery & Equipment, nec
NAICS 336399 All Other Motor Vehicle Part Manufacturing
NAICS 332999 All Other Miscellaneous Fabricated Metal Product Manufacturing
NAICS 333319 Other Commercial & Service Industry Machinery Manufacturing
NAICS 33271 Machine Shops
NAICS 333999 All Other General Purpose Machinery Manufacturing

ELECTRONIC & OTHER ELECTRICAL EQUIPMENT & COMPONENTS, EXCEPT COMPUTER EQUIPMENT

3612 Power, Distribution, & Specialty Transformers
NAICS 335311 Power, Distribution, & Specialty Transformer Manufacturing

3613 Switchgear & Switchboard Apparatus
NAICS 335313 Switchgear & Switchboard Apparatus Manufacturing

3621 Motors & Generators
NAICS 335312 Motor & Generator Manufacturing

3624 Carbon & Graphite Products
NAICS 335991 Carbon & Graphite Product Manufacturing

3625 Relays & Industrial Controls
NAICS 335314 Relay & Industrial Control Manufacturing

3629 Electrical Industrial Apparatus, nec
NAICS 335999 All Other Miscellaneous Electrical Equipment & Component Manufacturing

3631 Household Cooking Equipment
NAICS 335221 Household Cooking Appliance Manufacturing

3632 Household Refrigerators & Home & Farm Freezers
NAICS 335222 Household Refrigerator & Home Freezer Manufacturing

3633 Household Laundry Equipment
NAICS 335224 Household Laundry Equipment Manufacturing

3634 Electric Housewares & Fans
NAICS 335211 Electric Housewares & Fan Manufacturing

3635 Household Vacuum Cleaners
NAICS 335212 Household Vacuum Cleaner Manufacturing

3639 Household Appliances, nec
NAICS 335212 Household Vacuum Cleaner Manufacturing
NAICS 333298 All Other Industrial Machinery Manufacturing
NAICS 335228 Other Household Appliance Manufacturing

3641 Electric Lamp Bulbs & Tubes
NAICS 33511 Electric Lamp Bulb & Part Manufacturing

3643 Current-carrying Wiring Devices
NAICS 335931 Current-carrying Wiring Device Manufacturing

3644 Noncurrent-carrying Wiring Devices
NAICS 335932 Noncurrent-carrying Wiring Device Manufacturing

3645 Residential Electric Lighting Fixtures
NAICS 335121 Residential Electric Lighting Fixture Manufacturing

3646 Commercial, Industrial, & Institutional Electric Lighting Fixtures
NAICS 335122 Commercial, Industrial, & Institutional Electric Lighting Fixture Manufacturing

3647 Vehicular Lighting Equipment
NAICS 336321 Vehicular Lighting Equipment Manufacturing

3648 Lighting Equipment, nec
NAICS 335129 Other Lighting Equipment Manufacturing

3651 Household Audio & Video Equipment
NAICS 33431 Audio & Video Equipment Manufacturing 3652
NAICS 51222 Integrated Record Production/distribution

3661 Telephone & Telegraph Apparatus
NAICS 33421 Telephone Apparatus Manufacturing
NAICS 334416 Electronic Coil, Transformer, & Other Inductor Manufacturing
NAICS 334418 Printed Circuit/electronics Assembly Manufacturing

3663 Radio & Television Broadcasting & Communication Equipment
NAICS 33422   Radio & Television Broadcasting & Wireless Communications Equipment Manufacturing

3669 Communications Equipment, nec
NAICS 33429   Other Communication Equipment Manufacturing

3671 Electron Tubes
NAICS 334411 Electron Tube Manufacturing

3672 Printed Circuit Boards
NAICS 334412 Printed Circuit Board Manufacturing

3674 Semiconductors & Related Devices
NAICS 334413 Semiconductor & Related Device Manufacturing

3675 Electronic Capacitors
NAICS 334414 Electronic Capacitor Manufacturing

3676 Electronic Resistors
NAICS 334415 Electronic Resistor Manufacturing

3677 Electronic Coils, Transformers, & Other Inductors
NAICS 334416 Electronic Coil, Transformer, & Other Inductor Manufacturing

3678 Electronic ConNECtors
NAICS 334417 Electronic ConNECtor Manufacturing

3679 Electronic Components, nec
NAICS 33422   Radio & Television Broadcasting & Wireless Communications Equipment Manufacturing
NAICS 334418 Printed Circuit/electronics Assembly Manufacturing
NAICS 336322 Other Motor Vehicle Electrical & Electronic Equipment Manufacturing
NAICS 334419 Other Electronic Component Manufacturing

3691 Storage Batteries
NAICS 335911 Storage Battery Manufacturing

3692 Primary Batteries, Dry & Wet
NAICS 335912 Dry & Wet Primary Battery Manufacturing

3694 Electrical Equipment for Internal Combustion Engines
NAICS 336322 Other Motor Vehicle Electrical & Electronic Equipment Manufacturing

3695 Magnetic & Optical Recording Media
NAICS 334613 Magnetic & Optical Recording Media Manufacturing

3699 Electrical Machinery, Equipment, & Supplies, nec
NAICS 333319 Other Commercial & Service Industry Machinery Manufacturing
NAICS 333618 Other Engine Equipment Manufacturing
NAICS 334119 Other Computer Peripheral Equipment Manufacturing Classify According to Function
NAICS 335129 Other Lighting Equipment Manufacturing
NAICS 335999 All Other Miscellaneous Electrical Equipment & Component Manufacturing

TRANSPORTATION EQUIPMENT

3711 Motor Vehicles & Passenger Car Bodies
NAICS 336111 Automobile Manufacturing
NAICS 336112 Light Truck & Utility Vehicle Manufacturing
NAICS 33612   Heavy Duty Truck Manufacturing
NAICS 336211 Motor Vehicle Body Manufacturing
NAICS 336992 Military Armored Vehicle, Tank, & Tank Component Manufacturing

3713 Truck & Bus Bodies
NAICS 336211 Motor Vehicle Body Manufacturing

3714 Motor Vehicle Parts & Accessories
NAICS 336211 Motor Vehicle Body Manufacturing
NAICS 336312 Gasoline Engine & Engine Parts Manufacturing
NAICS 336322 Other Motor Vehicle Electrical & Electronic Equipment Manufacturing
NAICS 33633   Motor Vehicle Steering & Suspension Components Manufacturing
NAICS 33634   Motor Vehicle Brake System Manufacturing
NAICS 33635   Motor Vehicle Transmission & Power Train Parts Manufacturing
NAICS 336399 All Other Motor Vehicle Parts Manufacturing

3715 Truck Trailers
NAICS 336212 Truck Trailer Manufacturing

3716 Motor Homes
NAICS 336213 Motor Home Manufacturing

3721 Aircraft
NAICS 336411 Aircraft Manufacturing

3724 Aircraft Engines & Engine Parts
NAICS 336412 Aircraft Engine & Engine Parts Manufacturing 3728
NAICS 336413 Other Aircraft Part & Auxiliary Equipment Manufacturing

3731 Ship Building & Repairing
NAICS 336611 Ship Building & Repairing

3732 Boat Building & Repairing
NAICS 81149   Other Personal & Household Goods Repair & Maintenance
NAICS 336612 Boat Building

3743 Railroad Equipment
NAICS 333911 Pump & Pumping Equipment Manufacturing
NAICS 33651   Railroad Rolling Stock Manufacturing

3751 Motorcycles, Bicycles, & Parts
NAICS 336991 Motorcycle, Bicycle, & Parts Manufacturing

3761 Guided Missiles & Space Vehicles
NAICS 336414 Guided Missile & Space Vehicle Manufacturing 3764

3769 Guided Missile Space Vehicle Parts & Auxiliary Equipment, nec
NAICS 336419 Other Guided Missile & Space Vehicle Parts & Auxiliary Equipment Manufacturing

3792 Travel Trailers & Campers
NAICS 336214 Travel Trailer & Camper Manufacturing

3795 Tanks & Tank Components
NAICS 336992 Military Armored Vehicle, Tank, & Tank Component Manufacturing

3799 Transportation Equipment, nec
NAICS 336214 Travel Trailer & Camper Manufacturing
NAICS 332212 Hand & Edge Tool Manufacturing
NAICS 336999 All Other Transportation Equipment Manufacturing

MEASURING, ANALYZING, & CONTROLLING INSTRUMENTS

3812 Search, Detection, Navigation, Guidance, Aeronautical, & Nautical Systems & Instruments
NAICS 334511 Search, Detection, Navigation, Guidance, Aeronautical, & Nautical System & Instrument Manufacturing

3821 Laboratory Apparatus & Furniture
NAICS 339111 Laboratory Apparatus & Furniture Manufacturing

3822 Automatic Controls for Regulating Residential & Commercial Environments & Appliances
NAICS 334512 Automatic Environmental Control Manufacturing for Regulating Residential, Commercial, & Appliance Use

3823 Industrial Instruments for Measurement, Display, & Control of Process Variables & Related Products
NAICS 334513 Instruments & Related Product Manufacturing for Measuring Displaying, & Controlling Industrial Process Variables

3824 Totalizing Fluid Meters & Counting Devices
NAICS 334514 Totalizing Fluid Meter & Counting Device Manufacturing

3825 Instruments for Measuring & Testing of Electricity & Electrical Signals
NAICS 334416 Electronic Coil, Transformer, & Other Inductor Manufacturing
NAICS 334515 Instrument Manufacturing for Measuring & Testing Electricity & Electrical Signals

3826 Laboratory Analytical Instruments
NAICS 334516 Analytical Laboratory Instrument Manufacturing

3827 Optical Instruments & Lenses
NAICS 333314 Optical Instrument & Lens Manufacturing

3829 Measuring & Controlling Devices, nec
NAICS 339112 Surgical & Medical Instrument Manufacturing
NAICS 334519 Other Measuring & Controlling Device Manufacturing

3841 Surgical & Medical Instruments & Apparatus
NAICS 339112 Surgical & Medical Instrument Manufacturing

3842 Orthopedic, Prosthetic, & Surgical Appliances & Supplies
NAICS 339113 Surgical Appliance & Supplies Manufacturing
NAICS 334510 Electromedical & Electrotherapeutic Apparatus Manufacturing

3843 Dental Equipment & Supplies
NAICS 339114 Dental Equipment & Supplies Manufacturing

3844 X-ray Apparatus & Tubes & Related Irradiation Apparatus
NAICS 334517 Irradiation Apparatus Manufacturing

3845 Electromedical & Electrotherapeutic Apparatus
NAICS 334517 Irradiation Apparatus Manufacturing
NAICS 334510 Electromedical & Electrotherapeutic Apparatus Manufacturing

3851 Ophthalmic Goods
NAICS 339115 Ophthalmic Goods Manufacturing

3861 Photographic Equipment & Supplies
NAICS 333315 Photographic & Photocopying Equipment Manufacturing
NAICS 325992 Photographic Film, Paper, Plate & Chemical Manufacturing

3873 Watches, Clocks, Clockwork Operated Devices & Parts
NAICS 334518 Watch, Clock, & Part Manufacturing

MISCELLANEOUS MANUFACTURING INDUSTRIES

3911 Jewelry, Precious Metal
NAICS 339911 Jewelry Manufacturing

3914 Silverware, Plated Ware, & Stainless Steel Ware
NAICS 332211 Cutlery & Flatware Manufacturing
NAICS 339912 Silverware & Plated Ware Manufacturing

3915 Jewelers' Findings & Materials, & Lapidary Work
NAICS 339913 Jewelers' Material & Lapidary Work Manufacturing

3931 Musical Instruments
NAICS 339992 Musical Instrument Manufacturing

3942 Dolls & Stuffed Toys
NAICS 339931 Doll & Stuffed Toy Manufacturing

3944 Games, Toys, & Children's Vehicles, Except Dolls & Bicycles
NAICS 336991 Motorcycle, Bicycle & Parts Manufacturing
NAICS 339932 Game, Toy, & Children's Vehicle Manufacturing

3949 Sporting & Athletic Goods, nec
NAICS 33992 Sporting & Athletic Good Manufacturing

3951 Pens, Mechanical Pencils & Parts
NAICS 339941 Pen & Mechanical Pencil Manufacturing

3952 Lead Pencils, Crayons, & Artist's Materials
NAICS 337139 Other Wood Furniture Manufacturing
NAICS 337139 Other Wood Furniture Manufacturing
NAICS 325998 All Other Miscellaneous Chemical Manufacturing
NAICS 339942 Lead Pencil & Art Good Manufacturing

3953 Marking Devices
NAICS 339943 Marking Device Manufacturing

3955 Carbon Paper & Inked Ribbons
NAICS 339944 Carbon Paper & Inked Ribbon Manufacturing

3961 Costume Jewelry & Costume Novelties, Except Precious Metals
NAICS 339914 Costume Jewelry & Novelty Manufacturing

3965 Fasteners, Buttons, Needles, & Pins
NAICS 339993 Fastener, Button, Needle & Pin Manufacturing

3991 Brooms & Brushes
NAICS 339994 Broom, Brush & Mop Manufacturing

3993 Signs & Advertising Specialties
NAICS 33995 Sign Manufacturing

3995 Burial Caskets
NAICS 339995 Burial Casket Manufacturing

3996 Linoleum, Asphalted-felt-base, & Other Hard Surface Floor Coverings, nec
NAICS 326192 Resilient Floor Covering Manufacturing

3999 Manufacturing Industries, nec
NAICS 337148 Other Nonwood Furniture Manufacturing
NAICS 321999 All Other Miscellaneous Wood Product Manufacturing
NAICS 31611 Leather & Hide Tanning & Finishing
NAICS 335121 Residential Electric Lighting Fixture Manufacturing
NAICS 325998 All Other Miscellaneous Chemical Product Manufacturing
NAICS 332999 All Other Miscellaneous Fabricated Metal Product Manufacturing
NAICS 326199 All Other Plastics Product Manufacturing
NAICS 323112 Commercial Flexographic Printing
NAICS 323111 Commercial Gravure Printing
NAICS 323110 Commercial Lithographic Printing
NAICS 323113 Commercial Screen Printing
NAICS 323119 Other Commercial Printing
NAICS 332212 Hand & Edge Tool Manufacturing
NAICS 339999 All Other Miscellaneous Manufacturing

Appendix: SIC/NAICS Conversion

TRANSPORTATION, COMMUNICATIONS, ELECTRIC, GAS, & SANITARY SERVICES

4011 Railroads, Line-haul Operating
NAICS 482111 Line-haul Railroads

4013 Railroad Switching & Terminal Establishments
NAICS 482112 Short Line Railroads
NAICS 48821 Support Activities for Rail Transportation

4111 Local & Suburban Transit
NAICS 485111 Mixed Mode Transit Systems
NAICS 485112 Commuter Rail Systems
NAICS 485113 Bus & Motor Vehicle Transit Systems
NAICS 485119 Other Urban Transit Systems
NAICS 485999 All Other Transit & Ground Passenger
Transportation

4119 Local Passenger Transportation, nec
NAICS 62191 Ambulance Service
NAICS 48541 School & Employee Bus Transportation
NAICS 48711 Scenic & Sightseeing Transportation , Land
NAICS 485991 Special Needs Transportation
NAICS 485999 All Other Transit & Ground Passenger
Transportation
NAICS 48532 Limousine Service

4121 Taxicabs
NAICS 48531 Taxi Service

4131 Intercity & Rural Bus Transportation
NAICS 48521 Interurban & Rural Bus Transportation

4141 Local Bus Charter Service
NAICS 48551 Charter Bus Industry

4142 Bus Charter Service, Except Local
NAICS 48551 Charter Bus Industry

4151 School Buses
NAICS 48541 School & Employee Bus Transportation

4173 Terminal & Service Facilities for Motor Vehicle Passenger Transportation
NAICS 48849 Other Support Activities for Road
Transportation

4212 Local Trucking Without Storage
NAICS 562111 Solid Waste Collection
NAICS 562112 Hazardous Waste Collection
NAICS 562119 Other Waste Collection
NAICS 48411 General Freight Trucking, Local
NAICS 48421 Used Household & Office Goods Moving
NAICS 48422 Specialized Freight Trucking, Local

4213 Trucking, Except Local
NAICS 484121 General Freight Trucking, Long-distance,
Truckload
NAICS 484122 General Freight Trucking, Long-distance, less
than Truckload
NAICS 48421 Used Household & Office Goods Moving
NAICS 48423 Specialized Freight Trucking, Long-distance

4214 Local Trucking with Storage
NAICS 48411 General Freight Trucking, Local
NAICS 48421 Used Household & Office Goods Moving
NAICS 48422 Specialized Freight Trucking, Local

4215 Couriers Services Except by Air
NAICS 49211 Couriers
NAICS 49221 Local Messengers & Local Delivery

4221 Farm Product Warehousing & Storage
NAICS 49313 Farm Product Storage Facilities

4222 Refrigerated Warehousing & Storage
NAICS 49312 Refrigerated Storage Facilities

4225 General Warehousing & Storage
NAICS 49311 General Warehousing & Storage Facilities
NAICS 53113 Lessors of Miniwarehouses & Self Storage
Units

4226 Special Warehousing & Storage, nec
NAICS 49312 Refrigerated Warehousing & Storage Facilities
NAICS 49311 General Warehousing & Storage Facilities
NAICS 49319 Other Warehousing & Storage Facilities

4231 Terminal & Joint Terminal Maintenance Facilities for Motor Freight Transportation
NAICS 48849 Other Support Activities for Road
Transportation

4311 United States Postal Service
NAICS 49111 Postal Service

4412 Deep Sea Foreign Transportation of Freight
NAICS 483111 Deep Sea Freight Transportation

4424 Deep Sea Domestic Transportation of Freight
NAICS 483113 Coastal & Great Lakes Freight Transportation

4432 Freight Transportation on the Great Lakes - St. Lawrence Seaway
NAICS 483113 Coastal & Great Lakes Freight Transportation

4449 Water Transportation of Freight, nec
NAICS 483211 Inland Water Freight Transportation

4481 Deep Sea Transportation of Passengers, Except by Ferry
NAICS 483112 Deep Sea Passenger Transportation
NAICS 483114 Coastal & Great Lakes Passenger
Transportation

4482 Ferries
NAICS 483114 Coastal & Great Lakes Passenger
Transportation
NAICS 483212 Inland Water Passenger Transportation

4489 Water Transportation of Passengers, nec
NAICS 483212 Inland Water Passenger Transportation
NAICS 48721 Scenic & Sightseeing Transportation, Water

4491 Marine Cargo Handling
NAICS 48831 Port & Harbor Operations
NAICS 48832 Marine Cargo Handling

4492 Towing & Tugboat Services
NAICS 483113 Coastal & Great Lakes Freight Transportation
NAICS 483211 Inland Water Freight Transportation
NAICS 48833 Navigational Services to Shipping

4493 Marinas
NAICS 71393 Marinas

4499 Water Transportation Services, nec
NAICS 532411 Commercial Air, Rail, & Water Transportation
Equipment Rental & Leasing
NAICS 48831 Port & Harbor Operations
NAICS 48833 Navigational Services to Shipping
NAICS 48839 Other Support Activities for Water
Transportation

4512 Air Transportation, Scheduled
NAICS 481111 Scheduled Passenger Air Transportation
NAICS 481112 Scheduled Freight Air Transportation

4513 Air Courier Services
NAICS 49211 Couriers

4522 Air Transportation, Nonscheduled
NAICS 62191 Ambulance Services
NAICS 481212 Nonscheduled Chartered Freight Air
Transportation
NAICS 481211 Nonscheduled Chartered Passenger Air
Transportation
NAICS 48122 Nonscheduled Speciality Air Transportation
NAICS 48799 Scenic & Sightseeing Transportation , Other

4581 Airports, Flying Fields, & Airport Terminal Services
NAICS 488111 Air Traffic Control
NAICS 488112 Airport Operations, Except Air Traffic Control
NAICS 56172   Janitorial Services
NAICS 48819   Other Support Activities for Air Transportation
4612 Crude Petroleum Pipelines
NAICS 48611   Pipeline Transportation of Crude Oil
4613 Refined Petroleum Pipelines
NAICS 48691   Pipeline Transportation of Refined Petroleum
              Products
4619 Pipelines, nec
NAICS 48699   All Other Pipeline Transportation
4724 Travel Agencies
NAICS 56151   Travel Agencies
4725 Tour Operators
NAICS 56152   Tour Operators
4729 Arrangement of Passenger Transportation, nec
NAICS 488999 All Other Support Activities for Transportation
NAICS 561599 All Other Travel Arrangement & Reservation
              Services
4731 Arrangement of Transportation of Freight & Cargo
NAICS 541618 Other Management Consulting Services
NAICS 48851   Freight Transportation Arrangement
4741 Rental of Railroad Cars
NAICS 532411 Commercial Air, Rail, & Water Transportation
              Equipment Rental & Leasing
NAICS 48821   Support Activities for Rail Transportation
4783 Packing & Crating
NAICS 488991 Packing & Crating
**4785 Fixed Facilities & Inspection & Weighing Services for
     Motor Vehicle Transportation**
NAICS 48839   Other Support Activities for Water
              Transportation
NAICS 48849   Other Support Activities for Road
              Transportation
4789 Transportation Services, nec
NAICS 488999 All Other Support Activities for Transportation
NAICS 48711   Scenic & Sightseeing Transportation, Land
NAICS 48821   Support Activities for Rail Transportation
4812 Radiotelephone Communications
NAICS 513321 Paging
NAICS 513322 Cellular & Other Wireless Telecommunications
NAICS 51333   Telecommunications Resellers
4813 Telephone Communications, Except Radiotelephone
NAICS 51331   Wired Telecommunications Carriers
NAICS 51333   Telecommunications Resellers
4822 Telegraph & Other Message Communications
NAICS 51331   Wired Telecommunications Carriers
4832 Radio Broadcasting Stations
NAICS 513111 Radio Networks
NAICS 513112 Radio Stations
4833 Television Broadcasting Stations
NAICS 51312   Television Broadcasting
4841 Cable & Other Pay Television Services
NAICS 51321   Cable Networks
NAICS 51322   Cable & Other Program Distribution
4899 Communications Services, nec
NAICS 513322 Cellular & Other Wireless Telecommunications
NAICS 51334   Satellite Telecommunications
NAICS 51339   Other Telecommunications
4911 Electric Services
NAICS 221111 Hydroelectric Power Generation
NAICS 221112 Fossil Fuel Electric Power Generation
NAICS 221113 Nuclear Electric Power Generation

NAICS 221119 Other Electric Power Generation
NAICS 221121 Electric Bulk Power Transmission & Control
NAICS 221122 Electric Power Distribution
4922 Natural Gas Transmission
NAICS 48621   Pipeline Transportation of Natural Gas
4923 Natural Gas Transmission & Distribution
NAICS 22121   Natural Gas Distribution
NAICS 48621   Pipeline Transportation of Natural Gas
4924 Natural Gas Distribution
NAICS 22121   Natural Gas Distribution
**4925 Mixed, Manufactured, or Liquefied Petroleum Gas
     Production And/or Distribution**
NAICS 22121   Natural Gas Distribution
4931 Electric & Other Services Combined
NAICS 221111 Hydroelectric Power Generation
NAICS 221112 Fossil Fuel Electric Power Generation
NAICS 221113 Nuclear Electric Power Generation
NAICS 221119 Other Electric Power Generation
NAICS 221121 Electric Bulk Power Transmission & Control
NAICS 221122 Electric Power Distribution
NAICS 22121   Natural Gas Distribution
4932 Gas & Other Services Combined
NAICS 22121   Natural Gas Distribution
4939 Combination Utilities, nec
NAICS 221111 Hydroelectric Power Generation
NAICS 221112 Fossil Fuel Electric Power Generation
NAICS 221113 Nuclear Electric Power Generation
NAICS 221119 Other Electric Power Generation
NAICS 221121 Electric Bulk Power Transmission & Control
NAICS 221122 Electric Power Distribution
NAICS 22121   Natural Gas Distribution
4941 Water Supply
NAICS 22131   Water Supply & Irrigation Systems
4952 Sewerage Systems
NAICS 22132   Sewage Treatment Facilities
4953 Refuse Systems
NAICS 562111 Solid Waste Collection
NAICS 562112 Hazardous Waste Collection
NAICS 56292   Materials Recovery Facilities
NAICS 562119 Other Waste Collection
NAICS 562211 Hazardous Waste Treatment & Disposal
NAICS 562212 Solid Waste Landfills
NAICS 562213 Solid Waste Combustors & Incinerators
NAICS 562219 Other Nonhazardous Waste Treatment &
              Disposal
4959 Sanitary Services, nec
NAICS 488112 Airport Operations, Except Air Traffic Control
NAICS 56291   Remediation Services
NAICS 56171   Exterminating & Pest Control Services
NAICS 562998 All Other Miscellaneous Waste Management
              Services
4961 Steam & Air-conditioning Supply
NAICS 22133   Steam & Air-conditioning Supply
4971 Irrigation Systems
NAICS 22131   Water Supply & Irrigation Systems

WHOLESALE TRADE

5012 Automobiles & Other Motor Vehicles
NAICS 42111   Automobile & Other Motor Vehicle
              Wholesalers

Appendix: SIC/NAICS Conversion

5013 Motor Vehicle Supplies & New Parts
- NAICS 44131   Automotive Parts & Accessories Stores - Retail
- NAICS 42112   Motor Vehicle Supplies & New Part Wholesalers

5014 Tires & Tubes
- NAICS 44132   Tire Dealers - Retail
- NAICS 42113   Tire & Tube Wholesalers

5015 Motor Vehicle Parts, Used
- NAICS 42114   Motor Vehicle Part Wholesalers

5021 Furniture
- NAICS 44211   Furniture Stores
- NAICS 42121   Furniture Wholesalers

5023 Home Furnishings
- NAICS 44221   Floor Covering Stores
- NAICS 42122   Home Furnishing Wholesalers

5031 Lumber, Plywood, Millwork, & Wood Panels
- NAICS 44419   Other Building Material Dealers
- NAICS 42131   Lumber, Plywood, Millwork, & Wood Panel Wholesalers

5032 Brick, Stone & Related Construction Materials
- NAICS 44419   Other Building Material Dealers
- NAICS 42132   Brick, Stone & Related Construction Material Wholesalers

5033 Roofing, Siding, & Insulation Materials
- NAICS 42133   Roofing, Siding, & Insulation Material Wholesalers

5039 Construction Materials, nec
- NAICS 44419   Other Building Material Dealers
- NAICS 42139   Other Construction Material Wholesalers

5043 Photographic Equipment & Supplies
- NAICS 42141   Photographic Equipment & Supplies Wholesalers

5044 Office Equipment
- NAICS 42142   Office Equipment Wholesalers

5045 Computers & Computer Peripheral Equipment & Software
- NAICS 42143   Computer & Computer Peripheral Equipment & Software Wholesalers
- NAICS 44312   Computer & Software Stores - Retail

5046 Commercial Equipment, nec
- NAICS 42144   Other Commercial Equipment Wholesalers

5047 Medical, Dental, & Hospital Equipment & Supplies
- NAICS 42145   Medical, Dental & Hospital Equipment & Supplies Wholesalers
- NAICS 446199 All Other Health & Personal Care Stores - Retail

5048 Ophthalmic Goods
- NAICS 42146   Ophthalmic Goods Wholesalers

5049 Professional Equipment & Supplies, nec
- NAICS 42149   Other Professional Equipment & Supplies Wholesalers
- NAICS 45321   Office Supplies & Stationery Stores - Retail

5051 Metals Service Centers & Offices
- NAICS 42151   Metals Service Centers & Offices

5052 Coal & Other Minerals & Ores
- NAICS 42152   Coal & Other Mineral & Ore Wholesalers

5063 Electrical Apparatus & Equipment Wiring Supplies, & Construction Materials
- NAICS 44419   Other Building Material Dealers
- NAICS 42161   Electrical Apparatus & Equipment, Wiring Supplies & Construction Material Wholesalers

5064 Electrical Appliances, Television & Radio Sets
- NAICS 42162   Electrical Appliance, Television & Radio Set Wholesalers

5065 Electronic Parts & Equipment, Not Elsewhere Classified
- NAICS 42169   Other Electronic Parts & Equipment Wholesalers

5072 Hardware
- NAICS 42171   Hardware Wholesalers

5074 Plumbing & Heating Equipment & Supplies
- NAICS 44419   Other Building Material Dealers
- NAICS 42172   Plumbing & Heating Equipment & Supplies Wholesalers

5075 Warm Air Heating & Air-conditioning Equipment & Supplies
- NAICS 42173   Warm Air Heating & Air-conditioning Equipment & Supplies Wholesalers

5078 Refrigeration Equipment & Supplies
- NAICS 42174   Refrigeration Equipment & Supplies Wholesalers

5082 Construction & Mining Machinery & Equipment
- NAICS 42181   Construction & Mining Machinery & Equipment Wholesalers

5083 Farm & Garden Machinery & Equipment
- NAICS 42182   Farm & Garden Machinery & Equipment Wholesalers
- NAICS 44421   Outdoor Power Equipment Stores - Retail

5084 Industrial Machinery & Equipment
- NAICS 42183   Industrial Machinery & Equipment Wholesalers

5085 Industrial Supplies
- NAICS 42183   Industrial Machinery & Equipment Wholesalers
- NAICS 42184   Industrial Supplies Wholesalers
- NAICS 81131   Commercial & Industrial Machinery & Equipment Repair & Maintenence

5087 Service Establishment Equipment & Supplies
- NAICS 42185   Service Establishment Equipment & Supplies Wholesalers
- NAICS 44612   Cosmetics, Beauty Supplies, & Perfume Stores

5088 Transportation Equipment & Supplies, Except Motor Vehicles
- NAICS 42186   Transportation Equipment & Supplies Wholesalers

5091 Sporting & Recreational Goods & Supplies
- NAICS 42191   Sporting & Recreational Goods & Supplies Wholesalers

5092 Toys & Hobby Goods & Supplies
- NAICS 42192   Toy & Hobby Goods & Supplies Wholesalers

5093 Scrap & Waste Materials
- NAICS 42193   Recyclable Material Wholesalers

5094 Jewelry, Watches, Precious Stones, & Precious Metals
- NAICS 42194   Jewelry, Watch , Precious Stone, & Precious Metal Wholesalers

5099 Durable Goods, nec
- NAICS 42199   Other Miscellaneous Durable Goods Wholesalers

5111 Printing & Writing Paper
- NAICS 42211   Printing & Writing Paper Wholesalers

5112 Stationery & Office Supplies
- NAICS 45321   Office Supplies & Stationery Stores
- NAICS 42212   Stationery & Office Supplies Wholesalers

5113 Industrial & Personal Service Paper
- NAICS 42213   Industrial & Personal Service Paper Wholesalers

5122 Drugs, Drug Proprietaries, & Druggists' Sundries
- NAICS 42221   Drugs, Drug Proprietaries, & Druggists' Sundries Wholesalers

5131 Piece Goods, Notions, & Other Dry Goods
NAICS 313311 Broadwoven Fabric Finishing Mills
NAICS 313312 Textile & Fabric Finishing Mills
NAICS 42231　Piece Goods, Notions, & Other Dry Goods
　　　　　　　Wholesalers
5136 Men's & Boys' Clothing & Furnishings
NAICS 42232　Men's & Boys' Clothing & Furnishings
　　　　　　　Wholesalers
5137 Women's Children's & Infants' Clothing & Accessories
NAICS 42233　Women's, Children's, & Infants' Clothing &
　　　　　　　Accessories Wholesalers
5139 Footwear
NAICS 42234　Footwear Wholesalers
5141 Groceries, General Line
NAICS 42241　General Line Grocery Wholesalers
5142 Packaged Frozen Foods
NAICS 42242　Packaged Frozen Food Wholesalers
5143 Dairy Products, Except Dried or Canned
NAICS 42243　Dairy Products Wholesalers
5144 Poultry & Poultry Products
NAICS 42244　Poultry & Poultry Product Wholesalers
5145 Confectionery
NAICS 42245　Confectionery Wholesalers
5146 Fish & Seafoods
NAICS 42246　Fish & Seafood Wholesalers
5147 Meats & Meat Products
NAICS 311612 Meat Processed from Carcasses
NAICS 42247　Meat & Meat Product Wholesalers
5148 Fresh Fruits & Vegetables
NAICS 42248　Fresh Fruit & Vegetable Wholesalers
5149 Groceries & Related Products, nec
NAICS 42249　Other Grocery & Related Product Wholesalers
5153 Grain & Field Beans
NAICS 42251　Grain & Field Bean Wholesalers
5154 Livestock
NAICS 42252　Livestock Wholesalers
5159 Farm-product Raw Materials, nec
NAICS 42259　Other Farm Product Raw Material Wholesalers
5162 Plastics Materials & Basic Forms & Shapes
NAICS 42261　Plastics Materials & Basic Forms & Shapes
　　　　　　　Wholesalers
5169 Chemicals & Allied Products, nec
NAICS 42269　Other Chemical & Allied Products Wholesalers
5171 Petroleum Bulk Stations & Terminals
NAICS 454311 Heating Oil Dealers
NAICS 454312 Liquefied Petroleum Gas Dealers
NAICS 42271　Petroleum Bulk Stations & Terminals
5172 Petroleum & Petroleum Products Wholesalers, Except Bulk Stations & Terminals
NAICS 42272　Petroleum & Petroleum Products Wholesalers
5181 Beer & Ale
NAICS 42281　Beer & Ale Wholesalers
5182 Wine & Distilled Alcoholic Beverages
NAICS 42282　Wine & Distilled Alcoholic Beverage
　　　　　　　Wholesalers
5191 Farm Supplies
NAICS 44422　Nursery & Garden Centers - Retail
NAICS 42291　Farm Supplies Wholesalers
5192 Books, Periodicals, & Newspapers
NAICS 42292　Book, Periodical & Newspaper Wholesalers
5193 Flowers, Nursery Stock, & Florists' Supplies
NAICS 42293　Flower, Nursery Stock & Florists' Supplies
　　　　　　　Wholesalers
NAICS 44422　Nursery & Garden Centers - Retail

5194 Tobacco & Tobacco Products
NAICS 42294　Tobacco & Tobacco Product Wholesalers
5198 Paint, Varnishes, & Supplies
NAICS 42295　Paint, Varnish & Supplies Wholesalers
NAICS 44412　Paint & Wallpaper Stores
5199 Nondurable Goods, nec
NAICS 54189　Other Services Related to Advertising
NAICS 42299　Other Miscellaneous Nondurable Goods
　　　　　　　Wholesalers

RETAIL TRADE

5211 Lumber & Other Building Materials Dealers
NAICS 44411　Home Centers
NAICS 42131　Lumber, Plywood, Millwork & Wood Panel
　　　　　　　Wholesalers
NAICS 44419　Other Building Material Dealers
5231 Paint, Glass, & Wallpaper Stores
NAICS 42295　Paint, Varnish & Supplies Wholesalers
NAICS 44419　Other Building Material Dealers
NAICS 44412　Paint & Wallpaper Stores
5251 Hardware Stores
NAICS 44413　Hardware Stores
5261 Retail Nurseries, Lawn & Garden Supply Stores
NAICS 44422　Nursery & Garden Centers
NAICS 453998 All Other Miscellaneous Store Retailers
NAICS 44421　Outdoor Power Equipment Stores
5271 Mobile Home Dealers
NAICS 45393　Manufactured Home Dealers
5311 Department Stores
NAICS 45211　Department Stores
5331 Variety Stores
NAICS 45299　All Other General Merchandise Stores
5399 Miscellaneous General Merchandise Stores
NAICS 45291　Warehouse Clubs & Superstores
NAICS 45299　All Other General Merchandise Stores
5411 Grocery Stores
NAICS 44711　Gasoline Stations with Convenience Stores
NAICS 44511　Supermarkets & Other Grocery Stores
NAICS 45291　Warehouse Clubs & Superstores
NAICS 44512　Convenience Stores
5421 Meat & Fish Markets, Including Freezer Provisioners
NAICS 45439　Other Direct Selling Establishments
NAICS 44521　Meat Markets
NAICS 44522　Fish & Seafood Markets
5431 Fruit & Vegetable Markets
NAICS 44523　Fruit & Vegetable Markets
5441 Candy, Nut, & Confectionery Stores
NAICS 445292 Confectionary & Nut Stores
5451 Dairy Products Stores
NAICS 445299 All Other Specialty Food Stores
5461 Retail Bakeries
NAICS 722213 Snack & Nonalcoholic Beverage Bars
NAICS 311811 Retail Bakeries
NAICS 445291 Baked Goods Stores
5499 Miscellaneous Food Stores
NAICS 44521　Meat Markets
NAICS 722211 Limited-service Restaurants
NAICS 446191 Food Supplement Stores
NAICS 445299 All Other Specialty Food Stores
5511 Motor Vehicle Dealers
NAICS 44111　New Car Dealers

Appendix: SIC/NAICS Conversion

5521 Motor Vehicle Dealers
NAICS 44112   Used Car Dealers
5531 Auto & Home Supply Stores
NAICS 44132   Tire Dealers
NAICS 44131   Automotive Parts & Accessories Stores
5541 Gasoline Service Stations
NAICS 44711   Gasoline Stations with Convenience Store
NAICS 44719   Other Gasoline Stations
5551 Boat Dealers
NAICS 441222 Boat Dealers
5561 Recreational Vehicle Dealers
NAICS 44121   Recreational Vehicle Dealers
5571 Motorcycle Dealers
NAICS 441221 Motorcycle Dealers
5599 Automotive Dealers, nec
NAICS 441229 All Other Motor Vehicle Dealers
5611 Men's & Boys' Clothing & Accessory Stores
NAICS 44811   Men's Clothing Stores
NAICS 44815   Clothing Accessories Stores
5621 Women's Clothing Stores
NAICS 44812   Women's Clothing Stores
5632 Women's Accessory & Specialty Stores
NAICS 44819   Other Clothing Stores
NAICS 44815   Clothing Accessories Stores
5641 Children's & Infants' Wear Stores
NAICS 44813   Children's & Infants' Clothing Stores
5651 Family Clothing Stores
NAICS 44814   Family Clothing Stores
5661 Shoe Stores
NAICS 44821   Shoe Stores
5699 Miscellaneous Apparel & Accessory Stores
NAICS 315   Included in Apparel Manufacturing Subsector
                Based on Type of Garment Produced
NAICS 44819   Other Clothing Stores
NAICS 44815   Clothing Accessories Stores
5712 Furniture Stores
NAICS 337133 Wood Household Furniture, Except
                Upholstered, Manufacturing
NAICS 337131 Wood Kitchen Cabinet & Counter Top
                Manufacturing
NAICS 337132 Upholstered Household Furniture
                Manufacturing
NAICS 44211   Furniture Stores
5713 Floor Covering Stores
NAICS 44221   Floor Covering Stores
5714 Drapery, Curtain, & Upholstery Stores
NAICS 442291 Window Treatment Stores
NAICS 45113   Sewing, Needlework & Piece Goods Stores
NAICS 314121 Curtain & Drapery Mills
5719 Miscellaneous Homefurnishings Stores
NAICS 442291 Window Treatment Stores
NAICS 442299 All Other Home Furnishings Stores
5722 Household Appliance Stores
NAICS 443111 Household Appliance Stores
5731 Radio, Television, & Consumer Electronics Stores
NAICS 443112 Radio, Television, & Other Electronics Stores
NAICS 44131   Automotive Parts & Accessories Stores
5734 Computer & Computer Software Stores
NAICS 44312   Computer & Software Stores
5735 Record & Prerecorded Tape Stores
NAICS 45122   Prerecorded Tape, Compact Disc & Record
                Stores

5736 Musical Instrument Stores
NAICS 45114   Musical Instrument & Supplies Stores
5812 Eating & Drinking Places
NAICS 72211   Full-service Restaurants
NAICS 722211 Limited-service Restaurants
NAICS 722212 Cafeterias
NAICS 722213 Snack & Nonalcoholic Beverage Bars
NAICS 72231   Foodservice Contractors
NAICS 72232   Caterers
NAICS 71111   Theater Companies & Dinner Theaters
5813 Drinking Places
NAICS 72241   Drinking Places
5912 Drug Stores & Proprietary Stores
NAICS 44611   Pharmacies & Drug Stores
5921 Liquor Stores
NAICS 44531   Beer, Wine & Liquor Stores
5932 Used Merchandise Stores
NAICS 522298 All Other Non-depository Credit
                Intermediation
NAICS 45331   Used Merchandise Stores
5941 Sporting Goods Stores & Bicycle Shops
NAICS 45111   Sporting Goods Stores
5942 Book Stores
NAICS 451211 Book Stores
5943 Stationery Stores
NAICS 45321   Office Supplies & Stationery Stores
5944 Jewelry Stores
NAICS 44831   Jewelry Stores
5945 Hobby, Toy, & Game Shops
NAICS 45112   Hobby, Toy & Game Stores
5946 Camera & Photographic Supply Stores
NAICS 44313   Camera & Photographic Supplies Stores
5947 Gift, Novelty, & Souvenir Shops
NAICS 45322   Gift, Novelty & Souvenir Stores
5948 Luggage & Leather Goods Stores
NAICS 44832   Luggage & Leather Goods Stores
5949 Sewing, Needlework, & Piece Goods Stores
NAICS 45113   Sewing, Needlework & Piece Goods Stores
5961 Catalog & Mail-order Houses
NAICS 45411   Electronic Shopping & Mail-order Houses
5962 Automatic Merchandising Machine Operator
NAICS 45421   Vending Machine Operators
5963 Direct Selling Establishments
NAICS 72233   Mobile Caterers
NAICS 45439   Other Direct Selling Establishments
5983 Fuel Oil Dealers
NAICS 454311 Heating Oil Dealers
5984 Liquefied Petroleum Gas Dealers
NAICS 454312 Liquefied Petroleum Gas Dealers
5989 Fuel Dealers, nec
NAICS 454319 Other Fuel Dealers
5992 Florists
NAICS 45311   Florists
5993 Tobacco Stores & Stands
NAICS 453991 Tobacco Stores
5994 News Dealers & Newsstands
NAICS 451212 News Dealers & Newsstands
5995 Optical Goods Stores
NAICS 339117 Eyeglass & Contact Lens Manufacturing
NAICS 44613   Optical Goods Stores
5999 Miscellaneous Retail Stores, nec
NAICS 44612   Cosmetics, Beauty Supplies & Perfume Stores
NAICS 446199 All Other Health & Personal Care Stores
NAICS 45391   Pet & Pet Supplies Stores

NAICS 45392   Art Dealers
NAICS 443111 Household Appliance Stores
NAICS 443112 Radio, Television & Other Electronics Stores
NAICS 44831   Jewelry Stores
NAICS 453999 All Other Miscellaneous Store Retailers

FINANCE, INSURANCE, & REAL ESTATE

6011 Federal Reserve Banks
NAICS 52111   Monetary Authorities-central Banks
6019 Central Reserve Depository Institutions, nec
NAICS 52232   Financial Transactions Processing, Reserve, &
              Clearing House Activities
6021 National Commercial Banks
NAICS 52211   Commercial Banking
NAICS 52221   Credit Card Issuing
NAICS 523991 Trust, Fiduciary & Custody Activities
6022 State Commercial Banks
NAICS 52211   Commercial Banking
NAICS 52221   Credit Card Issuing
NAICS 52219   Other Depository Intermediation
NAICS 523991 Trust, Fiduciary & Custody Activities
6029 Commercial Banks, nec
NAICS 52211   Commercial Banking
6035 Savings Institutions, Federally Chartered
NAICS 52212   Savings Institutions
6036 Savings Institutions, Not Federally Chartered
NAICS 52212   Savings Institutions
6061 Credit Unions, Federally Chartered
NAICS 52213   Credit Unions
6062 Credit Unions, Not Federally Chartered
NAICS 52213   Credit Unions
6081 Branches & Agencies of Foreign Banks
NAICS 522293 International Trade Financing
NAICS 52211   Commercial Banking
NAICS 522298 All Other Non-depository Credit
              Intermediation
6082 Foreign Trade & International Banking Institutions
NAICS 522293 International Trade Financing
6091 Nondeposit Trust Facilities
NAICS 523991 Trust, Fiduciary, & Custody Activities
6099 Functions Related to Deposit Banking, nec
NAICS 52232   Financial Transactions Processing, Reserve, &
              Clearing House Activities
NAICS 52313   Commodity Contracts Dealing
NAICS 523991 Trust, Fiduciary, & Custody Activities
NAICS 523999 Miscellaneous Financial Investment Activities
NAICS 52239   Other Activities Related to Credit
              Intermediation
6111 Federal & Federally Sponsored Credit Agencies
NAICS 522293 International Trade Financing
NAICS 522294 Secondary Market Financing
NAICS 522298 All Other Non-depository Credit
              Intermediation
6141 Personal Credit Institutions
NAICS 52221   Credit Card Issuing
NAICS 52222   Sales Financing
NAICS 522291 Consumer Lending
6153 Short-term Business Credit Institutions, Except
  Agricultural
NAICS 52222   Sales Financing
NAICS 52232   Financial Transactions Processing, Reserve, &
              Clearing House Activities

NAICS 522298 All Other Non-depository Credit
              Intermediation
6159 Miscellaneous Business Credit Institutions
NAICS 52222   Sales Financing
NAICS 532   Included in Rental & Leasing Services
              Subsector by Type of Equipment & Method of
              Operation
NAICS 522293 International Trade Financing
NAICS 522298 All Other Non-depository Credit
              Intermediation
6162 Mortgage Bankers & Loan Correspondents
NAICS 522292 Real Estate Credit
NAICS 52239   Other Activities Related to Credit
              Intermediation
6163 Loan Brokers
NAICS 52231   Mortgage & Other Loan Brokers
6211 Security Brokers, Dealers, & Flotation Companies
NAICS 52311   Investment Banking & Securities Dealing
NAICS 52312   Securities Brokerage
NAICS 52391   Miscellaneous Intermediation
NAICS 523999 Miscellaneous Financial Investment Activities
6221 Commodity Contracts Brokers & Dealers
NAICS 52313   Commodity Contracts Dealing
NAICS 52314   Commodity Brokerage
6231 Security & Commodity Exchanges
NAICS 52321   Securities & Commodity Exchanges
6282 Investment Advice
NAICS 52392   Portfolio Management
NAICS 52393   Investment Advice
6289 Services Allied with the Exchange of Securities or
  Commodities, nec
NAICS 523991 Trust, Fiduciary, & Custody Activities
NAICS 523999 Miscellaneous Financial Investment Activities
6311 Life Insurance
NAICS 524113 Direct Life Insurance Carriers
NAICS 52413   Reinsurance Carriers
6321 Accident & Health Insurance
NAICS 524114 Direct Health & Medical Insurance Carriers
NAICS 52519   Other Insurance Funds
NAICS 52413   Reinsurance Carriers
6324 Hospital & Medical Service Plans
NAICS 524114 Direct Health & Medical Insurance Carriers
NAICS 52519   Other Insurance Funds
NAICS 52413   Reinsurance Carriers
6331 Fire, Marine, & Casualty Insurance
NAICS 524126 Direct Property & Casualty Insurance Carriers
NAICS 52519   Other Insurance Funds
NAICS 52413   Reinsurance Carriers
6351 Surety Insurance
NAICS 524126 Direct Property & Casualty Insurance Carriers
NAICS 52413   Reinsurance Carriers
6361 Title Insurance
NAICS 524127 Direct Title Insurance Carriers
NAICS 52413   Reinsurance Carriers
6371 Pension, Health, & Welfare Funds
NAICS 52392   Portfolio Management
NAICS 524292 Third Party Administration for Insurance &
              Pension Funds
NAICS 52511   Pension Funds
NAICS 52512   Health & Welfare Funds
6399 Insurance Carriers, nec
NAICS 524128 Other Direct Insurance Carriers

Appendix: SIC/NAICS Conversion

6411 Insurance Agents, Brokers, & Service
NAICS 52421   Insurance Agencies & Brokerages
NAICS 524291 Claims Adjusters
NAICS 524292 Third Party Administrators for Insurance &
Pension Funds
NAICS 524298 All Other Insurance Related Activities
6512 Operators of Nonresidential Buildings
NAICS 71131   Promoters of Performing Arts, Sports & Similar
Events with Facilities
NAICS 53112   Lessors of Nonresidential Buildings
6513 Operators of Apartment Buildings
NAICS 53111   Lessors of Residential Buildings & Dwellings
6514 Operators of Dwellings Other than Apartment Buildings
NAICS 53111   Lessors of Residential Buildings & Dwellings
6515 Operators of Residential Mobile Home Sites
NAICS 53119   Lessors of Other Real Estate Property
6517 Lessors of Railroad Property
NAICS 53119   Lessors of Other Real Estate Property
6519 Lessors of Real Property, nec
NAICS 53119   Lessors of Other Real Estate Property
6531 Real Estate Agents & Managers
NAICS 53121   Offices of Real Estate Agents & Brokers
NAICS 81399   Other Similar Organizations
NAICS 531311 Residential Property Managers
NAICS 531312 Nonresidential Property Managers
NAICS 53132   Offices of Real Estate Appraisers
NAICS 81222   Cemeteries & Crematories
NAICS 531399 All Other Activities Related to Real Estate
6541 Title Abstract Offices
NAICS 541191 Title Abstract & Settlement Offices
6552 Land Subdividers & Developers, Except Cemeteries
NAICS 23311   Land Subdivision & Land Development
6553 Cemetery Subdividers & Developers
NAICS 81222   Cemeteries & Crematories
6712 Offices of Bank Holding Companies
NAICS 551111 Offices of Bank Holding Companies
6719 Offices of Holding Companies, nec
NAICS 551112 Offices of Other Holding Companies
6722 Management Investment Offices, Open-end
NAICS 52591   Open-end Investment Funds
**6726 Unit Investment Trusts, Face-amount Certificate Offices, &
Closed-end Management Investment Offices**
NAICS 52599   Other Financial Vehicles
6732 Education, Religious, & Charitable Trusts
NAICS 813211 Grantmaking Foundations
6733 Trusts, Except Educational, Religious, & Charitable
NAICS 52392   Portfolio Management
NAICS 523991 Trust, Fiduciary, & Custody Services
NAICS 52519   Other Insurance Funds
NAICS 52592   Trusts, Estates, & Agency Accounts
6792 Oil Royalty Traders
NAICS 523999 Miscellaneous Financial Investment Activities
NAICS 53311   Owners & Lessors of Other Non-financial
Assets
6794 Patent Owners & Lessors
NAICS 53311   Owners & Lessors of Other Non-financial
Assets
6798 Real Estate Investment Trusts
NAICS 52593   Real Estate Investment Trusts
6799 Investors, nec
NAICS 52391   Miscellaneous Intermediation
NAICS 52392   Portfolio Management
NAICS 52313   Commodity Contracts Dealing
NAICS 523999 Miscellaneous Financial Investment Activities

SERVICE INDUSTRIES

7011 Hotels & Motels
NAICS 72111   Hotels & Motels
NAICS 72112   Casino Hotels
NAICS 721191 Bed & Breakfast Inns
NAICS 721199 All Other Traveler Accommodation
7021 Rooming & Boarding Houses
NAICS 72131   Rooming & Boarding Houses
7032 Sporting & Recreational Camps
NAICS 721214 Recreational & Vacation Camps
7033 Recreational Vehicle Parks & Campsites
NAICS 721211 Rv & Campgrounds
**7041 Organization Hotels & Lodging Houses, on Membership
Basis**
NAICS 72111   Hotels & Motels
NAICS 72131   Rooming & Boarding Houses
7211 Power Laundries, Family & Commercial
NAICS 812321 Laundries, Family & Commercial
7212 Garment Pressing, & Agents for Laundries
NAICS 812391 Garment Pressing & Agents for Laundries
7213 Linen Supply
NAICS 812331 Linen Supply
7215 Coin-operated Laundry & Drycleaning
NAICS 81231   Coin-operated Laundries & Drycleaners
7216 Drycleaning Plants, Except Rug Cleaning
NAICS 812322 Drycleaning Plants
7217 Carpet & Upholstery Cleaning
NAICS 56174   Carpet & Upholstery Cleaning Services
7218 Industrial Launderers
NAICS 812332 Industrial Launderers
7219 Laundry & Garment Services, nec
NAICS 812331 Linen Supply
NAICS 81149   Other Personal & Household Goods Repair &
Maintenance
NAICS 812399 All Other Laundry Services
7221 Photographic Studios, Portrait
NAICS 541921 Photographic Studios, Portrait
7231 Beauty Shops
NAICS 812112 Beauty Salons
NAICS 812113 Nail Salons
NAICS 611511 Cosmetology & Barber Schools
7241 Barber Shops
NAICS 812111 Barber Shops
NAICS 611511 Cosmetology & Barber Schools
7251 Shoe Repair Shops & Shoeshine Parlors
NAICS 81143   Footwear & Leather Goods Repair
7261 Funeral Services & Crematories
NAICS 81221   Funeral Homes
NAICS 81222   Cemeteries & Crematories
7291 Tax Return Preparation Services
NAICS 541213 Tax Preparation Services
7299 Miscellaneous Personal Services, nec
NAICS 62441   Child Day Care Services
NAICS 812191 Diet & Weight Reducing Centers
NAICS 53222   Formal Wear & Costume Rental
NAICS 812199 Other Personal Care Services
NAICS 81299   All Other Personal Services
7311 Advertising Agencies
NAICS 54181   Advertising Agencies
7312 Outdoor Advertising Services
NAICS 54185   Display Advertising

7313 Radio, Television, & Publishers' Advertising Representatives
NAICS 54184   Media Representatives

7319 Advertising, nec
NAICS 481219 Other Nonscheduled Air Transportation
NAICS 54183   Media Buying Agencies
NAICS 54185   Display Advertising
NAICS 54187   Advertising Material Distribution Services
NAICS 54189   Other Services Related to Advertising

7322 Adjustment & Collection Services
NAICS 56144   Collection Agencies
NAICS 561491 Repossession Services

7323 Credit Reporting Services
NAICS 56145   Credit Bureaus

7331 Direct Mail Advertising Services
NAICS 54186   Direct Mail Advertising

7334 Photocopying & Duplicating Services
NAICS 561431 Photocopying & Duplicating Services

7335 Commercial Photography
NAICS 48122   Nonscheduled Speciality Air Transportation
NAICS 541922 Commercial Photography

7336 Commercial Art & Graphic Design
NAICS 54143   Commercial Art & Graphic Design Services

7338 Secretarial & Court Reporting Services
NAICS 56141   Document Preparation Services
NAICS 561492 Court Reporting & Stenotype Services

7342 Disinfecting & Pest Control Services
NAICS 56172   Janitorial Services
NAICS 56171   Exterminating & Pest Control Services

7349 Building Cleaning & Maintenance Services, nec
NAICS 56172   Janitorial Services

7352 Medical Equipment Rental & Leasing
NAICS 532291 Home Health Equipment Rental
NAICS 53249   Other Commercial & Industrial Machinery & Equipment Rental & Leasing

7353 Heavy Construction Equipment Rental & Leasing
NAICS 23499   All Other Heavy Construction
NAICS 532412 Construction, Mining & Forestry Machinery & Equipment Rental & Leasing

7359 Equipment Rental & Leasing, nec
NAICS 53221   Consumer Electronics & Appliances Rental
NAICS 53231   General Rental Centers
NAICS 532299 All Other Consumer Goods Rental
NAICS 532412 Construction, Mining & Forestry Machinery & Equipment Rental & Leasing
NAICS 532411 Commercial Air, Rail, & Water Transportation Equipment Rental & Leasing
NAICS 562991 Septic Tank & Related Services
NAICS 53242   Office Machinery & Equipment Rental & Leasing
NAICS 53249   Other Commercial & Industrial Machinery & Equipment Rental & Leasing

7361 Employment Agencies
NAICS 541612 Human Resources & Executive Search Consulting Services
NAICS 56131   Employment Placement Agencies

7363 Help Supply Services
NAICS 56132   Temporary Help Services
NAICS 56133   Employee Leasing Services

7371 Computer Programming Services
NAICS 541511 Custom Computer Programming Services

7372 Prepackaged Software
NAICS 51121   Software Publishers
NAICS 334611 Software Reproducing

7373 Computer Integrated Systems Design
NAICS 541512 Computer Systems Design Services

7374 Computer Processing & Data Preparation & Processing Services
NAICS 51421   Data Processing Services

7375 Information Retrieval Services
NAICS 514191 On-line Information Services

7376 Computer Facilities Management Services
NAICS 541513 Computer Facilities Management Services

7377 Computer Rental & Leasing
NAICS 53242   Office Machinery & Equipment Rental & Leasing

7378 Computer Maintenance & Repair
NAICS 44312   Computer & Software Stores
NAICS 811212 Computer & Office Machine Repair & Maintenance

7379 Computer Related Services, nec
NAICS 541512 Computer Systems Design Services
NAICS 541519 Other Computer Related Services

7381 Detective, Guard, & Armored Car Services
NAICS 561611 Investigation Services
NAICS 561612 Security Guards & Patrol Services
NAICS 561613 Armored Car Services

7382 Security Systems Services
NAICS 561621 Security Systems Services

7383 News Syndicates
NAICS 51411   New Syndicates

7384 Photofinishing Laboratories
NAICS 812921 Photo Finishing Laboratories
NAICS 812922 One-hour Photo Finishing

7389 Business Services, nec
NAICS 51224   Sound Recording Studios
NAICS 51229   Other Sound Recording Industries
NAICS 541199 All Other Legal Services
NAICS 81299   All Other Personal Services
NAICS 54137   Surveying & Mapping Services
NAICS 54141   Interior Design Services
NAICS 54142   Industrial Design Services
NAICS 54134   Drafting Services
NAICS 54149   Other Specialized Design Services
NAICS 54189   Other Services Related to Advertising
NAICS 54193   Translation & Interpretation Services
NAICS 54135   Building Inspection Services
NAICS 54199   All Other Professional, Scientific & Technical Services
NAICS 71141   Agents & Managers for Artists, Athletes, Entertainers & Other Public Figures
NAICS 561422 Telemarketing Bureaus
NAICS 561432 Private Mail Centers
NAICS 561439 Other Business Service Centers
NAICS 561491 Repossession Services
NAICS 56191   Packaging & Labeling Services
NAICS 56179   Other Services to Buildings & Dwellings
NAICS 561599 All Other Travel Arrangement & Reservation Services
NAICS 56192   Convention & Trade Show Organizers
NAICS 561591 Convention & Visitors Bureaus
NAICS 52232   Financial Transactions, Processing, Reserve & Clearing House Activities
NAICS 561499 All Other Business Support Services
NAICS 56199   All Other Support Services

7513 Truck Rental & Leasing, Without Drivers
NAICS 53212   Truck, Utility Trailer & Rv Rental & Leasing

Appendix: SIC/NAICS Conversion

7514 Passenger Car Rental
NAICS 532111 Passenger Cars Rental
7515 Passenger Car Leasing
NAICS 532112 Passenger Cars Leasing
7519 Utility Trailer & Recreational Vehicle Rental
NAICS 53212 Truck, Utility Trailer & Rv Rental & Leasing
7521 Automobile Parking
NAICS 81293 Parking Lots & Garages
7532 Top, Body, & Upholstery Repair Shops & Paint Shops
NAICS 811121 Automotive Body, Paint, & Upholstery Repair
            & Maintenance
7533 Automotive Exhaust System Repair Shops
NAICS 811112 Automotive Exhaust System Repair
7534 Tire Retreading & Repair Shops
NAICS 326212 Tire Retreading
NAICS 811198 All Other Automotive Repair & Maintenance
7536 Automotive Glass Replacement Shops
NAICS 811122 Automotive Glass Replacement Shops
7537 Automotive Transmission Repair Shops
NAICS 811113 Automotive Transmission Repair
7538 General Automotive Repair Shops
NAICS 811111 General Automotive Repair
7539 Automotive Repair Shops, nec
NAICS 811118 Other Automotive Mechanical & Electrical
            Repair & Maintenance
7542 Carwashes
NAICS 811192 Car Washes
7549 Automotive Services, Except Repair & Carwashes
NAICS 811191 Automotive Oil Change & Lubrication Shops
NAICS 48841 Motor Vehicle Towing
NAICS 811198 All Other Automotive Repair & Maintenance
7622 Radio & Television Repair Shops
NAICS 811211 Consumer Electronics Repair & Maintenance
NAICS 443112 Radio, Television & Other Electronics Stores
7623 Refrigeration & Air-conditioning Services & Repair Shops
NAICS 443111 Household Appliance Stores
NAICS 81131 Commercial & Industrial Machinery &
            Equipment Repair & Maintenance
NAICS 811412 Appliance Repair & Maintenance
7629 Electrical & Electronic Repair Shops, nec
NAICS 443111 Household Appliance Stores
NAICS 811212 Computer & Office Machine Repair &
            Maintenance
NAICS 811213 Communication Equipment Repair &
            Maintenance
NAICS 811219 Other Electronic & Precision Equipment
            Repair & Maintenance
NAICS 811412 Appliance Repair & Maintenance
NAICS 811211 Consumer Electronics Repair & Maintenance
7631 Watch, Clock, & Jewelry Repair
NAICS 81149 Other Personal & Household Goods Repair &
            Maintenance
7641 Reupholster & Furniture Repair
NAICS 81142 Reupholstery & Furniture Repair
7692 Welding Repair
NAICS 81149 Other Personal & Household Goods Repair &
            Maintenance
7694 Armature Rewinding Shops
NAICS 81131 Commercial & Industrial Machinery &
            Equipment Repair & Maintenance
NAICS 335312 Motor & Generator Manufacturing
7699 Repair Shops & Related Services, nec
NAICS 561622 Locksmiths
NAICS 562991 Septic Tank & Related Services

NAICS 56179 Other Services to Buildings & Dwellings
NAICS 48839 Other Supporting Activities for Water
            Transportation
NAICS 45111 Sporting Goods Stores
NAICS 81131 Commercial & Industrial Machinery &
            Equipment Repair & Maintenance
NAICS 11521 Support Activities for Animal Production
NAICS 811212 Computer & Office Machine Repair &
            Maintenance
NAICS 811219 Other Electronic & Precision Equipment
            Repair & Maintenance
NAICS 811411 Home & Garden Equipment Repair &
            Maintenance
NAICS 811412 Appliance Repair & Maintenance
NAICS 81143 Footwear & Leather Goods Repair
NAICS 81149 Other Personal & Household Goods Repair &
            Maintenance
7812 Motion Picture & Video Tape Production
NAICS 51211 Motion Picture & Video Production
7819 Services Allied to Motion Picture Production
NAICS 512191 Teleproduction & Other Post-production
            Services
NAICS 56131 Employment Placement Agencies
NAICS 53222 Formal Wear & Costumes Rental
NAICS 53249 Other Commercial & Industrial Machinery &
            Equipment Rental & Leasing
NAICS 541214 Payroll Services
NAICS 71151 Independent Artists, Writers, & Performers
NAICS 334612 Prerecorded Compact Disc , Tape, & Record
            Manufacturing
NAICS 512199 Other Motion Picture & Video Industries
7822 Motion Picture & Video Tape Distribution
NAICS 42199 Other Miscellaneous Durable Goods
            Wholesalers
NAICS 51212 Motion Picture & Video Distribution
7829 Services Allied to Motion Picture Distribution
NAICS 512199 Other Motion Picture & Video Industries
NAICS 51212 Motion Picture & Video Distribution
7832 Motion Picture Theaters, Except Drive-ins.
NAICS 512131 Motion Picture Theaters, Except Drive-in
7833 Drive-in Motion Picture Theaters
NAICS 512132 Drive-in Motion Picture Theaters
7841 Video Tape Rental
NAICS 53223 Video Tapes & Disc Rental
7911 Dance Studios, Schools, & Halls
NAICS 71399 All Other Amusement & Recreation Industries
NAICS 61161 Fine Arts Schools
7922 Theatrical Producers & Miscellaneous Theatrical Services
NAICS 56131 Employment Placement Agencies
NAICS 71111 Theater Companies & Dinner Theaters
NAICS 71141 Agents & Managers for Artists, Athletes,
            Entertainers & Other Public Figures
NAICS 71112 Dance Companies
NAICS 71131 Promoters of Performing Arts, Sports, &
            Similar Events with Facilities
NAICS 71132 Promoters of Performing Arts, Sports, &
            Similar Events Without Facilities
NAICS 51229 Other Sound Recording Industries
NAICS 53249 Other Commercial & Industrial Machinery &
            Equipment Rental & Leasing
**7929 Bands, Orchestras, Actors, & Other Entertainers &
    Entertainment Groups**
NAICS 71113 Musical Groups & Artists
NAICS 71151 Independent Artists, Writers, & Performers

NAICS 71119   Other Performing Arts Companies
7933 Bowling Centers
NAICS 71395   Bowling Centers
7941 Professional Sports Clubs & Promoters
NAICS 711211   Sports Teams & Clubs
NAICS 71141   Agents & Managers for Artists, Athletes, Entertainers , & Other Public Figures
NAICS 71132   Promoters of Arts, Sports & Similar Events Without Facilities
NAICS 71131   Promoters of Arts, Sports, & Similar Events with Facilities
NAICS 711219 Other Spectator Sports
7948 Racing, Including Track Operations
NAICS 711212 Race Tracks
NAICS 711219 Other Spectator Sports
7991 Physical Fitness Facilities
NAICS 71394   Fitness & Recreational Sports Centers
7992 Public Golf Courses
NAICS 71391   Golf Courses & Country Clubs
7993 Coin Operated Amusement Devices
NAICS 71312   Amusement Arcades
NAICS 71329   Other Gambling Industries
NAICS 71399   All Other Amusement & Recreation Industries
7996 Amusement Parks
NAICS 71311   Amusement & Theme Parks
7997 Membership Sports & Recreation Clubs
NAICS 48122   Nonscheduled Speciality Air Transportation
NAICS 71391   Golf Courses & Country Clubs
NAICS 71394   Fitness & Recreational Sports Centers
NAICS 71399   All Other Amusement & Recreation Industries
7999 Amusement & Recreation Services, nec
NAICS 561599 All Other Travel Arrangement & Reservation Services
NAICS 48799   Scenic & Sightseeing Transportation, Other
NAICS 71119   Other Performing Arts Companies
NAICS 711219 Other Spectator Sports
NAICS 71392   Skiing Facilities
NAICS 71394   Fitness & Recreational Sports Centers
NAICS 71321   Casinos
NAICS 71329   Other Gambling Industries
NAICS 71219   Nature Parks & Other Similar Institutions
NAICS 61162   Sports & Recreation Instruction
NAICS 532292 Recreational Goods Rental
NAICS 48711   Scenic & Sightseeing Transportation, Land
NAICS 48721   Scenic & Sightseeing Transportation, Water
NAICS 71399   All Other Amusement & Recreation Industries
8011 Offices & Clinics of Doctors of Medicine
NAICS 621493 Freestanding Ambulatory Surgical & Emergency Centers
NAICS 621491 Hmo Medical Centers
NAICS 621112 Offices of Physicians, Mental Health Specialists
NAICS 621111 Offices of Physicians
8021 Offices & Clinics of Dentists
NAICS 62121   Offices of Dentists
8031 Offices & Clinics of Doctors of Osteopathy
NAICS 621111 Offices of Physicians
NAICS 621112 Offices of Physicians, Mental Health Specialists
8041 Offices & Clinics of Chiropractors
NAICS 62131   Offices of Chiropractors
8042 Offices & Clinics of Optometrists
NAICS 62132   Offices of Optometrists
8043 Offices & Clinics of Podiatrists
NAICS 621391 Offices of Podiatrists

8049 Offices & Clinics of Health Practitioners, nec
NAICS 62133   Offices of Mental Health Practitioners
NAICS 62134   Offices of Physical, Occupational, & Speech Therapists & Audiologists
NAICS 621399 Offices of All Other Miscellaneous Health Practitioners
8051 Skilled Nursing Care Facilities
NAICS 623311 Continuing Care Retirement Communities
NAICS 62311   Nursing Care Facilities
8052 Intermediate Care Facilities
NAICS 623311 Continuing Care Retirement Communities
NAICS 62321   Residential Mental Retardation Facilities
NAICS 62311   Nursing Care Facilities
8059 Nursing & Personal Care Facilities, nec
NAICS 623311 Continuing Care Retirement Communities
NAICS 62311   Nursing Care Facilities
8062 General Medical & Surgical Hospitals
NAICS 62211   General Medical & Surgical Hospitals
8063 Psychiatric Hospitals
NAICS 62221   Psychiatric & Substance Abuse Hospitals
8069 Specialty Hospitals, Except Psychiatric
NAICS 62211   General Medical & Surgical Hospitals
NAICS 62221   Psychiatric & Substance Abuse Hospitals
NAICS 62231   Specialty Hospitals
8071 Medical Laboratories
NAICS 621512 Diagnostic Imaging Centers
NAICS 621511 Medical Laboratories
8072 Dental Laboratories
NAICS 339116 Dental Laboratories
8082 Home Health Care Services
NAICS 62161   Home Health Care Services
8092 Kidney Dialysis Centers
NAICS 621492 Kidney Dialysis Centers
8093 Specialty Outpatient Facilities, nec
NAICS 62141   Family Planning Centers
NAICS 62142   Outpatient Mental Health & Substance Abuse Centers
NAICS 621498 All Other Outpatient Care Facilities
8099 Health & Allied Services, nec
NAICS 621991 Blood & Organ Banks
NAICS 54143   Graphic Design Services
NAICS 541922 Commercial Photography
NAICS 62141   Family Planning Centers
NAICS 621999 All Other Miscellaneous Ambulatory Health Care Services
8111 Legal Services
NAICS 54111   Offices of Lawyers
8211 Elementary & Secondary Schools
NAICS 61111   Elementary & Secondary Schools
8221 Colleges, Universities, & Professional Schools
NAICS 61131   Colleges, Universities & Professional Schools
8222 Junior Colleges & Technical Institutes
NAICS 61121   Junior Colleges
8231 Libraries
NAICS 51412   Libraries & Archives
8243 Data Processing Schools
NAICS 611519 Other Technical & Trade Schools
NAICS 61142   Computer Training
8244 Business & Secretarial Schools
NAICS 61141   Business & Secretarial Schools
8249 Vocational Schools, nec
NAICS 611513 Apprenticeship Training
NAICS 611512 Flight Training
NAICS 611519 Other Technical & Trade Schools

8299 Schools & Educational Services, nec
NAICS 48122   Nonscheduled speciality Air Transportation
NAICS 611512 Flight Training
NAICS 611692 Automobile Driving Schools
NAICS 61171   Educational Support Services
NAICS 611691 Exam Preparation & Tutoring
NAICS 61161   Fine Arts Schools
NAICS 61163   Language Schools
NAICS 61143   Professional & Management Development
              Training Schools
NAICS 611699 All Other Miscellaneous Schools & Instruction

8322 Individual & Family Social Services
NAICS 62411   Child & Youth Services
NAICS 62421   Community Food Services
NAICS 624229 Other Community Housing Services
NAICS 62423   Emergency & Other Relief Services
NAICS 62412   Services for the Elderly & Persons with
              Disabilities
NAICS 624221 Temporary Shelters
NAICS 92215   Parole Offices & Probation Offices
NAICS 62419   Other Individual & Family Services

8331 Job Training & Vocational Rehabilitation Services
NAICS 62431   Vocational Rehabilitation Services

8351 Child Day Care Services
NAICS 62441   Child Day Care Services

8361 Residential Care
NAICS 623312 Homes for the Elderly
NAICS 62322   Residential Mental Health & Substance Abuse
              Facilities
NAICS 62399   Other Residential Care Facilities

8399 Social Services, nec
NAICS 813212 Voluntary Health Organizations
NAICS 813219 Other Grantmaking & Giving Services
NAICS 813311 Human Rights Organizations
NAICS 813312 Environment, Conservation & Wildlife
              Organizations
NAICS 813319 Other Social Advocacy Organizations

8412 Museums & Art Galleries
NAICS 71211   Museums
NAICS 71212   Historical Sites

8422 Arboreta & Botanical or Zoological Gardens
NAICS 71213   Zoos & Botanical Gardens
NAICS 71219   Nature Parks & Other Similar Institutions

8611 Business Associations
NAICS 81391   Business Associations

8621 Professional Membership Organizations
NAICS 81392   Professional Organizations

8631 Labor Unions & Similar Labor Organizations
NAICS 81393   Labor Unions & Similar Labor Organizations

8641 Civic, Social, & Fraternal Associations
NAICS 81341   Civic & Social Organizations
NAICS 81399   Other Similar Organizations
NAICS 92115   American Indian & Alaska Native Tribal
              Governments
NAICS 62411   Child & Youth Services

8651 Political Organizations
NAICS 81394   Political Organizations

8661 Religious Organizations
NAICS 81311   Religious Organizations

8699 Membership Organizations, nec
NAICS 81341   Civic & Social Organizations
NAICS 81391   Business Associations
NAICS 813312 Environment, Conservation, & Wildlife
              Organizations

NAICS 561599 All Other Travel Arrangement & Reservation
              Services
NAICS 81399   Other Similar Organizations

8711 Engineering Services
NAICS 54133   Engineering Services

8712 Architectural Services
NAICS 54131   Architectural Services

8713 Surveying Services
NAICS 48122   Nonscheduled Air Speciality Transportation
NAICS 54136   Geophysical Surveying & Mapping Services
NAICS 54137   Surveying & Mapping Services

8721 Accounting, Auditing, & Bookkeeping Services
NAICS 541211 Offices of Certified Public Accountants
NAICS 541214 Payroll Services
NAICS 541219 Other Accounting Services

8731 Commercial Physical & Biological Research
NAICS 54171   Research & Development in the Physical
              Sciences & Engineering Sciences
NAICS 54172   Research & Development in the Life Sciences

**8732 Commercial Economic, Sociological, & Educational
      Research**
NAICS 54173   Research & Development in the Social Sciences
              & Humanities
NAICS 54191   Marketing Research & Public Opinion Polling

8733 Noncommercial Research Organizations
NAICS 54171   Research & Development in the Physical
              Sciences & Engineering Sciences
NAICS 54172   Research & Development in the Life Sciences
NAICS 54173   Research & Development in the Social Sciences
              & Humanities

8734 Testing Laboratories
NAICS 54194   Veterinary Services
NAICS 54138   Testing Laboratories

8741 Management Services
NAICS 56111   Office Administrative Services
NAICS 23   Included in Construction Sector by Type of
              Construction

8742 Management Consulting Services
NAICS 541611 Administrative Management & General
              Management Consulting Services
NAICS 541612 Human Resources & Executive Search Services
NAICS 541613 Marketing Consulting Services
NAICS 541614 Process, Physical, Distribution & Logistics
              Consulting Services

8743 Public Relations Services
NAICS 54182   Public Relations Agencies

8744 Facilities Support Management Services
NAICS 56121   Facilities Support Services

8748 Business Consulting Services, nec
NAICS 61171   Educational Support Services
NAICS 541618 Other Management Consulting Services
NAICS 54169   Other Scientific & Technical Consulting
              Services

8811 Private Households
NAICS 81411   Private Households

8999 Services, nec
NAICS 71151   Independent Artists, Writers, & Performers
NAICS 51221   Record Production
NAICS 54169   Other Scientific & Technical Consulting
              Services
NAICS 51223   Music Publishers
NAICS 541612 Human Resources & Executive Search
              Consulting Services
NAICS 514199 All Other Information Services

NAICS 54162   Environmental Consulting Services

PUBLIC ADMINISTRATION

9111 Executive Offices
NAICS 92111   Executive Offices
9121 Legislative Bodies
NAICS 92112   Legislative Bodies
9131 Executive & Legislative Offices, Combined
NAICS 92114   Executive & Legislative Offices, Combined
9199 General Government, nec
NAICS 92119   All Other General Government
9211 Courts
NAICS 92211   Courts
9221 Police Protection
NAICS 92212   Police Protection
9222 Legal Counsel & Prosecution
NAICS 92213   Legal Counsel & Prosecution
9223 Correctional Institutions
NAICS 92214   Correctional Institutions
9224 Fire Protection
NAICS 92216   Fire Protection
9229 Public Order & Safety, nec
NAICS 92219   All Other Justice, Public Order, & Safety
9311 Public Finance, Taxation, & Monetary Policy
NAICS 92113   Public Finance
9411 Administration of Educational Programs
NAICS 92311   Administration of Education Programs
9431 Administration of Public Health Programs
NAICS 92312   Administration of Public Health Programs
9441 Administration of Social, Human Resource & Income Maintenance Programs
NAICS 92313   Administration of Social, Human Resource & Income Maintenance Programs
9451 Administration of Veteran's Affairs, Except Health Insurance
NAICS 92314   Administration of Veteran's Affairs
9511 Air & Water Resource & Solid Waste Management
NAICS 92411   Air & Water Resource & Solid Waste Management
9512 Land, Mineral, Wildlife, & Forest Conservation
NAICS 92412   Land, Mineral, Wildlife, & Forest Conservation
9531 Administration of Housing Programs
NAICS 92511   Administration of Housing Programs
9532 Administration of Urban Planning & Community & Rural Development
NAICS 92512   Administration of Urban Planning & Community & Rural Development
9611 Administration of General Economic Programs
NAICS 92611   Administration of General Economic Programs
9621 Regulations & Administration of Transportation Programs
NAICS 488111   Air Traffic Control
NAICS 92612   Regulation & Administration of Transportation Programs
9631 Regulation & Administration of Communications, Electric, Gas, & Other Utilities
NAICS 92613   Regulation & Administration of Communications, Electric, Gas, & Other Utilities
9641 Regulation of Agricultural Marketing & Commodity
NAICS 92614   Regulation of Agricultural Marketing & Commodity

9651 Regulation, Licensing, & Inspection of Miscellaneous Commercial Sectors
NAICS 92615   Regulation, Licensing, & Inspection of Miscellaneous Commercial Sectors
9661 Space Research & Technology
NAICS 92711   Space Research & Technology
9711 National Security
NAICS 92811   National Security
9721 International Affairs
NAICS 92812   International Affairs
9999 Nonclassifiable Establishments
NAICS 99999   Unclassified Establishments

Appendix: SIC/NAICS Conversion

NAICS TO SIC CONVERSION GUIDE

AGRICULTURE, FORESTRY, FISHING, & HUNTING

11111 Soybean Farming
SIC 0116 Soybeans
11112 Oilseed Farming
SIC 0119 Cash Grains, nec
11113 Dry Pea & Bean Farming
SIC 0119 Cash Grains, nec
11114 Wheat Farming
SIC 0111 Wheat
11115 Corn Farming
SIC 0115 Corn
SIC 0119 Cash Grains, nec
11116 Rice Farming
SIC 0112 Rice
111191 Oilseed & Grain Combination Farming
SIC 0119 Cash Grains, nec
111199 All Other Grain Farming
SIC 0119 Cash Grains, nec
111211 Potato Farming
SIC 0134 Irish Potatoes
111219 Other Vegetable & Melon Farming
SIC 0161 Vegetables & Melons
SIC 0139 Field Crops Except Cash Grains
11131 Orange Groves
SIC 0174 Citrus Fruits
11132 Citrus Groves
SIC 0174 Citrus Fruits
111331 Apple Orchards
SIC 0175 Deciduous Tree Fruits
111332 Grape Vineyards
SIC 0172 Grapes
111333 Strawberry Farming
SIC 0171 Berry Crops
111334 Berry Farming
SIC 0171 Berry Crops
111335 Tree Nut Farming
SIC 0173 Tree Nuts
111336 Fruit & Tree Nut Combination Farming
SIC 0179 Fruits & Tree Nuts, nec
111339 Other Noncitrus Fruit Farming
SIC 0175 Deciduous Tree Fruits
SIC 0179 Fruit & Tree Nuts, nec
111411 Mushroom Production
SIC 0182 Food Crops Grown Under Cover
111419 Other Food Crops Grown Under Cover
SIC 0182 Food Crops Grown Under Cover
111421 Nursery & Tree Production
SIC 0181 Ornamental Floriculture & Nursery Products
SIC 0811 Timber Tracts
111422 Floriculture Production
SIC 0181 Ornamental Floriculture & Nursery Products
11191 Tobacco Farming
SIC 0132 Tobacco
11192 Cotton Farming
SIC 0131 Cotton
11193 Sugarcane Farming
SIC 0133 Sugarcane & Sugar Beets

11194 Hay Farming
SIC 0139 Field Crops, Except Cash Grains, nec
111991 Sugar Beet Farming
SIC 0133 Sugarcane & Sugar Beets
111992 Peanut Farming
SIC 0139 Field Crops, Except Cash Grains, nec
111998 All Other Miscellaneous Crop Farming
SIC 0139 Field Crops, Except Cash Grains, nec
SIC 0191 General Farms, Primarily Crop
SIC 0831 Forest Products
SIC 0919 Miscellaneous Marine Products
SIC 2099 Food Preparations, nec
112111 Beef Cattle Ranching & Farming
SIC 0212 Beef Cattle, Except Feedlots
SIC 0241 Dairy Farms
112112 Cattle Feedlots
SIC 0211 Beef Cattle Feedlots
11212 Dairy Cattle & Milk Production
SIC 0241 Dairy Farms
11213 Dual Purpose Cattle Ranching & Farming
No SIC equivalent
11221 Hog & Pig Farming
SIC 0213 Hogs
11231 Chicken Egg Production
SIC 0252 Chicken Eggs
11232 Broilers & Other Meat Type Chicken Production
SIC 0251 Broiler, Fryers, & Roaster Chickens
11233 Turkey Production
SIC 0253 Turkey & Turkey Eggs
11234 Poultry Hatcheries
SIC 0254 Poultry Hatcheries
11239 Other Poultry Production
SIC 0259 Poultry & Eggs, nec
11241 Sheep Farming
SIC 0214 Sheep & Goats
11242 Goat Farming
SIC 0214 Sheep & Goats
112511 Finfish Farming & Fish Hatcheries
SIC 0273 Animal Aquaculture
SIC 0921 Fish Hatcheries & Preserves
112512 Shellfish Farming
SIC 0273 Animal Aquaculture
SIC 0921 Fish Hatcheries & Preserves
112519 Other Animal Aquaculture
SIC 0273 Animal Aquaculture
11291 Apiculture
SIC 0279 Animal Specialties, nec
11292 Horse & Other Equine Production
SIC 0272 Horses & Other Equines
11293 Fur-Bearing Animal & Rabbit Production
SIC 0271 Fur-Bearing Animals & Rabbits
11299 All Other Animal Production
SIC 0219 General Livestock, Except Dairy & Poultry
SIC 0279 Animal Specialties, nec
SIC 0291 General Farms, Primarily Livestock & Animal
　　　Specialties;
11311 Timber Tract Operations
SIC 0811 Timber Tracts
11321 Forest Nurseries & Gathering of Forest Products
SIC 0831 Forest Nurseries & Gathering of Forest Products
11331 Logging
SIC 2411 Logging

114111 Finfish Fishing
SIC 0912 Finfish
114112 Shellfish Fishing
SIC 0913 Shellfish
114119 Other Marine Fishing
SIC 0919 Miscellaneous Marine Products
11421 Hunting & Trapping
SIC 0971 Hunting & Trapping, & Game Propagation;
115111 Cotton Ginning
SIC 0724 Cotton Ginning
115112 Soil Preparation, Planting, & Cultivating
SIC 0711 Soil Preparation Services
SIC 0721 Crop Planting, Cultivating, & Protecting
115113 Crop Harvesting, Primarily by Machine
SIC 0722 Crop Harvesting, Primarily by Machine
115114 Other Postharvest Crop Activities
SIC 0723 Crop Preparation Services For Market, Except Cotton Ginning
115115 Farm Labor Contractors & Crew Leaders
SIC 0761 Farm Labor Contractors & Crew Leaders
115116 Farm Management Services
SIC 0762 Farm Management Services
11521 Support Activities for Animal Production
SIC 0751 Livestock Services, Except Veterinary
SIC 0752 Animal Specialty Services, Except Veterinary
SIC 7699 Repair Services, nec
11531 Support Activities for Forestry
SIC 0851 Forestry Services

MINING

211111 Crude Petroleum & Natural Gas Extraction
SIC 1311 Crude Petroleum & Natural Gas
211112 Natural Gas Liquid Extraction
SIC 1321 Natural Gas Liquids
212111 Bituminous Coal & Lignite Surface Mining
SIC 1221 Bituminous Coal & Lignite Surface Mining
212112 Bituminous Coal Underground Mining
SIC 1222 Bituminous Coal Underground Mining
212113 Anthracite Mining
SIC 1231 Anthracite Mining
21221 Iron Ore Mining
SIC 1011 Iron Ores
212221 Gold Ore Mining
SIC 1041 Gold Ores
212222 Silver Ore Mining
SIC 1044 Silver Ores
212231 Lead Ore & Zinc Ore Mining
SIC 1031 Lead & Zinc Ores
212234 Copper Ore & Nickel Ore Mining
SIC 1021 Copper Ores
212291 Uranium-Radium-Vanadium Ore Mining
SIC 1094 Uranium-Radium-Vanadium Ores
212299 All Other Metal Ore Mining
SIC 1061 Ferroalloy Ores, Except Vanadium
SIC 1099 Miscellaneous Metal Ores, nec
212311 Dimension Stone Mining & Quarrying
SIC 1411 Dimension Stone
212312 Crushed & Broken Limestone Mining & Quarrying
SIC 1422 Crushed & Broken Limestone
212313 Crushed & Broken Granite Mining & Quarrying
SIC 1423 Crushed & Broken Granite

212319 Other Crushed & Broken Stone Mining & Quarrying
SIC 1429 Crushed & Broken Stone, nec
SIC 1499 Miscellaneous Nonmetallic Minerals, Except Fuels
212321 Construction Sand & Gravel Mining
SIC 1442 Construction Sand & Gravel
212322 Industrial Sand Mining
SIC 1446 Industrial Sand
212324 Kaolin & Ball Clay Mining
SIC 1455 Kaolin & Ball Clay
212325 Clay & Ceramic & Refractory Minerals Mining
SIC 1459 Clay, Ceramic, & Refractory Minerals, nec
212391 Potash, Soda, & Borate Mineral Mining
SIC 1474 Potash, Soda, & Borate Minerals
212392 Phosphate Rock Mining
SIC 1475 Phosphate Rock
212393 Other Chemical & Fertilizer Mineral Mining
SIC 1479 Chemical & Fertilizer Mineral Mining, nec
212399 All Other Nonmetallic Mineral Mining
SIC 1499 Miscellaneous Nonmetallic Minerals, Except Fuels
213111 Drilling Oil & Gas Wells
SIC 1381 Drilling Oil & Gas Wells
213112 Support Activities for Oil & Gas Operations
SIC 1382 Oil & Gas Field Exploration Services
SIC 1389 Oil & Gas Field Services, nec
213113 Other Gas & Field Support Activities
SIC 1389 Oil & Gas Field Services, nec
213114 Support Activities for Coal Mining
SIC 1241 Coal Mining Services
213115 Support Activities for Metal Mining
SIC 1081 Metal Mining Services
213116 Support Activities for Nonmetallic Minerals, Except Fuels
SIC 1481 Nonmetallic Minerals Services, Except Fuels

UTILITIES

221111 Hydroelectric Power Generation
SIC 4911 Electric Services
SIC 4931 Electric & Other Services Combined
SIC 4939 Combination Utilities, nec
221112 Fossil Fuel Electric Power Generation
SIC 4911 Electric Services
SIC 4931 Electric & Other Services Combined
SIC 4939 Combination Utilities, nec
221113 Nuclear Electric Power Generation
SIC 4911 Electric Services
SIC 4931 Electric & Other Services Combined
SIC 4939 Combination Utilities, nec
221119 Other Electric Power Generation
SIC 4911 Electric Services
SIC 4931 Electric & Other Services Combined
SIC 4939 Combination Utilities, nec
221121 Electric Bulk Power Transmission & Control
SIC 4911 Electric Services
SIC 4931 Electric & Other Services Combined
SIC 4939 Combination Utilities, NEC
221122 Electric Power Distribution
SIC 4911 Electric Services
SIC 4931 Electric & Other Services Combined
SIC 4939 Combination Utilities, nec
22121 Natural Gas Distribution
SIC 4923 Natural Gas Transmission & Distribution
SIC 4924 Natural Gas Distribution

SIC 4925 Mixed, Manufactured, or Liquefied Petroleum Gas
Production and/or Distribution
SIC 4931 Electronic & Other Services Combined
SIC 4932 Gas & Other Services Combined
SIC 4939 Combination Utilities, nec
22131 Water Supply & Irrigation Systems
SIC 4941 Water Supply
SIC 4971 Irrigation Systems
22132 Sewage Treatment Facilities
SIC 4952 Sewerage Systems
22133 Steam & Air-Conditioning Supply
SIC 4961 Steam & Air-Conditioning Supply

CONSTRUCTION

23311 Land Subdivision & Land Development
SIC 6552 Land Subdividers & Developers, Except Cemeteries
23321 Single Family Housing Construction
SIC 1521 General contractors-Single-Family Houses
SIC 1531 Operative Builders
23322 Multifamily Housing Construction
SIC 1522 General Contractors-Residential Building, Other
Than Single-Family
SIC 1531 Operative Builders
23331 Manufacturing & Industrial Building Construction
SIC 1531 Operative Builders
SIC 1541 General Contractors-Industrial Buildings &
Warehouses
23332 Commercial & Institutional Building Construction
SIC 1522 General Contractors-Residential Building Other than
Single-Family
SIC 1531 Operative Builders
SIC 1541 General Contractors-Industrial Buildings &
Warehouses
SIC 1542 General Contractor-Nonresidential Buildings, Other
than Industrial Buildings & Warehouses
23411 Highway & Street Construction
SIC 1611 Highway & Street Construction, Except Elevated
Highways
23412 Bridge & Tunnel Construction
SIC 1622 Bridge, Tunnel, & Elevated Highway Construction
2349 Other Heavy Construction
23491 Water, Sewer, & Pipeline Construction
SIC 1623 Water, Sewer, Pipeline, & Communications & Power
Line Construction
**23492 Power & Communication Transmission Line
Construction**
SIC 1623 Water, Sewer, Pipelines, & Communications & Power
Line Construction
23493 Industrial Nonbuilding Structure Construction
SIC 1629 Heavy Construction, nec
23499 All Other Heavy Construction
SIC 1629 Heavy Construction, nec
SIC 7353 Construction Equipment Rental & Leasing
23511 Plumbing, Heating & Air-Conditioning Contractors
SIC 1711 Plumbing, Heating & Air-Conditioning
23521 Painting & Wall Covering Contractors
SIC 1721 Painting & Paper Hanging
SIC 1799 Special Trade Contractors, nec
23531 Electrical Contractors
SIC 1731 Electrical Work

23541 Masonry & Stone Contractors
SIC 1741 Masonry, Stone Setting & Other Stone Work
23542 Drywall, Plastering, Acoustical & Insulation Contractors
SIC 1742 Plastering, Drywall, Acoustical, & Insulation Work
SIC 1743 Terrazzo, Tile, Marble & Mosaic work
SIC 1771 Concrete Work
23543 Tile, Marble, Terrazzo & Mosaic Contractors
SIC 1743 Terrazzo, Tile, Marble, & Mosaic Work
23551 Carpentry Contractors
SIC 1751 Carpentry Work
23552 Floor Laying & Other Floor Contractors
SIC 1752 Floor Laying & Other Floor Work, nec
23561 Roofing, Siding & Sheet Metal Contractors
SIC 1761 Roofing, Siding, & Sheet Metal Work
23571 Concrete Contractors
SIC 1771 Concrete Work
23581 Water Well Drilling Contractors
SIC 1781 Water Well Drilling
23591 Structural Steel Erection Contractors
SIC 1791 Structural Steel Erection
23592 Glass & Glazing Contractors
SIC 1793 Glass & Glazing Work
SIC 1799 Specialty Trade Contractors, nec
23593 Excavation Contractors
SIC 1794 Excavation Work
23594 Wrecking & Demolition Contractors
SIC 1795 Wrecking & Demolition Work
**23595 Building Equipment & Other Machinery Installation
Contractors**
SIC 1796 Installation of Erection of Building Equipment, nec
23599 All Other Special Trade Contractors
SIC 1799 Special Trade Contractors, nec

FOOD MANUFACTURING

311111 Dog & Cat Food Manufacturing
SIC 2047 Dog & Cat Food
311119 Other Animal Food Manufacturing
SIC 2048 Prepared Feeds & Feed Ingredients for Animals &
Fowls, Except Dogs & Cats
311211 Flour Milling
SIC 2034 Dehydrated Fruits, Vegetables & Soup Mixes
SIC 2041 Flour & Other Grain Mill Products
311212 Rice Milling
SIC 2044 Rice Milling
311213 Malt Manufacturing
SIC 2083 Malt
311221 Wet Corn Milling
SIC 2046 Wet Corn Milling
311222 Soybean Processing
SIC 2075 Soybean Oil Mills
SIC 2079 Shortening, Table Oils, Margarine, & Other Edible
Fats & Oils, nec
311223 Other Oilseed Processing
SIC 2074 Cottonseed Oil Mills
SIC 2079 Shortening, Table Oils, Margarine & Other Edible
Fats & Oils, nec
SIC 2076 Vegetable Oil Mills, Except Corn, Cottonseed, &
Soybean
311225 Edible Fats & Oils Manufacturing
SIC 2077 Animal & Marine Fats & Oil, nec
SIC 2074 Cottonseed Oil Mills
SIC 2075 Soybean Oil Mills

SIC 2076 Vegetable Oil Mills, Except Corn, Cottonseed, & Soybean
SIC 2079 Shortening, Table Oils, Margarine, & Other Edible Fats & Oils, nec

31123 Breakfast Cereal Manufacturing
SIC 2043 Cereal Breakfast Foods

311311 Sugarcane Mills
SIC 2061 Cane Sugar, Except Refining

311312 Cane Sugar Refining
SIC 2062 Cane Sugar Refining

311313 Beet Sugar Manufacturing
SIC 2063 Beet Sugar

31132 Chocolate & Confectionery Manufacturing from Cacao Beans
SIC 2066 Chocolate & Cocoa Products

31133 Confectionery Manufacturing from Purchased Chocolate
SIC 2064 Candy & Other Confectionery Products

31134 Non-Chocolate Confectionery Manufacturing
SIC 2064 Candy & Other Confectionery Products
SIC 2067 Chewing Gum
SIC 2099 Food Preparations, nec

311411 Frozen Fruit, Juice & Vegetable Processing
SIC 2037 Frozen Fruits, Fruit Juices, & Vegetables

311412 Frozen Specialty Food Manufacturing
SIC 2038 Frozen Specialties, NEC

311421 Fruit & Vegetable Canning
SIC 2033 Canned Fruits, Vegetables, Preserves, Jams, & Jellies
SIC 2035 Pickled Fruits & Vegetables, Vegetable Sauces, & Seasonings & Salad Dressings

311422 Specialty Canning
SIC 2032 Canned Specialties

311423 Dried & Dehydrated Food Manufacturing
SIC 2034 Dried & Dehydrated Fruits, Vegetables & Soup Mixes
SIC 2099 Food Preparation, nec

311511 Fluid Milk Manufacturing
SIC 2026 Fluid Milk

311512 Creamery Butter Manufacturing
SIC 2021 Creamery Butter

311513 Cheese Manufacturing
SIC 2022 Natural, Processed, & Imitation Cheese

311514 Dry, Condensed, & Evaporated Milk Manufacturing
SIC 2023 Dry, Condensed & Evaporated Dairy Products

31152 Ice Cream & Frozen Dessert Manufacturing
SIC 2024 Ice Cream & Frozen Desserts

311611 Animal Slaughtering
SIC 0751 Livestock Services, Except Veterinary
SIC 2011 Meat Packing Plants
SIC 2048 Prepared Feeds & Feed Ingredients for Animals & Fowls, Except Dogs & Cats

311612 Meat Processed from Carcasses
SIC 2013 Sausages & Other Prepared Meats
SIC 5147 Meat & Meat Products

311613 Rendering & Meat By-product Processing
SIC 2077 Animal & Marine Fats & Oils

311615 Poultry Processing
SIC 2015 Poultry Slaughtering & Processing

311711 Seafood Canning
SIC 2077 Animal & Marine Fats & Oils
SIC 2091 Canned & Cured Fish & Seafood

311712 Fresh & Frozen Seafood Processing
SIC 2077 Animal & Marine Fats & Oils
SIC 2092 Prepared Fresh or Frozen Fish & Seafood

311811 Retail Bakeries
SIC 5461 Retail Bakeries

311812 Commercial Bakeries
SIC 2051 Bread & Other Bakery Products, Except Cookies & Crackers
SIC 2052 Cookies & Crackers

311813 Frozen Bakery Product Manufacturing
SIC 2053 Frozen Bakery Products, Except Bread

311821 Cookie & Cracker Manufacturing
SIC 2052 Cookies & Crackers

311822 Flour Mixes & Dough Manufacturing from Purchased Flour
SIC 2045 Prepared Flour Mixes & Doughs

311823 Pasta Manufacturing
SIC 2098 Macaroni, Spaghetti, Vermicelli & Noodles

31183 Tortilla Manufacturing
SIC 2099 Food Preparations, nec

311911 Roasted Nuts & Peanut Butter Manufacturing
SIC 2068 Salted & Roasted Nuts & Seeds
SIC 2099 Food Preparations, nec

311919 Other Snack Food Manufacturing
SIC 2052 Cookies & Crackers
SIC 2096 Potato Chips, Corn Chips, & Similar Snacks

31192 Coffee & Tea Manufacturing
SIC 2043 Cereal Breakfast Foods
SIC 2095 Roasted Coffee
SIC 2099 Food Preparations, nec

31193 Flavoring Syrup & Concentrate Manufacturing
SIC 2087 Flavoring Extracts & Flavoring Syrups

311941 Mayonnaise, Dressing & Other Prepared Sauce Manufacturing
SIC 2035 Pickled Fruits & Vegetables, Vegetable Seasonings, & Sauces & Salad Dressings
SIC 2099 Food Preparations, nec

311942 Spice & Extract Manufacturing
SIC 2087 Flavoring Extracts & Flavoring Syrups
SIC 2095 Roasted Coffee
SIC 2099 Food Preparations, nec
SIC 2899 Chemical Preparations, nec

311991 Perishable Prepared Food Manufacturing
SIC 2099 Food Preparations, nec

311999 All Other Miscellaneous Food Manufacturing
SIC 2015 Poultry Slaughtering & Processing
SIC 2032 Canned Specialties
SIC 2087 Flavoring Extracts & Flavoring Syrups
SIC 2099 Food Preparations, nec

BEVERAGE & TOBACCO PRODUCT MANUFACTURING

312111 Soft Drink Manufacturing
SIC 2086 Bottled & Canned Soft Drinks & Carbonated Water

312112 Bottled Water Manufacturing
SIC 2086 Bottled & Canned Soft Drinks & Carbonated Water

312113 Ice Manufacturing
SIC 2097 Manufactured Ice

31212 Breweries
SIC 2082 Malt Beverages

31213 Wineries
SIC 2084 Wines, Brandy, & Brandy Spirits

31214 Distilleries
SIC 2085 Distilled & Blended Liquors

31221 Tobacco Stemming & Redrying
SIC 2141 Tobacco Stemming & Redrying
312221 Cigarette Manufacturing
SIC 2111 Cigarettes
312229 Other Tobacco Product Manufacturing
SIC 2121 Cigars
SIC 2131 Chewing & Smoking Tobacco & Snuff
SIC 2141 Tobacco Stemming & Redrying

TEXTILE MILLS

313111 Yarn Spinning Mills
SIC 2281 Yarn Spinning Mills
SIC 2299 Textile Goods, nec
313112 Yarn Texturing, Throwing & Twisting Mills
SIC 2282 Yarn Texturing, Throwing, Winding Mills
313113 Thread Mills
SIC 2284 Thread Mills
SIC 2299 Textile Goods, NEC
31321 Broadwoven Fabric Mills
SIC 2211 Broadwoven Fabric Mills, Cotton
SIC 2221 Broadwoven Fabric Mills, Manmade Fiber & Silk
SIC 2231 Broadwoven Fabric Mills, Wool
SIC 2299 Textile Goods, nec
313221 Narrow Fabric Mills
SIC 2241 Narrow Fabric & Other Smallware Mills: Cotton, Wool, Silk & Manmade Fiber
SIC 2299 Textile Goods, nec
313222 Schiffli Machine Embroidery
SIC 2397 Schiffli Machine Embroideries
31323 Nonwoven Fabric Mills
SIC 2297 Nonwoven Fabrics
SIC 2299 Textile Goods, nec
313241 Weft Knit Fabric Mills
SIC 2257 Weft Knit Fabric Mills
SIC 2259 Knitting Mills nec
313249 Other Knit Fabric & Lace Mills
SIC 2258 Lace & Warp Knit Fabric Mills
SIC 2259 Knitting Mills nec
313311 Broadwoven Fabric Finishing Mills
SIC 2231 Broadwoven Fabric Mills, Wool
SIC 2261 Finishers of Broadwoven Fabrics of Cotton
SIC 2262 Finishers of Broadwoven Fabrics of Manmade Fiber & Silk
SIC 2269 Finishers of Textiles, nec
SIC 5131 Piece Goods & Notions
313312 Textile & Fabric Finishing Mills
SIC 2231 Broadwoven Fabric Mills, Wool
SIC 2257 Weft Knit Fabric Mills
SIC 2258 Lace & Warp Knit Fabric Mills
SIC 2269 Finishers of Textiles, nec
SIC 2282 Yarn Texturizing, Throwing, Twisting, & Winding Mills
SIC 2284 Thread Mills
SIC 2299 Textile Goods, nec
SIC 5131 Piece Goods & Notions
31332 Fabric Coating Mills
SIC 2295 Coated Fabrics, Not Rubberized
SIC 3069 Fabricated Rubber Products, nec

TEXTILE PRODUCT MILLS

31411 Carpet & Rug Mills
SIC 2273 Carpets & Rugs
314121 Curtain & Drapery Mills
SIC 2391 Curtains & Draperies
SIC 5714 Drapery, Curtain, & Upholstery Stores
314129 Other Household Textile Product Mills
SIC 2392 Housefurnishings, Except Curtains & Draperies
314911 Textile Bag Mills
SIC 2392 Housefurnishings, Except Curtains & Draperies
SIC 2393 Textile Bags
314912 Canvas & Related Product Mills
SIC 2394 Canvas & Related Products
314991 Rope, Cordage & Twine Mills
SIC 2298 Cordage & Twine
314992 Tire Cord & Tire Fabric Mills
SIC 2296 Tire Cord & Fabrics
314999 All Other Miscellaneous Textile Product Mills
SIC 2299 Textile Goods, nec
SIC 2395 Pleating, Decorative & Novelty Stitching, & Tucking for the Trade
SIC 2396 Automotive Trimmings, Apparel Findings, & Related Products
SIC 2399 Fabricated Textile Products, nec

APPAREL MANUFACTURING

315111 Sheer Hosiery Mills
SIC 2251 Women's Full-Length & Knee-Length Hosiery, Except socks
SIC 2252 Hosiery, nec
315119 Other Hosiery & Sock Mills
SIC 2252 Hosiery, nec
315191 Outerwear Knitting Mills
SIC 2253 Knit Outerwear Mills
SIC 2259 Knitting Mills, nec
315192 Underwear & Nightwear Knitting Mills
SIC 2254 Knit Underwear & Nightwear Mills
SIC 2259 Knitting Mills, nec
315211 Men's & Boys' Cut & Sew Apparel Contractors
SIC 2311 Men's & Boys' Suits, Coats, & Overcoats
SIC 2321 Men's & Boys' Shirts, Except Work Shirts
SIC 2322 Men's & Boys' Underwear & Nightwear
SIC 2325 Men's & Boys' Trousers & Slacks
SIC 2326 Men's & Boys' Work Clothing
SIC 2329 Men's & Boys' Clothing, nec
SIC 2341 Women's, Misses', Children's, & Infants' Underwear & Nightwear
SIC 2361 Girls', Children's, & Infants' Dresses, Blouses & Shirts
SIC 2369 Girls', Children's, & Infants' Outerwear, nec
SIC 2384 Robes & Dressing Gowns
SIC 2385 Waterproof Outerwear
SIC 2389 Apparel & Accessories, nec
SIC 2395 Pleating, Decorative & Novelty Stitching, & Tucking for the Trade
315212 Women's & Girls' Cut & Sew Apparel Contractors
SIC 2331 Women's, Misses', & Juniors' Blouses & Shirts
SIC 2335 Women's, Misses' & Juniors' Dresses
SIC 2337 Women's, Misses', & Juniors' Suits, Skirts, & Coats
SIC 2339 Women's, Misses', & Juniors' Outerwear, nec

SIC 2341 Women's, Misses', Children's, & Infants' Underwear & Nightwear

SIC 2342 Brassieres, Girdles, & Allied Garments

SIC 2361 Girls', Children's, & Infants' Dresses, Blouses, & Shirts

SIC 2369 Girls', Children's, & Infants' Outerwear, nec

SIC 2384 Robes & Dressing Gowns

SIC 2385 Waterproof Outerwear

SIC 2389 Apparel & Accessories, nec

SIC 2395 Pleating, Decorative & Novelty Stitching, & Tucking for the Trade

315221 Men's & Boys' Cut & Sew Underwear & Nightwear Manufacturing

SIC 2322 Men's & Boys' Underwear & Nightwear

SIC 2341 Women's, Misses', Children's, & Infants' Underwear & Nightwear

SIC 2369 Girls', Children's, & Infants' Outerwear, nec

SIC 2384 Robes & Dressing Gowns

315222 Men's & Boys' Cut & Sew Suit, Coat & Overcoat Manufacturing

SIC 2311 Men's & Boys' Suits, Coats, & Overcoats

SIC 2369 Girls', Children's, & Infants' Outerwear, nec

SIC 2385 Waterproof Outerwear

315223 Men's & Boys' Cut & Sew Shirt Manufacturing

SIC 2321 Men's & Boys' Shirts, Except Work Shirts

SIC 2361 Girls', Children's, & Infants' Dresses, Blouses, & Shirts

315224 Men's & Boys' Cut & Sew Trouser, Slack & Jean Manufacturing

SIC 2325 Men's & Boys' Trousers & Slacks

SIC 2369 Girls', Children's, & Infants' Outerwear, NEC

315225 Men's & Boys' Cut & Sew Work Clothing Manufacturing

SIC 2326 Men's & Boys' Work Clothing

315228 Men's & Boys' Cut & Sew Other Outerwear Manufacturing

SIC 2329 Men's & Boys' Clothing, nec

SIC 2369 Girls', Children's, & Infants' Outerwear, nec

SIC 2385 Waterproof Outerwear

315231 Women's & Girls' Cut & Sew Lingerie, Loungewear & Nightwear Manufacturing

SIC 2341 Women's, Misses', Children's, & Infants' Underwear & Nightwear

SIC 2342 Brassieres, Girdles, & Allied Garments

SIC 2369 Girls', Children's, & Infants' Outerwear, nec

SIC 2384 Robes & Dressing Gowns

SIC 2389 Apparel & Accessories, NEC

315232 Women's & Girls' Cut & Sew Blouse & Shirt Manufacturing

SIC 2331 Women's, Misses', & Juniors' Blouses & Shirts

SIC 2361 Girls', Children's, & Infants' Dresses, Blouses & Shirts

315233 Women's & Girls' Cut & Sew Dress Manufacturing

SIC 2335 Women's, Misses', & Juniors' Dresses

SIC 2361 Girls', Children's, & Infants' Dresses, Blouses & Shirts

315234 Women's & Girls' Cut & Sew Suit, Coat, Tailored Jacket & Skirt Manufacturing

SIC 2337 Women's, Misses', & Juniors' Suits, Skirts, & Coats

SIC 2369 Girls', Children's, & Infants' Outerwear, nec

SIC 2385 Waterproof Outerwear

315238 Women's & Girls' Cut & Sew Other Outerwear Manufacturing

SIC 2339 Women's, Misses', & Juniors' Outerwear, nec

SIC 2369 Girls', Children's, & Infants' Outerwear, nec

SIC 2385 Waterproof Outerwear

315291 Infants' Cut & Sew Apparel Manufacturing

SIC 2341 Women's, Misses', Children's, & Infants' Underwear & Nightwear

SIC 2361 Girls', Children's, & Infants' Dresses, Blouses, & Shirts

SIC 2369 Girls', Children's, & Infants' Outerwear, nec

SIC 2385 Waterproof Outerwear

315292 Fur & Leather Apparel Manufacturing

SIC 2371 Fur Goods

SIC 2386 Leather & Sheep-lined Clothing

315299 All Other Cut & Sew Apparel Manufacturing

SIC 2329 Men's & Boys' Outerwear, nec

SIC 2339 Women's, Misses', & Juniors' Outerwear, nec

SIC 2389 Apparel & Accessories, nec

315991 Hat, Cap & Millinery Manufacturing

SIC 2353 Hats, Caps, & Millinery

315992 Glove & Mitten Manufacturing

SIC 2381 Dress & Work Gloves, Except Knit & All-Leather

SIC 3151 Leather Gloves & Mittens

315993 Men's & Boys' Neckwear Manufacturing

SIC 2323 Men's & Boys' Neckwear

315999 Other Apparel Accessories & Other Apparel Manufacturing

SIC 2339 Women's, Misses', & Juniors' Outerwear, nec

SIC 2385 Waterproof Outerwear

SIC 2387 Apparel Belts

SIC 2389 Apparel & Accessories, nec

SIC 2396 Automotive Trimmings, Apparel Findings, & Related Products

SIC 2399 Fabricated Textile Products, nec

LEATHER & ALLIED PRODUCT MANUFACTURING

31611 Leather & Hide Tanning & Finishing

SIC 3111 Leather Tanning & Finishing

SIC 3999 Manufacturing Industries, nec

316211 Rubber & Plastics Footwear Manufacturing

SIC 3021 Rubber & Plastics Footwear

316212 House Slipper Manufacturing

SIC 3142 House Slippers

316213 Men's Footwear Manufacturing

SIC 3143 Men's Footwear, Except Athletic

316214 Women's Footwear Manufacturing

SIC 3144 Women's Footwear, Except Athletic

316219 Other Footwear Manufacturing

SIC 3149 Footwear Except Rubber, NEC

316991 Luggage Manufacturing

SIC 3161 Luggage

316992 Women's Handbag & Purse Manufacturing

SIC 3171 Women's Handbags & Purses

316993 Personal Leather Good Manufacturing

SIC 3172 Personal Leather Goods, Except Women's Handbags & Purses

316999 All Other Leather Good Manufacturing

SIC 3131 Boot & Shoe Cut Stock & Findings

SIC 3199 Leather Goods, nec

WOOD PRODUCT MANUFACTURING

321113 Sawmills
SIC 2421 Sawmills & Planing Mills, General
SIC 2429 Special Product Sawmills, nec
321114 Wood Preservation
SIC 2491 Wood Preserving
321211 Hardwood Veneer & Plywood Manufacturing
SIC 2435 Hardwood Veneer & Plywood
321212 Softwood Veneer & Plywood Manufacturing
SIC 2436 Softwood Veneer & Plywood
321213 Engineered Wood Member Manufacturing
SIC 2439 Structural Wood Members, nec
321214 Truss Manufacturing
SIC 2439 Structural Wood Members, nec
321219 Reconstituted Wood Product Manufacturing
SIC 2493 Reconstituted Wood Products
321911 Wood Window & Door Manufacturing
SIC 2431 Millwork
321912 Hardwood Dimension Mills
SIC 2426 Hardwood Dimension & Flooring Mills
321913 Softwood Cut Stock, Resawing Lumber, & Planing
SIC 2421 Sawmills & Planing Mills, General
SIC 2429 Special Product Sawmills, nec
SIC 2439 Structural Wood Members, nec
321914 Other Millwork
SIC 2421 Sawmills & Planing Mills, General
SIC 2426 Hardwood Dimension & Flooring Mills
SIC 2431 Millwork
32192 Wood Container & Pallet Manufacturing
SIC 2441 Nailed & Lock Corner Wood Boxes & Shook
SIC 2448 Wood Pallets & Skids
SIC 2449 Wood Containers, NEC
SIC 2499 Wood Products, nec
321991 Manufactured Home Manufacturing
SIC 2451 Mobile Homes
321992 Prefabricated Wood Building Manufacturing
SIC 2452 Prefabricated Wood Buildings & Components
321999 All Other Miscellaneous Wood Product Manufacturing
SIC 2426 Hardwood Dimension & Flooring Mills
SIC 2499 Wood Products, nec
SIC 3131 Boot & Shoe Cut Stock & Findings
SIC 3999 Manufacturing Industries, nec
SIC 2421 Sawmills & Planing Mills, General
SIC 2429 Special Product Sawmills, nec

PAPER MANUFACTURING

32211 Pulp Mills
SIC 2611 Pulp Mills
322121 Paper Mills
SIC 2611 Pulp Mills
SIC 2621 Paper Mills
322122 Newsprint Mills
SIC 2621 Paper Mills
32213 Paperboard Mills
SIC 2611 Pulp Mills
SIC 2631 Paperboard Mills
322211 Corrugated & Solid Fiber Box Manufacturing
SIC 2653 Corrugated & Solid Fiber Boxes
322212 Folding Paperboard Box Manufacturing
SIC 2657 Folding Paperboard Boxes, Including Sanitary

322213 Setup Paperboard Box Manufacturing
SIC 2652 Setup Paperboard Boxes
322214 Fiber Can, Tube, Drum, & Similar Products Manufacturing
SIC 2655 Fiber Cans, Tubes, Drums, & Similar Products
322215 Non-Folding Sanitary Food Container Manufacturing
SIC 2656 Sanitary Food Containers, Except Folding
SIC 2679 Converted Paper & Paperboard Products, NEC
322221 Coated & Laminated Packaging Paper & Plastics Film Manufacturing
SIC 2671 Packaging Paper & Plastics Film, Coated & Laminated
322222 Coated & Laminated Paper Manufacturing
SIC 2672 Coated & Laminated Paper, nec
SIC 2679 Converted Paper & Paperboard Products, nec
322223 Plastics, Foil, & Coated Paper Bag Manufacturing
SIC 2673 Plastics, Foil, & Coated Paper Bags
322224 Uncoated Paper & Multiwall Bag Manufacturing
SIC 2674 Uncoated Paper & Multiwall Bags
322225 Laminated Aluminum Foil Manufacturing for Flexible Packaging Uses
SIC 3497 Metal Foil & Leaf
322231 Die-Cut Paper & Paperboard Office Supplies Manufacturing
SIC 2675 Die-Cut Paper & Paperboard & Cardboard
SIC 2679 Converted Paper & Paperboard Products, nec
322232 Envelope Manufacturing
SIC 2677 Envelopes
322233 Stationery, Tablet, & Related Product Manufacturing
SIC 2678 Stationery, Tablets, & Related Products
322291 Sanitary Paper Product Manufacturing
SIC 2676 Sanitary Paper Products
322292 Surface-Coated Paperboard Manufacturing
SIC 2675 Die-Cut Paper & Paperboard & Cardboard
322298 All Other Converted Paper Product Manufacturing
SIC 2675 Die-Cut Paper & Paperboard & Cardboard
SIC 2679 Converted Paper & Paperboard Products, NEC

PRINTING & RELATED SUPPORT ACTIVITIES

323110 Commercial Lithographic Printing
SIC 2752 Commercial Printing, Lithographic
SIC 2771 Greeting Cards
SIC 2782 Blankbooks, Loose-leaf Binders & Devices
SIC 3999 Manufacturing Industries, nec
323111 Commercial Gravure Printing
SIC 2754 Commercial Printing, Gravure
SIC 2771 Greeting Cards
SIC 2782 Blankbooks, Loose-leaf Binders & Devices
SIC 3999 Manufacturing Industries, nec
323112 Commercial Flexographic Printing
SIC 2759 Commercial Printing, NEC
SIC 2771 Greeting Cards
SIC 2782 Blankbooks, Loose-leaf Binders & Devices
SIC 3999 Manufacturing Industries, nec
323113 Commercial Screen Printing
SIC 2396 Automotive Trimmings, Apparel Findings, & Related Products
SIC 2759 Commercial Printing, nec
SIC 2771 Greeting Cards
SIC 2782 Blankbooks, Loose-leaf Binders & Devices
SIC 3999 Manufacturing Industries, nec

323114 Quick Printing
SIC 2752 Commercial Printing, Lithographic
SIC 2759 Commercial Printing, nec
323115 Digital Printing
SIC 2759 Commercial Printing, nec
323116 Manifold Business Form Printing
SIC 2761 Manifold Business Forms
323117 Book Printing
SIC 2732 Book Printing
323118 Blankbook, Loose-leaf Binder & Device Manufacturing
SIC 2782 Blankbooks, Loose-leaf Binders & Devices
323119 Other Commercial Printing
SIC 2759 Commercial Printing, nec
SIC 2771 Greeting Cards
SIC 2782 Blankbooks, Loose-leaf Binders & Devices
SIC 3999 Manufacturing Industries, nec
323121 Tradebinding & Related Work
SIC 2789 Bookbinding & Related Work
323122 Prepress Services
SIC 2791 Typesetting
SIC 2796 Platemaking & Related Services

PETROLEUM & COAL PRODUCTS MANUFACTURING

32411 Petroleum Refineries
SIC 2911 Petroleum Refining
324121 Asphalt Paving Mixture & Block Manufacturing
SIC 2951 Asphalt Paving Mixtures & Blocks
324122 Asphalt Shingle & Coating Materials Manufacturing
SIC 2952 Asphalt Felts & Coatings
324191 Petroleum Lubricating Oil & Grease Manufacturing
SIC 2992 Lubricating Oils & Greases
324199 All Other Petroleum & Coal Products Manufacturing
SIC 2999 Products of Petroleum & Coal, nec
SIC 3312 Blast Furnaces & Steel Mills

CHEMICAL MANUFACTURING

32511 Petrochemical Manufacturing
SIC 2865 Cyclic Organic Crudes & Intermediates, & Organic
        Dyes & Pigments
SIC 2869 Industrial Organic Chemicals, nec
32512 Industrial Gas Manufacturing
SIC 2813 Industrial Gases
SIC 2869 Industrial Organic Chemicals, nec
325131 Inorganic Dye & Pigment Manufacturing
SIC 2816 Inorganic Pigments
SIC 2819 Industrial Inorganic Chemicals, nec
325132 Organic Dye & Pigment Manufacturing
SIC 2865 Cyclic Organic Crudes & Intermediates, & Organic
        Dyes & Pigments
325181 Alkalies & Chlorine Manufacturing
SIC 2812 Alkalies & Chlorine
325182 Carbon Black Manufacturing
SIC 2816 Inorganic pigments
SIC 2895 Carbon Black
325188 All Other Basic Inorganic Chemical Manufacturing
SIC 2819 Industrial Inorganic Chemicals, nec
SIC 2869 Industrial Organic Chemicals, nec

325191 Gum & Wood Chemical Manufacturing
SIC 2861 Gum & Wood Chemicals
325192 Cyclic Crude & Intermediate Manufacturing
SIC 2865 Cyclic Organic Crudes & Intermediates & Organic
        Dyes & Pigments
325193 Ethyl Alcohol Manufacturing
SIC 2869 Industrial Organic Chemicals
325199 All Other Basic Organic Chemical Manufacturing
SIC 2869 Industrial Organic Chemicals, nec
SIC 2899 Chemical & Chemical Preparations, nec
325211 Plastics Material & Resin Manufacturing
SIC 2821 Plastics Materials, Synthetic & Resins, &
        Nonvulcanizable Elastomers
325212 Synthetic Rubber Manufacturing
SIC 2822 Synthetic Rubber
325221 Cellulosic Manmade Fiber Manufacturing
SIC 2823 Cellulosic Manmade Fibers
325222 Noncellulosic Organic Fiber Manufacturing
SIC 2824 Manmade Organic Fibers, Except Cellulosic
325311 Nitrogenous Fertilizer Manufacturing
SIC 2873 Nitrogenous Fertilizers
325312 Phosphatic Fertilizer Manufacturing
SIC 2874 Phosphatic Fertilizers
325314 Fertilizer Manufacturing
SIC 2875 Fertilizers, Mixing Only
32532 Pesticide & Other Agricultural Chemical Manufacturing
SIC 2879 Pesticides & Agricultural Chemicals, nec
325411 Medicinal & Botanical Manufacturing
SIC 2833 Medicinal Chemicals & Botanical Products
325412 Pharmaceutical Preparation Manufacturing
SIC 2834 Pharmaceutical Preparations
SIC 2835 In-Vitro & In-Vivo Diagnostic Substances
325413 In-Vitro Diagnostic Substance Manufacturing
SIC 2835 In-Vitro & In-Vivo Diagnostic Substances
325414 Biological Product Manufacturing
SIC 2836 Biological Products, Except Diagnostic Substance
32551 Paint & Coating Manufacturing
SIC 2851 Paints, Varnishes, Lacquers, Enamels & Allied
        Products
SIC 2899 Chemicals & Chemical Preparations, nec
32552 Adhesive & Sealant Manufacturing
SIC 2891 Adhesives & Sealants
325611 Soap & Other Detergent Manufacturing
SIC 2841 Soaps & Other Detergents, Except Specialty Cleaners
SIC 2844 Toilet Preparations
325612 Polish & Other Sanitation Good Manufacturing
SIC 2842 Specialty Cleaning, Polishing, & Sanitary Preparations
325613 Surface Active Agent Manufacturing
SIC 2843 Surface Active Agents, Finishing Agents, Sulfonated
        Oils, & Assistants
32562 Toilet Preparation Manufacturing
SIC 2844 Perfumes, Cosmetics, & Other Toilet Preparations
32591 Printing Ink Manufacturing
SIC 2893 Printing Ink
32592 Explosives Manufacturing
SIC 2892 Explosives
325991 Custom Compounding of Purchased Resin
SIC 3087 Custom Compounding of Purchased Plastics Resin
**325992 Photographic Film, Paper, Plate & Chemical
        Manufacturing**
SIC 3861 Photographic Equipment & Supplies

325998 All Other Miscellaneous Chemical Product Manufacturing
SIC 2819 Industrial Inorganic Chemicals, nec
SIC 2899 Chemicals & Chemical Preparations, nec
SIC 3952 Lead Pencils & Art Goods
SIC 3999 Manufacturing Industries, nec

PLASTICS & RUBBER PRODUCTS MANUFACTURING

326111 Unsupported Plastics Bag Manufacturing
SIC 2673 Plastics, Foil, & Coated Paper Bags

326112 Unsupported Plastics Packaging Film & Sheet Manufacturing
SIC 2671 Packaging Paper & Plastics Film, Coated, & Laminated

326113 Unsupported Plastics Film & Sheet Manufacturing
SIC 3081 Unsupported Plastics Film & Sheets

326121 Unsupported Plastics Profile Shape Manufacturing
SIC 3082 Unsupported Plastics Profile Shapes
SIC 3089 Plastics Product, nec

326122 Plastics Pipe & Pipe Fitting Manufacturing
SIC 3084 Plastics Pipe
SIC 3089 Plastics Products, nec

32613 Laminated Plastics Plate, Sheet & Shape Manufacturing
SIC 3083 Laminated Plastics Plate, Sheet & Profile Shapes

32614 Polystyrene Foam Product Manufacturing
SIC 3086 Plastics Foam Products

32615 Urethane & Other Foam Product Manufacturing
SIC 3086 Plastics Foam Products

32616 Plastics Bottle Manufacturing
SIC 3085 Plastics Bottles

326191 Plastics Plumbing Fixture Manufacturing
SIC 3088 Plastics Plumbing Fixtures

326192 Resilient Floor Covering Manufacturing
SIC 3069 Fabricated Rubber Products, nec
SIC 3996 Linoleum, Asphalted-Felt-Base, & Other Hard Surface Floor Coverings, nec

326199 All Other Plastics Product Manufacturing
SIC 3089 Plastics Products, nec
SIC 3999 Manufacturing Industries, nec

326211 Tire Manufacturing
SIC 3011 Tires & Inner Tubes

326212 Tire Retreading
SIC 7534 Tire Retreading & Repair Shops

32622 Rubber & Plastics Hoses & Belting Manufacturing
SIC 3052 Rubber & Plastics Hose & Belting

326291 Rubber Product Manufacturing for Mechanical Use
SIC 3061 Molded, Extruded, & Lathe-Cut Mechanical Rubber Goods

326299 All Other Rubber Product Manufacturing
SIC 3069 Fabricated Rubber Products, nec

NONMETALLIC MINERAL PRODUCT MANUFACTURING

327111 Vitreous China Plumbing Fixture & China & Earthenware Fittings & Bathroom Accessories Manufacturing
SIC 3261 Vitreous China Plumbing Fixtures & China & Earthenware Fittings & Bathroom Accessories

327112 Vitreous China, Fine Earthenware & Other Pottery Product Manufacturing
SIC 3262 Vitreous China Table & Kitchen Articles
SIC 3263 Fine Earthenware Table & Kitchen Articles
SIC 3269 Pottery Products, nec

327113 Porcelain Electrical Supply Manufacturing
SIC 3264 Porcelain Electrical Supplies

327121 Brick & Structural Clay Tile Manufacturing
SIC 3251 Brick & Structural Clay Tile

327122 Ceramic Wall & Floor Tile Manufacturing
SIC 3253 Ceramic Wall & Floor Tile

327123 Other Structural Clay Product Manufacturing
SIC 3259 Structural Clay Products, nec

327124 Clay Refractory Manufacturing
SIC 3255 Clay Refractories

327125 Nonclay Refractory Manufacturing
SIC 3297 Nonclay Refractories

327211 Flat Glass Manufacturing
SIC 3211 Flat Glass

327212 Other Pressed & Blown Glass & Glassware Manufacturing
SIC 3229 Pressed & Blown Glass & Glassware, nec

327213 Glass Container Manufacturing
SIC 3221 Glass Containers

327215 Glass Product Manufacturing Made of Purchased Glass
SIC 3231 Glass Products Made of Purchased Glass

32731 Hydraulic Cement Manufacturing
SIC 3241 Cement, Hydraulic

32732 Ready-Mix Concrete Manufacturing
SIC 3273 Ready-Mixed Concrete

327331 Concrete Block & Brick Manufacturing
SIC 3271 Concrete Block & Brick

327332 Concrete Pipe Manufacturing
SIC 3272 Concrete Products, Except Block & Brick

32739 Other Concrete Product Manufacturing
SIC 3272 Concrete Products, Except Block & Brick

32741 Lime Manufacturing
SIC 3274 Lime

32742 Gypsum & Gypsum Product Manufacturing
SIC 3275 Gypsum Products
SIC 3299 Nonmetallic Mineral Products, nec

32791 Abrasive Product Manufacturing
SIC 3291 Abrasive Products

327991 Cut Stone & Stone Product Manufacturing
SIC 3281 Cut Stone & Stone Products

327992 Ground or Treated Mineral & Earth Manufacturing
SIC 3295 Minerals & Earths, Ground or Otherwise Treated

327993 Mineral Wool Manufacturing
SIC 3296 Mineral Wool

327999 All Other Miscellaneous Nonmetallic Mineral Product Manufacturing
SIC 3272 Concrete Products, Except Block & Brick
SIC 3292 Asbestos Products
SIC 3299 Nonmetallic Mineral Products, nec

PRIMARY METAL MANUFACTURING

331111 Iron & Steel Mills
SIC 3312 Steel Works, Blast Furnaces , & Rolling Mills
SIC 3399 Primary Metal Products, nec

331112 Electrometallurgical Ferroalloy Product Manufacturing
SIC 3313 Electrometallurgical Products, Except Steel

33121 Iron & Steel Pipes & Tubes Manufacturing from Purchased Steel
SIC 3317 Steel Pipe & Tubes
331221 Cold-Rolled Steel Shape Manufacturing
SIC 3316 Cold-Rolled Steel Sheet, Strip & Bars
331222 Steel Wire Drawing
SIC 3315 Steel Wiredrawing & Steel Nails & Spikes
331311 Alumina Refining
SIC 2819 Industrial Inorganic Chemicals, nec
331312 Primary Aluminum Production
SIC 3334 Primary Production of Aluminum
331314 Secondary Smelting & Alloying of Aluminum
SIC 3341 Secondary Smelting & Refining of Nonferrous Metals
SIC 3399 Primary Metal Products, nec
331315 Aluminum Sheet, Plate & Foil Manufacturing
SIC 3353 Aluminum Sheet, Plate, & Foil
331316 Aluminum Extruded Product Manufacturing
SIC 3354 Aluminum Extruded Products
331319 Other Aluminum Rolling & Drawing
SIC 3355 Aluminum Rolling & Drawing, nec
SIC 3357 Drawing & Insulating of Nonferrous Wire
331411 Primary Smelting & Refining of Copper
SIC 3331 Primary Smelting & Refining of Copper
331419 Primary Smelting & Refining of Nonferrous Metal
SIC 3339 Primary Smelting & Refining of Nonferrous Metals, Except Copper & Aluminum
331421 Copper Rolling, Drawing & Extruding
SIC 3351 Rolling, Drawing, & Extruding of Copper
331422 Copper Wire Drawing
SIC 3357 Drawing & Insulating of Nonferrous Wire
331423 Secondary Smelting, Refining, & Alloying of Copper
SIC 3341 Secondary Smelting & Refining of Nonferrous Metals
SIC 3399 Primary Metal Products, nec
331491 Nonferrous Metal Rolling, Drawing & Extruding
SIC 3356 Rolling, Drawing & Extruding of Nonferrous Metals, Except Copper & Aluminum
SIC 3357 Drawing & Insulating of Nonferrous Wire
331492 Secondary Smelting, Refining, & Alloying of Nonferrous Metal
SIC 3313 Electrometallurgical Products, Except Steel
SIC 3341 Secondary Smelting & Reining of Nonferrous Metals
SIC 3399 Primary Metal Products, nec
331511 Iron Foundries
SIC 3321 Gray & Ductile Iron Foundries
SIC 3322 Malleable Iron Foundries
331512 Steel Investment Foundries
SIC 3324 Steel Investment Foundries
331513 Steel Foundries,
SIC 3325 Steel Foundries, nec
331521 Aluminum Die-Castings
SIC 3363 Aluminum Die-Castings
331522 Nonferrous Die-Castings
SIC 3364 Nonferrous Die-Castings, Except Aluminum
331524 Aluminum Foundries
SIC 3365 Aluminum Foundries
331525 Copper Foundries
SIC 3366 Copper Foundries
331528 Other Nonferrous Foundries
SIC 3369 Nonferrous Foundries, Except Aluminum & Copper

FABRICATED METAL PRODUCT MANUFACTURING

332111 Iron & Steel Forging
SIC 3462 Iron & Steel Forgings
332112 Nonferrous Forging
SIC 3463 Nonferrous Forgings
332114 Custom Roll Forming
SIC 3449 Miscellaneous Structural Metal Work
332115 Crown & Closure Manufacturing
SIC 3466 Crowns & Closures
332116 Metal Stamping
SIC 3469 Metal Stampings, nec
332117 Powder Metallurgy Part Manufacturing
SIC 3499 Fabricated Metal Products, nec
332211 Cutlery & Flatware Manufacturing
SIC 3421 Cutlery
SIC 3914 Silverware, Plated Ware, & Stainless Steel Ware
332212 Hand & Edge Tool Manufacturing
SIC 3423 Hand & Edge Tools, Except Machine Tools & Handsaws
SIC 3523 Farm Machinery & Equipment
SIC 3524 Lawn & Garden Tractors & Home Lawn & Garden Equipment
SIC 3545 Cutting Tools, Machine Tools Accessories, & Machinist Precision Measuring Devices
SIC 3799 Transportation Equipment, nec
SIC 3999 Manufacturing Industries, nec
332213 Saw Blade & Handsaw Manufacturing
SIC 3425 Saw Blades & Handsaws
332214 Kitchen Utensil, Pot & Pan Manufacturing
SIC 3469 Metal Stampings, nec
332311 Prefabricated Metal Building & Component Manufacturing
SIC 3448 Prefabricated Metal Buildings & Components
332312 Fabricated Structural Metal Manufacturing
SIC 3441 Fabricated Structural Metal
SIC 3449 Miscellaneous Structural Metal Work
332313 Plate Work Manufacturing
SIC 3443 Fabricated Plate Work
332321 Metal Window & Door Manufacturing
SIC 3442 Metal Doors, Sash, Frames, Molding & Trim
SIC 3449 Miscellaneous Structural Metal Work
332322 Sheet Metal Work Manufacturing
SIC 3444 Sheet Metal Work
332323 Ornamental & Architectural Metal Work Manufacturing
SIC 3446 Architectural & Ornamental Metal Work
SIC 3449 Miscellaneous Structural Metal Work
SIC 3523 Farm Machinery & Equipment
33241 Power Boiler & Heat Exchanger Manufacturing
SIC 3443 Fabricated Plate Work
33242 Metal Tank Manufacturing
SIC 3443 Fabricated Plate Work
332431 Metal Can Manufacturing
SIC 3411 Metal Cans
332439 Other Metal Container Manufacturing
SIC 3412 Metal Shipping Barrels, Drums, Kegs, & Pails
SIC 3429 Hardware, nec
SIC 3444 Sheet Metal Work
SIC 3499 Fabricated Metal Products, nec
SIC 3537 Industrial Trucks, Tractors, Trailers, & Stackers
33251 Hardware Manufacturing
SIC 3429 Hardware, nec
SIC 3499 Fabricated Metal Products, nec

332611 Steel Spring Manufacturing
SIC 3493 Steel Springs, Except Wire

332612 Wire Spring Manufacturing
SIC 3495 Wire Springs

332618 Other Fabricated Wire Product Manufacturing
SIC 3315 Steel Wiredrawing & Steel Nails & Spikes
SIC 3399 Primary Metal Products, nec
SIC 3496 Miscellaneous Fabricated Wire Products

33271 Machine Shops
SIC 3599 Industrial & Commercial Machinery & Equipment,
nec

332721 Precision Turned Product Manufacturing
SIC 3451 Screw Machine Products

332722 Bolt, Nut, Screw, Rivet & Washer Manufacturing
SIC 3452 Bolts, Nuts, Screws, Rivets, & Washers

332811 Metal Heat Treating
SIC 3398 Metal Heat Treating

332812 Metal Coating, Engraving , & Allied Services to Manufacturers
SIC 3479 Coating, Engraving, & Allied Services, nec

332813 Electroplating, Plating, Polishing, Anodizing & Coloring
SIC 3399 Primary Metal Products, nec
SIC 3471 Electroplating, Plating, Polishing, Anodizing, & Coloring

332911 Industrial Valve Manufacturing
SIC 3491 Industrial Valves

332912 Fluid Power Valve & Hose Fitting Manufacturing
SIC 3492 Fluid Power Valves & Hose Fittings
SIC 3728 Aircraft Parts & Auxiliary Equipment, nec

332913 Plumbing Fixture Fitting & Trim Manufacturing
SIC 3432 Plumbing Fixture Fittings & Trim

332919 Other Metal Valve & Pipe Fitting Manufacturing
SIC 3429 Hardware, nec
SIC 3494 Valves & Pipe Fittings, nec
SIC 3499 Fabricated Metal Products, nec

332991 Ball & Roller Bearing Manufacturing
SIC 3562 Ball & Roller Bearings

332992 Small Arms Ammunition Manufacturing
SIC 3482 Small Arms Ammunition

332993 Ammunition Manufacturing
SIC 3483 Ammunition, Except for Small Arms

332994 Small Arms Manufacturing
SIC 3484 Small Arms

332995 Other Ordnance & Accessories Manufacturing
SIC 3489 Ordnance & Accessories, nec

332996 Fabricated Pipe & Pipe Fitting Manufacturing
SIC 3498 Fabricated Pipe & Pipe Fittings

332997 Industrial Pattern Manufacturing
SIC 3543 Industrial Patterns

332998 Enameled Iron & Metal Sanitary Ware Manufacturing
SIC 3431 Enameled Iron & Metal Sanitary Ware

332999 All Other Miscellaneous Fabricated Metal Product Manufacturing
SIC 3291 Abrasive Products
SIC 3432 Plumbing Fixture Fittings & Trim
SIC 3494 Valves & Pipe Fittings, nec
SIC 3497 Metal Foil & Leaf
SIC 3499 Fabricated Metal Products, NEC
SIC 3537 Industrial Trucks, Tractors, Trailers, & Stackers
SIC 3599 Industrial & Commercial Machinery & Equipment,
nec
SIC 3999 Manufacturing Industries, nec

MACHINERY MANUFACTURING

333111 Farm Machinery & Equipment Manufacturing
SIC 3523 Farm Machinery & Equipment

333112 Lawn & Garden Tractor & Home Lawn & Garden Equipment Manufacturing
SIC 3524 Lawn & Garden Tractors & Home Lawn & Garden
Equipment

33312 Construction Machinery Manufacturing
SIC 3531 Construction Machinery & Equipment

333131 Mining Machinery & Equipment Manufacturing
SIC 3532 Mining Machinery & Equipment, Except Oil & Gas
Field Machinery & Equipment

333132 Oil & Gas Field Machinery & Equipment Manufacturing
SIC 3533 Oil & Gas Field Machinery & Equipment

33321 Sawmill & Woodworking Machinery Manufacturing
SIC 3553 Woodworking Machinery

33322 Rubber & Plastics Industry Machinery Manufacturing
SIC 3559 Special Industry Machinery, nec

333291 Paper Industry Machinery Manufacturing
SIC 3554 Paper Industries Machinery

333292 Textile Machinery Manufacturing
SIC 3552 Textile Machinery

333293 Printing Machinery & Equipment Manufacturing
SIC 3555 Printing Trades Machinery & Equipment

333294 Food Product Machinery Manufacturing
SIC 3556 Food Products Machinery

333295 Semiconductor Machinery Manufacturing
SIC 3559 Special Industry Machinery, nec

333298 All Other Industrial Machinery Manufacturing
SIC 3559 Special Industry Machinery, nec
SIC 3639 Household Appliances, nec

333311 Automatic Vending Machine Manufacturing
SIC 3581 Automatic Vending Machines

333312 Commercial Laundry, Drycleaning & Pressing Machine Manufacturing
SIC 3582 Commercial Laundry, Drycleaning & Pressing
Machines

333313 Office Machinery Manufacturing
SIC 3578 Calculating & Accounting Machinery, Except
Electronic Computers
SIC 3579 Office Machines, nec

333314 Optical Instrument & Lens Manufacturing
SIC 3827 Optical Instruments & Lenses

333315 Photographic & Photocopying Equipment Manufacturing
SIC 3861 Photographic Equipment & Supplies

333319 Other Commercial & Service Industry Machinery Manufacturing
SIC 3559 Special Industry Machinery, nec
SIC 3589 Service Industry Machinery, nec
SIC 3599 Industrial & Commercial Machinery & Equipment,
nec
SIC 3699 Electrical Machinery, Equipment & Supplies, nec

333411 Air Purification Equipment Manufacturing
SIC 3564 Industrial & Commercial Fans & Blowers & Air
Purification Equipment

333412 Industrial & Commercial Fan & Blower Manufacturing
SIC 3564 Industrial & Commercial Fans & Blowers & Air
Purification Equipment

333414 Heating Equipment Manufacturing
SIC 3433 Heating Equipment, Except Electric & Warm Air
Furnaces

SIC 3634 Electric Housewares & Fans

333415 Air-Conditioning & Warm Air Heating Equipment & Commercial & Industrial Refrigeration Equipment Manufacturing
SIC 3443 Fabricated Plate Work
SIC 3585 Air-Conditioning & Warm Air Heating Equipment & Commercial & Industrial Refrigeration Equipment

333511 Industrial Mold Manufacturing
SIC 3544 Special Dies & Tools, Die Sets, Jigs & Fixtures, & Industrial Molds

333512 Machine Tool Manufacturing
SIC 3541 Machine Tools, Metal Cutting Type

333513 Machine Tool Manufacturing
SIC 3542 Machine Tools, Metal Forming Type

333514 Special Die & Tool, Die Set, Jig & Fixture Manufacturing
SIC 3544 Special Dies & Tools, Die Sets, Jigs & Fixtures, & Industrial Molds

333515 Cutting Tool & Machine Tool Accessory Manufacturing
SIC 3545 Cutting Tools, Machine Tool Accessories, & Machinists' Precision Measuring Devices

333516 Rolling Mill Machinery & Equipment Manufacturing
SIC 3547 Rolling Mill Machinery & Equipment

333518 Other Metalworking Machinery Manufacturing
SIC 3549 Metalworking Machinery, nec

333611 Turbine & Turbine Generator Set Unit Manufacturing
SIC 3511 Steam, Gas, & Hydraulic Turbines, & Turbine Generator Set Units

333612 Speed Changer, Industrial High-Speed Drive & Gear Manufacturing
SIC 3566 Speed Changers, Industrial High-Speed Drives, & Gears

333613 Mechanical Power Transmission Equipment Manufacturing
SIC 3568 Mechanical Power Transmission Equipment, nec

333618 Other Engine Equipment Manufacturing
SIC 3519 Internal Combustion Engines, nec
SIC 3699 Electrical Machinery, Equipment & Supplies, nec

333911 Pump & Pumping Equipment Manufacturing
SIC 3561 Pumps & Pumping Equipment
SIC 3743 Railroad Equipment

333912 Air & Gas Compressor Manufacturing
SIC 3563 Air & Gas Compressors

333913 Measuring & Dispensing Pump Manufacturing
SIC 3586 Measuring & Dispensing Pumps

333921 Elevator & Moving Stairway Manufacturing
SIC 3534 Elevators & Moving Stairways

333922 Conveyor & Conveying Equipment Manufacturing
SIC 3523 Farm Machinery & Equipment
SIC 3535 Conveyors & Conveying Equipment

333923 Overhead Traveling Crane, Hoist & Monorail System Manufacturing
SIC 3536 Overhead Traveling Cranes, Hoists, & Monorail Systems
SIC 3531 Construction Machinery & Equipment

333924 Industrial Truck, Tractor, Trailer & Stacker Machinery Manufacturing
SIC 3537 Industrial Trucks, Tractors, Trailers, & Stackers

333991 Power-Driven Hand Tool Manufacturing
SIC 3546 Power-Driven Handtools

333992 Welding & Soldering Equipment Manufacturing
SIC 3548 Electric & Gas Welding & Soldering Equipment

333993 Packaging Machinery Manufacturing
SIC 3565 Packaging Machinery

333994 Industrial Process Furnace & Oven Manufacturing
SIC 3567 Industrial Process Furnaces & Ovens

333995 Fluid Power Cylinder & Actuator Manufacturing
SIC 3593 Fluid Power Cylinders & Actuators

333996 Fluid Power Pump & Motor Manufacturing
SIC 3594 Fluid Power Pumps & Motors

333997 Scale & Balance Manufacturing
SIC 3596 Scales & Balances, Except Laboratory

333999 All Other General Purpose Machinery Manufacturing
SIC 3599 Industrial & Commercial Machinery & Equipment, nec
SIC 3569 General Industrial Machinery & Equipment, nec

COMPUTER & ELECTRONIC PRODUCT MANUFACTURING

334111 Electronic Computer Manufacturing
SIC 3571 Electronic Computers

334112 Computer Storage Device Manufacturing
SIC 3572 Computer Storage Devices

334113 Computer Terminal Manufacturing
SIC 3575 Computer Terminals

334119 Other Computer Peripheral Equipment Manufacturing
SIC 3577 Computer Peripheral Equipment, nec
SIC 3578 Calculating & Accounting Machines, Except Electronic Computers
SIC 3699 Electrical Machinery, Equipment & Supplies, nec

33421 Telephone Apparatus Manufacturing
SIC 3661 Telephone & Telegraph Apparatus

33422 Radio & Television Broadcasting & Wireless Communications Equipment Manufacturing
SIC 3663 Radio & Television Broadcasting & Communication Equipment
SIC 3679 Electronic Components, nec

33429 Other Communications Equipment Manufacturing
SIC 3669 Communications Equipment, nec

33431 Audio & Video Equipment Manufacturing
SIC 3651 Household Audio & Video Equipment

334411 Electron Tube Manufacturing
SIC 3671 Electron Tubes

334412 Printed Circuit Board Manufacturing
SIC 3672 Printed Circuit Boards

334413 Semiconductor & Related Device Manufacturing
SIC 3674 Semiconductors & Related Devices

334414 Electronic Capacitor Manufacturing
SIC 3675 Electronic Capacitors

334415 Electronic Resistor Manufacturing
SIC 3676 Electronic Resistors

334416 Electronic Coil, Transformer, & Other Inductor Manufacturing
SIC 3661 Telephone & Telegraph Apparatus
SIC 3677 Electronic Coils, Transformers, & Other Inductors
SIC 3825 Instruments for Measuring & Testing of Electricity & Electrical Signals

334417 Electronic Connector Manufacturing
SIC 3678 Electronic Connectors

334418 Printed Circuit/Electronics Assembly Manufacturing
SIC 3679 Electronic Components, nec
SIC 3661 Telephone & Telegraph Apparatus

334419 Other Electronic Component Manufacturing
SIC 3679 Electronic Components, nec

334510 Electromedical & Electrotherapeutic Apparatus Manufacturing
SIC 3842 Orthopedic, Prosthetic & Surgical Appliances & Supplies
SIC 3845 Electromedical & Electrotherapeutic Apparatus

334511 Search, Detection, Navigation, Guidance, Aeronautical, & Nautical System & Instrument Manufacturing
SIC 3812 Search, Detection, Navigation, Guidance, Aeronautical, & Nautical Systems & Instruments

334512 Automatic Environmental Control Manufacturing for Residential, Commercial & Appliance Use
SIC 3822 Automatic Controls for Regulating Residential & Commercial Environments & Appliances

334513 Instruments & Related Products Manufacturing for Measuring, Displaying, & Controlling Industrial Process Variables
SIC 3823 Industrial Instruments for Measurement, Display, & Control of Process Variables; & Related Products

334514 Totalizing Fluid Meter & Counting Device Manufacturing
SIC 3824 Totalizing Fluid Meters & Counting Devices

334515 Instrument Manufacturing for Measuring & Testing Electricity & Electrical Signals
SIC 3825 Instruments for Measuring & Testing of Electricity & Electrical Signals

334516 Analytical Laboratory Instrument Manufacturing
SIC 3826 Laboratory Analytical Instruments

334517 Irradiation Apparatus Manufacturing
SIC 3844 X-Ray Apparatus & Tubes & Related Irradiation Apparatus
SIC 3845 Electromedical & Electrotherapeutic Apparatus

334518 Watch, Clock, & Part Manufacturing
SIC 3495 Wire Springs
SIC 3579 Office Machines, nec
SIC 3873 Watches, Clocks, Clockwork Operated Devices, & Parts

334519 Other Measuring & Controlling Device Manufacturing
SIC 3829 Measuring & Controlling Devices, nec

334611 Software Reproducing
SIC 7372 Prepackaged Software

334612 Prerecorded Compact Disc , Tape, & Record Reproducing
SIC 3652 Phonograph Records & Prerecorded Audio Tapes & Disks
SIC 7819 Services Allied to Motion Picture Production

334613 Magnetic & Optical Recording Media Manufacturing
SIC 3695 Magnetic & Optical Recording Media

ELECTRICAL EQUIPMENT, APPLIANCE, & COMPONENT MANUFACTURING

33511 Electric Lamp Bulb & Part Manufacturing
SIC 3641 Electric Lamp Bulbs & Tubes

335121 Residential Electric Lighting Fixture Manufacturing
SIC 3645 Residential Electric Lighting Fixtures
SIC 3999 Manufacturing Industries, nec

335122 Commercial, Industrial & Institutional Electric Lighting Fixture Manufacturing
SIC 3646 Commercial, Industrial, & Institutional Electric Lighting Fixtures

335129 Other Lighting Equipment Manufacturing
SIC 3648 Lighting Equipment, nec
SIC 3699 Electrical Machinery, Equipment, & Supplies, nec

335211 Electric Housewares & Fan Manufacturing
SIC 3634 Electric Housewares & Fans

335212 Household Vacuum Cleaner Manufacturing
SIC 3635 Household Vacuum Cleaners
SIC 3639 Household Appliances, nec

335221 Household Cooking Appliance Manufacturing
SIC 3631 Household Cooking Equipment

335222 Household Refrigerator & Home Freezer Manufacturing
SIC 3632 Household Refrigerators & Home & Farm Freezers

335224 Household Laundry Equipment Manufacturing
SIC 3633 Household Laundry Equipment

335228 Other Household Appliance Manufacturing
SIC 3639 Household Appliances, nec

335311 Power, Distribution & Specialty Transformer Manufacturing
SIC 3548 Electric & Gas Welding & Soldering Equipment
SIC 3612 Power, Distribution, & Speciality Transformers

335312 Motor & Generator Manufacturing
SIC 3621 Motors & Generators
SIC 7694 Armature Rewinding Shops

335313 Switchgear & Switchboard Apparatus Manufacturing
SIC 3613 Switchgear & Switchboard Apparatus

335314 Relay & Industrial Control Manufacturing
SIC 3625 Relays & Industrial Controls

335911 Storage Battery Manufacturing
SIC 3691 Storage Batteries

335912 Dry & Wet Primary Battery Manufacturing
SIC 3692 Primary Batteries, Dry & Wet

335921 Fiber-Optic Cable Manufacturing
SIC 3357 Drawing & Insulating of Nonferrous Wire

335929 Other Communication & Energy Wire Manufacturing
SIC 3357 Drawing & Insulating of Nonferrous Wire

335931 Current-Carrying Wiring Device Manufacturing
SIC 3643 Current-Carrying Wiring Devices

335932 Noncurrent-Carrying Wiring Device Manufacturing
SIC 3644 Noncurrent-Carrying Wiring Devices

335991 Carbon & Graphite Product Manufacturing
SIC 3624 Carbon & Graphite Products

335999 All Other Miscellaneous Electrical Equipment & Component Manufacturing
SIC 3629 Electrical Industrial Apparatus, nec
SIC 3699 Electrical Machinery, Equipment, & Supplies, nec

TRANSPORTATION EQUIPMENT MANUFACTURING

336111 Automobile Manufacturing
SIC 3711 Motor Vehicles & Passenger Car Bodies

336112 Light Truck & Utility Vehicle Manufacturing
SIC 3711 Motor Vehicles & Passenger Car Bodies

33612 Heavy Duty Truck Manufacturing
SIC 3711 Motor Vehicles & Passenger Car Bodies

336211 Motor Vehicle Body Manufacturing
SIC 3711 Motor Vehicles & Passenger Car Bodies
SIC 3713 Truck & Bus Bodies
SIC 3714 Motor Vehicle Parts & Accessories

336212 Truck Trailer Manufacturing
SIC 3715 Truck Trailers

336213 Motor Home Manufacturing
SIC 3716 Motor Homes
336214 Travel Trailer & Camper Manufacturing
SIC 3792 Travel Trailers & Campers
SIC 3799 Transportation Equipment, nec
336311 Carburetor, Piston, Piston Ring & Valve Manufacturing
SIC 3592 Carburetors, Pistons, Piston Rings, & Valves
336312 Gasoline Engine & Engine Parts Manufacturing
SIC 3714 Motor Vehicle Parts & Accessories
336321 Vehicular Lighting Equipment Manufacturing
SIC 3647 Vehicular Lighting Equipment
336322 Other Motor Vehicle Electrical & Electronic Equipment Manufacturing
SIC 3679 Electronic Components, nec
SIC 3694 Electrical Equipment for Internal Combustion Engines
SIC 3714 Motor Vehicle Parts & Accessories
33633 Motor Vehicle Steering & Suspension Components Manufacturing
SIC 3714 Motor Vehicle Parts & Accessories
33634 Motor Vehicle Brake System Manufacturing
SIC 3292 Asbestos Products
SIC 3714 Motor Vehicle Parts & Accessories
33635 Motor Vehicle Transmission & Power Train Parts Manufacturing
SIC 3714 Motor Vehicle Parts & Accessories
33636 Motor Vehicle Fabric Accessories & Seat Manufacturing
SIC 2396 Automotive Trimmings, Apparel Findings, & Related Products
SIC 2399 Fabricated Textile Products, nec
SIC 2531 Public Building & Related Furniture
33637 Motor Vehicle Metal Stamping
SIC 3465 Automotive Stampings
336391 Motor Vehicle Air-Conditioning Manufacturing
SIC 3585 Air-Conditioning & Warm Air Heating Equipment & Commercial & Industrial Refrigeration Equipment
336399 All Other Motor Vehicle Parts Manufacturing
SIC 3519 Internal Combustion Engines, nec
SIC 3599 Industrial & Commercial Machinery & Equipment, NEC
SIC 3714 Motor Vehicle Parts & Accessories
336411 Aircraft Manufacturing
SIC 3721 Aircraft
336412 Aircraft Engine & Engine Parts Manufacturing
SIC 3724 Aircraft Engines & Engine Parts
336413 Other Aircraft Part & Auxiliary Equipment Manufacturing
SIC 3728 Aircraft Parts & Auxiliary Equipment, nec
336414 Guided Missile & Space Vehicle Manufacturing
SIC 3761 Guided Missiles & Space Vehicles
336415 Guided Missile & Space Vehicle Propulsion Unit & Propulsion Unit Parts Manufacturing
SIC 3764 Guided Missile & Space Vehicle Propulsion Units & Propulsion Unit Parts
336419 Other Guided Missile & Space Vehicle Parts & Auxiliary Equipment Manufacturing
SIC 3769 Guided Missile & Space Vehicle Parts & Auxiliary Equipment
33651 Railroad Rolling Stock Manufacturing
SIC 3531 Construction Machinery & Equipment
SIC 3743 Railroad Equipment
336611 Ship Building & Repairing
SIC 3731 Ship Building & Repairing

336612 Boat Building
SIC 3732 Boat Building & Repairing
336991 Motorcycle, Bicycle, & Parts Manufacturing
SIC 3944 Games, Toys, & Children's Vehicles, Except Dolls & Bicycles
SIC 3751 Motorcycles, Bicycles & Parts
336992 Military Armored Vehicle, Tank & Tank Component Manufacturing
SIC 3711 Motor Vehicles & Passenger Car Bodies
SIC 3795 Tanks & Tank Components
336999 All Other Transportation Equipment Manufacturing
SIC 3799 Transportation Equipment, nec

FURNITURE & RELATED PRODUCT MANUFACTURING

337121 Upholstered Household Furniture Manufacturing
SIC 2512 Wood Household Furniture, Upholstered
SIC 2515 Mattress, Foundations, & Convertible Beds
SIC 5712 Furniture
337122 Nonupholstered Wood Household Furniture Manufacturing
SIC 2511 Wood Household Furniture, Except Upholstered
SIC 5712 Furniture Stores
337124 Metal Household Furniture Manufacturing
SIC 2514 Metal Household Furniture
337125 Household Furniture Manufacturing
SIC 2519 Household Furniture, NEC
337127 Institutional Furniture Manufacturing
SIC 2531 Public Building & Related Furniture
SIC 2599 Furniture & Fixtures, nec
SIC 3952 Lead Pencils, Crayons, & Artist's Materials
SIC 3999 Manufacturing Industries, nec
337129 Wood Television, Radio, & Sewing Machine Cabinet Manufacturing
SIC 2517 Wood Television, Radio, Phonograph, & Sewing Machine Cabinets
337131 Wood Kitchen & Counter Top Manufacturing
SIC 2434 Wood Kitchen Cabinets
SIC 2541 Wood Office & Store Fixtures, Partitions, Shelving, & Lockers
SIC 5712 Furniture Stores
337132 Upholstered Wood Household Furniture Manufacturing
SIC 2515 Mattresses, Foundations, & Convertible Beds
SIC 5712 Furniture Stores
337133 Wood Household Furniture
SIC 5712 Furniture Stores
337134 Wood Office Furniture Manufacturing
SIC 2521 Wood Office Furniture
337135 Custom Architectural Woodwork, Millwork, & Fixtures
SIC 2541 Wood Office & Store Fixtures, Partitions, Shelving, and Lockers
337139 Other Wood Furniture Manufacturing
SIC 2426 Hardwood Dimension & Flooring Mills
SIC 2499 Wood Products, nec
SIC 2517 Wood Television, Radio, Phonograph, & Sewing Machine Cabinets
SIC 2531 Public Building & Related Furniture
SIC 2541 Wood Office & Store Fixtures, Partitions., Shelving, & Lockers
SIC 2599 Furniture & Fixtures, nec
SIC 3952 Lead Pencils, Crayons, & Artist's Materials

337141 Nonwood Office Furniture Manufacturing
SIC 2522 Office Furniture, Except Wood
337143 Household Furniture Manufacturing
SIC 2519 Household Furniture, NEC
337145 Nonwood Showcase, Partition, Shelving, & Locker Manufacturing
SIC 2542 Office & Store Fixtures, Partitions, Shelving, & Lockers, Except Wood
337148 Other Nonwood Furniture Manufacturing
SIC 2499 Wood Products, NEC
SIC 2531 Public Building & Related Furniture
SIC 2599 Furniture & Fixtures, nec
SIC 3499 Fabricated Metal Products, nec
SIC 3952 Lead Pencils, Crayons, & Artist's Materials
SIC 3999 Manufacturing Industries, nec
337212 Custom Architectural Woodwork & Millwork Manufacturing
SIC 2541 Wood Office & Store Fixtures, Partitions, Shelving, & Lockers
337214 Nonwood Office Furniture Manufacturing
SIC 2522 Office Furniture, Except Wood
337215 Showcase, Partition, Shelving, & Locker Manufacturing
SIC 2542 Office & Store Fixtures, Partitions, Shelving & Lockers, Except Wood
SIC 2541 Wood Office & Store Fixtures, Partitions, Shelving, & Lockers
SIC 2426 Hardwood Dimension & Flooring Mills
SIC 3499 Fabricated Metal Products, nec
33791 Mattress Manufacturing
SIC 2515 Mattresses, Foundations & Convertible Beds
33792 Blind & Shade Manufacturing
SIC 2591 Drapery Hardware & Window Blinds & Shades

MISCELLANEOUS MANUFACTURING

339111 Laboratory Apparatus & Furniture Manufacturing
SIC 3829 Measuring & Controlling Devices, nec
339112 Surgical & Medical Instrument Manufacturing
SIC 3841 Surgical & Medical Instruments & Apparatus
SIC 3829 Measuring & Controlling Devices, nec
339113 Surgical Appliance & Supplies Manufacturing
SIC 2599 Furniture & Fixtures, nec
SIC 3842 Orthopedic, Prosthetic, & Surgical Appliances & Supplies
339114 Dental Equipment & Supplies Manufacturing
SIC 3843 Dental Equipment & Supplies
339115 Ophthalmic Goods Manufacturing
SIC 3851 Opthalmic Goods
SIC 5995 Optical Goods Stores
339116 Dental Laboratories
SIC 8072 Dental Laboratories 339117 Eyeglass & Contact Lens Manufacturing
SIC 5995 Optical Goods Stores
339911 Jewelry Manufacturing
SIC 3469 Metal Stamping, nec
SIC 3479 Coating, Engraving, & Allied Services, nec
SIC 3911 Jewelry, Precious Metal
339912 Silverware & Plated Ware Manufacturing
SIC 3479 Coating, Engraving, & Allied Services, nec
SIC 3914 Silverware, Plated Ware, & Stainless Steel Ware
339913 Jewelers' Material & Lapidary Work Manufacturing
SIC 3915 Jewelers' Findings & Materials, & Lapidary Work

339914 Costume Jewelry & Novelty Manufacturing
SIC 3479 Coating, Engraving, & Allied Services, nec
SIC 3499 Fabricated Metal Products, nec
SIC 3961 Costume Jewelry & Costume Novelties, Except Precious Metal
33992 Sporting & Athletic Goods Manufacturing
SIC 3949 Sporting & Athletic Goods, nec
339931 Doll & Stuffed Toy Manufacturing
SIC 3942 Dolls & Stuffed Toys
339932 Game, Toy, & Children's Vehicle Manufacturing
SIC 3944 Games, Toys, & Children's Vehicles, Except Dolls & Bicycles
339941 Pen & Mechanical Pencil Manufacturing
SIC 3951 Pens, Mechanical Pencils, & Parts
339942 Lead Pencil & Art Good Manufacturing
SIC 2531 Public Buildings & Related Furniture
SIC 3579 Office Machines, nec
SIC 3952 Lead Pencils, Crayons, & Artists' Materials
339943 Marking Device Manufacturing
SIC 3953 Marking Devices
339944 Carbon Paper & Inked Ribbon Manufacturing
SIC 3955 Carbon Paper & Inked Ribbons
33995 Sign Manufacturing
SIC 3993 Signs & Advertising Specialties
339991 Gasket, Packing, & Sealing Device Manufacturing
SIC 3053 Gaskets, Packing, & Sealing Devices
339992 Musical Instrument Manufacturing
SIC 3931 Musical Instruments
339993 Fastener, Button, Needle & Pin Manufacturing
SIC 3965 Fasteners, Buttons, Needles, & Pins
SIC 3131 Boat & Shoe Cut Stock & Findings
339994 Broom, Brush & Mop Manufacturing
SIC 3991 Brooms & Brushes
SIC 2392 Housefurnishings, Except Curtains & Draperies
339995 Burial Casket Manufacturing
SIC 3995 Burial Caskets
339999 All Other Miscellaneous Manufacturing
SIC 2499 Wood Products, NEC
SIC 3999 Manufacturing Industries, nec

WHOLESALE TRADE

42111 Automobile & Other Motor Vehicle Wholesalers
SIC 5012 Automobiles & Other Motor Vehicles
42112 Motor Vehicle Supplies & New Part Wholesalers
SIC 5013 Motor Vehicle Supplies & New Parts
42113 Tire & Tube Wholesalers
SIC 5014 Tires & Tubes
42114 Motor Vehicle Part Wholesalers
SIC 5015 Motor Vehicle Parts, Used
42121 Furniture Wholesalers
SIC 5021 Furniture
42122 Home Furnishing Wholesalers
SIC 5023 Homefurnishings
42131 Lumber, Plywood, Millwork & Wood Panel Wholesalers
SIC 5031 Lumber, Plywood, Millwork, & Wood Panels
SIC 5211 Lumber & Other Building Materials Dealers - Retail
42132 Brick, Stone & Related Construction Material Wholesalers
SIC 5032 Brick, Stone, & Related Construction Materials
42133 Roofing, Siding, & Insulation Material Wholesalers
SIC 5033 Roofing, Siding, & Insulation Materials

42139 Other Construction Material Wholesalers
SIC 5039 Construction Materials, nec

42141 Photographic Equipment & Supplies Wholesalers
SIC 5043 Photographic Equipment & Supplies

42142 Office Equipment Wholesalers
SIC 5044 Office Equipment

42143 Computer & Computer Peripheral Equipment & Software Wholesalers
SIC 5045 Computers & Computer Peripherals Equipment & Software

42144 Other Commercial Equipment Wholesalers
SIC 5046 Commercial Equipment, nec

42145 Medical, Dental & Hospital Equipment & Supplies Wholesalers
SIC 5047 Medical, Dental & Hospital Equipment & Supplies

42146 Ophthalmic Goods Wholesalers
SIC 5048 Ophthalmic Goods

42149 Other Professional Equipment & Supplies Wholesalers
SIC 5049 Professional Equipment & Supplies, nec

42151 Metal Service Centers & Offices
SIC 5051 Metals Service Centers & Offices

42152 Coal & Other Mineral & Ore Wholesalers
SIC 5052 Coal & Other Mineral & Ores

42161 Electrical Apparatus & Equipment, Wiring Supplies & Construction Material Wholesalers
SIC 5063 Electrical Apparatus & Equipment, Wiring Supplies & Construction Materials

42162 Electrical Appliance, Television & Radio Set Wholesalers
SIC 5064 Electrical Appliances, Television & Radio Sets

42169 Other Electronic Parts & Equipment Wholesalers
SIC 5065 Electronic Parts & Equipment, nec

42171 Hardware Wholesalers
SIC 5072 Hardware

42172 Plumbing & Heating Equipment & Supplies Wholesalers
SIC 5074 Plumbing & Heating Equipment & Supplies

42173 Warm Air Heating & Air-Conditioning Equipment & Supplies Wholesalers
SIC 5075 Warm Air Heating & Air-Conditioning Equipment & Supplies

42174 Refrigeration Equipment & Supplies Wholesalers
SIC 5078 Refrigeration Equipment & Supplies

42181 Construction & Mining Machinery & Equipment Wholesalers
SIC 5082 Construction & Mining Machinery & Equipment

42182 Farm & Garden Machinery & Equipment Wholesalers
SIC 5083 Farm & Garden Machinery & Equipment

42183 Industrial Machinery & Equipment Wholesalers
SIC 5084 Industrial Machinery & Equipment
SIC 5085 Industrial Supplies

42184 Industrial Supplies Wholesalers
SIC 5085 Industrial Supplies

42185 Service Establishment Equipment & Supplies Wholesalers
SIC 5087 Service Establishment Equipment & Supplies Wholesalers

42186 Transportation Equipment & Supplies Wholesalers
SIC 5088 Transportation Equipment and Supplies, Except Motor Vehicles

42191 Sporting & Recreational Goods & Supplies Wholesalers
SIC 5091 Sporting & Recreational Goods & Supplies

42192 Toy & Hobby Goods & Supplies Wholesalers
SIC 5092 Toys & Hobby Goods & Supplies

42193 Recyclable Material Wholesalers
SIC 5093 Scrap & Waste Materials

42194 Jewelry, Watch, Precious Stone & Precious Metal Wholesalers
SIC 5094 Jewelry, Watches, Precious Stones, & Precious Metals

42199 Other Miscellaneous Durable Goods Wholesalers
SIC 5099 Durable Goods, nec
SIC 7822 Motion Picture & Video Tape Distribution

42211 Printing & Writing Paper Wholesalers
SIC 5111 Printing & Writing Paper

42212 Stationary & Office Supplies Wholesalers
SIC 5112 Stationery & Office Supplies

42213 Industrial & Personal Service Paper Wholesalers
SIC 5113 Industrial & Personal Service Paper

42221 Drug, Drug Proprietaries & Druggists' Sundries Wholesalers
SIC 5122 Drugs, Drug Proprietaries, & Druggists' Sundries

42231 Piece Goods, Notions & Other Dry Goods Wholesalers
SIC 5131 Piece Goods, Notions, & Other Dry Goods

42232 Men's & Boys' Clothing & Furnishings Wholesalers
SIC 5136 Men's & Boys' Clothing & Furnishings

42233 Women's, Children's, & Infants' & Accessories Wholesalers
SIC 5137 Women's, Children's, & Infants' Clothing & Accessories

42234 Footwear Wholesalers
SIC 5139 Footwear

42241 General Line Grocery Wholesalers
SIC 5141 Groceries, General Line

42242 Packaged Frozen Food Wholesalers
SIC 5142 Packaged Frozen Foods

42243 Dairy Product Wholesalers
SIC 5143 Dairy Products, Except Dried or Canned

42244 Poultry & Poultry Product Wholesalers
SIC 5144 Poultry & Poultry Products

42245 Confectionery Wholesalers
SIC 5145 Confectionery

42246 Fish & Seafood Wholesalers
SIC 5146 Fish & Seafoods

42247 Meat & Meat Product Wholesalers
SIC 5147 Meats & Meat Products

42248 Fresh Fruit & Vegetable Wholesalers
SIC 5148 Fresh Fruits & Vegetables

42249 Other Grocery & Related Products Wholesalers
SIC 5149 Groceries & Related Products, nec

42251 Grain & Field Bean Wholesalers
SIC 5153 Grain & Field Beans

42252 Livestock Wholesalers
SIC 5154 Livestock

42259 Other Farm Product Raw Material Wholesalers
SIC 5159 Farm-Product Raw Materials, nec

42261 Plastics Materials & Basic Forms & Shapes Wholesalers
SIC 5162 Plastics Materials & Basic Forms & Shapes

42269 Other Chemical & Allied Products Wholesalers
SIC 5169 Chemicals & Allied Products, nec

42271 Petroleum Bulk Stations & Terminals
SIC 5171 Petroleum Bulk Stations & Terminals

42272 Petroleum & Petroleum Products Wholesalers
SIC 5172 Petroleum & Petroleum Products Wholesalers, Except Bulk Stations & Terminals

42281 Beer & Ale Wholesalers
SIC 5181 Beer & Ale

42282 Wine & Distilled Alcoholic Beverage Wholesalers
SIC 5182 Wine & Distilled Alcoholic Beverages
42291 Farm Supplies Wholesalers
SIC 5191 Farm Supplies
42292 Book, Periodical & Newspaper Wholesalers
SIC 5192 Books, Periodicals, & Newspapers
42293 Flower, Nursery Stock & Florists' Supplies Wholesalers
SIC 5193 Flowers, Nursery Stock, & Florists' Supplies
42294 Tobacco & Tobacco Product Wholesalers
SIC 5194 Tobacco & Tobacco Products
42295 Paint, Varnish & Supplies Wholesalers
SIC 5198 Paints, Varnishes, & Supplies
SIC 5231 Paint, Glass & Wallpaper Stores
42299 Other Miscellaneous Nondurable Goods Wholesalers
SIC 5199 Nondurable Goods, nec

RETAIL TRADE

44111 New Car Dealers
SIC 5511 Motor Vehicle Dealers, New and Used
44112 Used Car Dealers
SIC 5521 Motor Vehicle Dealers, Used Only
44121 Recreational Vehicle Dealers
SIC 5561 Recreational Vehicle Dealers
441221 Motorcycle Dealers
SIC 5571 Motorcycle Dealers
441222 Boat Dealers
SIC 5551 Boat Dealers
441229 All Other Motor Vehicle Dealers
SIC 5599 Automotive Dealers, NEC
44131 Automotive Parts & Accessories Stores
SIC 5013 Motor Vehicle Supplies & New Parts
SIC 5731 Radio, Television, & Consumer Electronics Stores
SIC 5531 Auto & Home Supply Stores
44132 Tire Dealers
SIC 5014 Tires & Tubes
SIC 5531 Auto & Home Supply Stores
44211 Furniture Stores
SIC 5021 Furniture
SIC 5712 Furniture Stores
44221 Floor Covering Stores
SIC 5023 Homefurnishings
SIC 5713 Floor Coverings Stores
442291 Window Treatment Stores
SIC 5714 Drapery, Curtain, & Upholstery Stores
SIC 5719 Miscellaneous Homefurnishings Stores
442299 All Other Home Furnishings Stores
SIC 5719 Miscellaneous Homefurnishings Stores
443111 Household Appliance Stores
SIC 5722 Household Appliance Stores
SIC 5999 Miscellaneous Retail Stores, nec
SIC 7623 Refrigeration & Air-Conditioning Service & Repair Shops
SIC 7629 Electrical & Electronic Repair Shops, nec
443112 Radio, Television & Other Electronics Stores
SIC 5731 Radio, Television, & Consumer Electronics Stores
SIC 5999 Miscellaneous Retail Stores, nec
SIC 7622 Radio & Television Repair Shops
44312 Computer & Software Stores
SIC 5045 Computers & Computer Peripheral Equipment & Software
SIC 7378 Computer Maintenance & Repair '
SIC 5734 Computer & Computer Software Stores

44313 Camera & Photographic Supplies Stores
SIC 5946 Camera & Photographic Supply Stores
44411 Home Centers
SIC 5211 Lumber & Other Building Materials Dealers
44412 Paint & Wallpaper Stores
SIC 5198 Paints, Varnishes, & Supplies
SIC 5231 Paint, Glass, & Wallpaper Stores
44413 Hardware Stores
SIC 5251 Hardware Stores
44419 Other Building Material Dealers
SIC 5031 Lumber, Plywood, Millwork, & Wood Panels
SIC 5032 Brick, Stone, & Related Construction Materials
SIC 5039 Construction Materials, nec
SIC 5063 Electrical Apparatus & Equipment, Wiring Supplies, & Construction Materials
SIC 5074 Plumbing & Heating Equipment & Supplies
SIC 5211 Lumber & Other Building Materials Dealers
SIC 5231 Paint, Glass, & Wallpaper Stores
44421 Outdoor Power Equipment Stores
SIC 5083 Farm & Garden Machinery & Equipment
SIC 5261 Retail Nurseries, Lawn & Garden Supply Stores
44422 Nursery & Garden Centers
SIC 5191 Farm Supplies
SIC 5193 Flowers, Nursery Stock, & Florists' Supplies
SIC 5261 Retail Nurseries, Lawn & Garden Supply Stores
44511 Supermarkets & Other Grocery Stores
SIC 5411 Grocery Stores
44512 Convenience Stores
SIC 5411 Grocery Stores
44521 Meat Markets
SIC 5421 Meat & Fish Markets, Including Freezer Provisioners
SIC 5499 Miscellaneous Food Stores
44522 Fish & Seafood Markets
SIC 5421 Meat & Fish Markets, Including Freezer Provisioners
44523 Fruit & Vegetable Markets
SIC 5431 Fruit & Vegetable Markets
445291 Baked Goods Stores
SIC 5461 Retail Bakeries
445292 Confectionery & Nut Stores
SIC 5441 Candy, Nut & Confectionery Stores
445299 All Other Specialty Food Stores
SIC 5499 Miscellaneous Food Stores
SIC 5451 Dairy Products Stores
44531 Beer, Wine & Liquor Stores
SIC 5921 Liquor Stores
44611 Pharmacies & Drug Stores
SIC 5912 Drug Stores & Proprietary Stores
44612 Cosmetics, Beauty Supplies & Perfume Stores
SIC 5087 Service Establishment Equipment & Supplies
SIC 5999 Miscellaneous Retail Stores, nec
44613 Optical Goods Stores
SIC 5995 Optical Goods Stores
446191 Food Supplement Stores
SIC 5499 Miscellaneous Food Stores
446199 All Other Health & Personal Care Stores
SIC 5047 Medical, Dental, & Hospital Equipment & Supplies
SIC 5999 Miscellaneous Retail Stores, nec
44711 Gasoline Stations with Convenience Stores
SIC 5541 Gasoline Service Station
SIC 5411 Grocery Stores
44719 Other Gasoline Stations
SIC 5541 Gasoline Service Station

44811 Men's Clothing Stores
SIC 5611 Men's & Boys' Clothing & Accessory Stores
44812 Women's Clothing Stores
SIC 5621 Women's Clothing Stores
44813 Children's & Infants' Clothing Stores
SIC 5641 Children's & Infants' Wear Stores
44814 Family Clothing Stores
SIC 5651 Family Clothing Stores
44815 Clothing Accessories Stores
SIC 5611 Men's & Boys' Clothing & Accessory Stores
SIC 5632 Women's Accessory & Specialty Stores
SIC 5699 Miscellaneous Apparel & Accessory Stores
44819 Other Clothing Stores
SIC 5699 Miscellaneous Apparel & Accessory Stores
SIC 5632 Women's Accessory & Specialty Stores
44821 Shoe Stores
SIC 5661 Shoe Stores
44831 Jewelry Stores
SIC 5999 Miscellaneous Retailer, nec
SIC 5944 Jewelry Stores
44832 Luggage & Leather Goods Stores
SIC 5948 Luggage & Leather Goods Stores
45111 Sporting Goods Stores
SIC 7699 Repair Shops & Related Services, NEC
SIC 5941 Sporting Goods Stores & Bicycle Shops
45112 Hobby, Toy & Game Stores
SIC 5945 Hobby, Toy, & Game Stores
45113 Sewing, Needlework & Piece Goods Stores
SIC 5714 Drapery, Curtain, & Upholstery Stores
SIC 5949 Sewing, Needlework, & Piece Goods Stores
45114 Musical Instrument & Supplies Stores
SIC 5736 Musical Instruments Stores
451211 Book Stores
SIC 5942 Book Stores
451212 News Dealers & Newsstands
SIC 5994 News Dealers & Newsstands
45122 Prerecorded Tape, Compact Disc & Record Stores
SIC 5735 Record & Prerecorded Tape Stores
45211 Department Stores
SIC 5311 Department Stores
45291 Warehouse Clubs & Superstores
SIC 5399 Miscellaneous General Merchandise Stores
SIC 5411 Grocery Stores
45299 All Other General Merchandise Stores
SIC 5399 Miscellaneous General Merchandise Stores
SIC 5331 Variety Stores
45311 Florists
SIC 5992 Florists
45321 Office Supplies & Stationery Stores
SIC 5049 Professional Equipment & Supplies, nec
SIC 5112 Stationery & Office Supplies
SIC 5943 Stationery Stores
45322 Gift, Novelty & Souvenir Stores
SIC 5947 Gift, Novelty, & Souvenir Shops
45331 Used Merchandise Stores
SIC 5932 Used Merchandise Stores
45391 Pet & Pet Supplies Stores
SIC 5999 Miscellaneous Retail Stores, NEC
45392 Art Dealers
SIC 5999 Miscellaneous Retail Stores, nec
45393 Manufactured Home Dealers
SIC 5271 Mobile Home Dealers

453991 Tobacco Stores
SIC 5993 Tobacco Stores & Stands
453999 All Other Miscellaneous Store Retailers
SIC 5999 Miscellaneous Retail Stores, nec
SIC 5261 Retail Nurseries, Lawn & Garden Supply Stores
45411 Electronic Shopping & Mail-Order Houses
SIC 5961 Catalog & Mail-Order Houses
45421 Vending Machine Operators
SIC 5962 Automatic Merchandise Machine Operators
454311 Heating Oil Dealers
SIC 5171 Petroleum Bulk Stations & Terminals
SIC 5983 Fuel Oil Dealers
454312 Liquefied Petroleum Gas Dealers
SIC 5171 Petroleum Bulk Stations & Terminals
SIC 5984 Liquefied Petroleum Gas Dealers
454319 Other Fuel Dealers
SIC 5989 Fuel Dealers, nec
45439 Other Direct Selling Establishments
SIC 5421 Meat & Fish Markets, Including Freezer Provisioners
SIC 5963 Direct Selling Establishments

TRANSPORTATION & WAREHOUSING

481111 Scheduled Passenger Air Transportation
SIC 4512 Air Transportation, Scheduled
481112 Scheduled Freight Air Transportation
SIC 4512 Air Transportation, Scheduled
481211 Nonscheduled Chartered Passenger Air Transportation
SIC 4522 Air Transportation, Nonscheduled
481212 Nonscheduled Chartered Freight Air Transportation
SIC 4522 Air Transportation, Nonscheduled
481219 Other Nonscheduled Air Transportation
SIC 7319 Advertising, nec
48122 Nonscheduled Speciality Air Transportation
SIC 0721 Crop Planting, Cultivating, & Protecting
SIC 1382 Oil & Gas Field Exploration Services
SIC 4522 Air Transportation, Nonscheduled
SIC 7335 Commercial Photography
SIC 7997 Membership Sports & Recreation Clubs
SIC 8299 Schools & Educational Services, nec
SIC 8713 Surveying Services
482111 Line-Haul Railroads
SIC 4011 Railroads, Line-Haul Operating
482112 Short Line Railroads
SIC 4013 Railroad Switching & Terminal Establishments
483111 Deep Sea Freight Transportation
SIC 4412 Deep Sea Foreign Transportation of Freight
483112 Deep Sea Passenger Transportation
SIC 4481 Deep Sea Transportation of Passengers, Except by Ferry
483113 Coastal & Great Lakes Freight Transportation
SIC 4424 Deep Sea Domestic Transportation of Freight
SIC 4432 Freight Transportation on the Great Lakes - St. Lawrence Seaway
SIC 4492 Towing & Tugboat Services
483114 Coastal & Great Lakes Passenger Transportation
SIC 4481 Deep Sea Transportation of Passengers, Except by Ferry
SIC 4482 Ferries
483211 Inland Water Freight Transportation
SIC 4449 Water Transportation of Freight, nec
SIC 4492 Towing & Tugboat Services

483212 Inland Water Passenger Transportation
SIC 4482 Ferries
SIC 4489 Water Transportation of Passengers, nec
48411 General Freight Trucking, Local
SIC 4212 Local Trucking without Storage
SIC 4214 Local Trucking with Storage
484121 General Freight Trucking, Long-Distance, Truckload
SIC 4213 Trucking, Except Local
484122 General Freight Trucking, Long-Distance, Less Than Truckload
SIC 4213 Trucking, Except Local
48421 Used Household & Office Goods Moving
SIC 4212 Local Trucking Without Storage
SIC 4213 Trucking, Except Local
SIC 4214 Local Trucking With Storage
48422 Specialized Freight Trucking, Local
SIC 4212 Local Trucking without Storage
SIC 4214 Local Trucking with Storage
48423 Specialized Freight Trucking, Long-Distance
SIC 4213 Trucking, Except Local
485111 Mixed Mode Transit Systems
SIC 4111 Local & Suburban Transit
485112 Commuter Rail Systems
SIC 4111 Local & Suburban Transit
485113 Bus & Motor Vehicle Transit Systems
SIC 4111 Local & Suburban Transit
485119 Other Urban Transit Systems
SIC 4111 Local & Suburban Transit
48521 Interurban & Rural Bus Transportation
SIC 4131 Intercity & Rural Bus Transportation
48531 Taxi Service
SIC 4121 Taxicabs
48532 Limousine Service
SIC 4119 Local Passenger Transportation, nec
48541 School & Employee Bus Transportation
SIC 4151 School Buses
SIC 4119 Local Passenger Transportation, nec
48551 Charter Bus Industry
SIC 4141 Local Charter Bus Service
SIC 4142 Bus Charter Services, Except Local
485991 Special Needs Transportation
SIC 4119 Local Passenger Transportation, nec
485999 All Other Transit & Ground Passenger Transportation
SIC 4111 Local & Suburban Transit
SIC 4119 Local Passenger Transportation, nec
48611 Pipeline Transportation of Crude Oil
SIC 4612 Crude Petroleum Pipelines
48621 Pipeline Transportation of Natural Gas
SIC 4922 Natural Gas Transmission
SIC 4923 Natural Gas Transmission & Distribution
48691 Pipeline Transportation of Refined Petroleum Products
SIC 4613 Refined Petroleum Pipelines
48699 All Other Pipeline Transportation
SIC 4619 Pipelines, nec
48711 Scenic & Sightseeing Transportation, Land
SIC 4119 Local Passenger Transportation, nec
SIC 4789 Transportation Services, nec
SIC 7999 Amusement & Recreation Services, nec
48721 Scenic & Sightseeing Transportation, Water
SIC 4489 Water Transportation of Passengers, nec
SIC 7999 Amusement & Recreation Services, nec
48799 Scenic & Sightseeing Transportation, Other
SIC 4522 Air Transportation, Nonscheduled
SIC 7999 Amusement & Recreation Services, nec

488111 Air Traffic Control
SIC 4581 Airports, Flying Fields, & Airport Terminal Services
SIC 9621 Regulation & Administration of Transportation Programs
488112 Airport Operations, except Air Traffic Control
SIC 4581 Airports, Flying Fields, & Airport Terminal Services
SIC 4959 Sanitary Services, nec
488119 Other Airport Operations
SIC 4581 Airports, Flying Fields, & Airport Terminal Services
SIC 4959 Sanitary Services, nec
48819 Other Support Activities for Air Transportation
SIC 4581 Airports, Flying Fields, & Airport Terminal Services
48821 Support Activities for Rail Transportation
SIC 4013 Railroad Switching & Terminal Establishments
SIC 4741 Rental of Railroad Cars
SIC 4789 Transportation Services, nec
48831 Port & Harbor Operations
SIC 4491 Marine Cargo Handling
SIC 4499 Water Transportation Services, nec
48832 Marine Cargo Handling
SIC 4491 Marine Cargo Handling
48833 Navigational Services to Shipping
SIC 4492 Towing & Tugboat Services
SIC 4499 Water Transportation Services, nec
48839 Other Support Activities for Water Transportation
SIC 4499 Water Transportation Services, nec
SIC 4785 Fixed Facilities & Inspection & Weighing Services for Motor Vehicle Transportation
SIC 7699 Repair Shops & Related Services, nec
48841 Motor Vehicle Towing
SIC 7549 Automotive Services, Except Repair & Carwashes
48849 Other Support Activities for Road Transportation
SIC 4173 Terminal & Service Facilities for Motor Vehicle Passenger Transportation
SIC 4231 Terminal & Joint Terminal Maintenance Facilities for Motor Freight Transportation
SIC 4785 Fixed Facilities & Inspection & Weighing Services for Motor Vehicle Transportation
48851 Freight Transportation Arrangement
SIC 4731 Arrangement of Transportation of Freight & Cargo
488991 Packing & Crating
SIC 4783 Packing & Crating
488999 All Other Support Activities for Transportation
SIC 4729 Arrangement of Passenger Transportation, nec
SIC 4789 Transportation Services, nec
49111 Postal Service
SIC 4311 United States Postal Service
49211 Couriers
SIC 4215 Courier Services, Except by Air
SIC 4513 Air Courier Services
49221 Local Messengers & Local Delivery
SIC 4215 Courier Services, Except by Air
49311 General Warehousing & Storage Facilities
SIC 4225 General Warehousing & Storage
SIC 4226 Special Warehousing & Storage, nec
49312 Refrigerated Storage Facilities
SIC 4222 Refrigerated Warehousing & Storage
SIC 4226 Special Warehousing & Storage, nec
49313 Farm Product Storage Facilities
SIC 4221 Farm Product Warehousing & Storage
49319 Other Warehousing & Storage Facilities
SIC 4226 Special Warehousing & Storage, nec

INFORMATION

51111 Newspaper Publishers
SIC 2711 Newspapers: Publishing or Publishing & Printing
51112 Periodical Publishers
SIC 2721 Periodicals: Publishing or Publishing & Printing
51113 Book Publishers
SIC 2731 Books: Publishing or Publishing & Printing
51114 Database & Directory Publishers
SIC 2741 Miscellaneous Publishing
511191 Greeting Card Publishers
SIC 2771 Greeting Cards
511199 All Other Publishers
SIC 2741 Miscellaneous Publishing
51121 Software Publishers
SIC 7372 Prepackaged Software
51211 Motion Picture & Video Production
SIC 7812 Motion Picture & Video Tape Production
51212 Motion Picture & Video Distribution
SIC 7822 Motion Picture & Video Tape Distribution
SIC 7829 Services Allied to Motion Picture Distribution
512131 Motion Picture Theaters, Except Drive-Ins.
SIC 7832 Motion Picture Theaters, Except Drive-In
512132 Drive-In Motion Picture Theaters
SIC 7833 Drive-In Motion Picture Theaters
512191 Teleproduction & Other Post-Production Services
SIC 7819 Services Allied to Motion Picture Production
512199 Other Motion Picture & Video Industries
SIC 7819 Services Allied to Motion Picture Production
SIC 7829 Services Allied to Motion Picture Distribution
51221 Record Production
SIC 8999 Services, nec
51222 Integrated Record Production/Distribution
SIC 3652 Phonograph Records & Prerecorded Audio Tapes & Disks
51223 Music Publishers
SIC 2731 Books: Publishing or Publishing & Printing
SIC 2741 Miscellaneous Publishing
SIC 8999 Services, nec
51224 Sound Recording Studios
SIC 7389 Business Services, nec
51229 Other Sound Recording Industries
SIC 7389 Business Services, nec
SIC 7922 Theatrical Producers & Miscellaneous Theatrical Services
513111 Radio Networks
SIC 4832 Radio Broadcasting Stations
513112 Radio Stations
SIC 4832 Radio Broadcasting Stations
51312 Television Broadcasting
SIC 4833 Television Broadcasting Stations
51321 Cable Networks
SIC 4841 Cable & Other Pay Television Services
51322 Cable & Other Program Distribution
SIC 4841 Cable & Other Pay Television Services
51331 Wired Telecommunications Carriers
SIC 4813 Telephone Communications, Except Radiotelephone
SIC 4822 Telegraph & Other Message Communications
513321 Paging
SIC 4812 Radiotelephone Communications
513322 Cellular & Other Wireless Telecommunications
SIC 4812 Radiotelephone Communications
SIC 4899 Communications Services, nec

51333 Telecommunications Resellers
SIC 4812 Radio Communications
SIC 4813 Telephone Communications, Except Radiotelephone
51334 Satellite Telecommunications
SIC 4899 Communications Services, NEC
51339 Other Telecommunications
SIC 4899 Communications Services, NEC
51411 News Syndicates
SIC 7383 News Syndicates
51412 Libraries & Archives
SIC 8231 Libraries
514191 On-Line Information Services
SIC 7375 Information Retrieval Services
514199 All Other Information Services
SIC 8999 Services, nec
51421 Data Processing Services
SIC 7374 Computer Processing & Data Preparation & Processing Services

FINANCE & INSURANCE

52111 Monetary Authorities - Central Bank
SIC 6011 Federal Reserve Banks
52211 Commercial Banking
SIC 6021 National Commercial Banks
SIC 6022 State Commercial Banks
SIC 6029 Commercial Banks, nec
SIC 6081 Branches & Agencies of Foreign Banks
52212 Savings Institutions
SIC 6035 Savings Institutions, Federally Chartered
SIC 6036 Savings Institutions, Not Federally Chartered
52213 Credit Unions
SIC 6061 Credit Unions, Federally Chartered
SIC 6062 Credit Unions, Not Federally Chartered
52219 Other Depository Credit Intermediation
SIC 6022 State Commercial Banks
52221 Credit Card Issuing
SIC 6021 National Commercial Banks
SIC 6022 State Commercial Banks
SIC 6141 Personal Credit Institutions
52222 Sales Financing
SIC 6141 Personal Credit Institutions
SIC 6153 Short-Term Business Credit Institutions, Except Agricultural .
SIC 6159 Miscellaneous Business Credit Institutions
522291 Consumer Lending
SIC 6141 Personal Credit Institutions
522292 Real Estate Credit
SIC 6162 Mortgage Bankers & Loan Correspondents
522293 International Trade Financing
SIC 6081 Branches & Agencies of Foreign Banks
SIC 6082 Foreign Trade & International Banking Institutions
SIC 6111 Federal & Federally-Sponsored Credit Agencies
SIC 6159 Miscellaneous Business Credit Institutions
522294 Secondary Market Financing
SIC 6111 Federal & Federally Sponsored Credit Agencies
522298 All Other Nondepository Credit Intermediation
SIC 5932 Used Merchandise Stores
SIC 6081 Branches & Agencies of Foreign Banks
SIC 6111 Federal & Federally-Sponsored Credit Agencies
SIC 6153 Short-Term Business Credit Institutions, Except Agricultural
SIC 6159 Miscellaneous Business Credit Institutions

52231   Mortgage & Other Loan Brokers
SIC 6163 Loan Brokers
52232   Financial Transactions Processing, Reserve, & Clearing House Activities
SIC 6019 Central Reserve Depository Institutions, nec
SIC 6099 Functions Related to Depository Banking, nec
SIC 6153 Short-Term Business Credit Institutions, Except Agricultural
SIC 7389 Business Services, nec
52239   Other Activities Related to Credit Intermediation
SIC 6099 Functions Related to Depository Banking, nec
SIC 6162 Mortgage Bankers & Loan Correspondents
52311   Investment Banking & Securities Dealing
SIC 6211 Security Brokers, Dealers, & Flotation Companies
52312   Securities Brokerage
SIC 6211 Security Brokers, Dealers, & Flotation Companies
52313   Commodity Contracts Dealing
SIC 6099 Functions Related to depository Banking, nec
SIC 6799 Investors, nec
SIC 6221 Commodity Contracts Brokers & Dealers
52314   Commodity Brokerage
SIC 6221 Commodity Contracts Brokers & Dealers
52321   Securities & Commodity Exchanges
SIC 6231 Security & Commodity Exchanges
52391   Miscellaneous Intermediation
SIC 6211 Securities Brokers, Dealers & Flotation Companies
SIC 6799 Investors, nec
52392   Portfolio Management
SIC 6282 Investment Advice
SIC 6371 Pension, Health, & Welfare Funds
SIC 6733 Trust, Except Educational, Religious, & Charitable
SIC 6799 Investors, nec
52393   Investment Advice
SIC 6282 Investment Advice
523991 Trust, Fiduciary & Custody Activities
SIC 6021 National Commercial Banks
SIC 6022 State Commercial Banks
SIC 6091 Nondepository Trust Facilities
SIC 6099 Functions Related to Depository Banking, nec
SIC 6289 Services Allied With the Exchange of Securities or Commodities, nec
SIC 6733 Trusts, Except Educational, Religious, & Charitable
523999 Miscellaneous Financial Investment Activities
SIC 6099 Functions Related to Depository Banking, nec
SIC 6211 Security Brokers, Dealers, & Flotation Companies
SIC 6289 Services Allied With the Exchange of Securities or Commodities, nec
SIC 6799 Investors, nec
SIC 6792 Oil Royalty Traders
524113 Direct Life Insurance Carriers
SIC 6311 Life Insurance
524114 Direct Health & Medical Insurance Carriers
SIC 6324 Hospital & Medical Service Plans
SIC 6321 Accident & Health Insurance
524126 Direct Property & Casualty Insurance Carriers
SIC 6331 Fire, Marine, & Casualty Insurance
SIC 6351 Surety Insurance
524127 Direct Title Insurance Carriers
SIC 6361 Title Insurance
524128 Other Direct Insurance Carriers
SIC 6399 Insurance Carriers, nec
52413   Reinsurance Carriers
SIC 6311 Life Insurance
SIC 6321 Accident & Health Insurance

SIC 6324 Hospital & Medical Service Plans
SIC 6331 Fire, Marine, & Casualty Insurance
SIC 6351 Surety Insurance
SIC 6361 Title Insurance
52421   Insurance Agencies & Brokerages
SIC 6411 Insurance Agents, Brokers & Service
524291 Claims Adjusters
SIC 6411 Insurance Agents, Brokers & Service
524292 Third Party Administration for Insurance & Pension Funds
SIC 6371 Pension, Health, & Welfare Funds
SIC 6411 Insurance Agents, Brokers & Service
524298 All Other Insurance Related Activities
SIC 6411 Insurance Agents, Brokers & Service
52511   Pension Funds
SIC 6371 Pension, Health, & Welfare Funds
52512   Health & Welfare Funds
SIC 6371 Pension, Health, & Welfare Funds
52519   Other Insurance Funds
SIC 6321 Accident & Health Insurance
SIC 6324 Hospital & Medical Service Plans
SIC 6331 Fire, Marine, & Casualty Insurance
SIC 6733 Trusts, Except Educational, Religious, & Charitable
52591   Open-End Investment Funds
SIC 6722 Management Investment Offices, Open-End
52592   Trusts, Estates, & Agency Accounts
SIC 6733 Trusts, Except Educational, Religious, & Charitable
52593   Real Estate Investment Trusts
SIC 6798 Real Estate Investment Trusts
52599   Other Financial Vehicles
SIC 6726 Unit Investment Trusts, Face-Amount Certificate Offices, & Closed-End Management Investment Offices

REAL ESTATE & RENTAL & LEASING

53111   Lessors of Residential Buildings & Dwellings
SIC 6513 Operators of Apartment Buildings
SIC 6514 Operators of Dwellings Other Than Apartment Buildings
53112   Lessors of Nonresidential Buildings
SIC 6512 Operators of Nonresidential Buildings
53113   Lessors of Miniwarehouses & Self Storage Units
SIC 4225 General Warehousing & Storage
53119   Lessors of Other Real Estate Property
SIC 6515 Operators of Residential Mobile Home Sites
SIC 6517 Lessors of Railroad Property
SIC 6519 Lessors of Real Property, nec
53121   Offices of Real Estate Agents & Brokers
SIC 6531 Real Estate Agents Managers
531311 Residential Property Managers
SIC 6531 Real Estate Agents & Managers
531312 Nonresidential Property Managers
SIC 6531 Real Estate Agents & Managers
53132   Offices of Real Estate Appraisers
SIC 6531 Real Estate Agents & Managers
531399 All Other Activities Related to Real Estate
SIC 6531 Real Estate Agents & Managers
532111 Passenger Car Rental
SIC 7514 Passenger Car Rental
532112 Passenger Car Leasing
SIC 7515 Passenger Car Leasing

53212   Truck, Utility Trailer, & RV Rental & Leasing
SIC 7513 Truck Rental & Leasing Without Drivers
SIC 7519 Utility Trailers & Recreational Vehicle Rental

53221   Consumer Electronics & Appliances Rental
SIC 7359 Equipment Rental & Leasing, nec

53222   Formal Wear & Costume Rental
SIC 7299 Miscellaneous Personal Services, nec
SIC 7819 Services Allied to Motion Picture Production

53223   Video Tape & Disc Rental
SIC 7841 Video Tape Rental

532291 Home Health Equipment Rental
SIC 7352 Medical Equipment Rental & Leasing

532292 Recreational Goods Rental
SIC 7999 Amusement & Recreation Services, nec

532299 All Other Consumer Goods Rental
SIC 7359 Equipment Rental & Leasing, nec

53231   General Rental Centers
SIC 7359 Equipment Rental & Leasing, nec

**532411 Commercial Air, Rail, & Water Transportation
         Equipment Rental & Leasing**
SIC 4499 Water Transportation Services, nec
SIC 4741 Rental of Railroad Cars
SIC 7359 Equipment Rental & Leasing, nec

**532412 Construction, Mining & Forestry Machinery &
         Equipment Rental & Leasing**
SIC 7353 Heavy Construction Equipment Rental & Leasing
SIC 7359 Equipment Rental & Leasing, nec

53242   Office Machinery & Equipment Rental & Leasing
SIC 7359 Equipment Rental & Leasing
SIC 7377 Computer Rental & Leasing

**53249   Other Commercial & Industrial Machinery &
         Equipment Rental & Leasing**
SIC 7352 Medical Equipment Rental & Leasing
SIC 7359 Equipment Rental & Leasing, nec
SIC 7819 Services Allied to Motion Picture Production
SIC 7922 Theatrical Producers & Miscellaneous Theatrical
         Services

53311   Owners & Lessors of Other Nonfinancial Assets
SIC 6792 Oil Royalty Traders
SIC 6794 Patent Owners & Lessors

PROFESSIONAL, SCIENTIFIC, & TECHNICAL SERVICES

54111   Offices of Lawyers
SIC 8111 Legal Services

541191 Title Abstract & Settlement Offices
SIC 6541 Title Abstract Offices

541199 All Other Legal Services
SIC 7389 Business Services, nec

541211 Offices of Certified Public Accountants
SIC 8721 Accounting, Auditing, & Bookkeeping Services

541213 Tax Preparation Services
SIC 7291 Tax Return Preparation Services

541214 Payroll Services
SIC 7819 Services Allied to Motion Picture Production
SIC 8721 Accounting, Auditing, & Bookkeeping Services

541219 Other Accounting Services
SIC 8721 Accounting, Auditing, & Bookkeeping Services

54131   Architectural Services
SIC 8712 Architectural Services

54132   Landscape Architectural Services
SIC 0781 Landscape Counseling & Planning

54133   Engineering Services
SIC 8711 Engineering Services

54134   Drafting Services
SIC 7389 Business Services, nec

54135   Building Inspection Services
SIC 7389 Business Services, nec

54136   Geophysical Surveying & Mapping Services
SIC 8713 Surveying Services
SIC 1081 Metal Mining Services
SIC 1382 Oil & Gas Field Exploration Services
SIC 1481 Nonmetallic Minerals Services, Except Fuels

54137   Surveying & Mapping Services
SIC 7389 Business Services, nec
SIC 8713 Surveying Services

54138   Testing Laboratories
SIC 8734 Testing Laboratories

54141   Interior Design Services
SIC 7389 Business Services, nec

54142   Industrial Design Services
SIC 7389 Business Services, nec

54143   Commercial Art & Graphic Design Services
SIC 7336 Commercial Art & Graphic Design
SIC 8099 Health & Allied Services, nec

54149   Other Specialized Design Services
SIC 7389 Business Services, nec

541511 Custom Computer Programming Services
SIC 7371 Computer Programming Services

541512 Computer Systems Design Services
SIC 7373 Computer Integrated Systems Design
SIC 7379 Computer Related Services, nec

541513 Computer Facilities Management Services
SIC 7376 Computer Facilities Management Services

541519 Other Computer Related Services
SIC 7379 Computer Related Services, nec

**541611 Administrative Management & General Management
         Consulting Services**
SIC 8742 Management Consulting Services

**541612 Human Resources & Executive Search Consulting
         Services**
SIC 8742 Management Consulting Services
SIC 7361 Employment Agencies
SIC 8999 Services, nec

541613 Marketing Consulting Services
SIC 8742 Management Consulting Services

**541614 Process, Physical, Distribution & Logistics Consulting
         Services**
SIC 8742 Management Consulting Services

541618 Other Management Consulting Services
SIC 4731 Arrangement of Transportation of Freight & Cargo
SIC 8748 Business Consulting Services, nec

54162   Environmental Consulting Services
SIC 8999 Services, nec

54169   Other Scientific & Technical Consulting Services
SIC 0781 Landscape Counseling & Planning
SIC 8748 Business Consulting Services, nec
SIC 8999 Services, nec

**54171   Research & Development in the Physical Sciences &
         Engineering Sciences**
SIC 8731 Commercial Physical & Biological Research
SIC 8733 Noncommercial Research Organizations

54172 Research & Development in the Life Sciences
SIC 8731 Commercial Physical & Biological Research
SIC 8733 Noncommercial Research Organizations

54173 Research & Development in the Social Sciences & Humanities
SIC 8732 Commercial Economic, Sociological, & Educational Research
SIC 8733 Noncommercial Research Organizations

54181 Advertising Agencies
SIC 7311 Advertising Agencies

54182 Public Relations Agencies
SIC 8743 Public Relations Services

54183 Media Buying Agencies
SIC 7319 Advertising, nec

54184 Media Representatives
SIC 7313 Radio, Television, & Publishers' Advertising Representatives

54185 Display Advertising
SIC 7312 Outdoor Advertising Services
SIC 7319 Advertising, nec

54186 Direct Mail Advertising
SIC 7331 Direct Mail Advertising Services

54187 Advertising Material Distribution Services
SIC 7319 Advertising, NEC

54189 Other Services Related to Advertising
SIC 7319 Advertising, nec
SIC 5199 Nondurable Goods, nec
SIC 7389 Business Services, nec

54191 Marketing Research & Public Opinion Polling
SIC 8732 Commercial Economic, Sociological, & Educational Research

541921 Photography Studios, Portrait
SIC 7221 Photographic Studios, Portrait

541922 Commercial Photography
SIC 7335 Commercial Photography
SIC 8099 Health & Allied Services, nec

54193 Translation & Interpretation Services
SIC 7389 Business Services, NEC

54194 Veterinary Services
SIC 0741 Veterinary Services for Livestock
SIC 0742 Veterinary Services for Animal Specialties
SIC 8734 Testing Laboratories

54199 All Other Professional, Scientific & Technical Services
SIC 7389 Business Services

MANAGEMENT OF COMPANIES & ENTERPRISES

551111 Offices of Bank Holding Companies
SIC 6712 Offices of Bank Holding Companies

551112 Offices of Other Holding Companies
SIC 6719 Offices of Holding Companies, nec

551114 Corporate, Subsidiary, & Regional Managing Offices
No SIC equivalent

ADMINISTRATIVE & SUPPORT, WASTE MANAGEMENT & REMEDIATION SERVICES

56111 Office Administrative Services
SIC 8741 Management Services

56121 Facilities Support Services
SIC 8744 Facilities Support Management Services

56131 Employment Placement Agencies
SIC 7361 Employment Agencies
SIC 7819 Services Allied to Motion Pictures Production
SIC 7922 Theatrical Producers & Miscellaneous Theatrical Services

56132 Temporary Help Services
SIC 7363 Help Supply Services

56133 Employee Leasing Services
SIC 7363 Help Supply Services

56141 Document Preparation Services
SIC 7338 Secretarial & Court Reporting

561421 Telephone Answering Services
SIC 7389 Business Services, nec

561422 Telemarketing Bureaus
SIC 7389 Business Services, nec

561431 Photocopying & Duplicating Services
SIC 7334 Photocopying & Duplicating Services

561432 Private Mail Centers
SIC 7389 Business Services, nec

561439 Other Business Service Centers
SIC 7334 Photocopying & Duplicating Services
SIC 7389 Business Services, nec

56144 Collection Agencies
SIC 7322 Adjustment & Collection Services

56145 Credit Bureaus
SIC 7323 Credit Reporting Services

561491 Repossession Services
SIC 7322 Adjustment & Collection
SIC 7389 Business Services, nec

561492 Court Reporting & Stenotype Services
SIC 7338 Secretarial & Court Reporting

561499 All Other Business Support Services
SIC 7389 Business Services, NEC

56151 Travel Agencies
SIC 4724 Travel Agencies

56152 Tour Operators
SIC 4725 Tour Operators

561591 Convention & Visitors Bureaus
SIC 7389 Business Services, nec

561599 All Other Travel Arrangement & Reservation Services
SIC 4729 Arrangement of Passenger Transportation, nec
SIC 7389 Business Services, nec
SIC 7999 Amusement & Recreation Services, nec
SIC 8699 Membership Organizations, nec

561611 Investigation Services
SIC 7381 Detective, Guard, & Armored Car Services

561612 Security Guards & Patrol Services
SIC 7381 Detective, Guard, & Armored Car Services

561613 Armored Car Services
SIC 7381 Detective, Guard, & Armored Car Services

561621 Security Systems Services
SIC 7382 Security Systems Services
SIC 1731 Electrical Work

561622 Locksmiths
SIC 7699 Repair Shops & Related Services, nec

56171 Exterminating & Pest Control Services
SIC 4959 Sanitary Services, NEC
SIC 7342 Disinfecting & Pest Control Services

56172 Janitorial Services
SIC 7342 Disinfecting & Pest Control Services
SIC 7349 Building Cleaning & Maintenance Services, nec
SIC 4581 Airports, Flying Fields, & Airport Terminal Services

56173   Landscaping Services
SIC 0782 Lawn & Garden Services
SIC 0783 Ornamental Shrub & Tree Services
56174   Carpet & Upholstery Cleaning Services
SIC 7217 Carpet & Upholstery Cleaning
56179   Other Services to Buildings & Dwellings
SIC 7389 Business Services, nec
SIC 7699 Repair Shops & Related Services, nec
56191   Packaging & Labeling Services
SIC 7389 Business Services, nec
56192   Convention & Trade Show Organizers
SIC 7389 Business Services, NEC
56199   All Other Support Services
SIC 7389 Business Services, nec
562111 Solid Waste Collection
SIC 4212 Local Trucking Without Storage
SIC 4953 Refuse Systems
562112 Hazardous Waste Collection
SIC 4212 Local Trucking Without Storage
SIC 4953 Refuse Systems
562119 Other Waste Collection
SIC 4212 Local Trucking Without Storage
SIC 4953 Refuse Systems
562211 Hazardous Waste Treatment & Disposal
SIC 4953 Refuse Systems
562212 Solid Waste Landfill
SIC 4953 Refuse Systems
562213 Solid Waste Combustors & Incinerators
SIC 4953 Refuse Systems
562219 Other Nonhazardous Waste Treatment & Disposal
SIC 4953 Refuse Systems
56291   Remediation Services
SIC 1799 Special Trade Contractors, nec
SIC 4959 Sanitary Services, nec
56292   Materials Recovery Facilities
SIC 4953 Refuse Systems
562991 Septic Tank & Related Services
SIC 7359 Equipment Rental & Leasing, nec
SIC 7699 Repair Shops & Related Services, nec
562998 All Other Miscellaneous Waste Management Services
SIC 4959 Sanitary Services, nec

EDUCATIONAL SERVICES

61111   Elementary & Secondary Schools
SIC 8211 Elementary & Secondary Schools
61121   Junior Colleges
SIC 8222 Junior Colleges & Technical Institutes
61131   Colleges, Universities & Professional Schools
SIC 8221 Colleges, Universities, & Professional Schools
61141   Business & Secretarial Schools
SIC 8244 Business & Secretarial Schools
61142   Computer Training
SIC 8243 Data Processing Schools
61143   Professional & Management Development Training Schools
SIC 8299 Schools & Educational Services, nec
611511 Cosmetology & Barber Schools
SIC 7231 Beauty Shops
SIC 7241 Barber Shops
611512 Flight Training
SIC 8249 Vocational Schools, nec
SIC 8299 Schools & Educational Services, nec

611513 Apprenticeship Training
SIC 8249 Vocational Schools, nec
611519 Other Technical & Trade Schools
SIC 8249 Vocational Schools, NEC
SIC 8243 Data Processing Schools
61161   Fine Arts Schools
SIC 8299 Schools & Educational Services, nec
SIC 7911 Dance Studios, Schools, & Halls
61162   Sports & Recreation Instruction
SIC 7999 Amusement & Recreation Services, nec
61163   Language Schools
SIC 8299 Schools & Educational Services, nec
611691 Exam Preparation & Tutoring
SIC 8299 Schools & Educational Services, nec
611692 Automobile Driving Schools
SIC 8299 Schools & Educational Services, nec
611699 All Other Miscellaneous Schools & Instruction
SIC 8299 Schools & Educational Services, nec
61171   Educational Support Services
SIC 8299 Schools & Educational Services nec
SIC 8748 Business Consulting Services, nec

HEALTH CARE & SOCIAL ASSISTANCE

621111 Offices of Physicians
SIC 8011 Offices & Clinics of Doctors of Medicine
SIC 8031 Offices & Clinics of Doctors of Osteopathy
621112 Offices of Physicians, Mental Health Specialists
SIC 8011 Offices & Clinics of Doctors of Medicine
SIC 8031 Offices & Clinics of Doctors of Osteopathy
62121   Offices of Dentists
SIC 8021 Offices & Clinics of Dentists
62131   Offices of Chiropractors
SIC 8041 Offices & Clinics of Chiropractors
62132   Offices of Optometrists
SIC 8042 Offices & Clinics of Optometrists
62133   Offices of Mental Health Practitioners
SIC 8049 Offices & Clinics of Health Practitioners, nec
62134   Offices of Physical, Occupational & Speech Therapists & Audiologists
SIC 8049 Offices & Clinics of Health Practitioners, nec
621391 Offices of Podiatrists
SIC 8043 Offices & Clinics of Podiatrists
621399 Offices of All Other Miscellaneous Health Practitioners
SIC 8049 Offices & Clinics of Health Practitioners, nec
62141   Family Planning Centers
SIC 8093 Speciality Outpatient Facilities, NEC
SIC 8099 Health & Allied Services, nec
62142   Outpatient Mental Health & Substance Abuse Centers
SIC 8093 Specialty Outpatient Facilities, nec
621491 HMO Medical Centers
SIC 8011 Offices & Clinics of Doctors of Medicine
621492 Kidney Dialysis Centers
SIC 8092 Kidney Dialysis Centers
621493 Freestanding Ambulatory Surgical & Emergency Centers
SIC 8011 Offices & Clinics of Doctors of Medicine
621498 All Other Outpatient Care Centers
SIC 8093 Specialty Outpatient Facilities, nec
621511 Medical Laboratories
SIC 8071 Medical Laboratories
621512 Diagnostic Imaging Centers
SIC 8071 Medical Laboratories

62161   Home Health Care Services
  SIC 8082 Home Health Care Services
62191   Ambulance Services
  SIC 4119 Local Passenger Transportation, nec
  SIC 4522 Air Transportation, Nonscheduled
621991 Blood & Organ Banks
  SIC 8099 Health & Allied Services, nec
621999 All Other Miscellaneous Ambulatory Health Care Services
  SIC 8099 Health & Allied Services, nec
62211   General Medical & Surgical Hospitals
  SIC 8062 General Medical & Surgical Hospitals
  SIC 8069 Specialty Hospitals, Except Psychiatric
62221   Psychiatric & Substance Abuse Hospitals
  SIC 8063 Psychiatric Hospitals
  SIC 8069 Specialty Hospitals, Except Psychiatric
62231   Specialty Hospitals
  SIC 8069 Specialty Hospitals, Except Psychiatric
62311   Nursing Care Facilities
  SIC 8051 Skilled Nursing Care Facilities
  SIC 8052 Intermediate Care Facilities
  SIC 8059 Nursing & Personal Care Facilities, nec
62321   Residential Mental Retardation Facilities
  SIC 8052 Intermediate Care Facilities
62322   Residential Mental Health & Substance Abuse Facilities
  SIC 8361 Residential Care
623311 Continuing Care Retirement Communities
  SIC 8051 Skilled Nursing Care Facilities
  SIC 8052 Intermediate Care Facilities
  SIC 8059 Nursing & Personal Care Facilities, nec
623312 Homes for the Elderly
  SIC 8361 Residential Care
62399   Other Residential Care Facilities
  SIC 8361 Residential Care
62411   Child & Youth Services
  SIC 8322 Individual & Family Social Services
  SIC 8641 Civic, Social, & Fraternal Organizations
62412   Services for the Elderly & Persons with Disabilities
  SIC 8322 Individual & Family Social Services
62419   Other Individual & Family Services
  SIC 8322 Individual & Family Social Services
62421   Community Food Services
  SIC 8322 Individual & Family Social Services
624221 Temporary Shelters
  SIC 8322 Individual & Family Social Services
624229 Other Community Housing Services
  SIC 8322 Individual & Family Social Services
62423   Emergency & Other Relief Services
  SIC 8322 Individual & Family Social Services
62431   Vocational Rehabilitation Services
  SIC 8331 Job Training & Vocational Rehabilitation Services
62441   Child Day Care Services
  SIC 8351 Child Day Care Services
  SIC 7299 Miscellaneous Personal Services, nec

ARTS, ENTERTAINMENT, & RECREATION

71111   Theater Companies & Dinner Theaters
  SIC 5812 Eating Places
  SIC 7922 Theatrical Producers & Miscellaneous Theatrical Services

71112   Dance Companies
  SIC 7922 Theatrical Producers & Miscellaneous Theatrical Services
71113   Musical Groups & Artists
  SIC 7929 Bands, Orchestras, Actors, & Entertainment Groups
71119   Other Performing Arts Companies
  SIC 7929 Bands, Orchestras, Actors, & Entertainment Groups
  SIC 7999 Amusement & Recreation Services, nec
711211 Sports Teams & Clubs
  SIC 7941 Professional Sports Clubs & Promoters
711212 Race Tracks
  SIC 7948 Racing, Including Track Operations
711219 Other Spectator Sports
  SIC 7941 Professional Sports Clubs & Promoters
  SIC 7948 Racing, Including Track Operations
  SIC 7999 Amusement & Recreation Services, nec
71131   Promoters of Performing Arts, Sports & Similar Events with Facilities
  SIC 6512 Operators of Nonresidential Buildings
  SIC 7922 Theatrical Procedures & Miscellaneous Theatrical Services
  SIC 7941 Professional Sports Clubs & Promoters
71132   Promoters of Performing Arts, Sports & Similar Events without Facilities
  SIC 7922 Theatrical Producers & Miscellaneous Theatrical Services
  SIC 7941 Professional Sports Clubs & Promoters
71141   Agents & Managers for Artists, Athletes, Entertainers & Other Public Figures
  SIC 7389 Business Services, nec
  SIC 7922 Theatrical Producers & Miscellaneous Theatrical Services
  SIC 7941 Professional Sports Clubs & Promoters
71151   Independent Artists, Writers, & Performers
  SIC 7819 Services Allied to Motion Picture Production
  SIC 7929 Bands, Orchestras, Actors, & Other Entertainers & Entertainment Services
  SIC 8999 Services, nec
71211   Museums
  SIC 8412 Museums & Art Galleries
71212   Historical Sites
  SIC 8412 Museums & Art Galleries
71213   Zoos & Botanical Gardens
  SIC 8422 Arboreta & Botanical & Zoological Gardens
71219   Nature Parks & Other Similar Institutions
  SIC 7999 Amusement & Recreation Services, nec
  SIC 8422 Arboreta & Botanical & Zoological Gardens
71311   Amusement & Theme Parks
  SIC 7996 Amusement Parks
71312   Amusement Arcades
  SIC 7993 Coin-Operated Amusement Devices
71321   Casinos
  SIC 7999 Amusement & Recreation Services, nec
71329   Other Gambling Industries
  SIC 7993 Coin-Operated Amusement Devices
  SIC 7999 Amusement & Recreation Services, nec
71391   Golf Courses & Country Clubs
  SIC 7992 Public Golf Courses
  SIC 7997 Membership Sports & Recreation Clubs
71392   Skiing Facilities
  SIC 7999 Amusement & Recreation Services, nec
71393   Marinas
  SIC 4493 Marinas

71394 Fitness & Recreational Sports Centers
SIC 7991 Physical Fitness Facilities
SIC 7997 Membership Sports & Recreation Clubs
SIC 7999 Amusement & Recreation Services, nec
71395 Bowling Centers
SIC 7933 Bowling Centers
71399 All Other Amusement & Recreation Industries
SIC 7911 Dance Studios, Schools, & Halls
SIC 7993 Amusement & Recreation Services, nec
SIC 7997 Membership Sports & Recreation Clubs
SIC 7999 Amusement & Recreation Services, nec

ACCOMMODATION & FOODSERVICES

72111 Hotels & Motels
SIC 7011 Hotels & Motels
SIC 7041 Organization Hotels & Lodging Houses, on
        Membership Basis
72112 Casino Hotels
SIC 7011 Hotels & Motels
721191 Bed & Breakfast Inns
SIC 7011 Hotels & Motels
721199 All Other Traveler Accommodation
SIC 7011 Hotels & Motels
721211 RV Parks & Campgrounds
SIC 7033 Recreational Vehicle Parks & Campgrounds
721214 Recreational & Vacation Camps
SIC 7032 Sporting & Recreational Camps
72131 Rooming & Boarding Houses
SIC 7021 Rooming & Boarding Houses
SIC 7041 Organization Hotels & Lodging Houses, on
        Membership Basis
72211 Full-Service Restaurants
SIC 5812 Eating Places
722211 Limited-Service Restaurants
SIC 5812 Eating Places
SIC 5499 Miscellaneous Food Stores
722212 Cafeterias
SIC 5812 Eating Places
722213 Snack & Nonalcoholic Beverage Bars
SIC 5812 Eating Places
SIC 5461 Retail Bakeries
72231 Foodservice Contractors
SIC 5812 Eating Places
72232 Caterers
SIC 5812 Eating Places
72233 Mobile Caterers
SIC 5963 Direct Selling Establishments
72241 Drinking Places
SIC 5813 Drinking Places

OTHER SERVICES

811111 General Automotive Repair
SIC 7538 General Automotive Repair Shops
811112 Automotive Exhaust System Repair
SIC 7533 Automotive Exhaust System Repair Shops
811113 Automotive Transmission Repair
SIC 7537 Automotive Transmission Repair Shops

811118 Other Automotive Mechanical & Electrical Repair &
        Maintenance
SIC 7539 Automotive Repair Shops, nec
811121 Automotive Body, Paint & Upholstery Repair &
        Maintenance
SIC 7532 Top, Body, & Upholstery Repair Shops & Paint
        Shops
811122 Automotive Glass Replacement Shops
SIC 7536 Automotive Glass Replacement Shops
811191 Automotive Oil Change & Lubrication Shops
SIC 7549 Automotive Services, Except Repair & Carwashes
811192 Car Washes
SIC 7542 Carwashes
811198 All Other Automotive Repair & Maintenance
SIC 7534 Tire Retreading & Repair Shops
SIC 7549 Automotive Services, Except Repair & Carwashes
811211 Consumer Electronics Repair & Maintenance
SIC 7622 Radio & Television Repair Shops
SIC 7629 Electrical & Electronic Repair Shops, nec
811212 Computer & Office Machine Repair & Maintenance
SIC 7378 Computer Maintenance & Repair
SIC 7629 Electrical & Electronic Repair Shops, nec
SIC 7699 Repair Shops & Related Services, nec
811213 Communication Equipment Repair & Maintenance
SIC 7622 Radio & Television Repair Shops
SIC 7629 Electrical & Electronic Repair Shops, nec
811219 Other Electronic & Precision Equipment Repair &
        Maintenance
SIC 7629 Electrical & Electronic Repair Shops, nec
SIC 7699 Repair Shops & Related Services, NEC
81131 Commercial & Industrial Machinery & Equipment
        Repair & Maintenance
SIC 7699 Repair Shops & Related Services, nec
SIC 7623 Refrigerator & Air-Conditioning Service & Repair
        Shops
SIC 7694 Armature Rewinding Shops
811411 Home & Garden Equipment Repair & Maintenance
SIC 7699 Repair Shops & Related Services, nec
811412 Appliance Repair & Maintenance
SIC 7623 Refrigeration & Air-Conditioning Service & Repair
        Shops
SIC 7629 Electrical & Electronic Repair Shops, NEC
SIC 7699 Repairs Shops & Related Services, nec
81142 Reupholstery & Furniture Repair
SIC 7641 Reupholstery & Furniture Repair
81143 Footwear & Leather Goods Repair
SIC 7251 Shoe Repair & Shoeshine Parlors
SIC 7699 Repair Shops & Related Services
81149 Other Personal & Household Goods Repair &
        Maintenance
SIC 3732 Boat Building & Repairing
SIC 7219 Laundry & Garment Services, nec
SIC 7631 Watch, Clock, & Jewelry Repair
SIC 7692 Welding Repair
SIC 7699 Repair Shops & Related Services, nec
812111 Barber Shops
SIC 7241 Barber Shops
812112 Beauty Salons
SIC 7231 Beauty Shops
812113 Nail Salons
SIC 7231 Beauty Shops
812191 Diet & Weight Reducing Centers
SIC 7299 Miscellaneous Personal Services, nec

812199 Other Personal Care Services
SIC 7299 Miscellaneous Personal Services, nec,
81221　Funeral Homes
SIC 7261 Funeral Services & Crematories
81222　Cemeteries & Crematories
SIC 6531 Real Estate Agents & Managers
SIC 6553 Cemetery Subdividers & Developers
SIC 7261 Funeral Services & Crematories
81231　Coin-Operated Laundries & Drycleaners
SIC 7215 Coin-Operated Laundry & Drycleaning
812321 Laundries, Family & Commercial
SIC 7211 Power Laundries, Family & Commercial
812322 Drycleaning Plants
SIC 7216 Drycleaning Plants, Except Rug Cleaning
812331 Linen Supply
SIC 7213 Linen Supply
SIC 7219 Laundry & Garment Services, nec,
812332 Industrial Launderers
SIC 7218 Industrial Launderers
812391 Garment Pressing, & Agents for Laundries
SIC 7212 Garment Pressing & Agents for Laundries
812399 All Other Laundry Services
SIC 7219 Laundry & Garment Services, NEC
81291　Pet Care Services
SIC 0752 Animal Speciality Services, Except Veterinary
812921 Photo Finishing Laboratories
SIC 7384 Photofinishing Laboratories
812922 One-Hour Photo Finishing
SIC 7384 Photofinishing Laboratories
81293　Parking Lots & Garages
SIC 7521 Automobile Parking
81299　All Other Personal Services
SIC 7299 Miscellaneous Personal Services, nec
SIC 7389 Miscellaneous Business Services
81311　Religious Organizations
SIC 8661 Religious Organizations
813211 Grantmaking Foundations
SIC 6732 Educational, Religious, & Charitable Trust
813212 Voluntary Health Organizations
SIC 8399 Social Services, nec
813219 Other Grantmaking & Giving Services
SIC 8399 Social Services, NEC
813311 Human Rights Organizations
SIC 8399 Social Services, nec
813312 Environment, Conservation & Wildlife Organizations
SIC 8399 Social Services, nec
SIC 8699 Membership Organizations, nec
813319 Other Social Advocacy Organizations
SIC 8399 Social Services, NEC
81341　Civic & Social Organizations
SIC 8641 Civic, Social, & Fraternal Organizations
SIC 8699 Membership Organizations, nec
81391　Business Associations
SIC 8611 Business Associations
SIC 8699 Membership Organizations, nec
81392　Professional Organizations
SIC 8621 Professional Membership Organizations
81393　Labor Unions & Similar Labor Organizations
SIC 8631 Labor Unions & Similar Labor Organizations
81394　Political Organizations
SIC 8651 Political Organizations
81399　Other Similar Organizations
SIC 6531 Real Estate Agents & Managers
SIC 8641 Civic, Social, & Fraternal Organizations

SIC 8699 Membership Organizations, nec
81411　Private Households
SIC 8811 Private Households

PUBLIC ADMINISTRATION

92111　Executive Offices
SIC 9111 Executive Offices
92112　Legislative Bodies
SIC 9121 Legislative Bodies
92113　Public Finance
SIC 9311 Public Finance, Taxation, & Monetary Policy
92114　Executive & Legislative Offices, Combined
SIC 9131 Executive & Legislative Offices, Combined
92115　American Indian & Alaska Native Tribal Governments
SIC 8641 Civic, Social, & Fraternal Organizations
92119　All Other General Government
SIC 9199 General Government, nec
92211　Courts
SIC 9211 Courts
92212　Police Protection
SIC 9221 Police Protection
92213　Legal Counsel & Prosecution
SIC 9222 Legal Counsel & Prosecution
92214　Correctional Institutions
SIC 9223 Correctional Institutions
92215　Parole Offices & Probation Offices
SIC 8322 Individual & Family Social Services
92216　Fire Protection
SIC 9224 Fire Protection
92219　All Other Justice, Public Order, & Safety
SIC 9229 Public Order & Safety, nec
92311　Administration of Education Programs
SIC 9411 Administration of Educational Programs
92312　Administration of Public Health Programs
SIC 9431 Administration of Public Health Programs
92313　Administration of Social, Human Resource & Income Maintenance Programs
SIC 9441 Administration of Social, Human Resource & Income Maintenance Programs
92314　Administration of Veteran's Affairs
SIC 9451 Administration of Veteran's Affairs, Except Health Insurance
92411　Air & Water Resource & Solid Waste Management
SIC 9511 Air & Water Resource & Solid Waste Management
92412　Land, Mineral, Wildlife, & Forest Conservation
SIC 9512 Land, Mineral, Wildlife, & Forest Conservation
92511　Administration of Housing Programs
SIC 9531 Administration of Housing Programs
92512　Administration of Urban Planning & Community & Rural Development
SIC 9532 Administration of Urban Planning & Community & Rural Development
92611　Administration of General Economic Programs
SIC 9611 Administration of General Economic Programs
92612　Regulation & Administration of Transportation Programs
SIC 9621 Regulations & Administration of Transportation Programs
92613　Regulation & Administration of Communications, Electric, Gas, & Other Utilities
SIC 9631 Regulation & Administration of Communications, Electric, Gas, & Other Utilities

92614 Regulation of Agricultural Marketing & Commodities
SIC 9641 Regulation of Agricultural Marketing & Commodities
**92615 Regulation, Licensing, & Inspection of Miscellaneous
Commercial Sectors**
SIC 9651 Regulation, Licensing, & Inspection of Miscellaneous
Commercial Sectors
92711 Space Research & Technology
SIC 9661 Space Research & Technology
92811 National Security
SIC 9711 National Security
92812 International Affairs
SIC 9721 International Affairs
99999 Unclassified Establishments
SIC 9999 Nonclassifiable Establishments

Appendix: NAICS/SIC Conversion

APPENDIX III

ANNOTATED SOURCE LIST

The following listing provides the names, publishers, addresses, telephone and fax numbers (if available), and frequency of publications for the primary sources used in *Market Share Reporter*.

20 20 Magazine, Jobson Publishing Corp., 100 Avenue of the Americas, 9th Fl., New York, NY 10013, *Telephone:* (212) 274-7000, *Fax*: (212) 431-0500, *Published*: monthly.

AAII Journal, American Association of Individual Investors, 625 N. Michigan Ave., Ste. 1900, Chicago, IL 60611, *Telephone:* (312) 280-0170, *Published*: monthly.

ABA Banking Journal, Simmons-Boardman Publishing Corp., 345 Hudson St., New York, NY 10014-4502, *Telephone:* (212) 620-7200.

Accountancy International, The American Institute of Certified Public Accountants, 1211 Avenue of the Americas, New York, NY 10036, *Telephone:* (212) 596-6200, *Fax:* (212) 596-6213. *Published:* monthly.

The Accountant, Lafferty Publications Ltd., IDA Tower, Pearse Street, Dublin 2, Ireland, *Telephone*: (353-1) 671-8022, *Fax:* (353-1) 671-8520, *Published*: monthly.

Advertising Age, Crain Communications, Inc., 220 E. 42nd St., New York, NY 10017, *Telephone:* (212) 210-0725, *Fax:* (212) 210-0111, *Published:* weekly.

Advisor Today, National Association of Insurance Advisors, 2901 Telestar Ct., Falls Church, VA, 22042-1205.

Adweek, BPI Communications, Merchandise Mart, Suite 936, Chicago, IL 60654, *Telephone:* (800) 722-6658, *Fax:* (312) 464-8540, *Published:* weekly.

Aerospace America, Advanstar Communications Inc., 7500 Old Oak Blvd., Cleveland OH 44130-3343, *Published:* monthly.

Aftermarket Business, Advanstar Communications, Inc., 7500 Old Oak Blvd., Cleveland, OH 44130-3343, *Published*: monthly.

AgLender, 11701 Boorman Dr., St. Louis, MO 63146, Telephone: (800) 535-2342.

Air Cargo World, Journal of Commerce Inc., 1230 National Press Building, Washington D.C. 20045, *Telphone*: (202) 783-1148, *Published*: monthly.

AISE Steel Technology, Three Gateway Center, Ste. 1900, Pittsburgh, PA 15222-1004, *Telephone*: (412) 281-4657.

American Ceramic Society Bulletin, American Ceramic Society, 735 Ceramic Place, Westerville, OH 43081-8720, *Published*: monthly, *Price*: $50 per year for nonmembers and libraries; included in membership dues.

American Clinical Laboratory, International Scientific Communications Inc., 30 Controls Drive, P.O. Box 870, Shelton, CT 06484-0870, *Telephone*: (203) 583926-9300, *Fax:* (203) 926-9310.

American Ink Maker, MacNair-Dorland Co., 445 Broadhollow Rd., Melville, NY 11747, *Telephone:* (212) 279-4456. *Published:* monthly.

American Laboratory, International Scientific Commuications Inc., 30 Controls Drive, P.O. Box 870, Shelton, CT 06484-0870, *Telephone:* (203) 926-9300, *Fax:* (203) 926-9310.

American Medical News, American Medical Assn., 515 N State St., Chicago IL 60610, *Telephone:* (312) 464-4440, *Fax:* (312) 464-4184, *Published:* 48x/yr.

American Metal Market, Capital Cities Media Inc., 825 7th Avenue, New York, NY 10019, *Telephone:* (800) 360-7600, *Published:* daily, except Saturdays, Sundays, and holidays, *Price:* $560 per year (U.S., Canada, and Mexico).

American Printer, Maclean Hunter Publishing Co., 29 N. Wacker Dr., Chicago, IL 60606. *Published:* monthly.

American Shipper, Howard Publications Inc., 33 South Hogan Street, P.O. Box 4728, Jacksonville, FL 32201, *Telephone:* (904) 365-2601, *Published:* monthly, *Price:* $35 per year.

Appliance, Dana Chase Publications Inc., 1110 Jorie Blvd., CS 9019, Ste. 203, Hinsdale, IL 60521, *Telephone:* (708) 990 - 3484, *Fax:* (708) 990 - 0078, *Published:* monthly, *Price:* $60.

Appliance Manufacturer, Business News Publishing Co., 755 W. Big Beaver Rd., Ste. 1000, Troy, MI 48084-4900, *Telephone:* (313) 362-3700, *Fax:* (313) 244-6439, *Published:* monthly.

AS&U (American School and University), North American Publishing Co., 401 N. Broad St., Philadelphia, PA 19106, *Telephone:* (215) 238-4200, *Fax:* (215) 238-4227, *Published:* monthly.

Assembly, Hitchcock Publishing Co., 191 S. Gary Ave., Carol Stream, IL 60188, *Telephone:* (708) 665 - 1000, *Fax:* (708) 462 - 2225.

ATI, Billian Publishing, 2100 Powers Ferry NW, Ste. 300, Atlanta, GA 30339, *Telephone:* (404) 955-5656, *Fax:* (404) 952-0669, *Published:* monthly.

Atlanta Business Chronicle, American City Business Journals, 1801 Peachtree Blvd., NE, Suite 15D, Atlanta, GA 30309, *Telephone:* (404) 249-1000, *Fax:* (404) 249-1048, *Published:* weekly.

Atlanta Journal-Constitution, 72 Marietta St., NW Atlanta, GA 30303, *Telephone:* (404) 526 - 5151, *Published:* daily.

Auto Body Repair News, Capital Cities/ABC/ Chilton Co., Chilton Way, Radnor PA 19089, *Published:* monthly.

Automatic Merchandiser, Johsnon Hill Press Inc., 1233 Janesville Ave., Fort Atkinson, WI 53538, *Telephone:* (414) 563-6388, *Fax:* (414) 563-1702, *Published:* 6x/yr.

Automotive Industries, Capital Cities/ABC/Chilton Co., Chilton Way, Radnor PA 19089, *Telephone:* (215) 961-4255, *Fax:* (215) 964 -4251.

Automotive News, Crain Communications Inc., 380 Woodbridge, Detroit, MI 48207 *Telephone:* (313) 446-6000, *Fax:* (313) 446-0347.

AVG, Meister Publishing Co., 37733 Euclid Ave., Willoughby, OH 44094-5992, *Telephone:* (216) 942-2000, *Fax:* (216) 942-0662. *Published:* monthly.

Baking Business, Sosland Publishing Co., 4800 Main St., Ste. 100, Kansas City, MO 64112, Telephone: (816) 756-1000, Fax: (*16) 756-0494.

Baltimore Business Journal, American City Business Journals, 117 Water St., Baltimore, MD 21202, *Telephone:* (410) 576-1161, *Fax:* (301) 383-321, *Published:* weekly.

Bank Network News, Miller Freeman Inc., 1515 Broadway, New York, NY 10036, *Telephone:* (212) 869-1300, *Fax:* (212) 302-6273.

The Banker, Greystoke Place, Feteer Lane, London. England EC4A IND, *Telephone*: (071) 405-6969, *Published:* monthly.

Banking Strategies, Bank Administration Institute, One North Franklin, Chicago, IL 60606, *Telephone:* (312) 553-4600, *Price:* $59.

Best's Review, A.M. Best Co. Inc., Ambest Rd., Oldwick, NJ 08858, *Telephone:* (908) 439-2200, *Fax:* (908) 439-3363, *Published:* monthly.

Beverage Industry, Advanstar Communications, Inc., 7500 Old Oak Blvd., Cleveland OH 44130, *Telephone:* (216) 243-8100, *Fax:* (216) 891-2651, *Published:* monthly, *Price:* $40 per year.

Beverage World, Keller International Publishing Corp., 150 Great Neck Rd., Great Neck, NY 11021, *Telephone:* (516) 829-9210, *Fax:* (516) 829-5414, *Published:* monthly.

Bicycle Retailer & Industry News, 502 W. Cordova Rd., Santa Fe., NM 87501, *Telephone*: (505) 988-5099, *Fax:* (505) 988-7224, *Published:* 18x/yr.

Billboard, BPI Communications, 1515 Broadway, 14th FL, New York, NY 10036, *Telephone*: (212) 764-7300, *Fax:* (212) 536-5358.

Bobbin, Bobbin Blenheim Media Corp., 1110 Shop Rd., PO Box 1986, Columbia, SC 29202, *Telephone:* (803) 771-7500, *Fax:* (803) 799-1461.

The Boston Globe, Globe Newspaper Co., P.O. Box 2378, Boston, MA 02107, *Telephone:* (617) 929-2000, *Published:* daily.

Brandweek, Adweek L.P., 1515 Broadway, New York, NY 10036, *Telephone:* (212) 536-5336. *Published:* weekly, except no issue in the last week of Dec.

Brill's Content, Brill Media Ventures, 521 Fifth Avenue, New York, NY 10175, *Published:* monthle, except for combined issues in December/January and July/August.

Broadcasting & Cable, Cahners Publishing Co., 1705 DeSales Street, N.W., Washington, DC 20036, *Telephone:* (800) 554-5729 or (202) 659-2340, *Fax:* (202) 331-1732.

Broiler Industry, Watt Publishing Co., 122 S. Wesley Ave., Mount Morris, IL 61054-1497, *Telephone:* (815) 734-4171, *Fax:* (815) 734-4201, *Published:* monthly.

BtoB, Crain Communications, Inc., 220 E. 42nd St., New York, NY 10017, *Telephone:* (212) 210-0725, *Fax:* (212) 210-0111, *Published:* weekly.

Builder, Hanley-Wood Inc., 655 15th St. N.W., Ste. 475, Washington, D.C. 20005, *Telephone:* (202) 737-0717, *Fax:* (202) 737-2439, *Published:* monthly.

Building Design & Construction, Cahners Publishing, 1350 E. Touhy Ave., Des Plaines, IL 60017-5080, *Telephone:* (708) 635-8800, *Published:* monthly.

Building Material Dealer, National Lumbermens Publishing Corp., 1405 Lilac Drive N, No. 131, Minneapolis, MN 55422, Telephone: (612) 544-1597, Fax: (612) 544-820, *Published:* monthly.

Business 2.0, Imagine Media Inc., 150 North Hill Drive, Brisbane, CA 94005, *Published:* monthly.

Business & Health, Medical Economics Publishing Co., 5 Paragon Dr., Montvale, NJ 07645-1184, *Telephone:* (201) 358-7208, *Published:* 14x/yr.

Business Communications Review, BCR Enterprises, Inc., 950 York Rd., Hinsdale, IL 60521, *Telephone:* (800) 227-1324, *Published:* monthly.

Business Insurance, Crain Communications, Inc., 740 N. Rush St., Chicago IL 60611, *Published:* monthly.

The Business Journal of Portland, P.O. Box 14490, Portland, OR 97293, *Telephone:* (503) 274-8733, *Fax:* (503) 227-2680.

Business News New Jersey, Business Journal of New Jersey Inc., 55 Park Place, P.O. Box 920, Morristown, NJ 07963-0920, *Telephone:* (201) 539-8230, *Fax:* (201) 530-2953.

Business Marketing, Crain Communications, 740 N. Rush St., Chicago, IL 60611, *Telephone*: (312) 649-5200, *Published:* monthly.

Business Week, McGraw-Hill Inc., 1221 Avenue of the Americas, New York, NY 10020. *Published:* weekly, *Price:* U.S.: $46.95 per year; Canada: $69 CDN per year.

C&EN, American Chemical Society, Dept. L-0011, Columbus, OH 43210, *Telephone:* (800) 333-9511 or (614) 447-3776. *Published:* weekly, except last week in December, *Price:* U.S.: $100 per year, $198 for 2 years; elsewhere: $148 per year, $274 for 2 years.

Canadian Grocer, Maclean Hunter Ltd., 77 Bay St., Toronto ON Canada M5W 1A7.

Candy Business, 10225 Berea Rd., Ste. B, Cleveland, OH, *Telephone*: (216) 631-8200, *Fax:* (216) 631-8210.

CCJ, Capital Cities/ABC/Chilton Co., Chilton Way, Radnor, PA 19089, *Telephone:* (215) 964-4000, *Fax:* (215) 964-4981.

Ceramic Bulletin, American Ceramic Society, 735 Ceramic Place, Westerville, OH 43081-8720, *Published:* monthly, *Price*: $50 for nonmembers and libraries, inccluded in membership dues.

Cereal Foods World, American Association of Cereal Chemists, 3340 Pilot Knob Rd., Saint Paul, MN 55121, *Telephone*: (612) 454-7250, *Published:* monthly.

Chain Drug Review, Racher Press Inc., 220 5th Ave., New York, NY 10001, Telephone: (212) 213-6000, *Published:* weekly.

Chain Store Age, Lebhar-Friedman Inc., 425 Park Ave., New York, NY 10022, *Telephone:* (212) 371-9400, *Fax:* (212) 319-4129. *Published:* monthly.

Chemical Engineering, McGraw-Hill Inc., 1221 Avenue of the Americas, New York, NY 10020, *Telephone:* (212) 512-2000. *Published:* monthly.

Chemical Week, Chemical Week Associates, P.O. Box 7721, Riverton, NJ 08077-7721, *Telephone:* (609) 786-0401, *Published:* weekly, except four combination issues (total of 49 issues), *Price:* U.S.: $99 per year; Canada: $129 per year. Single copies $8 in U.S. and $10 elsewhere.

The Chicago Tribune, 435 N. Michigan Ave., Chicago, IL 60611, *Telephone:* (312) 222-3232. *Published:* daily.

Child Care Information Exchange, Exchange Press Inc., P.O. 2890, Redmond, WA 98073, *Telephone:* (800) 221-2864, *Published:* bimonthly, *Price:* $35 per year.

The Christian Science Monitor, Christian Science Publishing Society, One Norway St., Boston, MA 02115, *Telephone:* (800) 456-2220, *Published:* daily, except weekends and holidays.

The Chronicle of Philanthropy, 1255 23rd Street, NW, Ste 775, Washington D.C. 20037, *Telephone:* (202) 466-1200, *Fax:* (202) 296-2691.

The Cincinnati Enquirer, 312 Elm St., Cincinnati, OH 45202, *Telephone:* (513) 721-2700, *Fax:* (513) 768-8330, *Published:* weekdays.

CIO, CIO Publishing, 492 Old Connecticut Path, P.O. Box 9208, Framingham, MA 01701-9208, *Telephone:* (508) 872-8200.

CMR, Schnell Publishing Co., Inc., 80 Broad St., New York, NY 1004-2203, *Telephone:* (212) 248-4177, *Fax:* (212) 248-4903, *Published:* weekly.

Communications of the ACM, Association for Computing Machinery, 1515 Broadway 17th Fl, New York, NY 10036, *Telephone:* (212) 869-7440, *Fax:* (212) 869-0481.

Computer Graphics World, PennWell Publishing Co., 1 Technology Park Drive, Westford, MA 01886, *Telephone:* (508) 692-0700, *Fax:* (508) 692-7806.

Computer Reseller News, CMP Media Inc., One Jericho Plaza, Jericho, New York 11753, *Published:* weekly, *Price*: $199; Canada $224

Computerworld, P.O. Box 2043, Marion, OH 43305-2403, *Telephone:* (800) 669-1002, *Published*: weekly.

Concrete Construction, The Aberdeen Group,426 S. Westgate, Addison, IL 60101-9929, *Telephone*: (708) 543-0870, *Published:* monthly.

Contemporary Long Term Care, Bill Communications Inc., P.O. Box 3599, Akron, OH 44309-3599, *Telephone:* (216) 867-4402, *Fax:* (216) 867-0019.

Convenience Store News, BMT Publications Inc., 7 Penn Plaza, New York, NY 10001-3900, *Telephone*: (212) 594-4120.

Crain's Chicago Business, Crain Communications Inc., 740 N. Rush St., Chicago, IL 60611, *Telephone:* (312) 649-5411.

Crain's Cleveland Business, Crain Communications, Inc., 1725 Merriman Rd., Ste. 300, Akron, OH 44313-5251, *Telephone:* (216) 836-9180, *Fax:* (216) 836-1005, *Published:* weekly.

Crain's Detroit Business, Crain Communications Inc., 1400 Woodbridge, Detroit, MI 48207-3187, *Telephone:* (313) 446-6000. *Published:* weekly, except semiweekly the fourth week in May.

Crain's New York Business, Crain Communications, Inc., 220 E. 42nd St., New York, NY 10017, *Telephone:* (212) 210-0100, *Fax:* (212) 210-0799. *Published:* weekly.

Credit Collections News, Faulkner & Grey, Eleven Penn Plaza, New York, NY 10001, *Telephone:* (800) 535-8403.

Dairy Foods, Gorman Publishing Co., 8750 W. Bryn Mawr Ave., Chicago, IL 60062, *Telephone:* (312) 693-3200. *Published:* monthly, except semimonthly in Aug.

Dairy Herd Management, Miller Publishing, 12400 Whitewater Dr., Minnetonka, MN 55345, *Telephone*: (612) 931-0211.

Dealernews, Advanstar Communications Inc., 1700 E. Dyer Rd. Ste 250, Santa Ana, CA 92705, *Telephone*: (714) 252-5300, *Published:* monthly.

Design News, Cahnres Publishing Co., 275 Washington St., Newton, MA 02158-1630, *Telephone*: (617) 964-3030.

Detroit Free Press, Knight-Ridder, Inc., 1 Herald Plaza, Miami, FL 33132, *Telephone:* (305) 376-3800, *Published:* daily.

Detroit News, Gannett Company Inc., Gannett Dr., White Plains, NY 10604-3498, *Published:* daily.

The Detroiter, Detroit Regional Chamber, One Woodward Avenue, Suite 1700, P.O. Box 33840, Detroit, MI 48322-0840, *Telephone:* (313) 593-0373, *Published*: monthly, *Price:* $14 chamber members; $18 nonmembers.

Discount Merchandiser, Schwartz Publications, 233 Park Ave. S., New York, NY 10003, *Telephone:* (212) 979-4860, *Fax:* (212) 979-7431, *Published:* monthly.

Discount Store News, Lebhar-Friedman Inc., 425 Park Ave, New York, NY 10022, *Telephone:* (212) 756-5100, *Fax:* (212) 756-5125, *Published:* weekly.

DNR, Cahners Publishing Co., 275 Washington St., Newton, MA 02158, *Telephone:* (617) 558-4243, *Fax:* (617) 558-4759, *Published:* 2x/mo.

Do-It-Yourself-Retailing, National Retail Hardware Assn., 5822 W. 74th St., Indianapolis, IN 46278-1756, *Telephone:* (317) 297-1190, *Fax:* (317) 328-4354, *Published:* monthly, *Price: $8; $2 single issue.*

Doane's Agricultural Report, 11701 Boorman Dr., St. Louis, MO 63146, *Telephone:* (800) 535-2342.

DSN Supercenter & Club Business, Lebhar-Friedman Inc., 425 Park Ave, New York, NY 10022, *Telephone:* (212) 756-5100, *Fax:* (212) 756-5125, *Published:* weekly.

DVM News Magazine, Advanstar Communications, Inc., 7500 Old Oak Blvd., Cleveland OH 44130, *Telephone:* (216) 243-8100, *Fax:* (216) 891-2651, *Published:* monthly.

E-Media Professional, Online Inc., 462 Danbury Road, Wilton, CT 06897-2126, *Published:* monthly, *Cost:* $55; $98 corporate.

East Bay Business Times, 6160 Stoneridge Mall, Ste 300, Pleasanton, CA 94588, *Telephone:* (925) 598-1830.

The Economist, The Economist Bldg, 111 W. 57th St., New York, NY 10019, *Telephone:* (212) 541-5730, *Fax:* (212) 541-9378, *Published:* weekly, *Cost:* $110; $3.50 per single issue.

Editor & Publisher, 11 W. 19th St., New York, NY 10011, *Telephone:* (212) 675-4380, *Fax:* (212) 929-1259, *Published:* weekly.

Egg Industry, Watt Publishing Co., 122 S. Wesley Ave., Mount Morris, IL 61054-1497, *Telephone:* (815) 734-4171, *Fax:* (815) 734-4201, *Published:* bimonthly.

Electronic Business, CMP Publications Inc., 8773 South Ridgeline Blvd., Highlands Ranch, CO, 80126-2329, *Telephone:* (516) 562-5000, *Fax:* (516) 562-5409, *Published:* monthly.

Electronic Design, 222 Rosewood Drive, Danvers, MA 01923.

Electronic Media, 740 N. Rush St., Chicago, IL 60611-2590.

Electronic Packaging & Production, Cahners Publishing Co., 1350 E. Touhy Ave., P.O. Box 5080, Des Plaines, IL 60017-5080, *Telephone:* (708) 635-8800, *Fax*: (708) 635-9950, *Published:* monthly.

Engineering & Mining Journal, Maclean Hunter Publishing Co., 29 Wacker Dr., Chicago, IL 60606, *Fax:* (312) 726-2574, *Published:* monthly.

ENR , McGraw-Hill Inc., Fulfillment Manager, ENR, P.O. Box 518, Highstown, NJ 08520, *Telephone:* (609) 426-7070 or (212) 512-3549, *Fax:* (212) 512-3150, *Published:* weekly, *Price:* U.S.: $89 per year; Canada: $75 per year. Single copies $5 in U.S.

ENT, 1300 Virginia Dr, Ste. 400, Ft. Washington PA 19034, Telephone: (215) 643-8000, *Fax:* (215) 643-3901, *Published:* semimonthly.

Entertainment Weekly, Time-Warner Inc., 1675 Broadway, New York, NY 10019, Published: weekly.

Equus, Fleet Street Publishing Corp., 656 Quince Orchard Rd., Gaithersburg, MD 20878, *Telephone*: (301) 977-3900, *Fax:* (301) 990-9015, *Published*: monthly, Price: $24 per year.

Farm Journal, 230 W. Washington Sq., Philadelphia, PA 19106, *Telephone:* (215) 829-4700, *Published:* 13x/yr, *Price:* $14 per year.

Feedstuffs, Miller Publishing Co., 12400 Whitewater Dr., Ste. 1600, Minnetonka, MN 55343, *Telephone:* (612) 931-0211.

The Financial Times, FT Publications Inc., 14 East 60th Street, New York, NY 21002, *Telephone:* (212) 752-4500, *Fax:* (212) 319-0704, *Published:* daily, except for Sundays and holidays, *Price:* $425.

Floor Covering Weekly, Hearst Business Communications Inc., 60 E 42nd St., Ste 234, New York, NY 10165-0006, *Telephone:* (212) 541-4080, *Fax:* (212) 541-4699, *Published*: weekly.

Floor Focus, 28 Old Stone Hill, Pound Ridge, NY 10576, *Telephone:* (914) 764-0556, *Fax:* (914) 764-0560.

Florist's Review, Florist's Review Enterprises, 3641 SW Plass Ave., Topeka, KS 66611-2588, *Telephone:* (913) 266-0888, *Published:* monthly.

Food & Beverage Marketing, Charleson Publishing Co., 505 8th Ave., Ste. 1403, New York, NY 10018, *Telephone:* (212) 695-0704, *Fax:* (212) 695-0748.

Food in Canada, Maclean Hunter, 77 Bay St., Toronto, ON Canada M5W 1A7.

Food Management, Chilton Co., One Chilton Way, Radnor, PA 19089, *Telephone:* (215) 964-4000. *Published:* monthly, *Price:* solicited only from professionals in field: $55 per year, $100 for 2 years; educational rate: $28 per year.

Footwear News, Fairchild Publications, 7 W. 34th St., New York, NY 10001, *Telephone:* (212) 630-4000, *Published:* weekly.

Forbes, Forbes, Inc., P.O. Box 10048, Des Moines, IA 50340-0048, *Telephone:* (800) 888-9896, *Published:* 27 issues per year, *Price:* U.S.: $54 per year; Canada: $95 per year (includes GST).

Forest Products Journal, Forest Products Society, 2801 Marshall Court, Madison, WI 53705-2295, *Published:* monthly, except combined issues in July/August and November/December, *Price:* U.S.: $115 per year; Canada/Mexico: $125; single copies $12 each plus shipping and handling.

Fortune, Time Inc., Time & Life Building, Rockefeller Center, New York, NY 10020-1393, *Published:* twice monthly, except two issues combined into a single issue at year-end, *Price:* U.S.: $57 per year; Canada: $65 per year.

Frozen Food Age, Maclean Hunter Media Inc., 4 Stamford Four, Stamford, CT 06901-1202, *Telephone:* (203) 325-3500, *Published:* weekly.

Fruit Grower, Meister Publishing Co., 37733 Euclid Ave., Willoughsby, OH 44094-5992.

Furniture Today, Cahners Publishing Co., 200 S. Main St., P.O. Box 2754, High Point, NC 27261, *Telephone:* (919) 889-0113, *Published:* weekly.

Garden Design, Evergreen Publishing, 4401 Connecticut Ave., NW, 5th Fl, Washington D.C. 20008-2302, *Telephone:* (202) 686-2752, *Published:* 6x/yr.

Global Cosmetics Industry, Advanstar Communications Inc., 270 Madison Ave., New York, NY 10016.

Global Finance, Global Finance Joint Venture, 11 W. 19th St. 2nd Fl., New York, NY 1011, *Telephone:* (212)337-5900, *Fax:* (212) 697-8331, *Published:* monthly.

Globe and Mail, 444 Front St. W., Toronto, ON, Canada M5V 2S9, *Telephone:* (416) 585-5000, *Fax:* (416) 585-5085, *Published:* Mon.-Sat. (Morn.).

Golfweek, Golfweek Ltd., P.O. Box 1458, Winter Haven, FL 33882, *Telephone:* (813) 294-5511, *Published:* weekly.

Government Executive, National Journal Inc., 1730 M St. NW, Ste. 1100, Washington D.C. 20036, *Telephone:* (202) 862-0600, *Published:* 12x/yr.

Graphic Arts Monthly, Cahners Publishing Company, 44 Cook St., Denver, CO 80206-5800, *Telephone:* (800)637-6089.

Greenhouse Grower, Meister Publishing, 37733 Euclid Ave., Willoughby, OH 44094-5922, *Telephone:* (216) 942-2000.

Grocery Headquarters, Delta Communications Inc., 455 N. Cityfront Plaza Drive, Chicago, IL 60611, *Telephone:* (312) 222-2000, *Fax:* (312) 222-2026, *Published:* monthly.

Grounds Maintenance, Intertec Publishing Co., 9800 Metcalf Ave., Overland Park, KS 66212-2215, *Published:* monthly.

H&HN, Chilton Co., 737 North Michigan Ave., Suite 700, Chicago, IL 60611, *Telephone*: (312) 440-6836, *Published*: monthly.

Healthcare Informatics, Wiesner Inc., Englewood, CO 80112, *Published:* monthly.

Heavy Construction News, Maclean Hunter Ltd., 777 Bay St., Tortonto, ON, Canada M5w 1A7, *Telephone:* (416) 596-5000.

HFN, 7 E. 12th St., New York, NY 10003. *Published:* weekly.

The High Point, 4250 Richmond Rd., Rm. 2203, Highland Hill, OH 44122, Telephone: (216) 987-2344.

Home Textiles Today, Cahners Publishing Co., 249 W. 17th St., New York, NY 10011, *Telephone:* (212) 337-6900, *Fax*: (212) 337-6922.

Hotel & Motel Management, Advanstar Communications, Inc., 7500 Old Oak Blvd., Cleveland, OH 44130, *Telephone:* (216) 826-2839.

Household and Personal Products Industry, Rodman Publishing, 17 S. Franklin Turnpike, Box 555, Ramsey, NJ 07446, *Telephone:* (201) 825-2552, *Fax:* (201) 825-0553, *Published:* monthly.

HPAC Engineering, 1100 Superior Ave., Cleveland, OH 44114.

ID, Magazine Publications Limited, 250 W 57th St., Ste. 215, New York, NY 10107-0001, *Telephone*: (212) 9560535, *Published*: 6x/yr.

IEEE Spectrum, Institute of Electrical and Electronics Engineers Inc., 345 E 47th St., New York, NY 10017, *Telephone*: (212) 705-7555, *Fax*: (212) 705-7589, *Published*: monthly.

Inc., Goldhirsh Group Inc., 38 Commercial Wharf, Boston, MA 02110, *Published*: monthly.

Industrial Distribution, Cahners Publishing Company, 275 Washington Street, Newton, MA 02158, *Telephone:* (617) 964-3030, *Published:* monthly.

Industrial Paint & Powder, Chilton Publications, 191 S. Gary Ave., Carol Stream, IL 60188, *Telephone*: (708) 665-1000, *Fax:* (708) 462-2225, *Published*: monthly.

The Industry Standard, Internet Industy Publishing, 315 Pacific Ave., San Francisco, CA 94111-1701, *Telephone:* (415) 733-5400, *Fax*: (415) 733-5401, *Published:* weekly.

INFORM, American Oil Chemists Society, P.O. Box 3489, Champaign, IL 61826-3489, *Telephone:* (217) 359-2344, *Fax:* (217) 351-8091.

Informationweek, CMP Publications Inc., 600 Community Drive, Manhasset, NY 11030, Telephone: (516) 365-4600.

Infoworld, Infoworld Publishing Co., 155 Bovet Rd., Ste. 800, San Mateo, CA 94402, *Telephone:* (415) 572-7341, *Published:* weekly.

Injection Molding, Abby Communications Inc., 10 Fairmont Ave., Chatham, NJ 07928, *Telephone:* (973) 635-5646, *Published*: monthly.

InTech, ISA Services Inc., 67 Alexander Dr., P.O. Box 12277 Research Triangle Park, NC 27709, *Telephone:* (919) 549-8411, *Fax:* (919) 549-8288, *Published*: monthly.

Interior Design, Cahners Publishing Co., 249 W. 17th St., New York, NY 10011, *Telephone:* (212) 463-6694.

Investor's Business Daily, P.O. Box 661750, Los Angeles, CA 90066-8950, *Published:* daily, except weekends and holidays, *Cost:* $128 per year.

JOM, The Minerals , Metals & Materials Society, 420 Commonwealth Drive, Warrendale, PA 15086, *Telephone*: (412) 776-9070.

Journal of Commerce, Journal of Commerce, Inc., Two World Trade Center, 27th Floor, New York, NY 10048, *Telephone:* (212) 837-7000, *Fax:* (212) 837-7035.

The Kansas City Star, Kansas City Star Co., 1729 Grand Ave., Kansas City, NO 64108, *Telephone:* (816) 234-4141, *Fax*: (816) 234-4926.

KM World, Knowledge Asset Media,16-18 Bayview Landing, P.O. 1358, Camden, ME 04843, *Telephone:* (207) 236-8524, *Published:* monthly.

Latin Trade, Freedom Communications Inc., 200 South Bicauyne Blvd., Suite 1150, Miami, FL 33131, *Published:* monthly.

Limousine & Chauffered Transportation, 21061 S. Western Ave., Torrance, CA 90501, *Telephone:* (310) 533-2400.

Lodging Hospitality, Penton Publishing, 1100 Superior Ave., Cleveland, OH 44114, *Telephone*: (216) 696-7000, *Fax*: (216) 696-7658.

Los Angeles Times, The Times Mirror Company, Times Mirror Square, Los Angeles, CA 90053, *Telephone:* (800) LA TIMES.

LP/GAS, Advanstar Communications Inc., 131 West First Street, Duluth, MN 55802-2065, *Published:* monthly, *Cost:* $40 one year.

The Manufacturing Confectioner, The Manufacturing Confectioner Publishing Company, 175 Rock Rd., Glen Rock, NJ 07452, *Telephone:* (201) 652-2655, *Fax:* (201) 652-3419, *Published:* 12 times per year, *Price:* $25 per year, single copies $10 each, except $25 for April and July issues.

Marketing Magazine, Maclean Hunter Canadian Publishing, P.O. Box 4541, Buffalo, NY 14240-4541, *Telephone:* (800) 567-0444, *Fax:* (416) 946-1679, *Price:* Canada: $59.50 per year, $98.50 for 2 years, $125 for 3 years; U.S.: $90 per year.

MB, 3033 Chimey Rd., Suite 300, Houston, TX 77056, *Published:* monthly, combined issues in Jan./Feb. and July/Aug.

Med Ad News, Engel Communications Inc., 820 Bear Tavern Rd., Ste. 302, West Trenton, NJ 08628, Telephone: (609) 530-0044, Fax: (609) 530-0207.

Mediaweek, ADWEEK, L.P., P.O. Box 1976, Danbury, CT 06813-1976, *Telephone:* (800) 722-6658, *Published:* weekly, except first week of July, last week of August, and Last two weeks of December, *Price:* U.S.: $95 per year, $170 for 2 years; Canada: $230 per year.

Medical & Healthcare Marketplace, Dorland Healthcare, 1500 Walnut St., Philadelphia, PA 19102.

Medical Marketing & Media, CPS Communications, 7200 West Camino Real, Ste. 215, Boca Raton, FL 33433, *Telephone:* (407) 368-9301, *Fax*: (407) 368-7870, *Published:* monthly, *Price*: $75 per year.

Men's Fitness, Weider Publications, 21100 Erwin St., Woodland Hills, CA 91367, *Telephone:* (818) 884-6800, *Published*: monthly.

Mexico Business Monthly, Caribbean UPDATE, 52 Maple Ave., Maplewood NJ 07040, Telephone: (800) 647-9990.

Michigan Retailer, Michigan Retailers Association, 221 North Pine Street, Lansing, MI 48933, *Published:* 10x/yr. *Cost:* $20.

Milling & Baking News, Sosland Publishing Co., 4800 Main St., Ste. 100, Kansas City, MO 64112, Telephone: (816) 756-1000, Fax: (*16) 756-0494.

Milwaukee Journal-Sentinel, Journal/Sentinel Inc., P.O. Box 371, 53201, *Telephone:* (414) 224-2000, *Published:* Mon-Sat.

Mining Engineering, Society for Mining, Metallurgy and Exploration Inc., 8307 Shaffer Parkway, Littleton CO 80127-5002, *Telephone:* (303) 973-9550, *Fax*: (303) 973-3845, *Published*: monthly.

MMR, Racher Press, 220 5th Ave., New York, NY 1001, *Telephone:* (212) 213-6000, *Fax:* (212) 213-6101, *Published:* biweekly.

MMR (Musical Merchandise Review), Larkin Publications, 485 7th Ave., Ste. 1400, New York, NY 10018, *Published:* monthly.

Modern Casting, American Foundrymen's Society, 505 State St., Des Plaines, IL 60016-8399, *Telephone:* (708) 824-0181.

Modern Materials Handling, Cahners Publishing, 275 Washington St., Newton, MA 02158, *Telephone:* (617) 964-3030, *Fax:* (617) 558-4402.

Modern Physician, Crain Communications Inc., 740 N. Rush St., Chicago, IL 60611-2590.

Modern Plastics, McGraw-Hill, Inc., Attn. Fulfillment Manager, P.O. Box 481, Highstown, NJ 08520, *Telephone:* (800) 525-5003, *Published:* monthly, *Price:* U.S.: $41.75 per year, $62.70 for 2 years, $83.50 for 3 years; Canada:$CDN 53 per year, $CDN 80 for 2 years, $CDN 106 for 3 years.

Motor Truck, Southam Magazine Group, P.O. Box 1144, Lewiston, NY 14092, *Published:* monthly.

Music Trades, P.O. Box 432, 80 West St., Englewood, NJ 07631, *Telephone:* (201) 871-1965, *Fax:* (201) 871-0455, *Published:* monthly.

National Home Center News, Lebhar-Friedman Inc., 425 Park Ave., New York, NY 10022, *Telephone*: (212) 756-5151, Fax: (212) 756-5295, *Published:* 2x/mo.

National Petroleum News, Hunter Publishing Limited Partnership, Circulation Dept., National Petroleum News, 25 Northwest Point Blvd., Suite 800, Elk Grove Village, IL 60007, *Telephone:* (708) 427-9512, *Published:* monthly, except semimonthly in June, *Price:* U.S.: $60 per year for those in petroleum marketing industry, $75 per year for others; Canada: $69 per year for those in petroleum marketing industry, $84 per year for others.

National Real Estate Investor, Communications Channels Inc., 6255 Barfield Rd., Atlanta, GA 30328, *Telephone:* (404) 256-9800, *Published:* monthly.

National Trade Data Bank, STAT-USA, U.S. Department of Commerce, Washington D.C., 20230, *Telephone:* (202) 482-1986, *Fax:* (202) 482-2164.

National Underwriter, The National Underwriter Co., 505 Gest St., Cincinnati, OH 45203, *Telephone:* (800) 543-0874, *Fax:* (800) 874-1916, *Published:* weekly, except last week in December, *Price:* U.S.: $77 per year, $130 for 2 years; Canada: $112 per year, $130 for 2 years.

Nation's Restaurant News, Lebhar-Friedman, Inc., Subscription Dept., P.O. Box 31179, Tampa, FL 33631-3179, *Telephone:* (800) 447-7133. *Published:* weekly on Mondays, except the first Monday in July and the last Monday in December, *Price:* $34.50 per year and $55 for 2 years for professionals in the field; $89 per year for those allied to field.

Network World, Network World, Inc., 161 Worcester Rd., Framingham, MA 01701-9172, *Telephone:* (508) 875-6400, *Published:* weekly.

The New York Times, New York Times Co., 229 W. 43rd St., New York, NY 10036, *Telephone:* (212) 556-1234. *Published:* daily.

Newsweek, The Newsweek Building, Livingston, NJ 07039-1666, *Telephone:* (800) 631-1040, *Published:* weekly, *Price:* U.S.: $41.08 per year; Canada: $61.88 per year (send to P.O. Box 4012, Postal Station A, Toronto, ON M5W 2K1).

Nonwovens Industry, Rodman Publishing Co., 17 S. Franklin Tpke., P.O. Box 55, Ramsey, NJ 07466, Telephone: (201) 825-2552, *Published:* monthly.

Nursery Retailer, Brantwood Publications, Inc., 3023 Eastland Blvd., Ste. 103, Clearwater, FL 34621-4106, *Telephone:* (813) 796-3877, *Fax:* (813) 791-4126, *Published:* 6x/yr.

OR Manager, 2170 S. Parker Rd., Ste. 300, Denver, CO 80231-5711, *Telephone:* (303) 755-6300.

PC Computing, Ziff-Davis Publishing, 950 Tower Ln., Foster City, CA 94404, *Telephone:* (415) 378-5600, *Published:* monthly.

PC Magazine, 28 E 28th St., New York, NY 10016-7930, *Telephone:* (212) 503-5255, *Published:* weekly.

Pensions & Investments, Crain Communications Inc., 220 E. 42nd St., New York, NY 10017, *Telephone:* (212) 210-0227, *Fax:* (212) 210-0117, *Published:* bi-weekly.

Pet Product News, Fancy Publications, P.O. Box 6050, Mission Viejo, CA 92690, *Telephone:* (213) 385-2222.

Pipeline & Gas Journal, Oildom Publishing Co. of Texas, Inc., 3314 Mercer St., Houston, TX 77027, *Telephone:* (713) 622-0676, *Fax:* (713) 623-4768, *Published:* monthly, *Price:* free to qualitifed subscribers; all others $15 per year.

Pit & Quarry, Edgell Communications, Inc., 7500 Old Oak Blvd., Cleveland, OH 44130, *Telephone:* (216) 243-8100, *Fax:* (216) 891-2726, *Published:* monthly.

Pittsburgh Post-Gazette, California Delta Newspaper Inc., 1650 Cavallo Rd., Antioch, CA 94509, *Telephone:* (510) 757-2525, *Fax:* (510) 754-9483.

Plastics News, Crain Communications, 965 E. Jefferson, Detroit, MI 48207-3185, *Published:* weekly.

Playthings, Geyer-McAllister Publications, Inc., 51 Madison Ave., New York, NY 10010, *Telephone:* (212) 689-4411, *Fax:* (212) 683-7929, *Published:* monthly, except semimonthly in May.

Pork, National Pork Producers Council, P.O. Box10383, Des Moines, IA 50306, *Telephone:* (515) 223-2600.

Poultry and Egg Marketing, Gannett Company Inc., 1 gannett Dr., White Plains, NY 10604-3498,*Telephone:* (914) 694-9300.

Power Engineering, PennWell Publishing Co., 1250 S. Grove Ave., Ste. 302, Barrington, IL 60010, *Telephone*: (708) 382-2450.

PR Week, PR Publications Ltd., 220 Fifth Ave., New York, NY 10001, *Telephone:* (212) 532-9200, *Fax:* (212) 532-9200, *Published*: 49x/yr.

Practical Accountant, Faulkner & Gray, Inc., 11 Penn Plaza, 17th Floor, New York, NY 10001, *Telephone:* (800) 535-8403 or (212) 967-7060, *Published:* monthly, *Price:* U.S.: $60 per year; Elsewhere: $79 per year.

Prepared Foods, Cahners Publishing Company, 44 Cook St., Denver, CO 80217-3377, *Telephone*: (303) 388-4511, *Published*: monthly.

Printing Impressions, North American Publishing Co., 401 N Broad St., Philadelphia, PA 19108, *Telephone*: (215) 238-5300, *Fax:* (215) 238-5457.

Professional Candy Buyer, Adams Business Media, 2101 S. Arlington Heights Rd., Arlington Heights, IL 60005-4142.

Progressive Grocer, 263 Tresser Blvd., Stamford, CT 06901, *Telephone:* (203) 325-3500, *Published:* monthly, *Price:* U.S.: $75 per year; Canada: $86 per year; single copies $9 each.

Provider, American Health Care Association, 5615 W. Cermak Rd., Cicero, IL 60650, *Published:* monthly.

Publishers Weekly, Cahners Publishing Company, ESP Computer Services, 19110 Van Ness Ave., Torrance, CA 90501-1170, *Telephone:* (800) 278-2991, *Published:* weekly, *Price:* U.S.: $129 per year; Canada: $177 per year (includes GST).

Pulp & Paper, Miller Freeman Inc., P.O. Box 1065, Skokie, IL 60076-8065, *Telephone:* (800) 682-8297, *Published:* monthly, *Price:* free to those in pulp, paper, and board manufacturing and paper converting firms; Others in U.S.: $100 per year.

Purchasing, Cahners Publishing Company, 44 Cook St., Denver, CO 80217-3377, *Telephone:* (303) 388-4511. *Published:* semimonthly, except monthly in January, February, July, August, December, and one extra issue in March and September, *Price:* U.S.: $84.95 per year; Canada: $133.95 per year; Mexico: $124.95 per year.

Railway Age, Simmons-Boardman Publishing, 345 Hudson St., New York, NY 10014, *Telephone:* (212) 620-7200, *Fax:* (212) 633-1165, *Published:* monthly.

RCR, RCR Publications, 777 East Speer Blvd., Denver, CO 80203.

Realtor, 430 N. Michigan Ave., Chicago, Il 60611-4087.

Refrigerated & Frozen Foods, Stagnito Communications, 1935 Sherman Rd., Northbrook, IL 60062, *Telephone:* (847) 205-5660, *Fax:* (847) 205-5680.

Restaurants & Institutions, Cahners Publishing Co., 1350 Touhy Ave., Cahners Plaza, Des Plaines, IL 60017-5080, *Telephone:* (312) 635-8800.

Rice Journal, Specialized Agricultural Publications Ltd., P.O. Box 95075 , Raleigh, NC 27625, *Telephone*: (919) 872-5040.

Risk, Society for Risk Analysis, 1313 Dolley Madison Blvd., Ste. 402, McLean, VA 22101, *Telephone:* (703) 790-1745.

Rock Products, Maclean Hunter Publishing Co., 29 N Wacker Drive, Chicago, IL 60606, *Telephone*: (312) 726-2802, *Fax:* (312) 726-2574.

Rolling Stone, 1290 Avenue of the Americas, New York City, NY 10104, *Telephone*: (212) 484-1616, *Fax:* (212) 767-8209.

Rough Notes, Rough Notes Co. Inc., 11690 Technologies Dr., Carmel, IN 46032-5600, *Published:* monthly, *Cost:* $25.

Rubber & Plastics News, Crain Communications, 1725 Merriman Road, Ste. 300, Akron, OH 44313, *Telephone:* (330) 836-9180, *Fax*: (33) 836-1005, *Published:* weekly.

Sacramento Business Journal, 1401 21st St., Sacramento, CA 95814-5221, *Telephone:* (916) 447-7661, *Fax:* (916) 444-7779, *Published:* weekly.

Security Management, America Society for Industrial Security, 1655 N Fort Myer Dr., Ste. 1200, Arlington, VA 22209, Telephone: (703) 522-5800.

The Shepard, Sheep & Farm Life Inc., 5696 Johnston Rd., New Washington, OH 44854, *Published:* monthly.

Shopping Center World, Communications Channels, Inc., 6255 Barfield Rd., Altanta, GA 30328, *Telephone:* (404) 256-9800.

Snack Food & Wholesale Bakery, Stagnito Publishing Co., 1935 Shermer Rd., Ste. 100, Northbrook, IL 60062-5354, *Telephone:* (708) 205-5660, *Fax:* (708) 205-5680, *Published:* monthly, *Price:* free to qualified subscribers; $45 per year to all others.

Sports Business Journal, Street & Smith, 112 S. Tyron, Ste. 1600, Charlotte, NC 28284, *Telephone:* (704) 371-3100.

Spray Technology & Marketing, Indsutry Publications, Inc., 389 Passaic Ave., Fairfield, NJ 07004, *Telephone:* (201) 227-5151, *Fax:* (201) 227-921, *Published:* monthly.

Stores, NRF Enterprises Inc., 100 West 31st St., New York, NY 10001, *Published:* monthly, *Price:* U.S./Canada: $49 per year, $80 for 2 years, $120 for 3 years.

Successful Farming, Meredith Corp., 1716 Locust St., Des Moines, IA 50309, *Telephone:* (515) 284-3000, *Fax:* (515) 284-2700.

Supermarket Business, Howfrey Communications, Inc., 1086 Teaneck Rd., Teaneck, NJ 07666, *Telephone:* (201) 833-1900, *Published:* monthly.

Supermarket News, Fairchild Publications, 7 W. 34th St., New York, NY 10001, *Telephone:* (212) 630-4750, *Fax:* (212) 630-4760.

Tampa Bay Business Journal, American City Business Journals, 405 Reo St. Ste 210, Tampa, FL 33609, *Telephone:* (813) 289-8225, *Published:* weekly, *Price:* $42.

Telephony, Intersec Publishing Corp., 9800 Metcalf, Overland Park, KS 66282-2960, *Published:* monthly.

Textile Asia, Tak Yan Commercial Bldg., 11th Fl., 30-32 D'Aguilar St., Hong Kong, *Telephone:* (5) 247467, *Published:* monthly.

Textile World, Maclean Hunter Publishing Co., Circulation Dept., 29 N. Wacker Dr., Chicago, IL 60606, *Price:* U.S./Canada: $45 per year, $75 for 2 years, $105 for 3 years.

Time, Time, Inc., Time & Life Bldg., Rockefeller Center, New York, NY 10020-1393, *Telephone:* (800) 843-8463, *Published:* weekly.

Times-Picauyne, Times-Picauyne Publishing Co., 800 Howard Ave., New Orleans, LA 70140, *Telephone:* (504) 826-3300, *Published:* daily.

Tire Business, Crain Commincations, Inc., 1725 Merriman Rd., Ste. 300, Akron, OH 44313-5251, *Telephone:* (216) 836-9180, *Fax:* (216) 836-1005.

Tooling & Production, Huebcore Communications Inc., 29100 Aurora Rd., Ste. 200, Solon, OH 44139, *Published:* monthly, *Price:* $90 per year.

Toronto Star, One Yong Street, Toronto, Ontario M5E 1E6, Telephone: (416) 367-2000, *Published:* daily.

Traffic World, Journal of Commerce Inc., Two World Trade Center, New York, NY 10048, *Published:* weekly, except last week of December, *Price:* $159 per year.

Transportation & Distribution, Penton Publishing, 1100 Superior Ave., Cleveland, OH 44114-2543, *Telephone*: (216) 696-7000, Fax: (216) 696-4135, Price: $45 per year.

TRENDS Magazine, American Animal Hospital Assn., 12575 W. Bayaud Ave., Lakewood, CO 80228, *Telephone:* (303) 986-2800, *Fax:* (303) 986-1700, *Published:* 6x/yr.

TWICE, Cahners Publishing, 249 W. 17th St., New York, NY 10010, *Telephone*: (212) 645-0067, *Price:* $35 per year.

U.S. News & World Report, 2400 N. St. NW, Washington, D.C. 20037, *Telephone:* (202) 955-2000, *Published:* weekly.

Upside, Upside Media Inc., 2015 Pioneer Court, San Mateo, CA 94403, *Telephone:* (650) 377-0950, *Fax:* (650) 377-1962, *Published*: monthly.

Urethane Technology, Crain Communications Inc., 1725 Merriman Rd., Ste. 300, Akron, OH 44313-5251, *Telephone:* (216) 836-9180, *Fax*: (216) 836-1005, *Published:* 6x/yr, Price: $83.

US Banker, Kalo Communications, 60 E. 42nd St., Ste. 3810, New York, NY 10165, Telephone: (212) 599-3310.

USA TODAY, Gannett Co., Inc., 1000 Wilson Blvd., Arlington, VA 22229, *Telephone:* (703) 276-3400. *Published:* Mon.-Fri.

VAR Business, CMP Media Inc., 1 Jericho Plaza A, Jericho NY 11753, *Telephone:* (516) 733-6700, *Published:* weekly.

Variety, 475 Park Ave., South, New York, NY 10016, *Telephone:* (212) 779-1100, *Fax:* (212) 779-0026. *Published:* weekly.

Vending Times, Vending Times Inc., 545 8th Ave., New York, NY 10018, *Telephone:* (212) 714-0101, *Fax:* (212) 564-0196, *Published:* monthly.

Veterinary Product News, 1905 Powers Ferry Rd., Ste. 120, Marietta, GA 30067, *Telephone:* (404) 988-9558, *Fax:* (404) 859-9166, *Published:* 9x/yr.

VM + SD, ST Publications Inc., 407 Gilbert Ave., Cincinnati, OH 45202, *Telephone:* (513) 421-2050, *Published:* monthly, *Price:* $39 per year.

Wall Street Journal, Dow Jones & Co. Inc., 200 Liberty St., New York, NY 10281, *Telephone:* (212) 416-2000. *Published:* Mon.-Fri.

Wallace's Farmer, Farm Progress Companies, 191 S. Gary Ave., Carol Stream, IL 60188, *Published:* 15x/yr.

WARD's Dealer Business, Ward's Communications, 28 W. Adams, Detroit, MI 48226, *Telephone:* (313) 962-4456. *Published:* monthly.

The Washington Post, The Washington Post, 1150 15th St., N.W., Washington, DC 20071, *Published:* weekly.

Washington Technology, Post-Newsweek, 8500 Leesburg Pike, Suite 7500, Vienna, VA 22182-2412, *Telephone*: (703) 848-2800, *Fax:* (703) 848-2353.

Waste Age, National Solid Waste Management Assn., 1730 Rhode Island Ave., NW, Ste. 1000, Washington D.C. 20036, *Telephone:* (202) 861-0708, *Fax:* (202) 659-0925.

Waste News, 1725 Merriman Rd., Akron, OH 44314, *Telephone:* (330) 836-9180.

Water Engineering & Management, Scranton Gillette Communications, 380 E Northwest Highway, Des Plaines, IL 60016, *Telephone*: (708) 298-6622.

Windows, Ziff-Davis, One Park Ave., New York, NY 10016, *Published:* monthly.

Wines & Vines, Hiaring Co., 1800 Lincoln Ave., San Rafael, CA 94901-1298, *Telephone:* (415) 453-9700, *Fax:* (415) 453-2517, *Published:* monthly, *Price:* $32 per year without directory; $77.50 per year including directory.

Wired, 520 3rd St., 4th Fl., San Francisco, CA 94107-1815, Telephone: (415) 276-5000, *Published*: monthly, *Price:* $39.95; Corporate: $80.

Wireless Week, P.O. Box 266008, Highlands Ranch, CO 80163-6008, *Telephone:* (303)470-4800.

Wood & Wood Products, Vance Publishing Corp., 400 Knightsbridge Pkway., Lincolnshire, IL 60069, *Telephone:* (708) 634-4347, *Fax:* (708) 634-4379, Published: monthly, except semimonthly in March.

Wood Digest, Johnson Hill Press, 1233 Janesville Ave., Fort Atkinson, WI 53538, *Telephone:* (414) 563-6388, *Fax:* (414) 563-1702.

Wood Technology, Miller Freeman Inc., 600 Harrison St., San Francisco, CA 94107, *Telephone:* (415) 905-2502, *Fax:* (415) 905-2630, *Published*: bimonthly.

World Oil, Gulf Publishing Co., 3301 Allen Pkwy., P.O. Box 2608, Houston, TX 77252-2608, *Telephone*: (713) 529-4301, *Fax:* (713) 520-4433.

WWD, Fairchild Publications, 7 E. 12th St., New York, NY 10003, *Telephone:* (212) 741-4000, *Fax:* (212) 337-3225. *Published:* weekly.

Yahoo!Internet Life, Ziff Davis Inc., Ona Park Ave., New York, NY 10016, *Published:* monthly, *Price:* $19.95.